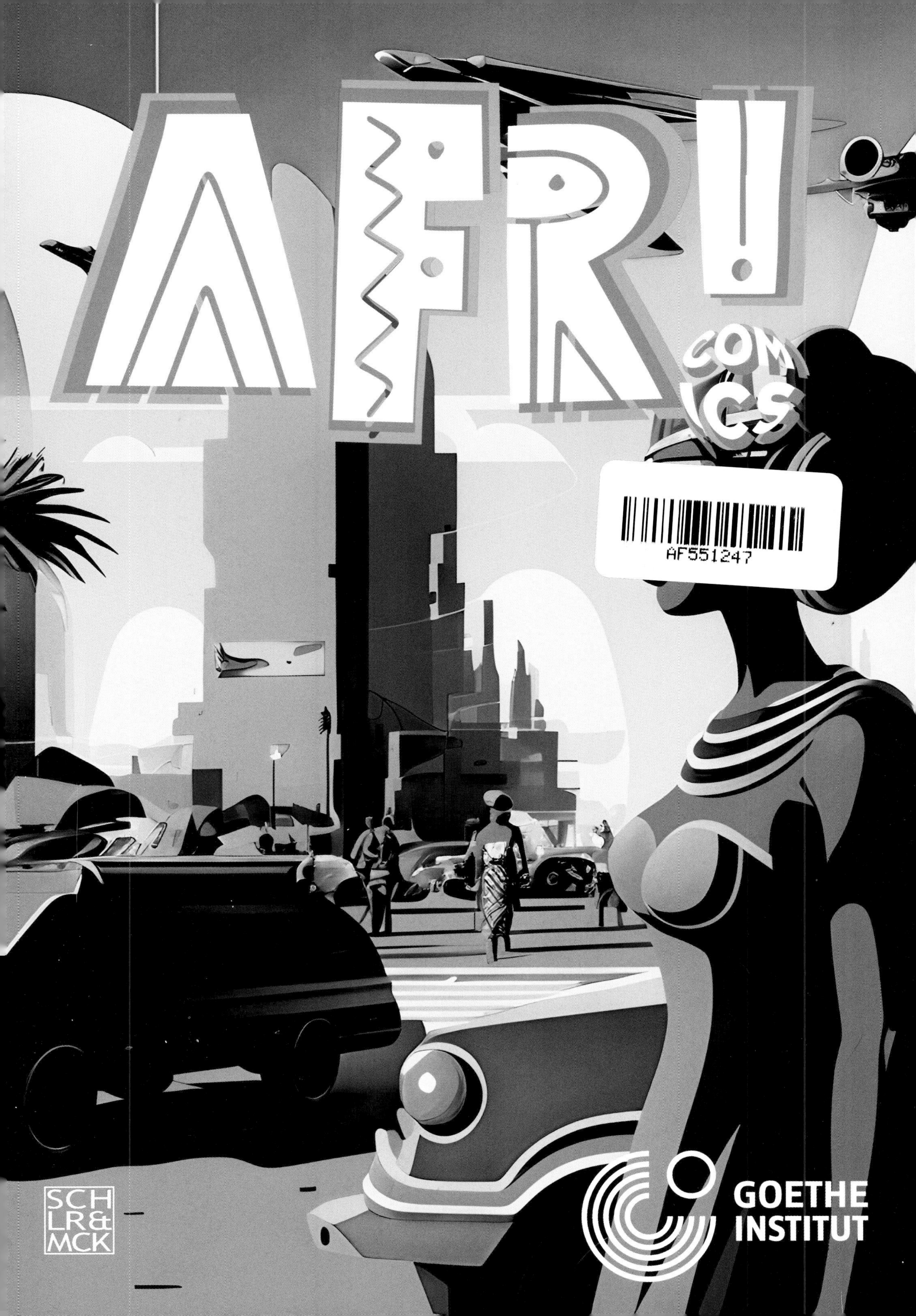
AFRI
COMICS
SCHLR&MCK
GOETHE
INSTITUT

Bibliographic information published by the Deutsche Nationalbibliothek

The Deutsche Nationalbibliothek lists this publication in the Deutsche Nationalbibliografie; detailed bibliographic data are available on the Internet at http://dnb.dnb.de .

This anthology is a part of the regional project AfriComics, carried out by the Region Sub-Saharan Africa of the Goethe-Institut e. V.

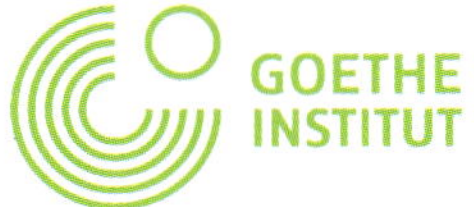

First Édition

Copy editing: Antonia Sümnich, Heike Friesel
Cover-Design: Derek Amoah
Printed by Standart Impressa
in Lithuania.

ISBN 978-3-89930-471-8

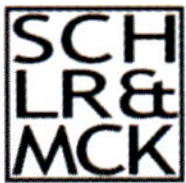

Contents

Dear readers,

The book in your hands is the result of a long and complex process, and all those who have contributed to it are very happy and proud to present you with this beautiful outcome of their work.

However, I would like to begin this preface not with technical details of the project but with a heartfelt thank you, especially to the participating artists whose works are gathered here. It is primarily thanks to them that the "AfriComics" project has been brought to a successful conclusion, and a vibrant network has emerged that gives continued opportunities for interaction and mutual support.

We must not forget all those who produced videos for the website in earlier phases of the project, designed and led workshops, and, of course, the participants in the many workshops of the first phase of the project. Without the active participation of all these creative and committed people, coming from a total of 21 different countries, this achievement would not have been possible. Our thanks also go to colleagues at participating Goethe-Institutes, who supported us from the beginning with trust, their knowledge of the host countries, and, of course, the necessary financial resources.

Africa's comic scene is as diverse as the vast continent itself, and the videos that were created at the beginning of the project in 2020 still provide a comprehensive insight into this diversity. From portraits of national comic icons, to practical short lectures on marketing strategies or character development methods, to comprehensive presentations on the development of African comics, this video collection is a treasure-trove of the world of comics in and from Africa.

But this was only the first step. When relaxation of Covid restrictions finally allowed physical meetings again, workshops were held in a total of 14 countries. Most of these were designed and led by two trainers who were able to combine their experiences and expertise from Germany and the respective host country in a fruitful collaboration. Some results and photographic impressions of these workshops can also be found on the aforementioned website:

www.goethe.de/africomics.

One of our central aims was to provide comic artists with opportunities for international networking. This was realized through the various workshops in the host countries, and on an international level during the joint meeting in Ghana in the summer of 2022. There selected artists from 15 countries came together to work on new comics on the theme of "Decolonize...!". With the guidance of Mikaël Ross from Germany and Akosua Hanson from Ghana, new ideas were developed, storyboards were elaborated, and discussed with other participants, modified, and presented to colleagues again. The seventeen comic artists formed a group during that week and continue to stay in touch and support each other.

As one finds everywhere, creating comics is a niche activity on the African continent, still gradually establishing itself. Myths and superheroes, fantasy, and the desire for alternative realities play a significant role in comic art here as elsewhere. However, in the stories presented here, one can easily recognize the distinctive role that ancestors play in the historical self-perception of many people in Africa. It is also clear that colonial history continues to be a heavy burden on societies economically, culturally, and not least psychologically, and yet a desire for harmonious and respectful co-existence is present in many stories.

Accra, Summer 2023
Heike Friesel

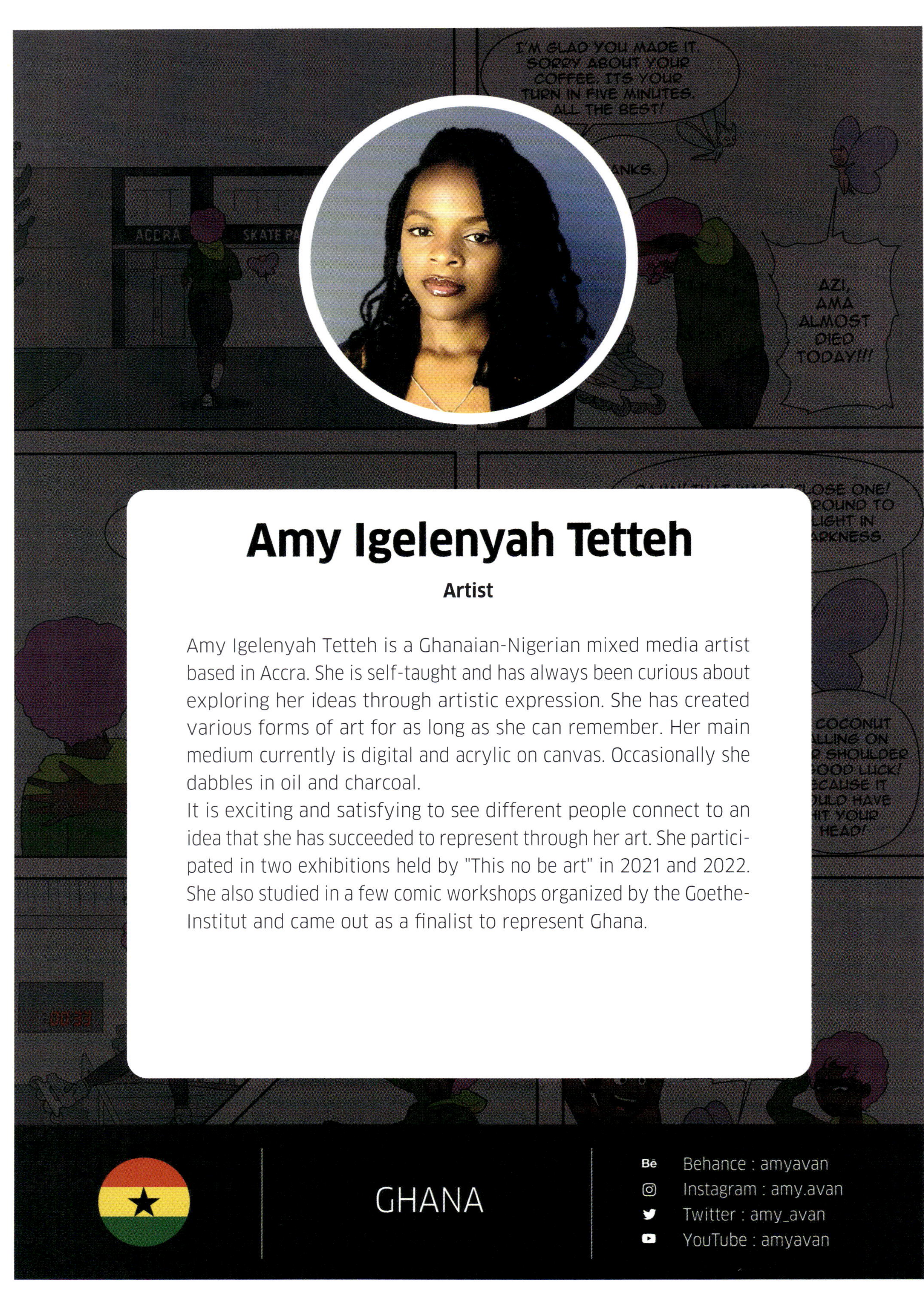

Amy Igelenyah Tetteh

Artist

Amy Igelenyah Tetteh is a Ghanaian-Nigerian mixed media artist based in Accra. She is self-taught and has always been curious about exploring her ideas through artistic expression. She has created various forms of art for as long as she can remember. Her main medium currently is digital and acrylic on canvas. Occasionally she dabbles in oil and charcoal.

It is exciting and satisfying to see different people connect to an idea that she has succeeded to represent through her art. She participated in two exhibitions held by "This no be art" in 2021 and 2022. She also studied in a few comic workshops organized by the Goethe-Institut and came out as a finalist to represent Ghana.

GHANA

Behance : amyavan
Instagram : amy.avan
Twitter : amy_avan
YouTube : amyavan

UNCHAINED

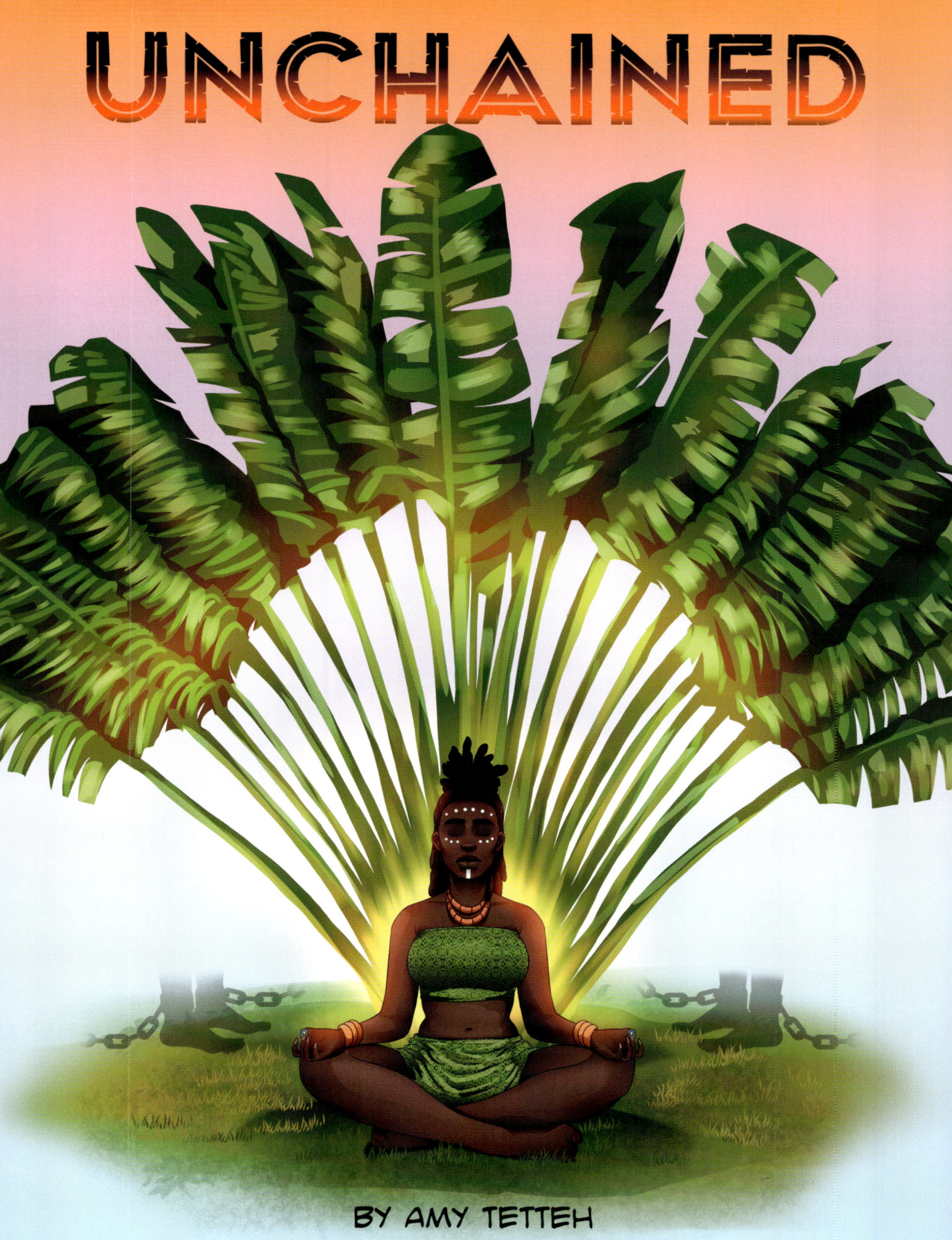

BY AMY TETTEH

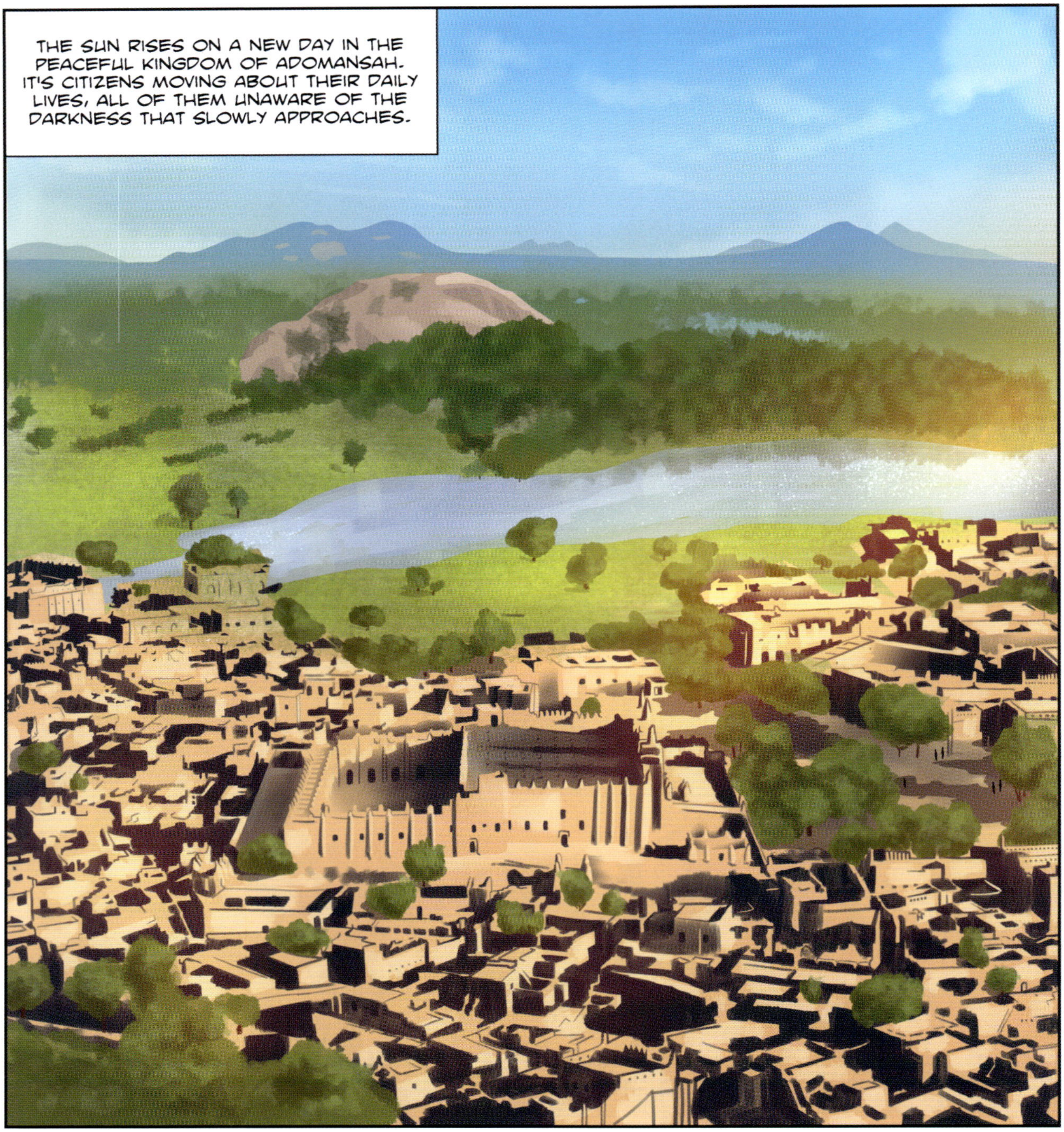

THE SUN RISES ON A NEW DAY IN THE PEACEFUL KINGDOM OF ADOMANSAH. IT'S CITIZENS MOVING ABOUT THEIR DAILY LIVES, ALL OF THEM UNAWARE OF THE DARKNESS THAT SLOWLY APPROACHES.

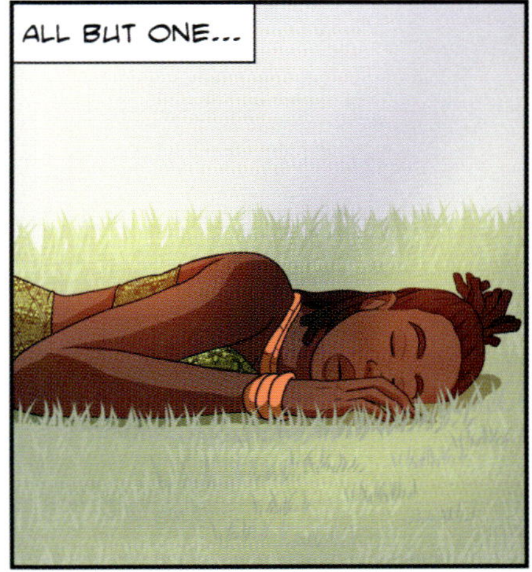

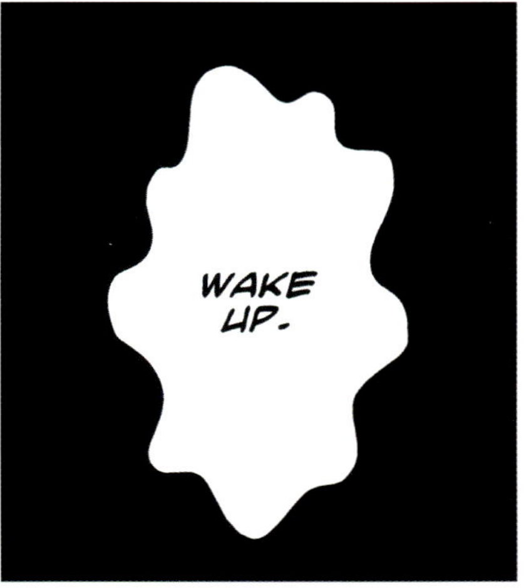

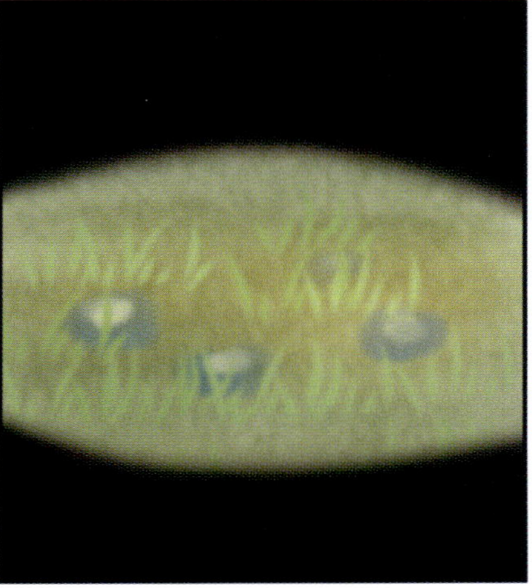

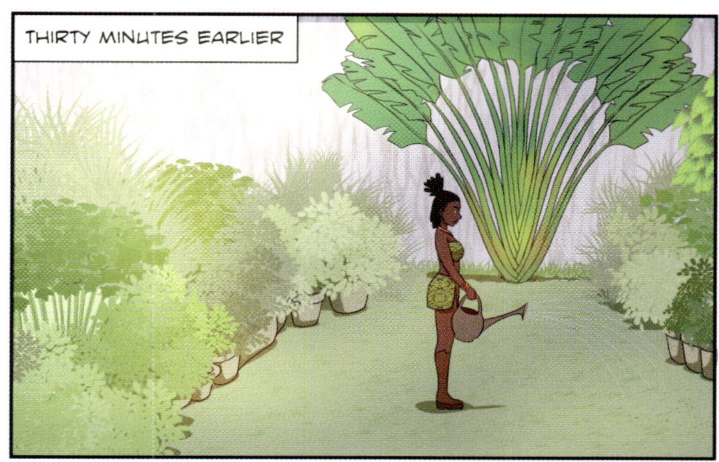
THIRTY MINUTES EARLIER

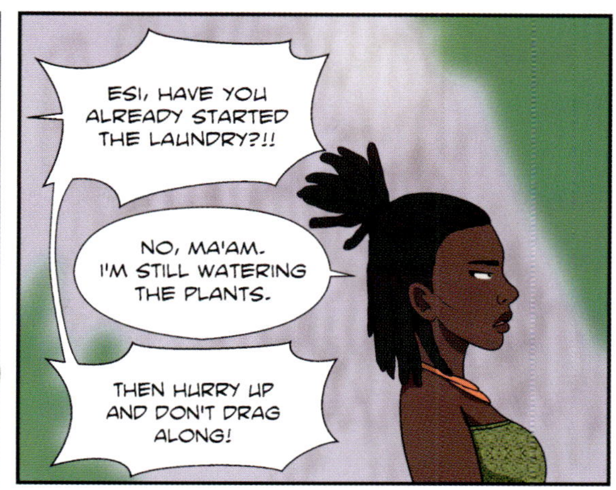
ESI, HAVE YOU ALREADY STARTED THE LAUNDRY?!!
NO, MA'AM. I'M STILL WATERING THE PLANTS.
THEN HURRY UP AND DON'T DRAG ALONG!

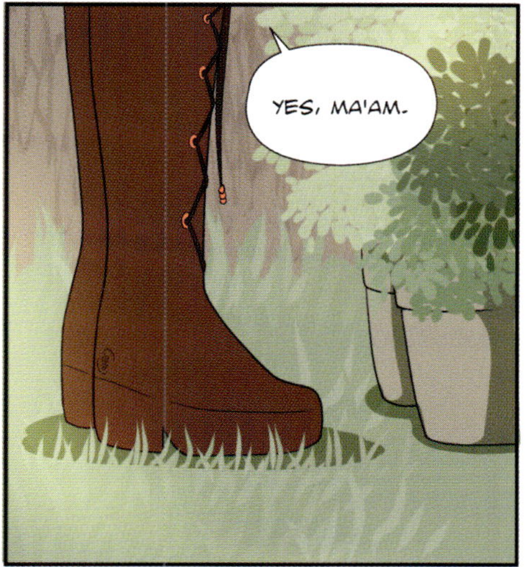
YES, MA'AM.

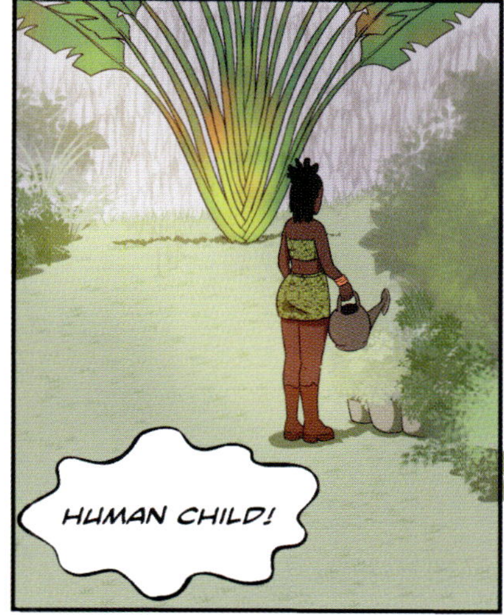
HUMAN CHILD!

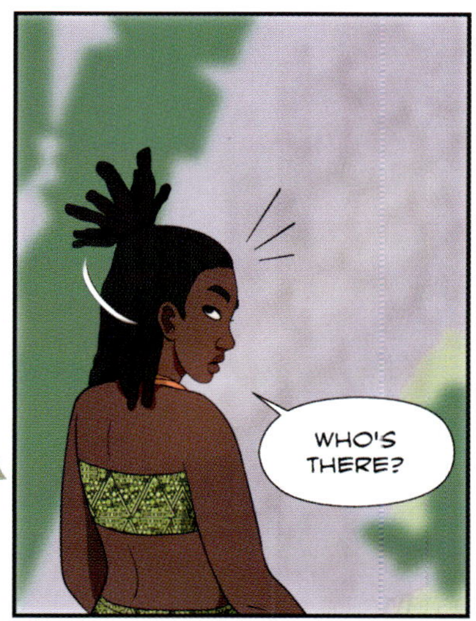
WHO'S THERE?

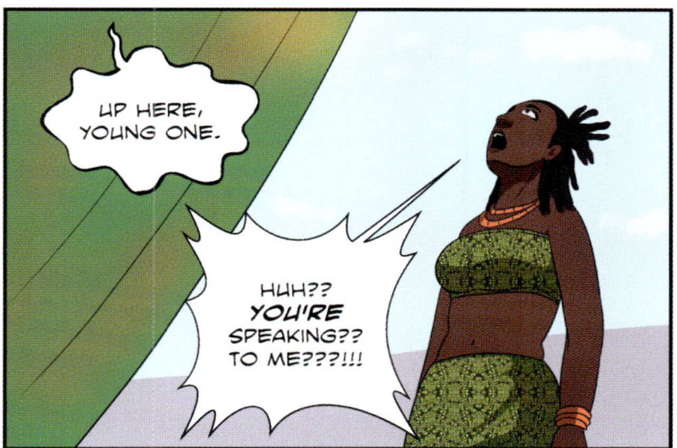
UP HERE, YOUNG ONE.
HUH?? **YOU'RE** SPEAKING?? TO ME???!!!

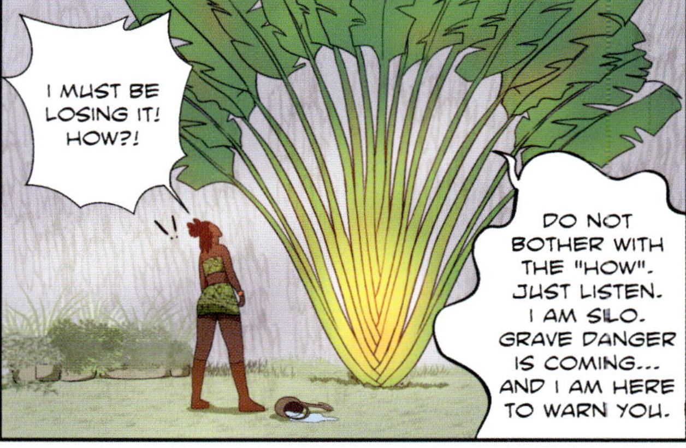
I MUST BE LOSING IT! HOW?!
!!
DO NOT BOTHER WITH THE "HOW". JUST LISTEN. I AM SILO. GRAVE DANGER IS COMING... AND I AM HERE TO WARN YOU.

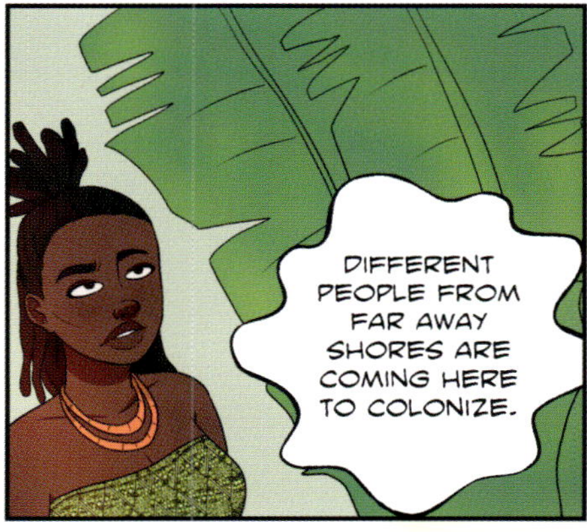
DIFFERENT PEOPLE FROM FAR AWAY SHORES ARE COMING HERE TO COLONIZE.

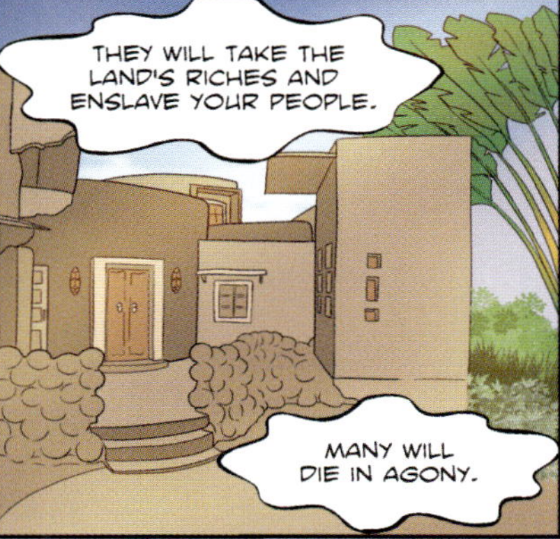
THEY WILL TAKE THE LAND'S RICHES AND ENSLAVE YOUR PEOPLE.
MANY WILL DIE IN AGONY.

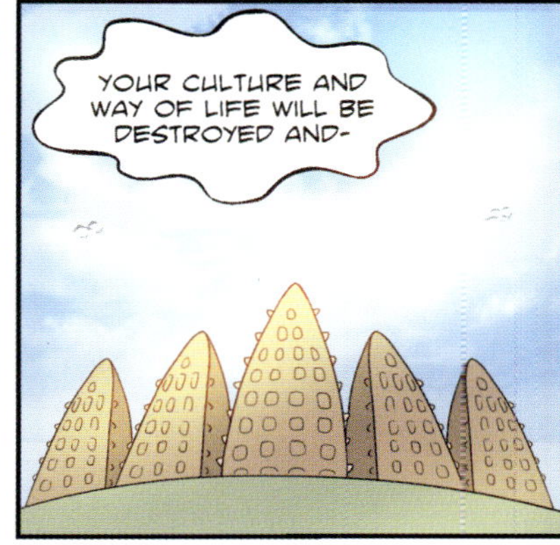
YOUR CULTURE AND WAY OF LIFE WILL BE DESTROYED AND-

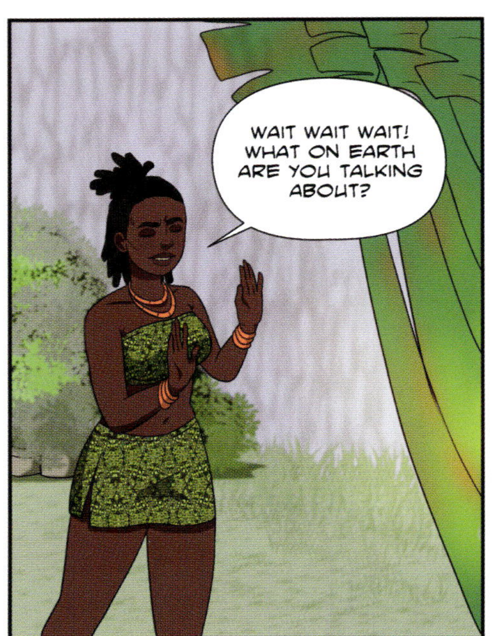
WAIT WAIT WAIT! WHAT ON EARTH ARE YOU TALKING ABOUT?

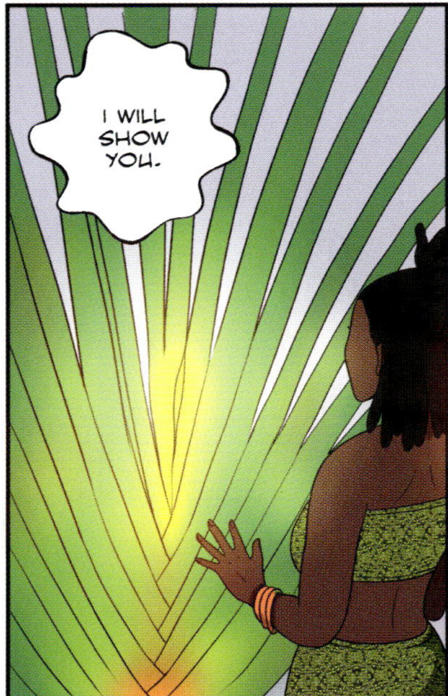
I WILL SHOW YOU.

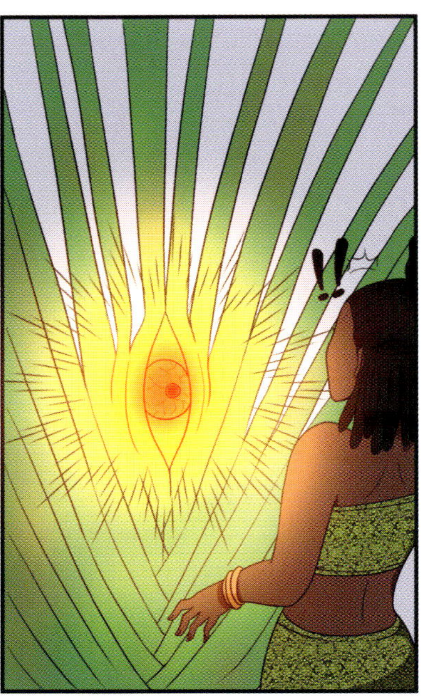
!!

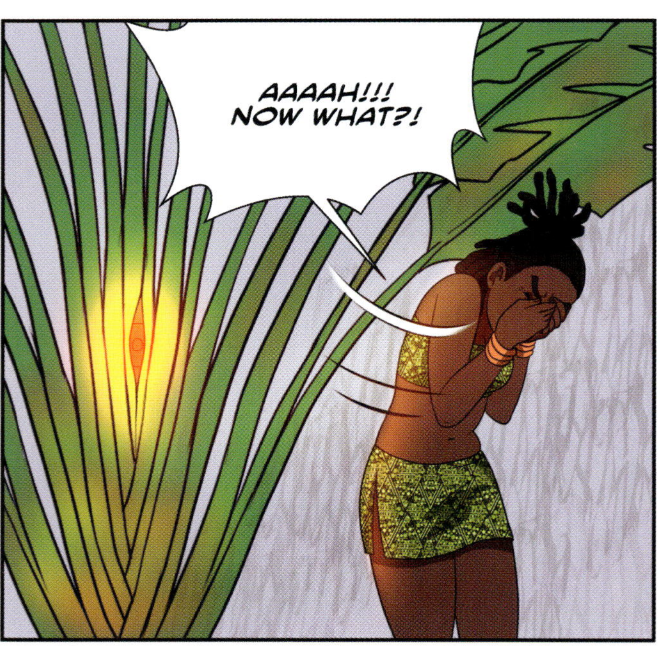
AAAAH!!! NOW WHAT?!

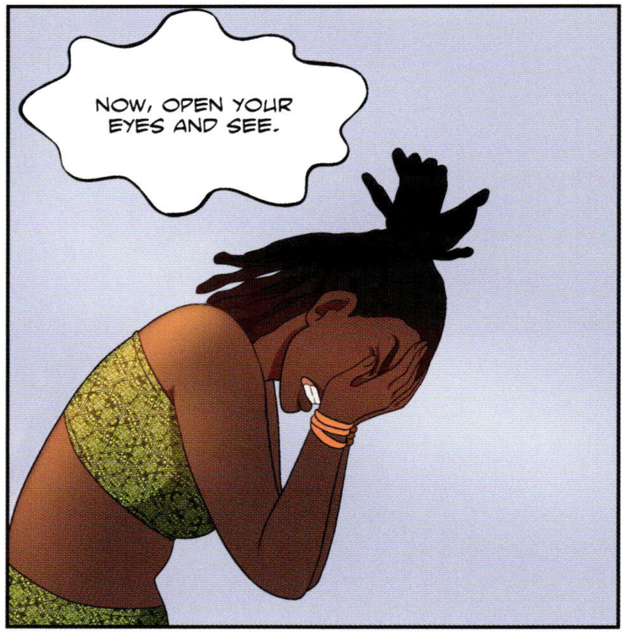
NOW, OPEN YOUR EYES AND SEE.

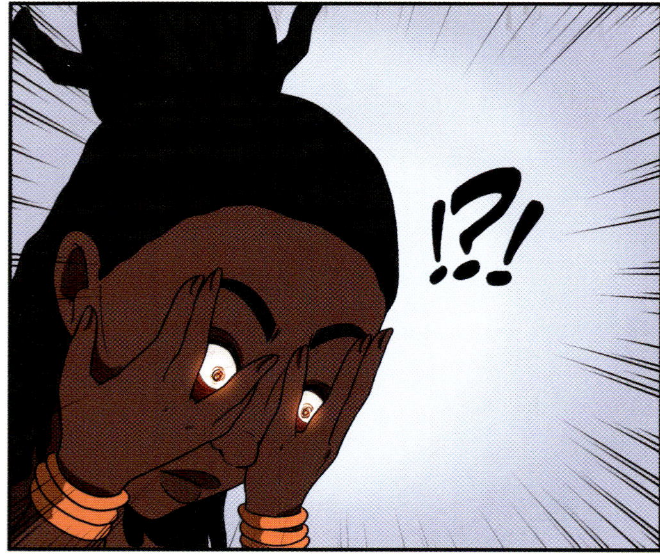
!?!

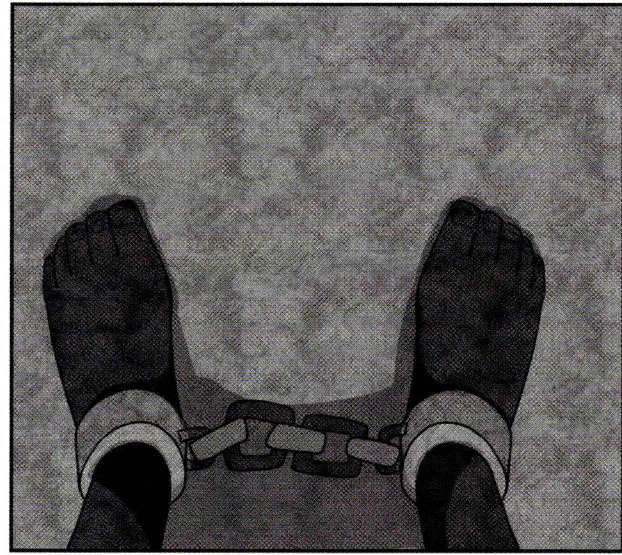

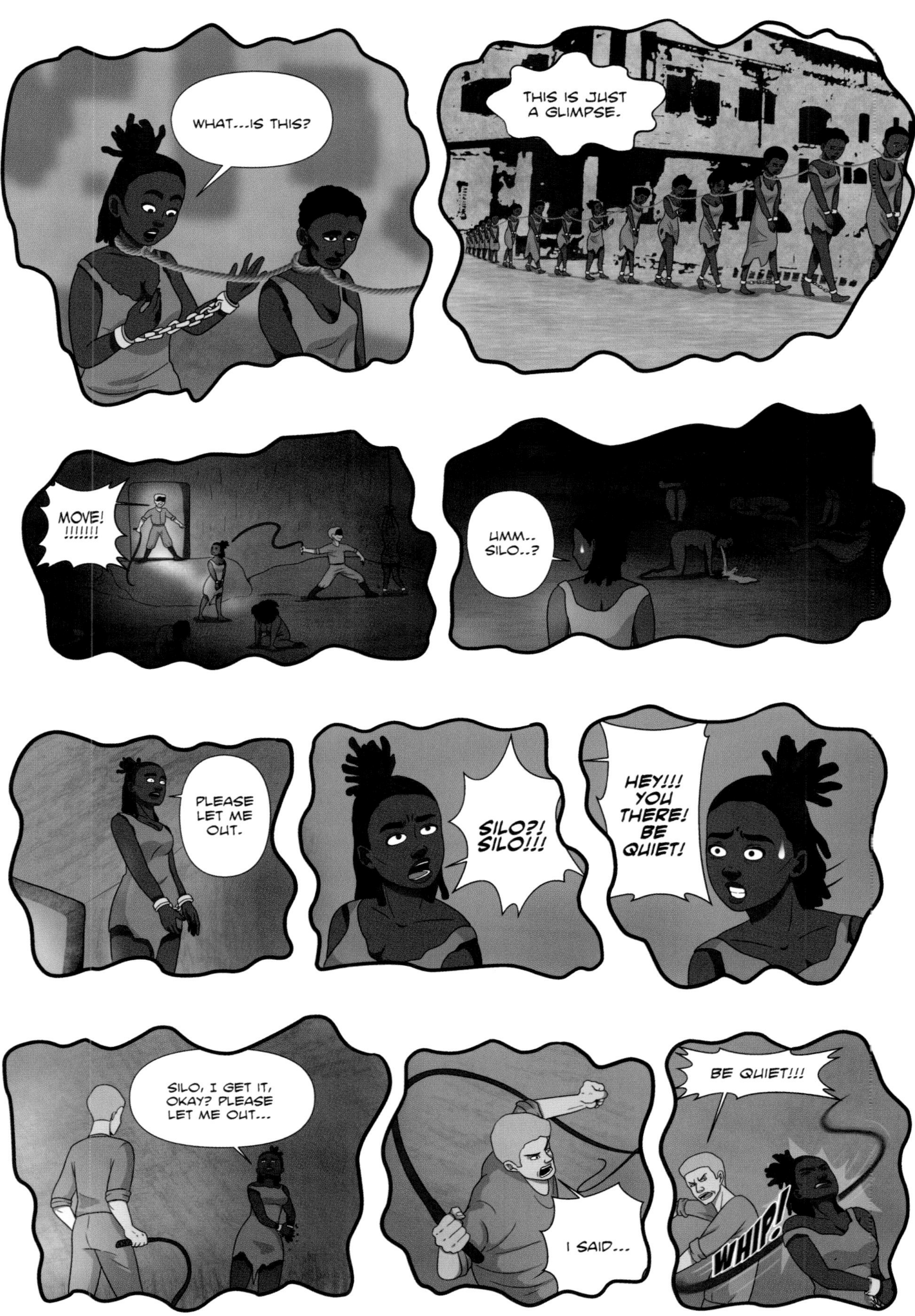
WHAT...IS THIS?
THIS IS JUST A GLIMPSE.
MOVE! !!!!!!!
UMM.. SILO..?
PLEASE LET ME OUT.
SILO?! SILO!!!
HEY!!! YOU THERE! BE QUIET!
SILO, I GET IT, OKAY? PLEASE LET ME OUT...
I SAID...
BE QUIET!!!
WHIP!

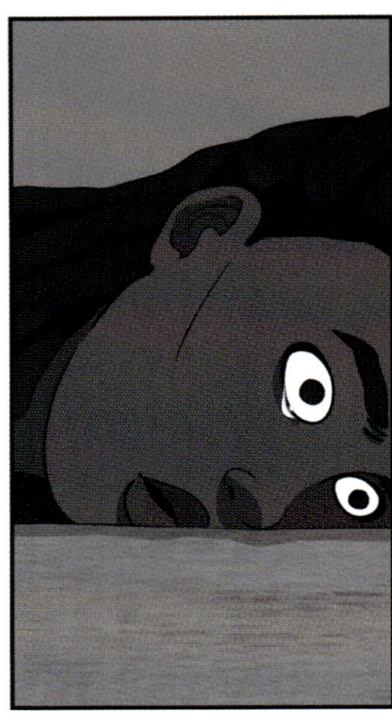

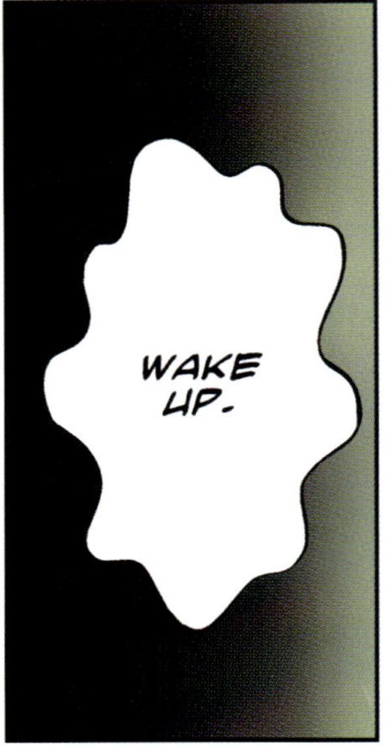
WAKE UP.

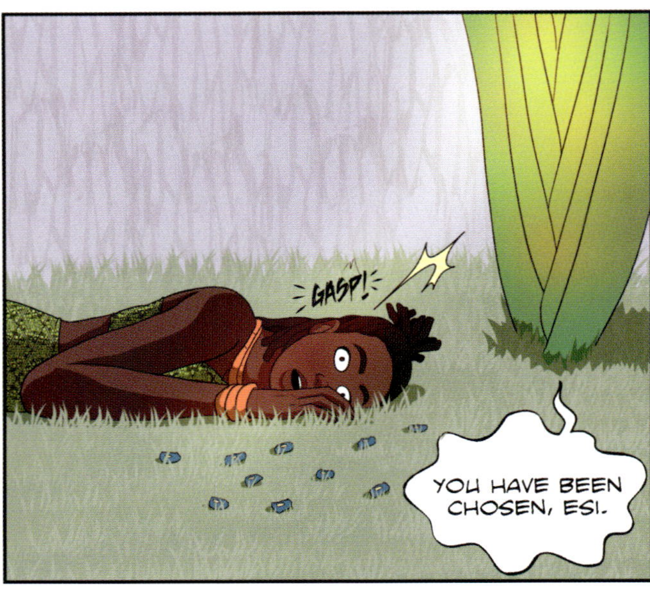
GASP!
YOU HAVE BEEN CHOSEN, ESI.

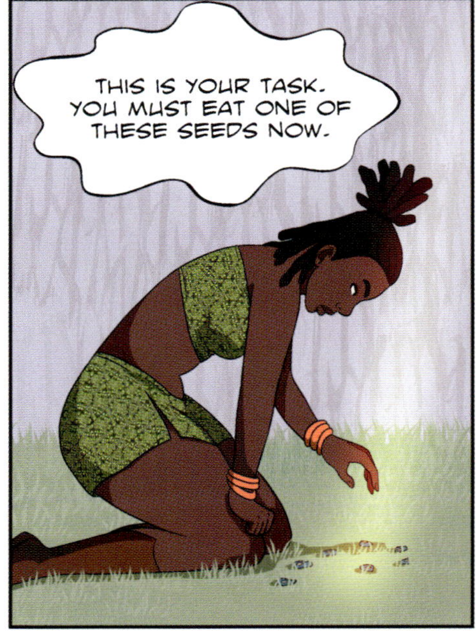
THIS IS YOUR TASK. YOU MUST EAT ONE OF THESE SEEDS NOW.

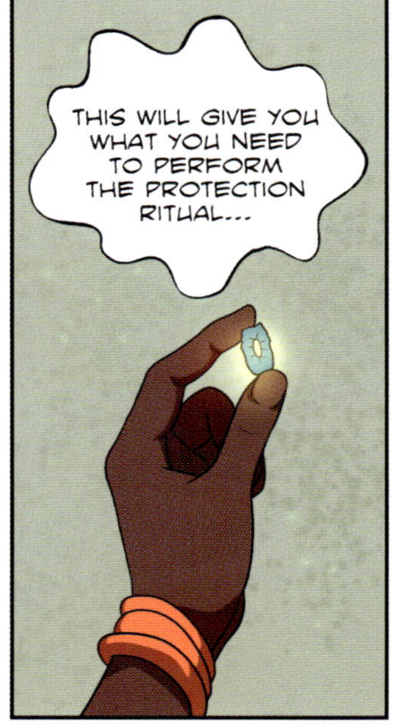
THIS WILL GIVE YOU WHAT YOU NEED TO PERFORM THE PROTECTION RITUAL...

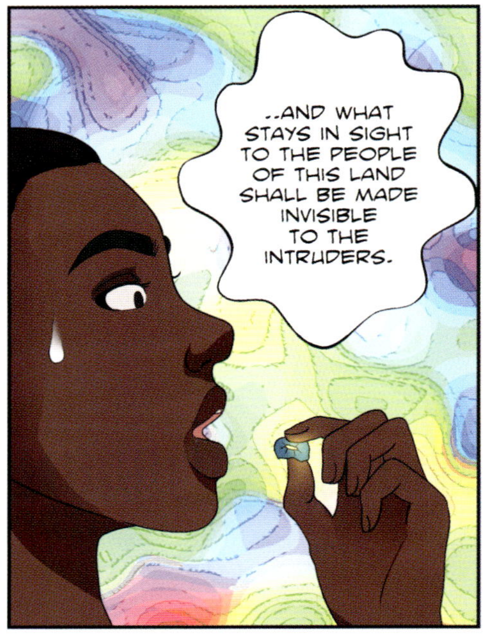
..AND WHAT STAYS IN SIGHT TO THE PEOPLE OF THIS LAND SHALL BE MADE INVISIBLE TO THE INTRUDERS.

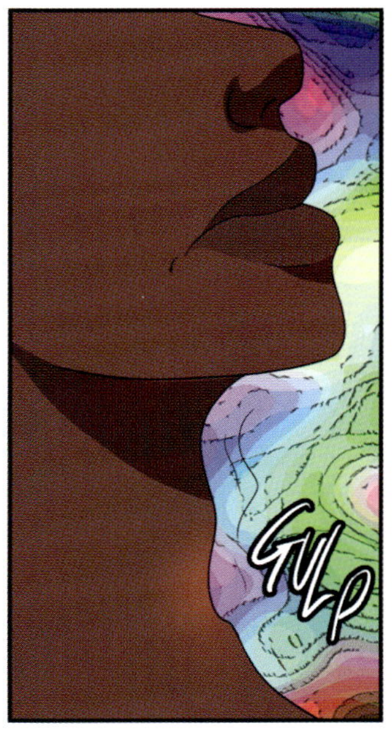
GULP

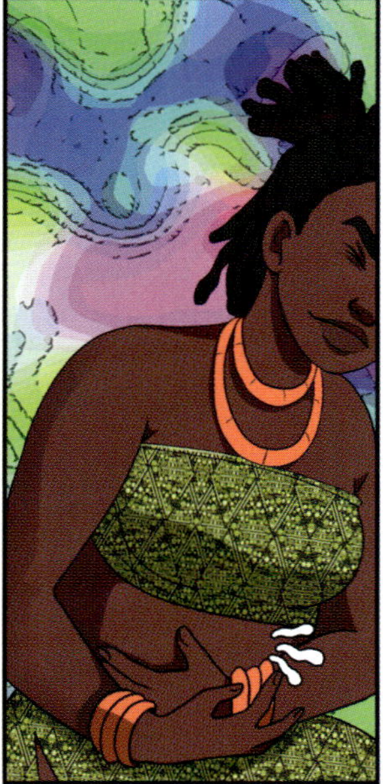

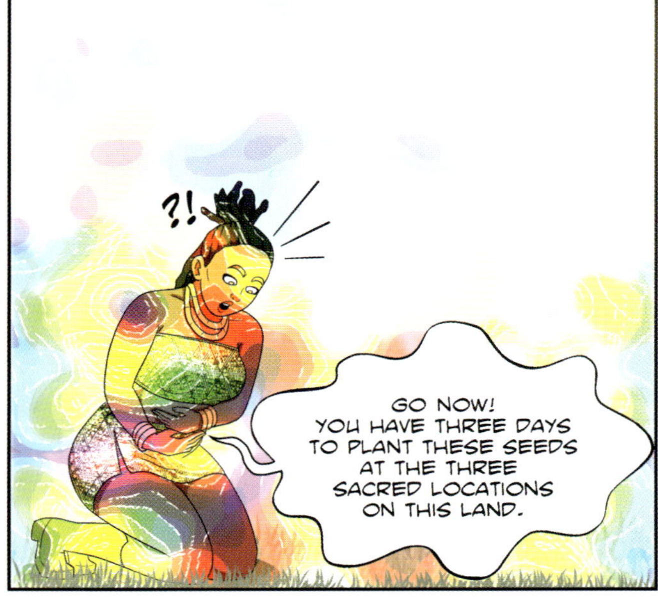
?!
GO NOW! YOU HAVE THREE DAYS TO PLANT THESE SEEDS AT THE THREE SACRED LOCATIONS ON THIS LAND.

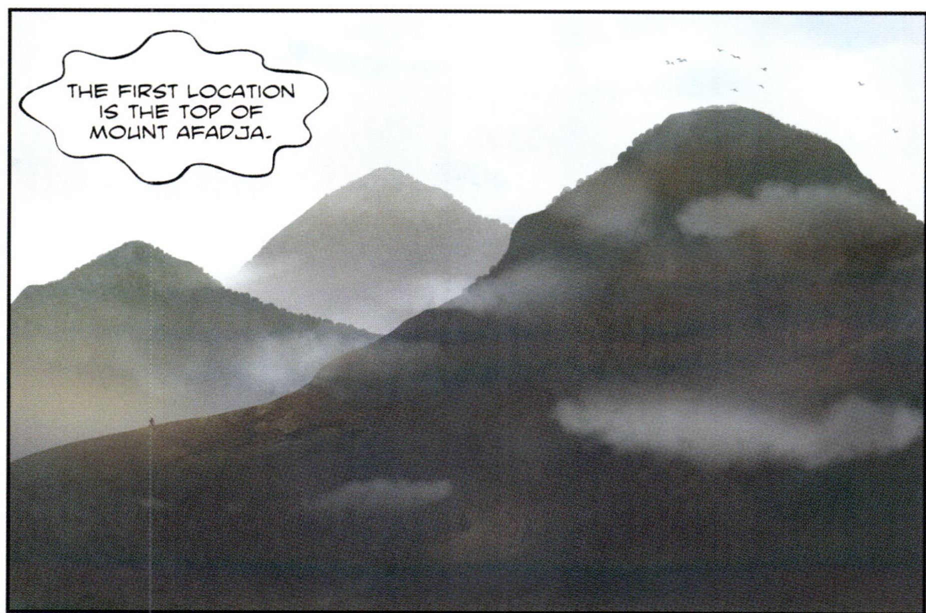
THE FIRST LOCATION
IS THE TOP OF
MOUNT AFADJA.

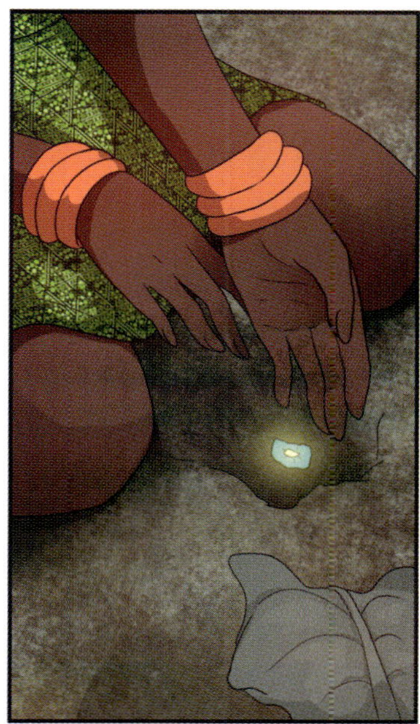

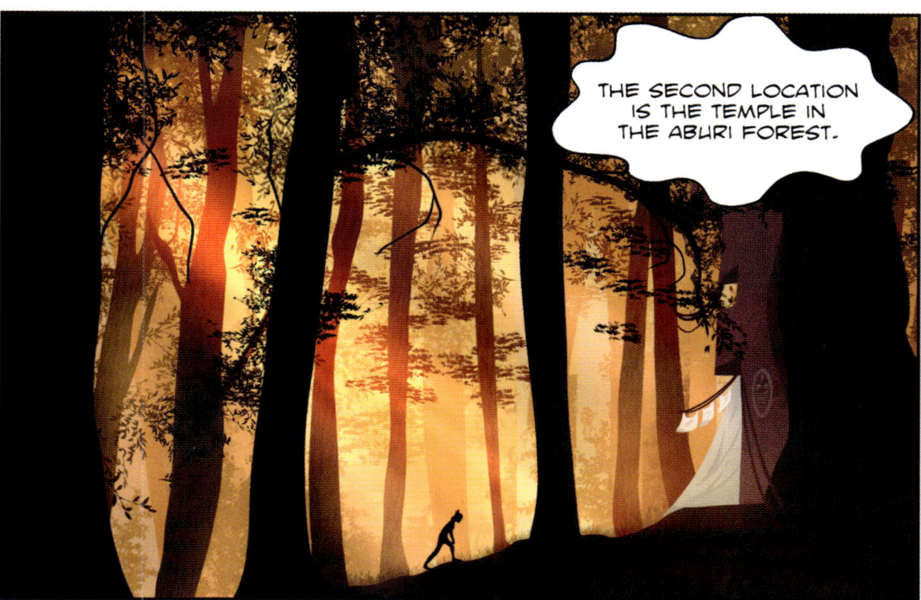
THE SECOND LOCATION
IS THE TEMPLE IN
THE ABURI FOREST.

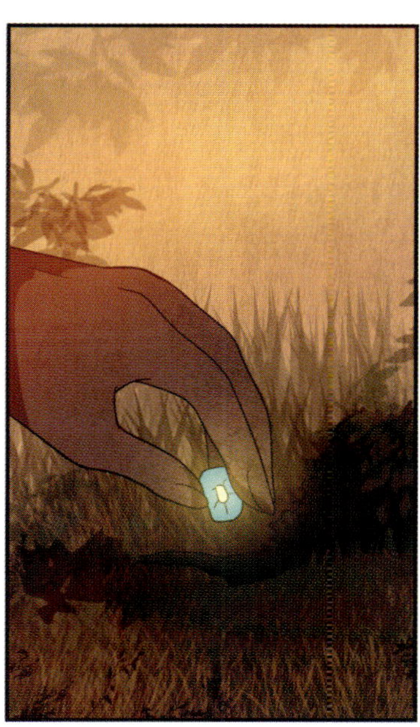

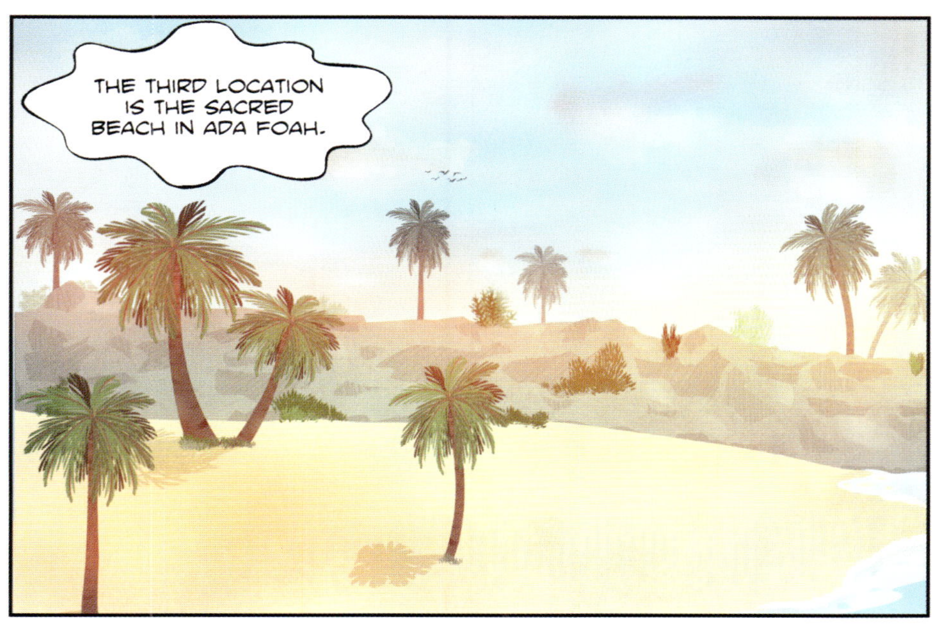
THE THIRD LOCATION
IS THE SACRED
BEACH IN ADA FOAH.

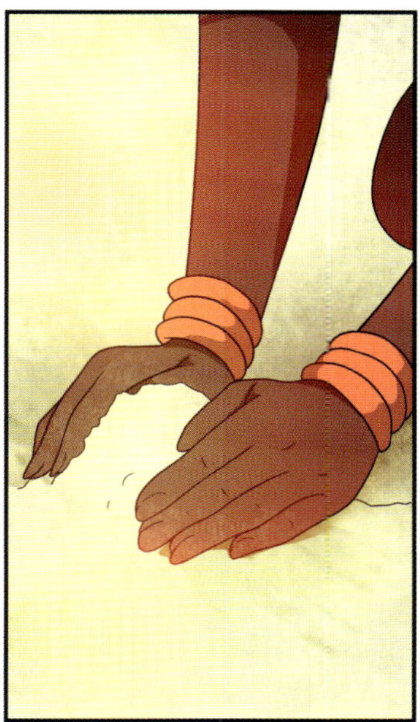

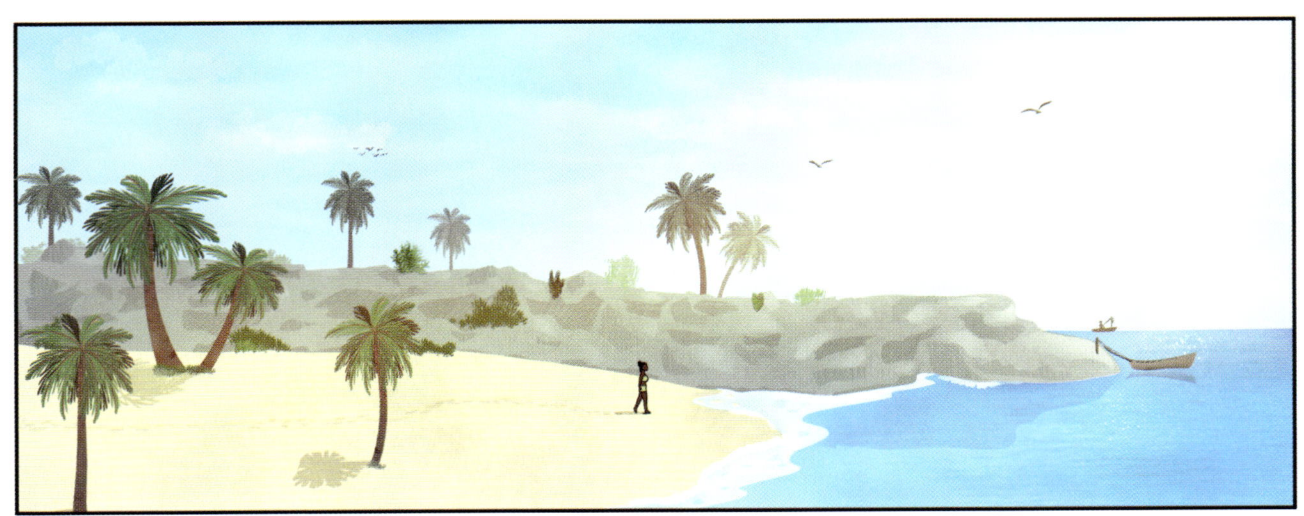

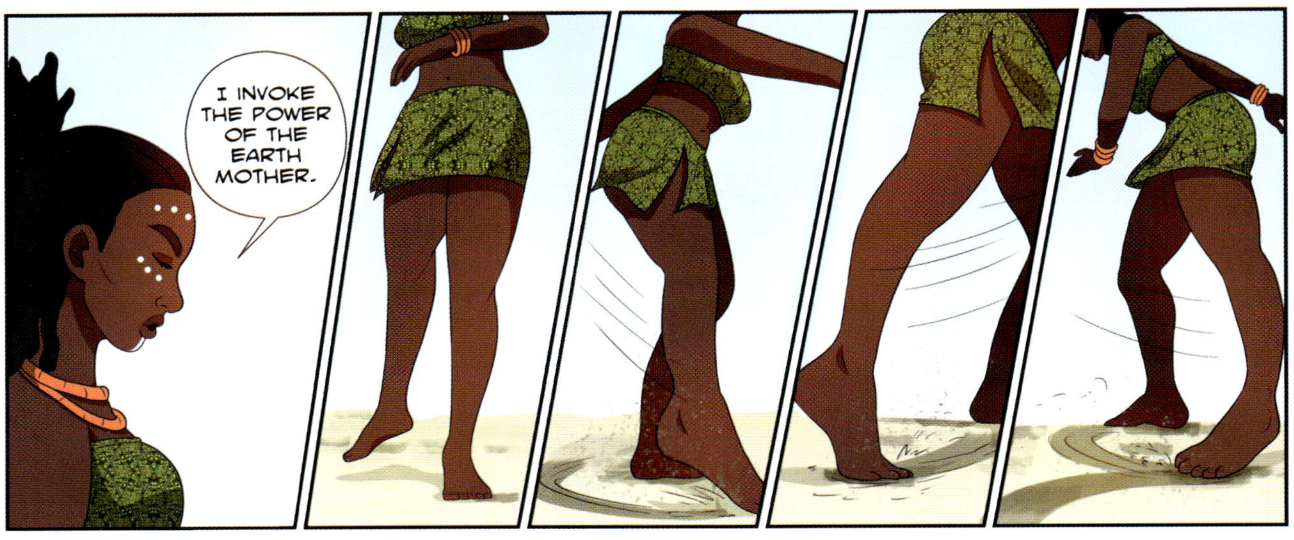
I INVOKE THE POWER OF THE EARTH MOTHER.

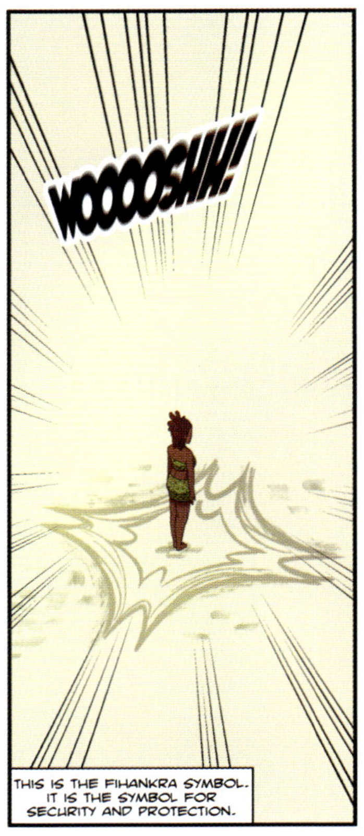
WOOOOSHH!
THIS IS THE FIHANKRA SYMBOL. IT IS THE SYMBOL FOR SECURITY AND PROTECTION.

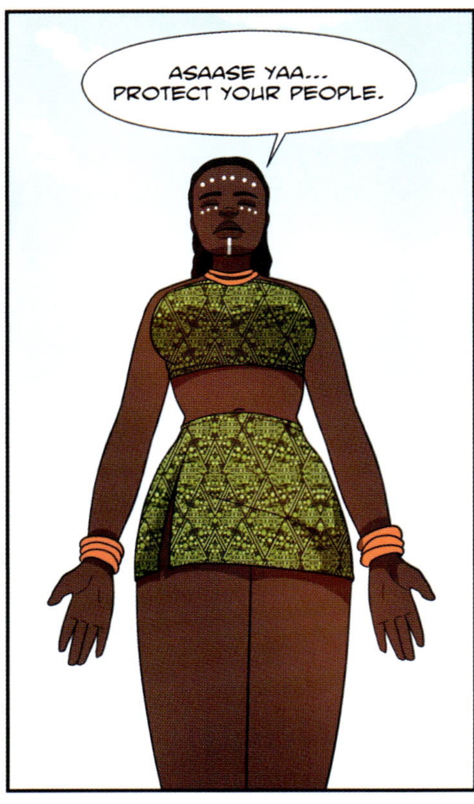
ASAASE YAA... PROTECT YOUR PEOPLE.

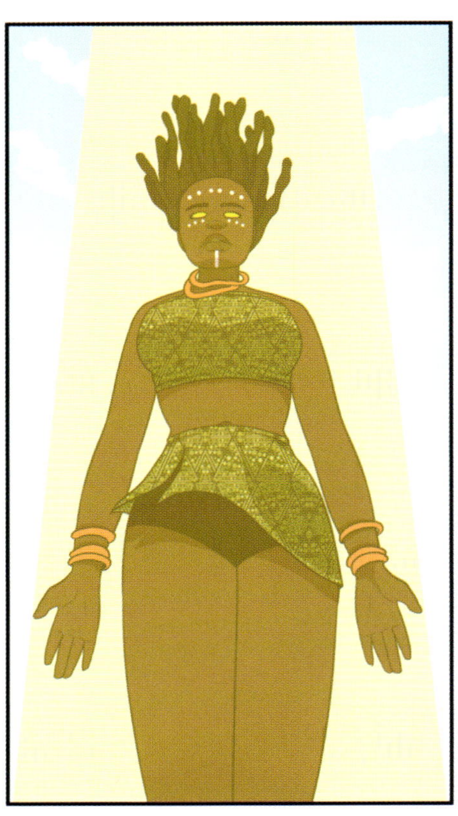

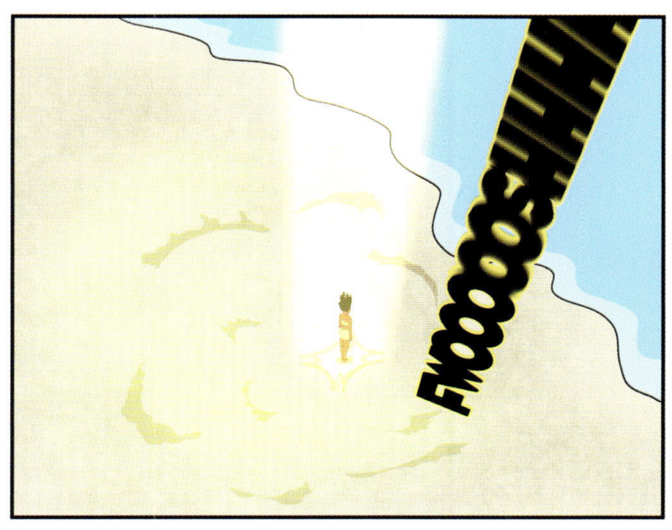
FWOOOOOSHHHH

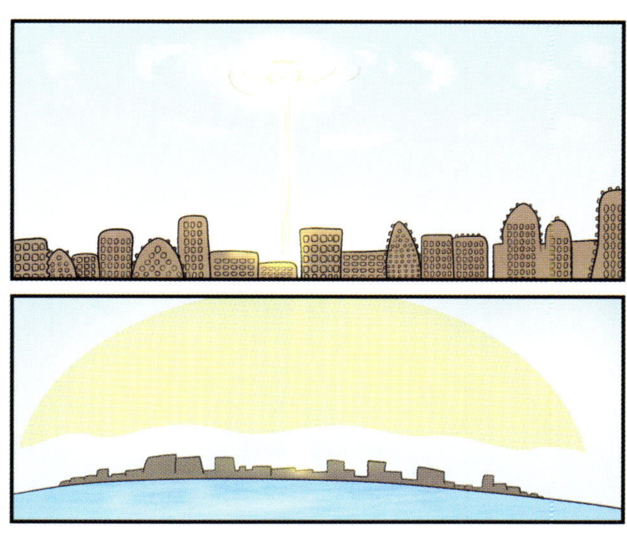

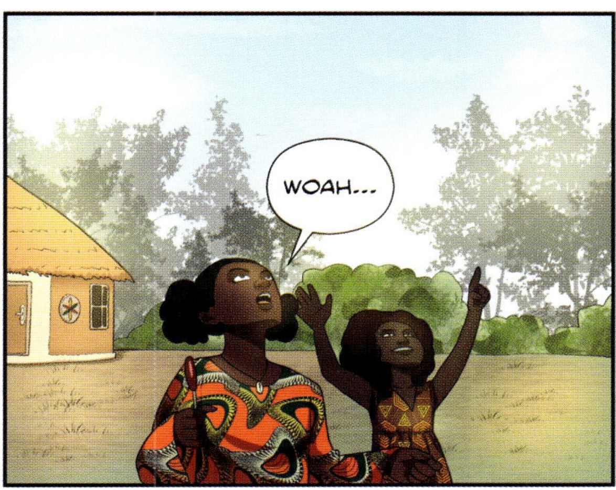
WOAH...

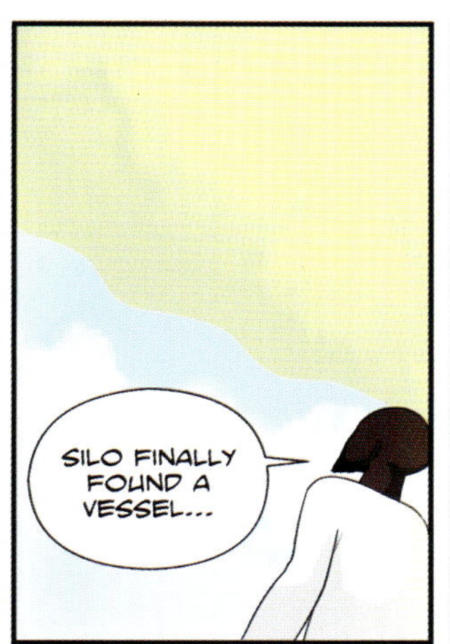
SILO FINALLY FOUND A VESSEL...

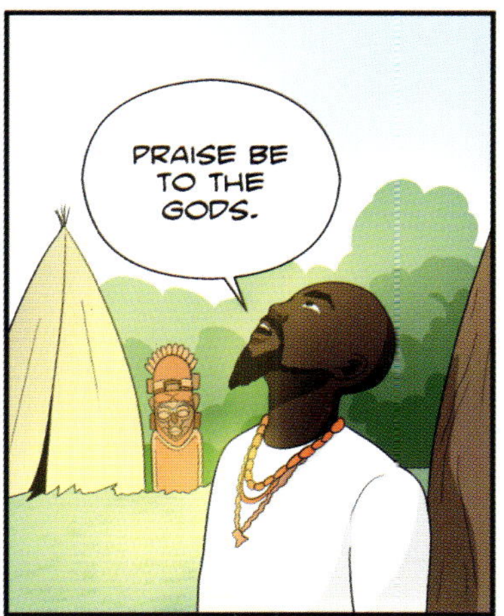
PRAISE BE TO THE GODS.

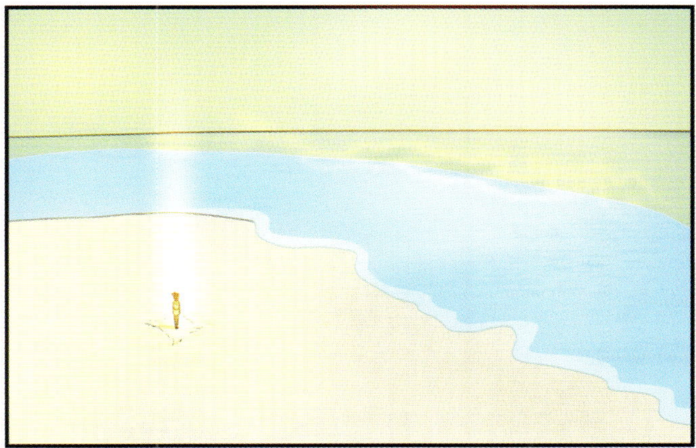

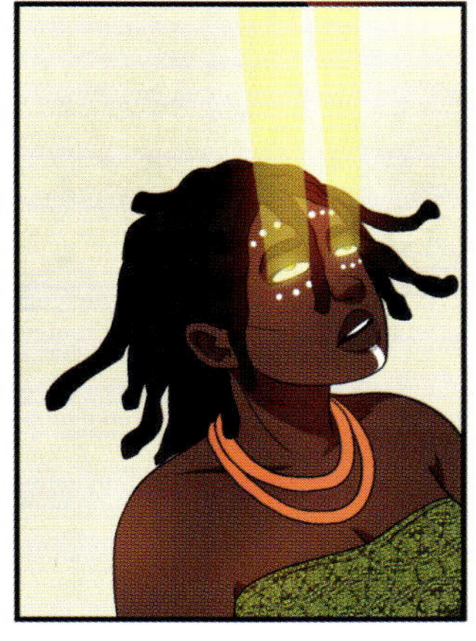

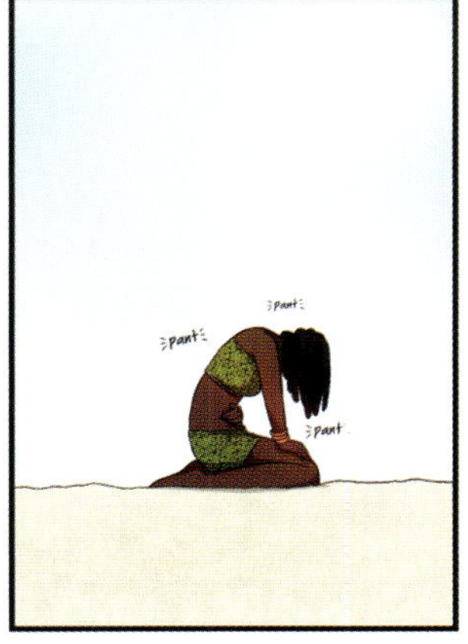
pant
pant
pant

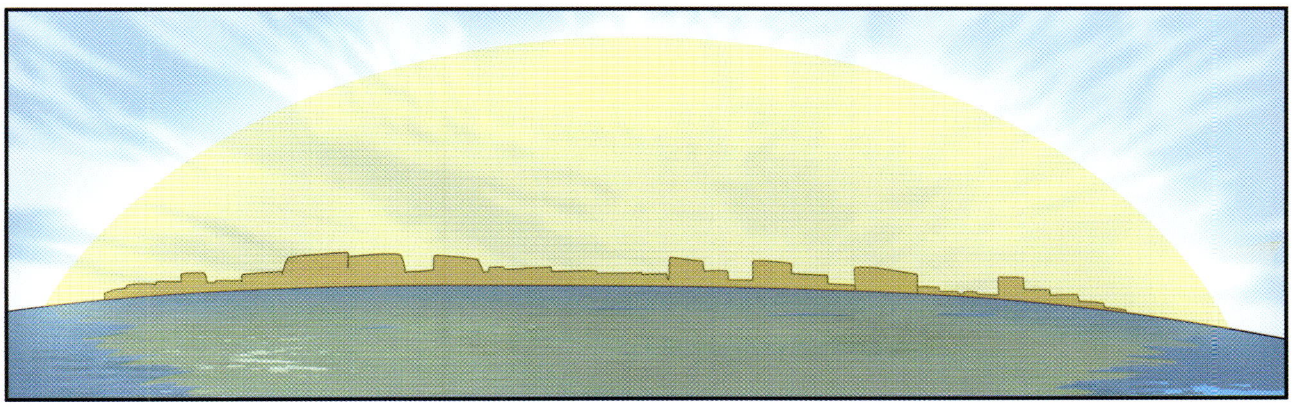

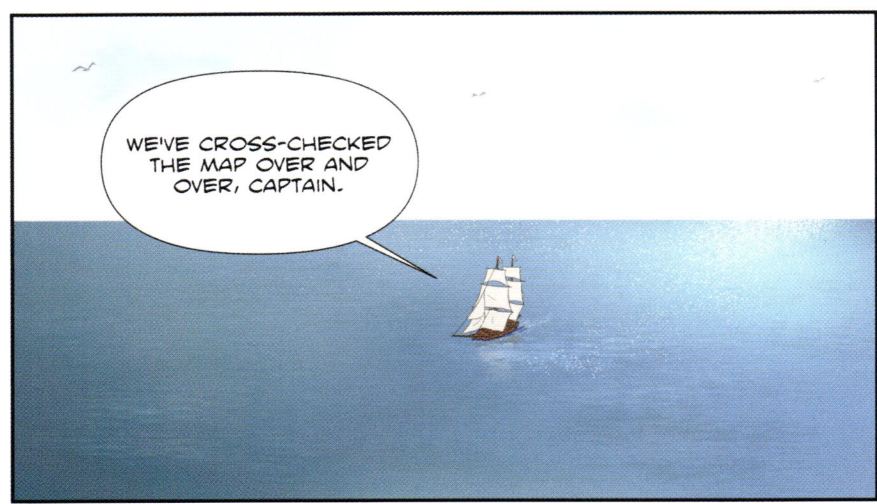
WE'VE CROSS-CHECKED THE MAP OVER AND OVER, CAPTAIN.

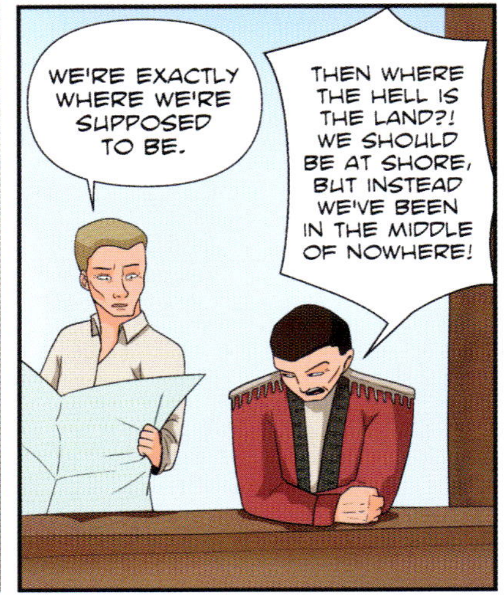
WE'RE EXACTLY WHERE WE'RE SUPPOSED TO BE.
THEN WHERE THE HELL IS THE LAND?! WE SHOULD BE AT SHORE, BUT INSTEAD WE'VE BEEN IN THE MIDDLE OF NOWHERE!

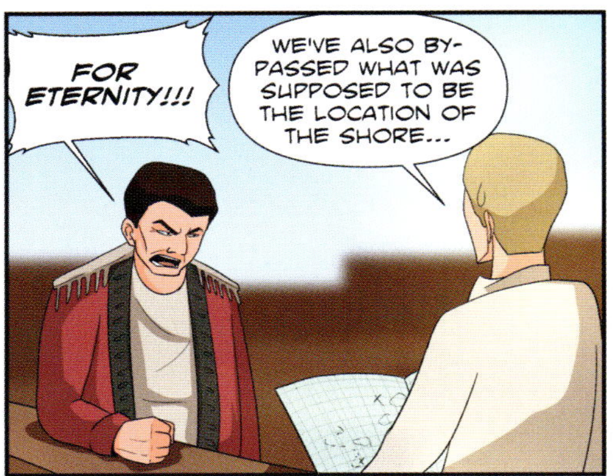
FOR ETERNITY!!!
WE'VE ALSO BY-PASSED WHAT WAS SUPPOSED TO BE THE LOCATION OF THE SHORE...

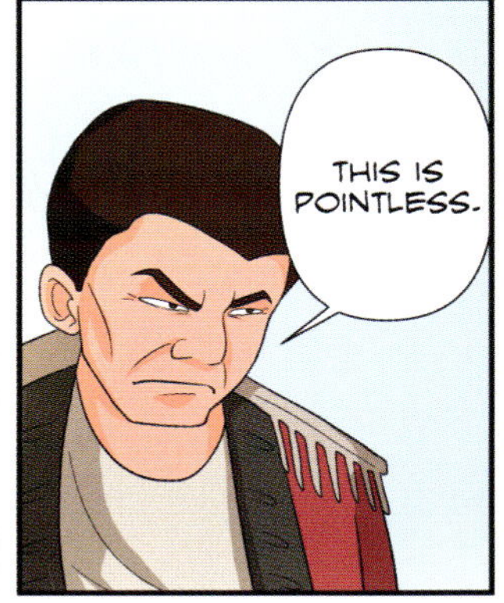
THIS IS POINTLESS.

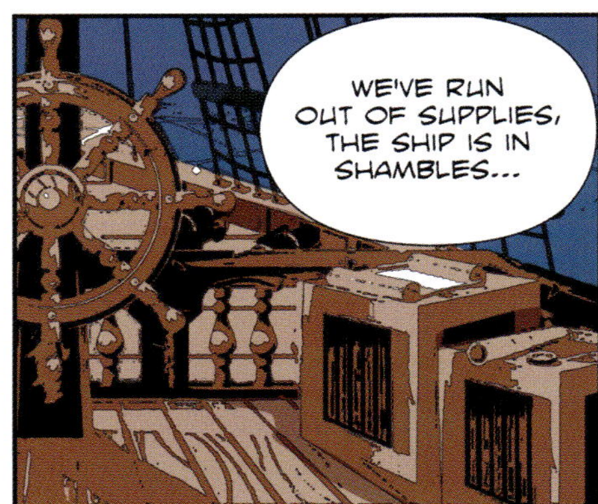
WE'VE RUN OUT OF SUPPLIES, THE SHIP IS IN SHAMBLES...

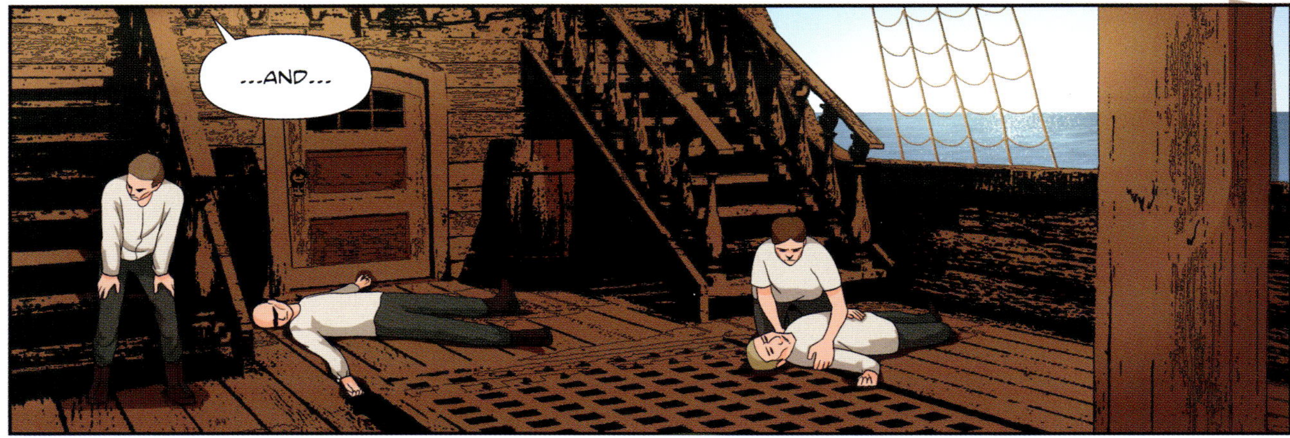
...AND...

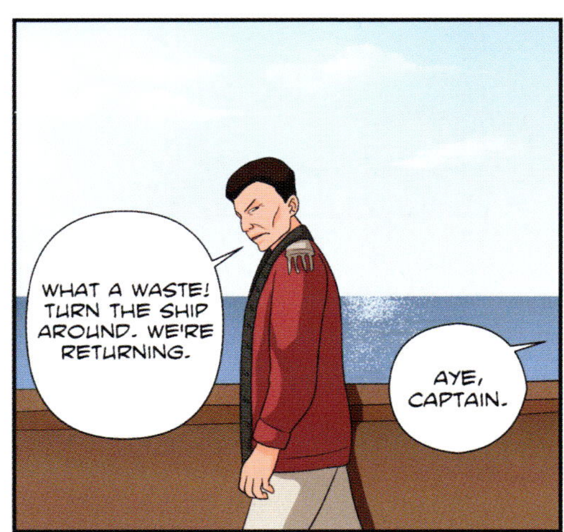
WHAT A WASTE! TURN THE SHIP AROUND. WE'RE RETURNING.
AYE, CAPTAIN.

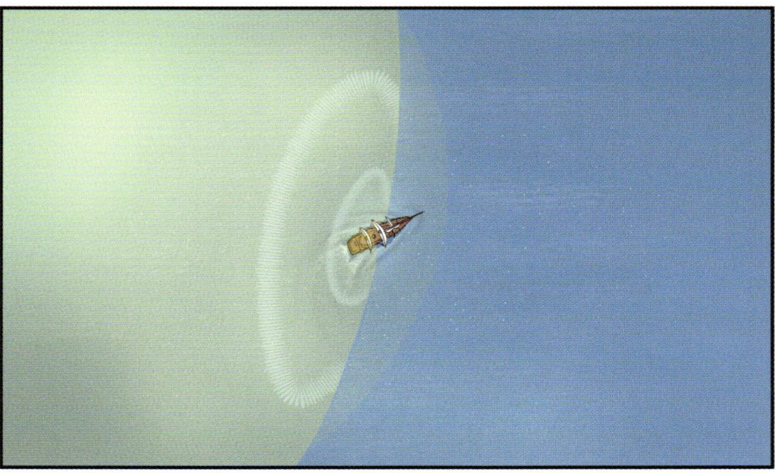

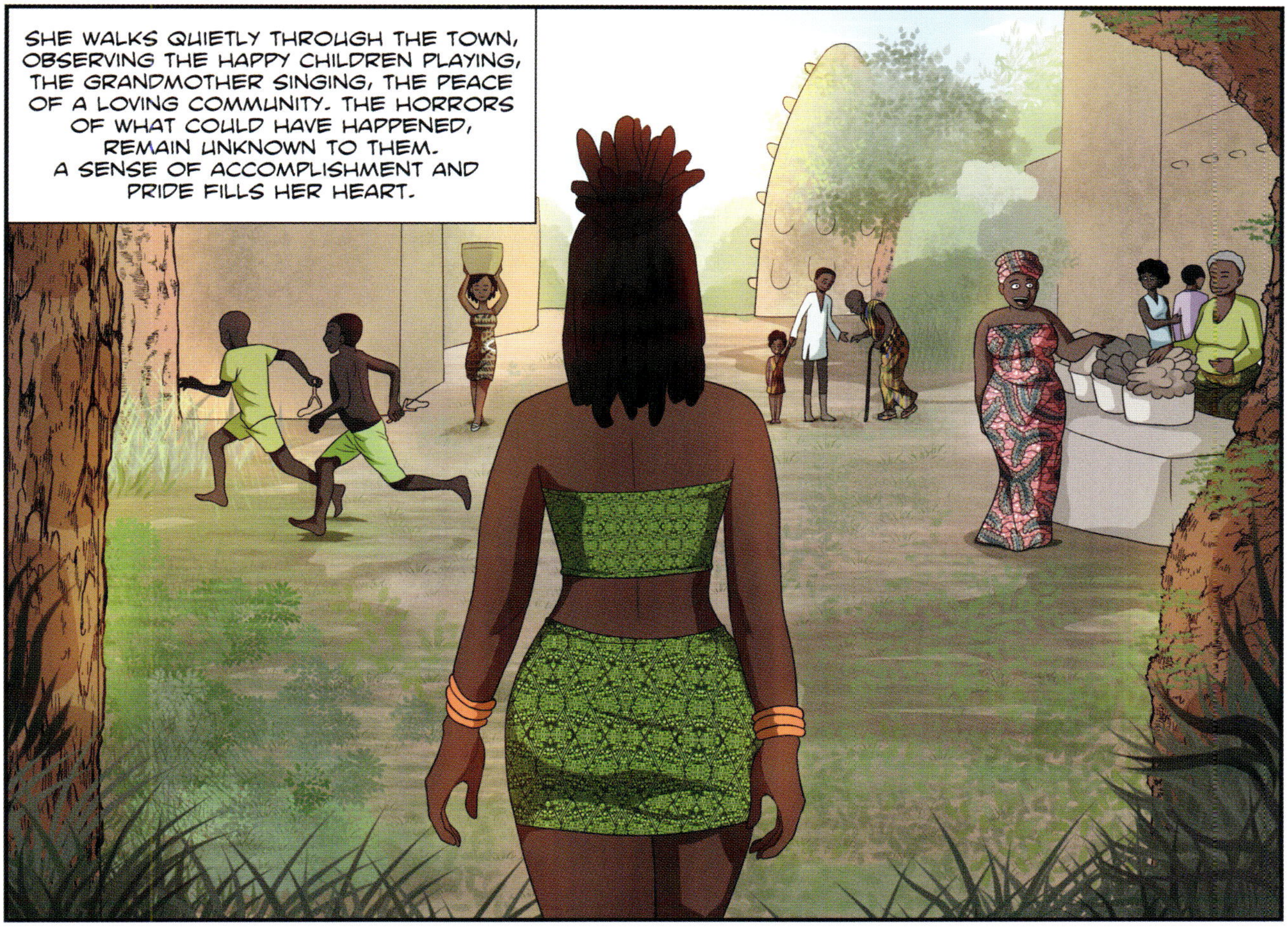

SHE WALKS QUIETLY THROUGH THE TOWN, OBSERVING THE HAPPY CHILDREN PLAYING, THE GRANDMOTHER SINGING, THE PEACE OF A LOVING COMMUNITY. THE HORRORS OF WHAT COULD HAVE HAPPENED, REMAIN UNKNOWN TO THEM.
A SENSE OF ACCOMPLISHMENT AND PRIDE FILLS HER HEART.

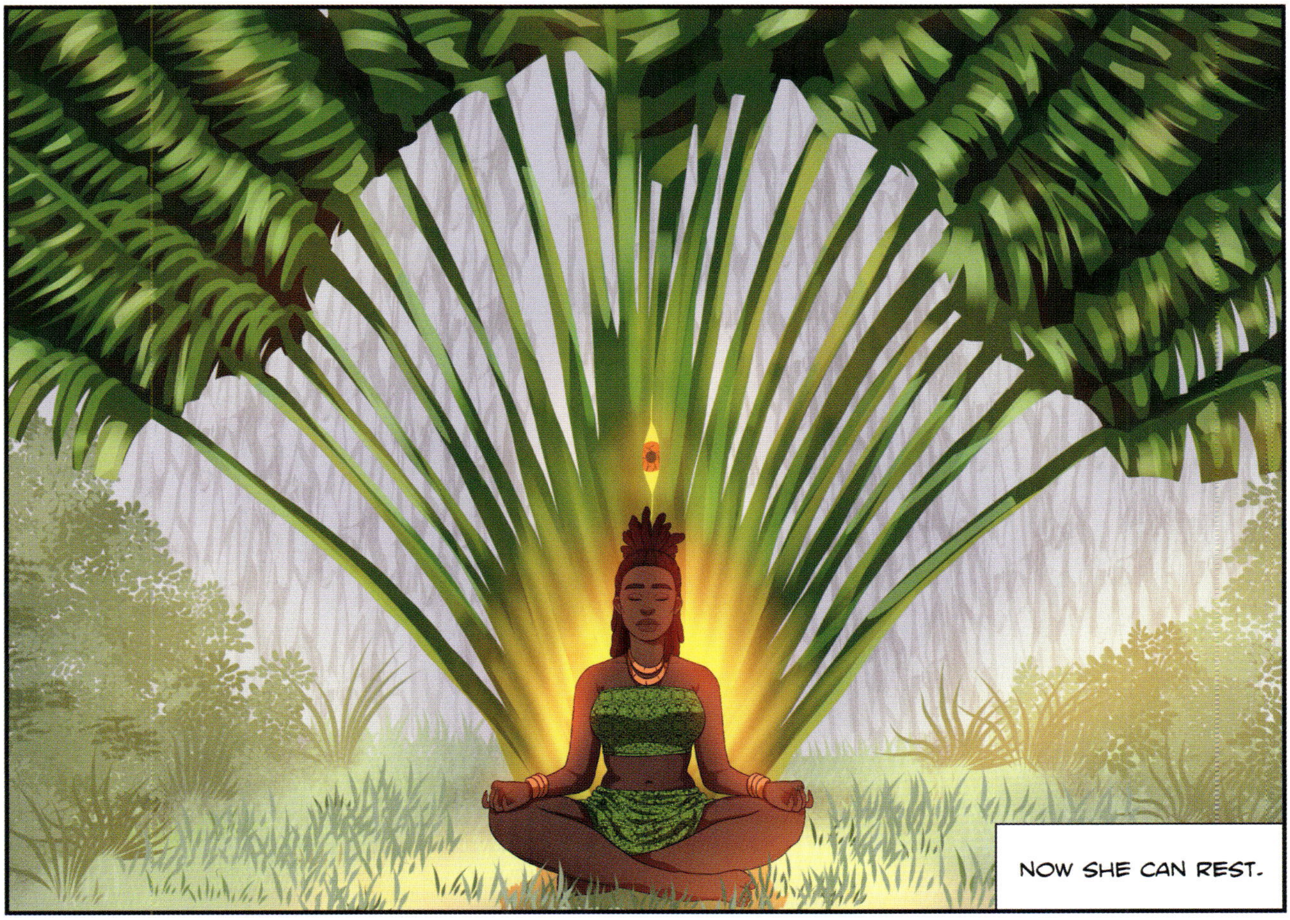

NOW SHE CAN REST.

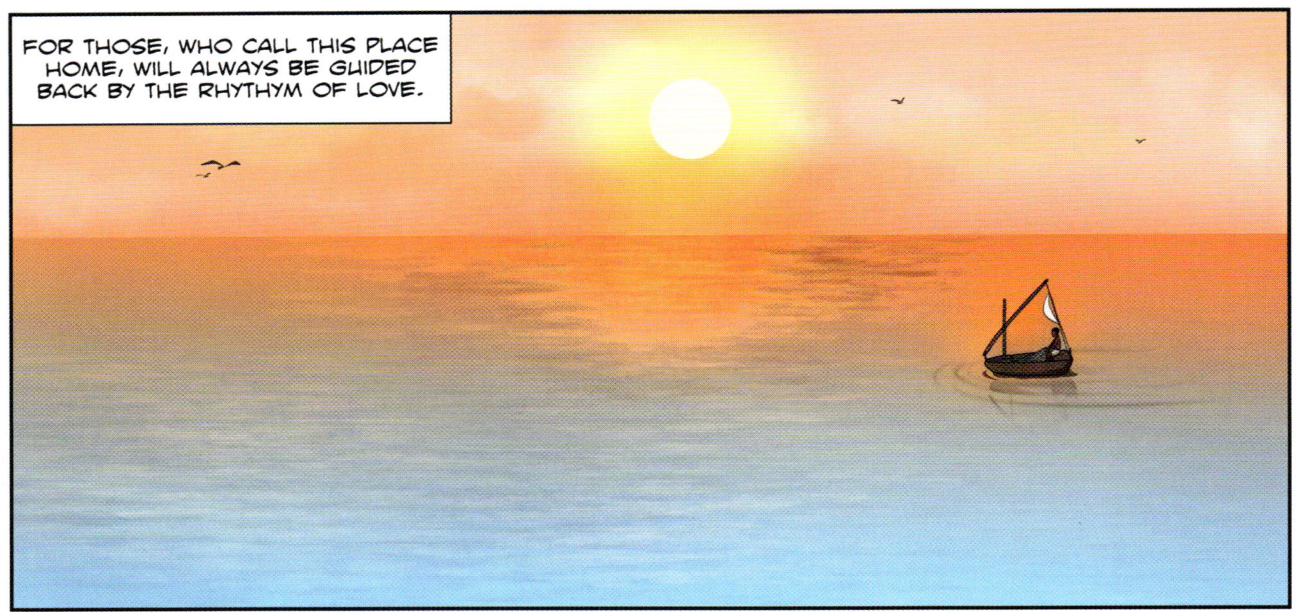
FOR THOSE, WHO CALL THIS PLACE HOME, WILL ALWAYS BE GUIDED BACK BY THE RHYTHYM OF LOVE.

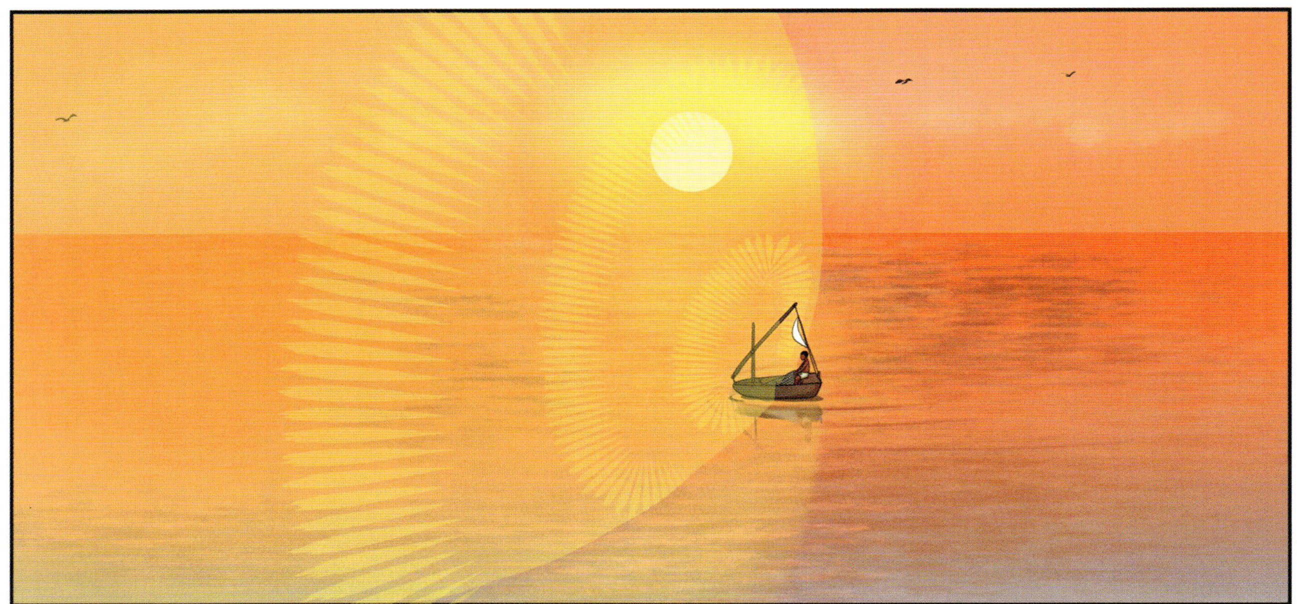

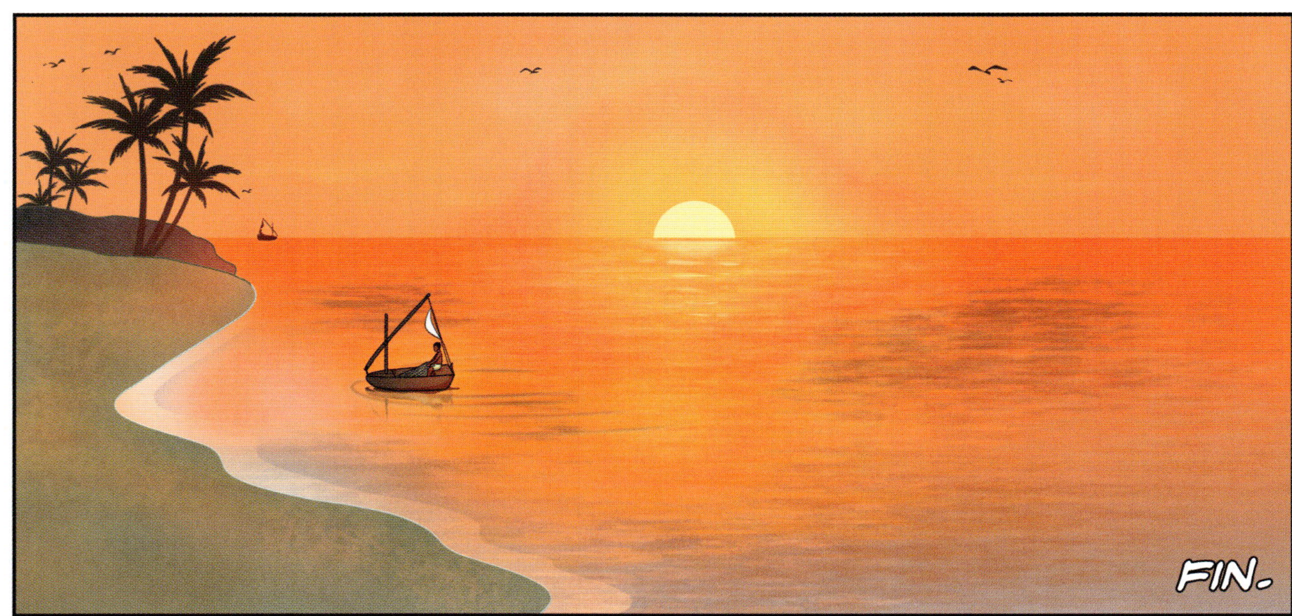
FIN.

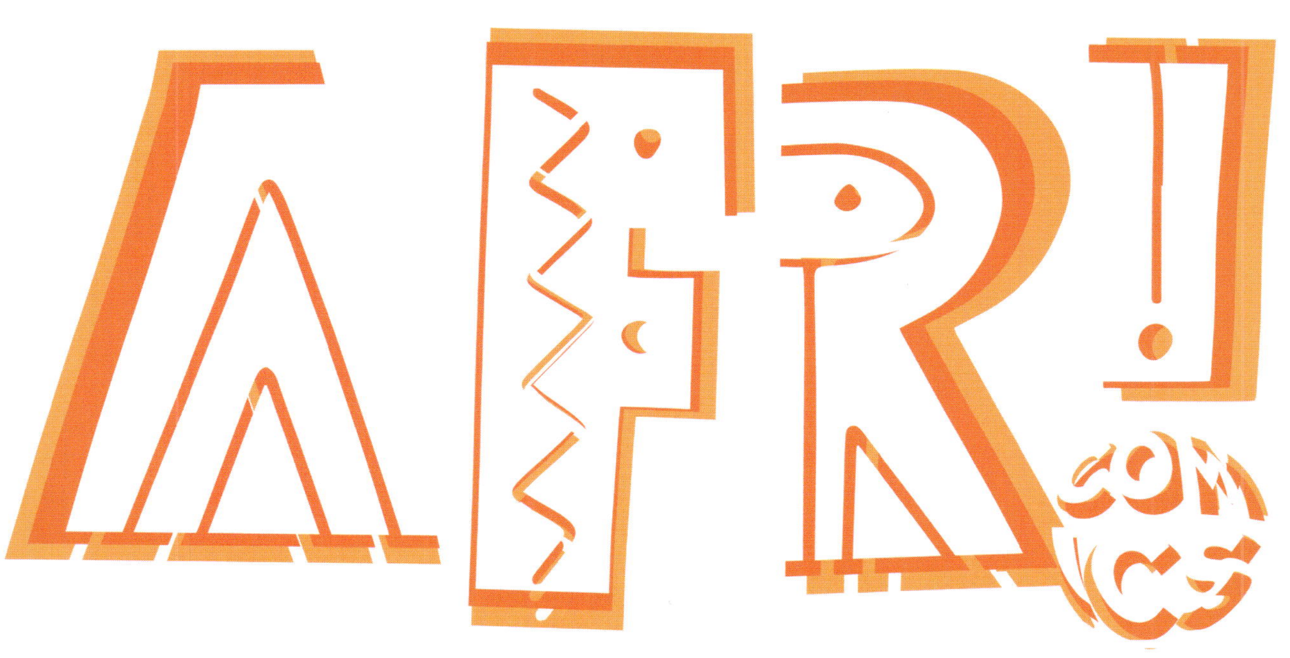
AFR!
COM
ICS

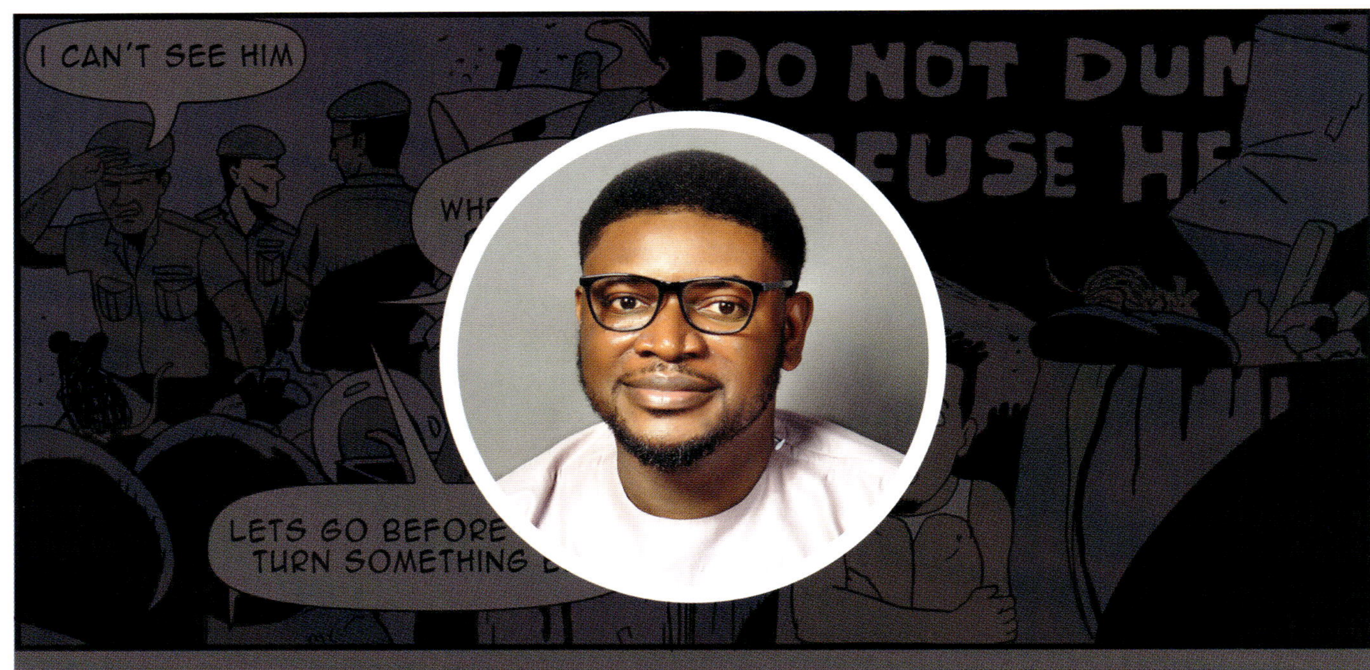

Baba Aminu Mustapha

Artist | Illustrator

A self-taught artist with a background in electrical computer engineering, Baba Aminu Mustapha from Nigeria has gained notoriety for his talent to illustrate stunning visual interpretations. He has collaborated with numerous people and organizations over the years, producing stunning illustrations that, particularly in children's books, have captured the attention of audiences all over the world.

In addition to his work as a freelance artist and illustrator Baba Aminu Mustapha hopes to run an animation studio that tells African stories to the world. He is dedicated to using his art to spread awareness of African society and culture, and he sees comics and animation as effective mediums for doing so. The goal of Baba Aminu Mustapha's work is to provide captivating, high-quality visual contents and stories that celebrate the diversity and depth of African traditions. He desires that his work will inspire and enlighten people around the world about the beauty and complexity of African stories and cultures.

He is a well-known person in the illustration community thanks to his commitment to his profession and his talent for producing exquisite works of art.

NIGERIA

Facebook : Baba9ja4life
Instagram : bamanimax
Twiter : babaminustapha
Website : www.bamanimax.com

THE RETURN

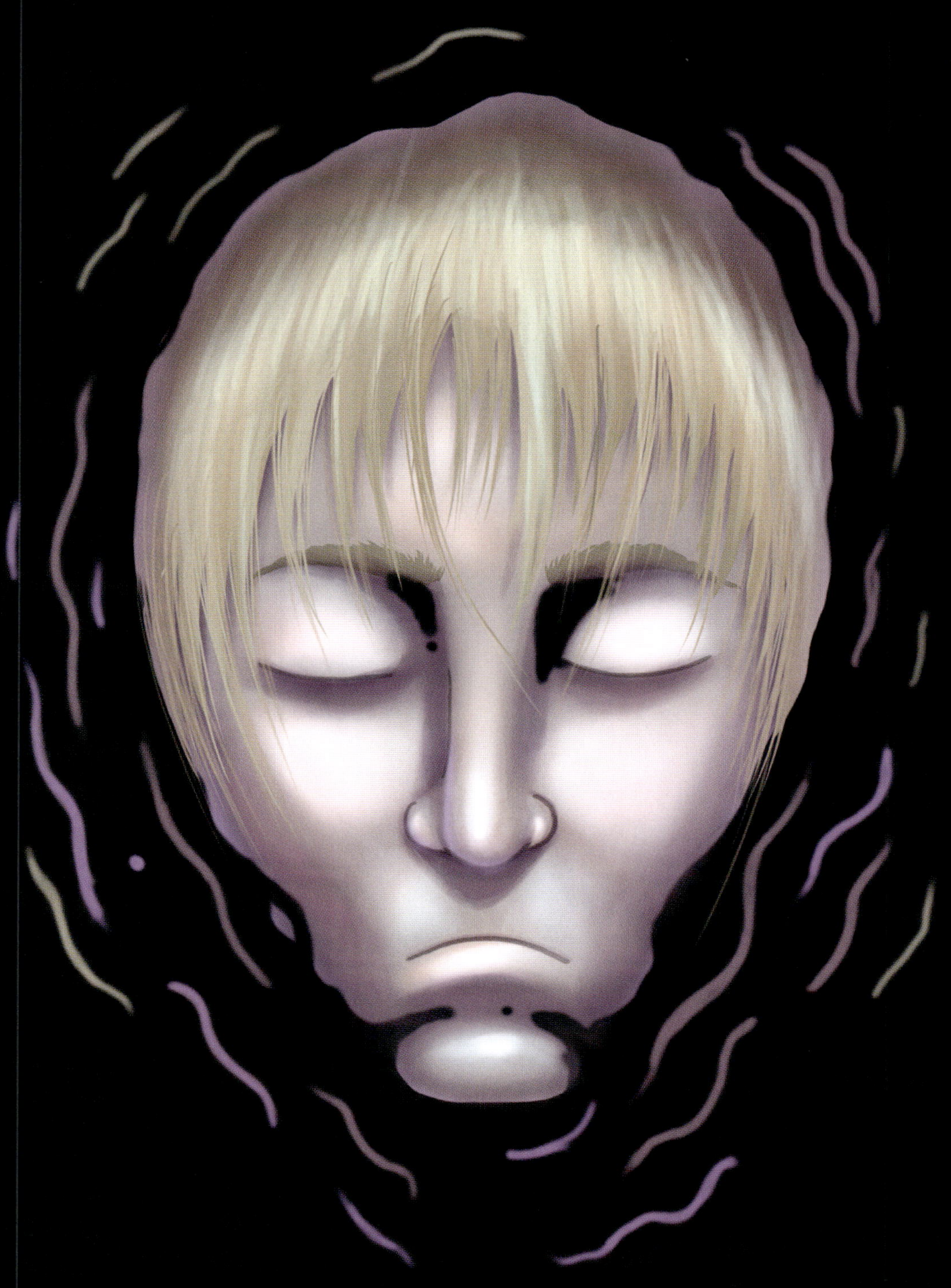

By: Baba Aminu Mustapha

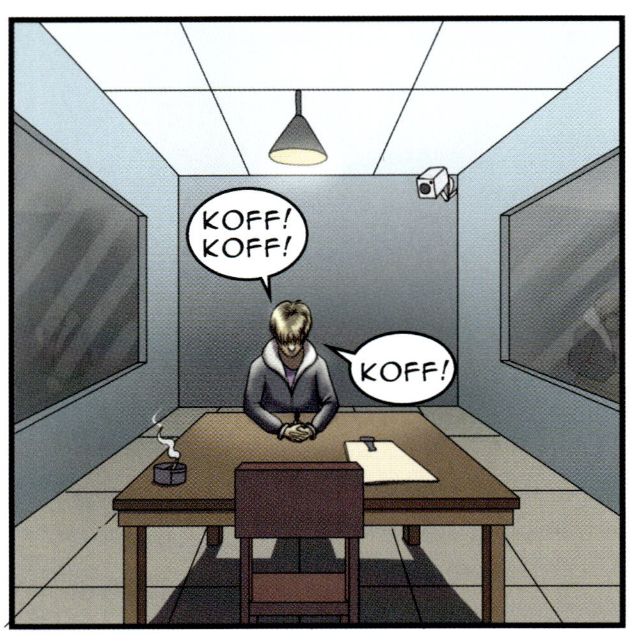
KOFF! KOFF!
KOFF!

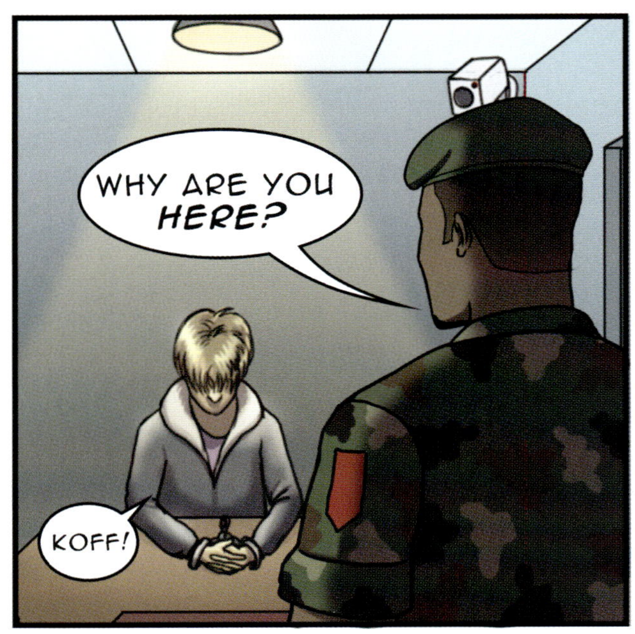
WHY ARE YOU *HERE?*
KOFF!

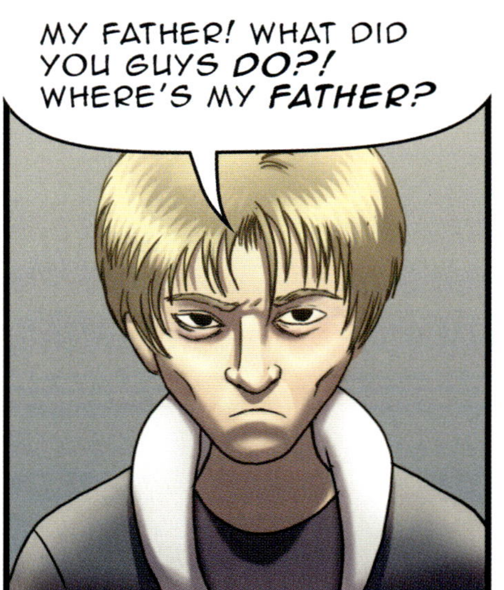
MY FATHER! WHAT DID YOU GUYS *DO?!* WHERE'S MY *FATHER?*

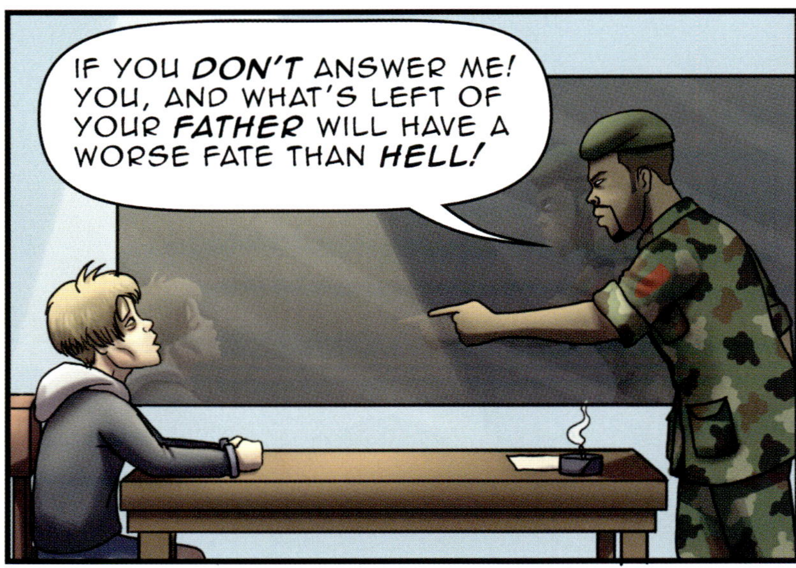
IF YOU *DON'T* ANSWER ME! YOU, AND WHAT'S LEFT OF YOUR *FATHER* WILL HAVE A WORSE FATE THAN *HELL!*

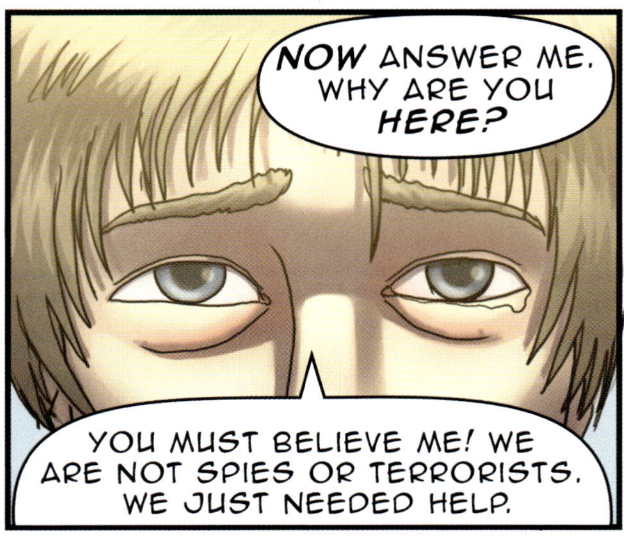
NOW ANSWER ME. WHY ARE YOU *HERE?*
YOU MUST BELIEVE ME! WE ARE NOT SPIES OR TERRORISTS. WE JUST NEEDED HELP.

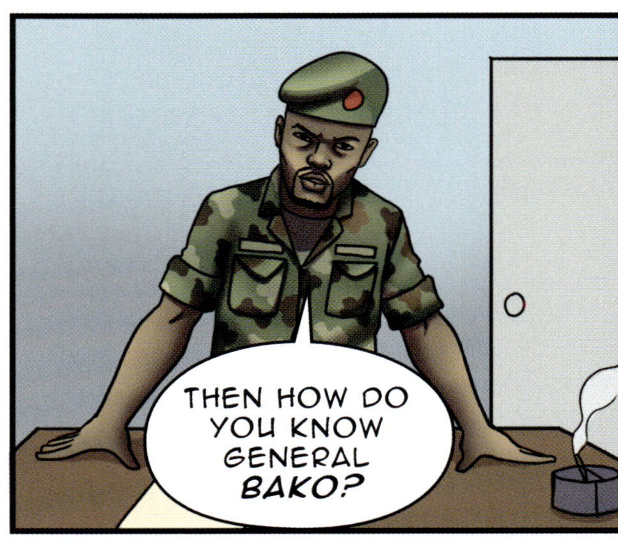
THEN HOW DO YOU KNOW GENERAL *BAKO?*

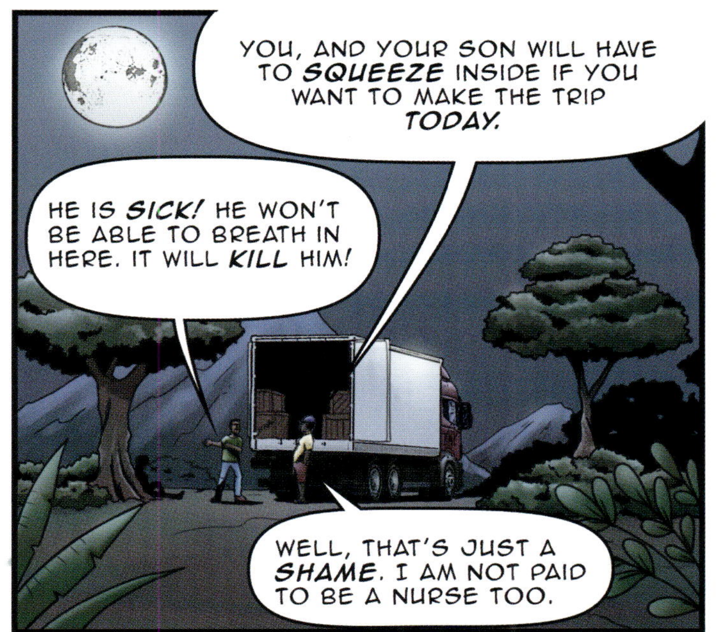
YOU, AND YOUR SON WILL HAVE TO SQUEEZE INSIDE IF YOU WANT TO MAKE THE TRIP TODAY.
HE IS SICK! HE WON'T BE ABLE TO BREATH IN HERE. IT WILL KILL HIM!
WELL, THAT'S JUST A SHAME. I AM NOT PAID TO BE A NURSE TOO.

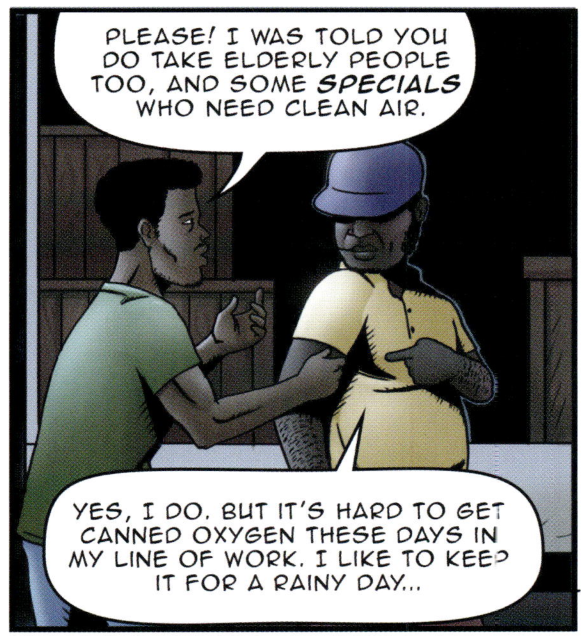
PLEASE! I WAS TOLD YOU DO TAKE ELDERLY PEOPLE TOO, AND SOME SPECIALS WHO NEED CLEAN AIR.
YES, I DO. BUT IT'S HARD TO GET CANNED OXYGEN THESE DAYS IN MY LINE OF WORK. I LIKE TO KEEP IT FOR A RAINY DAY...

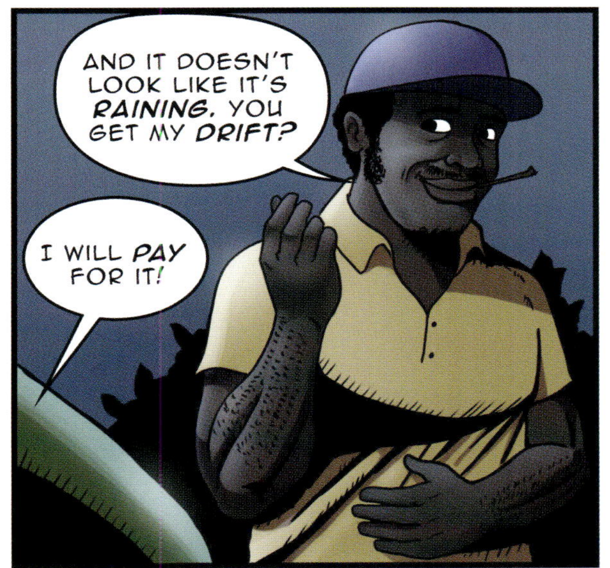
AND IT DOESN'T LOOK LIKE IT'S RAINING. YOU GET MY DRIFT?
I WILL PAY FOR IT!

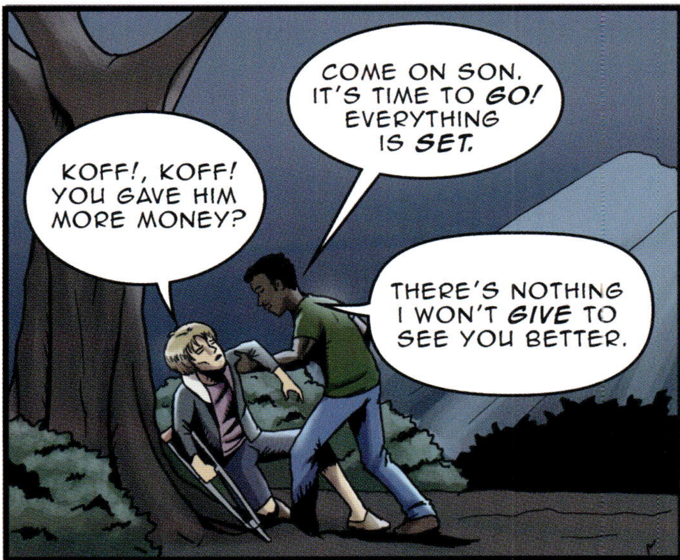
COME ON SON. IT'S TIME TO GO! EVERYTHING IS SET.
KOFF!, KOFF! YOU GAVE HIM MORE MONEY?
THERE'S NOTHING I WON'T GIVE TO SEE YOU BETTER.

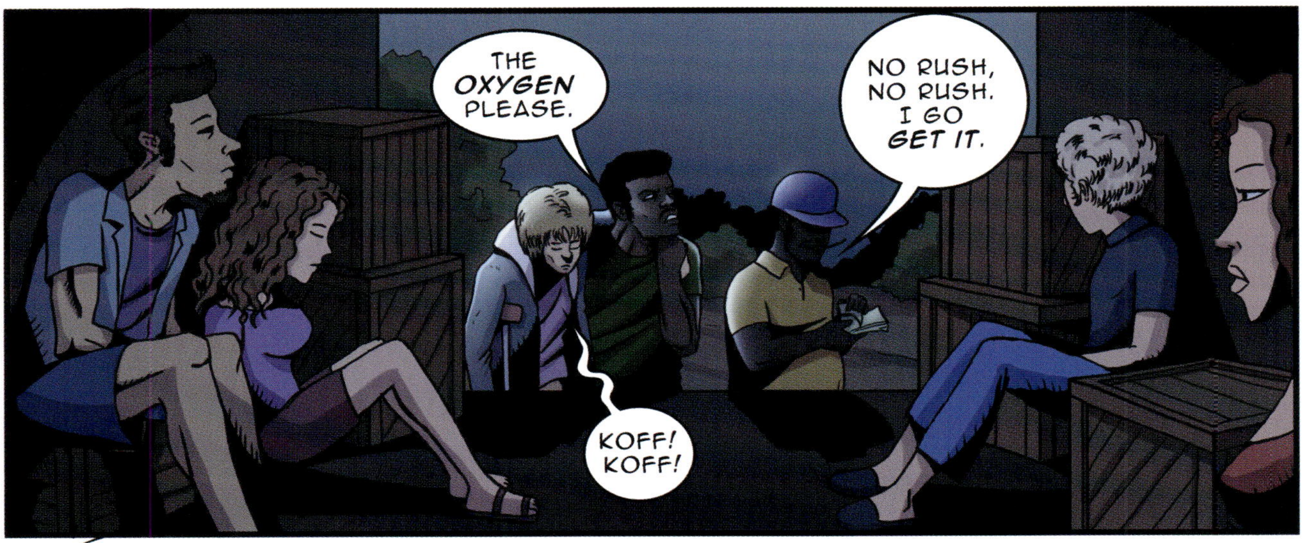
THE OXYGEN PLEASE.
KOFF! KOFF!
NO RUSH, NO RUSH. I GO GET IT.

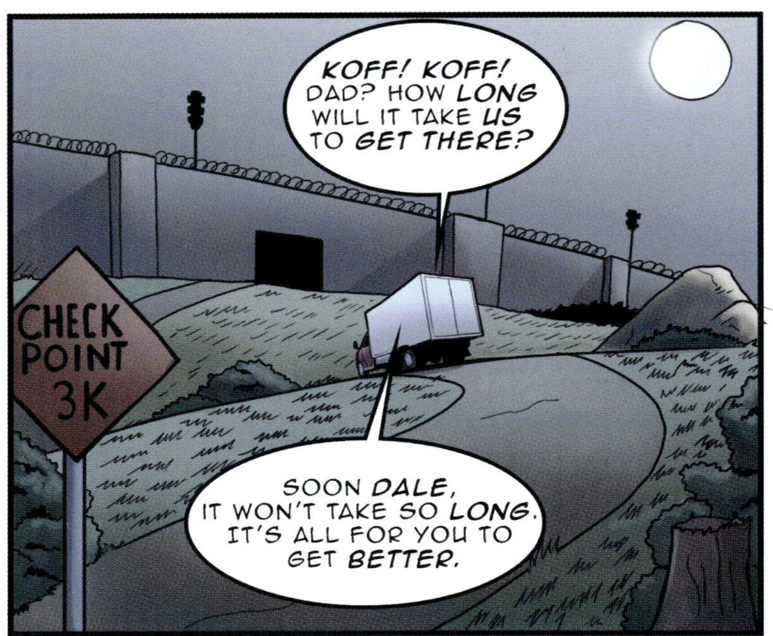
KOFF! KOFF! DAD? HOW LONG WILL IT TAKE US TO GET THERE?
CHECK POINT 3K
SOON DALE, IT WON'T TAKE SO LONG. IT'S ALL FOR YOU TO GET BETTER.

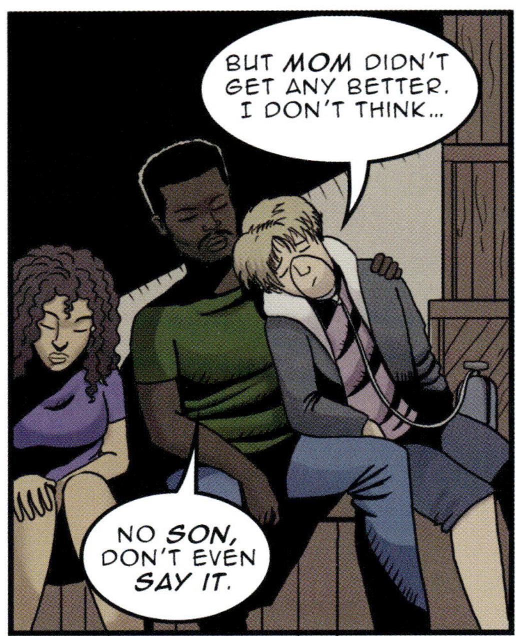
BUT MOM DIDN'T GET ANY BETTER. I DON'T THINK...
NO SON, DON'T EVEN SAY IT.

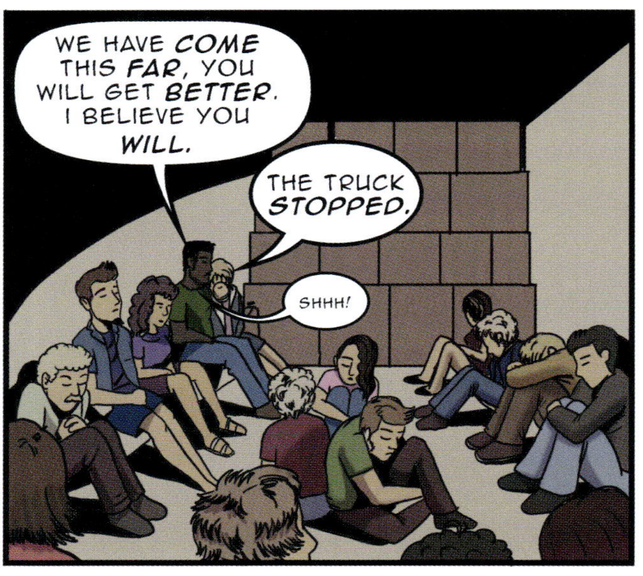
WE HAVE COME THIS FAR, YOU WILL GET BETTER. I BELIEVE YOU WILL.
THE TRUCK STOPPED.
SHHH!

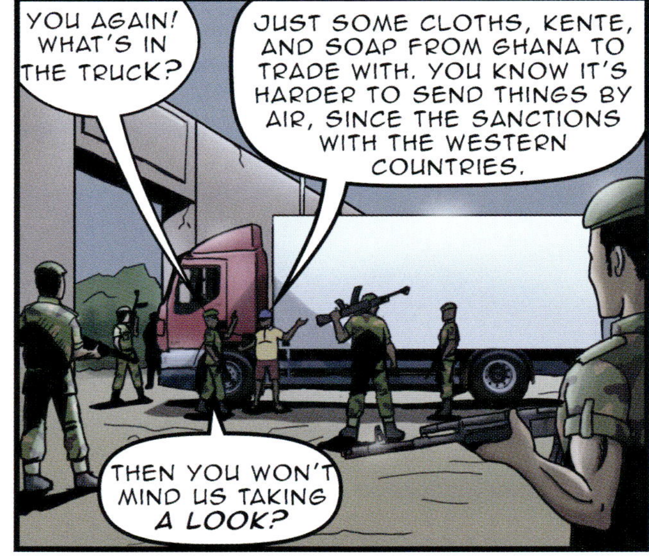
YOU AGAIN! WHAT'S IN THE TRUCK?
JUST SOME CLOTHS, KENTE, AND SOAP FROM GHANA TO TRADE WITH. YOU KNOW IT'S HARDER TO SEND THINGS BY AIR, SINCE THE SANCTIONS WITH THE WESTERN COUNTRIES.
THEN YOU WON'T MIND US TAKING A LOOK?

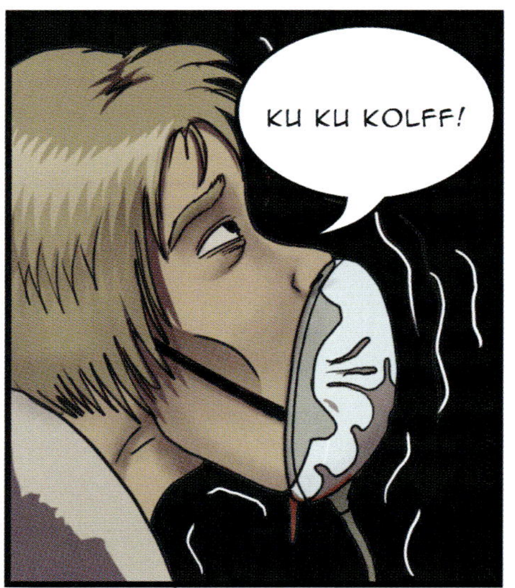
KU KU KOLFF!

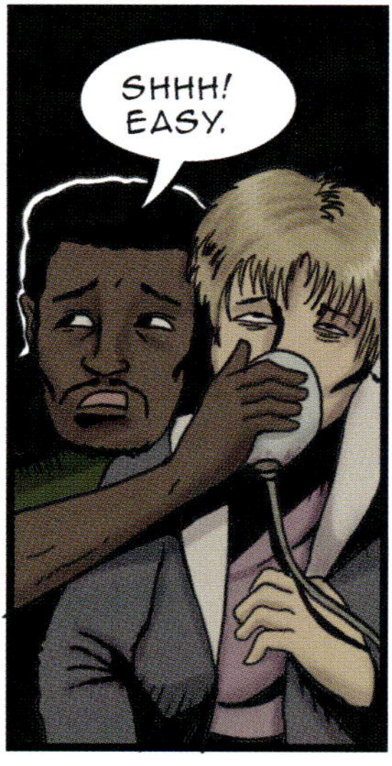
SHHH! EASY.

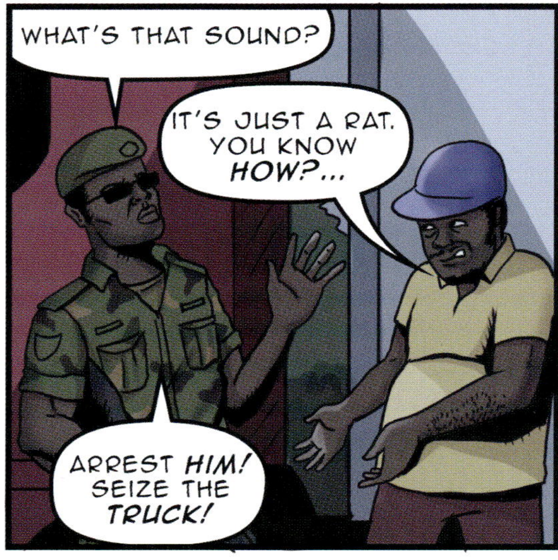
WHAT'S THAT SOUND?
IT'S JUST A RAT. YOU KNOW HOW?...
ARREST HIM! SEIZE THE TRUCK!

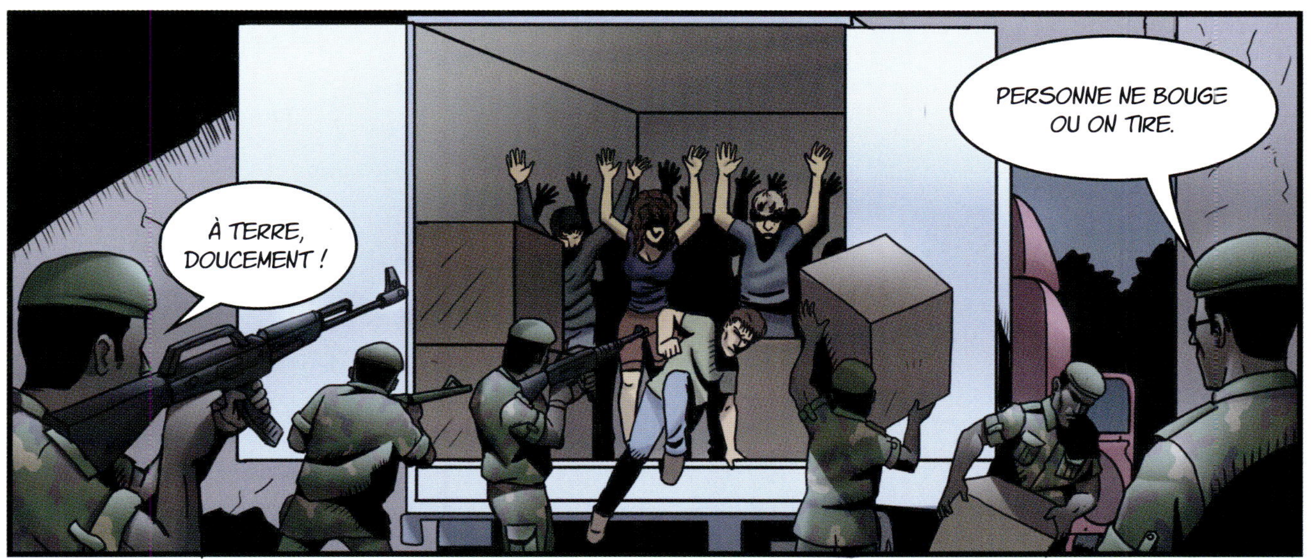
À TERRE, DOUCEMENT !
PERSONNE NE BOUGE OU ON TIRE.

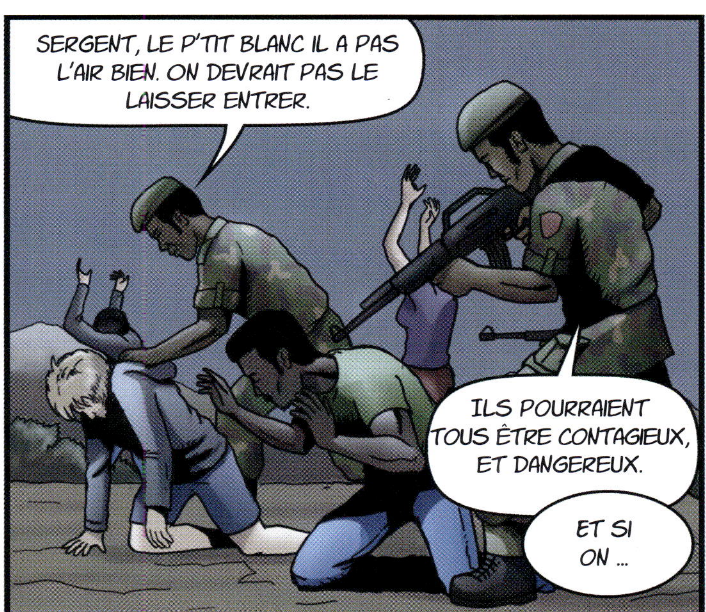
SERGENT, LE P'TIT BLANC IL A PAS L'AIR BIEN. ON DEVRAIT PAS LE LAISSER ENTRER.
ILS POURRAIENT TOUS ÊTRE CONTAGIEUX, ET DANGEREUX.
ET SI ON ...

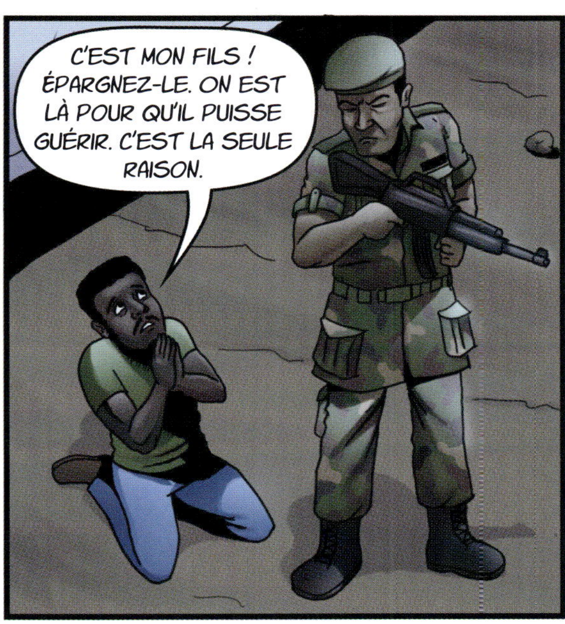
C'EST MON FILS ! ÉPARGNEZ-LE. ON EST LÀ POUR QU'IL PUISSE GUÉRIR. C'EST LA SEULE RAISON.

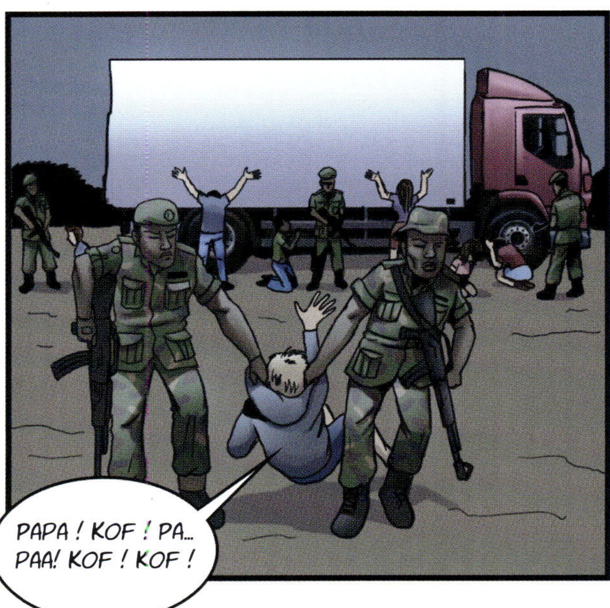
PAPA ! KOF ! PA... PAA! KOF ! KOF !

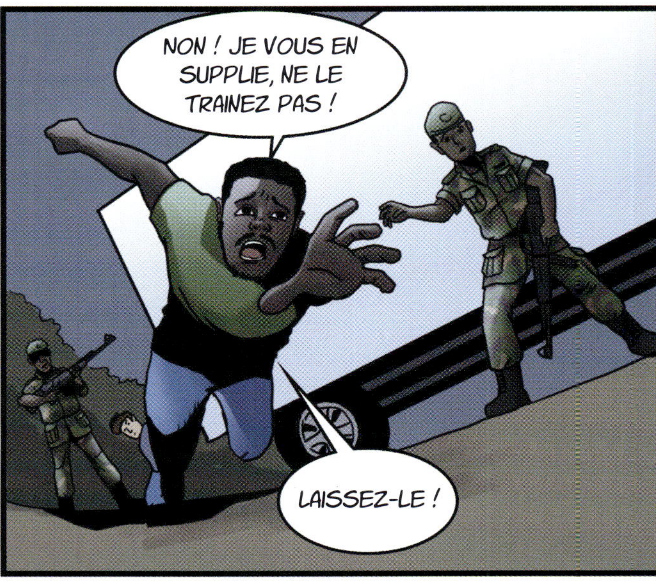
NON ! JE VOUS EN SUPPLIE, NE LE TRAINEZ PAS !
LAISSEZ-LE !

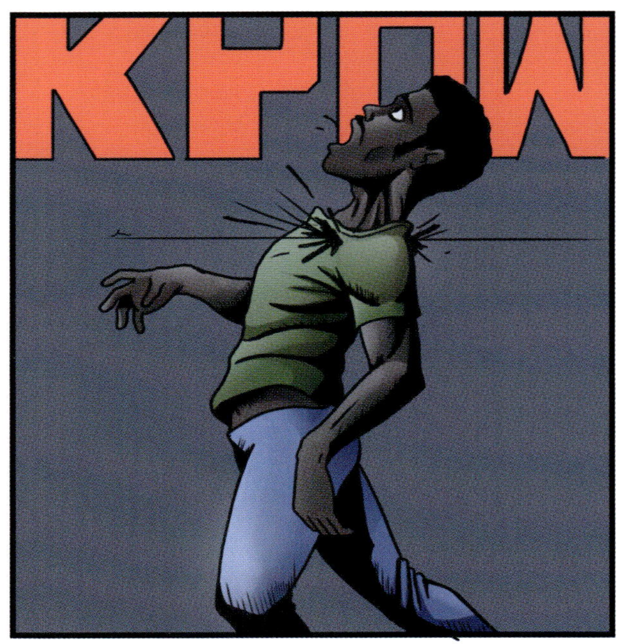
KPOW

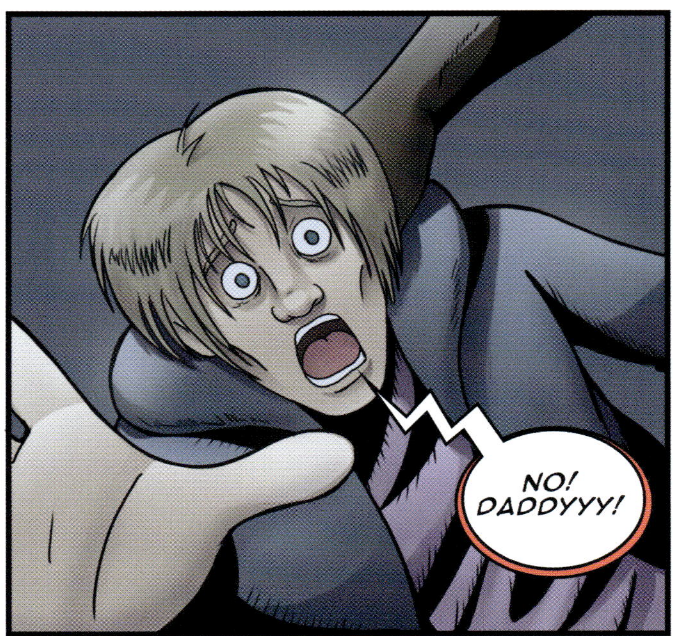
NO! DADDYYY!

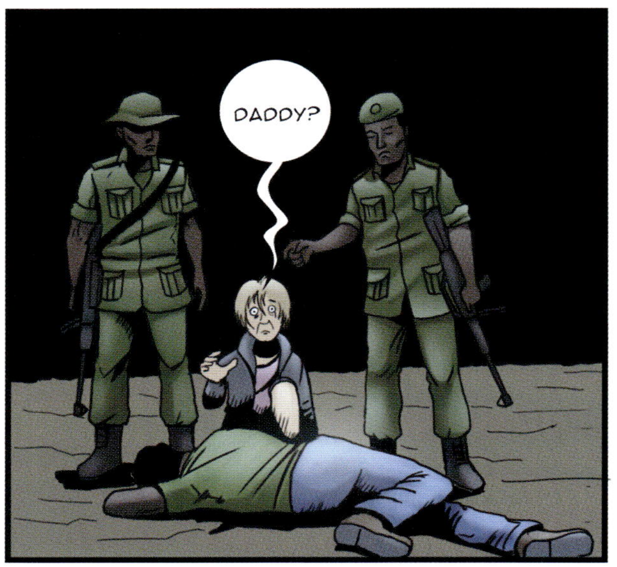
DADDY?

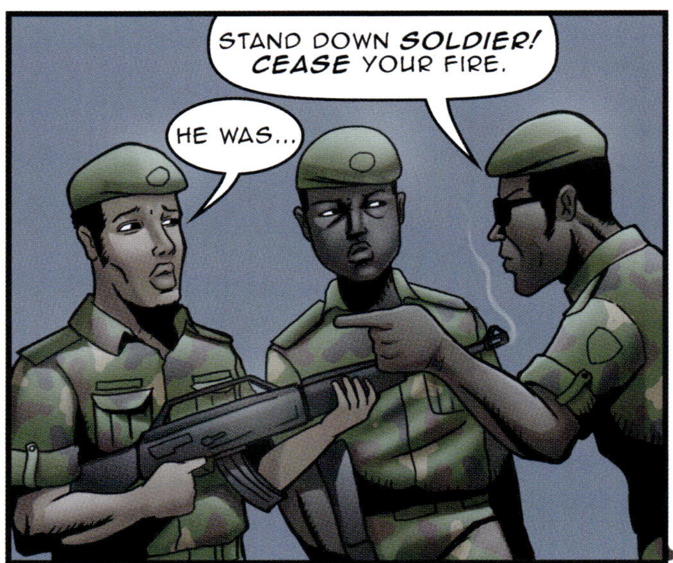
STAND DOWN SOLDIER! CEASE YOUR FIRE.
HE WAS...

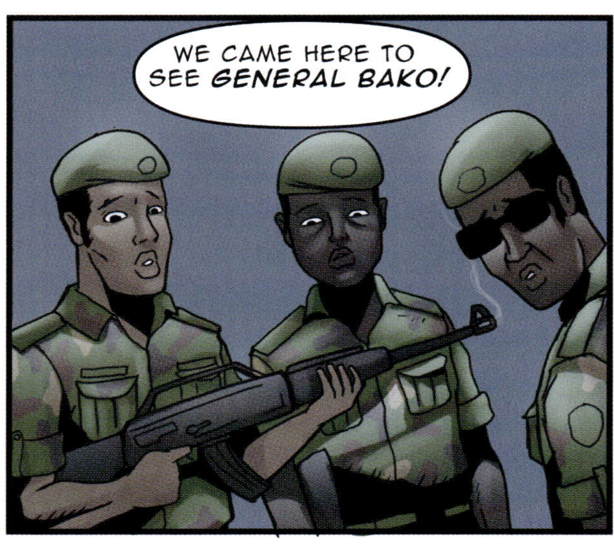
WE CAME HERE TO SEE GENERAL BAKO!

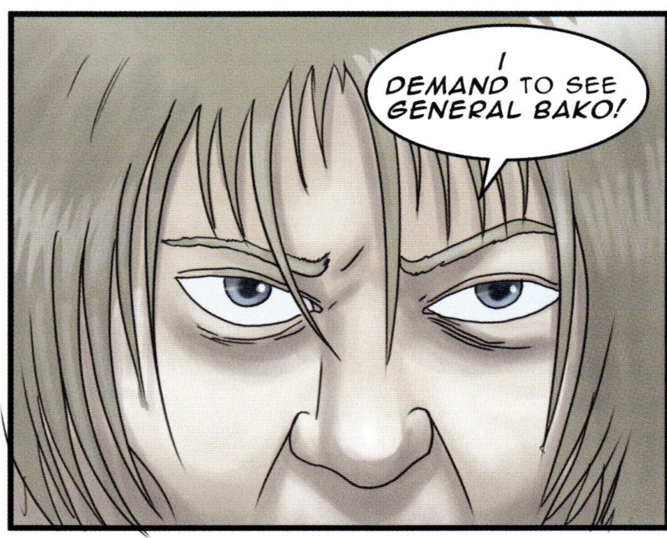
I DEMAND TO SEE GENERAL BAKO!

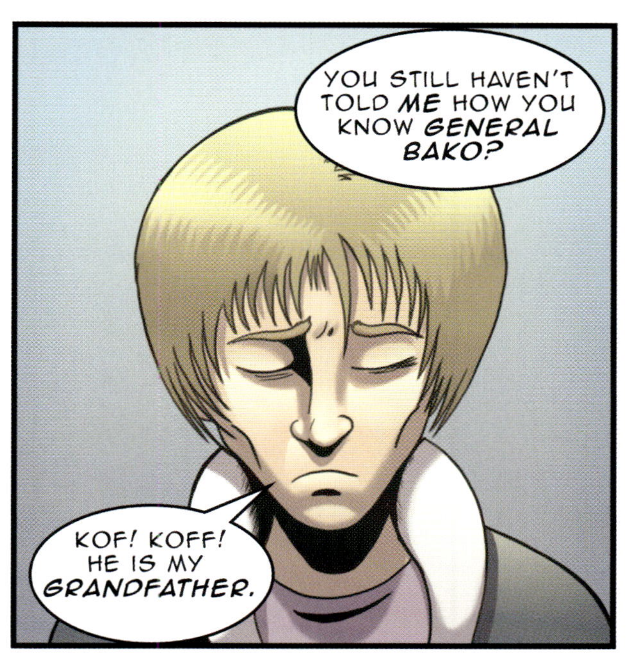
YOU STILL HAVEN'T TOLD ME HOW YOU KNOW GENERAL BAKO?
KOF! KOFF! HE IS MY GRANDFATHER.

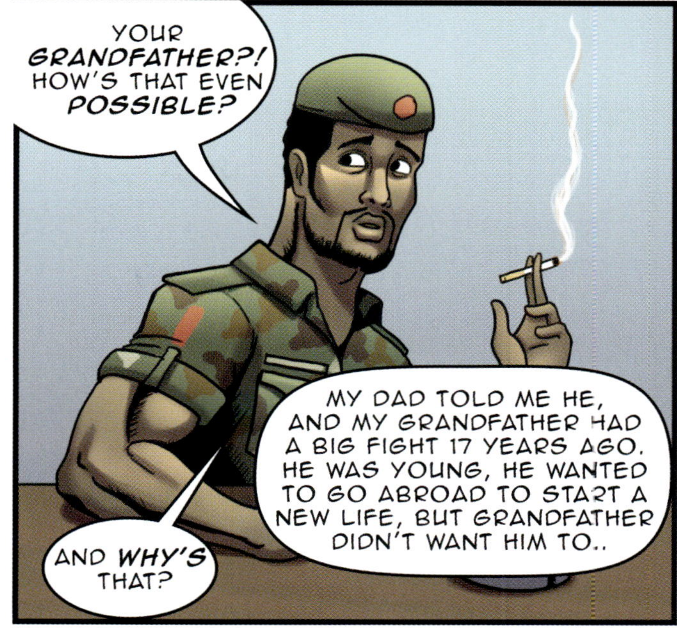
YOUR GRANDFATHER?! HOW'S THAT EVEN POSSIBLE?
MY DAD TOLD ME HE, AND MY GRANDFATHER HAD A BIG FIGHT 17 YEARS AGO. HE WAS YOUNG, HE WANTED TO GO ABROAD TO START A NEW LIFE, BUT GRANDFATHER DIDN'T WANT HIM TO..
AND WHY'S THAT?

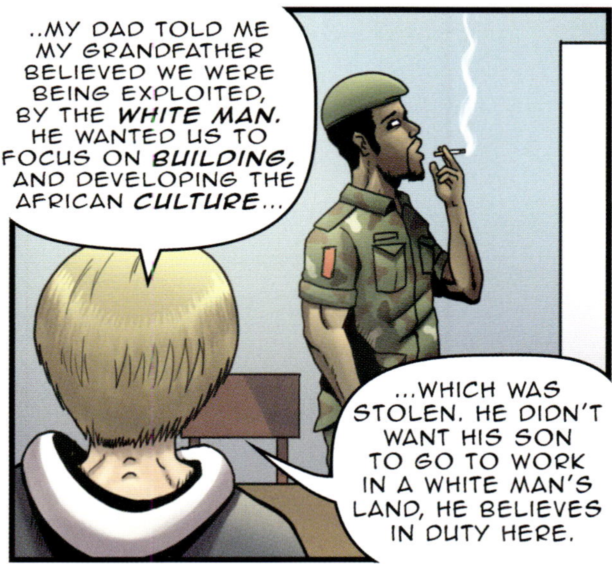
..MY DAD TOLD ME MY GRANDFATHER BELIEVED WE WERE BEING EXPLOITED, BY THE WHITE MAN. HE WANTED US TO FOCUS ON BUILDING, AND DEVELOPING THE AFRICAN CULTURE...
...WHICH WAS STOLEN. HE DIDN'T WANT HIS SON TO GO TO WORK IN A WHITE MAN'S LAND, HE BELIEVES IN DUTY HERE.

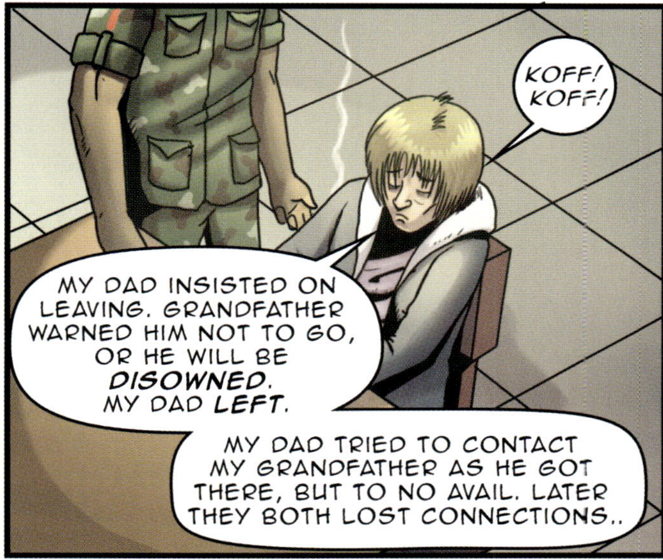
KOFF! KOFF!
MY DAD INSISTED ON LEAVING. GRANDFATHER WARNED HIM NOT TO GO, OR HE WILL BE DISOWNED. MY DAD LEFT.
MY DAD TRIED TO CONTACT MY GRANDFATHER AS HE GOT THERE, BUT TO NO AVAIL. LATER THEY BOTH LOST CONNECTIONS..

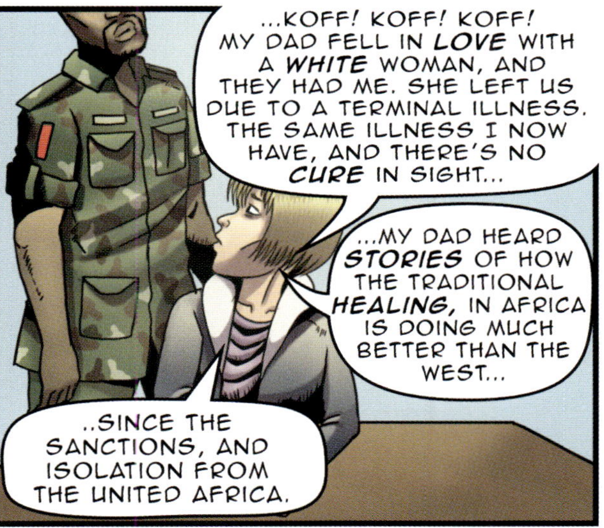
...KOFF! KOFF! KOFF! MY DAD FELL IN LOVE WITH A WHITE WOMAN, AND THEY HAD ME. SHE LEFT US DUE TO A TERMINAL ILLNESS. THE SAME ILLNESS I NOW HAVE, AND THERE'S NO CURE IN SIGHT...
...MY DAD HEARD STORIES OF HOW THE TRADITIONAL HEALING, IN AFRICA IS DOING MUCH BETTER THAN THE WEST...
..SINCE THE SANCTIONS, AND ISOLATION FROM THE UNITED AFRICA.

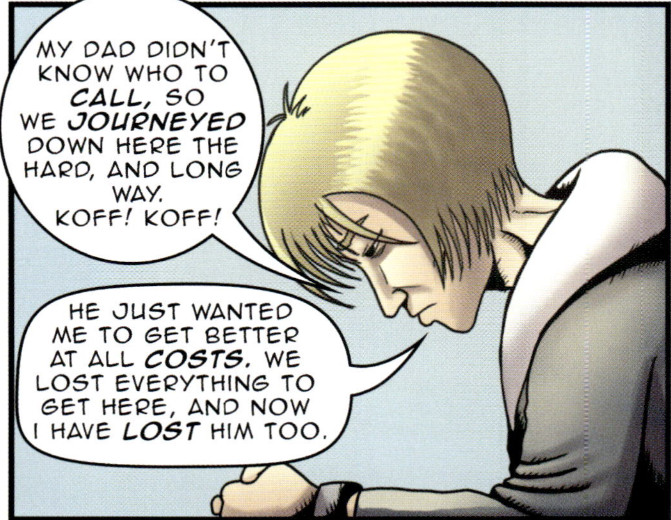
MY DAD DIDN'T KNOW WHO TO CALL, SO WE JOURNEYED DOWN HERE THE HARD, AND LONG WAY. KOFF! KOFF!
HE JUST WANTED ME TO GET BETTER AT ALL COSTS. WE LOST EVERYTHING TO GET HERE, AND NOW I HAVE LOST HIM TOO.

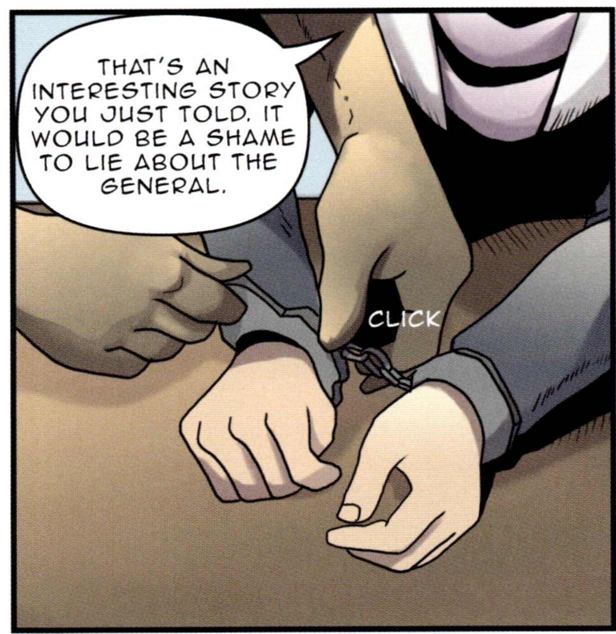
THAT'S AN INTERESTING STORY YOU JUST TOLD. IT WOULD BE A SHAME TO LIE ABOUT THE GENERAL.
CLICK

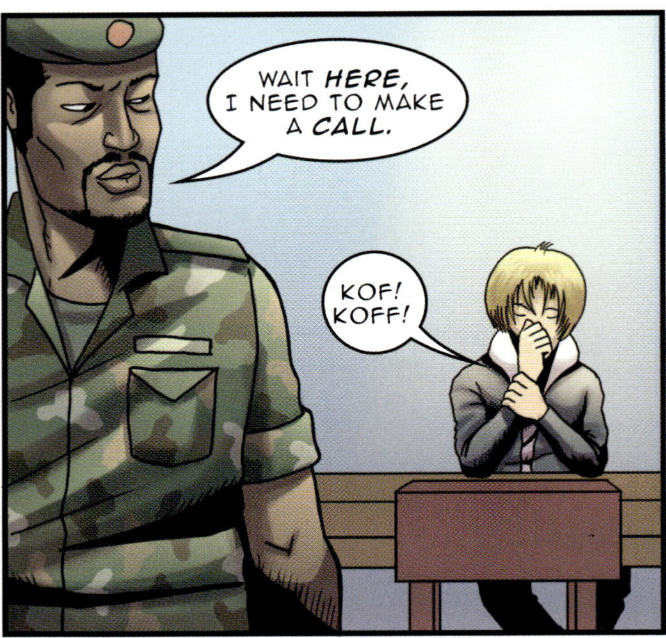
WAIT HERE, I NEED TO MAKE A CALL.
KOF! KOFF!

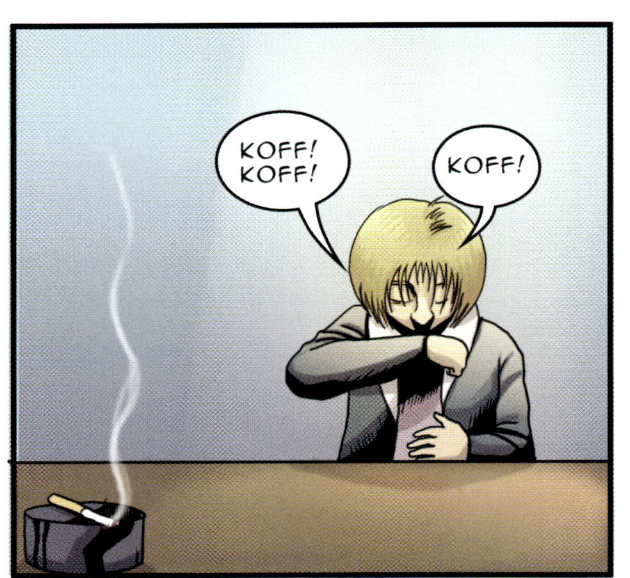
KOFF! KOFF!
KOFF!

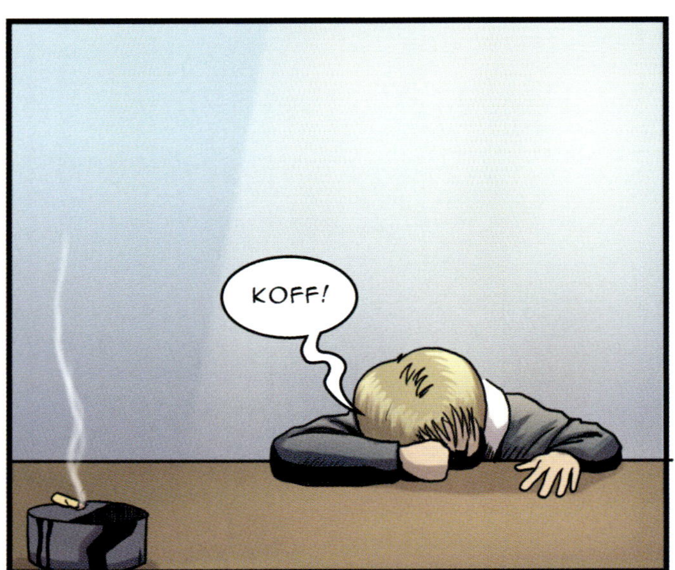
KOFF!

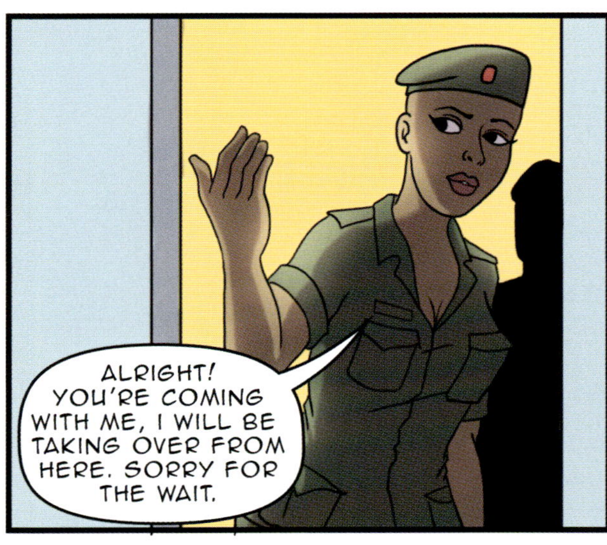
ALRIGHT! YOU'RE COMING WITH ME, I WILL BE TAKING OVER FROM HERE. SORRY FOR THE WAIT.

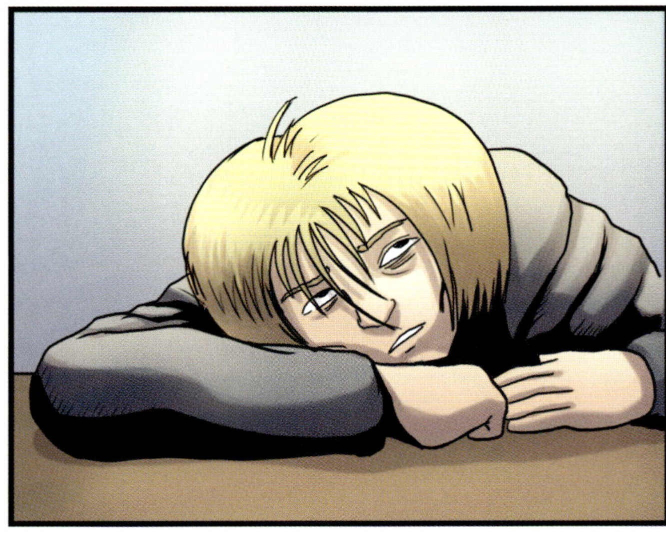

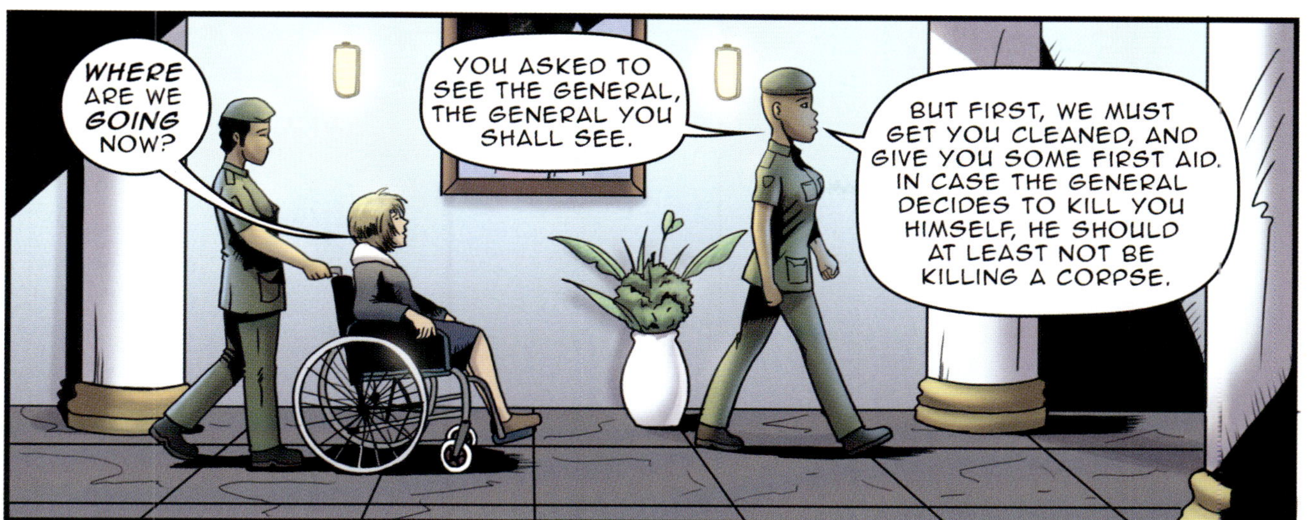
WHERE ARE WE GOING NOW?
YOU ASKED TO SEE THE GENERAL, THE GENERAL YOU SHALL SEE.
BUT FIRST, WE MUST GET YOU CLEANED, AND GIVE YOU SOME FIRST AID. IN CASE THE GENERAL DECIDES TO KILL YOU HIMSELF, HE SHOULD AT LEAST NOT BE KILLING A CORPSE.

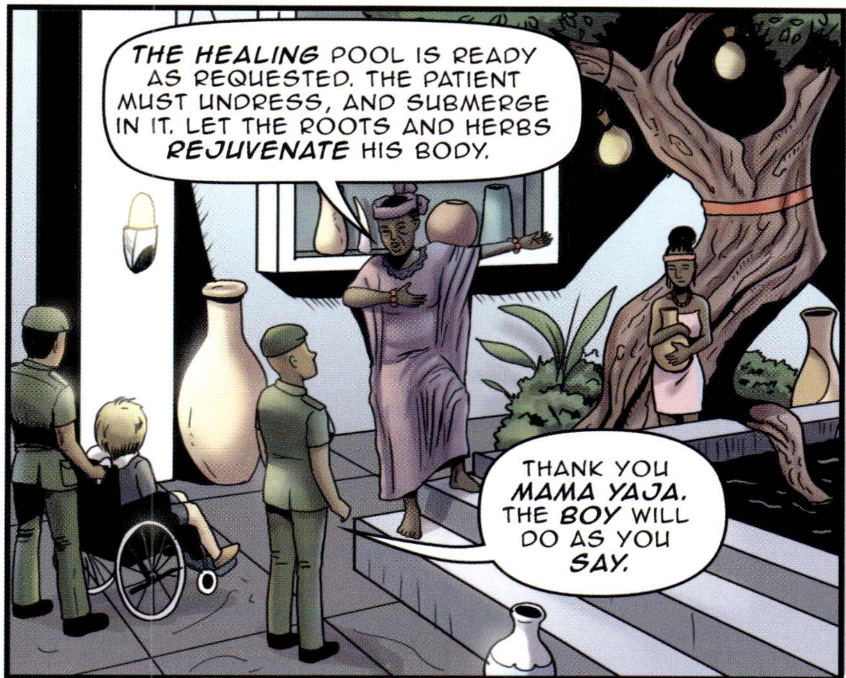
THE HEALING POOL IS READY AS REQUESTED. THE PATIENT MUST UNDRESS, AND SUBMERGE IN IT. LET THE ROOTS AND HERBS REJUVENATE HIS BODY.
THANK YOU MAMA YAJA. THE BOY WILL DO AS YOU SAY.

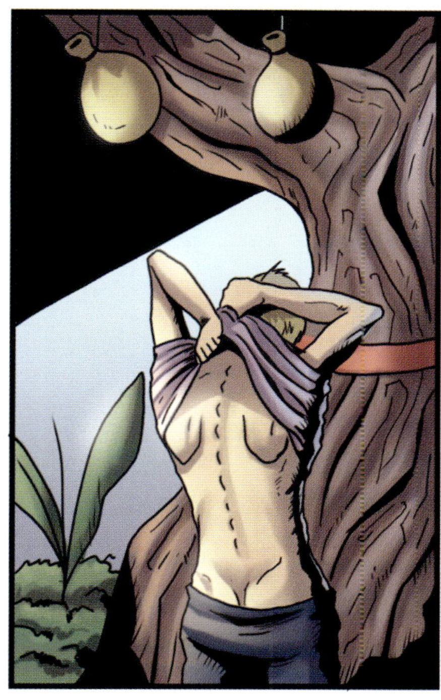

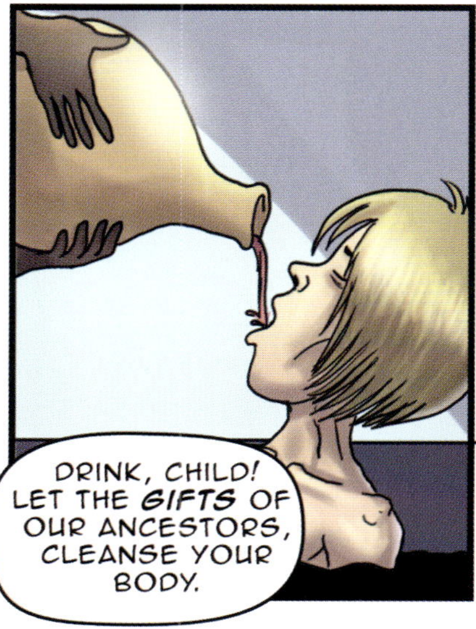
DRINK, CHILD! LET THE GIFTS OF OUR ANCESTORS, CLEANSE YOUR BODY.

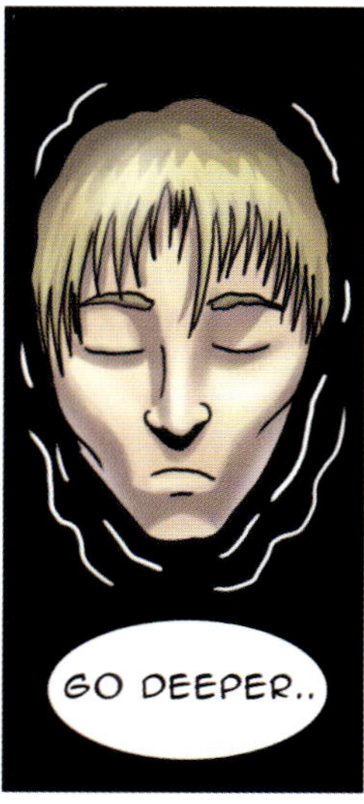
GO DEEPER..

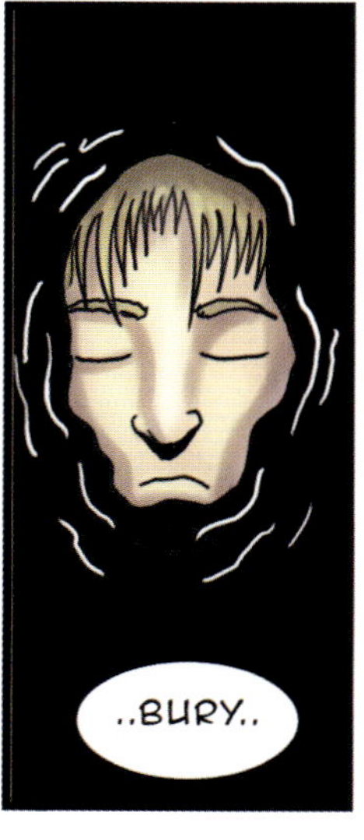
..BURY..

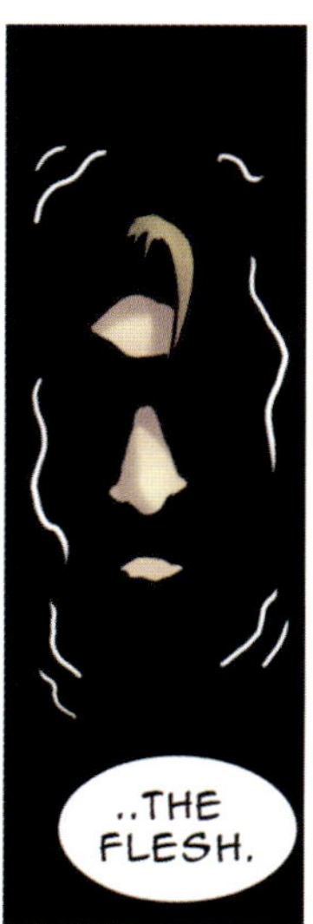
..THE FLESH.

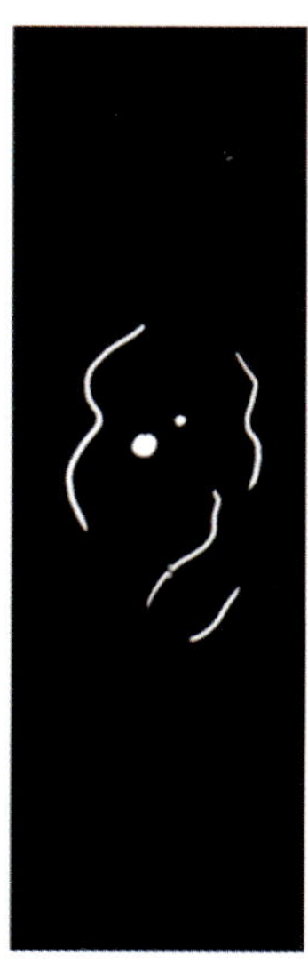

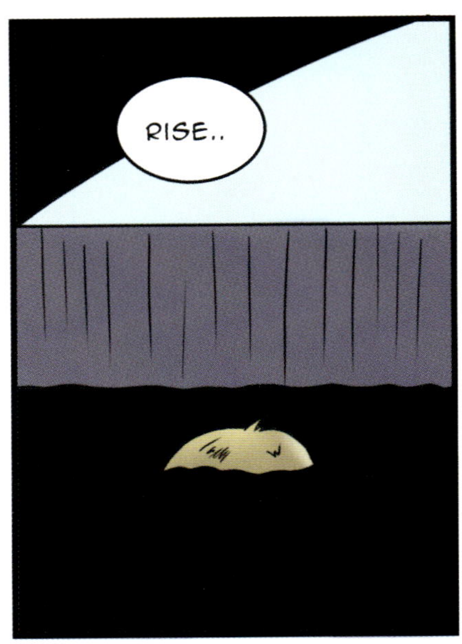
RISE..

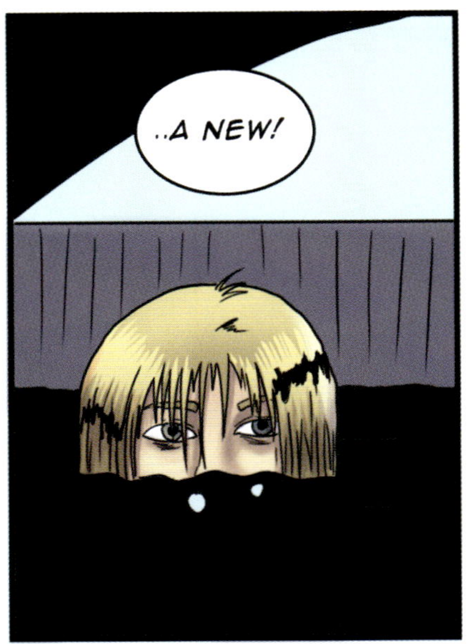
..A NEW!

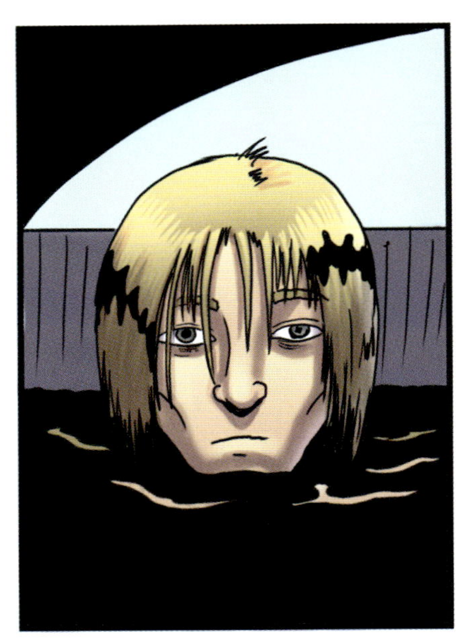

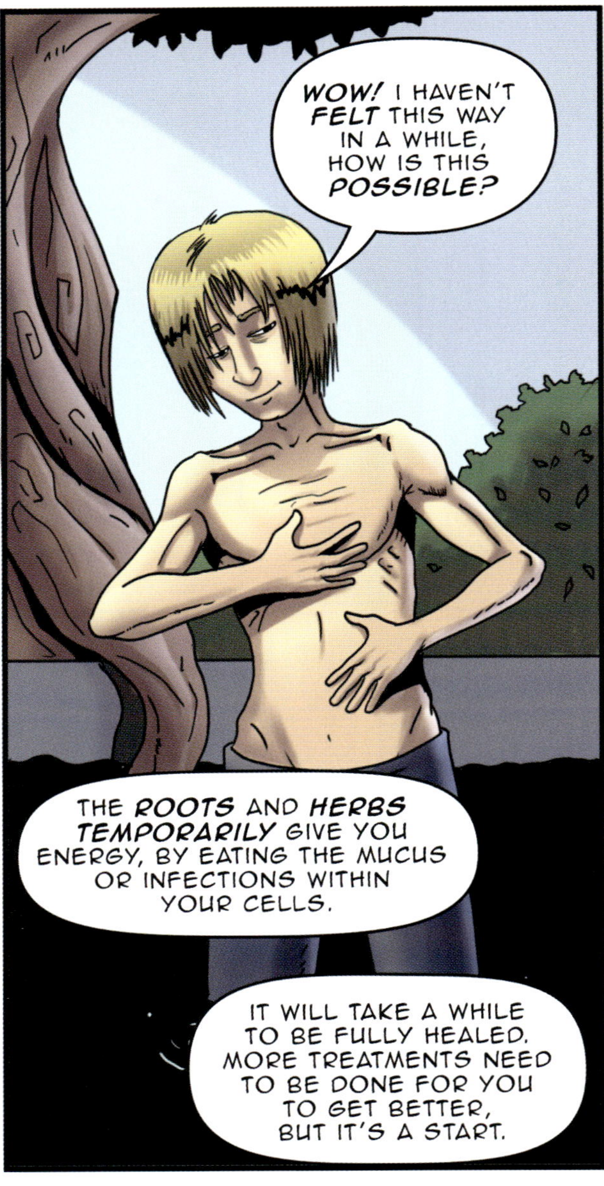
WOW! I HAVEN'T FELT THIS WAY IN A WHILE, HOW IS THIS POSSIBLE?
THE ROOTS AND HERBS TEMPORARILY GIVE YOU ENERGY, BY EATING THE MUCUS OR INFECTIONS WITHIN YOUR CELLS.
IT WILL TAKE A WHILE TO BE FULLY HEALED. MORE TREATMENTS NEED TO BE DONE FOR YOU TO GET BETTER, BUT IT'S A START.

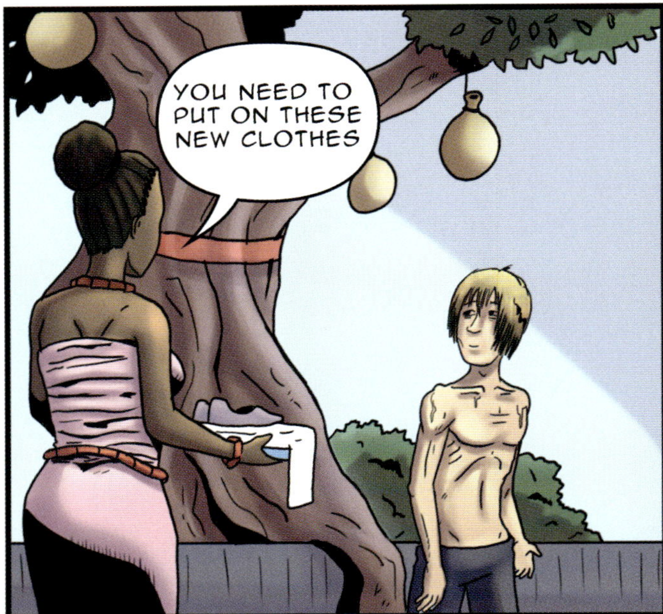
YOU NEED TO PUT ON THESE NEW CLOTHES

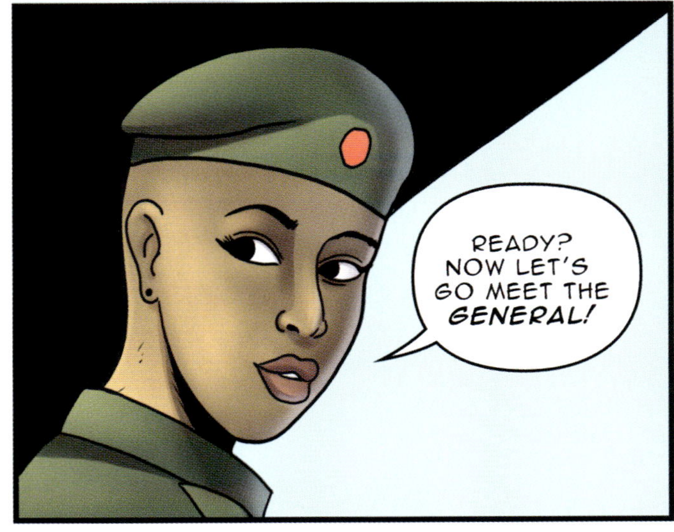
READY? NOW LET'S GO MEET THE GENERAL!

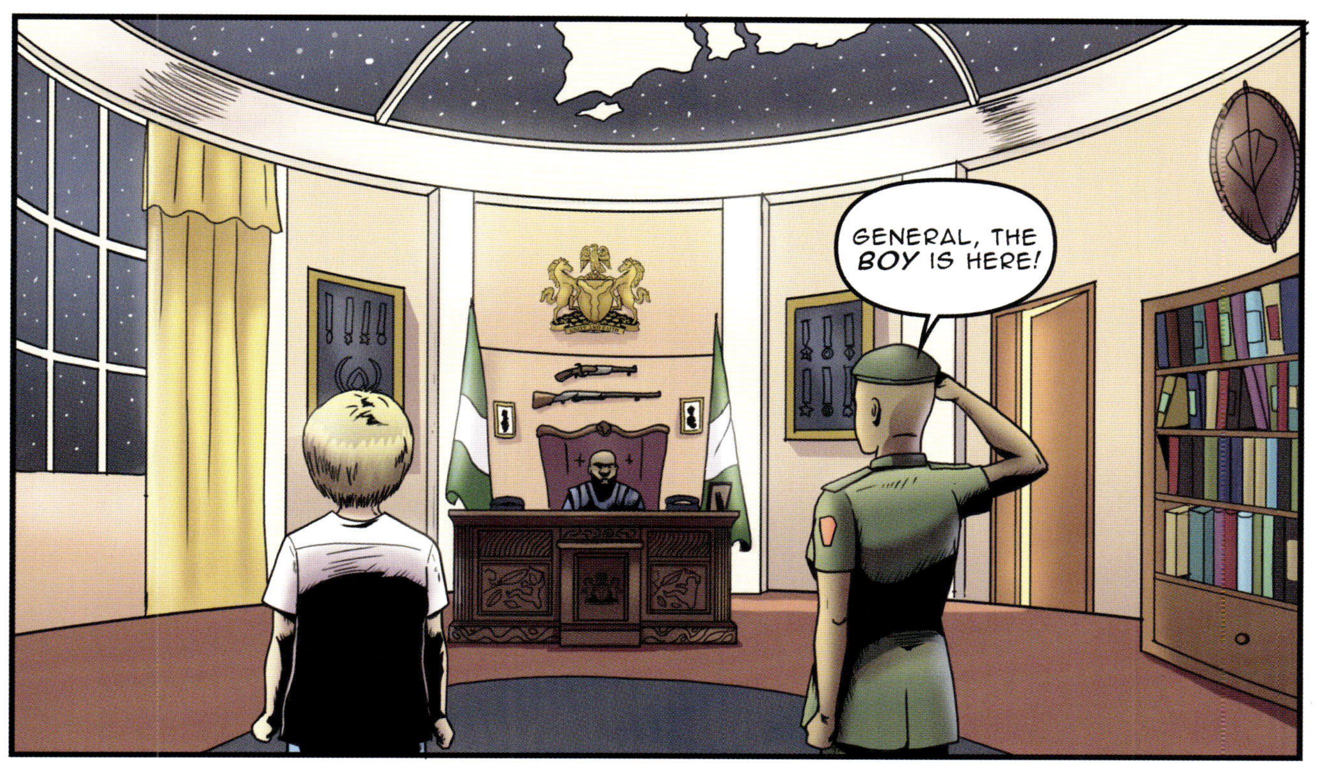
GENERAL, THE BOY IS HERE!

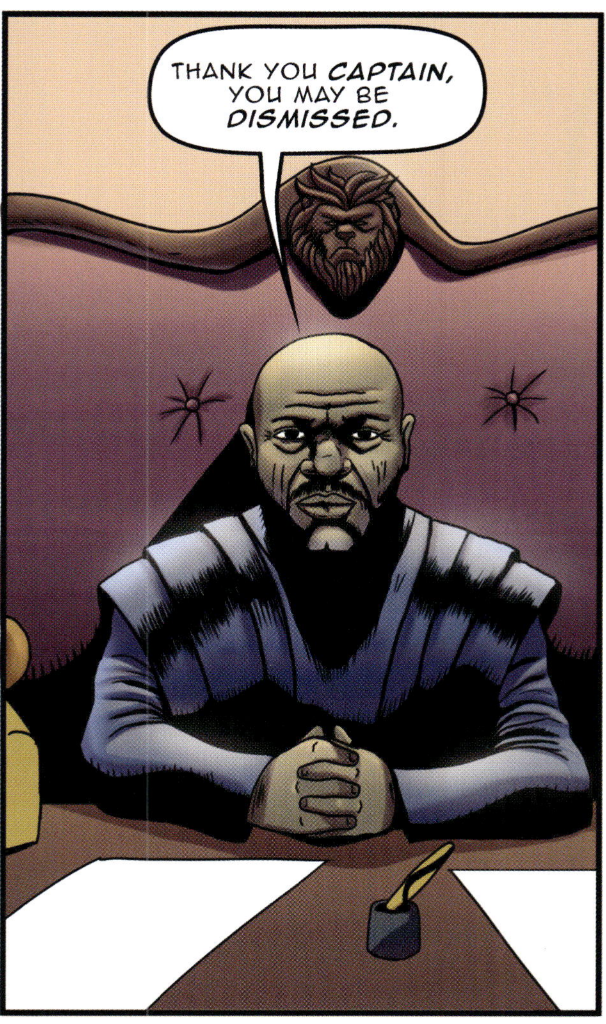
THANK YOU CAPTAIN, YOU MAY BE DISMISSED.

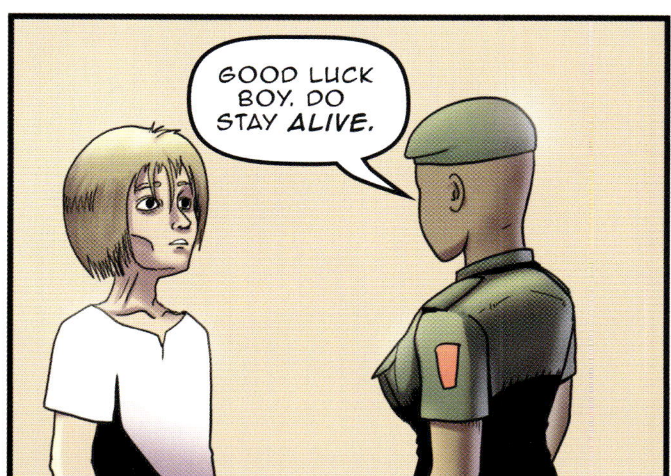
GOOD LUCK BOY. DO STAY ALIVE.

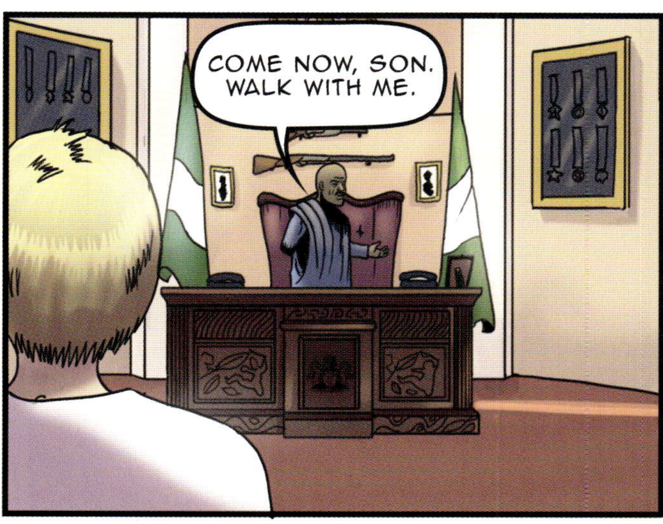
COME NOW, SON. WALK WITH ME.

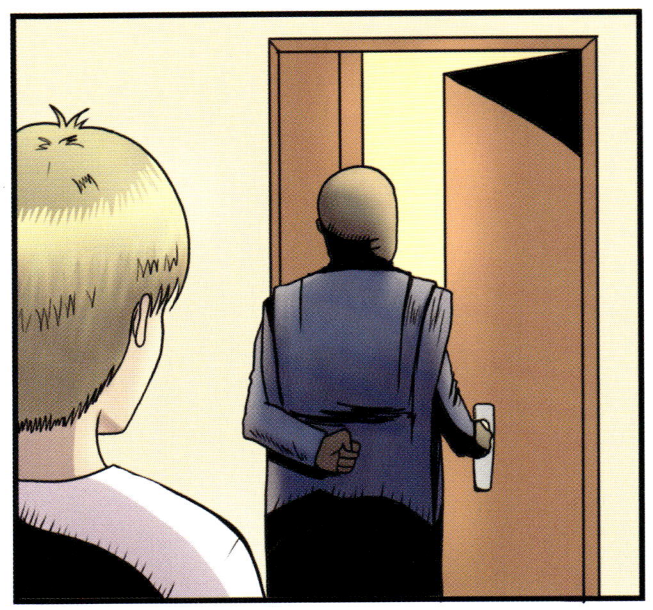

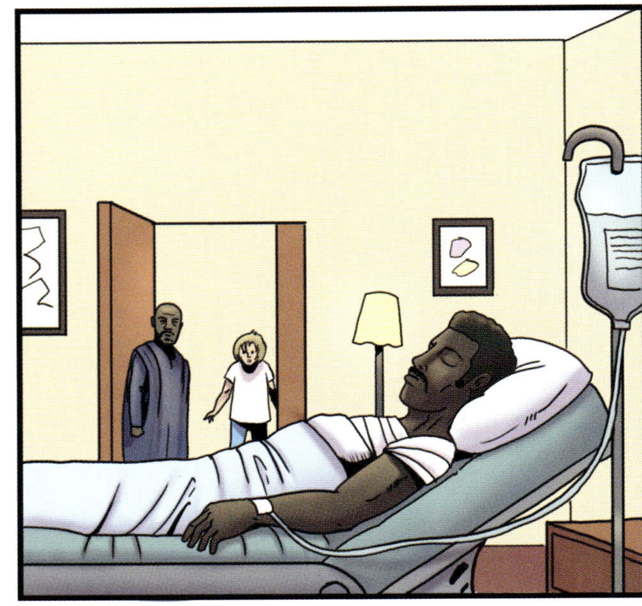

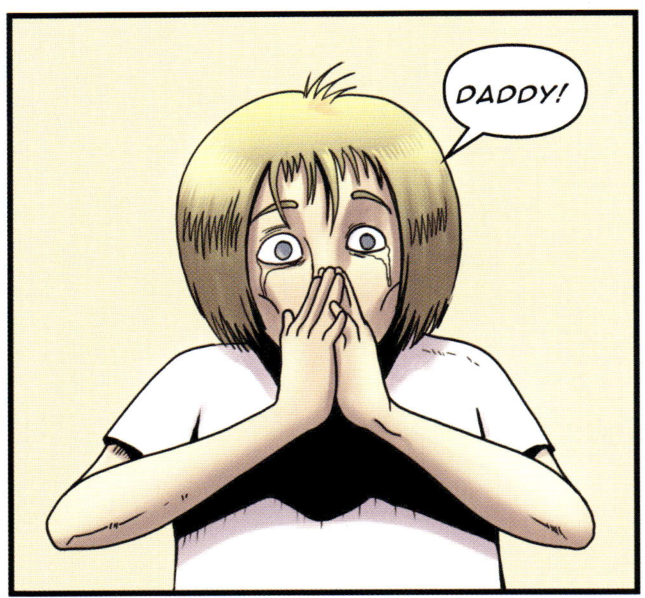
DADDY!

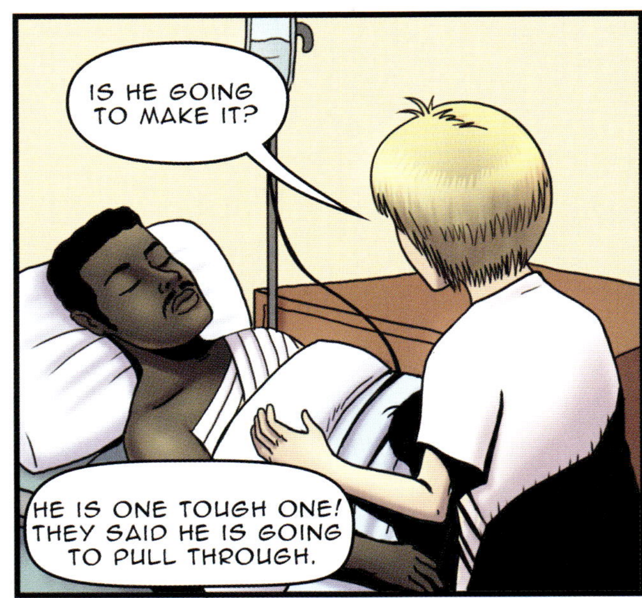
IS HE GOING TO MAKE IT?
HE IS ONE TOUGH ONE! THEY SAID HE IS GOING TO PULL THROUGH.

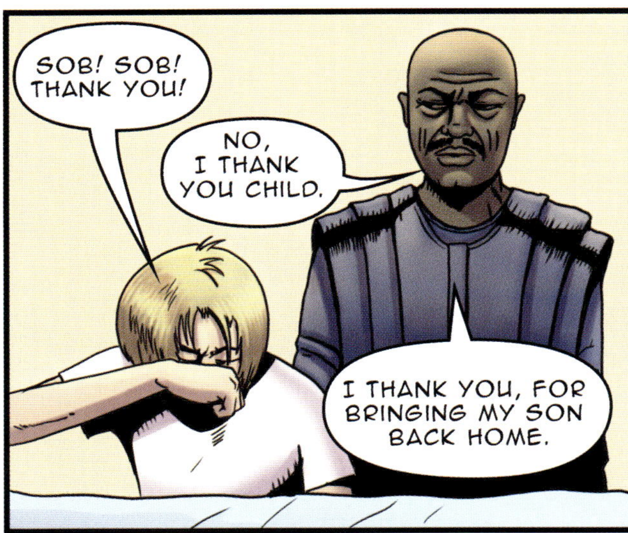
SOB! SOB! THANK YOU!
NO, I THANK YOU CHILD.
I THANK YOU, FOR BRINGING MY SON BACK HOME.

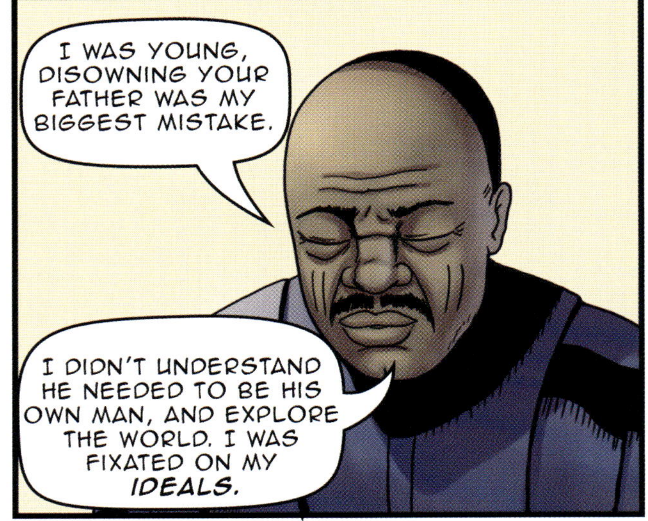
I WAS YOUNG, DISOWNING YOUR FATHER WAS MY BIGGEST MISTAKE.
I DIDN'T UNDERSTAND HE NEEDED TO BE HIS OWN MAN, AND EXPLORE THE WORLD. I WAS FIXATED ON MY IDEALS.

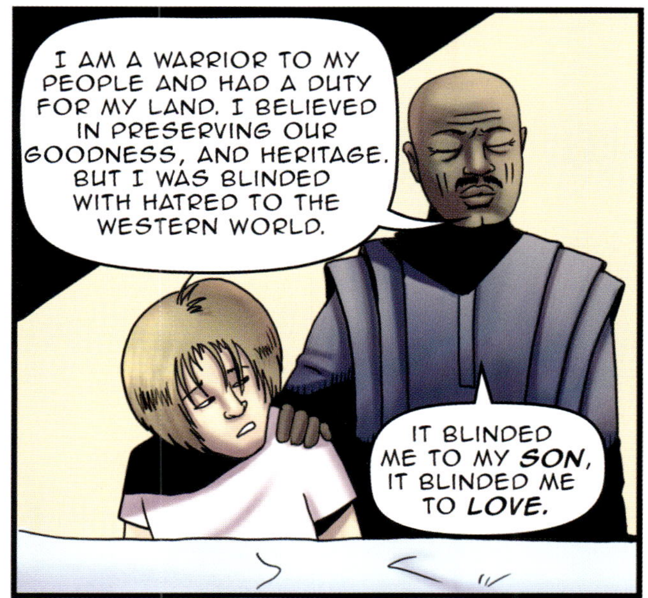
I AM A WARRIOR TO MY PEOPLE AND HAD A DUTY FOR MY LAND. I BELIEVED IN PRESERVING OUR GOODNESS, AND HERITAGE. BUT I WAS BLINDED WITH HATRED TO THE WESTERN WORLD.
IT BLINDED ME TO MY ***SON***, IT BLINDED ME TO ***LOVE.***

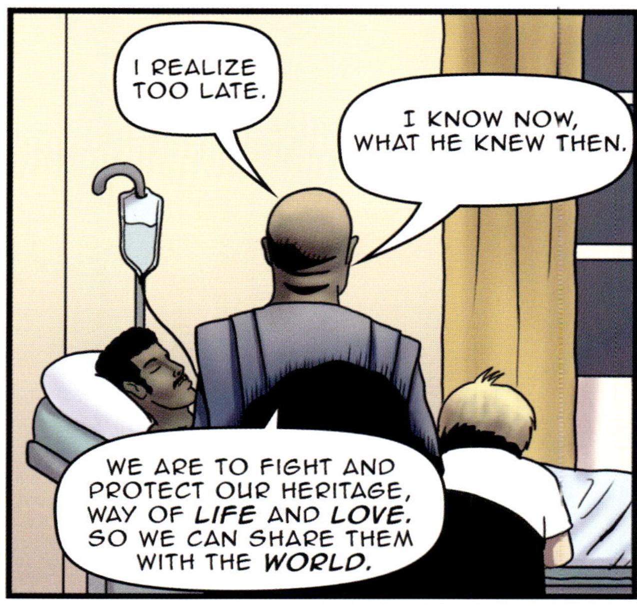
I REALIZE TOO LATE.
I KNOW NOW, WHAT HE KNEW THEN.
WE ARE TO FIGHT AND PROTECT OUR HERITAGE, WAY OF ***LIFE*** AND ***LOVE.*** SO WE CAN SHARE THEM WITH THE ***WORLD.***

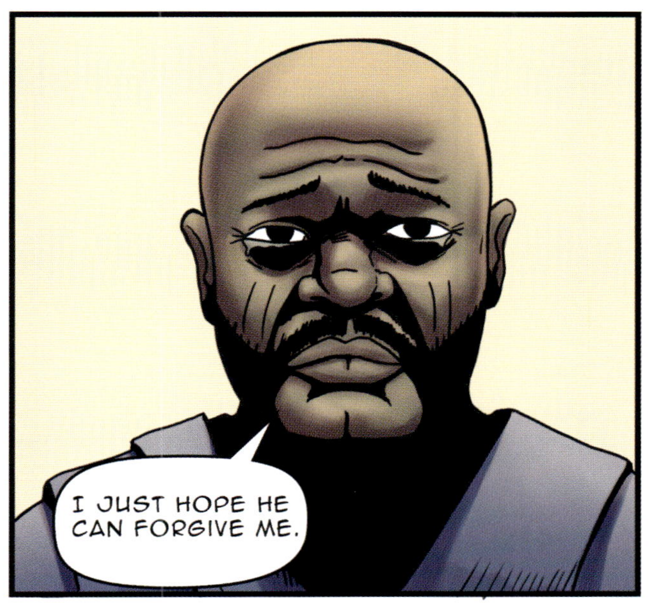
I JUST HOPE HE CAN FORGIVE ME.

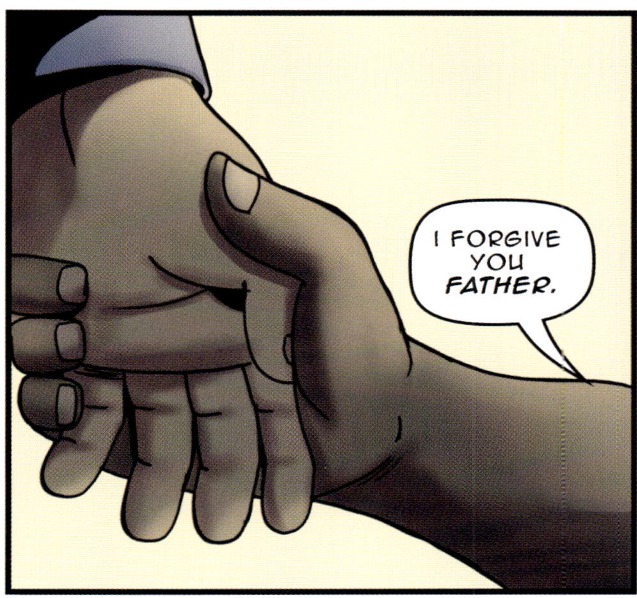
I FORGIVE YOU ***FATHER.***

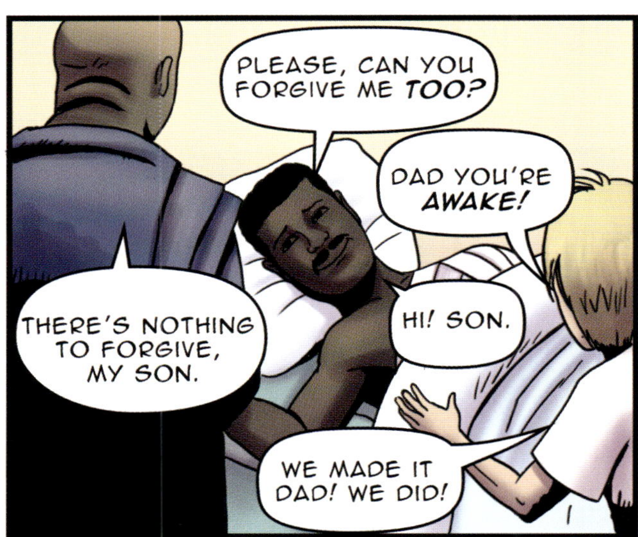
PLEASE, CAN YOU FORGIVE ME ***TOO?***
THERE'S NOTHING TO FORGIVE, MY SON.
DAD YOU'RE ***AWAKE!***
HI! SON.
WE MADE IT DAD! WE DID!

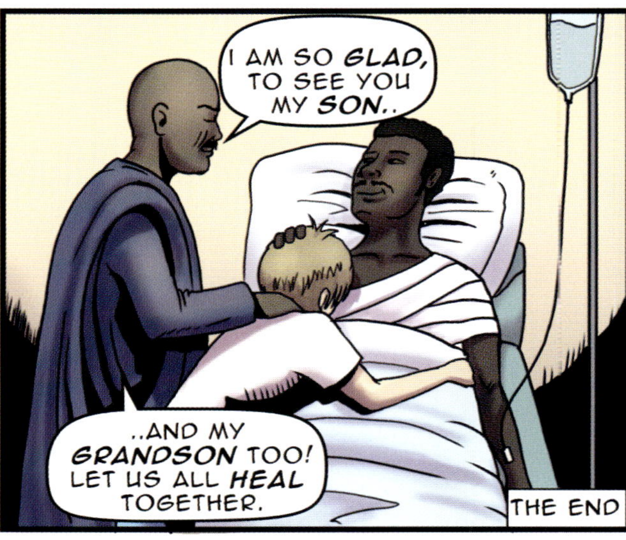
I AM SO ***GLAD***, TO SEE YOU MY ***SON***..
..AND MY ***GRANDSON*** TOO! LET US ALL ***HEAL*** TOGETHER.
THE END

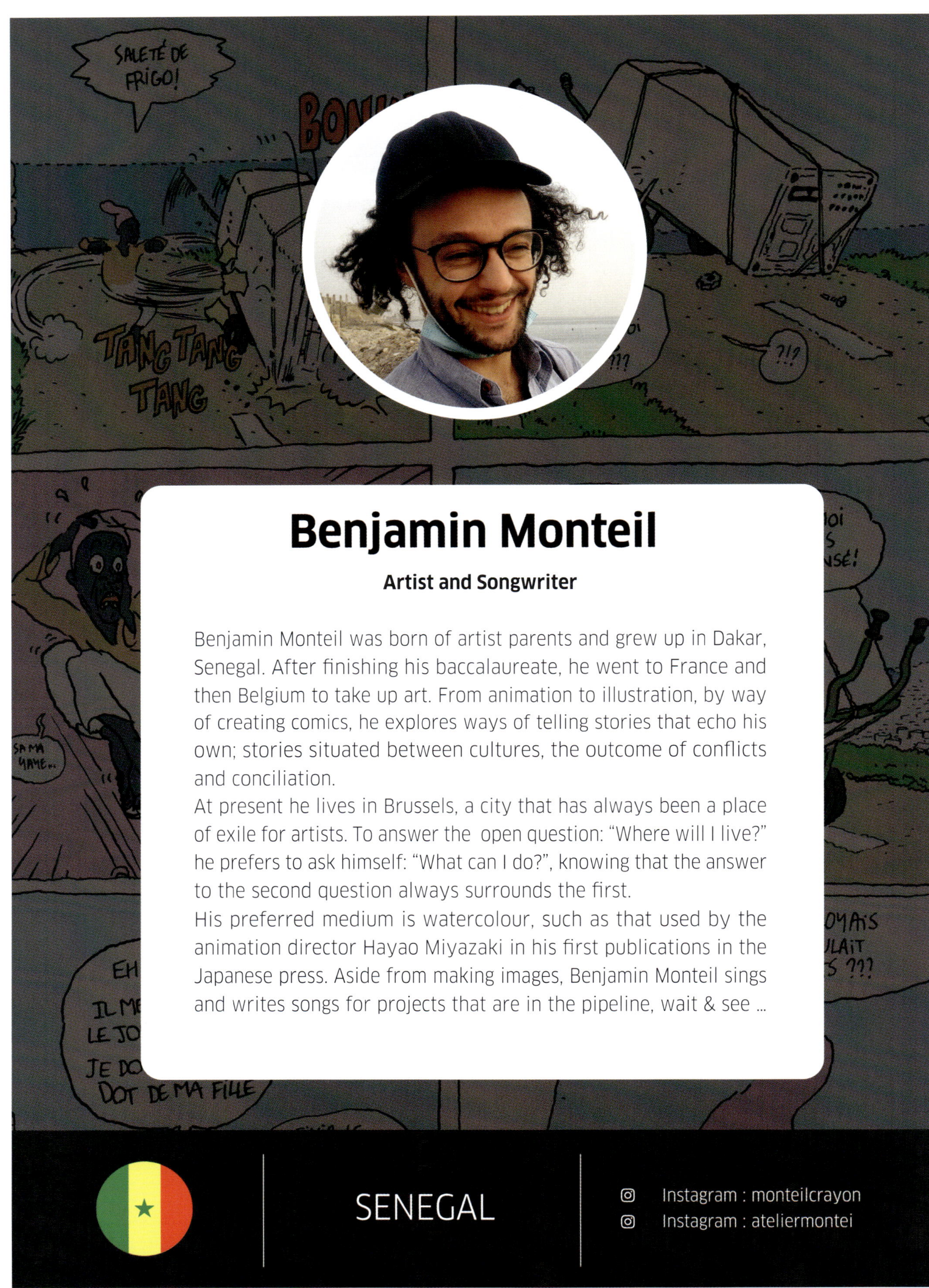

Benjamin Monteil

Artist and Songwriter

Benjamin Monteil was born of artist parents and grew up in Dakar, Senegal. After finishing his baccalaureate, he went to France and then Belgium to take up art. From animation to illustration, by way of creating comics, he explores ways of telling stories that echo his own; stories situated between cultures, the outcome of conflicts and conciliation.

At present he lives in Brussels, a city that has always been a place of exile for artists. To answer the open question: “Where will I live?” he prefers to ask himself: “What can I do?”, knowing that the answer to the second question always surrounds the first.

His preferred medium is watercolour, such as that used by the animation director Hayao Miyazaki in his first publications in the Japanese press. Aside from making images, Benjamin Monteil sings and writes songs for projects that are in the pipeline, wait & see ...

SENEGAL

Instagram : monteilcrayon
Instagram : ateliermontei

THE RUBBER TREE

MONTEIL

= FLASHBACK / = NARRATIVE TIME

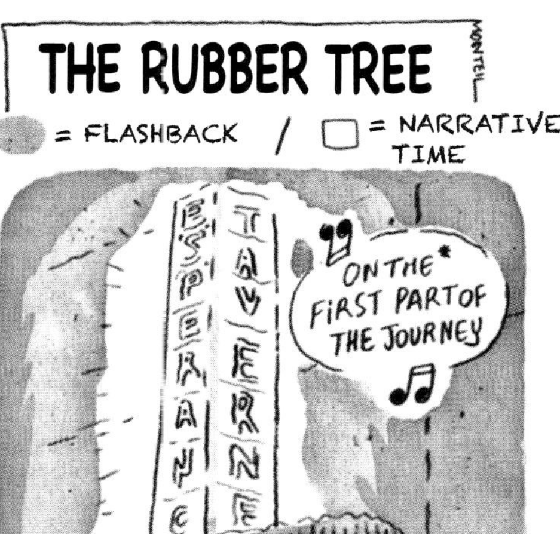

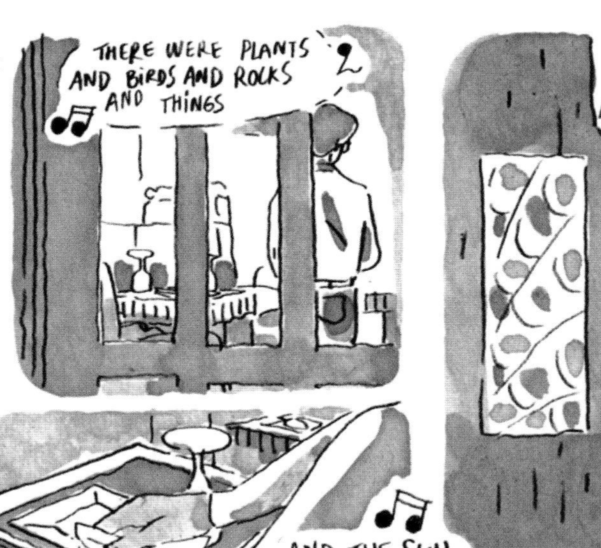

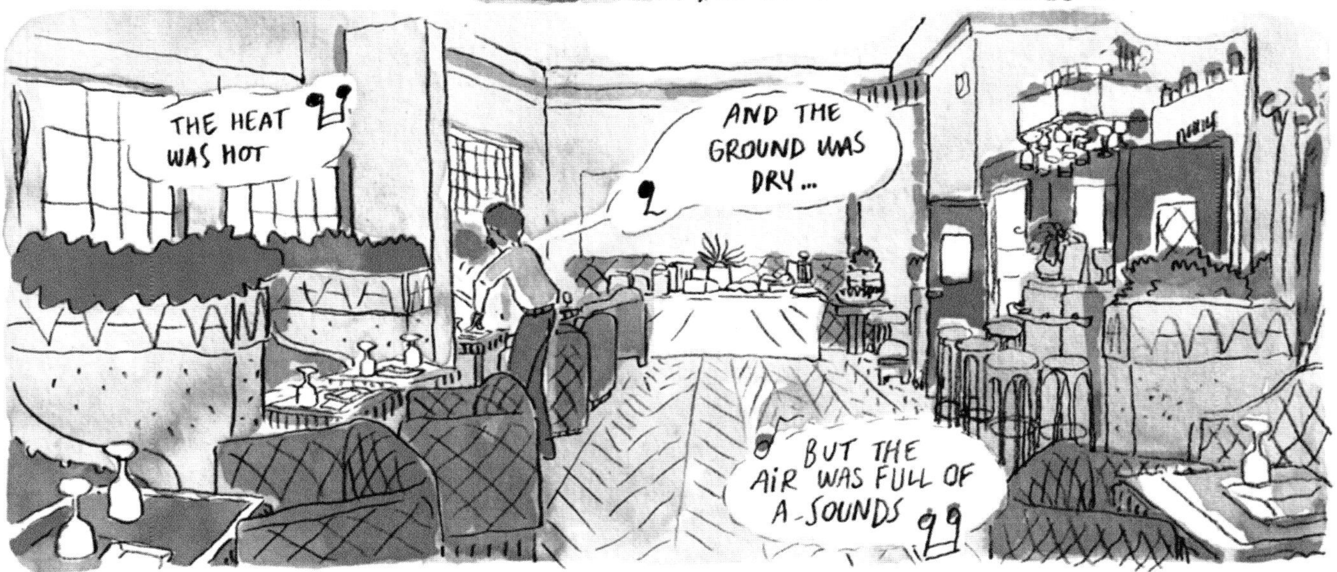

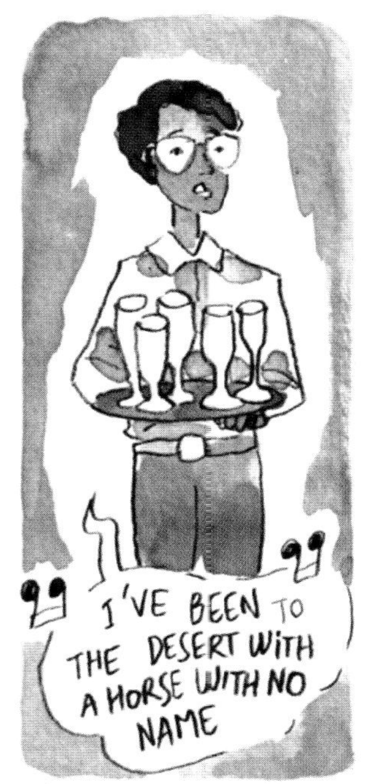

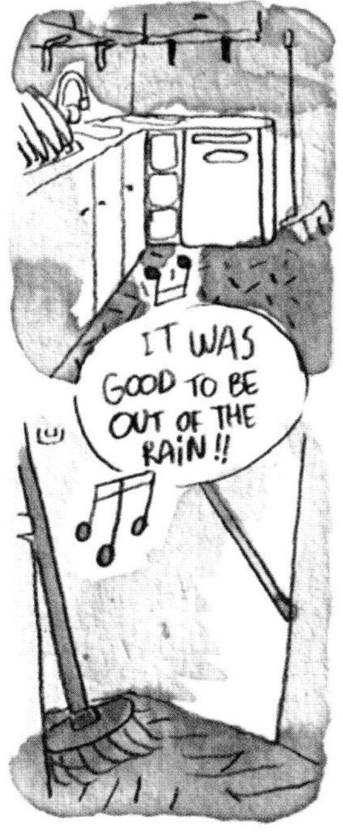

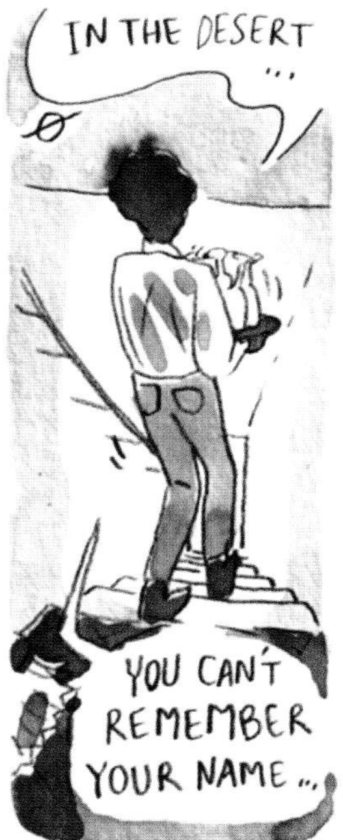

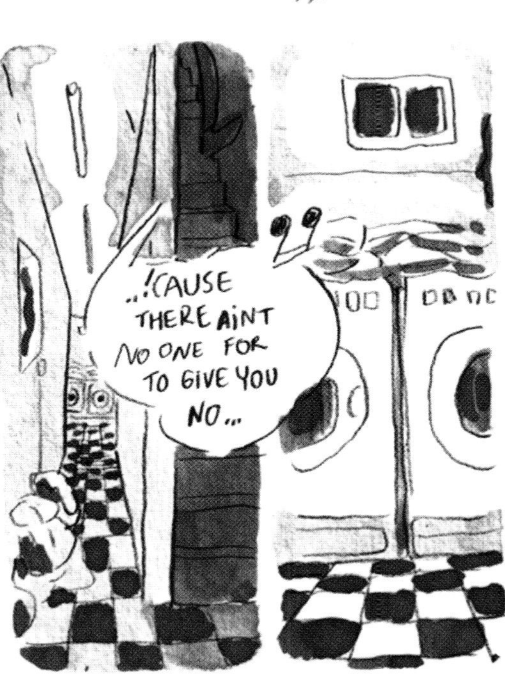

* "HORSE WITH NO NAME", TAKEN UP BY HORACE ANDY

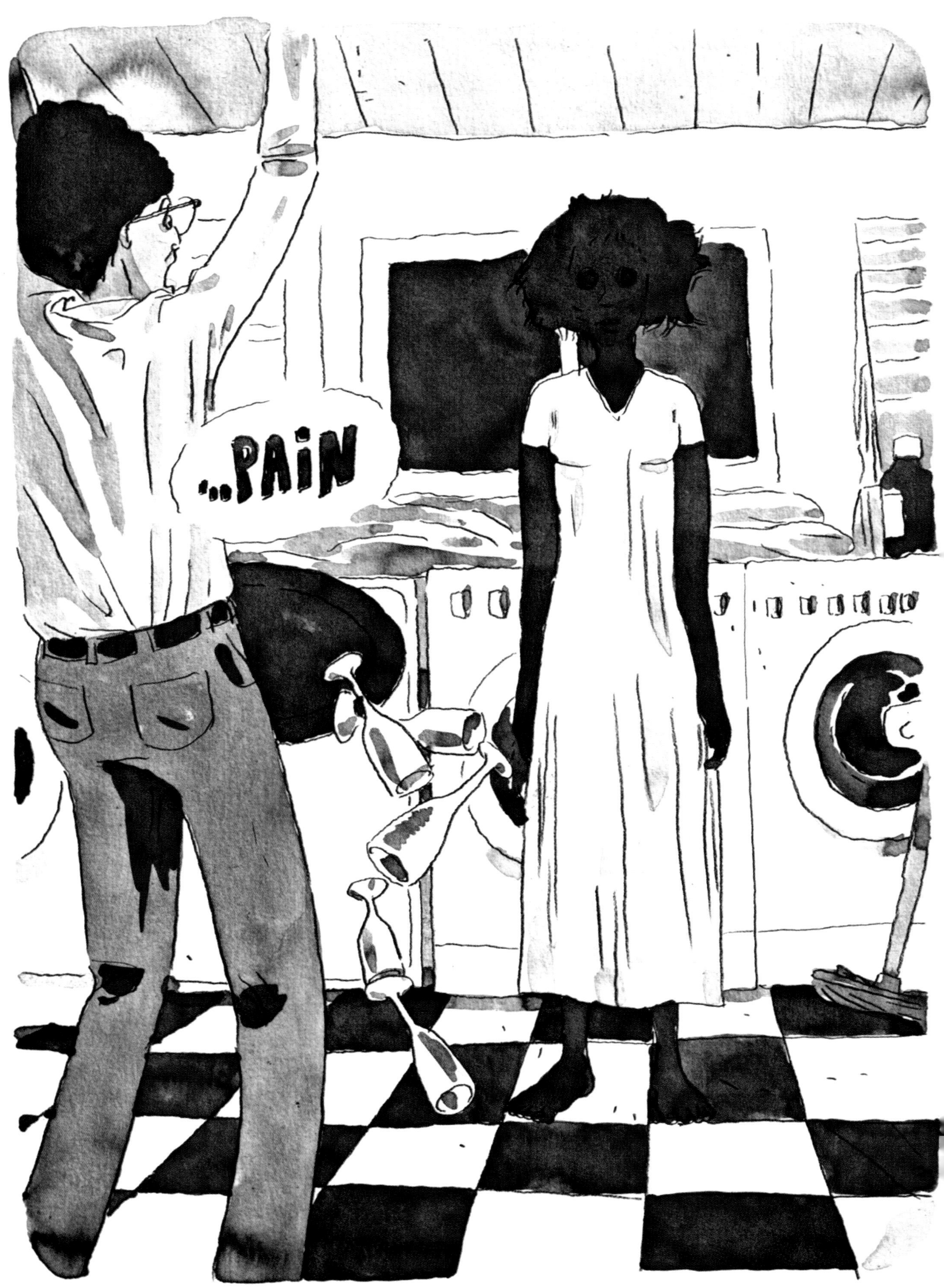
...PAIN

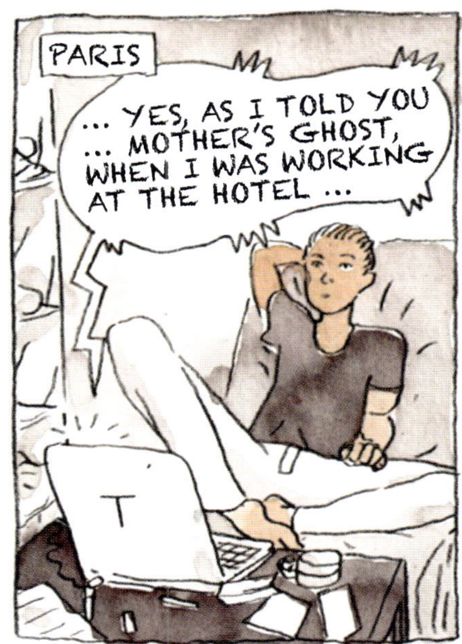
PARIS
... YES, AS I TOLD YOU ... MOTHER'S GHOST, WHEN I WAS WORKING AT THE HOTEL ...

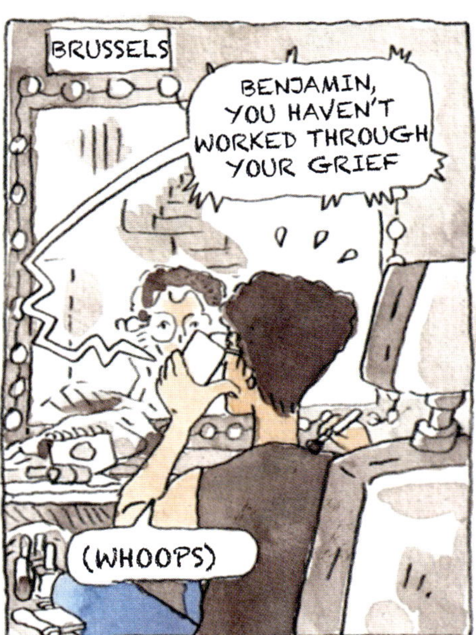
BRUSSELS
BENJAMIN, YOU HAVEN'T WORKED THROUGH YOUR GRIEF
(WHOOPS)

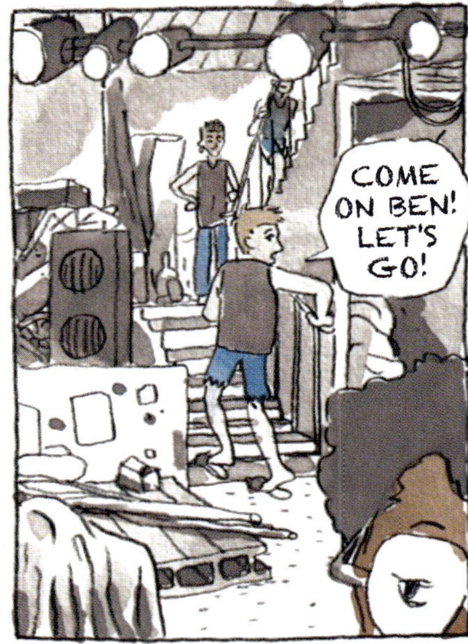
COME ON BEN! LET'S GO!

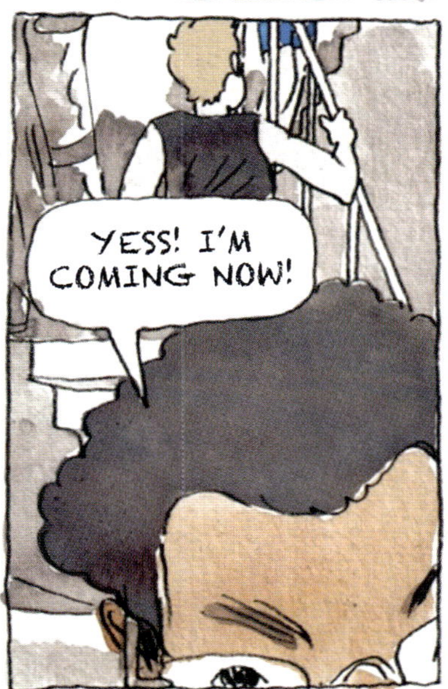
YESS! I'M COMING NOW!

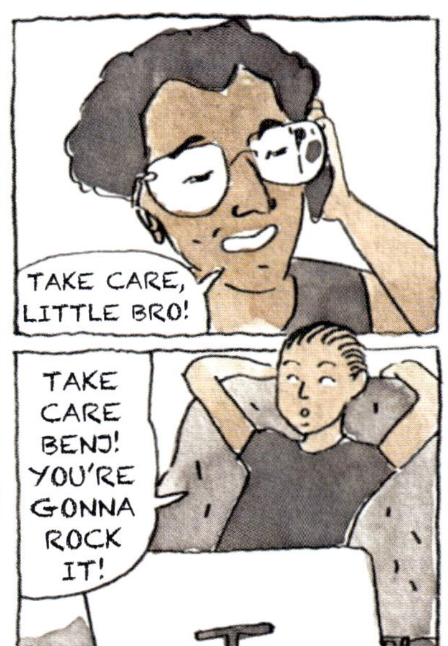
TAKE CARE, LITTLE BRO!
TAKE CARE BENJ! YOU'RE GONNA ROCK IT!

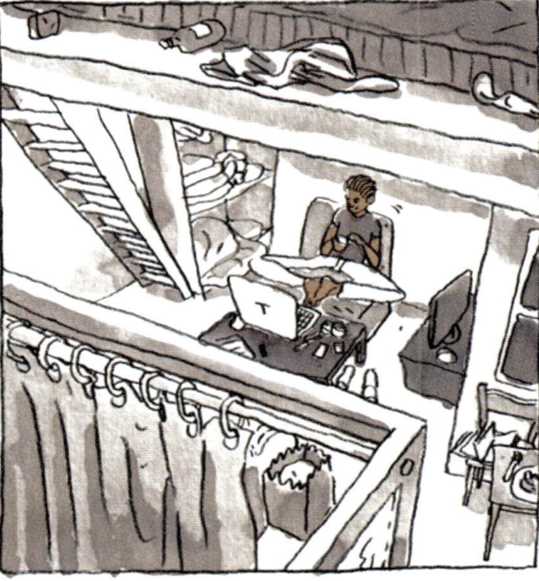

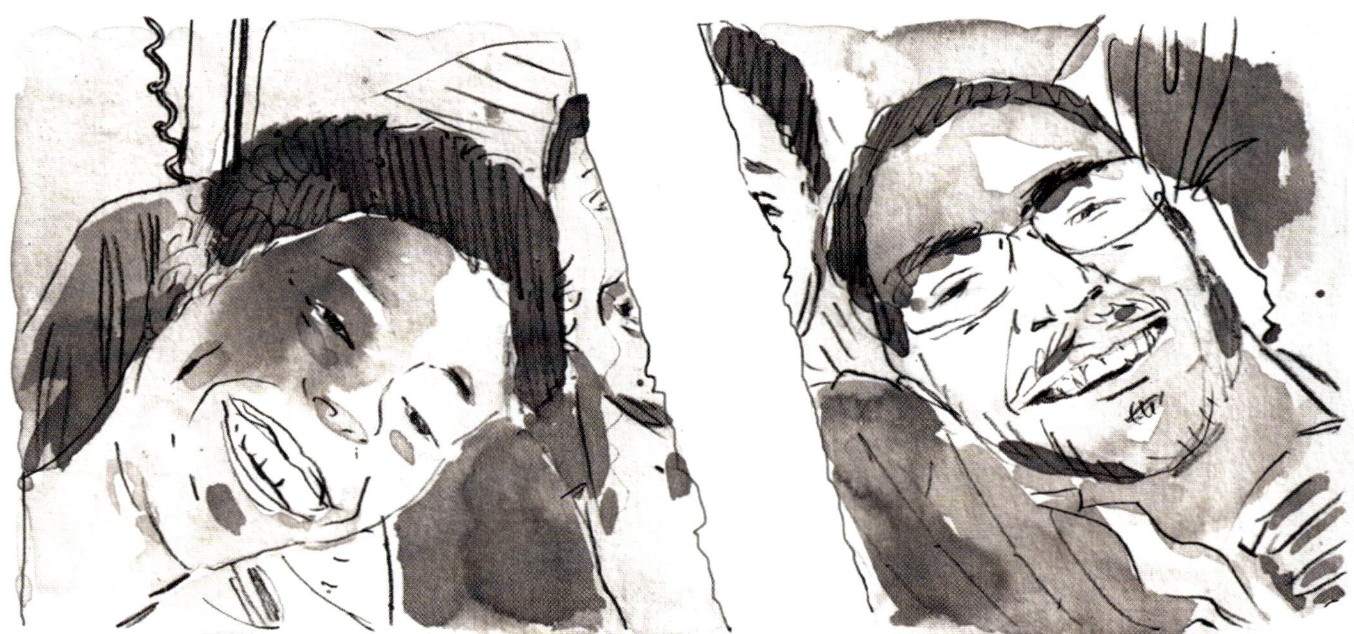

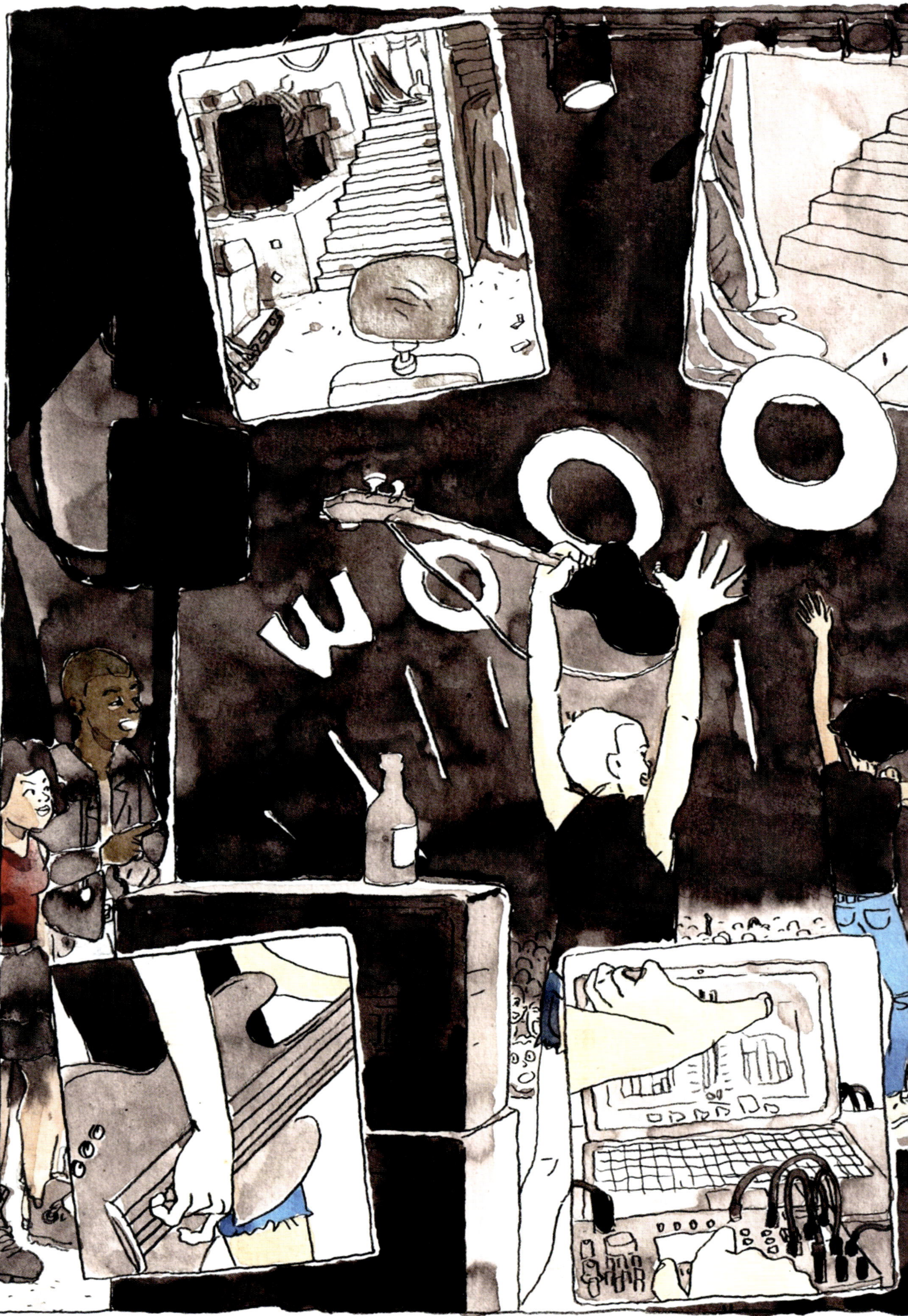
WOOO

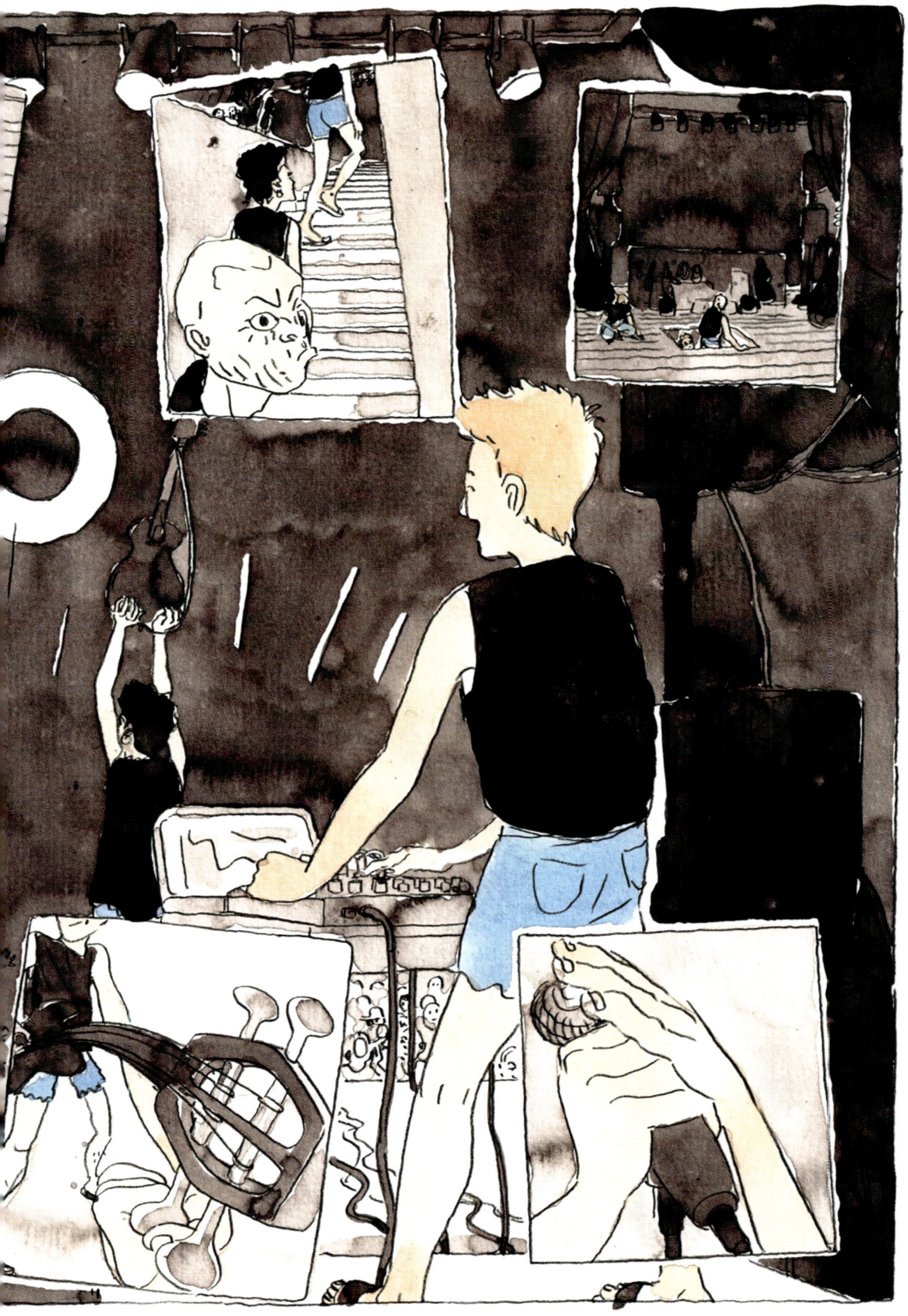

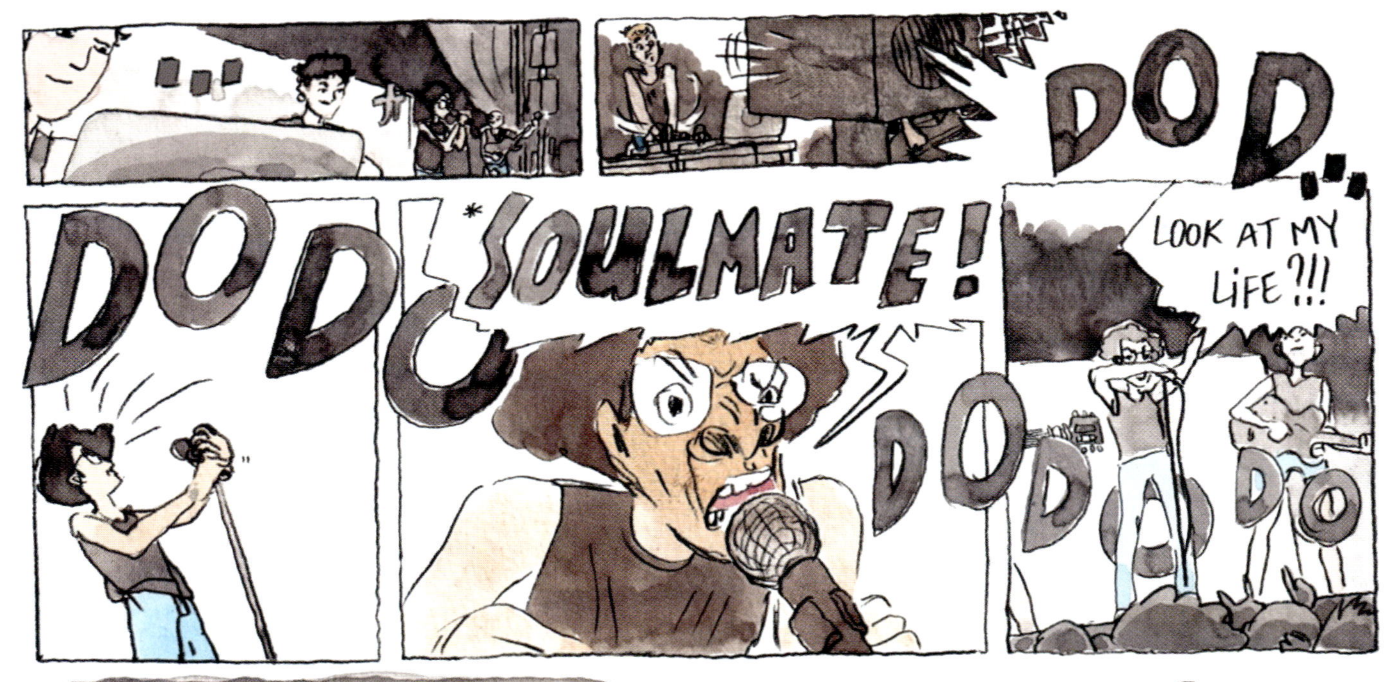

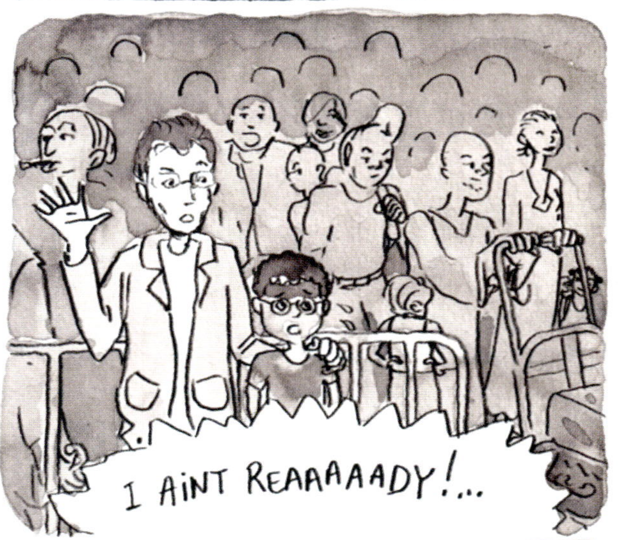

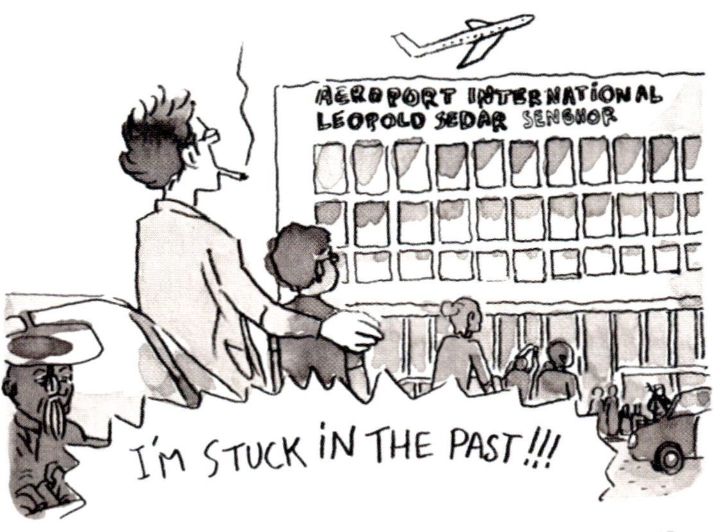

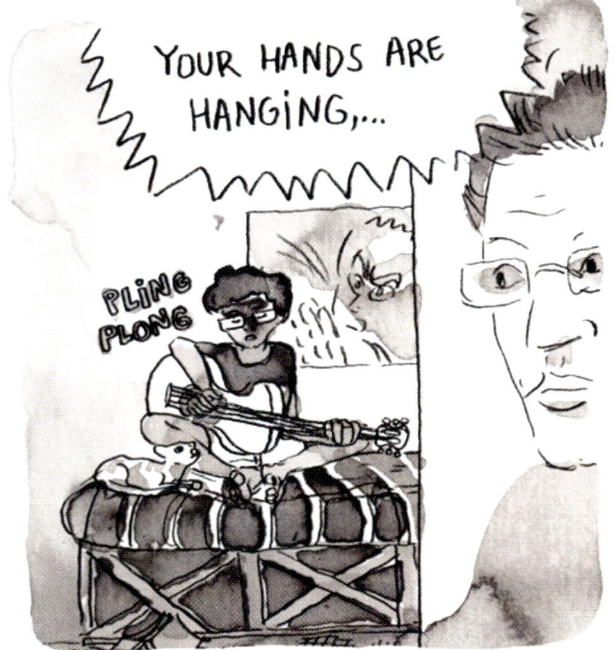

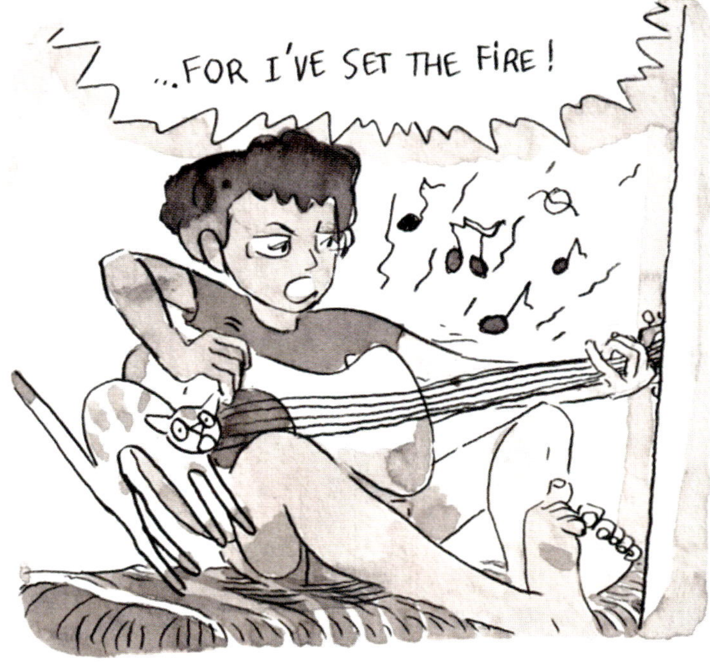

* 'ADOLESCENT CRISIS' ROCK MUSIC

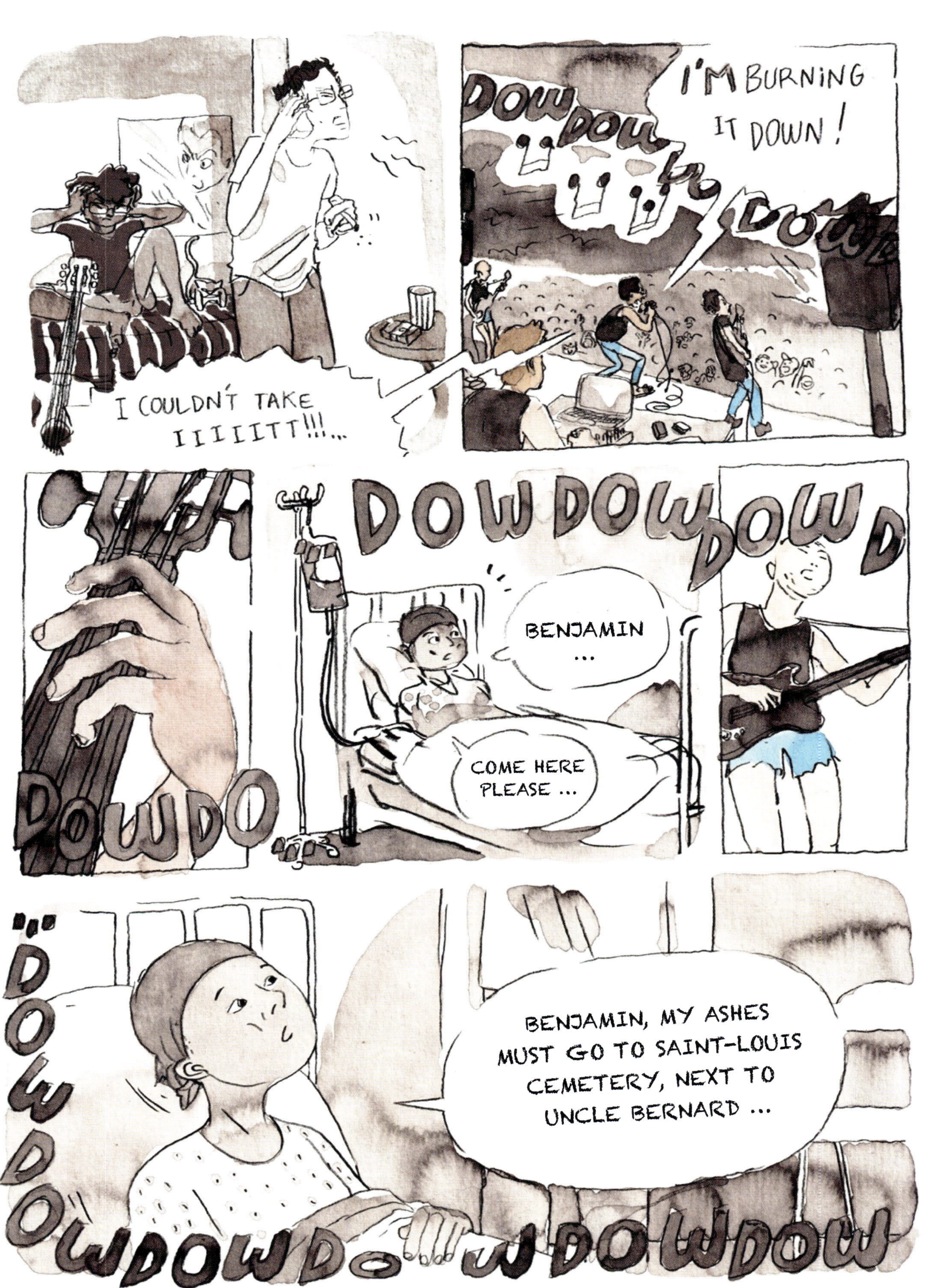
I COULDN'T TAKE IIIIITT!!!...
DOW DOW
I'M BURNING IT DOWN!
DOW
DOW DOW DOWD
DOWDO
BENJAMIN ...
COME HERE PLEASE ...
DOW
BENJAMIN, MY ASHES MUST GO TO SAINT-LOUIS CEMETERY, NEXT TO UNCLE BERNARD ...
DOWDOWDOWDO WDOWDOW

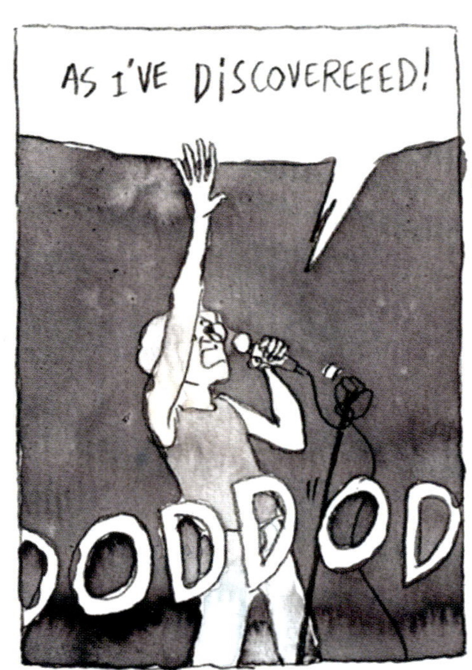

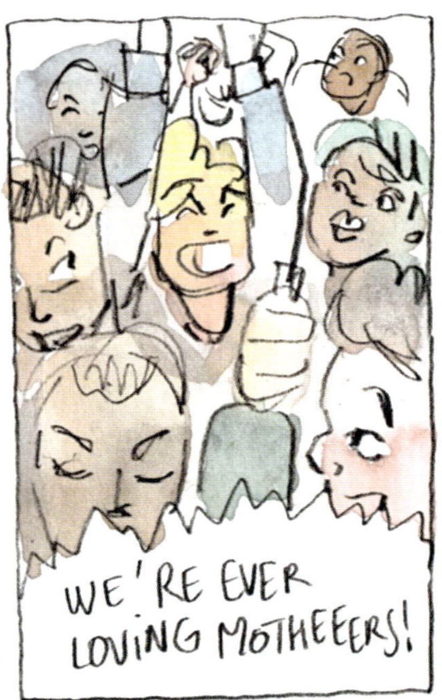

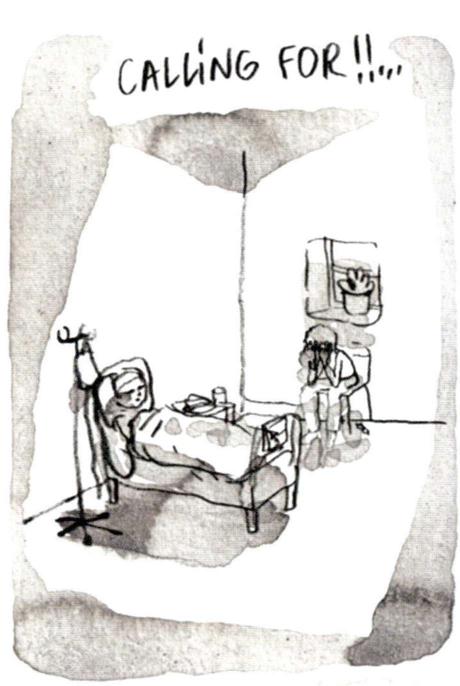

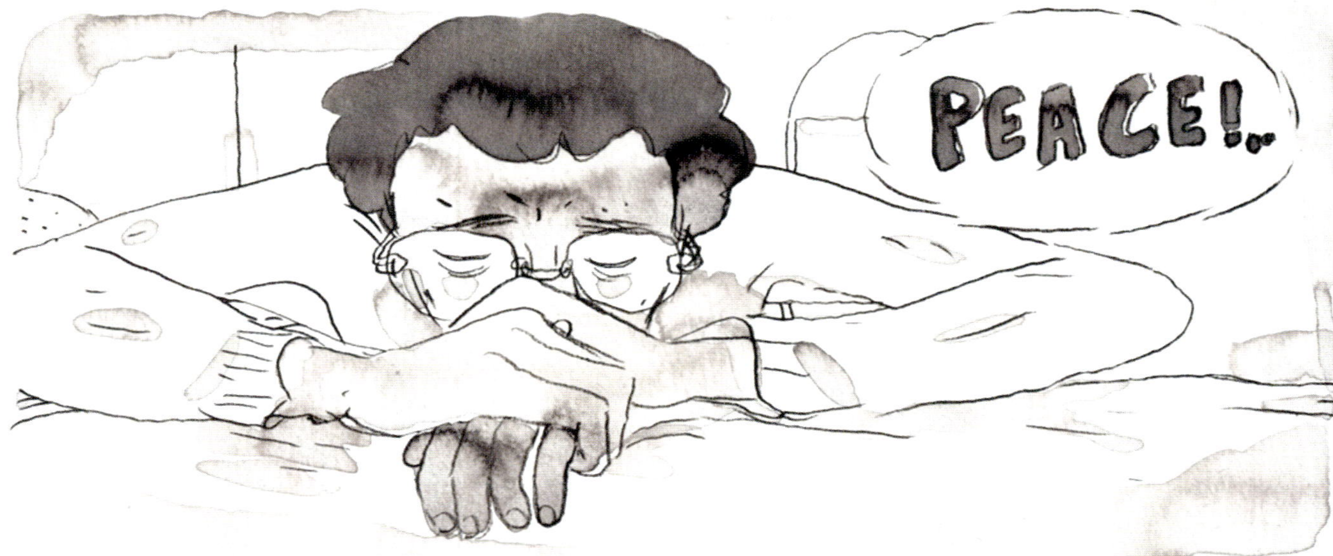

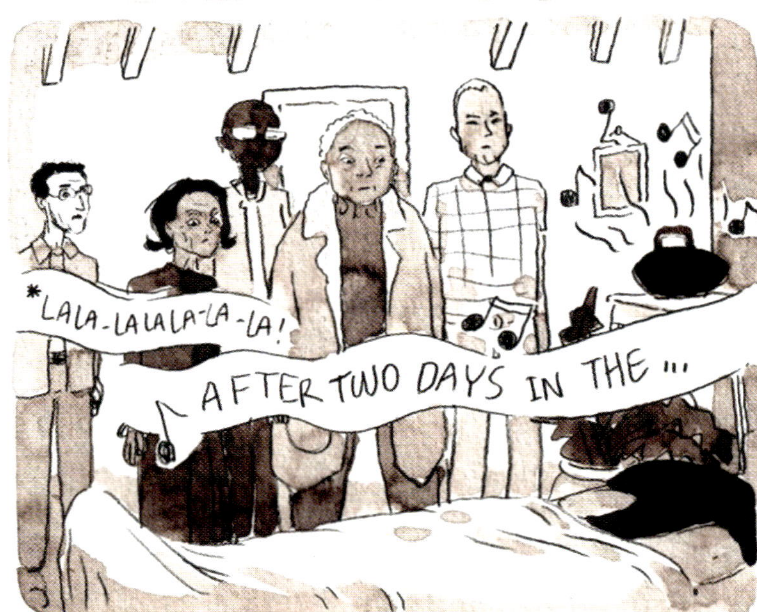

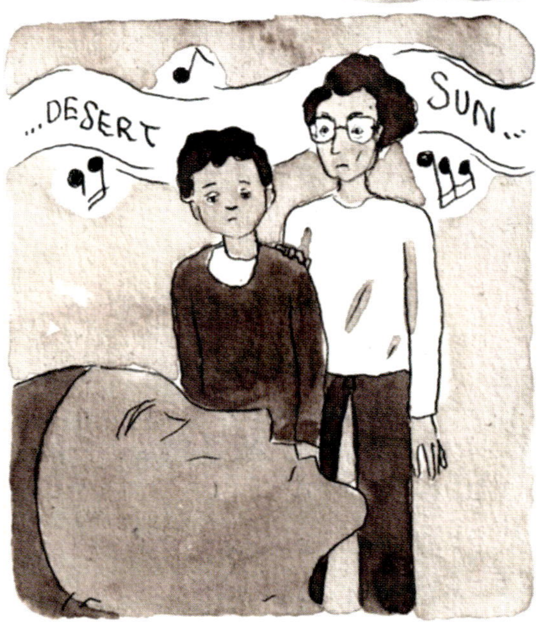

* HORACE ANDY, AGAIN

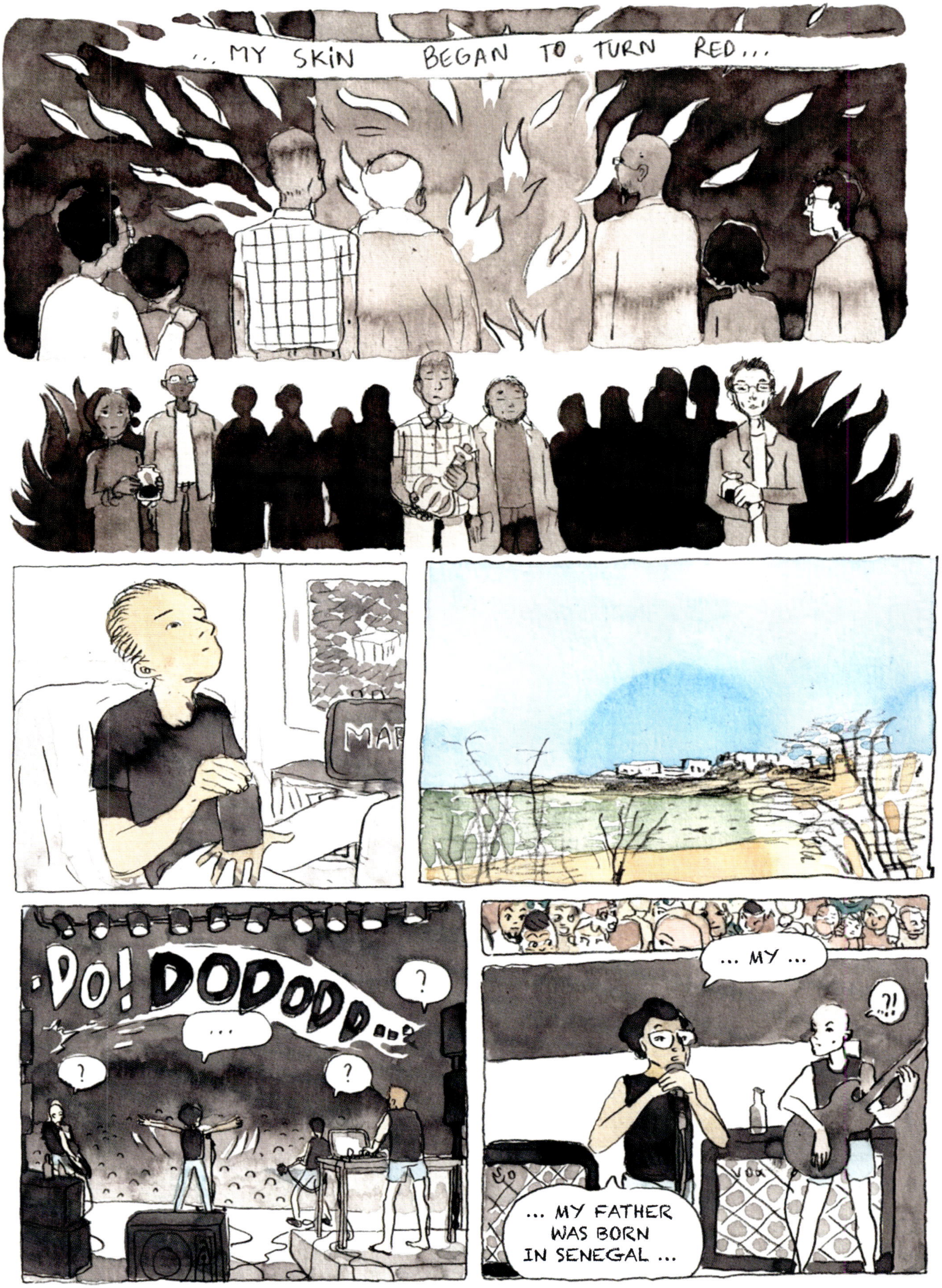

... MY SKIN BEGAN TO TURN RED...

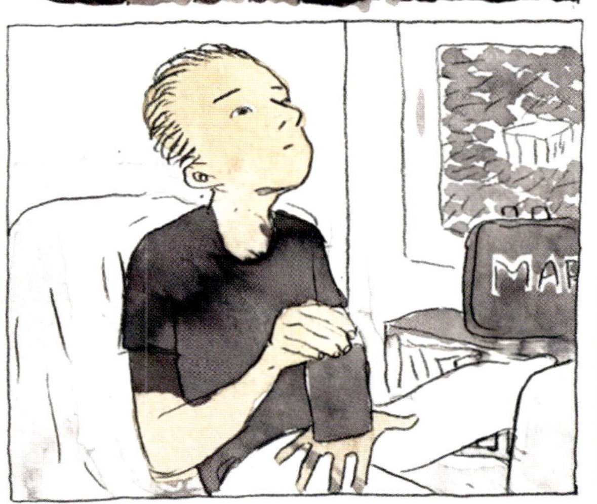

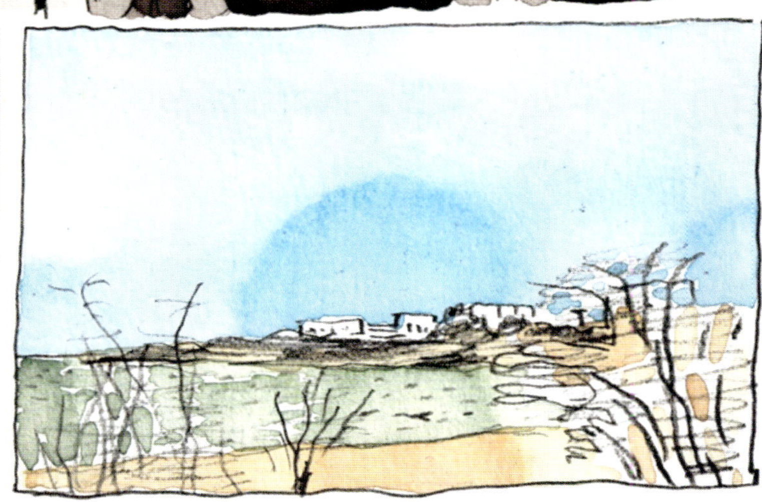

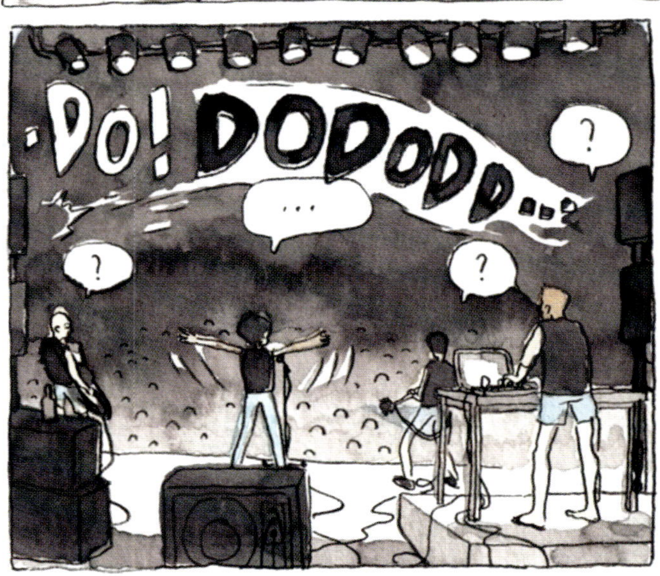

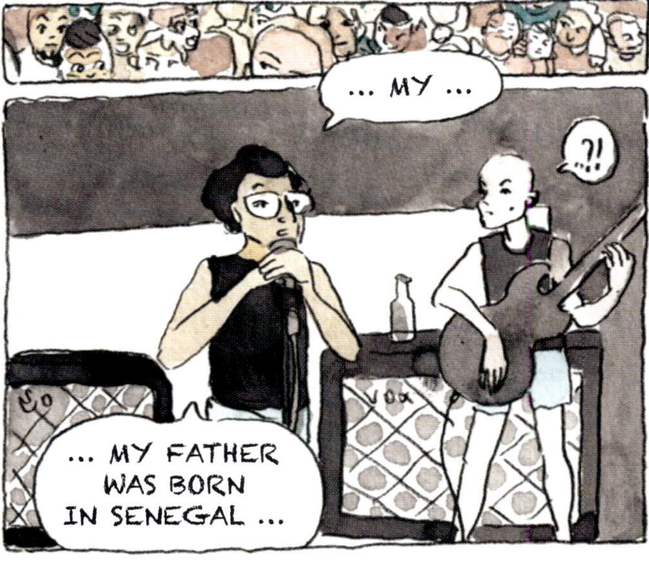

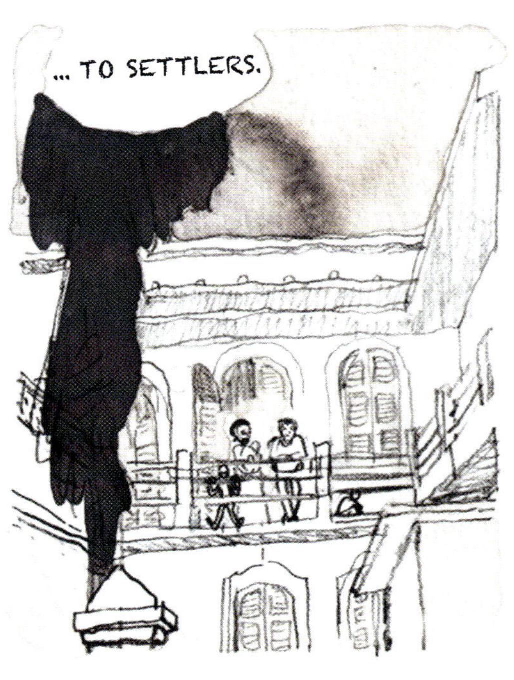

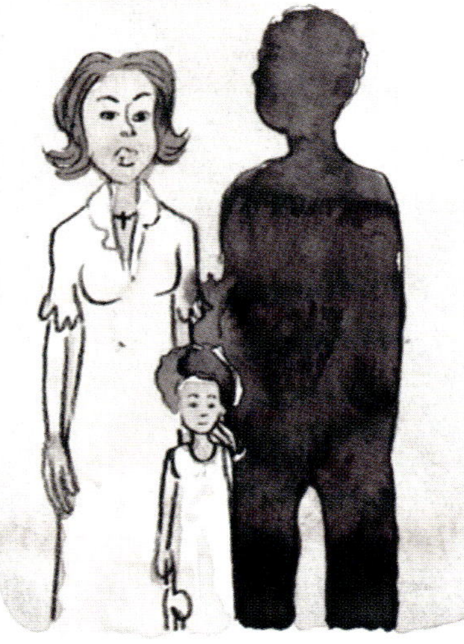

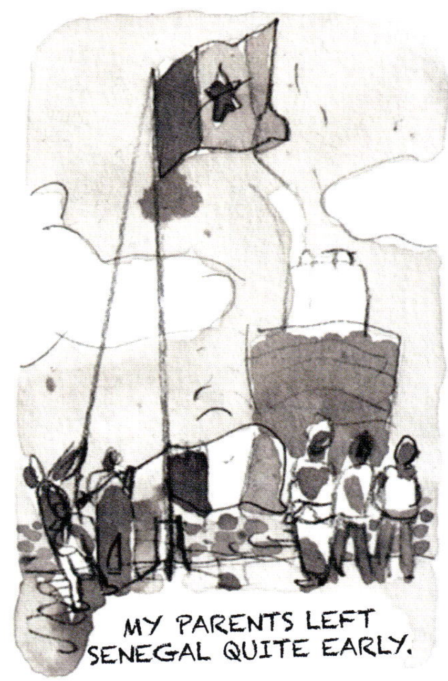

MY FATHER FOLLOWED HIS FAMILY AFTER THE END OF COLONISATION.

LITTLE DAD

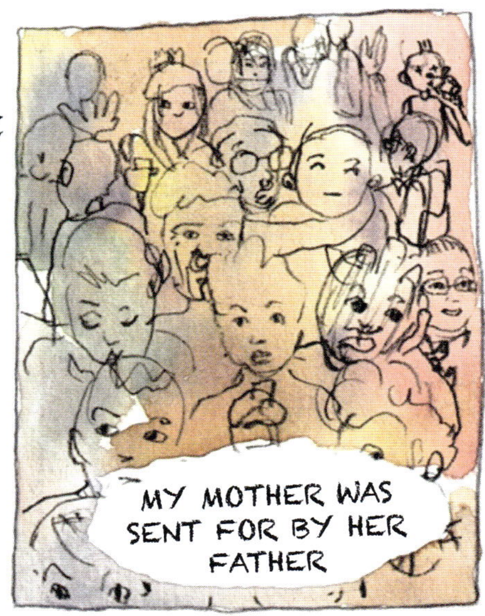

WHO HAD LEFT SENEGAL AT HER BIRTH (SEE FRAME 2) TO TRY HIS LUCK IN FRANCE.

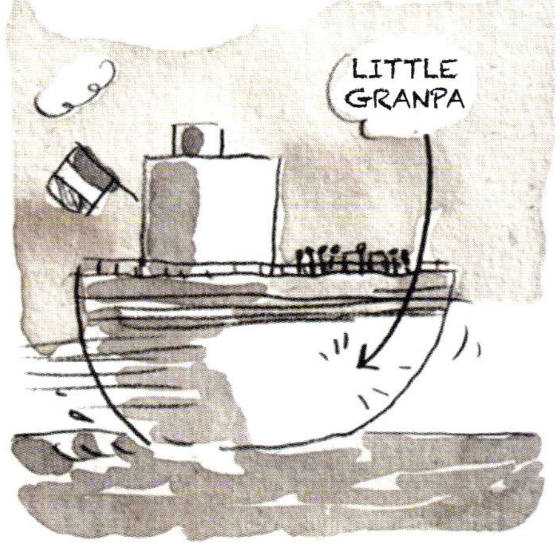

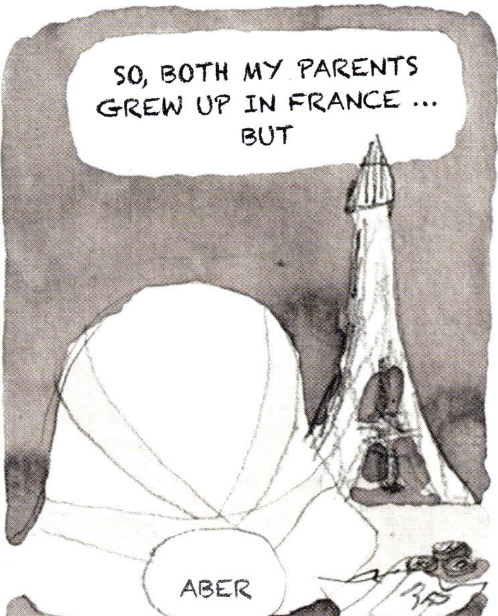

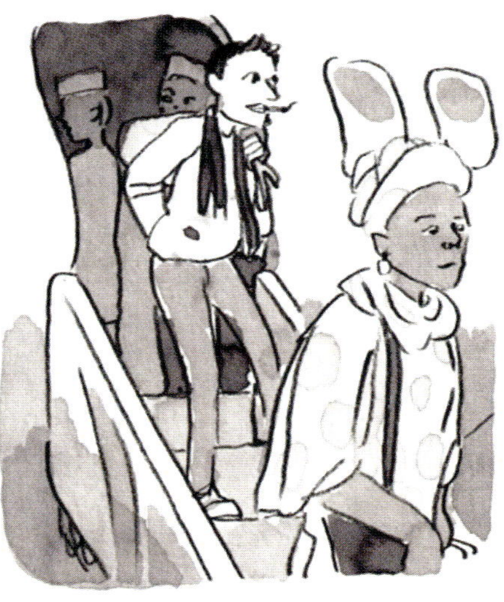

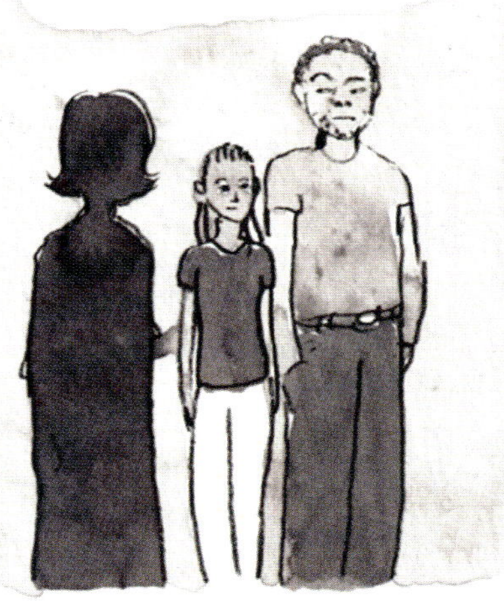

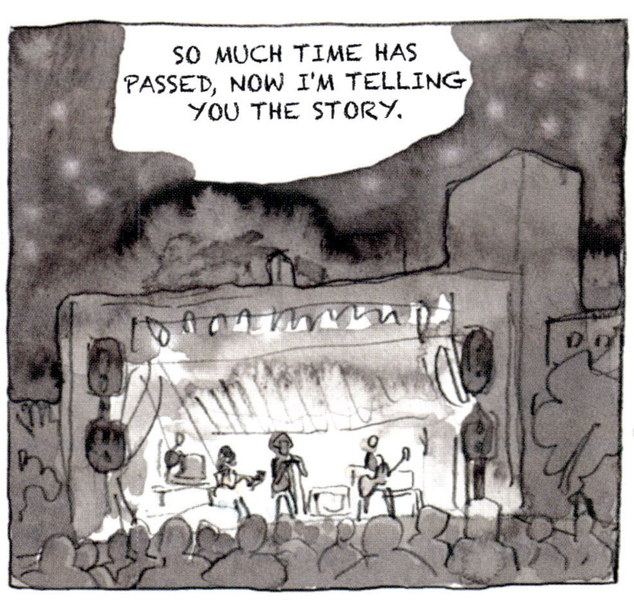
SO MUCH TIME HAS PASSED, NOW I'M TELLING YOU THE STORY.

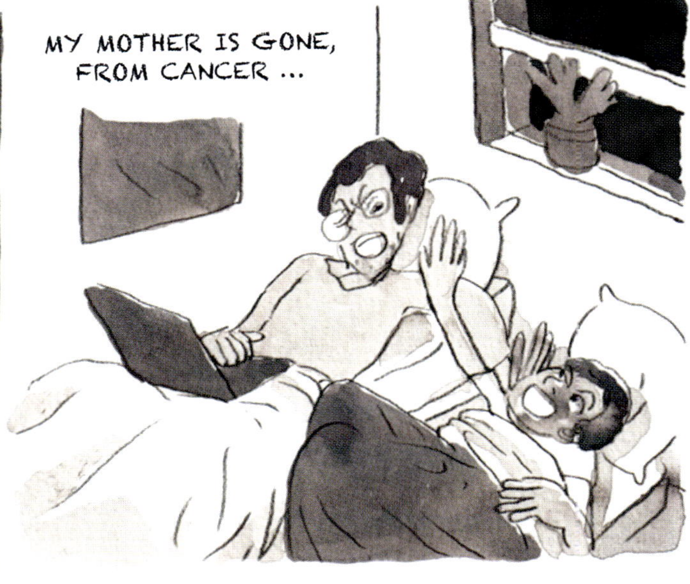
MY MOTHER IS GONE, FROM CANCER ...

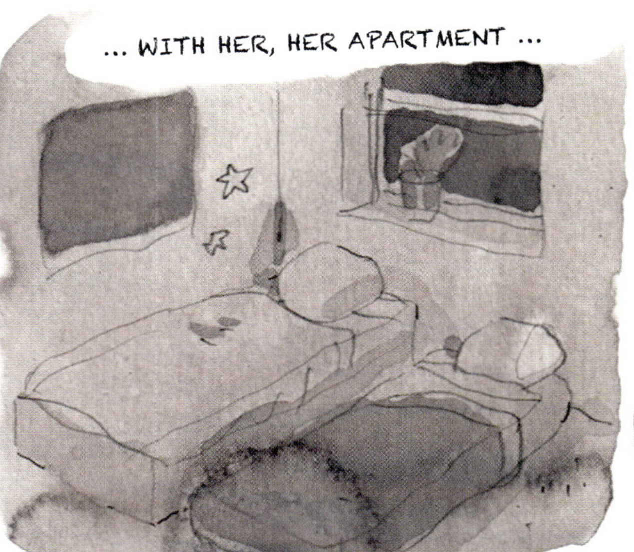
... WITH HER, HER APARTMENT ...

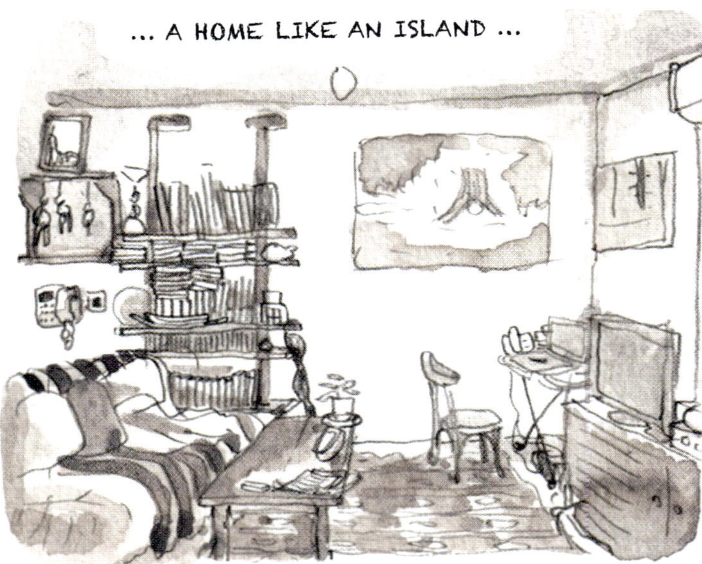
... A HOME LIKE AN ISLAND ...

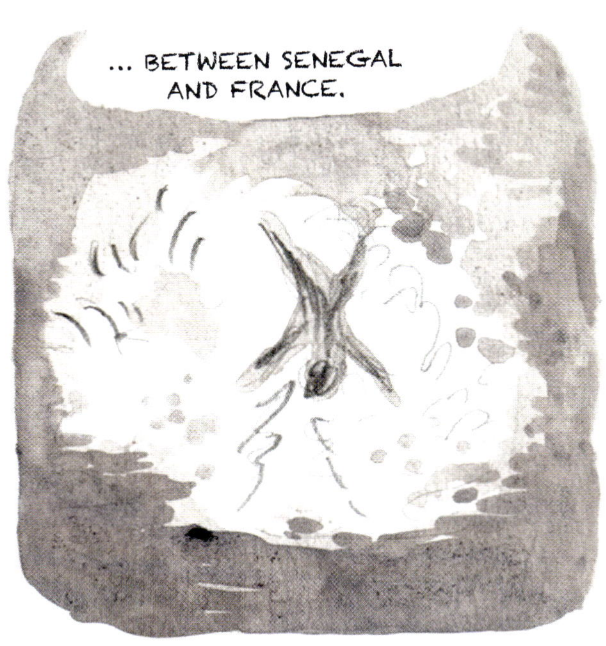
... BETWEEN SENEGAL AND FRANCE.

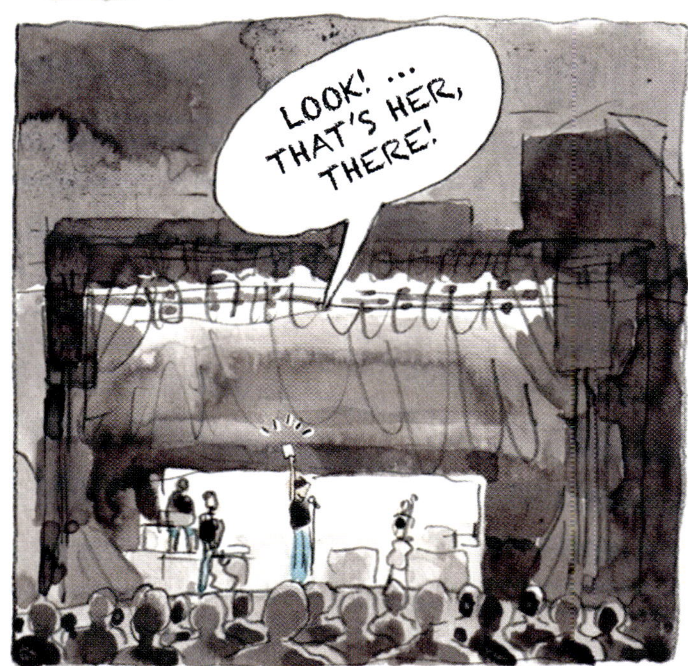
LOOK! ... THAT'S HER, THERE!

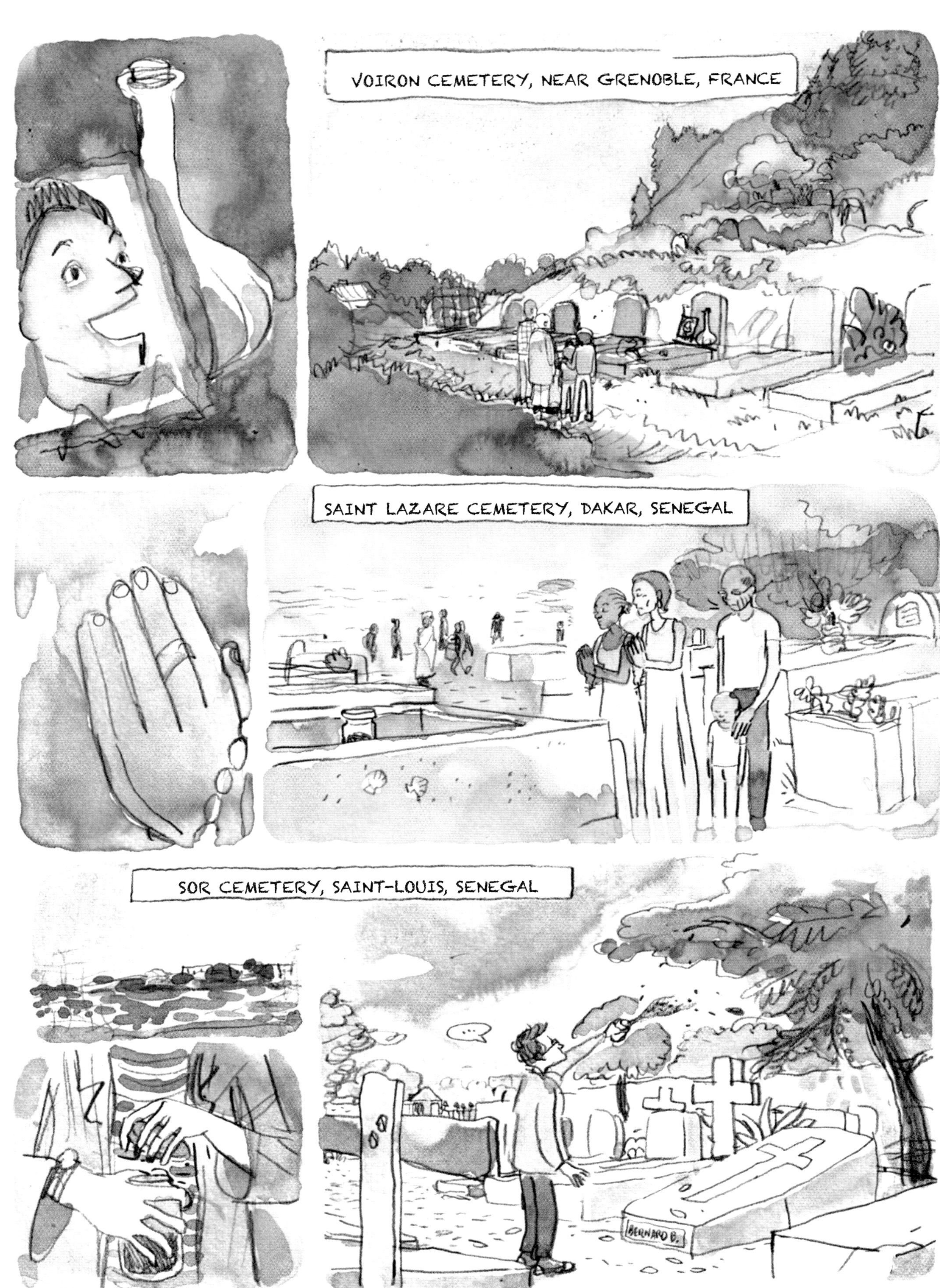
VOIRON CEMETERY, NEAR GRENOBLE, FRANCE
SAINT LAZARE CEMETERY, DAKAR, SENEGAL
SOR CEMETERY, SAINT-LOUIS, SENEGAL
...
BERNARD B.

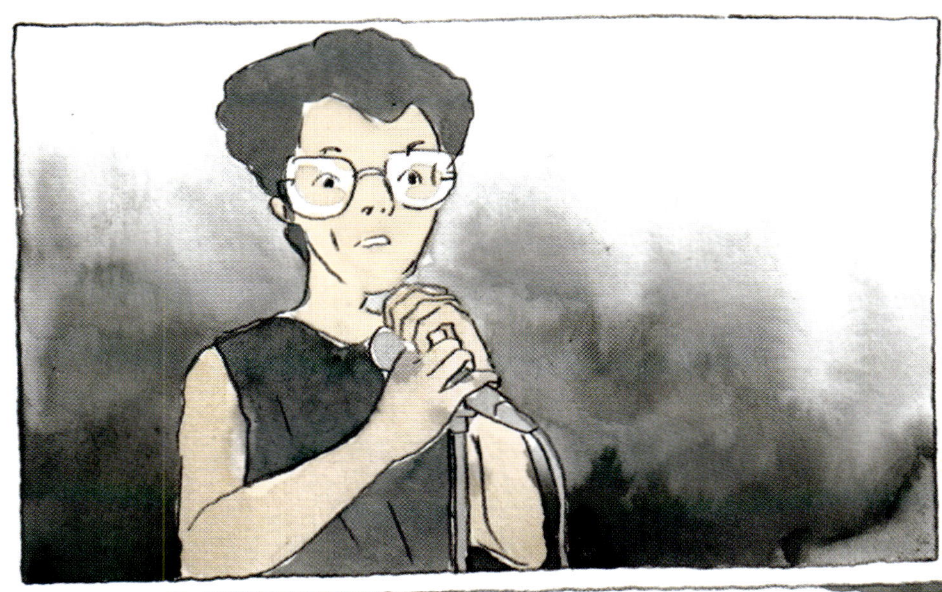

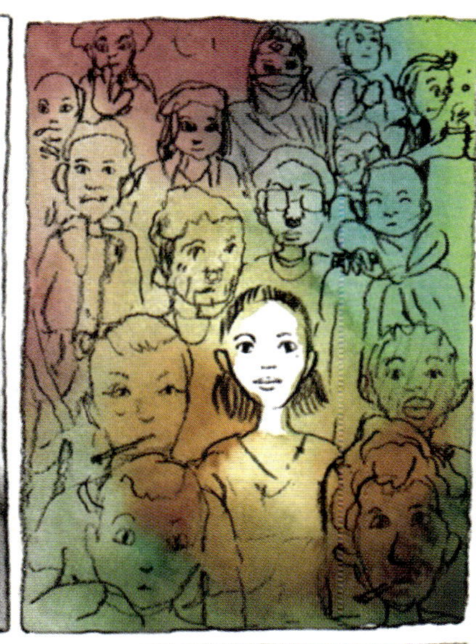

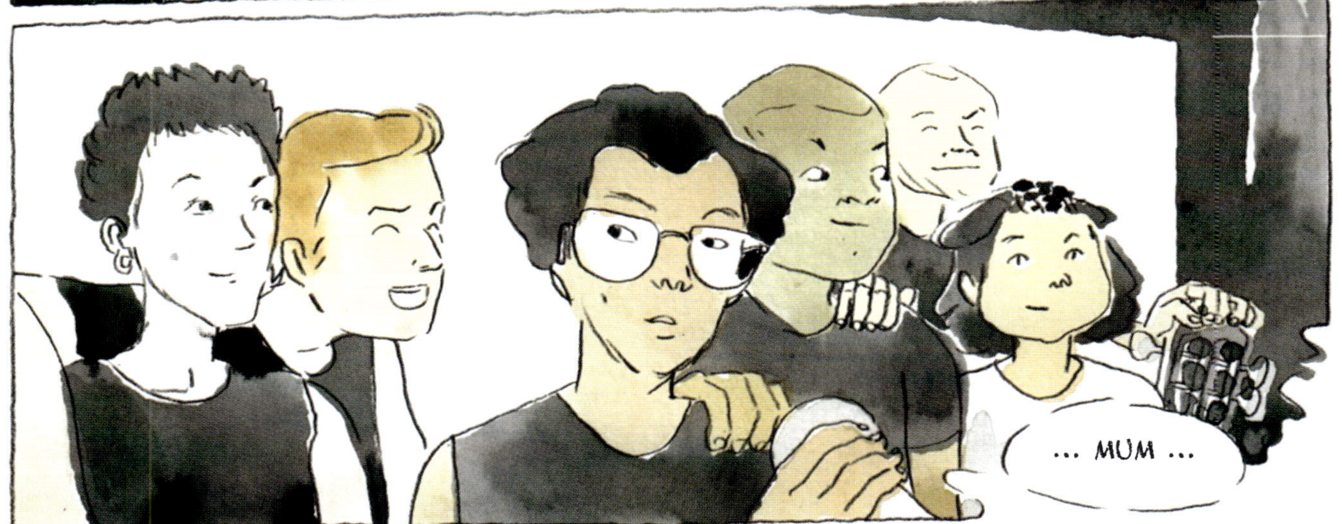
... MUM ...

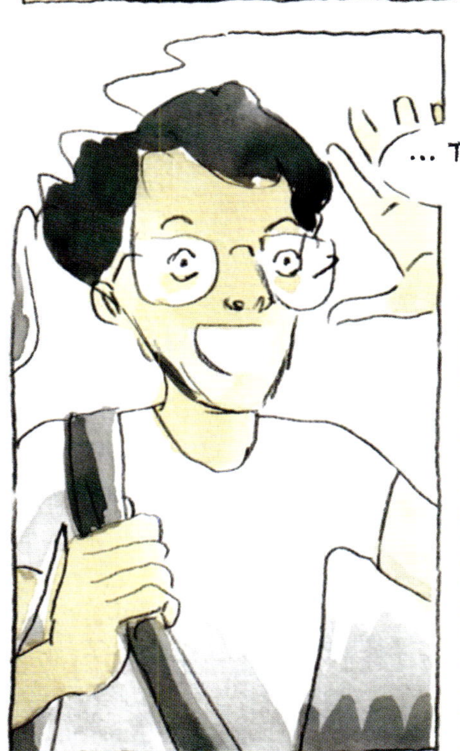
... THERE ARE SO MANY QUESTIONS ...

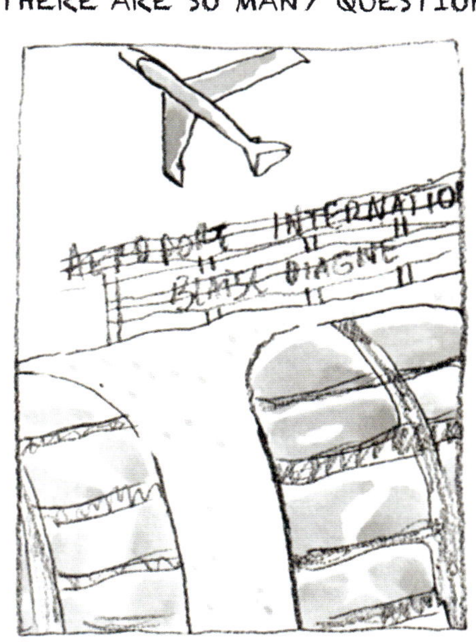

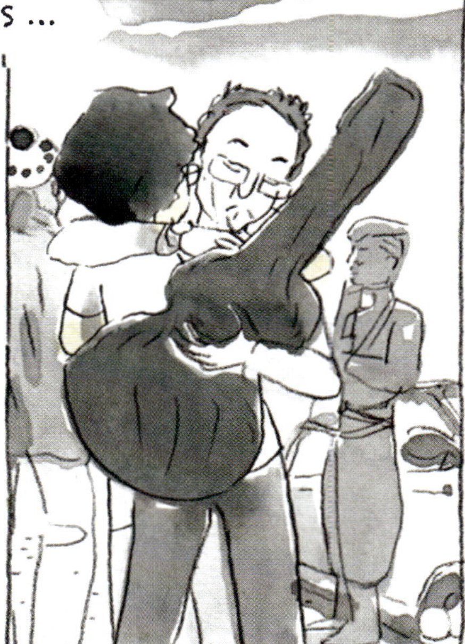

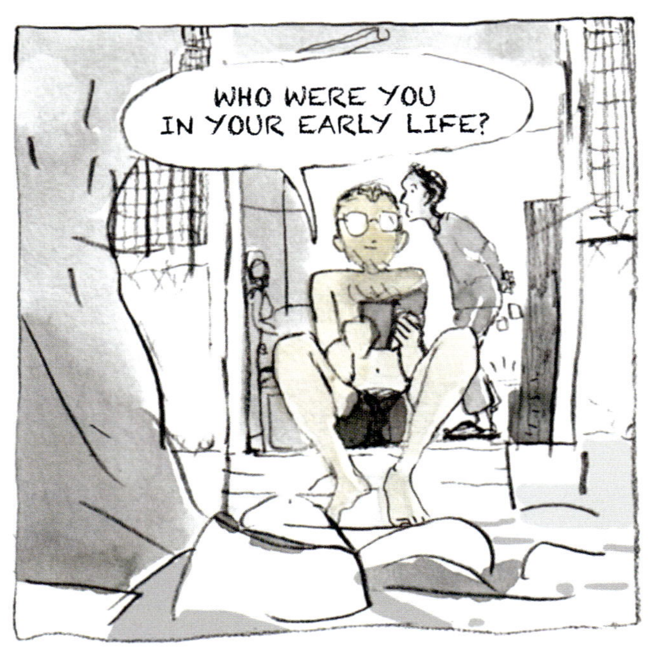
WHO WERE YOU
IN YOUR EARLY LIFE?

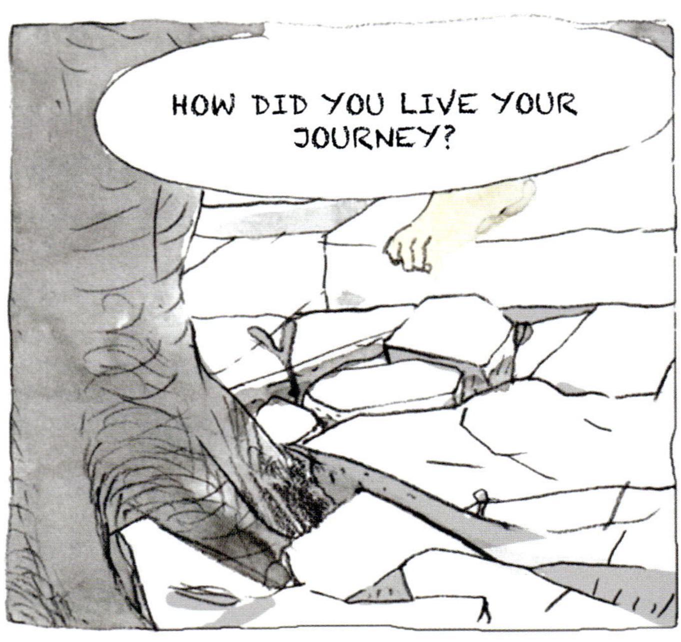
HOW DID YOU LIVE YOUR
JOURNEY?

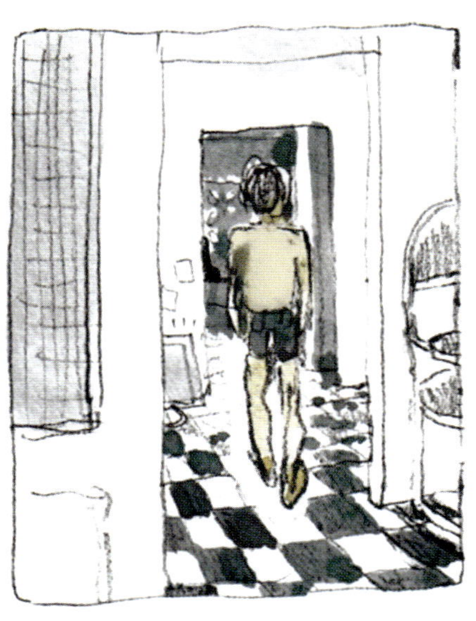

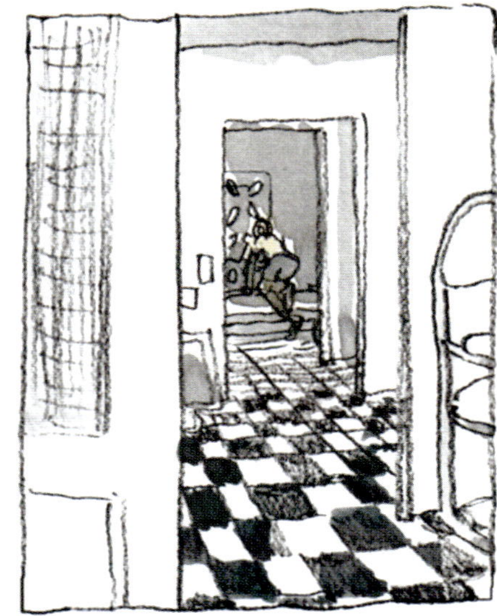

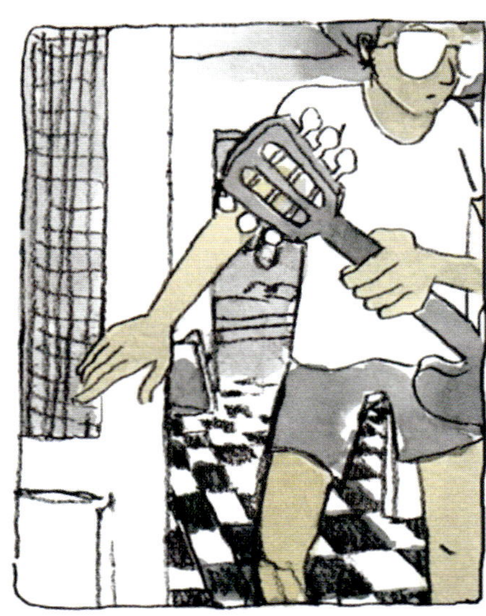

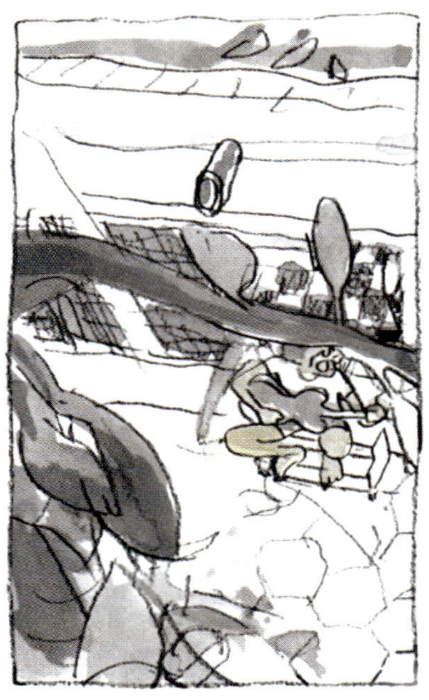

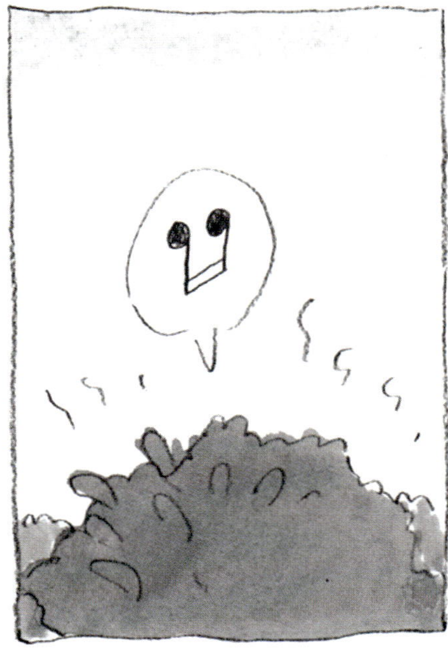

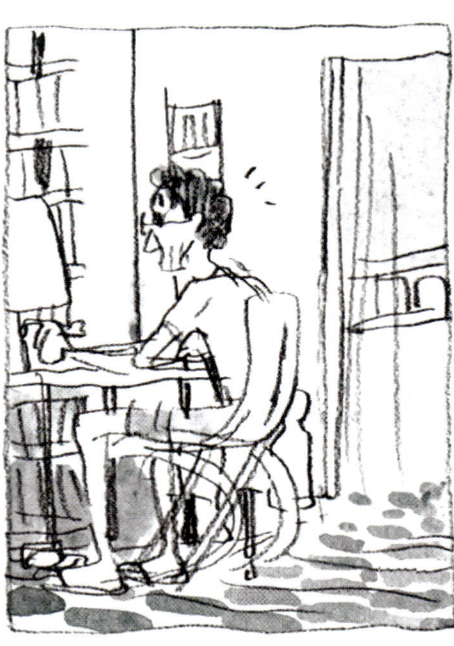

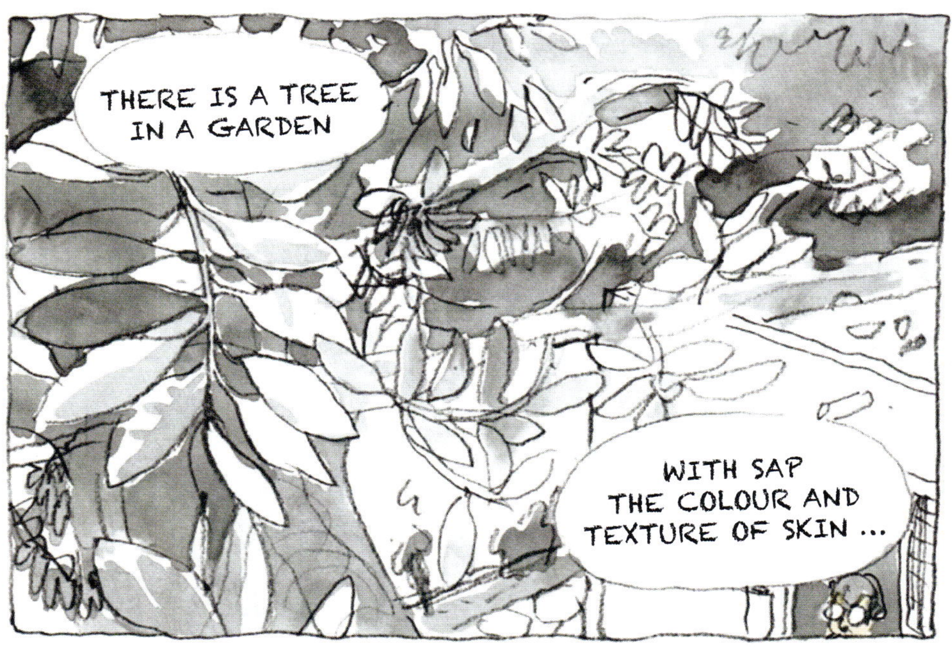
THERE IS A TREE IN A GARDEN
WITH SAP THE COLOUR AND TEXTURE OF SKIN ...

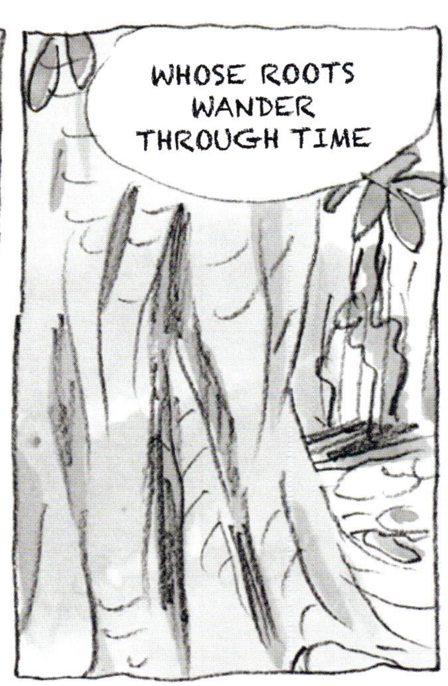
WHOSE ROOTS WANDER THROUGH TIME

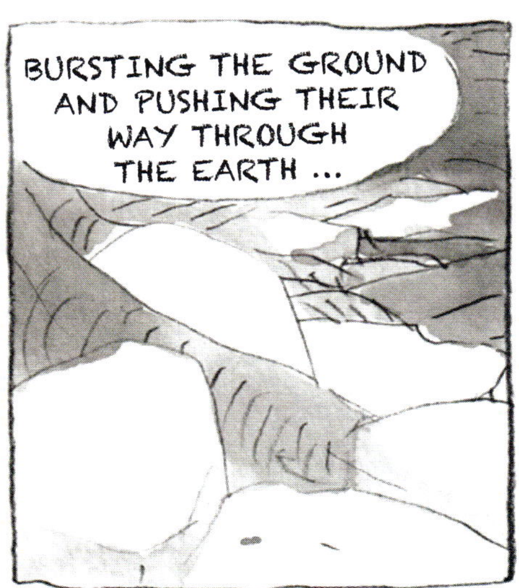
BURSTING THE GROUND AND PUSHING THEIR WAY THROUGH THE EARTH ...

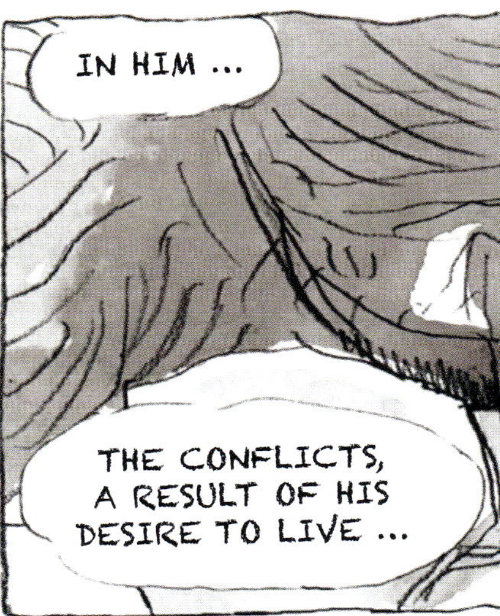
IN HIM ...
THE CONFLICTS, A RESULT OF HIS DESIRE TO LIVE ...

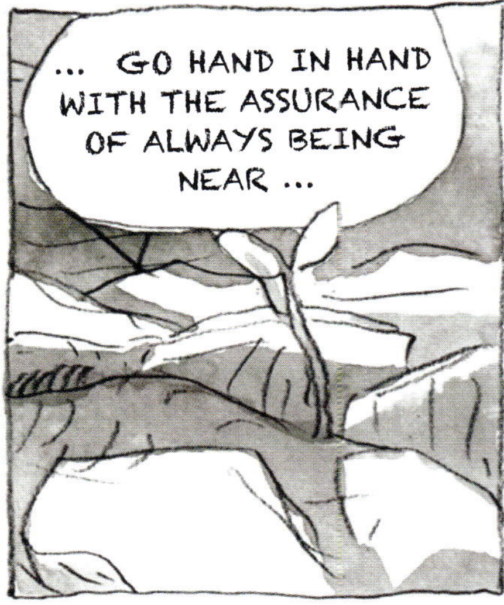
... GO HAND IN HAND WITH THE ASSURANCE OF ALWAYS BEING NEAR ...

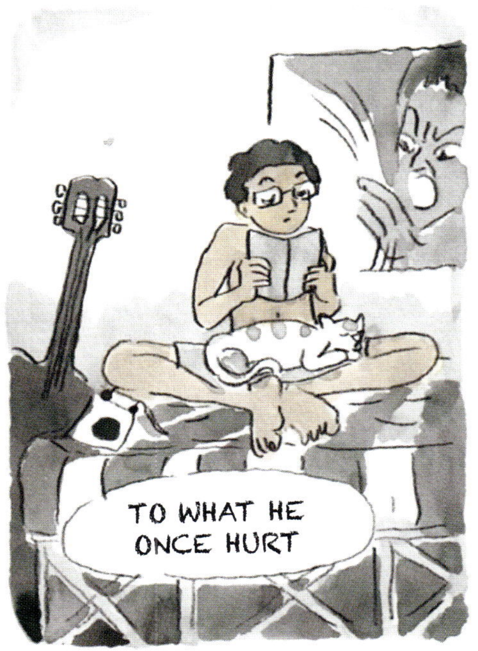
TO WHAT HE ONCE HURT

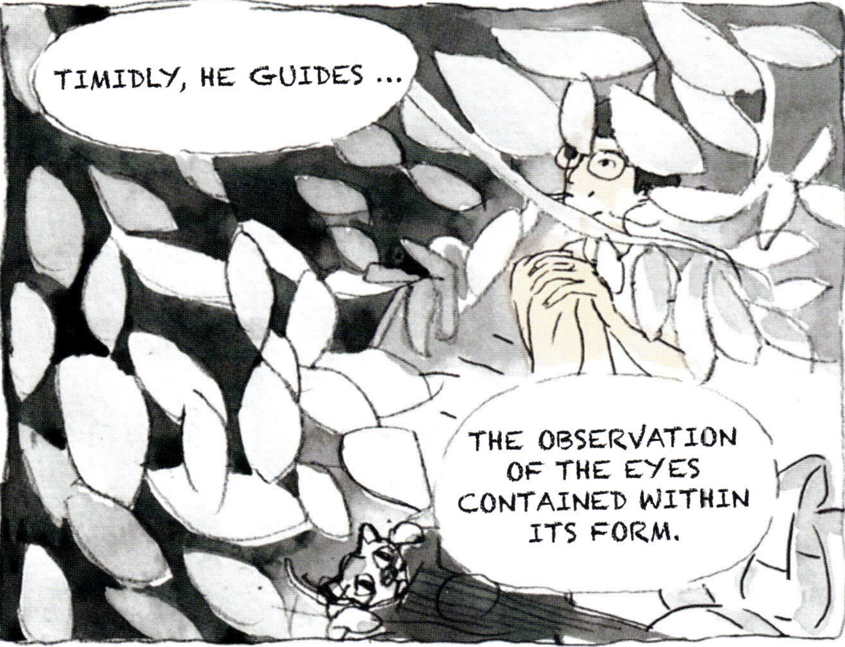
TIMIDLY, HE GUIDES ...
THE OBSERVATION OF THE EYES CONTAINED WITHIN ITS FORM.

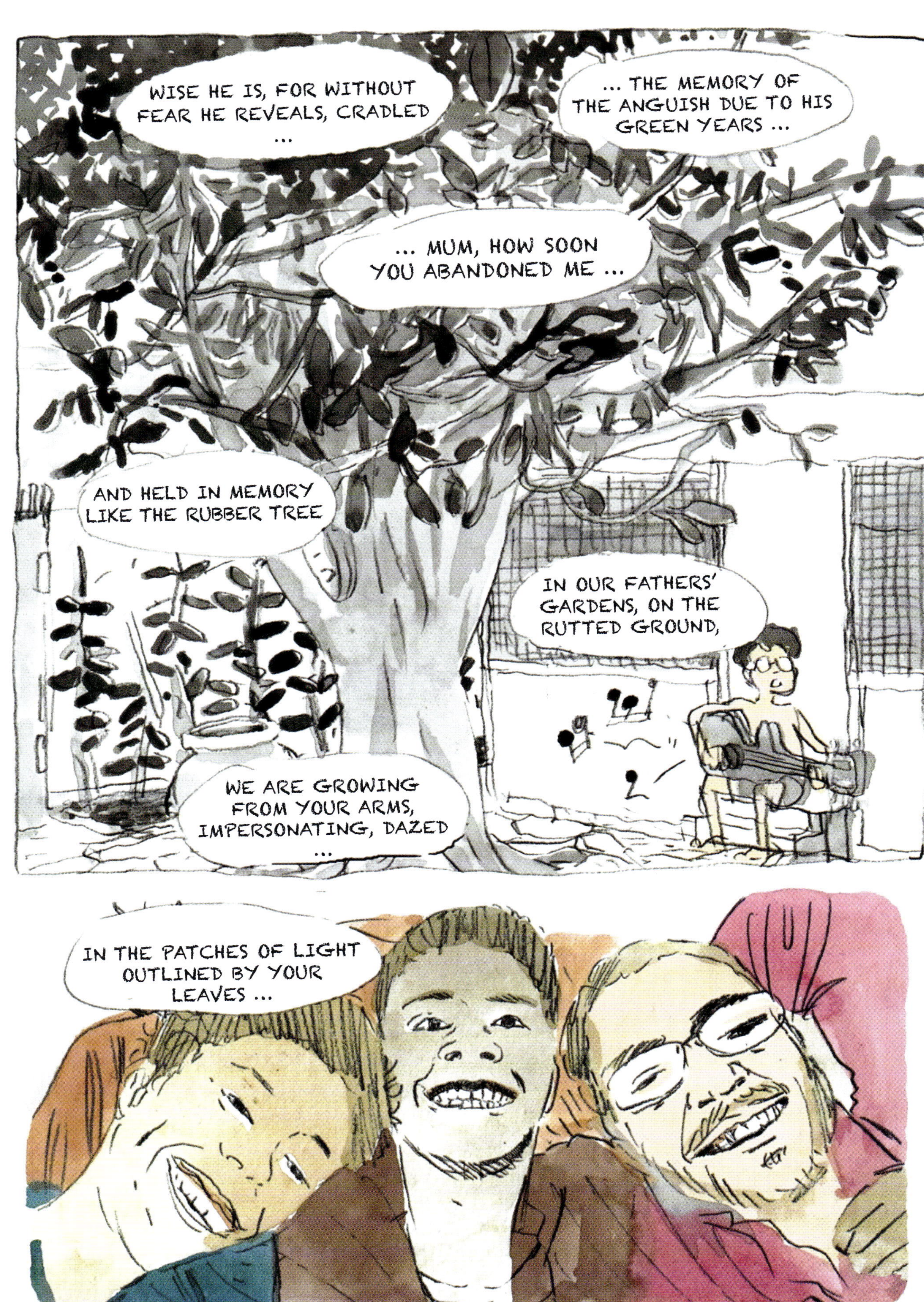
WISE HE IS, FOR WITHOUT FEAR HE REVEALS, CRADLED ...
... THE MEMORY OF THE ANGUISH DUE TO HIS GREEN YEARS ...
... MUM, HOW SOON YOU ABANDONED ME ...
AND HELD IN MEMORY LIKE THE RUBBER TREE
IN OUR FATHERS' GARDENS, ON THE RUTTED GROUND,
WE ARE GROWING FROM YOUR ARMS, IMPERSONATING, DAZED ...
IN THE PATCHES OF LIGHT OUTLINED BY YOUR LEAVES ...

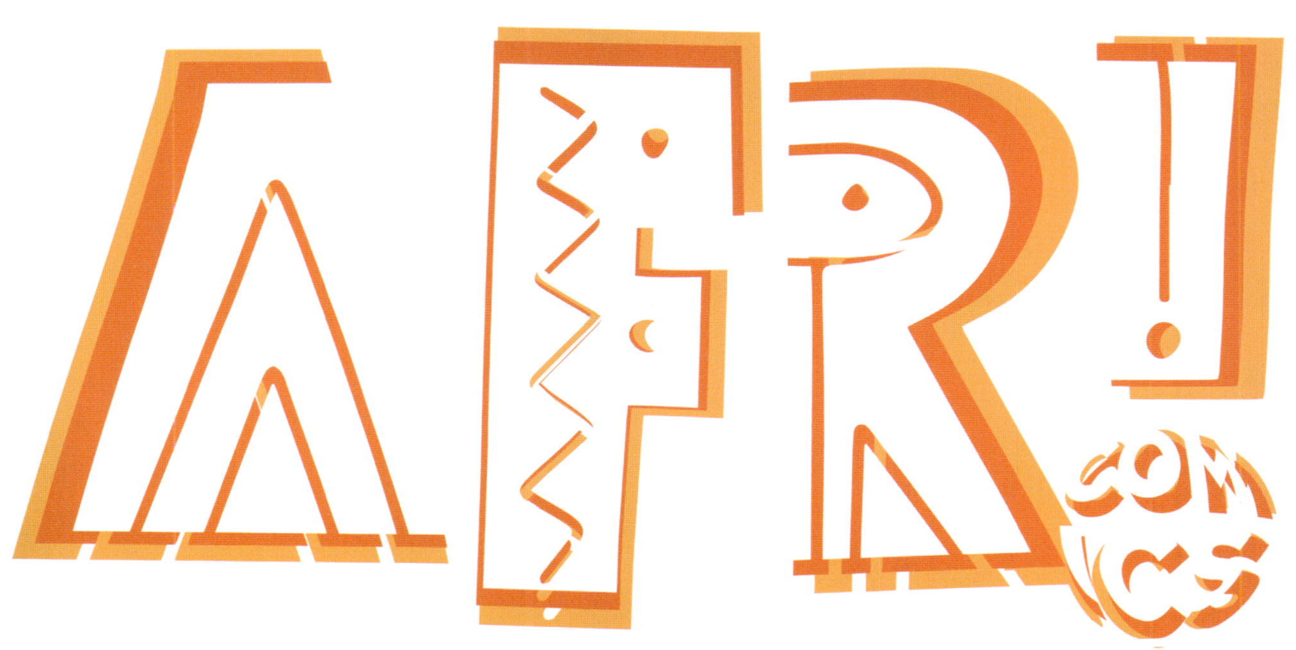
AFR!
COMICS

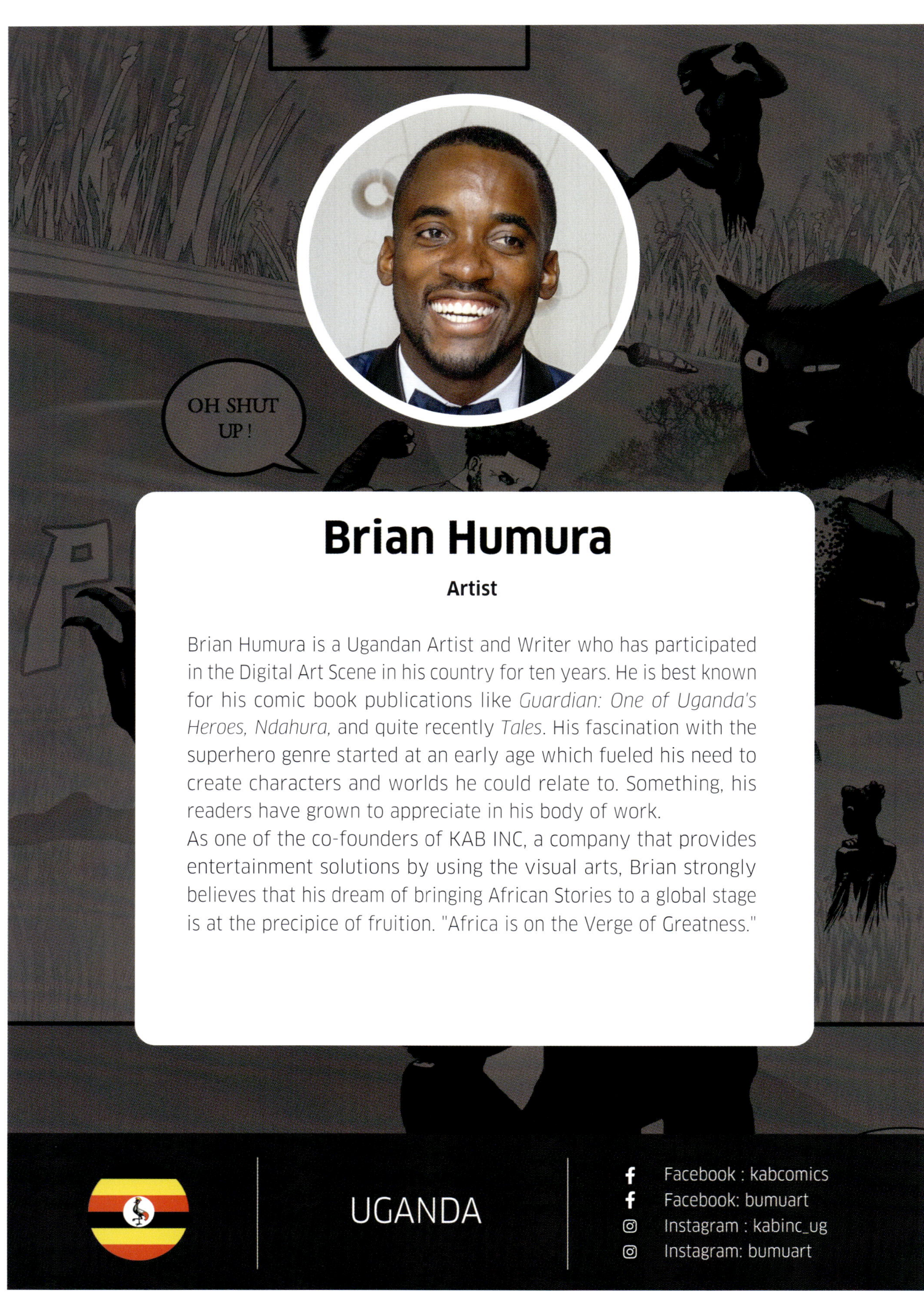

Brian Humura

Artist

Brian Humura is a Ugandan Artist and Writer who has participated in the Digital Art Scene in his country for ten years. He is best known for his comic book publications like *Guardian: One of Uganda's Heroes*, *Ndahura*, and quite recently *Tales*. His fascination with the superhero genre started at an early age which fueled his need to create characters and worlds he could relate to. Something, his readers have grown to appreciate in his body of work.
As one of the co-founders of KAB INC, a company that provides entertainment solutions by using the visual arts, Brian strongly believes that his dream of bringing African Stories to a global stage is at the precipice of fruition. "Africa is on the Verge of Greatness."

UGANDA

Facebook : kabcomics
Facebook: bumuart
Instagram : kabinc_ug
Instagram: bumuart

BRIAN HUMURA'S

THE COG

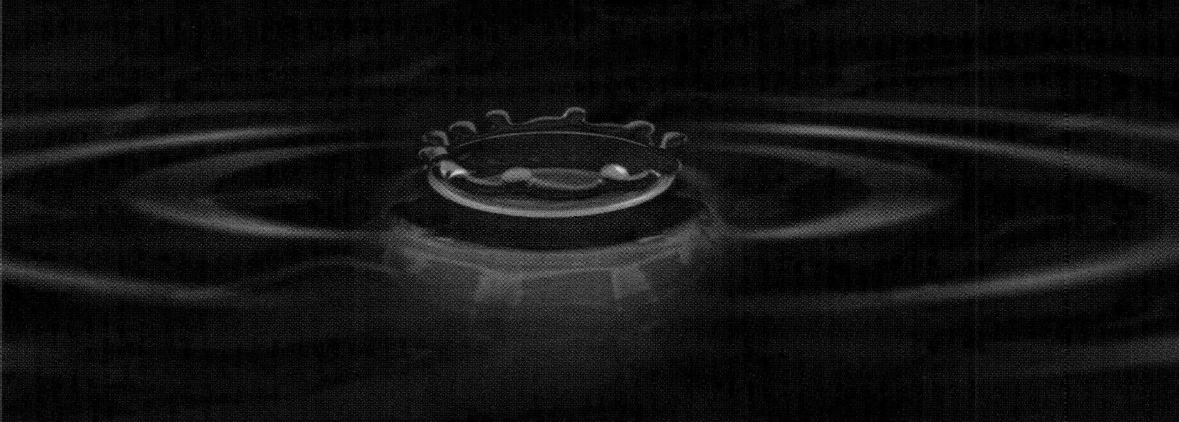

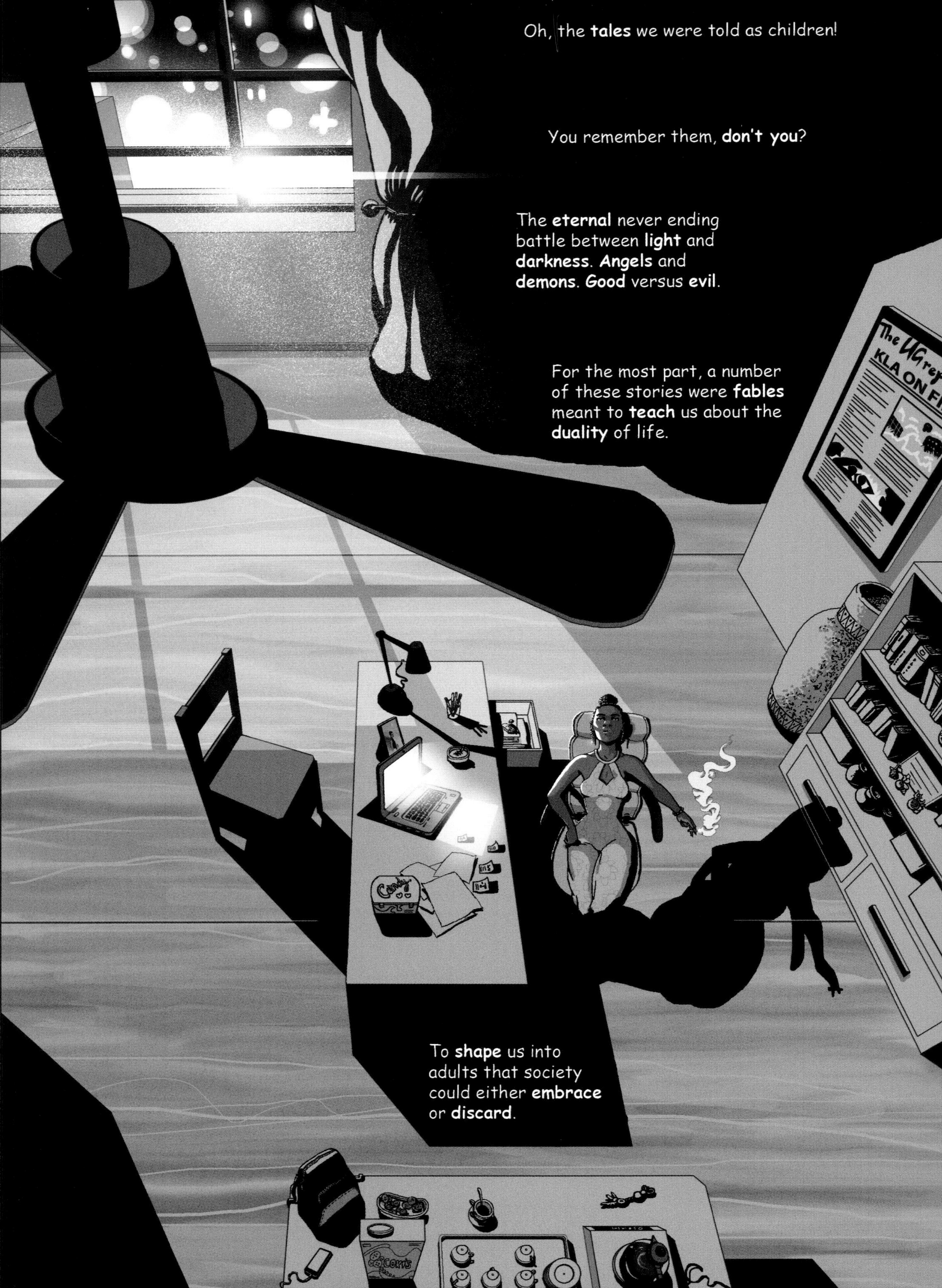
Oh, the **tales** we were told as children!
You remember them, **don't you**?
The **eternal** never ending battle between **light** and **darkness**. **Angels** and **demons**. **Good** versus **evil**.
For the most part, a number of these stories were **fables** meant to **teach** us about the **duality** of life.
To **shape** us into adults that society could either **embrace** or **discard**.

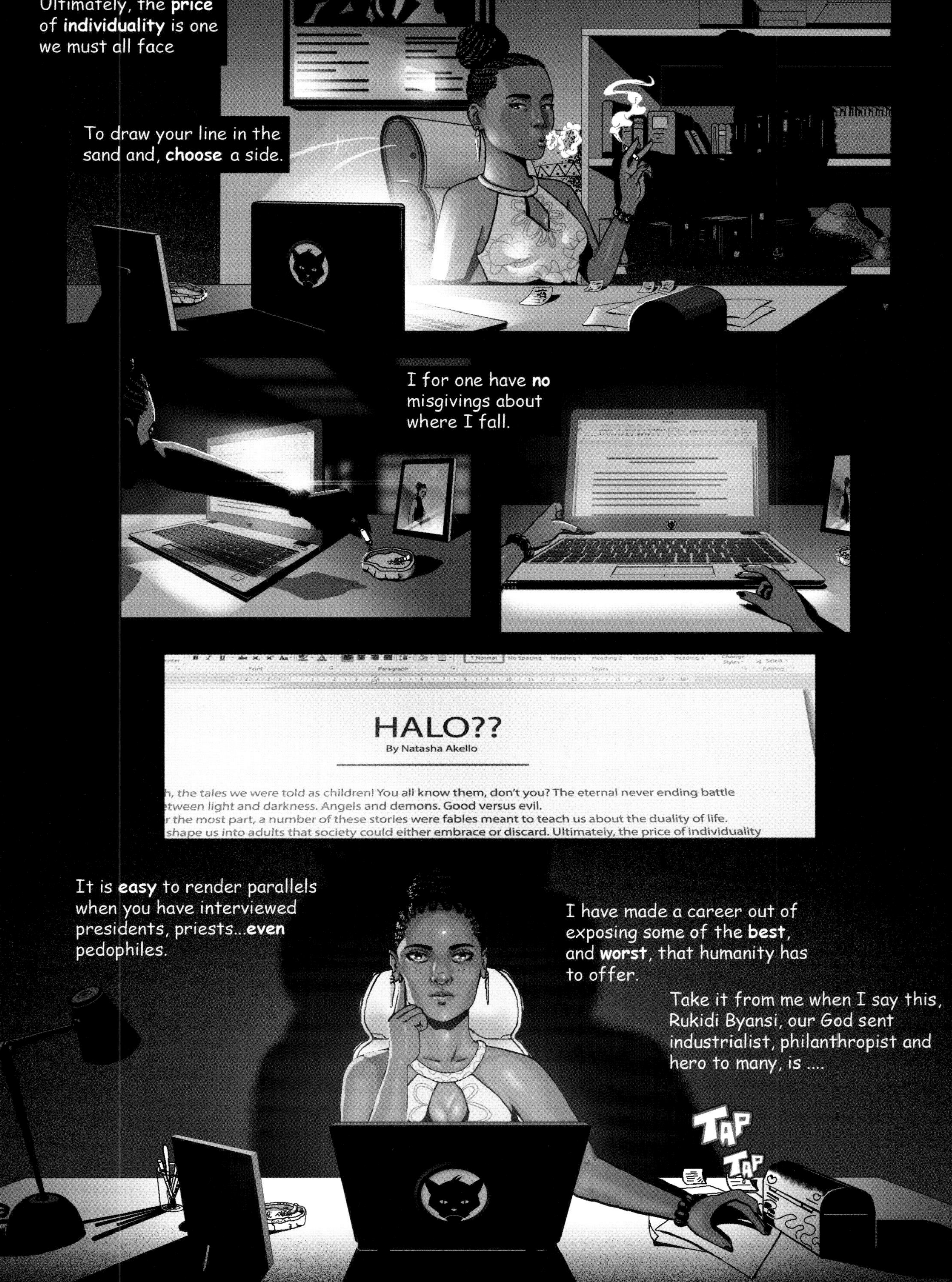

Ultimately, the **price** of **individuality** is one we must all face
To draw your line in the sand and, **choose** a side.
I for one have **no** misgivings about where I fall.
HALO??
By Natasha Akello
h, the tales we were told as children! You all know them, don't you? The eternal never ending battle
tween light and darkness. Angels and demons. Good versus evil.
r the most part, a number of these stories were fables meant to teach us about the duality of life.
shape us into adults that society could either embrace or discard. Ultimately, the price of individuality
It is **easy** to render parallels when you have interviewed presidents, priests...**even** pedophiles.
I have made a career out of exposing some of the **best**, and **worst**, that humanity has to offer.
Take it from me when I say this, Rukidi Byansi, our God sent industrialist, philanthropist and hero to many, is ....
TAP
TAP

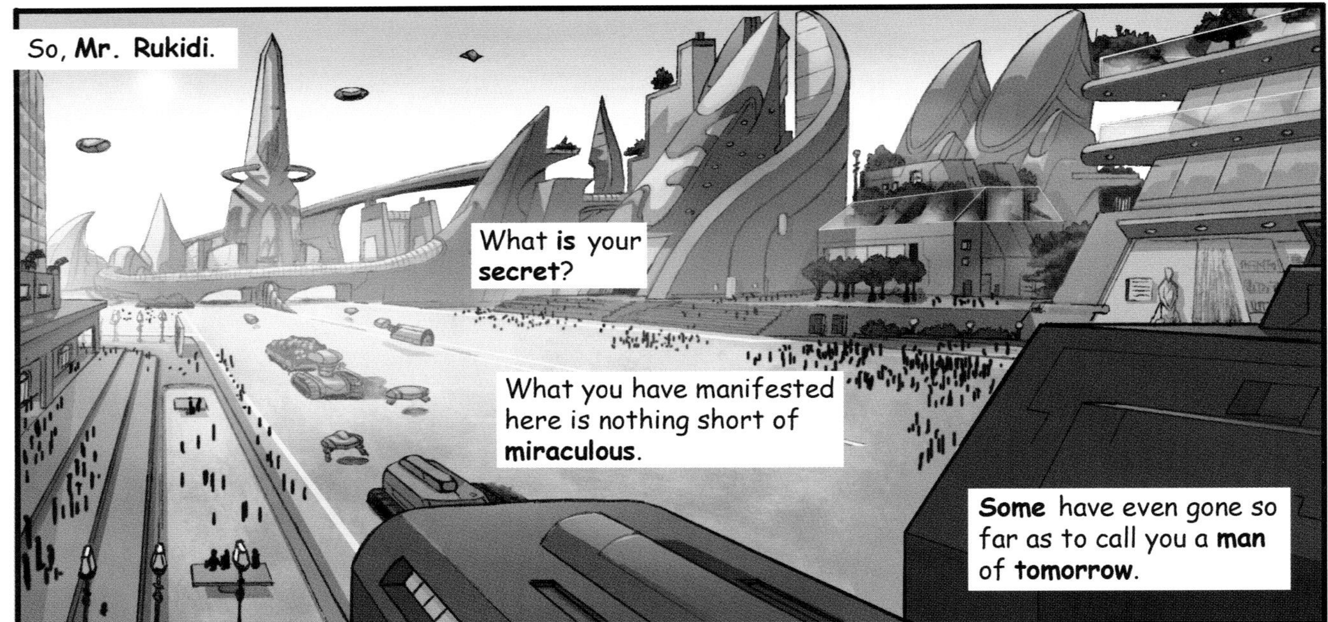
So, **Mr. Rukidi**.
What **is** your **secret**?
What you have manifested here is nothing short of **miraculous**.
Some have even gone so far as to call you a **man** of **tomorrow**.

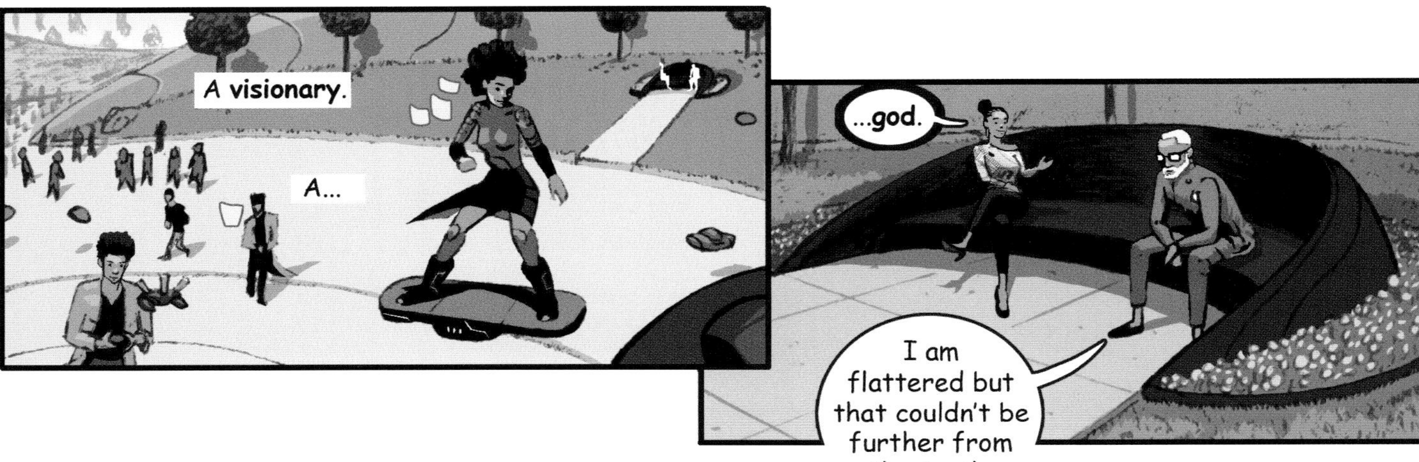
A **visionary**.
A...
...**god**.
I am flattered but that couldn't be further from the truth.

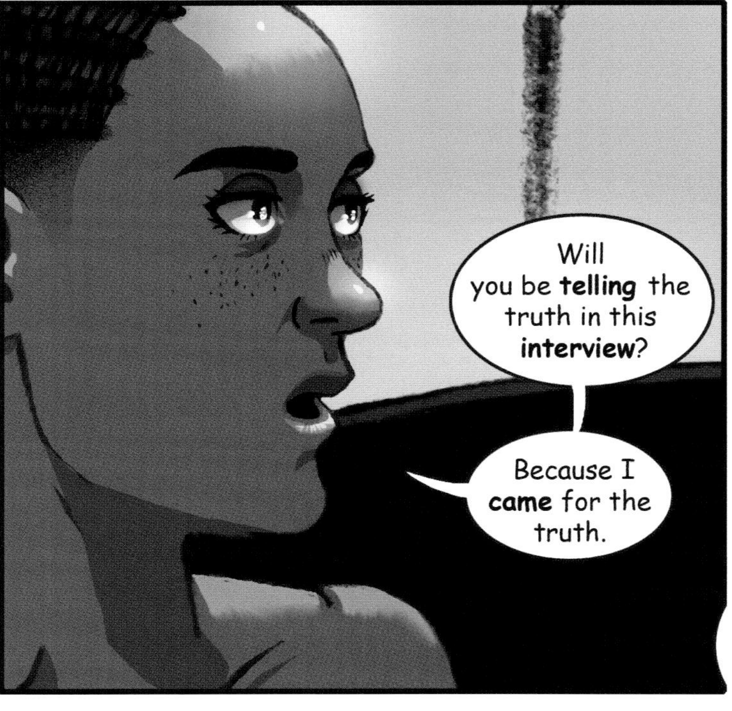
Will you be **telling** the truth in this **interview**?
Because I **came** for the truth.

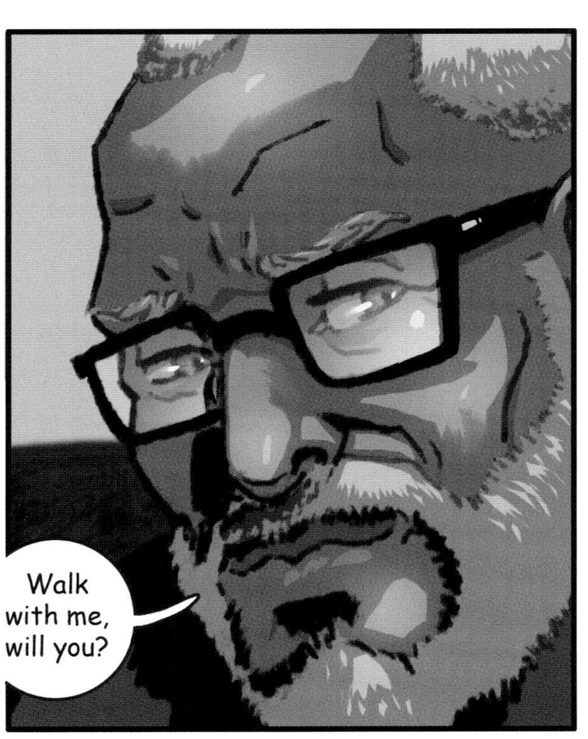
Walk with me, will you?

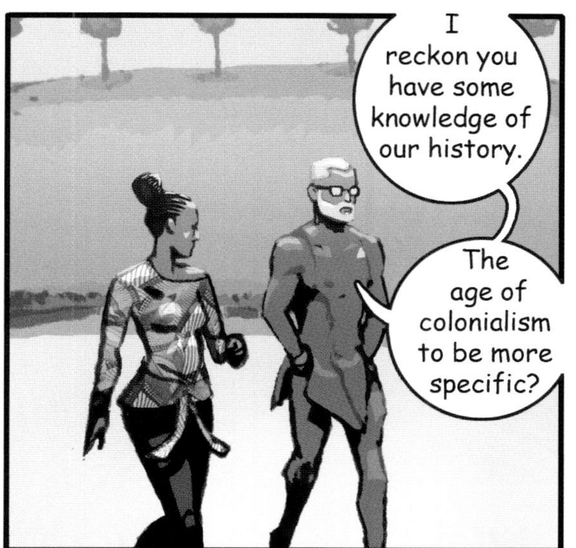
I reckon you have some knowledge of our history.
The age of colonialism to be more specific?

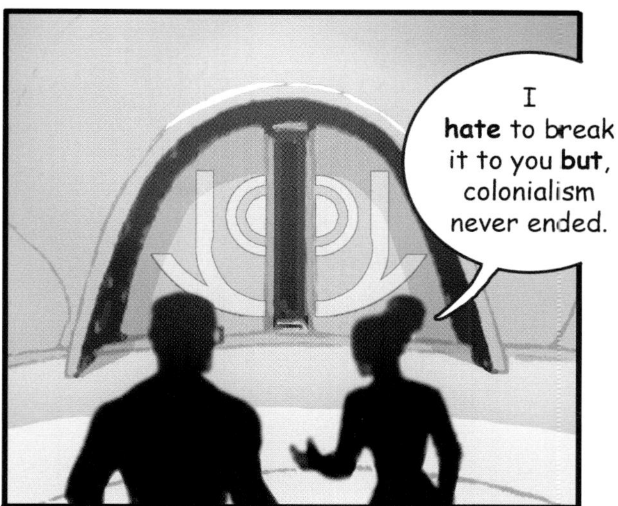
I **hate** to break it to you **but**, colonialism never ended.

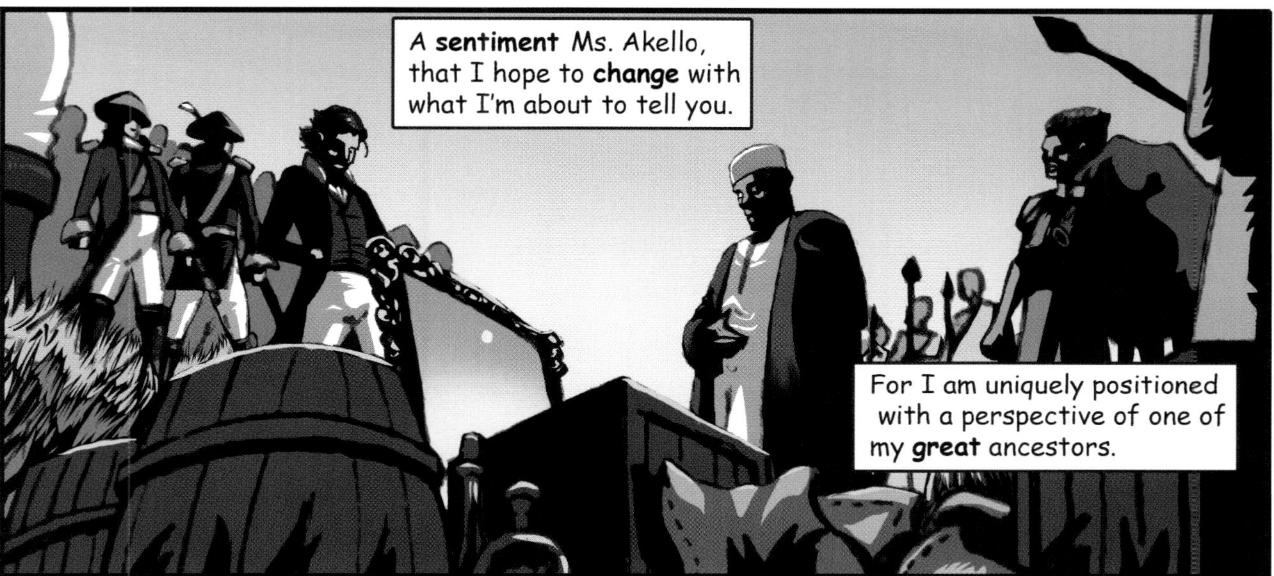
A **sentiment** Ms. Akello, that I hope to **change** with what I'm about to tell you.
For I am uniquely positioned with a perspective of one of my **great** ancestors.

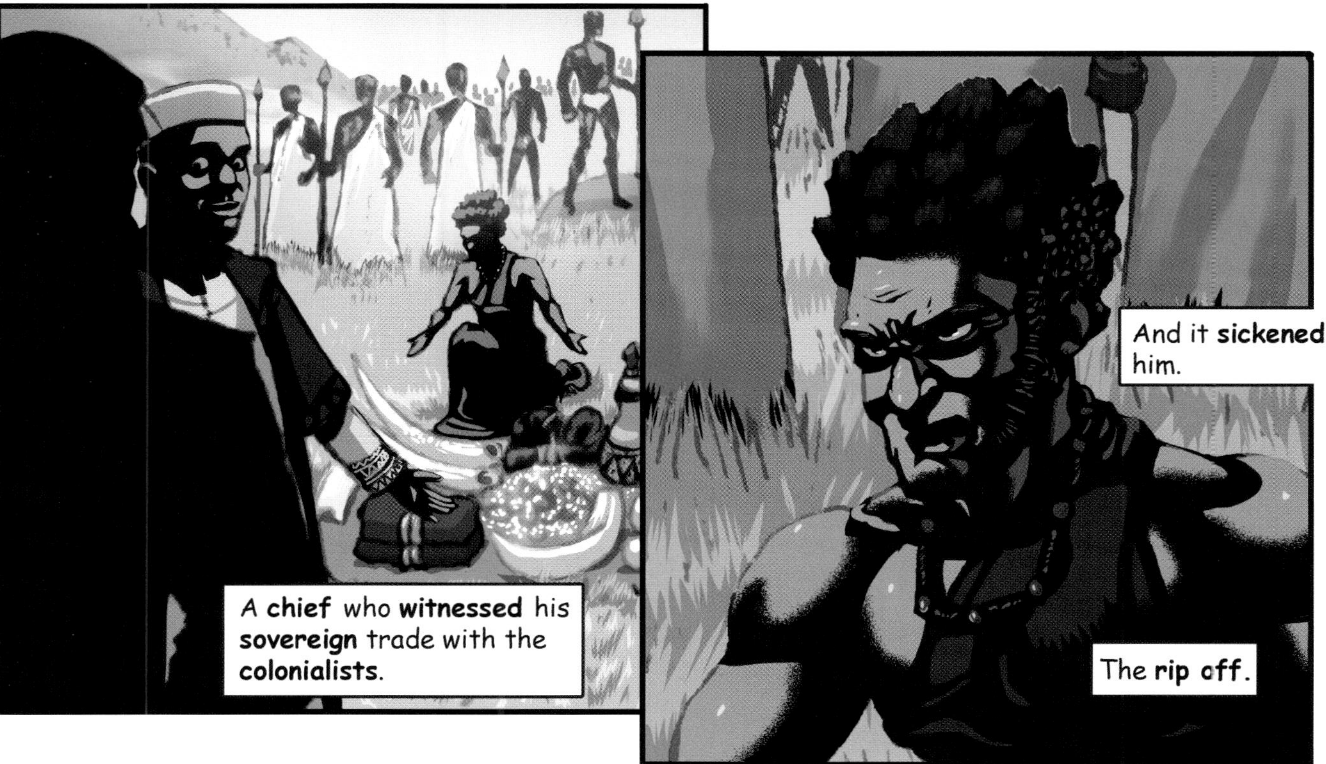
A **chief** who **witnessed** his **sovereign** trade with the **colonialists**.
And it **sickened** him.
The **rip off**.

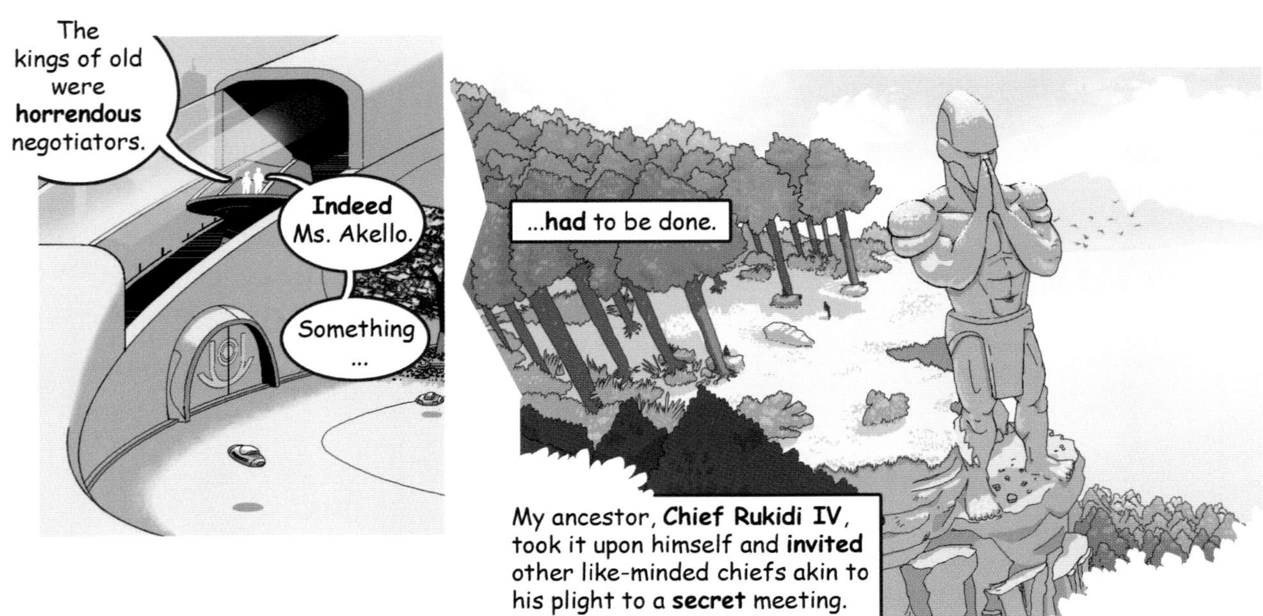
The kings of old were **horrendous** negotiators.
Indeed Ms. Akello.
Something ...
...**had** to be done.
My ancestor, **Chief Rukidi IV**, took it upon himself and **invited** other like-minded chiefs akin to his plight to a **secret** meeting.

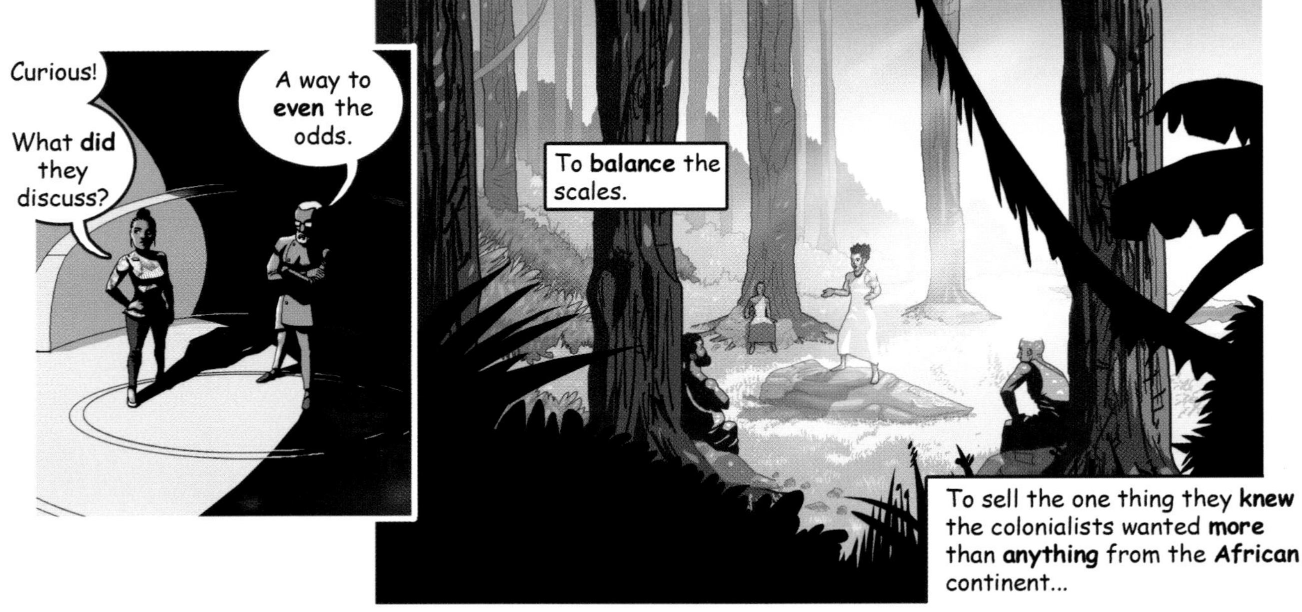
Curious!
What **did** they discuss?
A way to **even** the odds.
To **balance** the scales.
To sell the one thing they **knew** the colonialists wanted **more** than **anything** from the **African** continent...

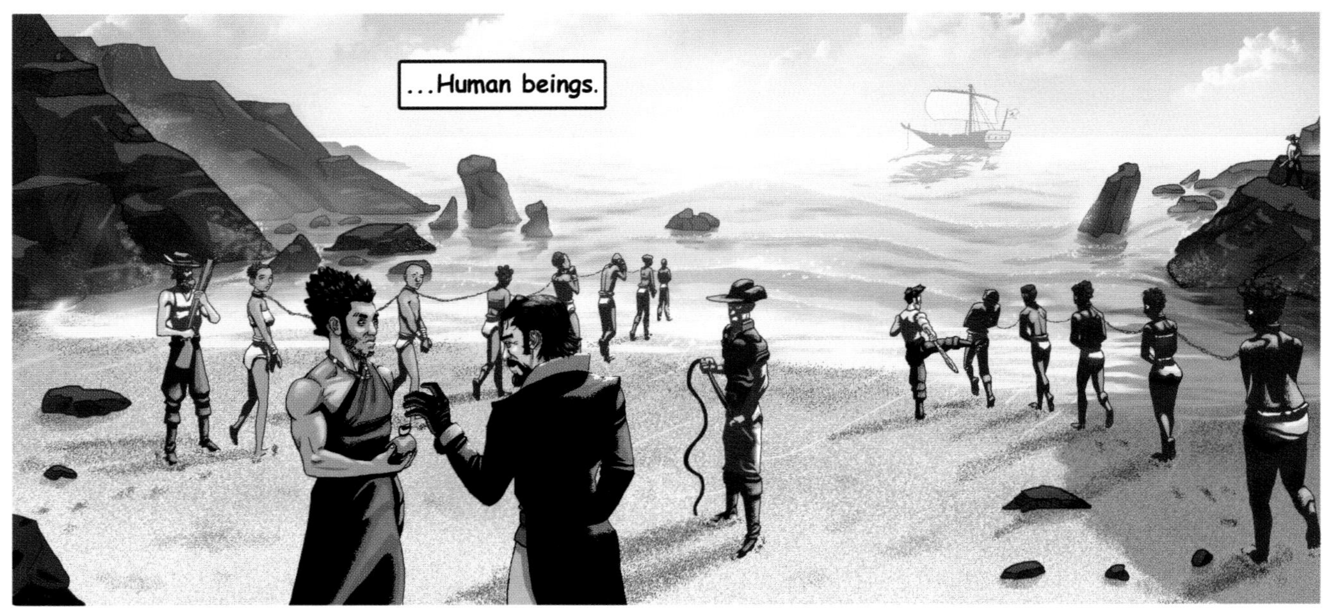
...**Human beings.**

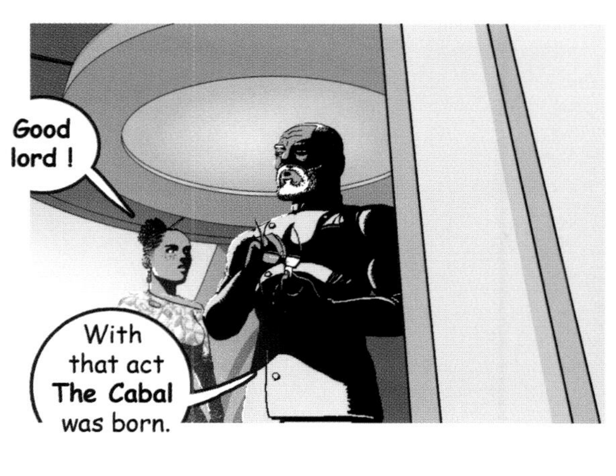

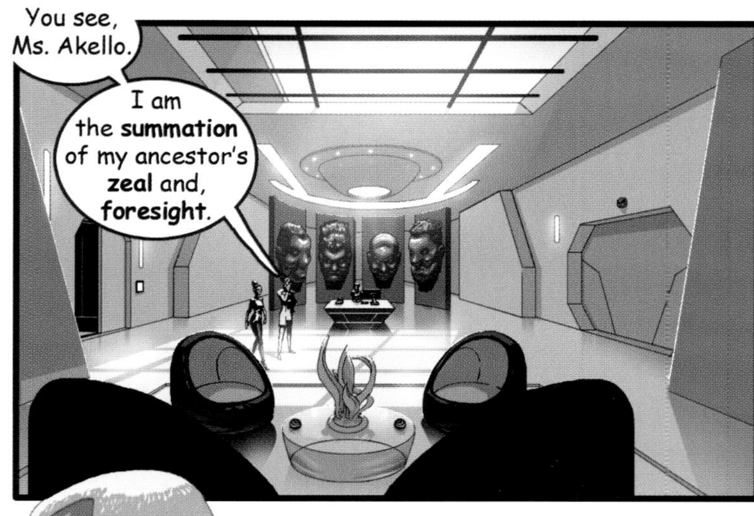

You sound **unencumbered** by your **admission**.

If **anything**, it's an **indicator** that **you**, Mr. Rukidi, are **unhinged**.

Hmm!

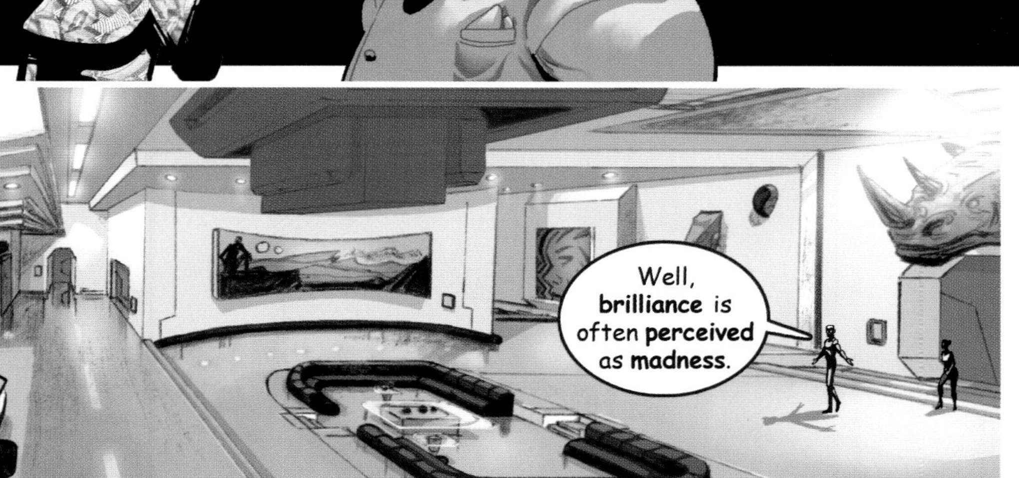

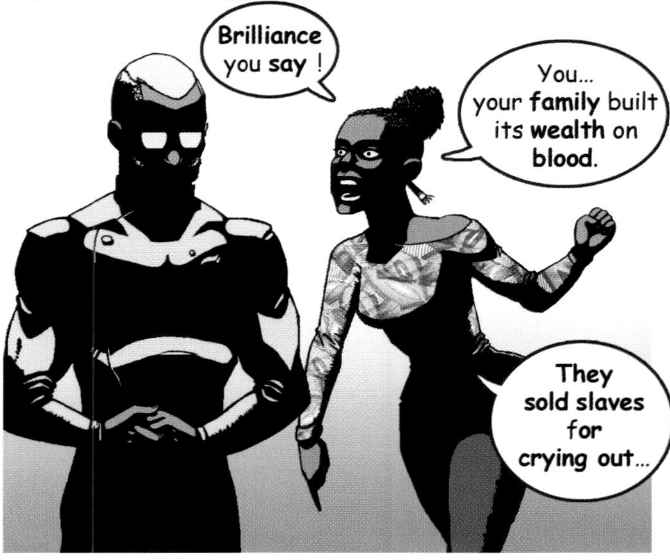

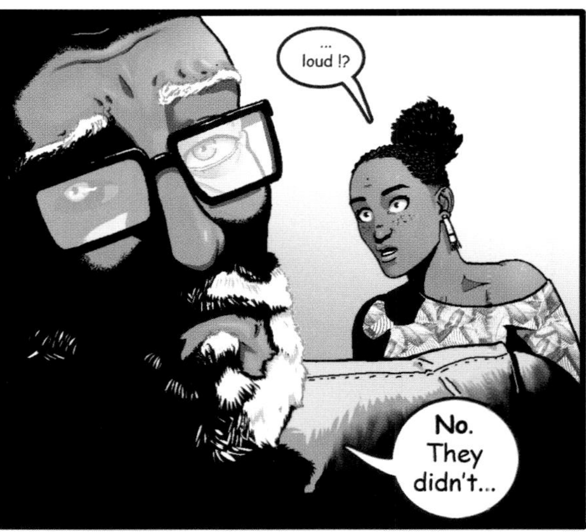

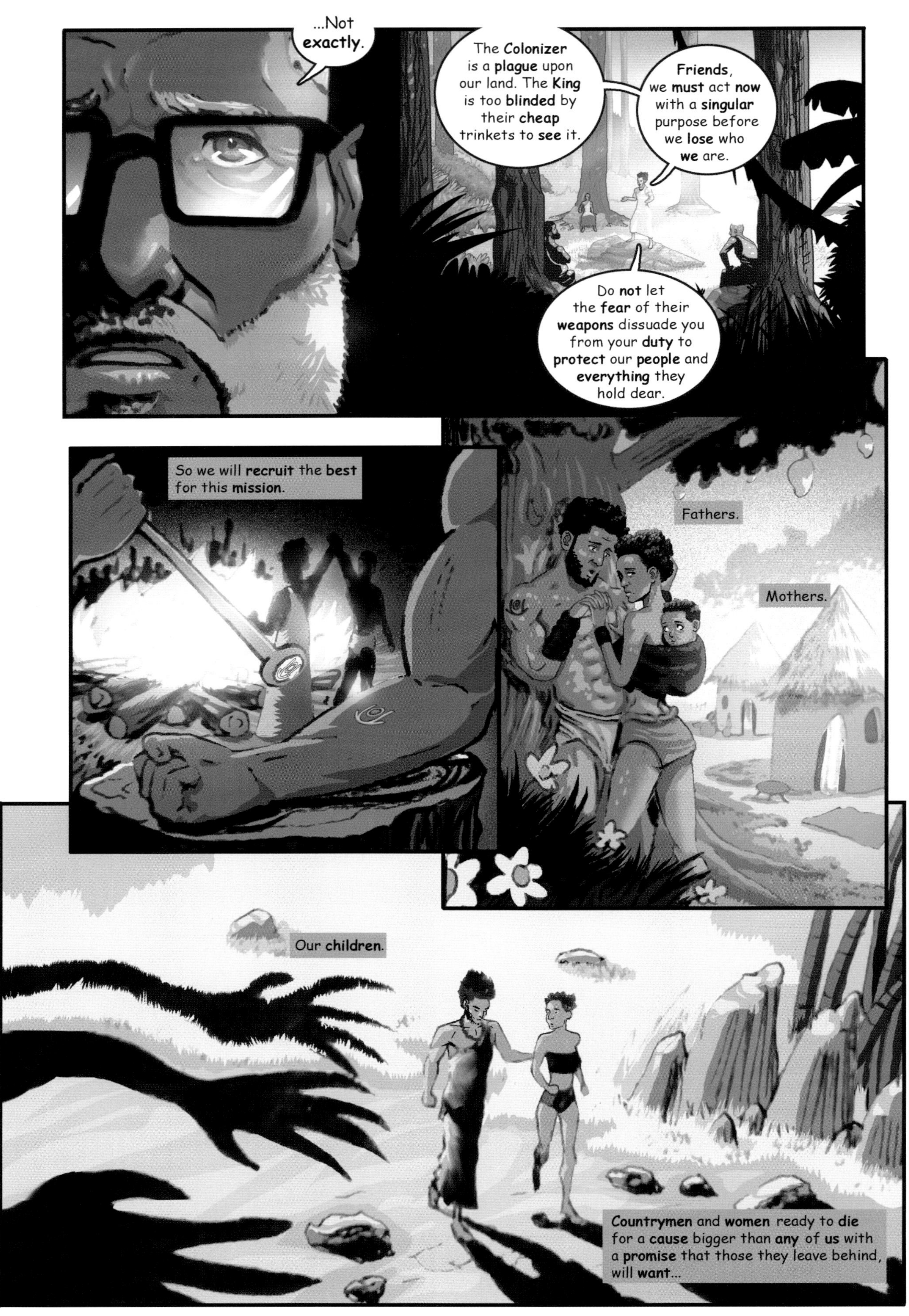
...Not exactly.
The Colonizer is a plague upon our land. The King is too blinded by their cheap trinkets to see it.
Friends, we must act now with a singular purpose before we lose who we are.
Do not let the fear of their weapons dissuade you from your duty to protect our people and everything they hold dear.
So we will recruit the best for this mission.
Fathers.
Mothers.
Our children.
Countrymen and women ready to die for a cause bigger than any of us with a promise that those they leave behind, will want...

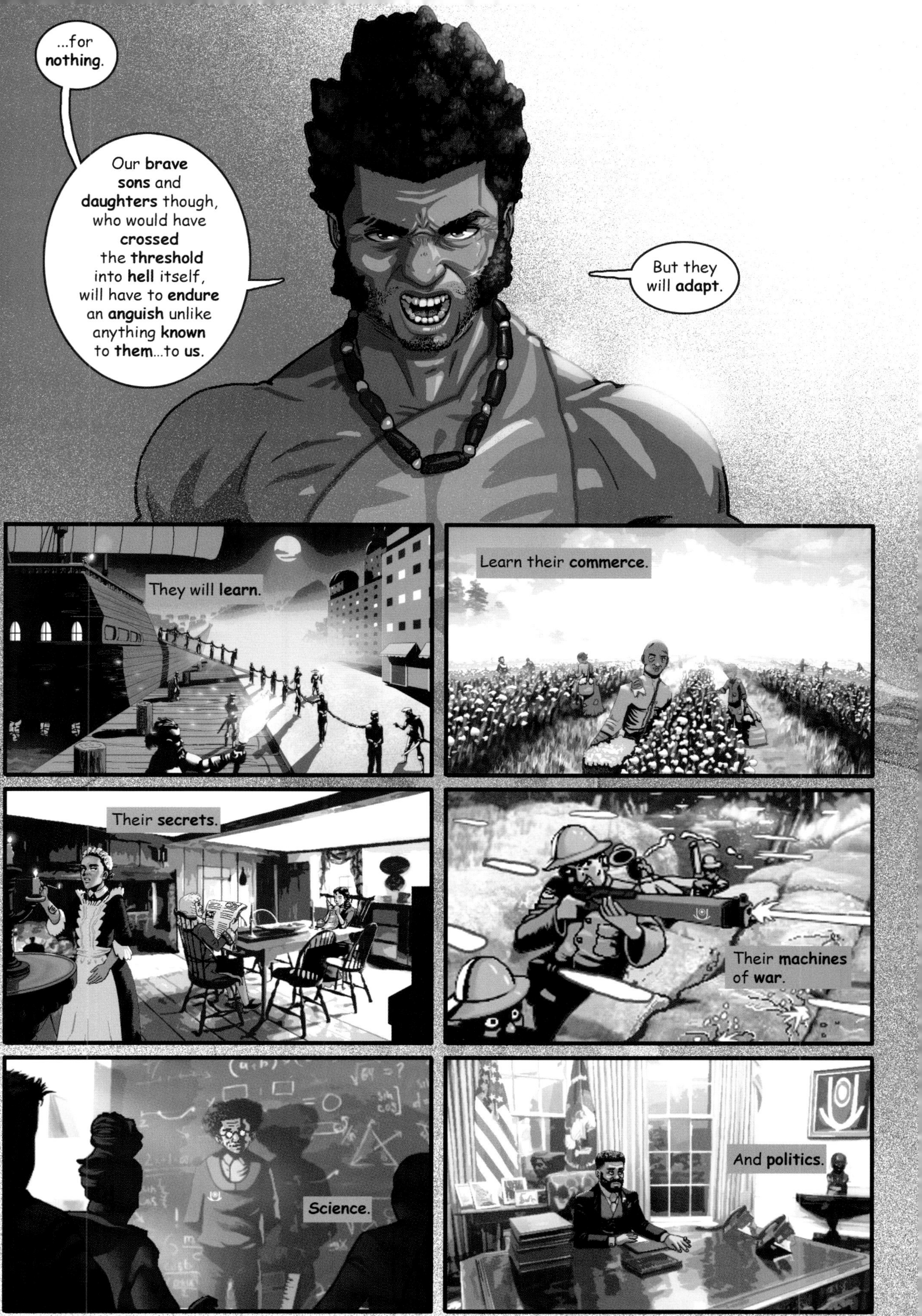

...for **nothing**.

Our **brave sons** and **daughters** though, who would have **crossed** the **threshold** into **hell** itself, will have to **endure** an **anguish** unlike anything **known** to **them**...to **us**.

But they will **adapt**.

They will **learn**.

Learn their **commerce**.

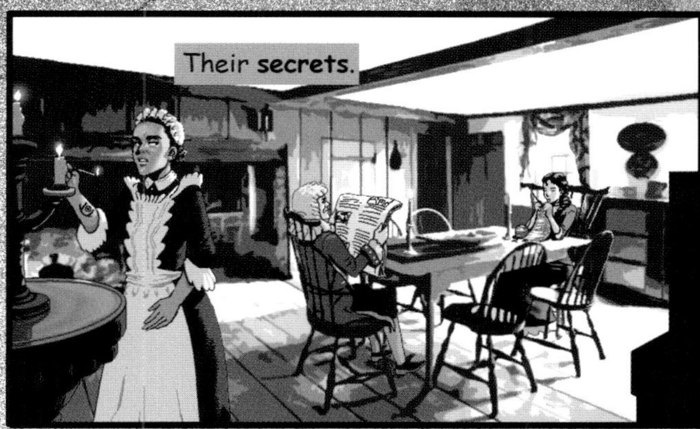

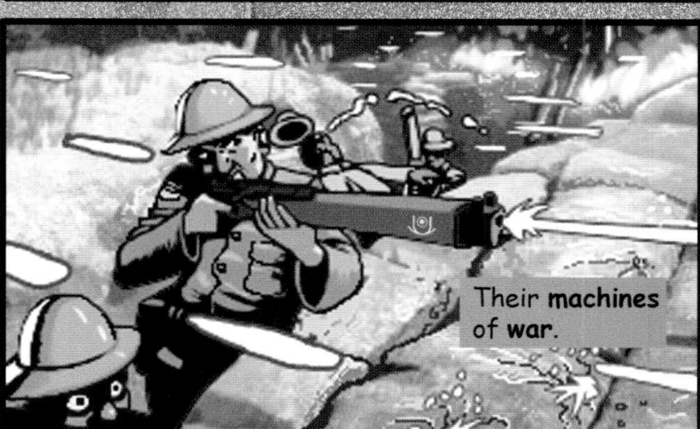

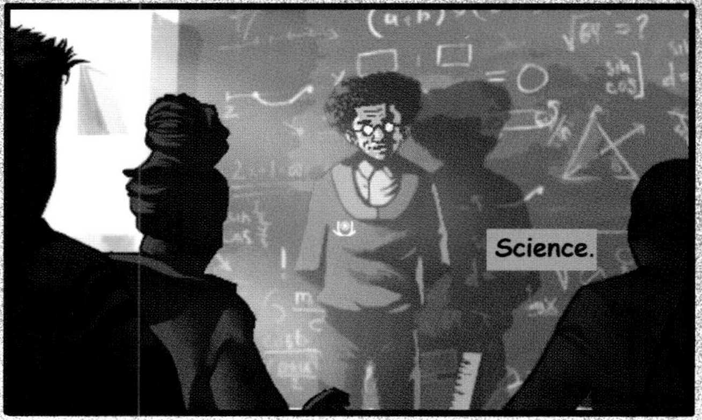

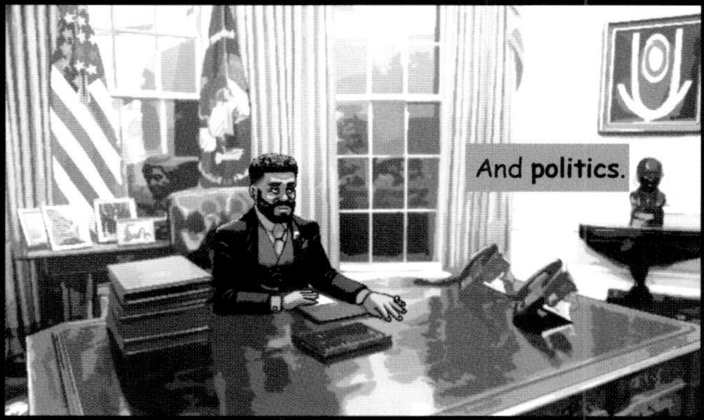

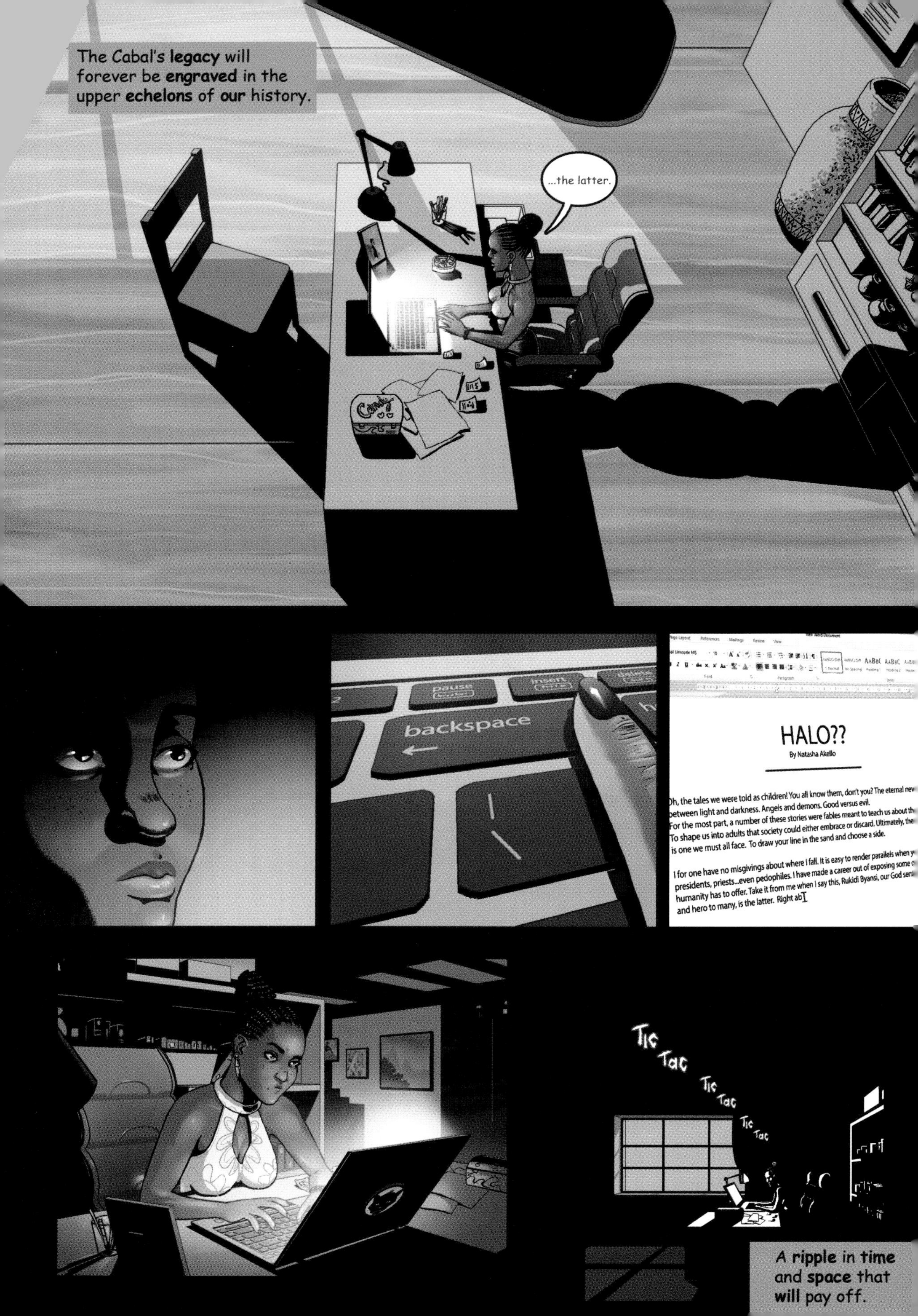

The Cabal's **legacy** will forever be **engraved** in the upper **echelons** of **our** history.

...the latter.

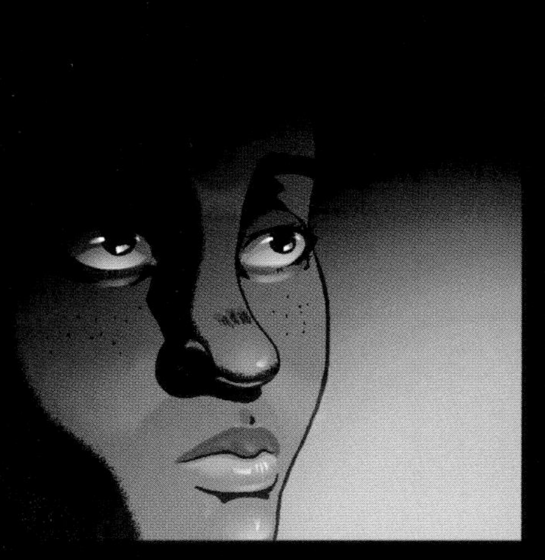

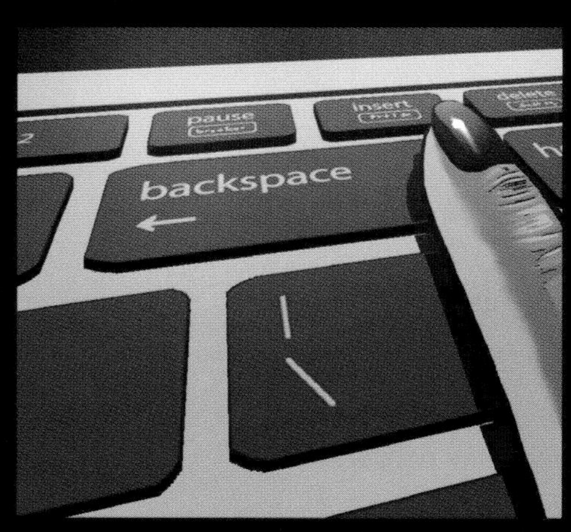

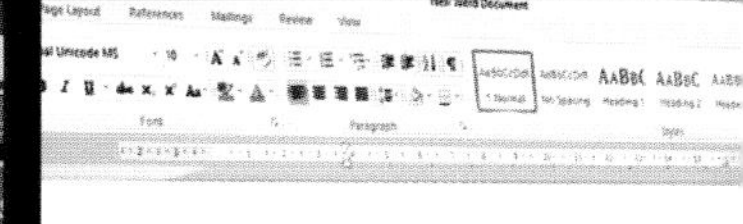

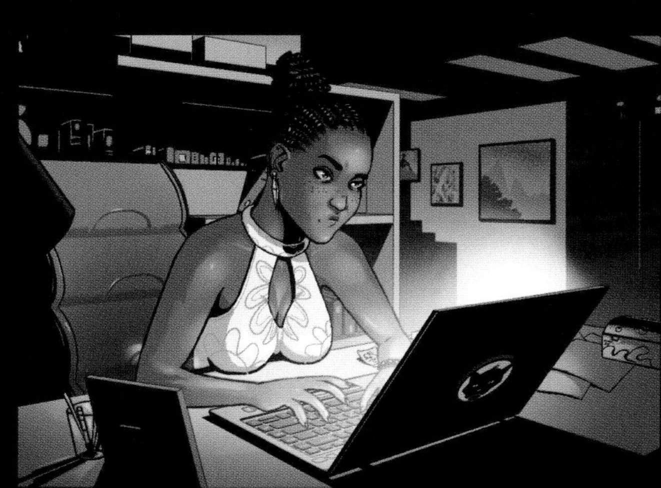

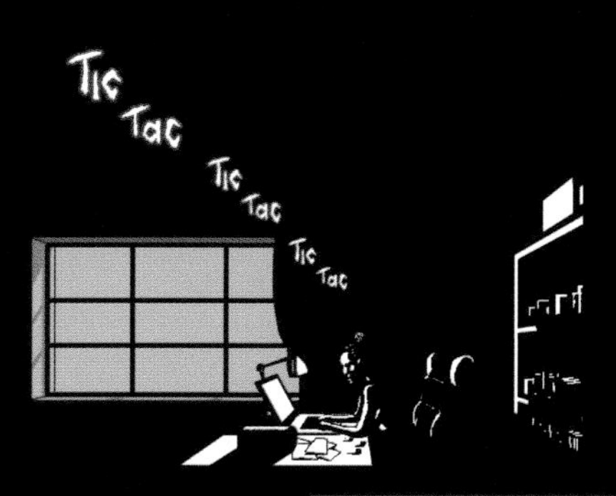

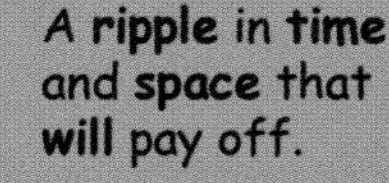

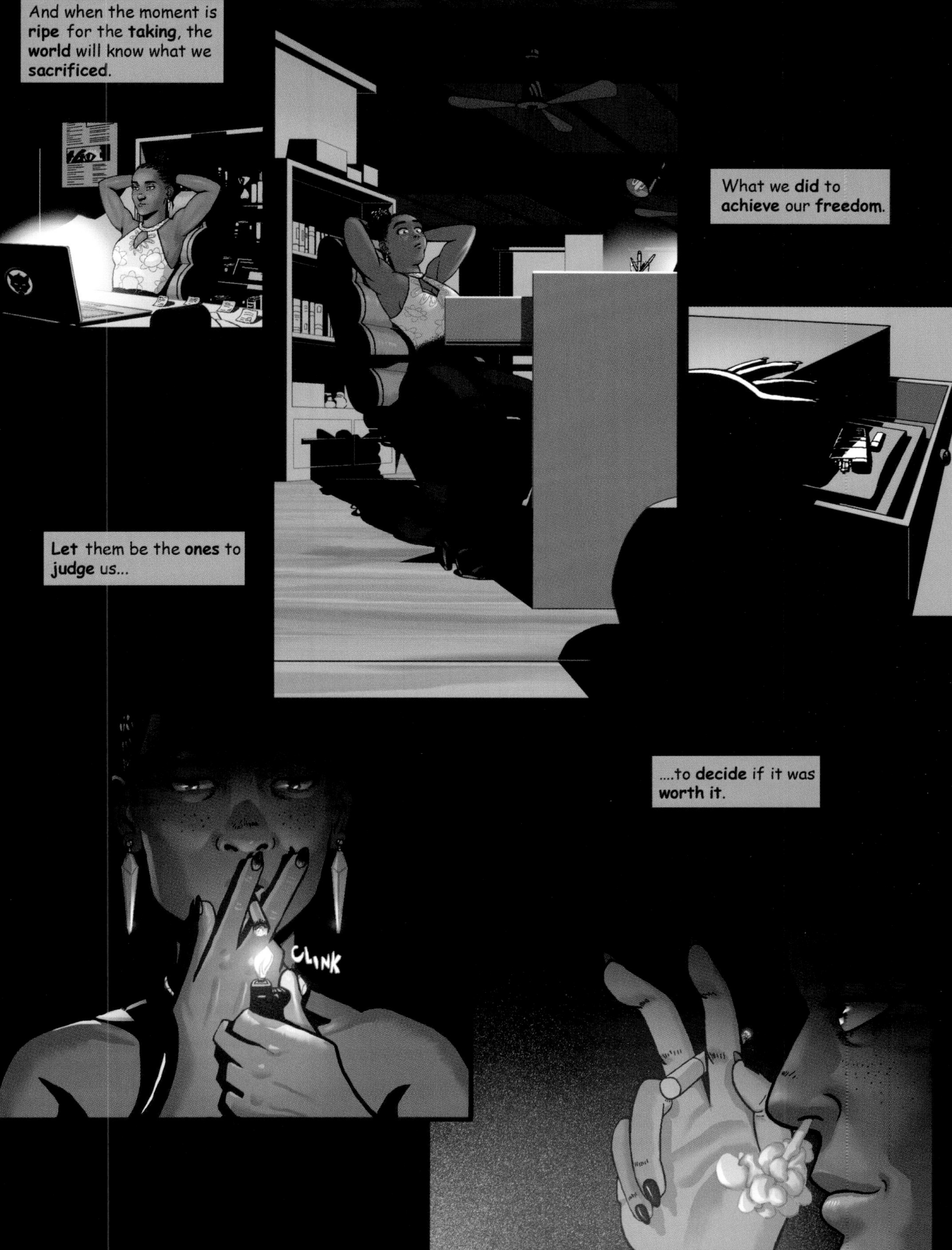

And when the moment is ripe for the taking, the world will know what we sacrificed.
What we did to achieve our freedom.
Let them be the ones to judge us...
CLINK
....to decide if it was worth it.

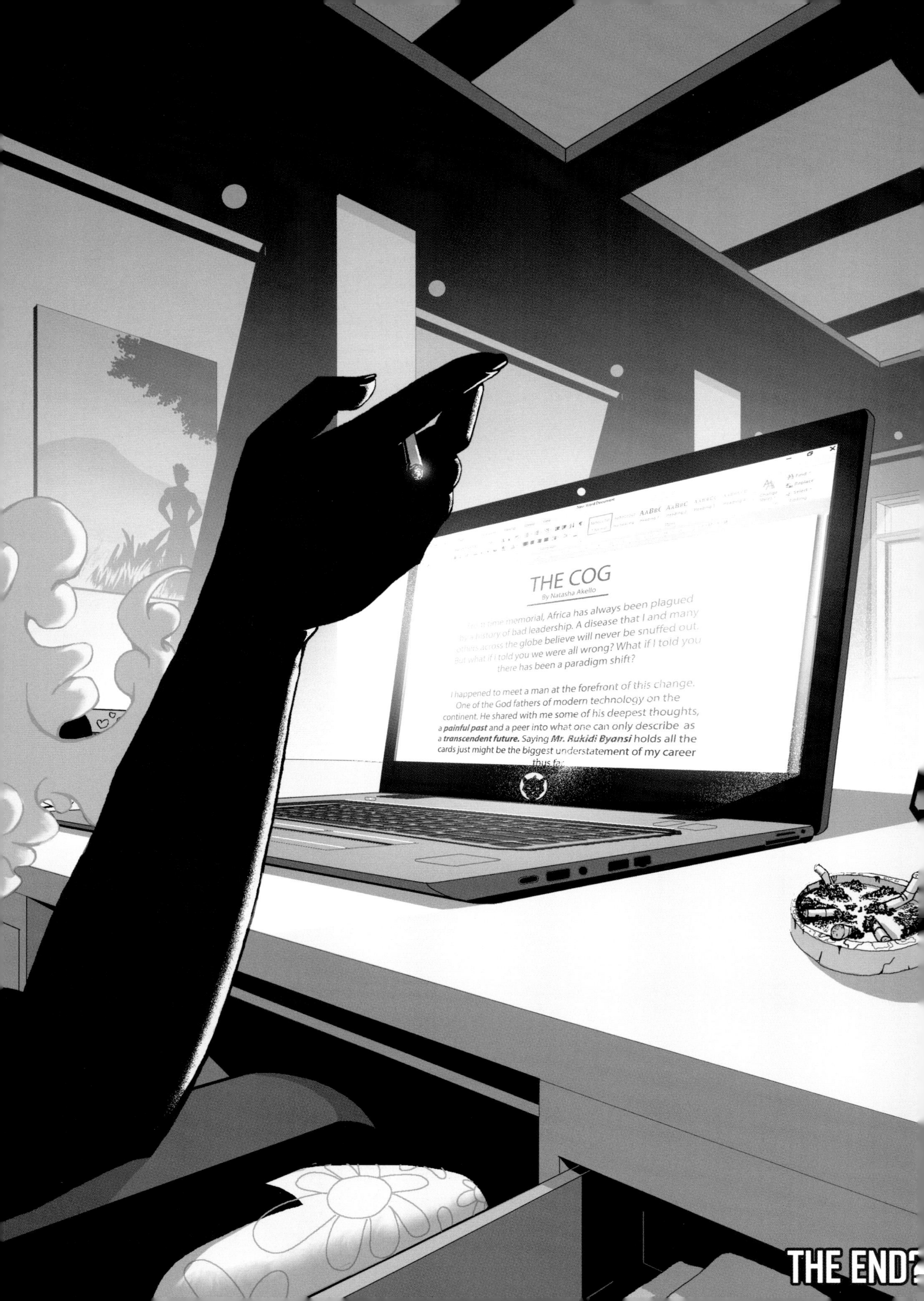
New Word Document
THE COG
By Natasha Akello
time memorial, Africa has always been plagued
by a history of bad leadership. A disease that I and many
others across the globe believe will never be snuffed out.
But what if I told you we were all wrong? What if I told you
there has been a paradigm shift?
I happened to meet a man at the forefront of this change.
One of the God fathers of modern technology on the
continent. He shared with me some of his deepest thoughts,
a **painful past** and a peer into what one can only describe as
a **transcendent future.** Saying **Mr. Rukidi Byansi** holds all the
cards just might be the biggest understatement of my career
thus far
THE END?

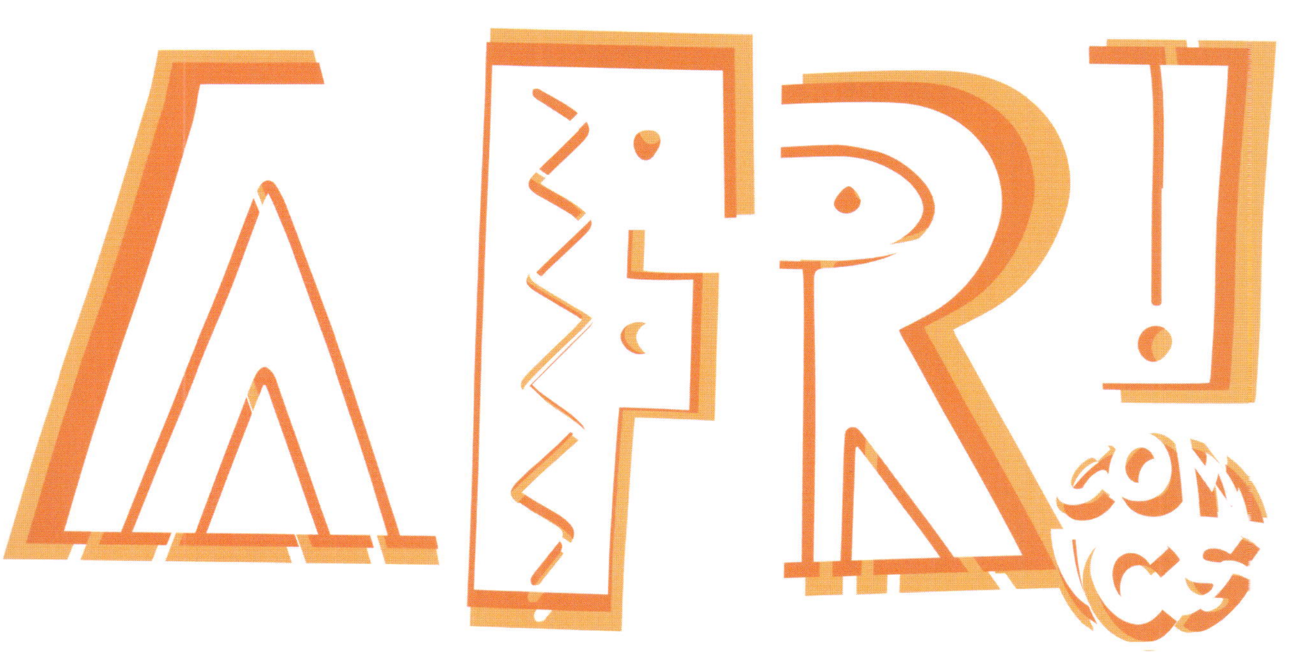
AFRI
COMICS

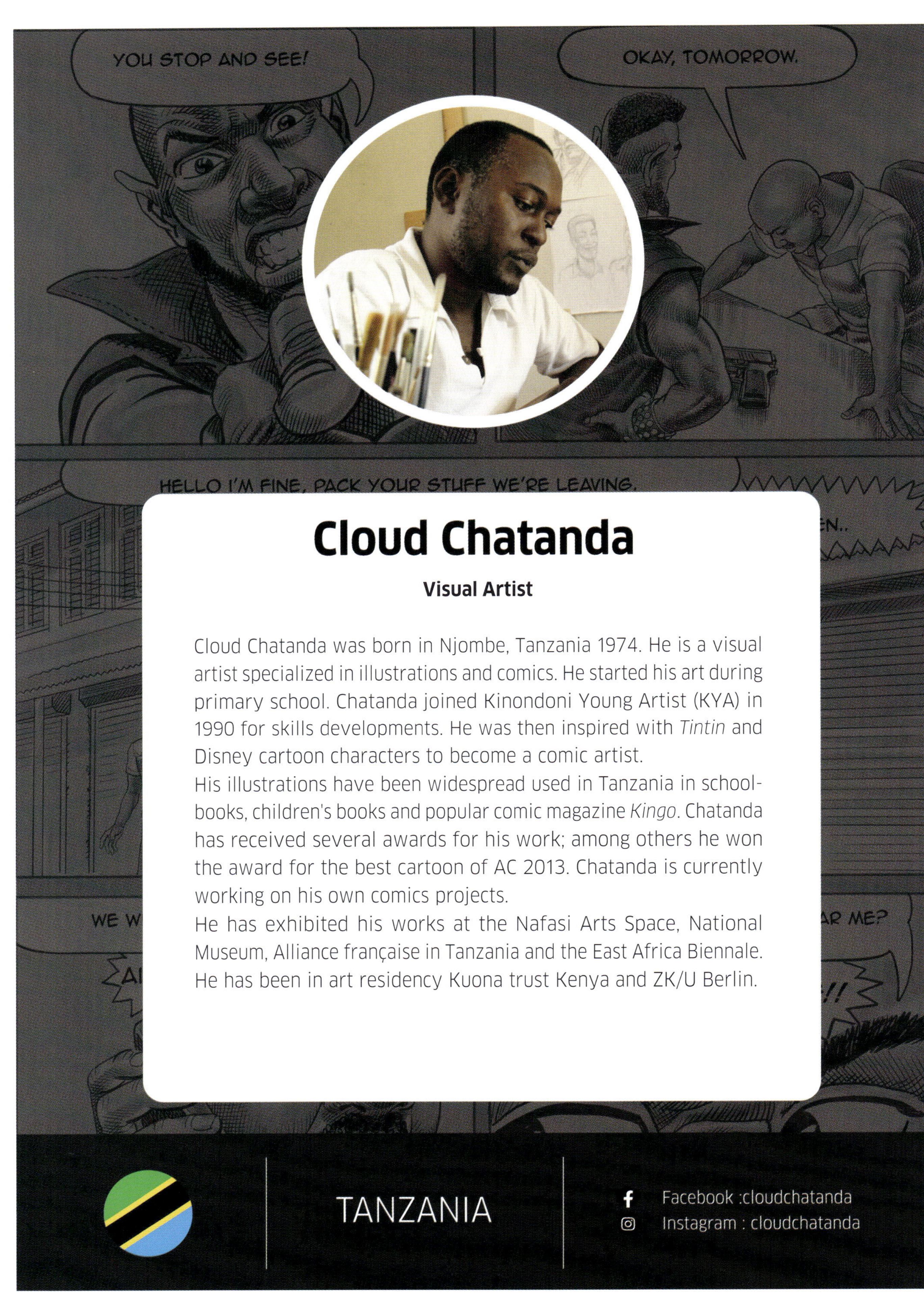

Cloud Chatanda

Visual Artist

Cloud Chatanda was born in Njombe, Tanzania 1974. He is a visual artist specialized in illustrations and comics. He started his art during primary school. Chatanda joined Kinondoni Young Artist (KYA) in 1990 for skills developments. He was then inspired with *Tintin* and Disney cartoon characters to become a comic artist.

His illustrations have been widespread used in Tanzania in school-books, children's books and popular comic magazine *Kingo*. Chatanda has received several awards for his work; among others he won the award for the best cartoon of AC 2013. Chatanda is currently working on his own comics projects.

He has exhibited his works at the Nafasi Arts Space, National Museum, Alliance française in Tanzania and the East Africa Biennale. He has been in art residency Kuona trust Kenya and ZK/U Berlin.

TANZANIA

Facebook :cloudchatanda
Instagram : cloudchatanda

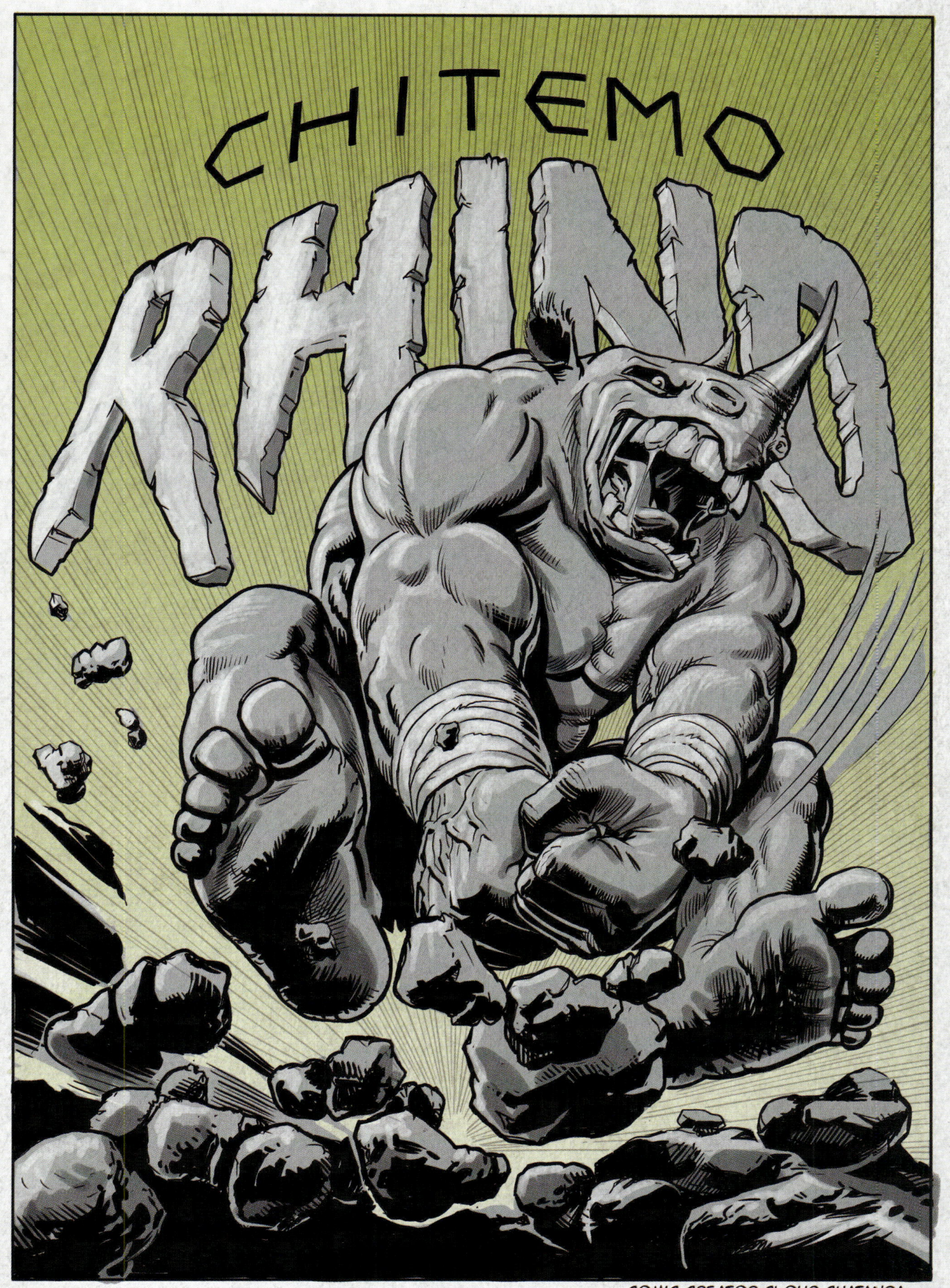
CHITEMO
RHINO
COMIC CREATOR CLOUD CHATANDA

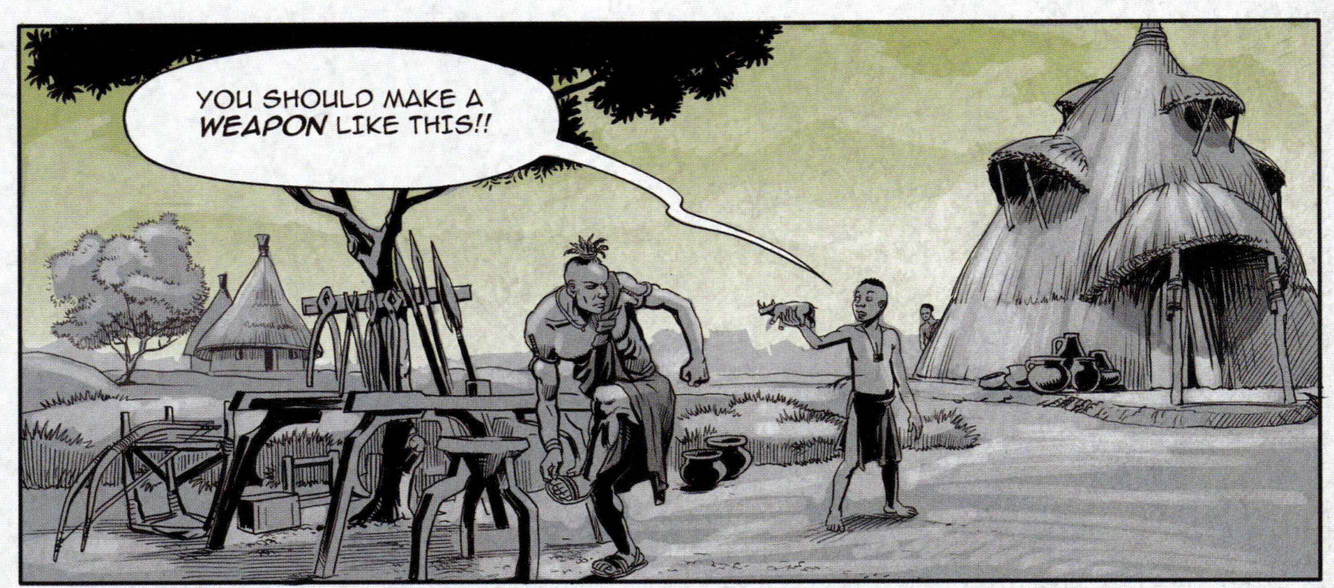
YOU SHOULD MAKE A
WEAPON LIKE THIS!!

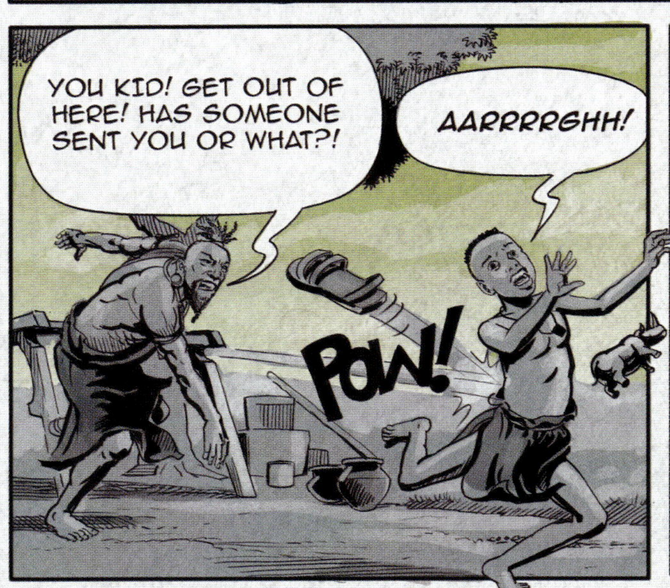
YOU KID! GET OUT OF HERE! HAS SOMEONE SENT YOU OR WHAT?!
AARRRRGHH!
POW!

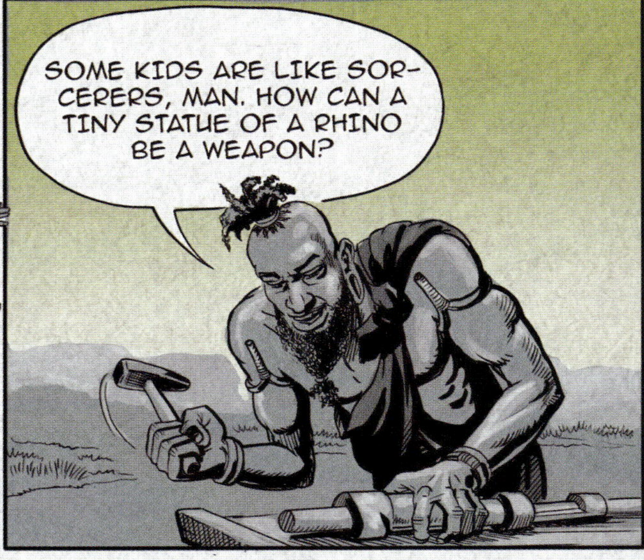
SOME KIDS ARE LIKE SORCERERS, MAN. HOW CAN A TINY STATUE OF A RHINO BE A WEAPON?

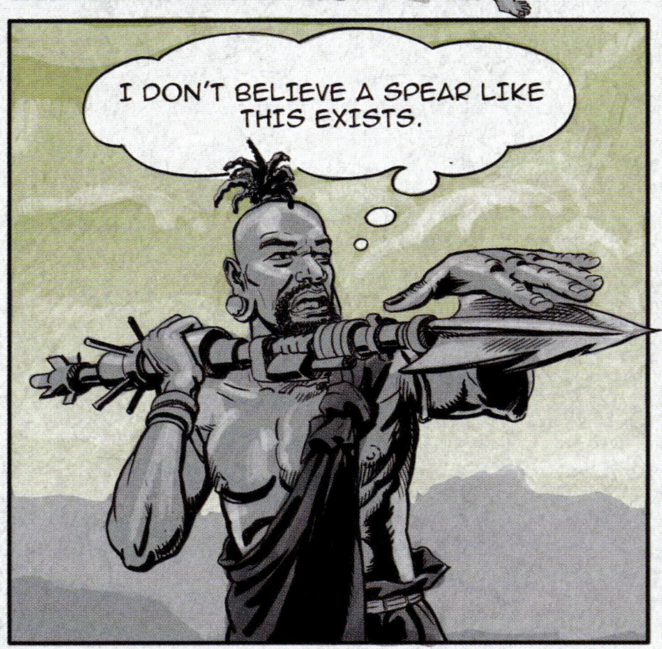
I DON'T BELIEVE A SPEAR LIKE THIS EXISTS.

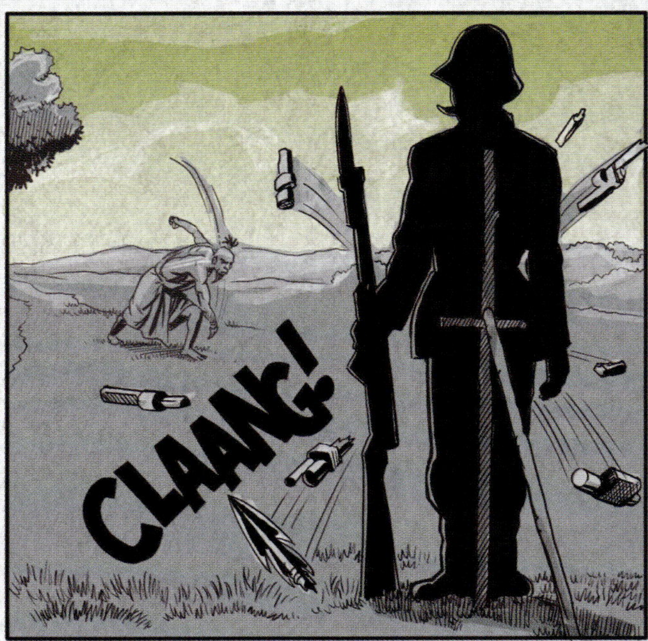
CLAANG!

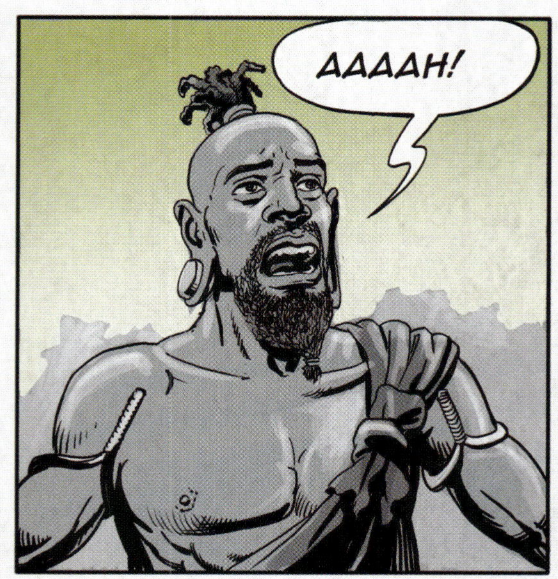
AAAAH!

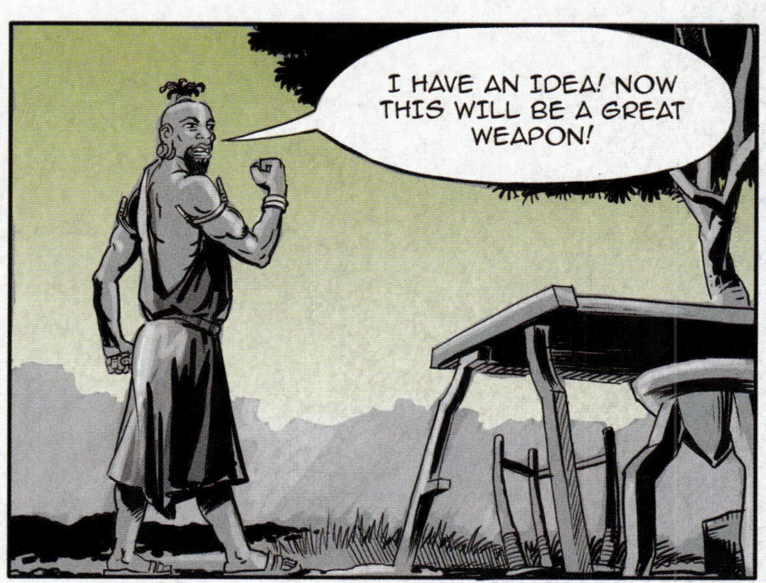
I HAVE AN IDEA! NOW THIS WILL BE A GREAT WEAPON!

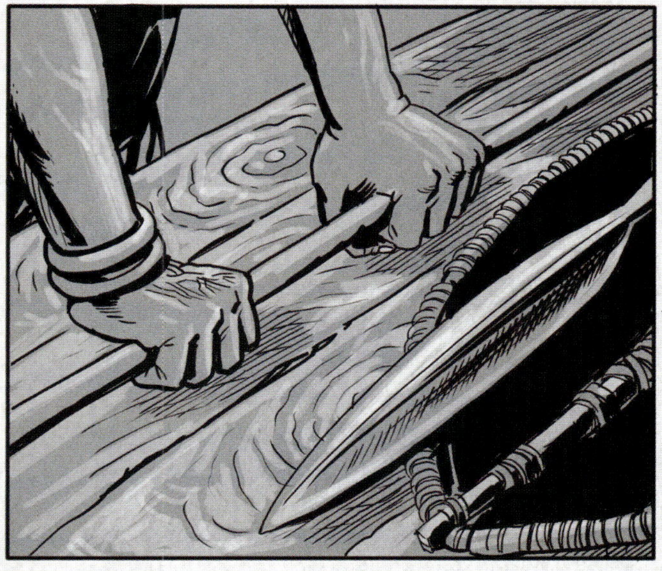

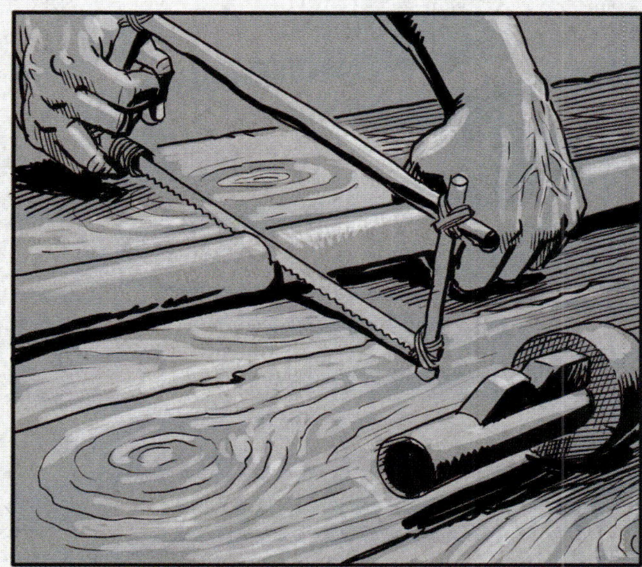

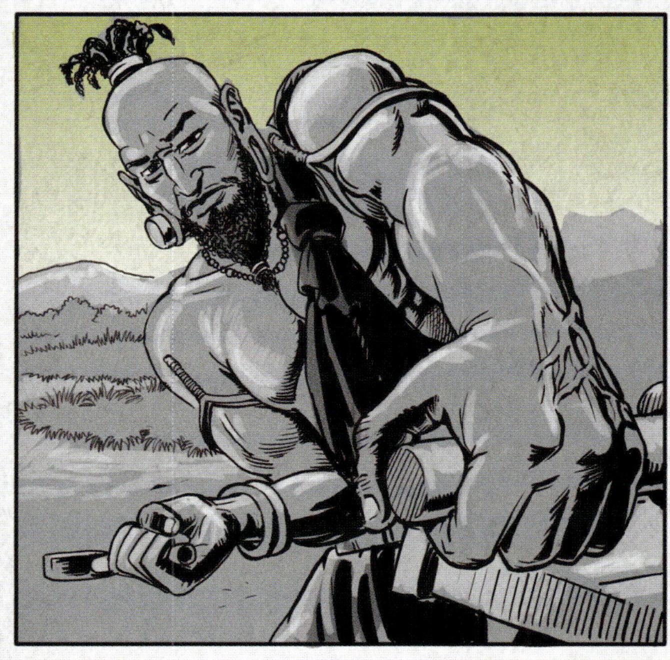

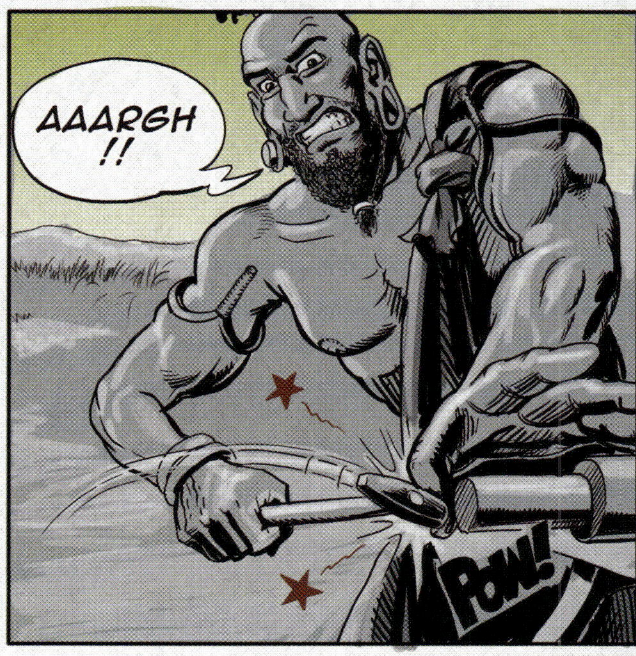
AAARGH !!
POW!

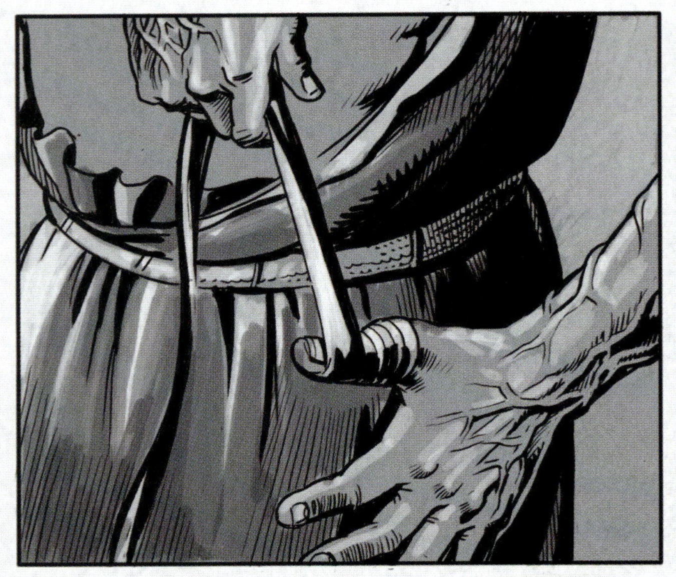
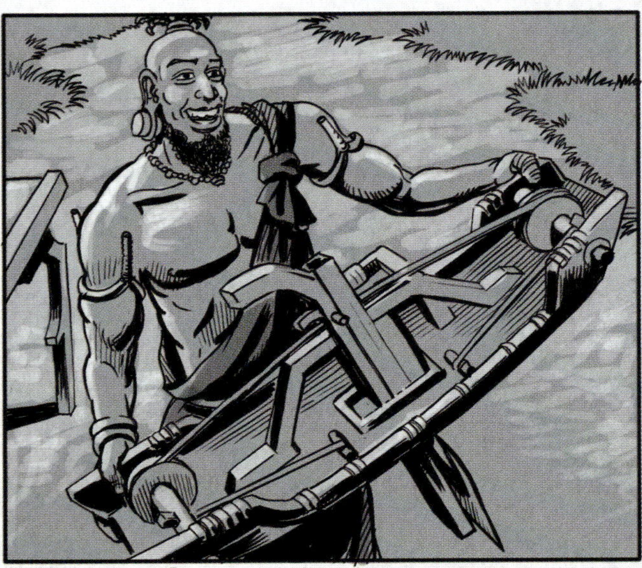
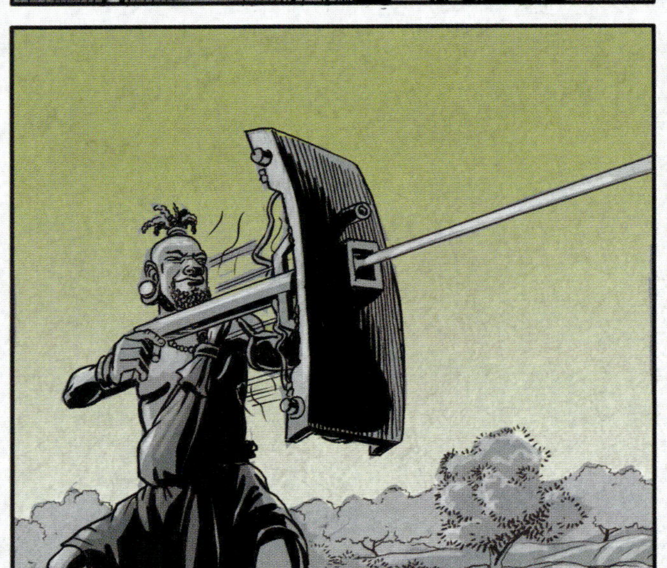
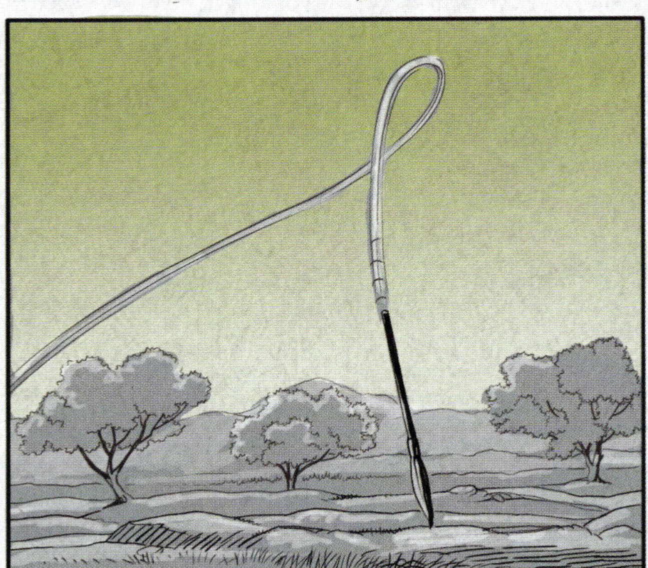
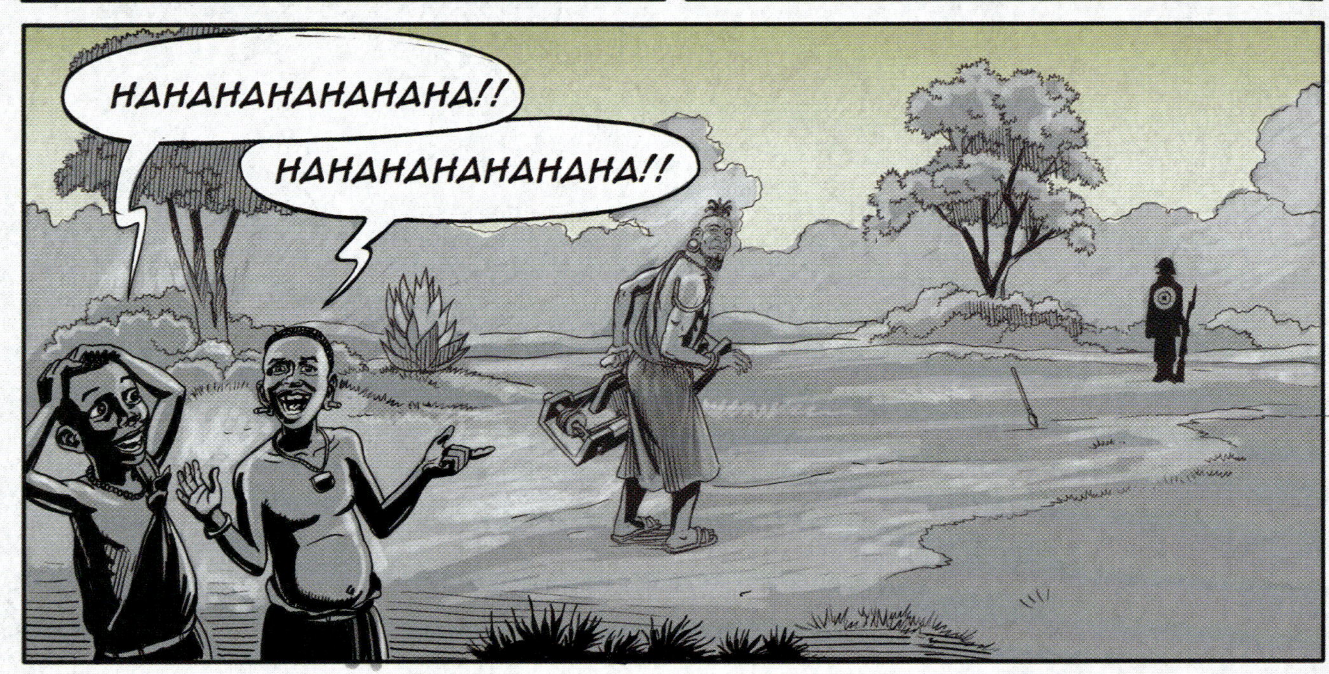
HAHAHAHAHAHAHA!!
HAHAHAHAHAHAHA!!

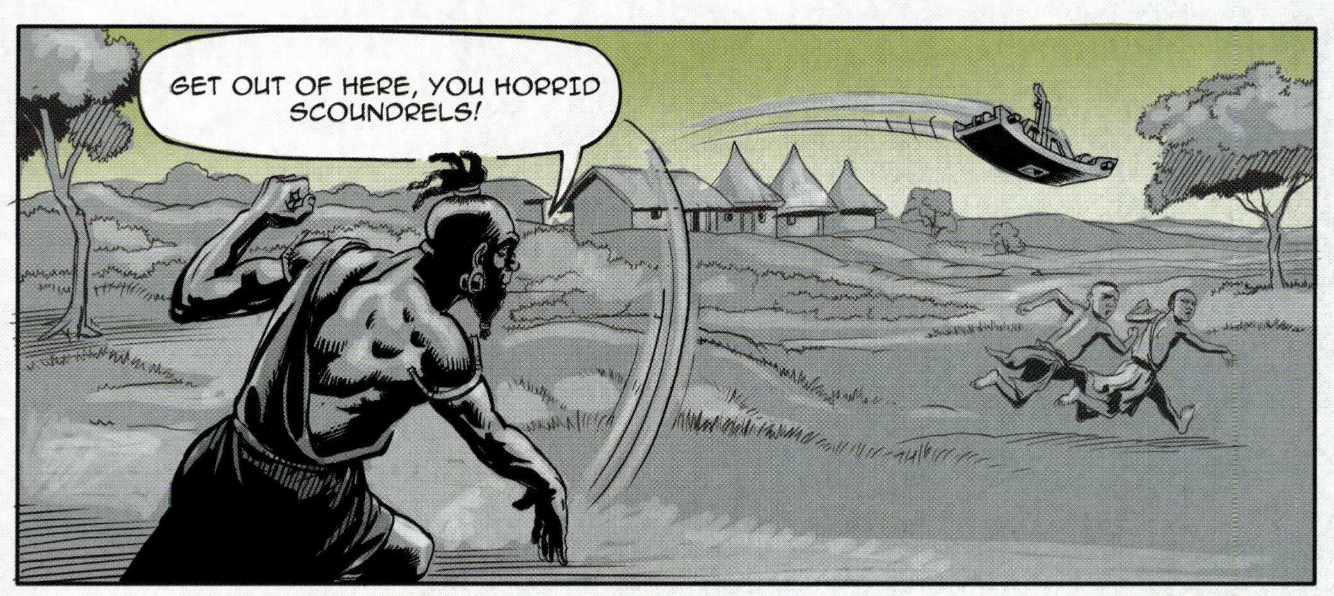
GET OUT OF HERE, YOU HORRID SCOUNDRELS!

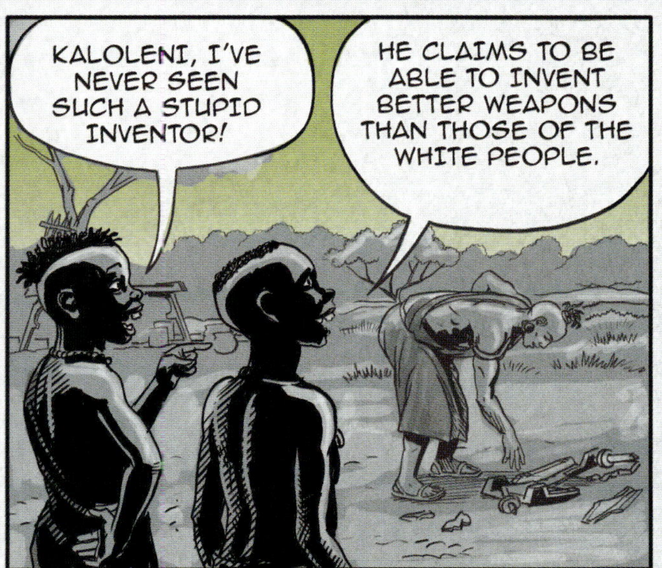
KALOLENI, I'VE NEVER SEEN SUCH A STUPID INVENTOR!
HE CLAIMS TO BE ABLE TO INVENT BETTER WEAPONS THAN THOSE OF THE WHITE PEOPLE.

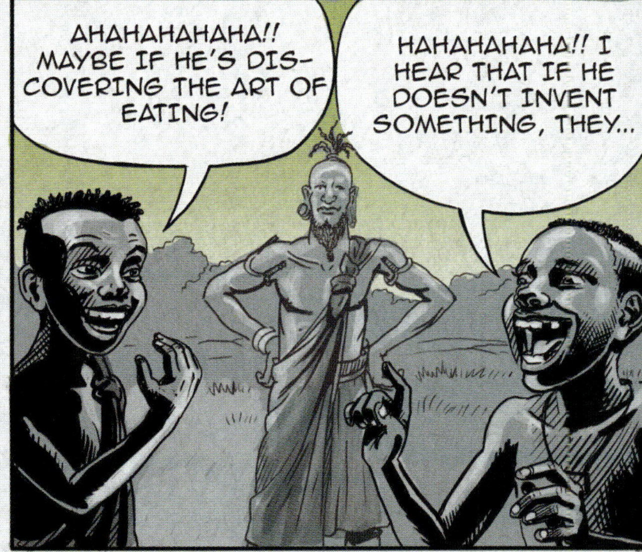
AHAHAHAHAHA!! MAYBE IF HE'S DIS-COVERING THE ART OF EATING!
HAHAHAHAHA!! I HEAR THAT IF HE DOESN'T INVENT SOMETHING, THEY...

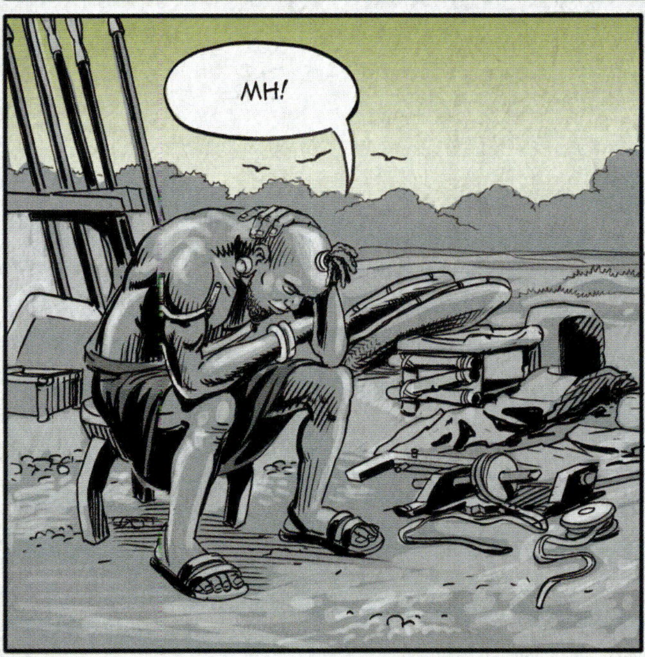
MH!

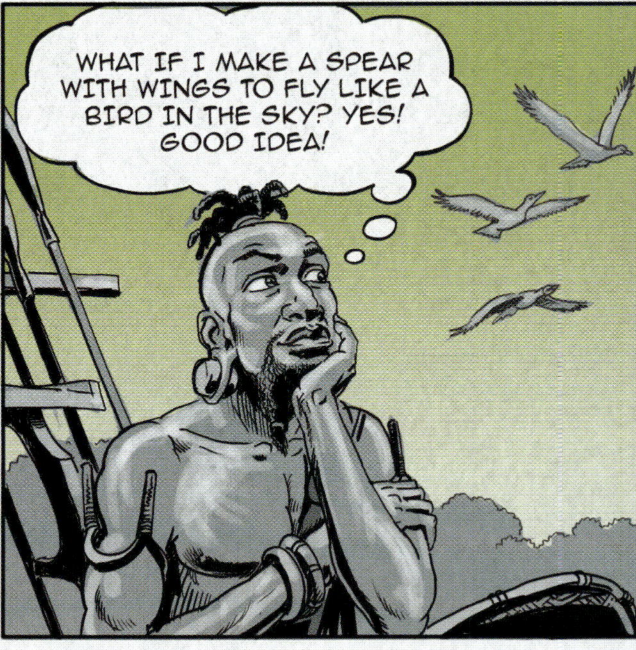
WHAT IF I MAKE A SPEAR WITH WINGS TO FLY LIKE A BIRD IN THE SKY? YES! GOOD IDEA!

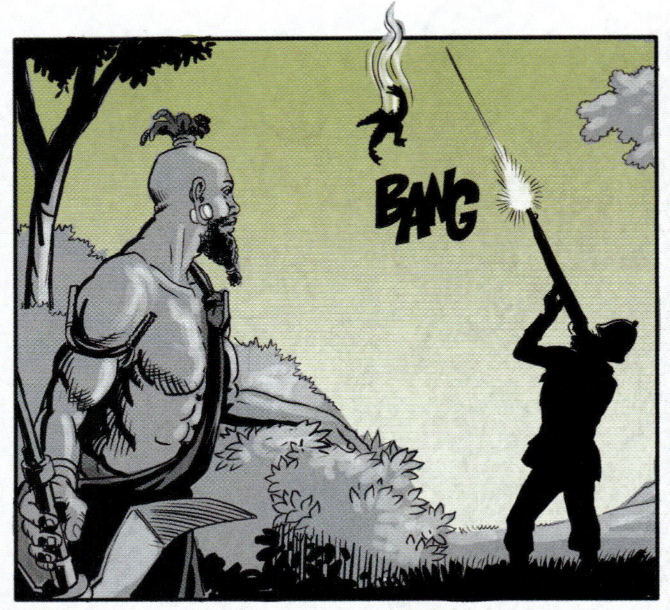
BANG

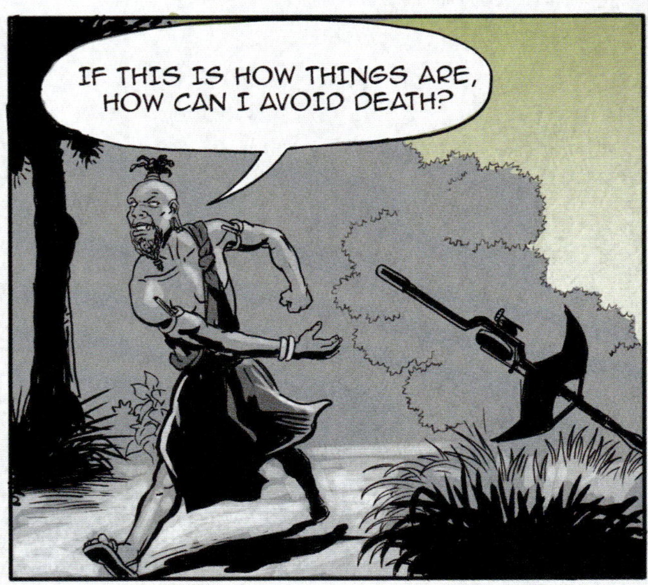
IF THIS IS HOW THINGS ARE, HOW CAN I AVOID DEATH?

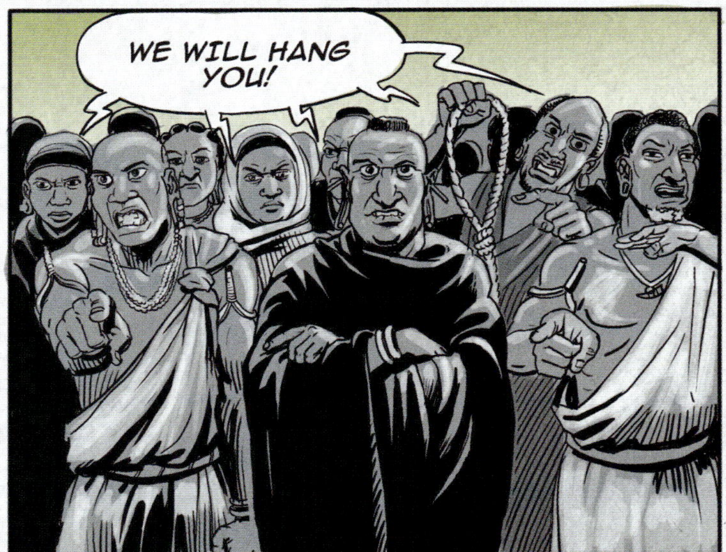
WE WILL HANG YOU!

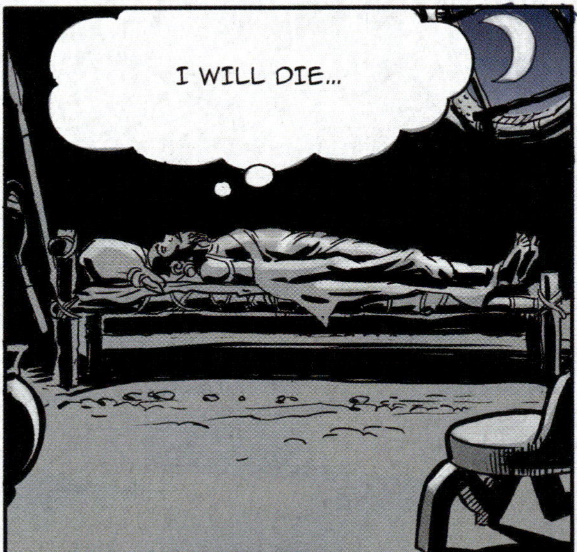
I WILL DIE...

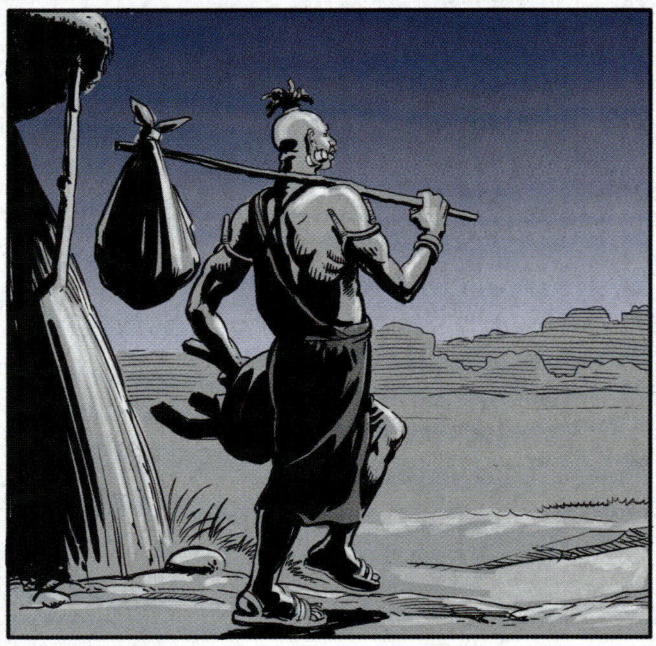

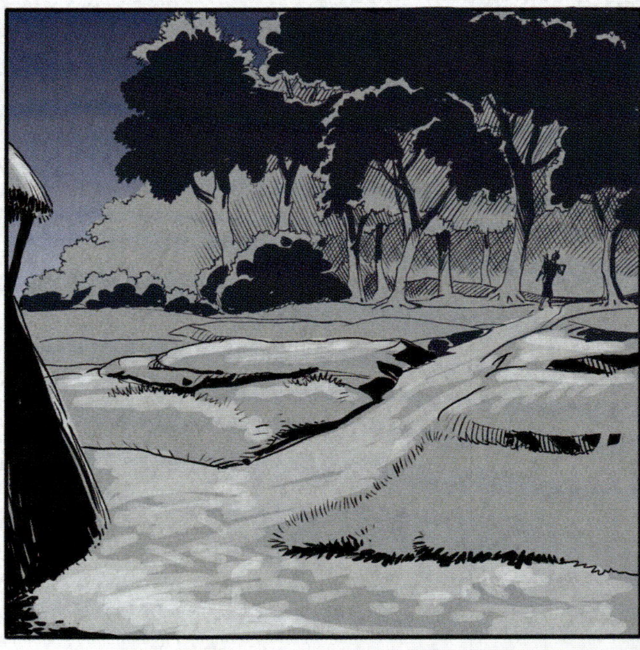

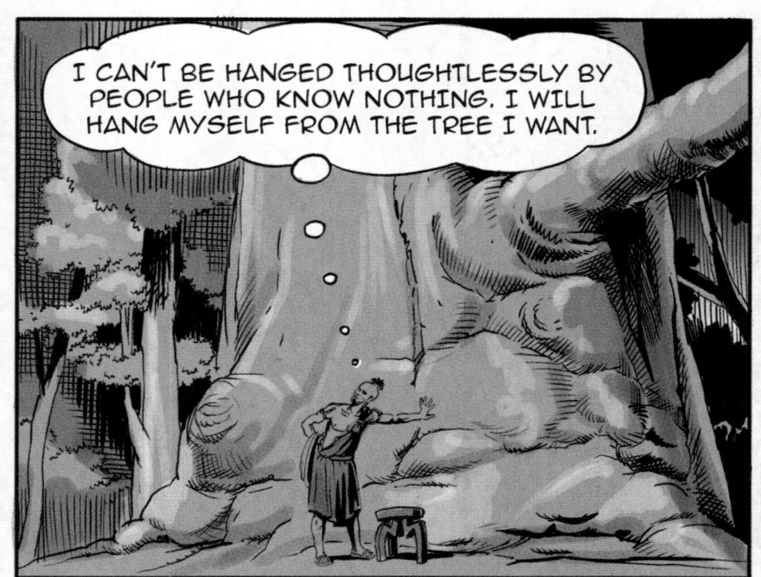
I CAN'T BE HANGED THOUGHTLESSLY BY PEOPLE WHO KNOW NOTHING. I WILL HANG MYSELF FROM THE TREE I WANT.

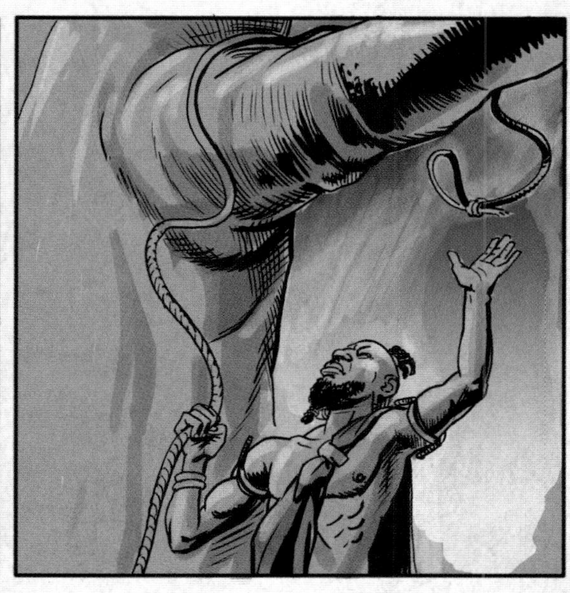

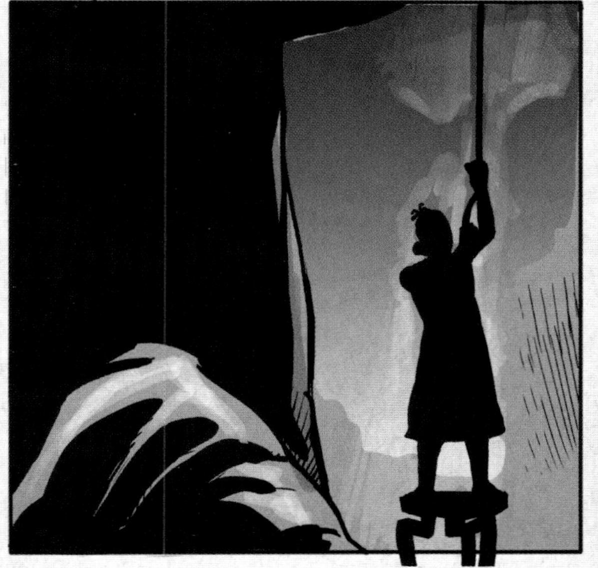

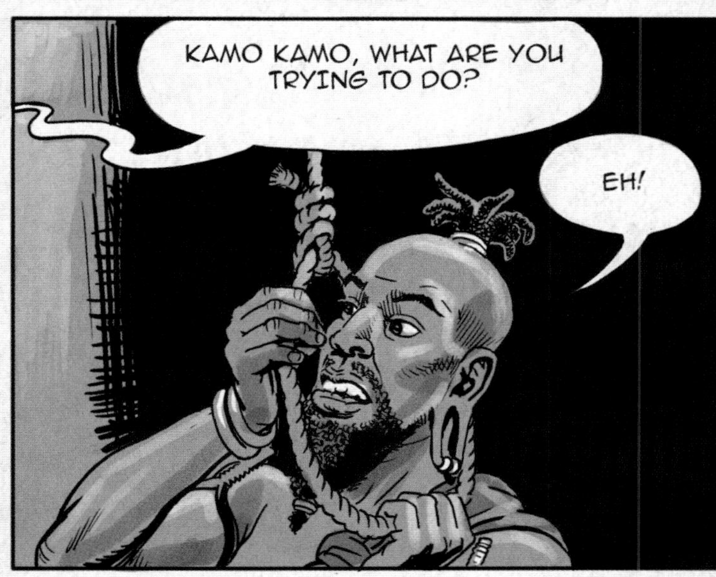
KAMO KAMO, WHAT ARE YOU TRYING TO DO?
EH!

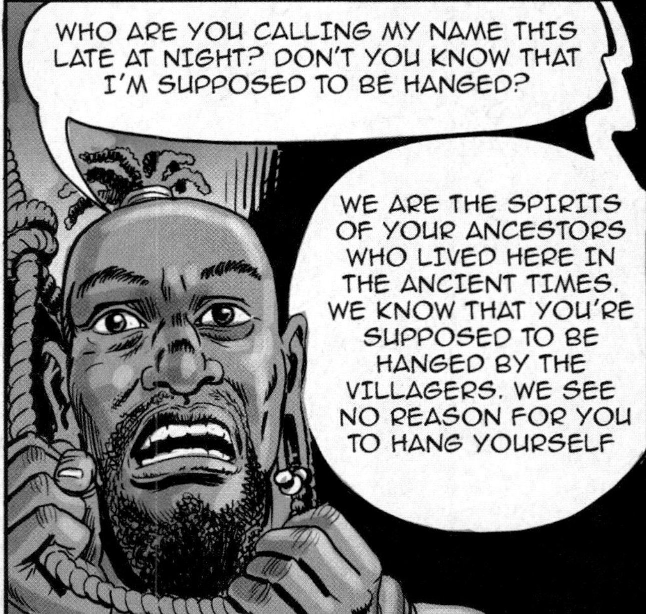
WHO ARE YOU CALLING MY NAME THIS LATE AT NIGHT? DON'T YOU KNOW THAT I'M SUPPOSED TO BE HANGED?
WE ARE THE SPIRITS OF YOUR ANCESTORS WHO LIVED HERE IN THE ANCIENT TIMES. WE KNOW THAT YOU'RE SUPPOSED TO BE HANGED BY THE VILLAGERS. WE SEE NO REASON FOR YOU TO HANG YOURSELF

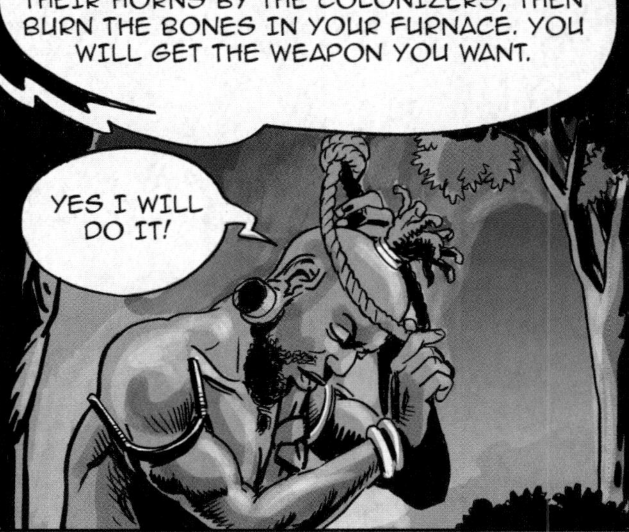
GO BACK TO THE VILLAGE AND COLLECT THE BONES OF EVERY RHINO KILLED FOR THEIR HORNS BY THE COLONIZERS, THEN BURN THE BONES IN YOUR FURNACE. YOU WILL GET THE WEAPON YOU WANT.
YES I WILL DO IT!

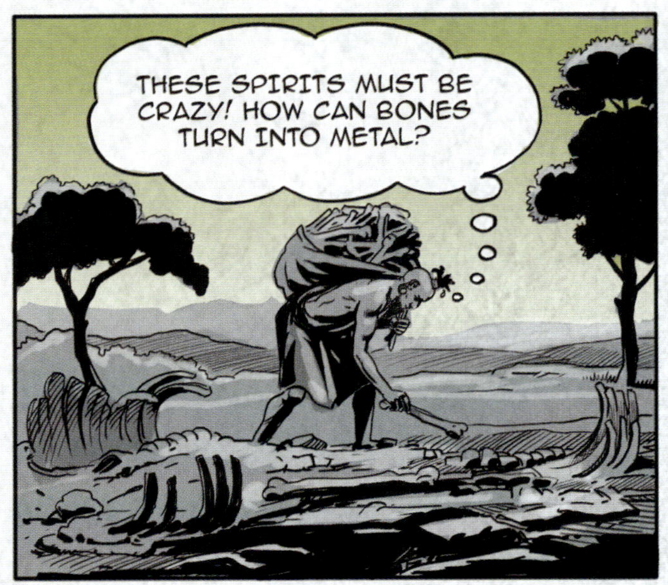
THESE SPIRITS MUST BE CRAZY! HOW CAN BONES TURN INTO METAL?

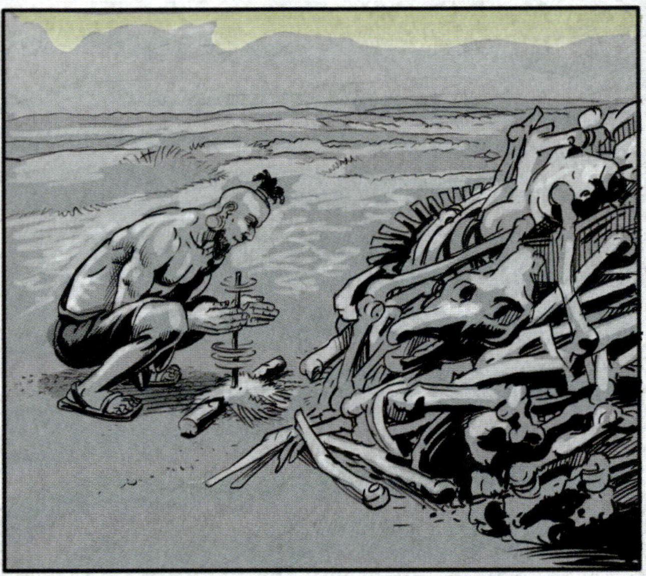

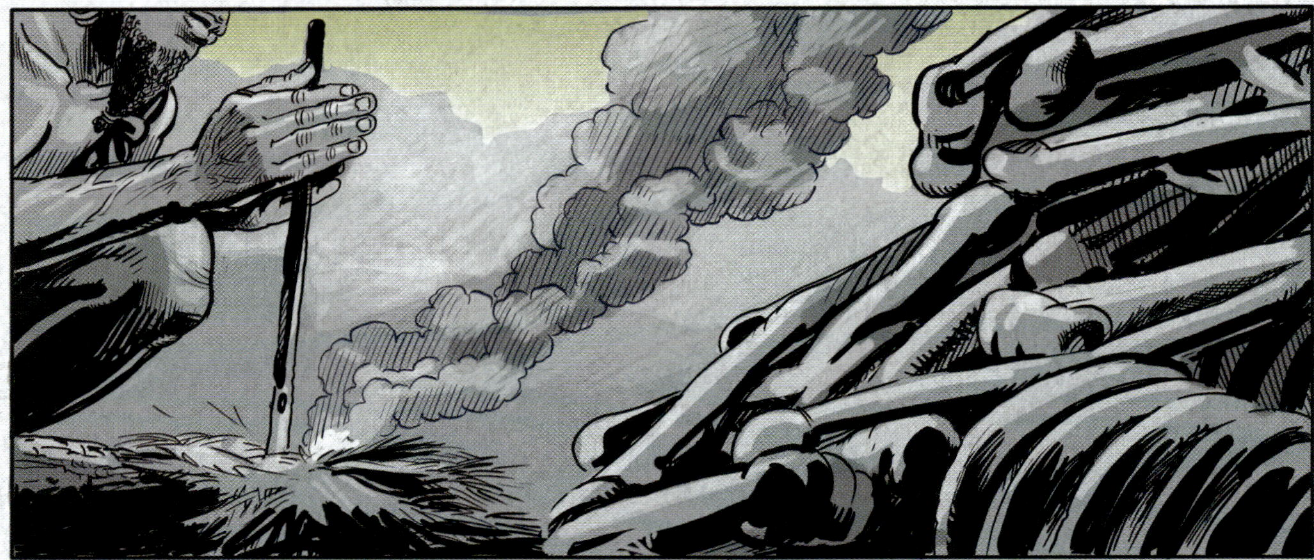

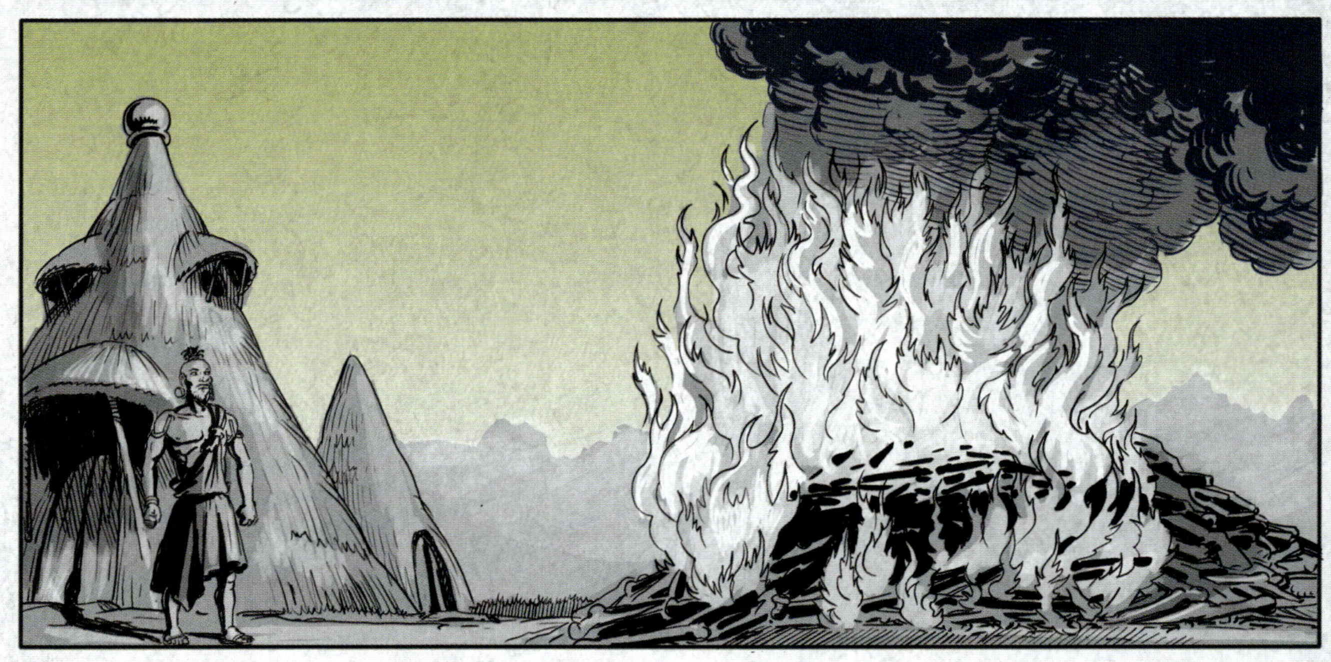

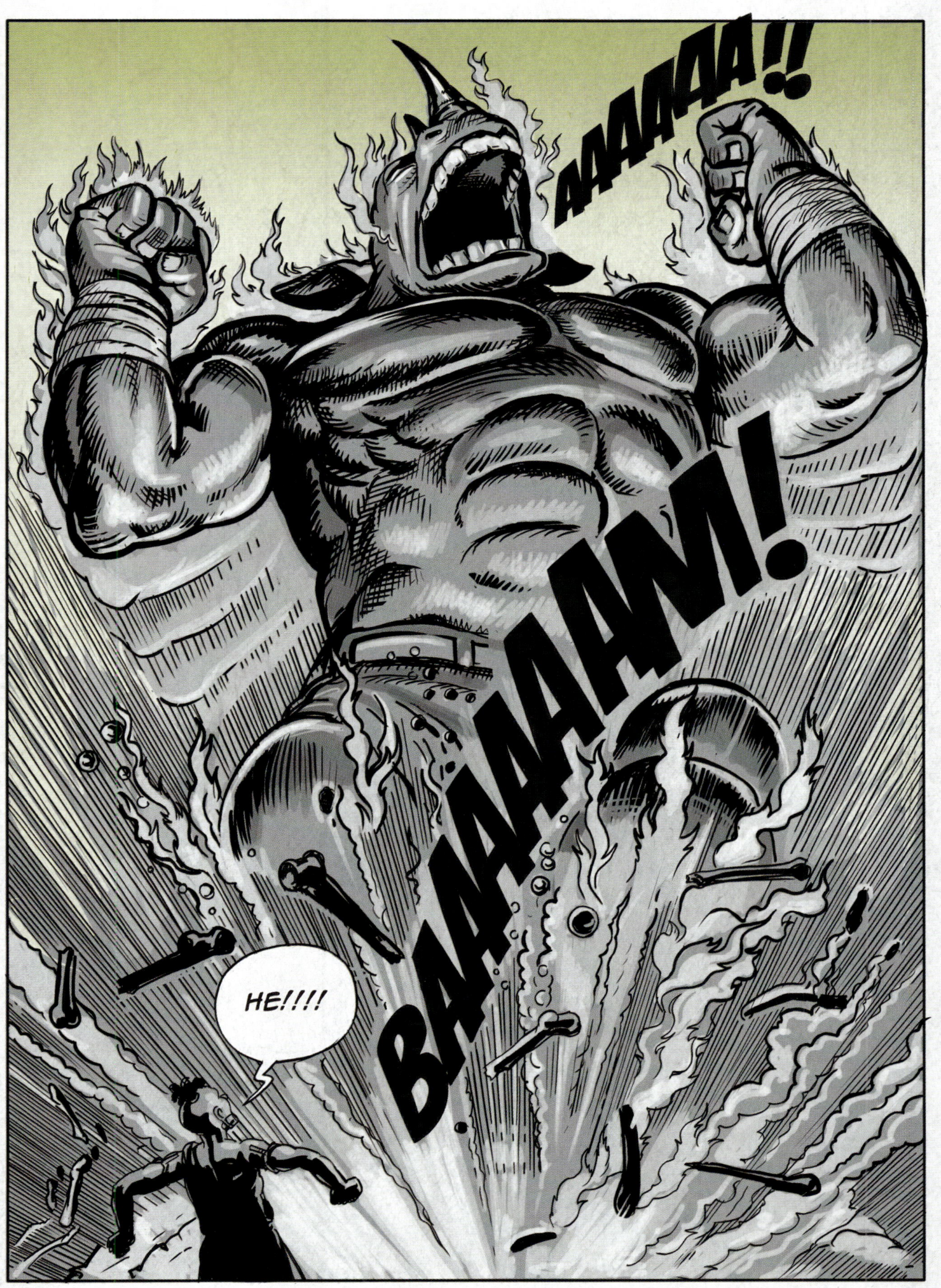
AAAAAA!!
BAAAAAM!
HE!!!!

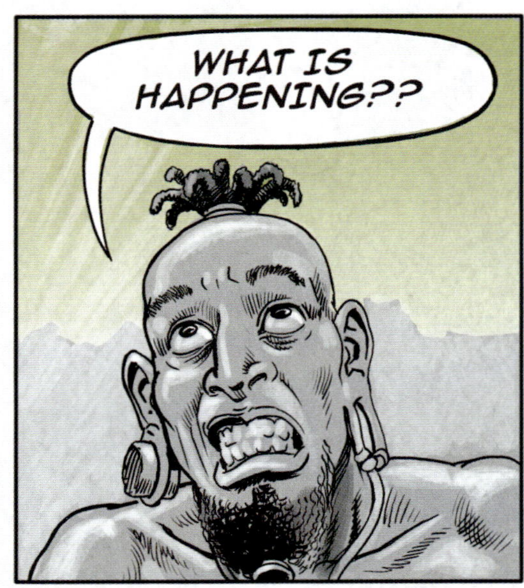
WHAT IS HAPPENING??

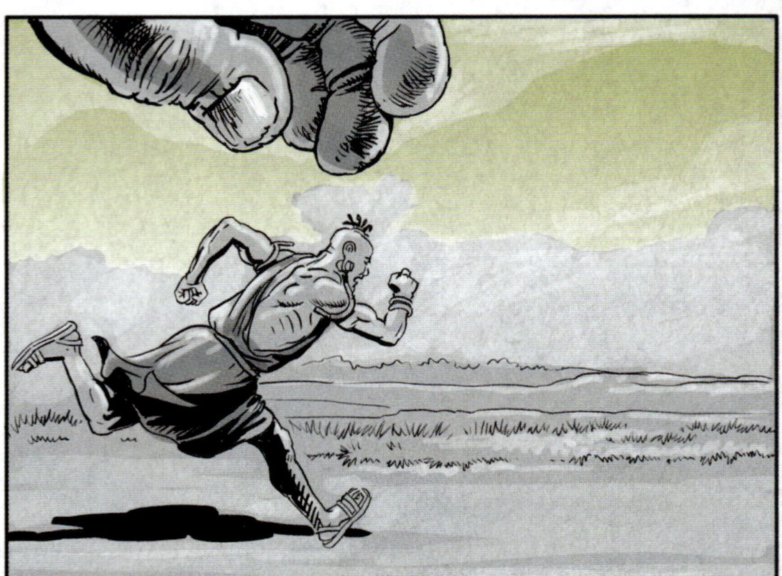

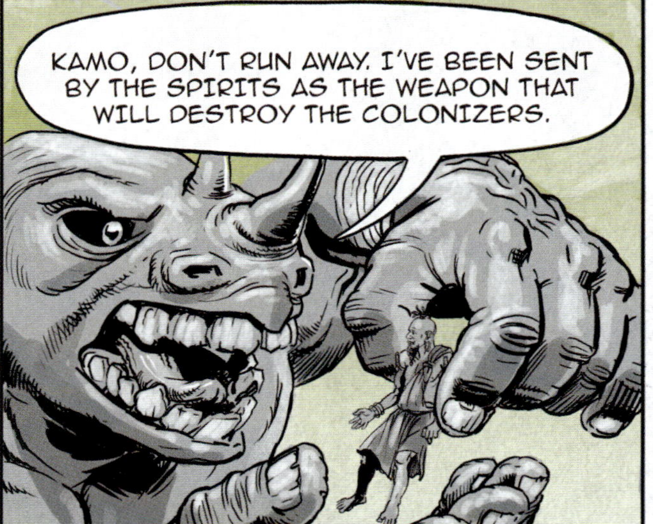
KAMO, DON'T RUN AWAY. I'VE BEEN SENT BY THE SPIRITS AS THE WEAPON THAT WILL DESTROY THE COLONIZERS.

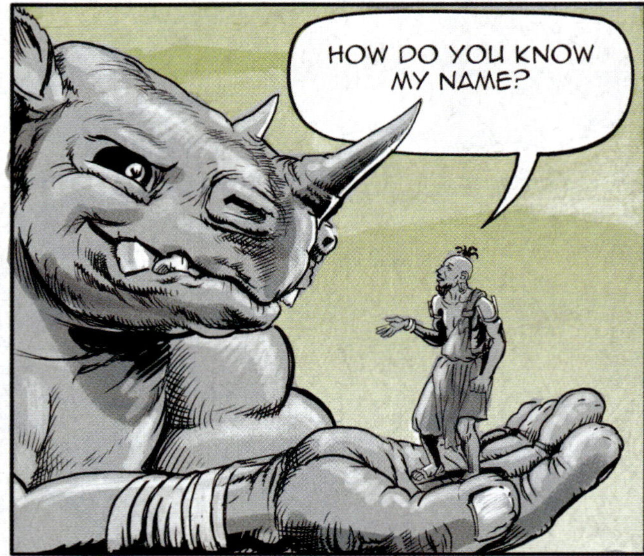
HOW DO YOU KNOW MY NAME?

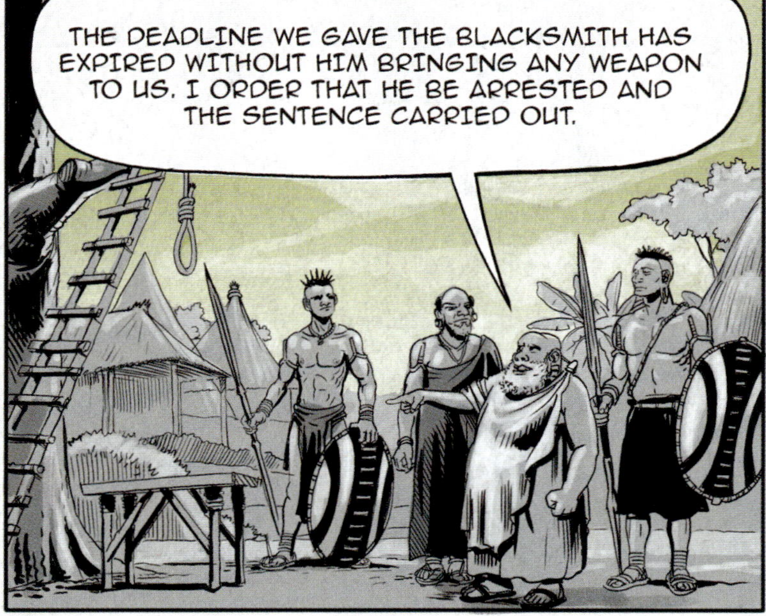
THE DEADLINE WE GAVE THE BLACKSMITH HAS EXPIRED WITHOUT HIM BRINGING ANY WEAPON TO US. I ORDER THAT HE BE ARRESTED AND THE SENTENCE CARRIED OUT.

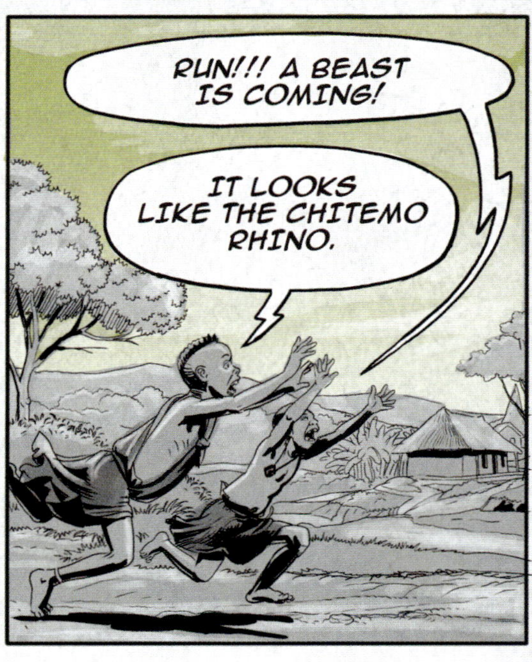
RUN!!! A BEAST IS COMING!
IT LOOKS LIKE THE CHITEMO RHINO.

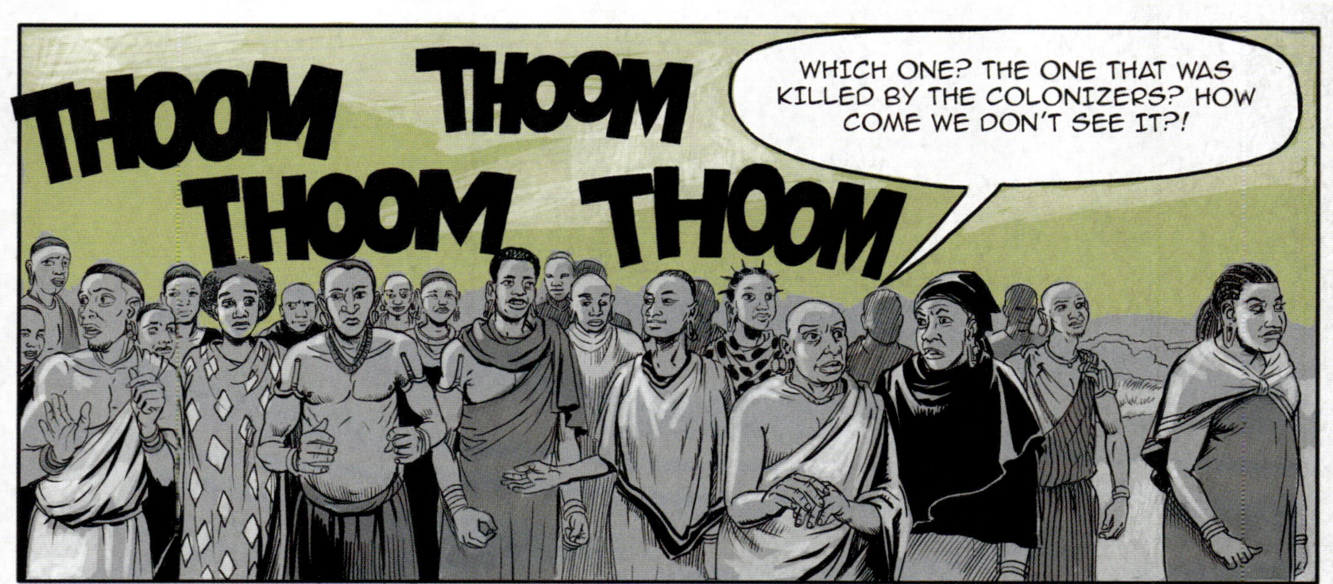
THOOM THOOM
THOOM THOOM
WHICH ONE? THE ONE THAT WAS KILLED BY THE COLONIZERS? HOW COME WE DON'T SEE IT?!

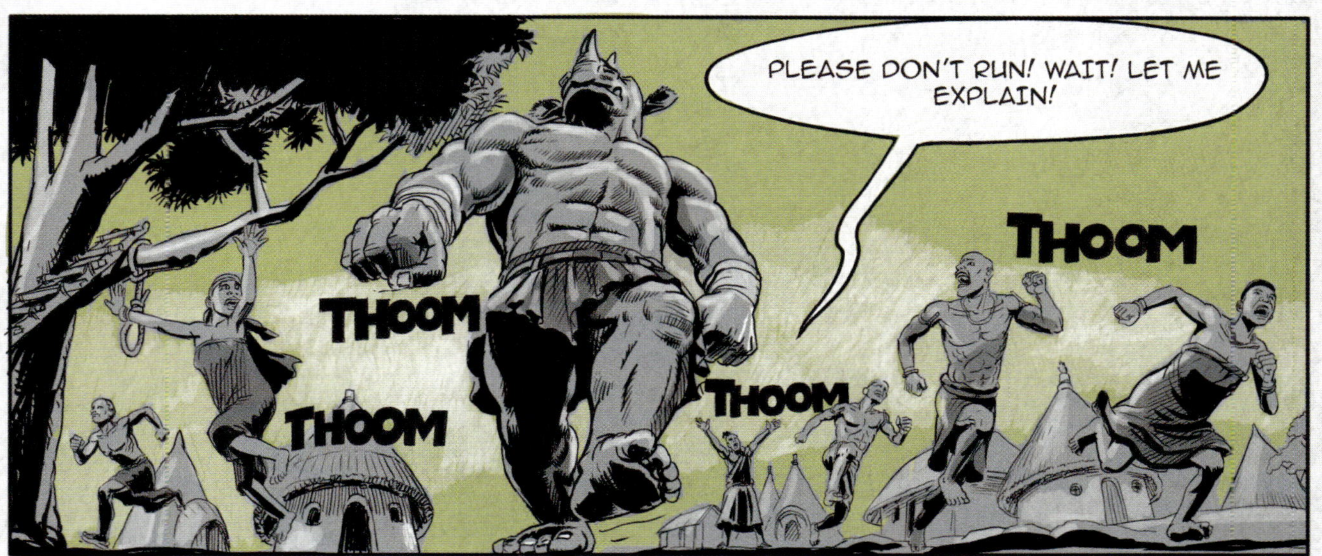
PLEASE DON'T RUN! WAIT! LET ME EXPLAIN!
THOOM
THOOM
THOOM
THOOM

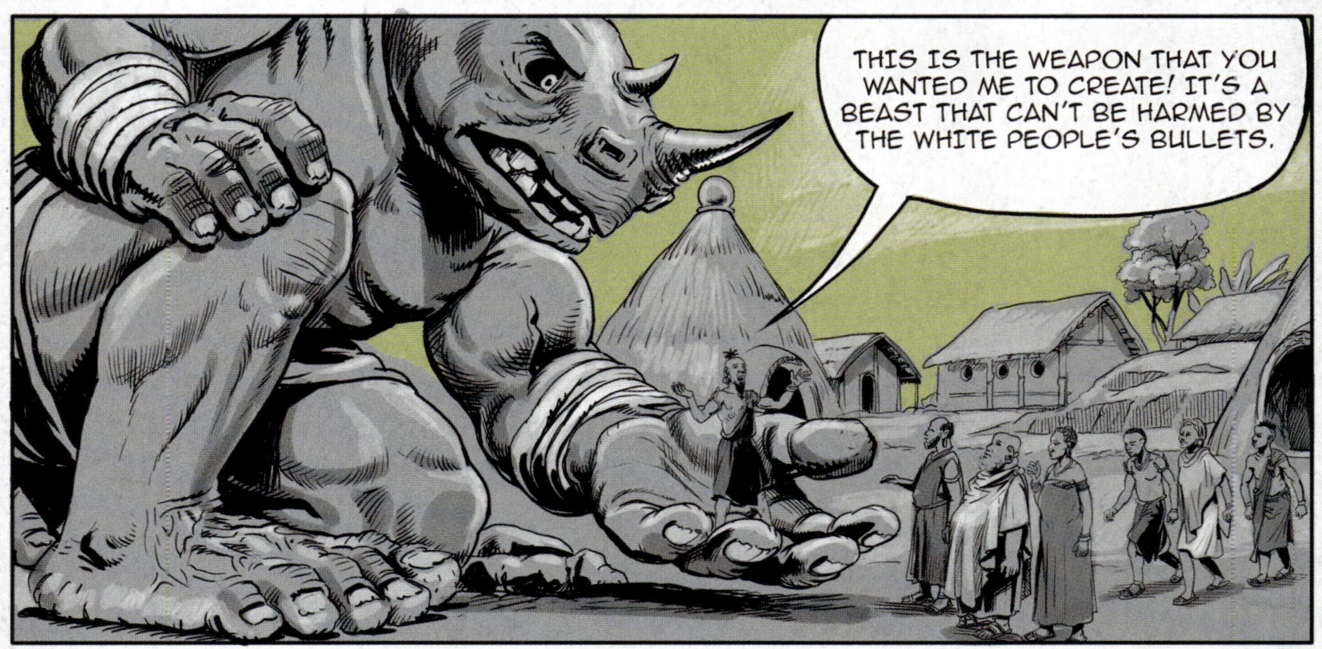
THIS IS THE WEAPON THAT YOU WANTED ME TO CREATE! IT'S A BEAST THAT CAN'T BE HARMED BY THE WHITE PEOPLE'S BULLETS.

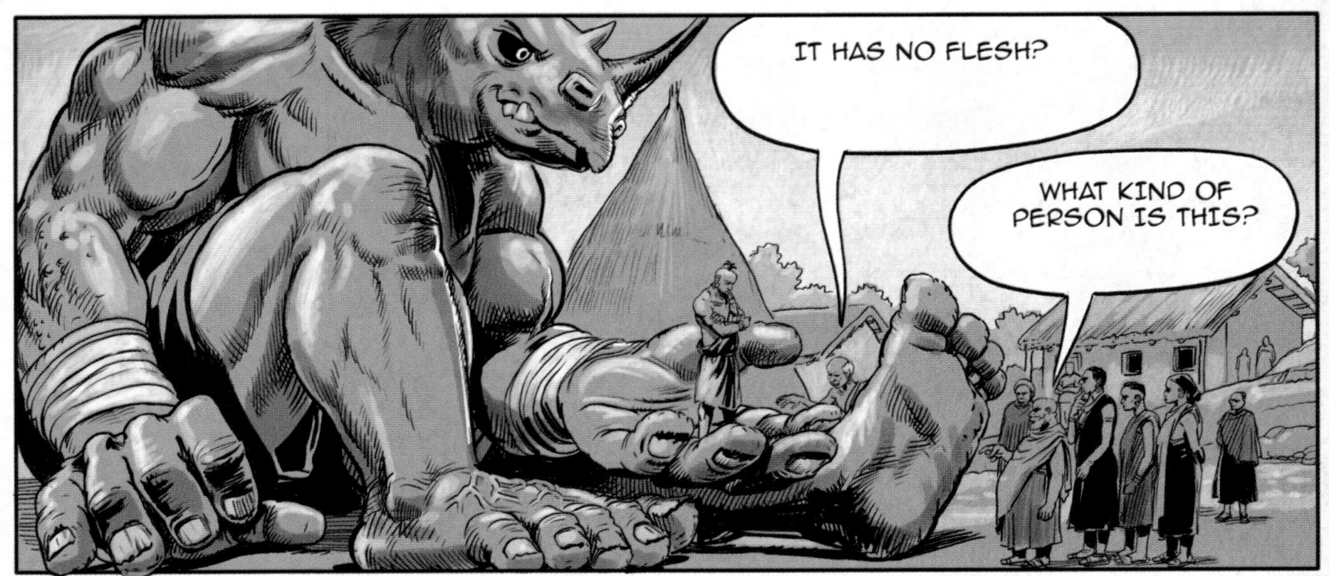
IT HAS NO FLESH?
WHAT KIND OF PERSON IS THIS?

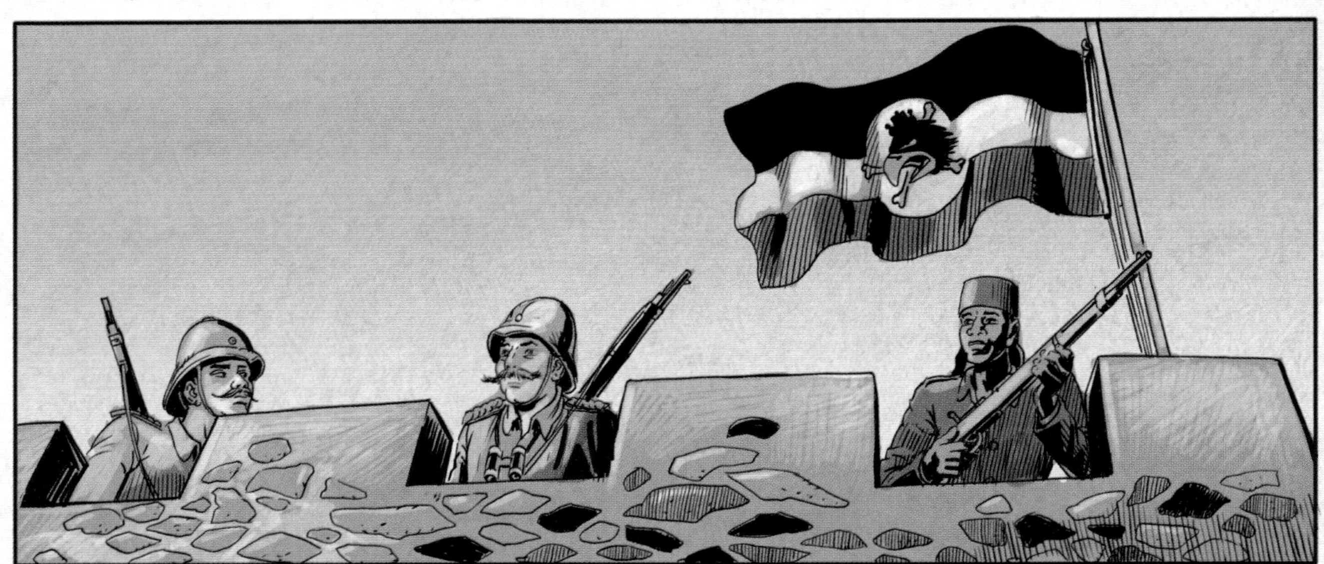

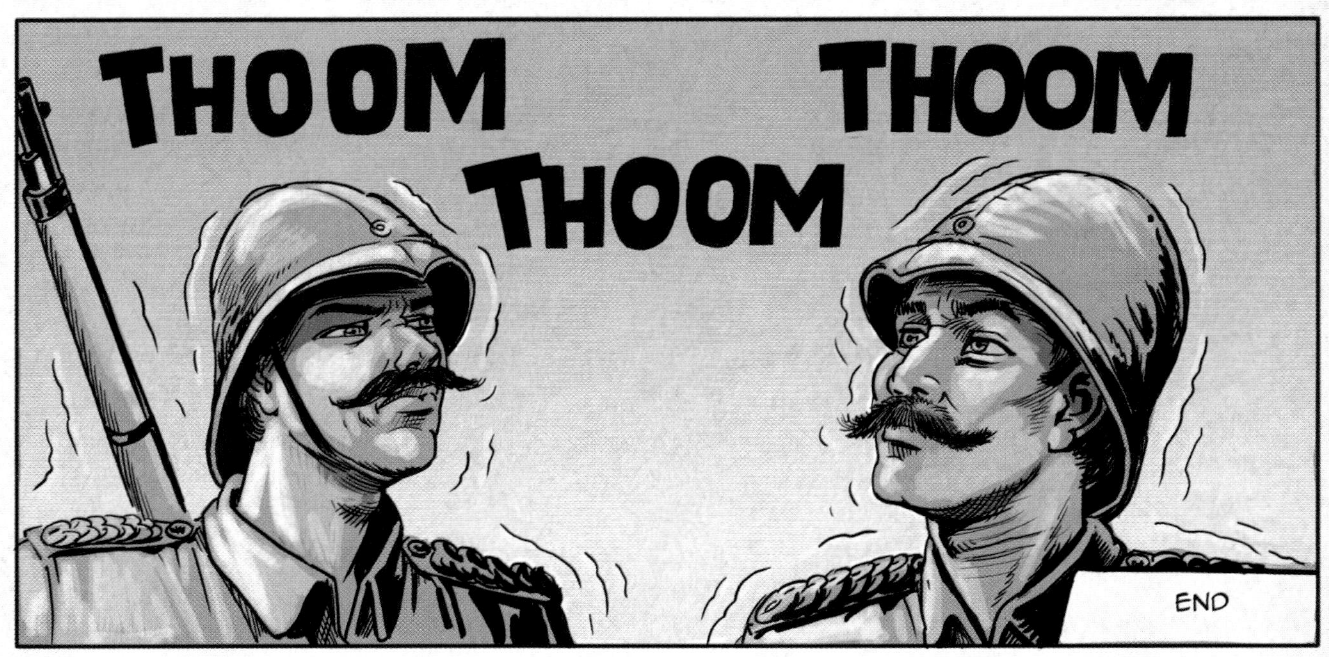
THOOM
THOOM
THOOM
END

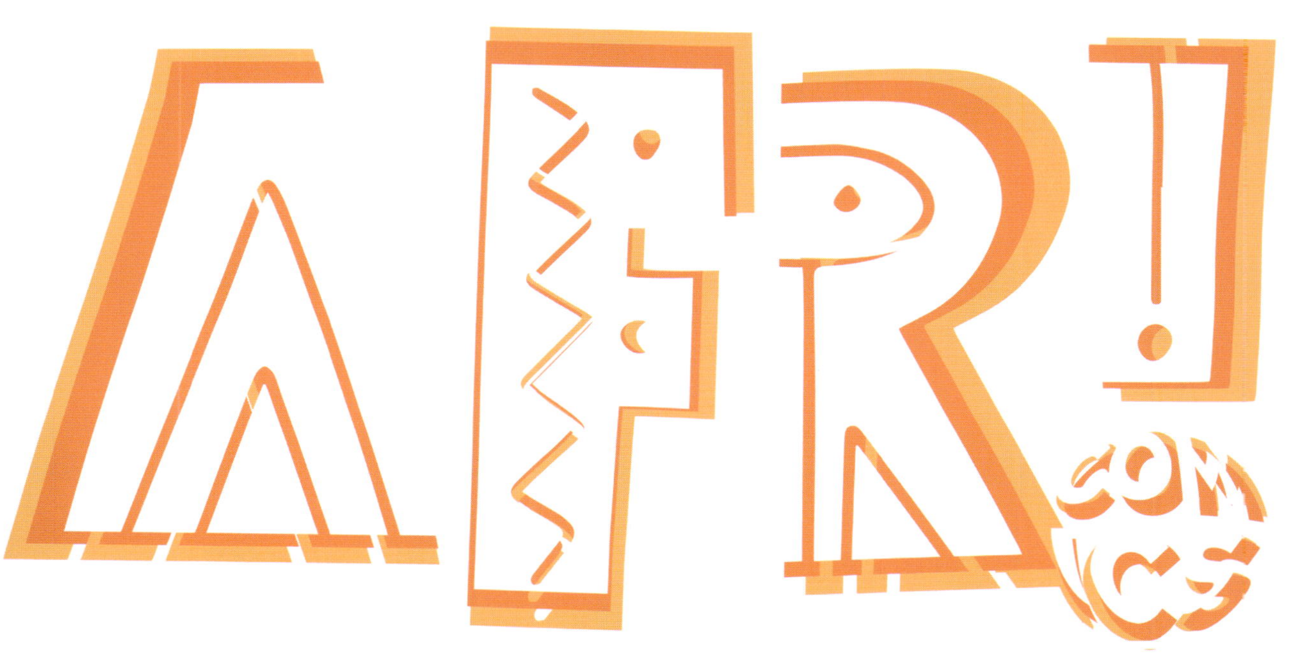
AFRI
COMICS

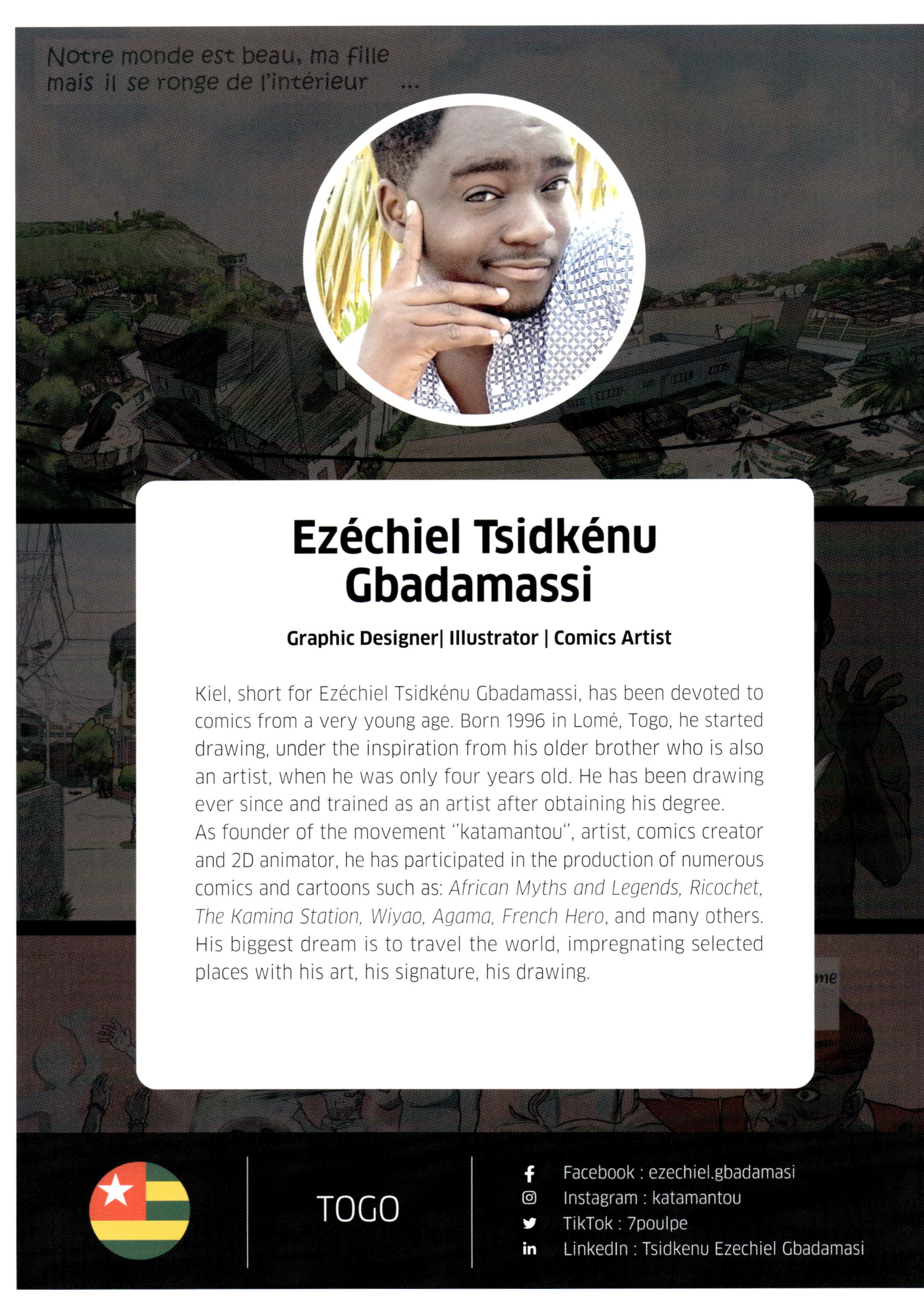

Ezéchiel Tsidkénu Gbadamassi

Graphic Designer| Illustrator | Comics Artist

Kiel, short for Ezéchiel Tsidkénu Gbadamassi, has been devoted to comics from a very young age. Born 1996 in Lomé, Togo, he started drawing, under the inspiration from his older brother who is also an artist, when he was only four years old. He has been drawing ever since and trained as an artist after obtaining his degree.
As founder of the movement "katamantou", artist, comics creator and 2D animator, he has participated in the production of numerous comics and cartoons such as: *African Myths and Legends, Ricochet, The Kamina Station, Wiyao, Agama, French Hero*, and many others. His biggest dream is to travel the world, impregnating selected places with his art, his signature, his drawing.

TOGO

Facebook : ezechiel.gbadamasi
Instagram : katamantou
TikTok : 7poulpe
LinkedIn : Tsidkenu Ezechiel Gbadamasi

KIEL

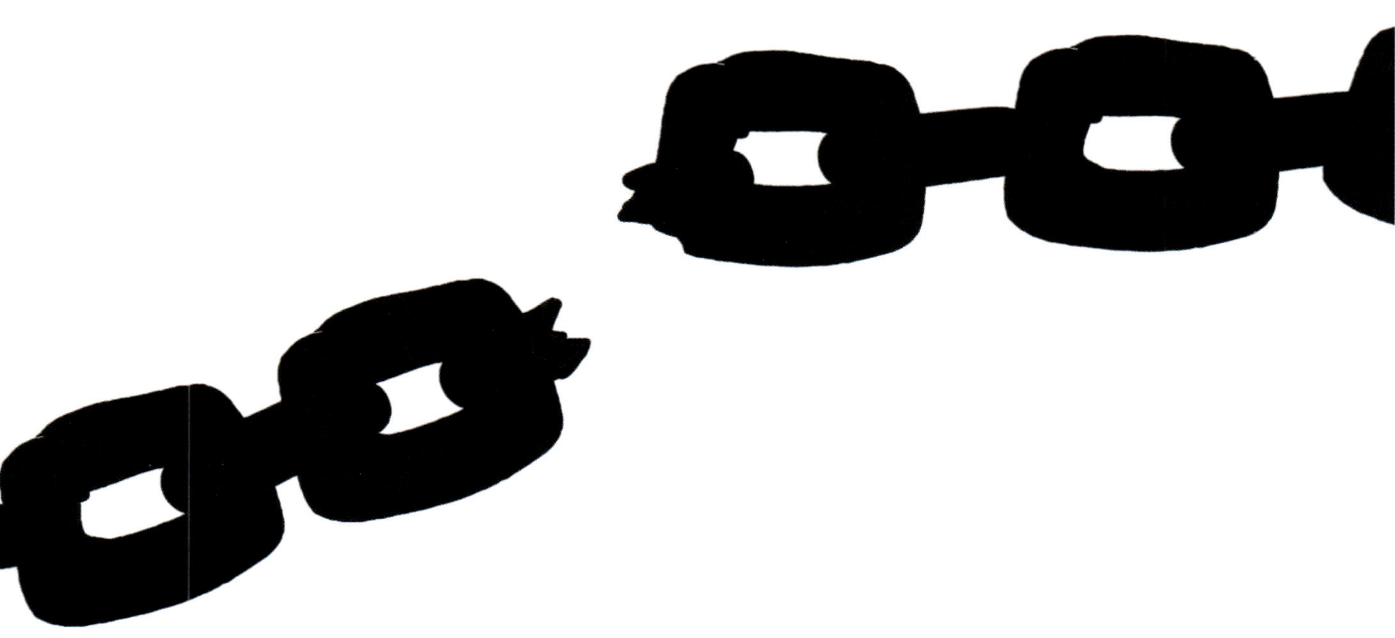

DECOLONIZER

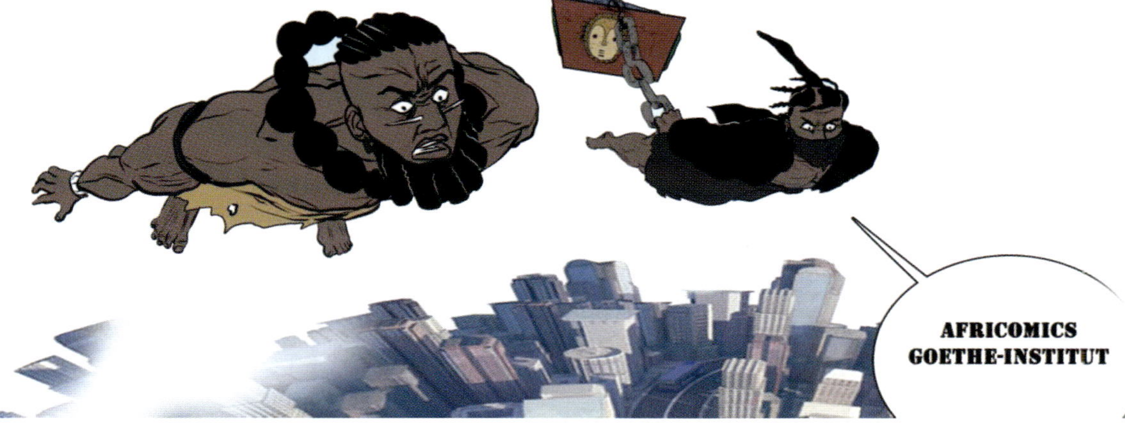

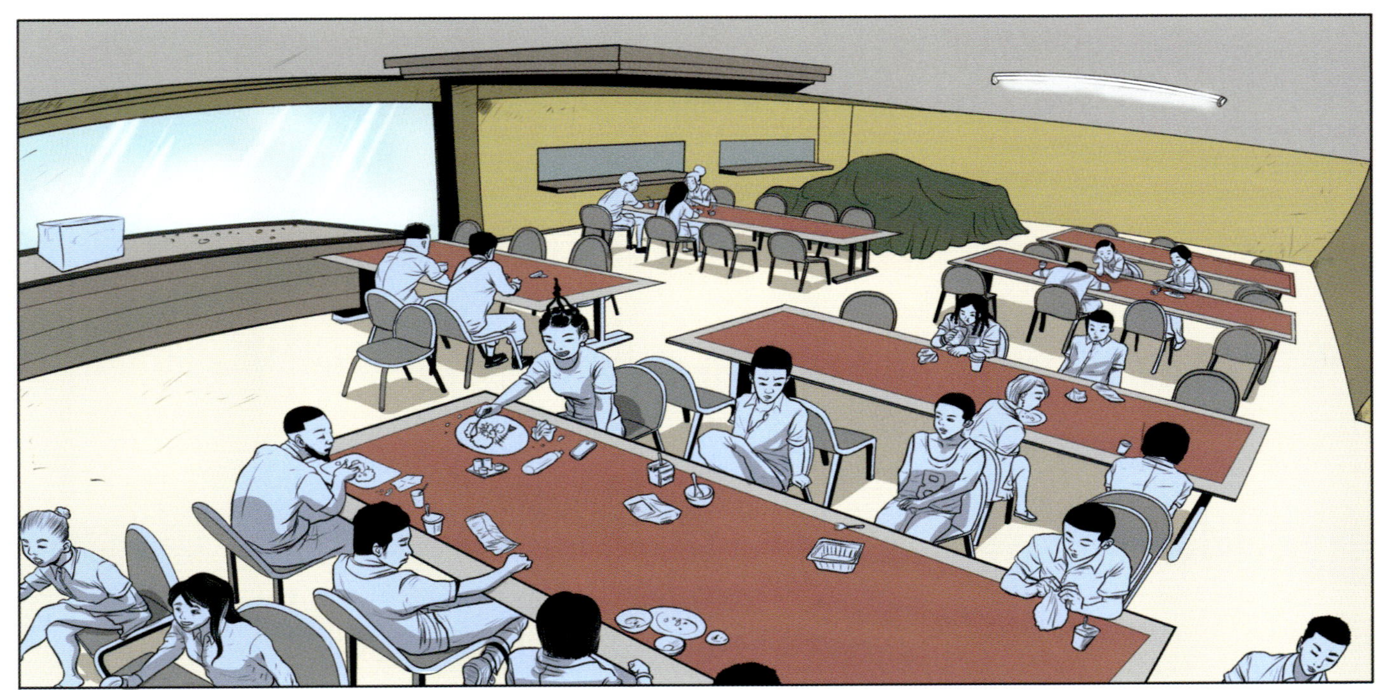

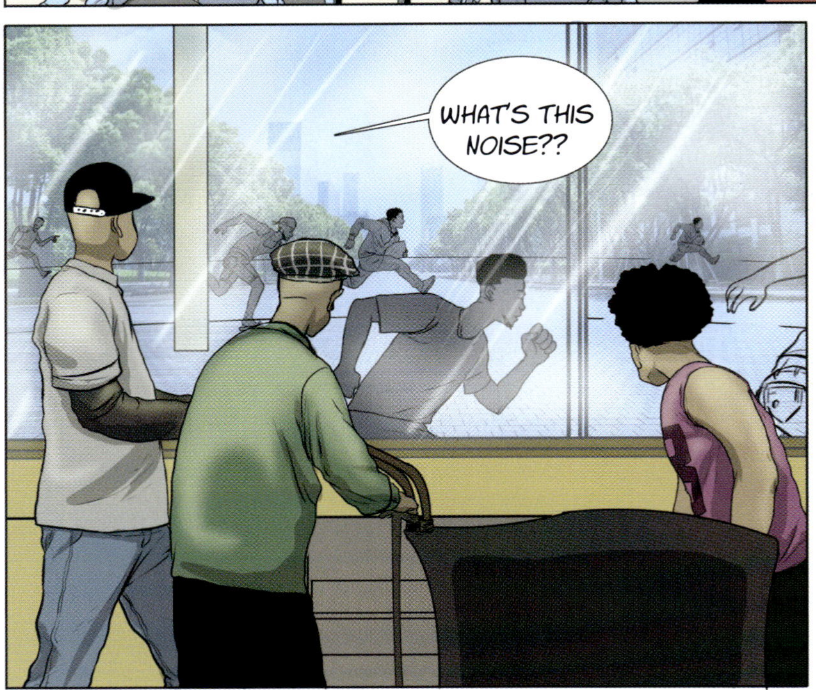
WHAT'S THIS NOISE??

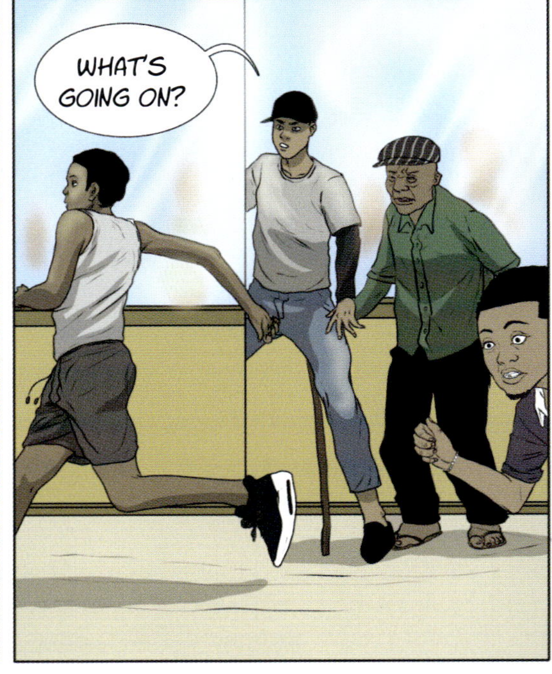
WHAT'S GOING ON?

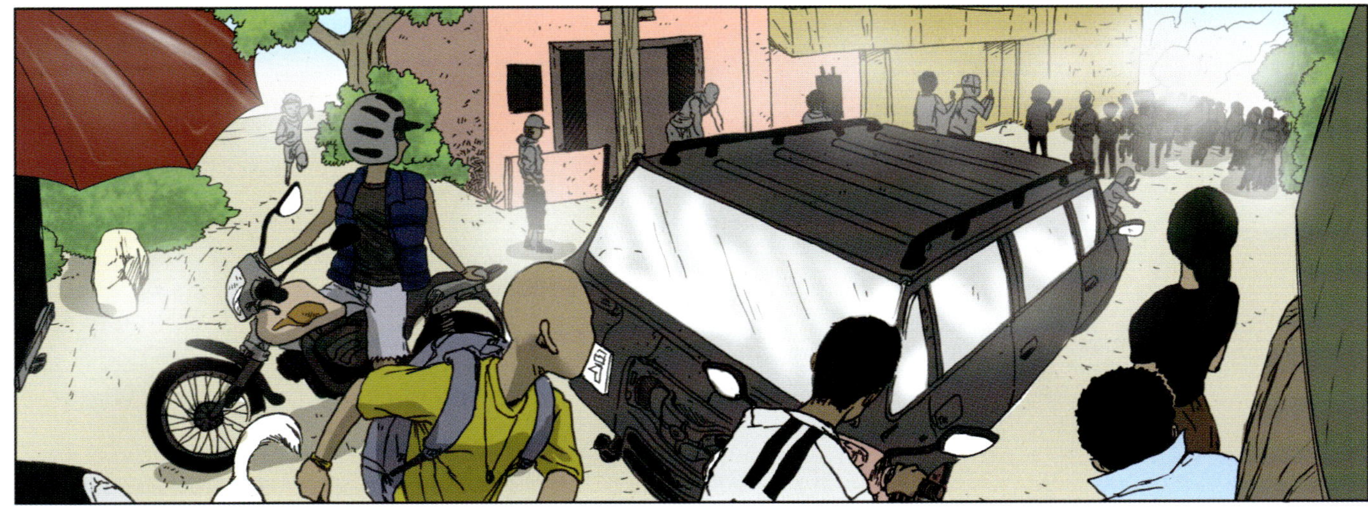

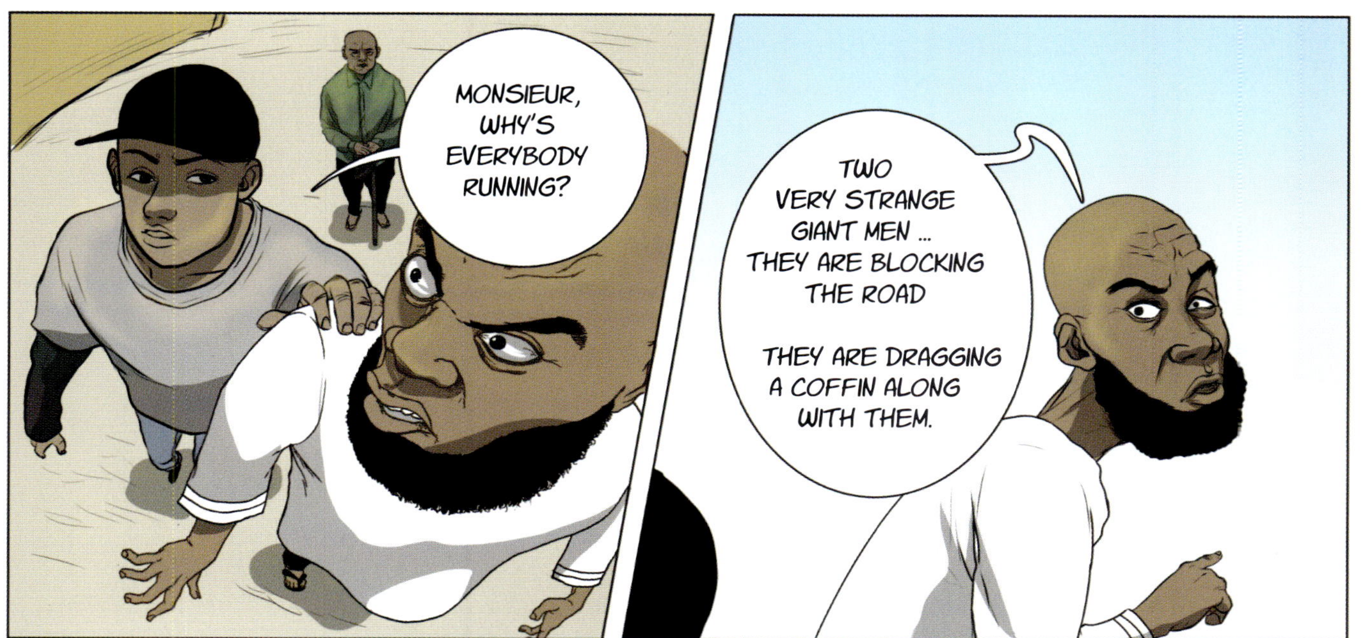
MONSIEUR, WHY'S EVERYBODY RUNNING?
TWO VERY STRANGE GIANT MEN ... THEY ARE BLOCKING THE ROAD
THEY ARE DRAGGING A COFFIN ALONG WITH THEM.

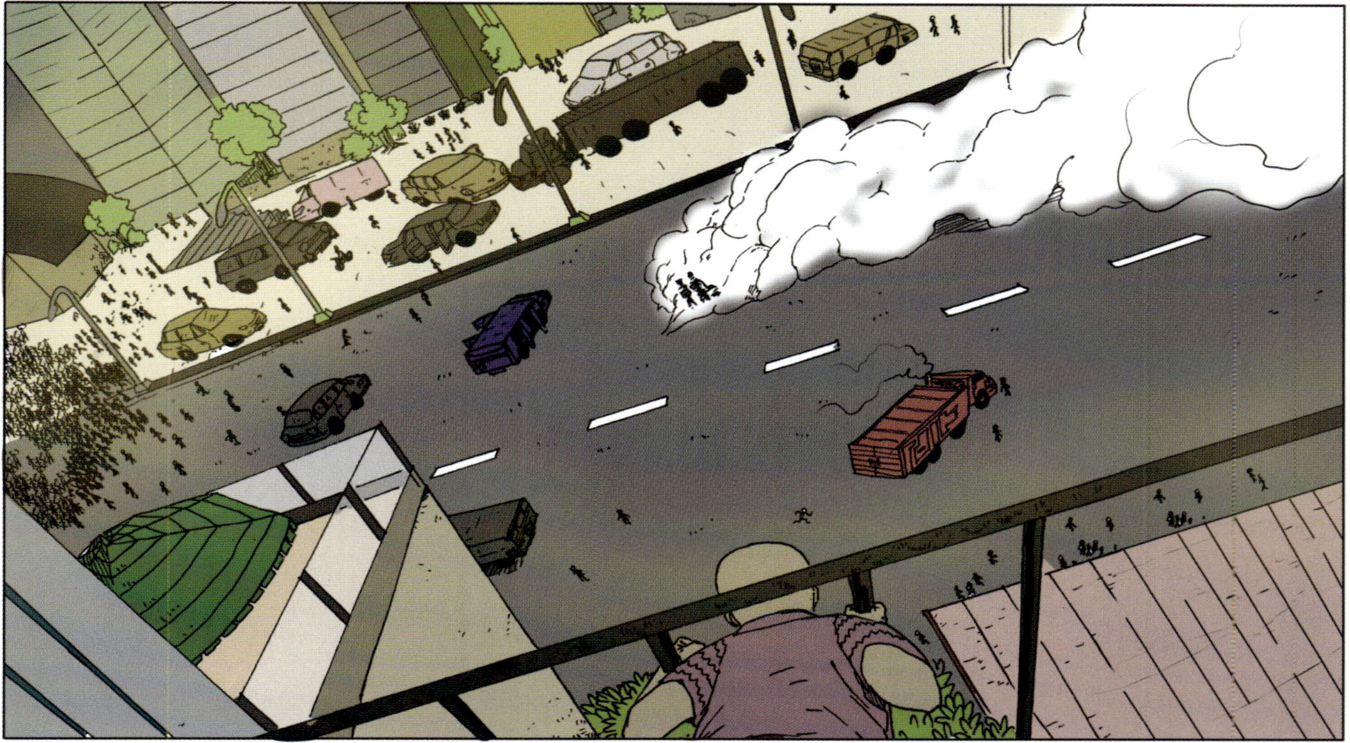

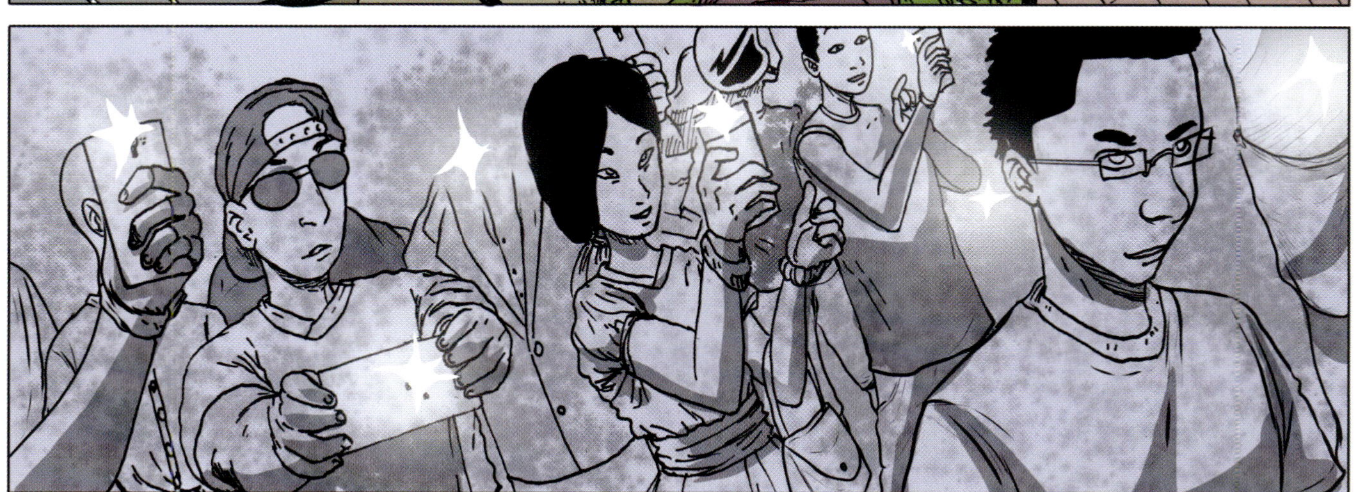

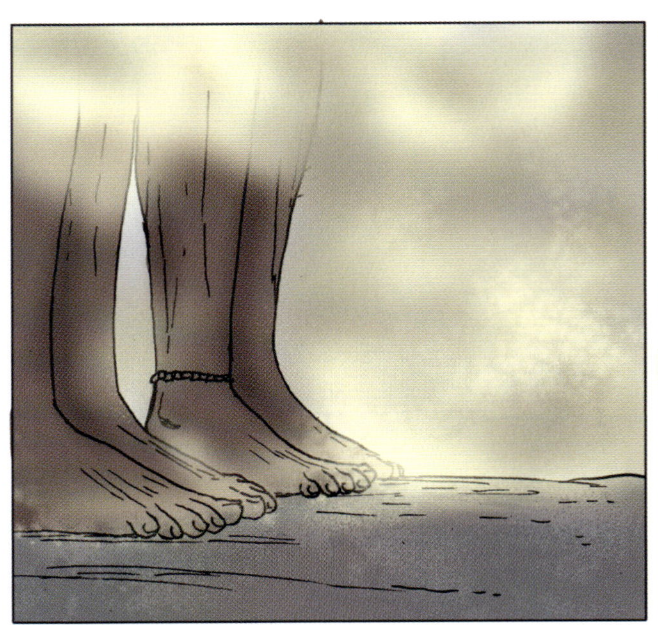

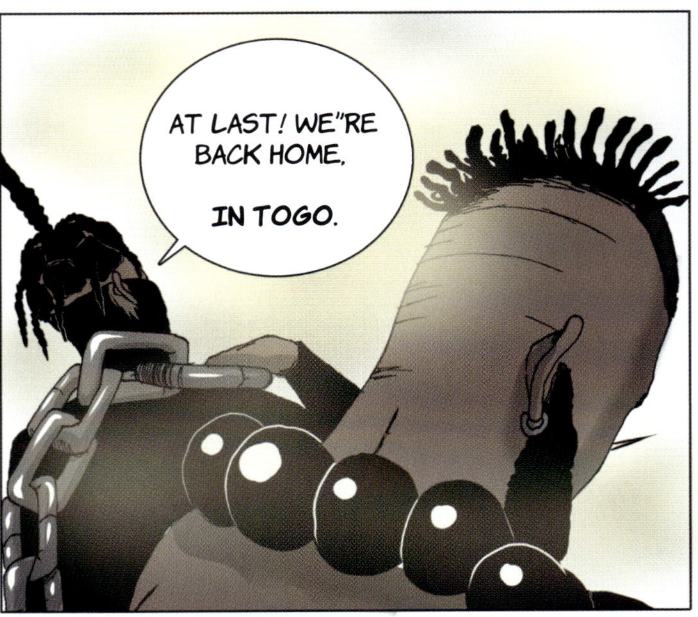
AT LAST! WE"RE BACK HOME,
IN TOGO.

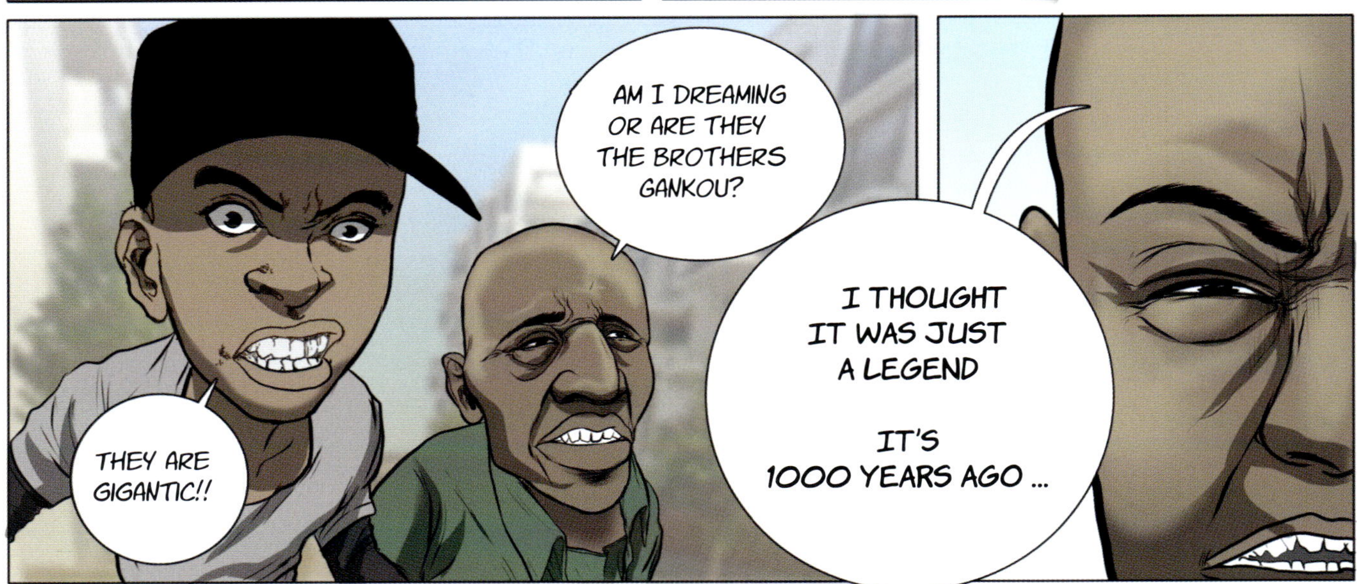
AM I DREAMING OR ARE THEY THE BROTHERS GANKOU?
THEY ARE GIGANTIC!!
I THOUGHT IT WAS JUST A LEGEND
IT'S 1000 YEARS AGO ...

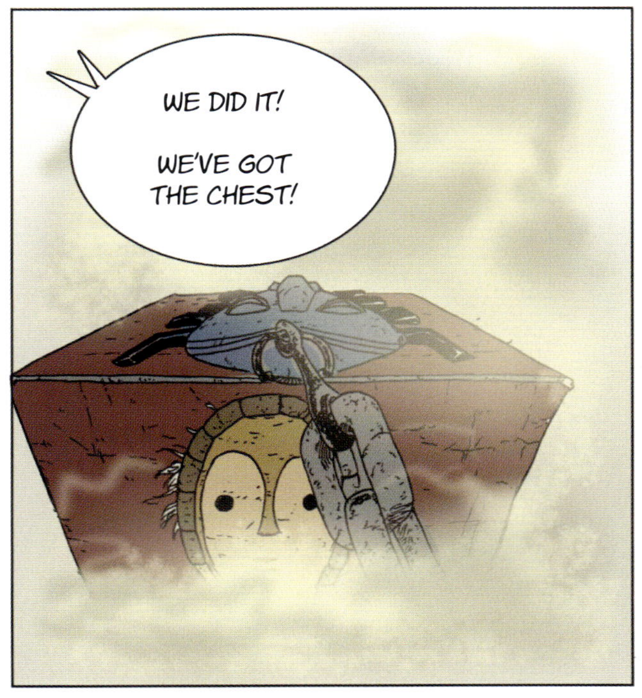
WE DID IT!
WE'VE GOT THE CHEST!

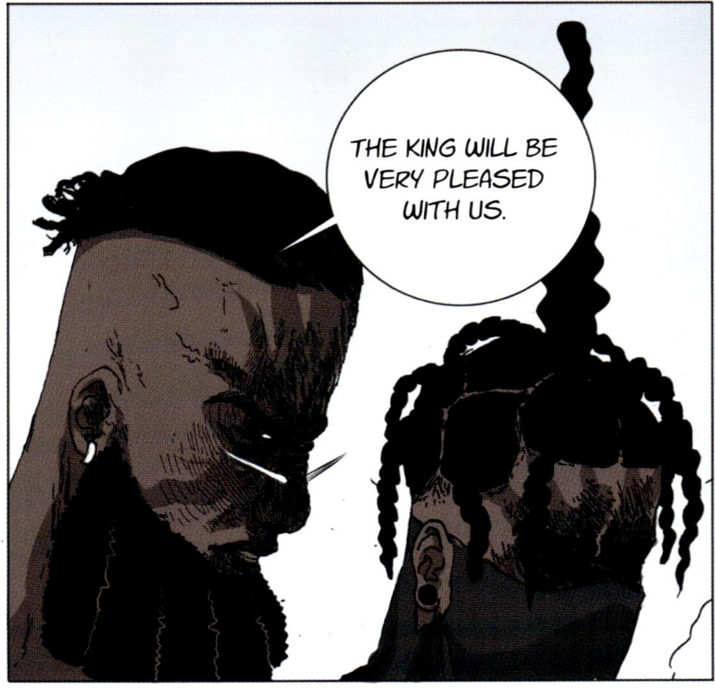
THE KING WILL BE VERY PLEASED WITH US.

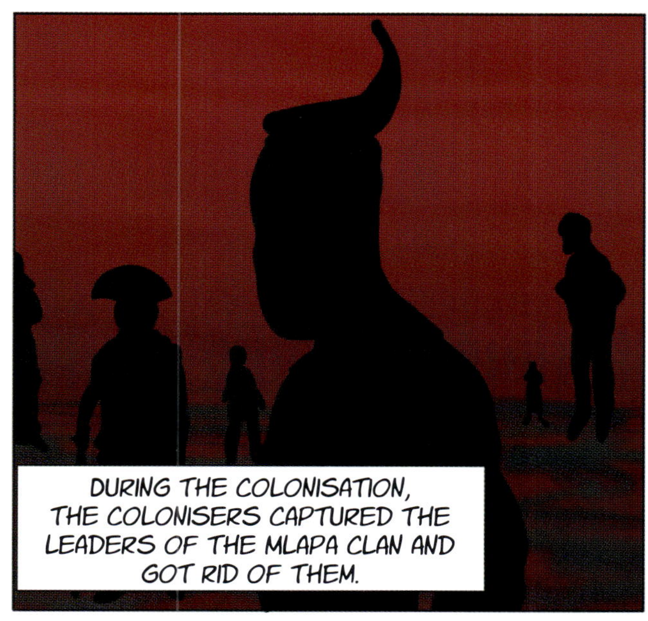
DURING THE COLONISATION, THE COLONISERS CAPTURED THE LEADERS OF THE MLAPA CLAN AND GOT RID OF THEM.

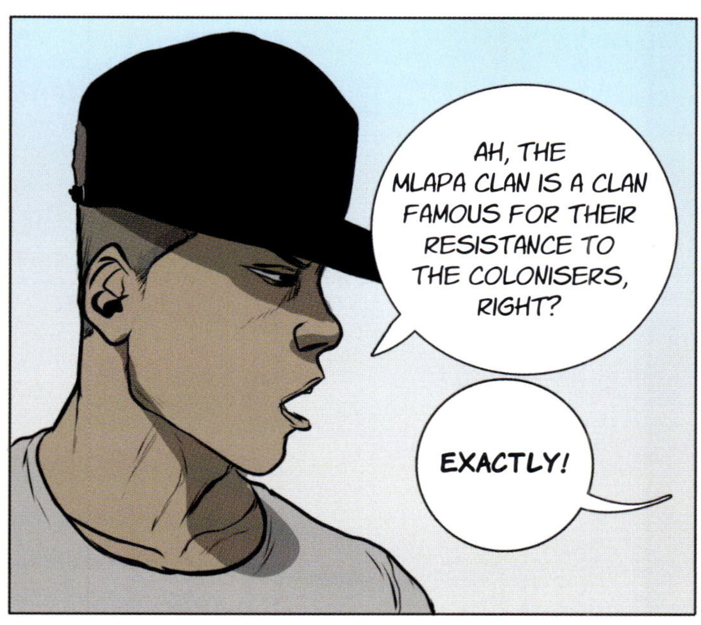
AH, THE MLAPA CLAN IS A CLAN FAMOUS FOR THEIR RESISTANCE TO THE COLONISERS, RIGHT?
EXACTLY!

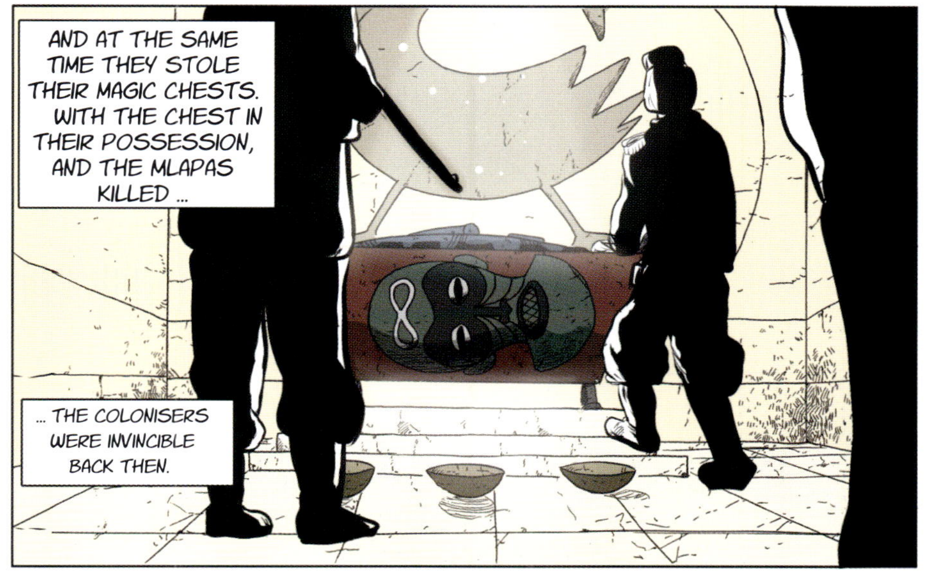
AND AT THE SAME TIME THEY STOLE THEIR MAGIC CHESTS. WITH THE CHEST IN THEIR POSSESSION, AND THE MLAPAS KILLED ...
... THE COLONISERS WERE INVINCIBLE BACK THEN.

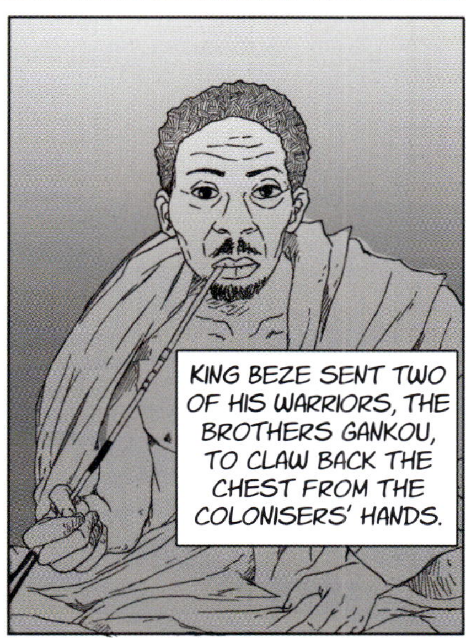
KING BEZE SENT TWO OF HIS WARRIORS, THE BROTHERS GANKOU, TO CLAW BACK THE CHEST FROM THE COLONISERS' HANDS.

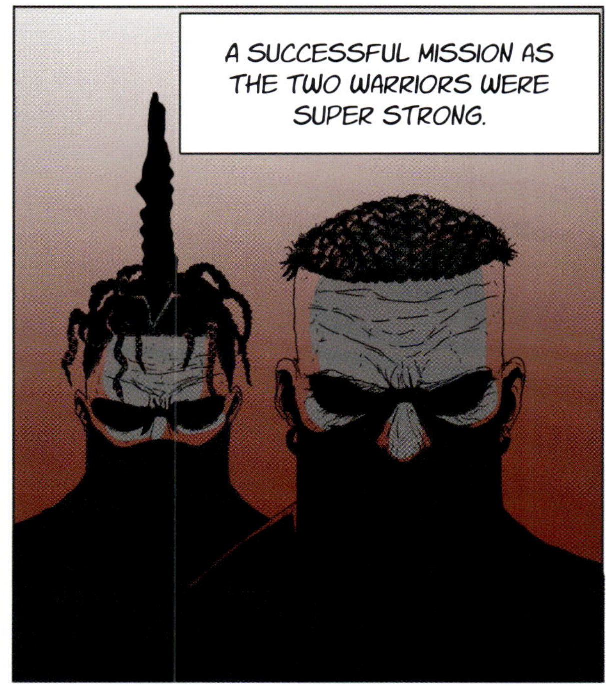
A SUCCESSFUL MISSION AS THE TWO WARRIORS WERE SUPER STRONG.

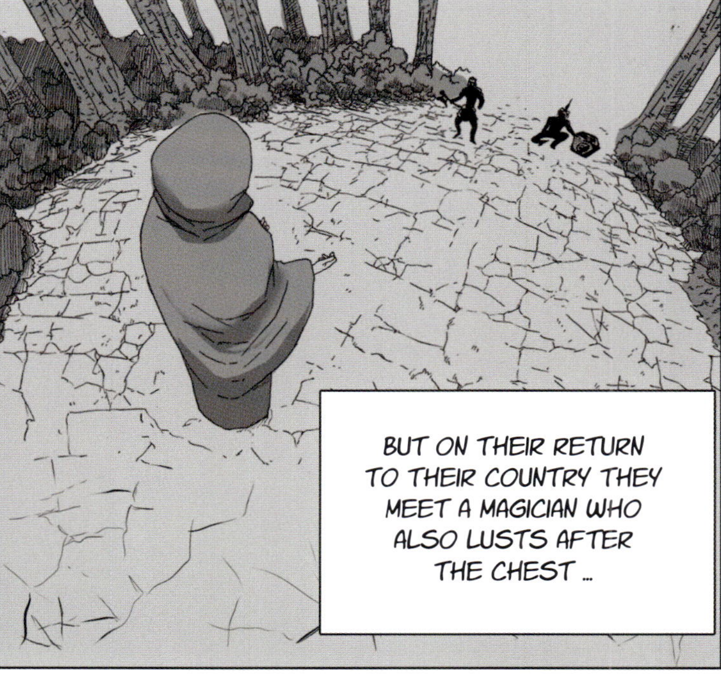
BUT ON THEIR RETURN TO THEIR COUNTRY THEY MEET A MAGICIAN WHO ALSO LUSTS AFTER THE CHEST ...

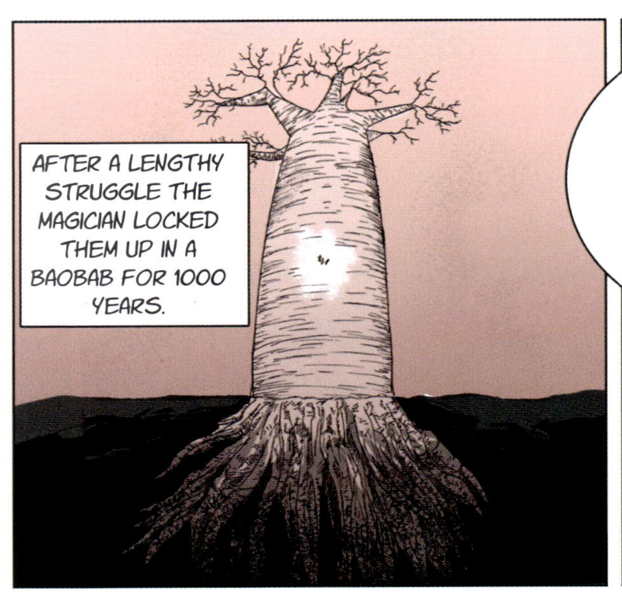
AFTER A LENGTHY STRUGGLE THE MAGICIAN LOCKED THEM UP IN A BAOBAB FOR 1000 YEARS.

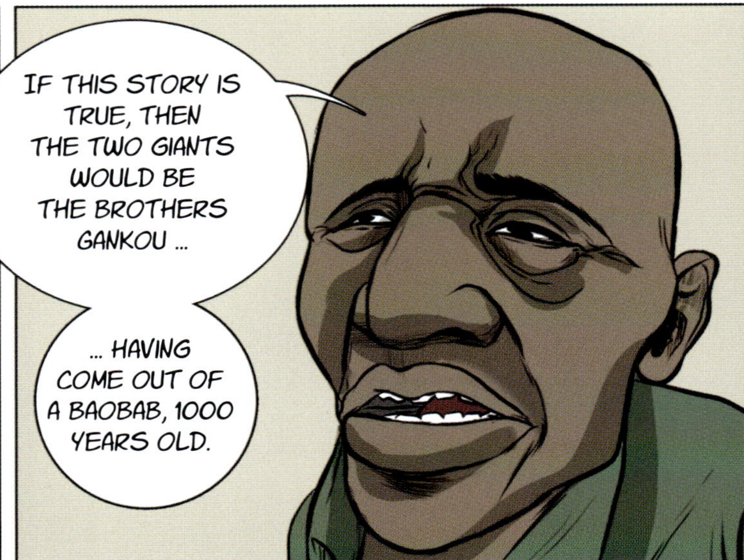
IF THIS STORY IS TRUE, THEN THE TWO GIANTS WOULD BE THE BROTHERS GANKOU ...
... HAVING COME OUT OF A BAOBAB, 1000 YEARS OLD.

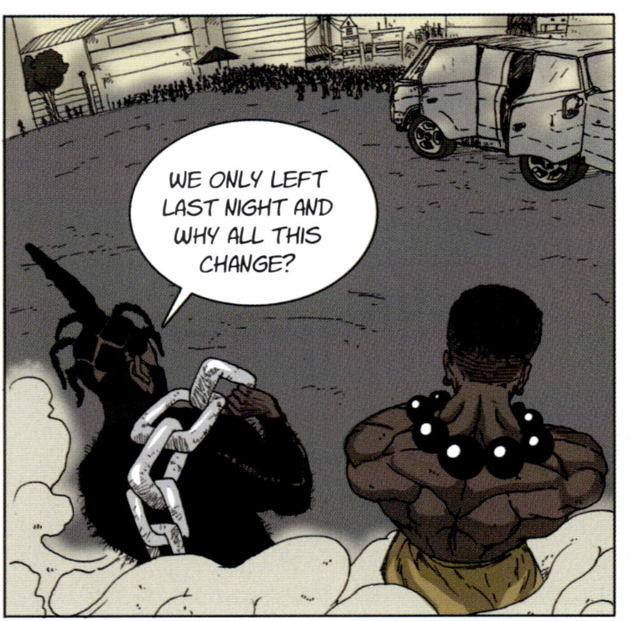
WE ONLY LEFT LAST NIGHT AND WHY ALL THIS CHANGE?

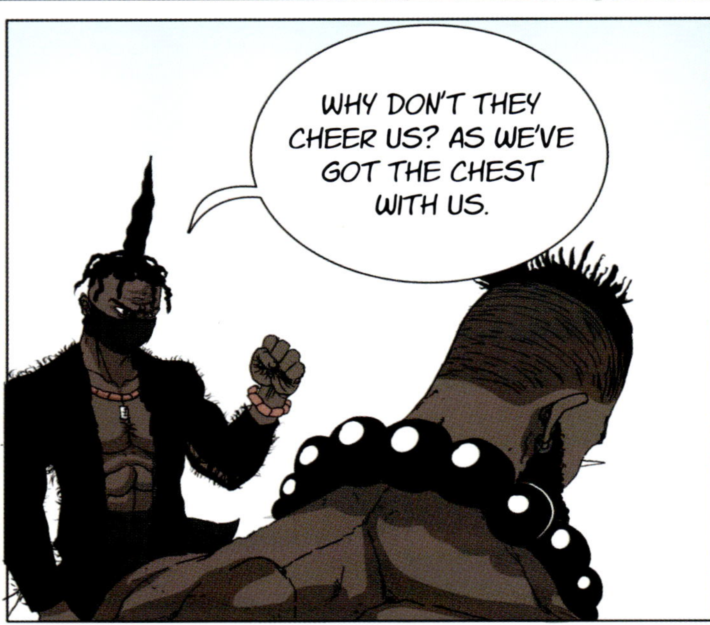
WHY DON'T THEY CHEER US? AS WE'VE GOT THE CHEST WITH US.

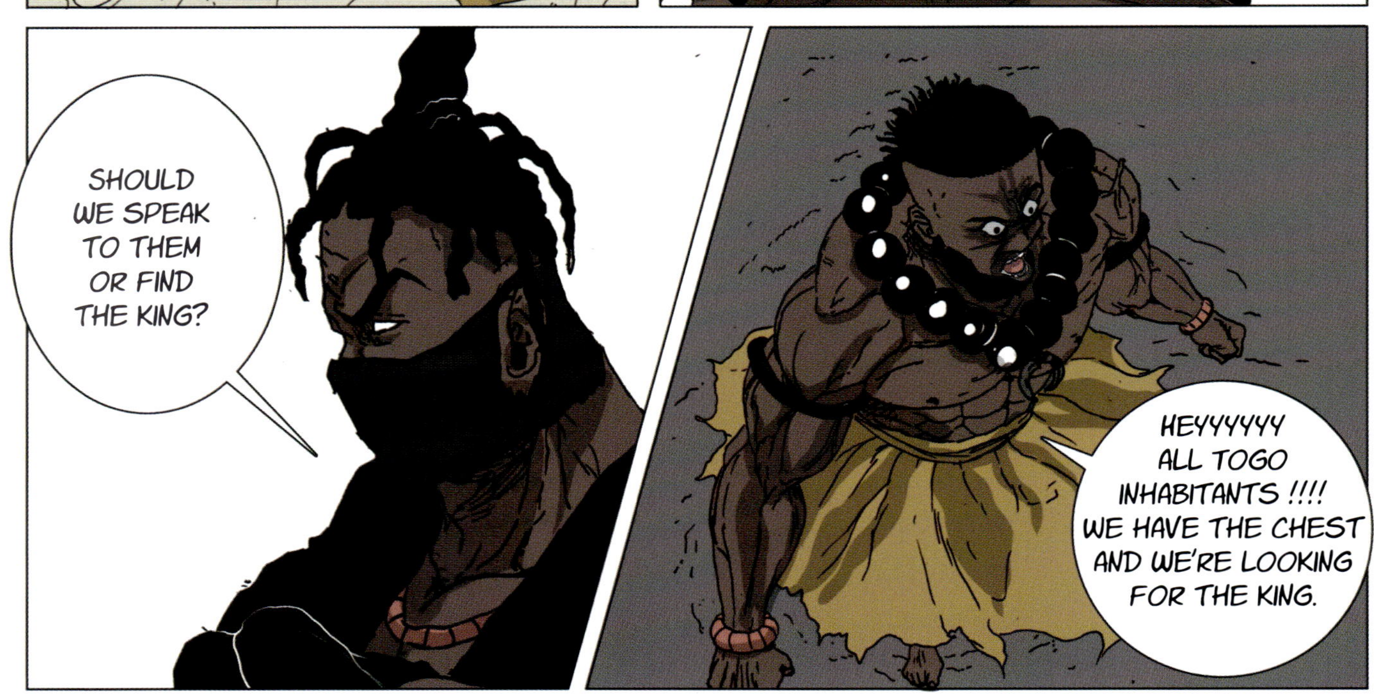
SHOULD WE SPEAK TO THEM OR FIND THE KING?
HEYYYYYY ALL TOGO INHABITANTS !!!! WE HAVE THE CHEST AND WE'RE LOOKING FOR THE KING.

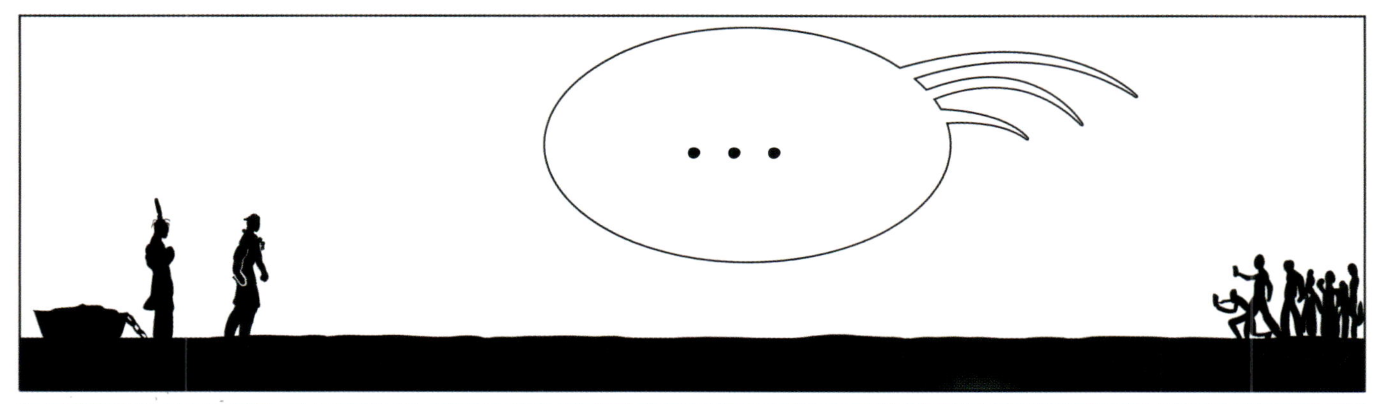
...

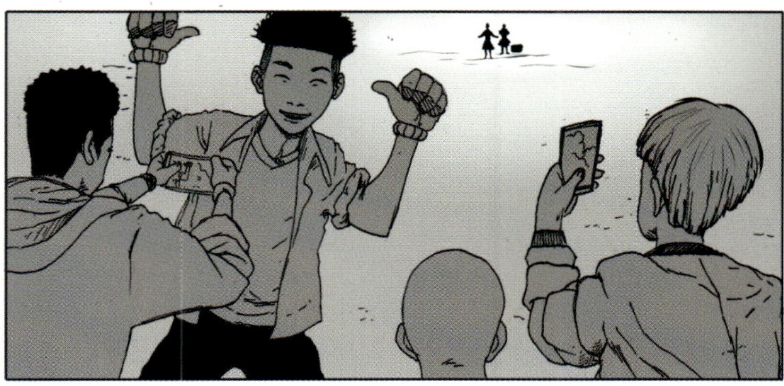

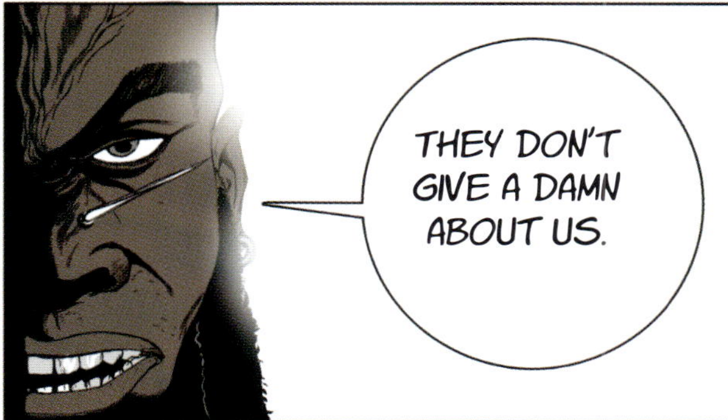
THEY DON'T GIVE A DAMN ABOUT US.

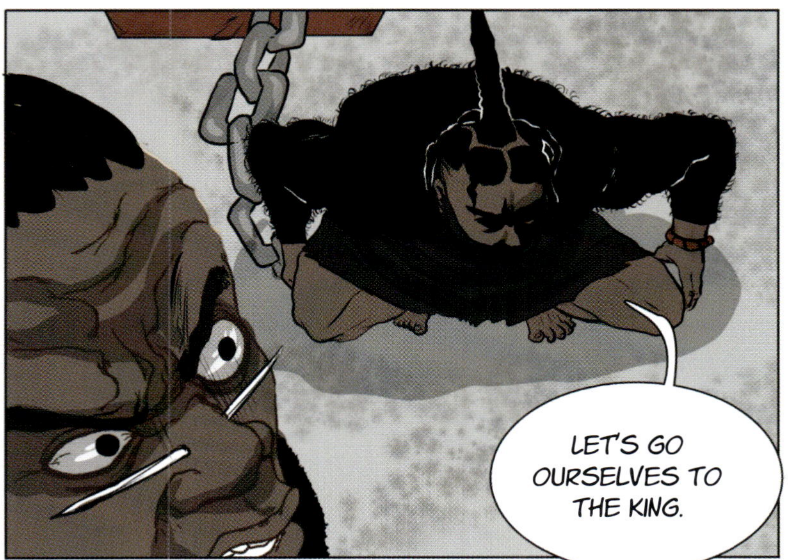
LET'S GO OURSELVES TO THE KING.

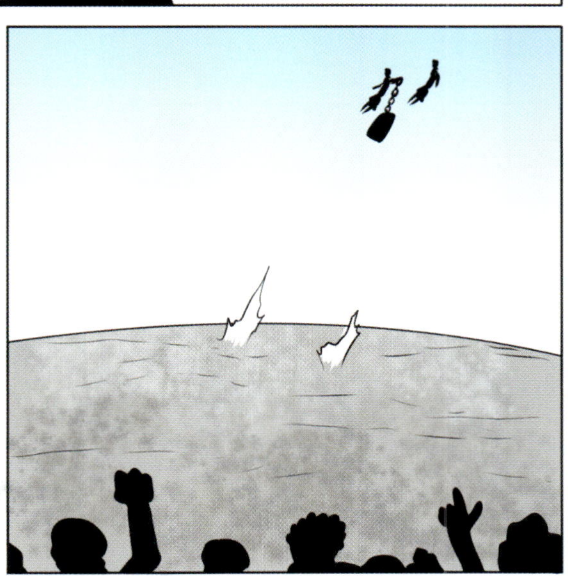

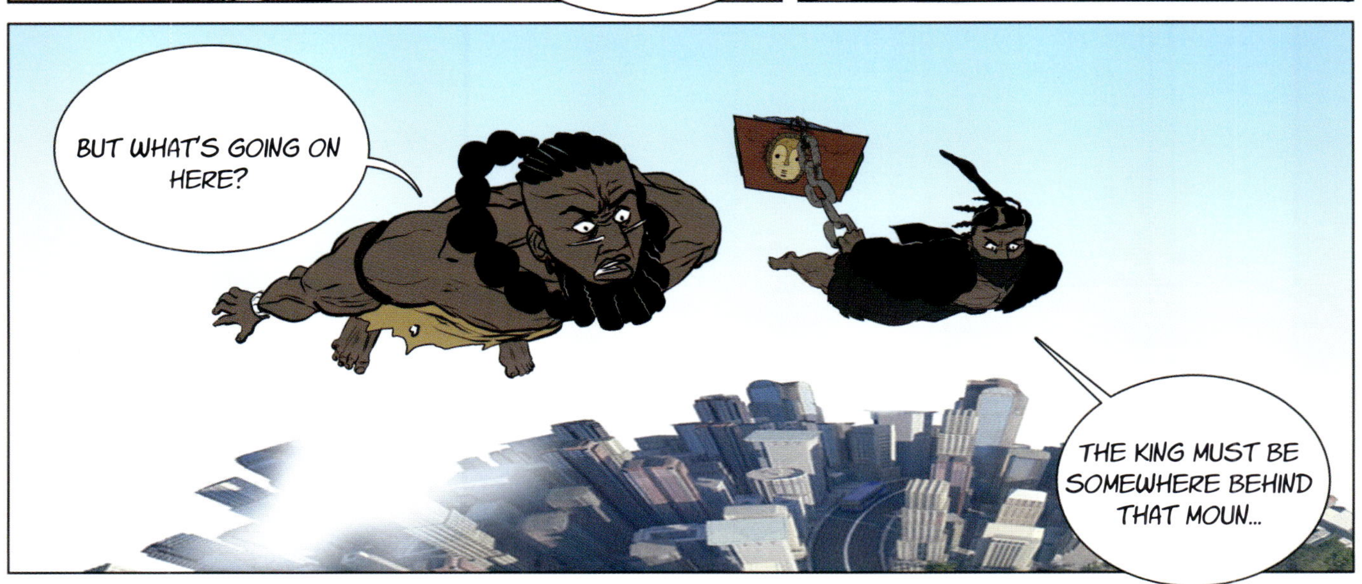
BUT WHAT'S GOING ON HERE?
THE KING MUST BE SOMEWHERE BEHIND THAT MOUN...

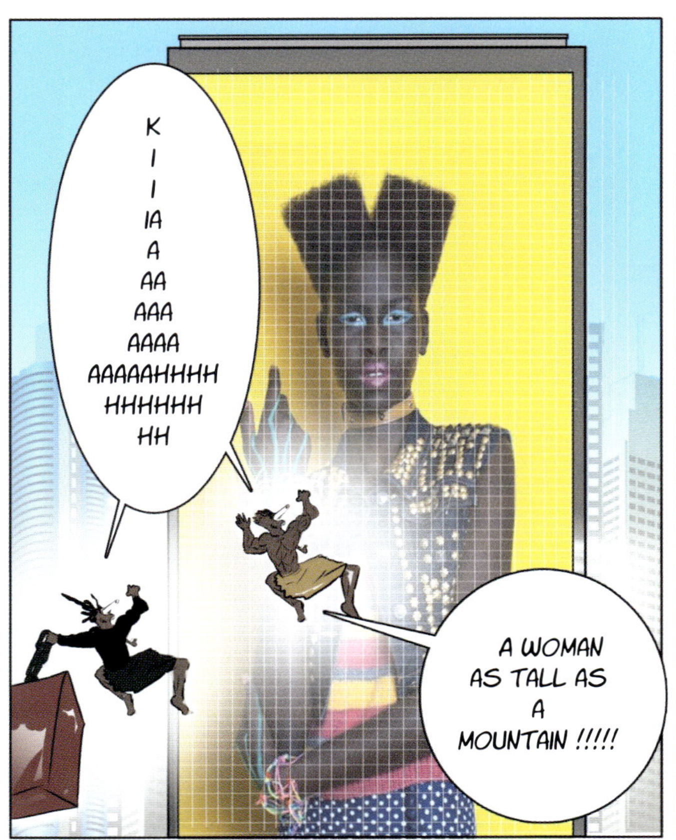
K
I
I
IA
A
AA
AAA
AAAA
AAAAAHHHH
HHHHHH
HH
A WOMAN AS TALL AS A MOUNTAIN !!!!!

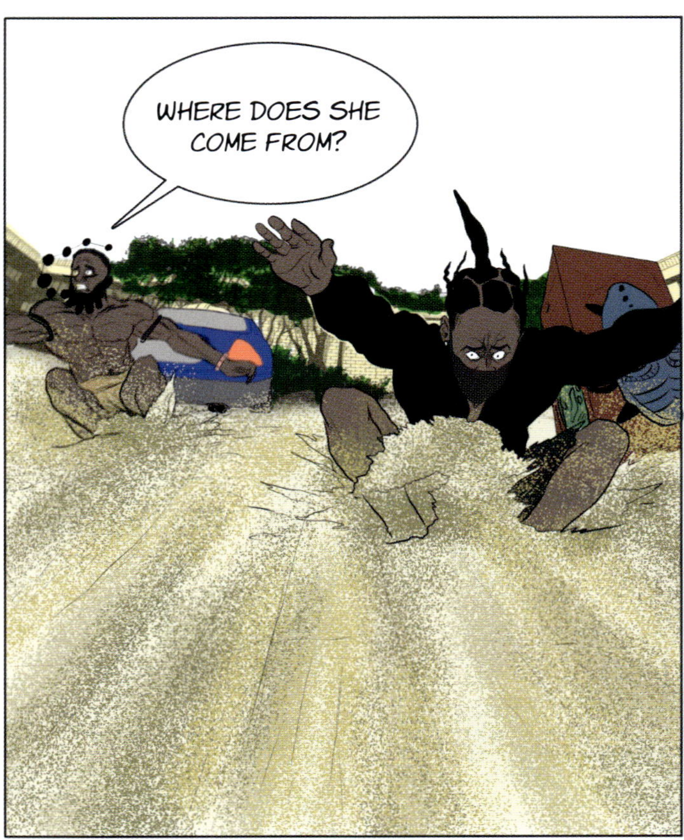
WHERE DOES SHE COME FROM?

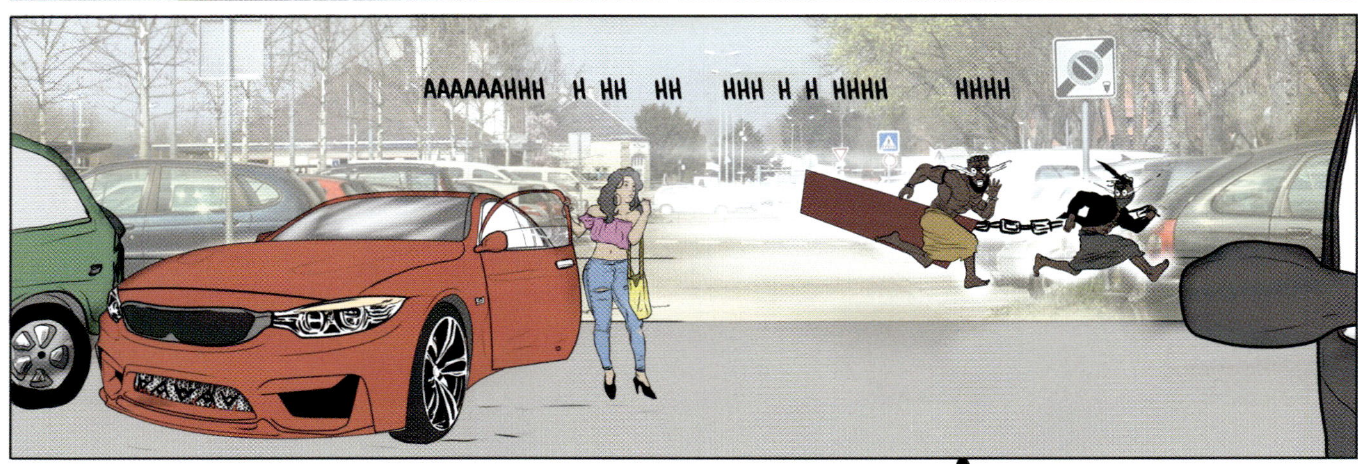
AAAAAAHHH H HH HH HHH H H HHHH HHHH

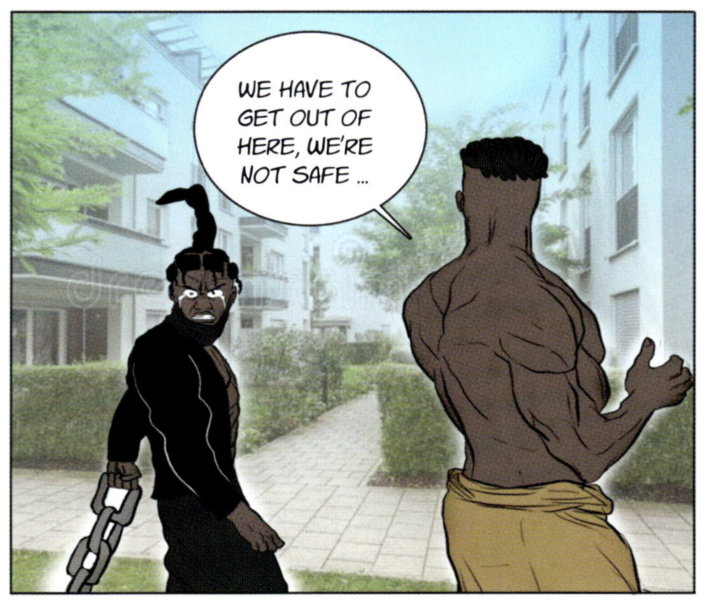
WE HAVE TO GET OUT OF HERE, WE'RE NOT SAFE ...

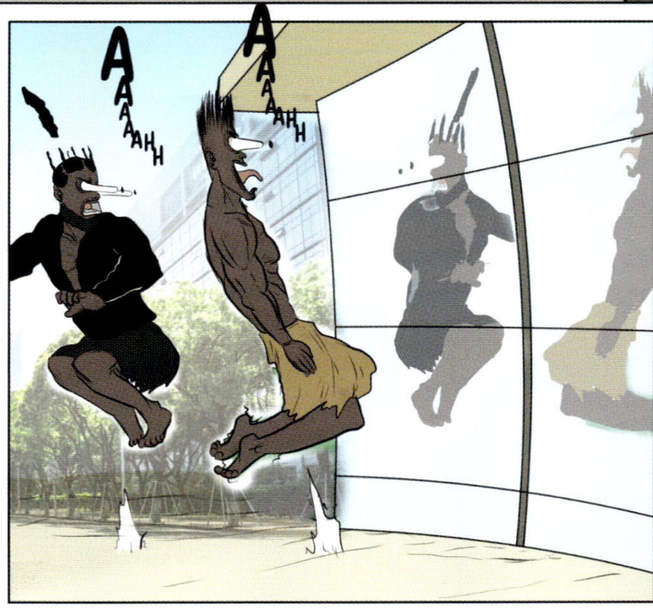
AAAAAHH
AAAAAHH

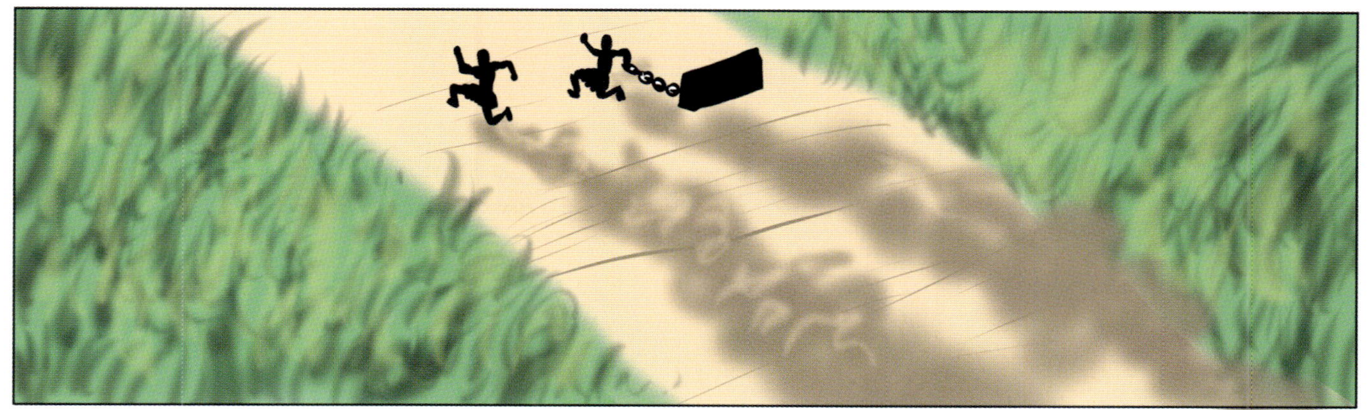

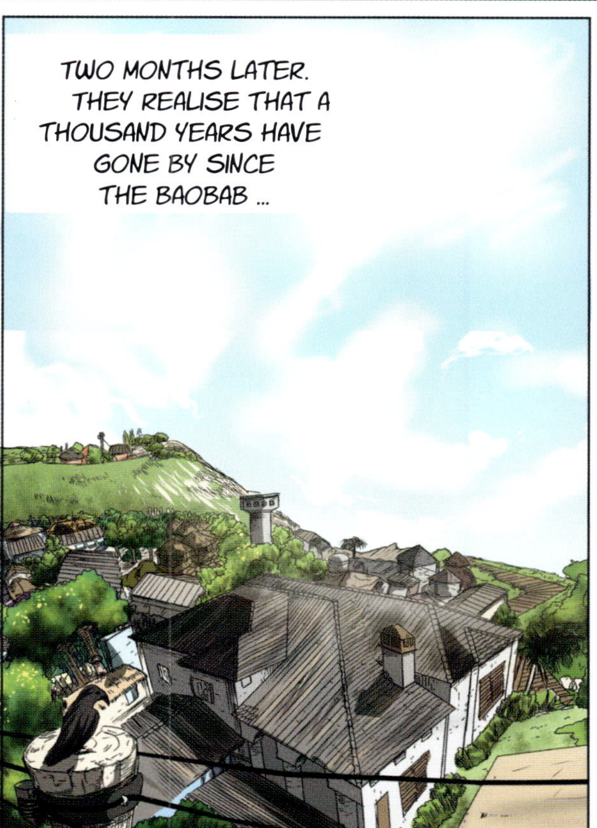
TWO MONTHS LATER.
THEY REALISE THAT A THOUSAND YEARS HAVE GONE BY SINCE THE BAOBAB ...

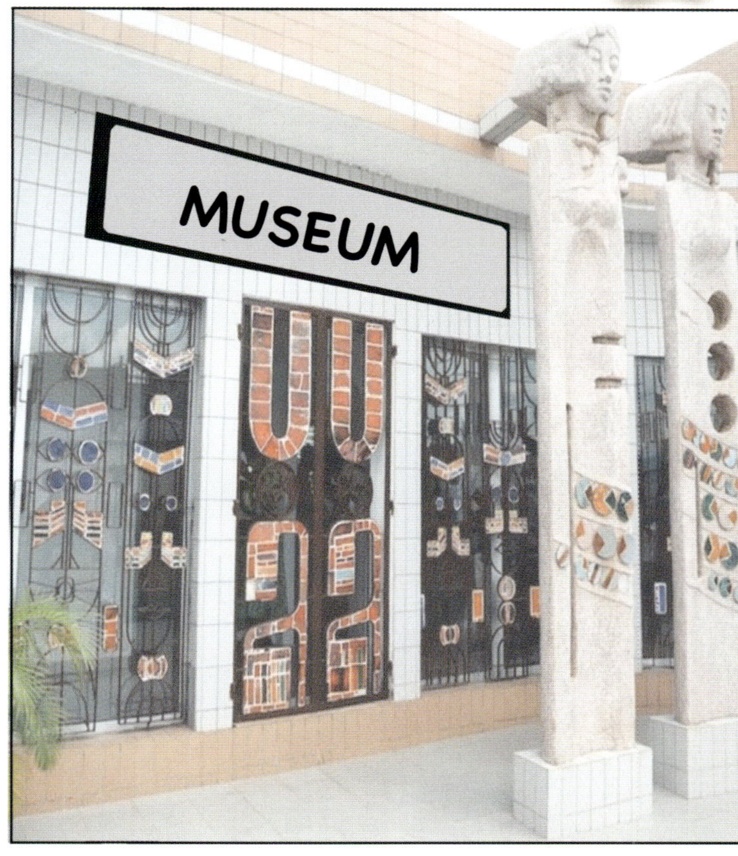
MUSEUM

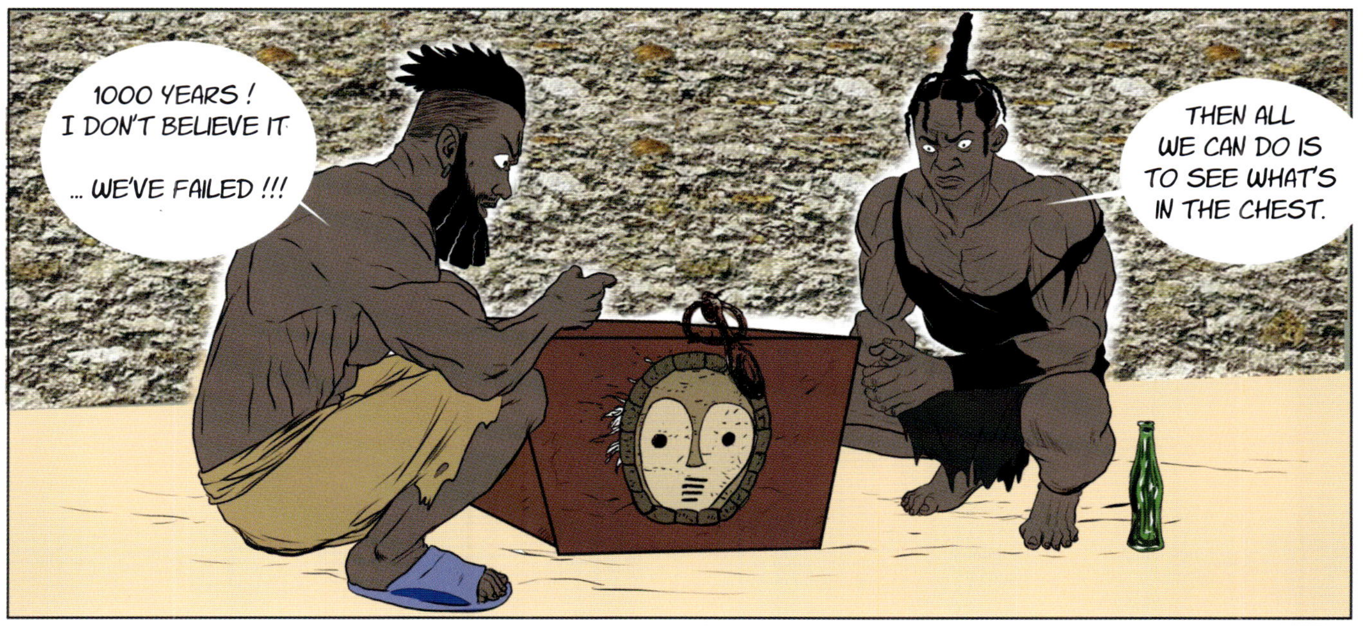
1000 YEARS ! I DON'T BELIEVE IT
... WE'VE FAILED !!!
THEN ALL WE CAN DO IS TO SEE WHAT'S IN THE CHEST.

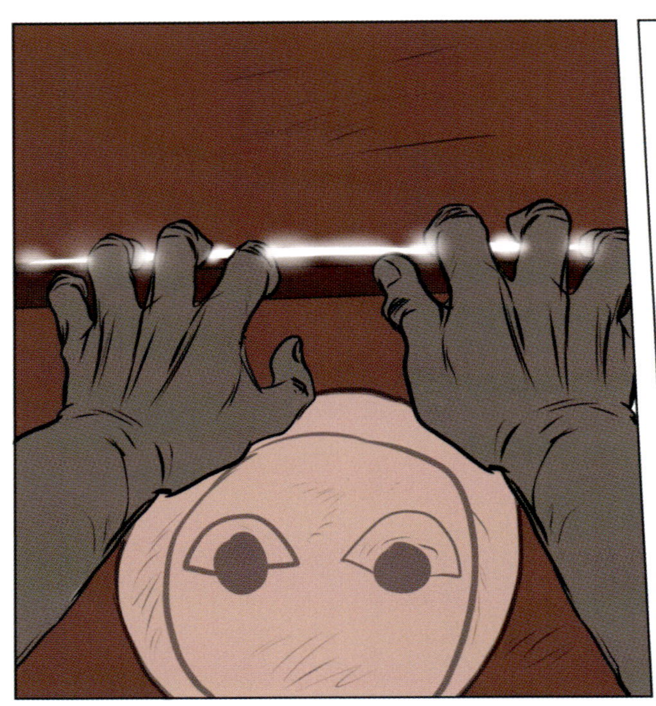

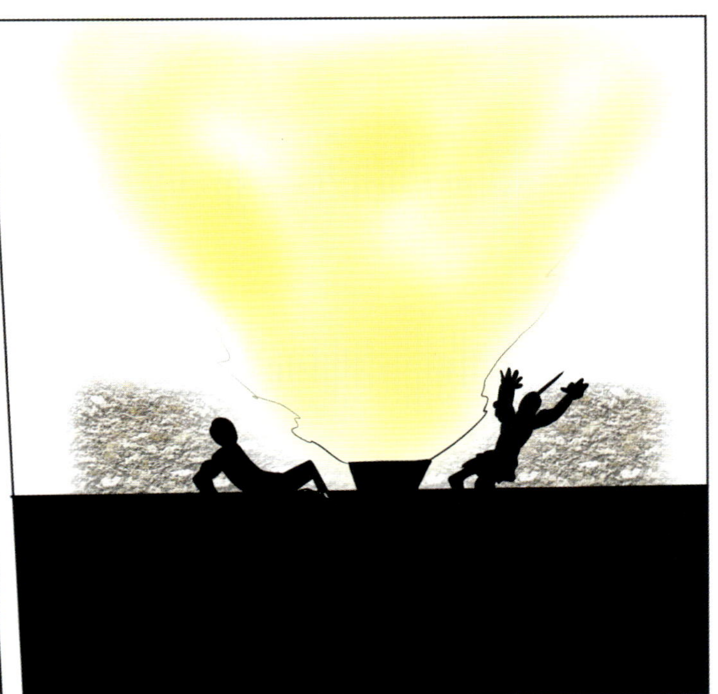

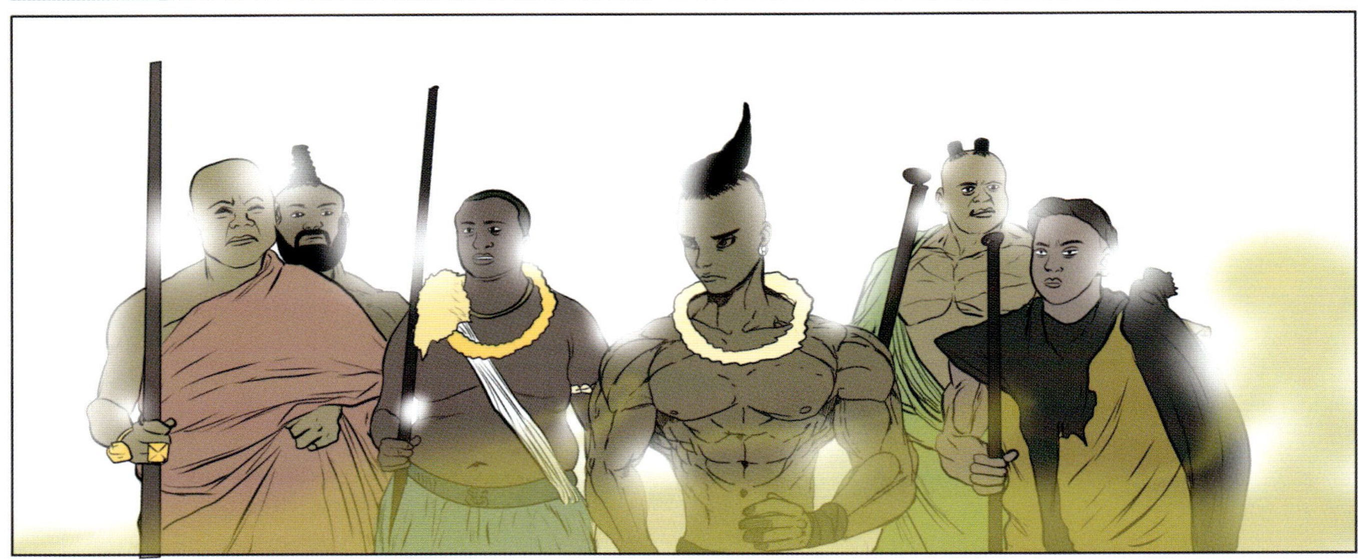

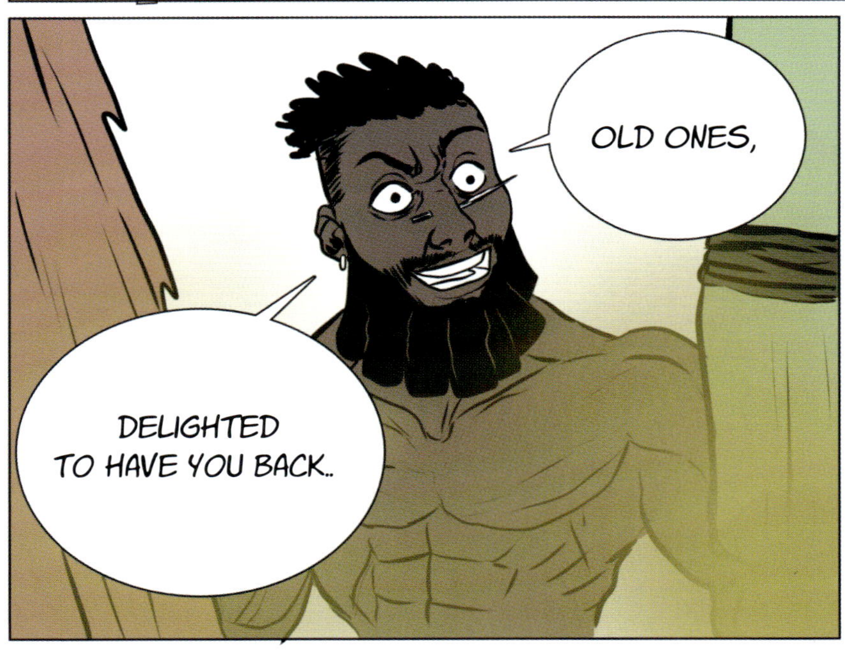
OLD ONES,
DELIGHTED TO HAVE YOU BACK..

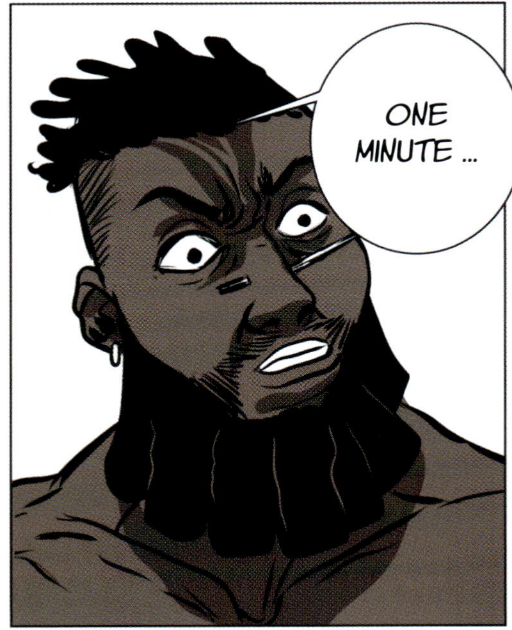
ONE MINUTE ...

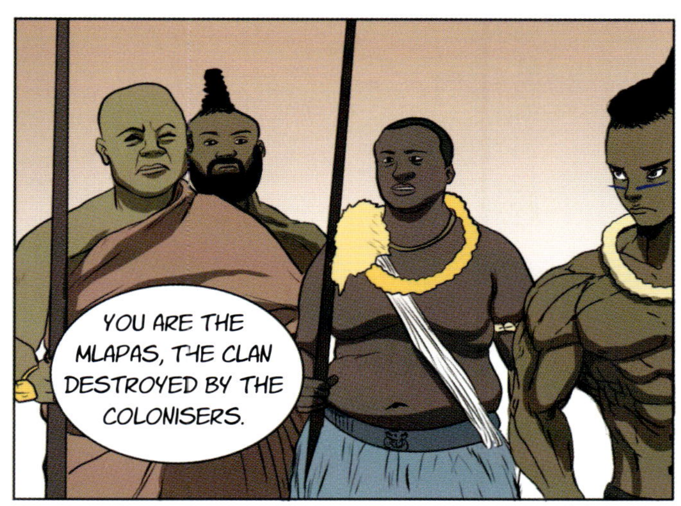
YOU ARE THE MLAPAS, THE CLAN DESTROYED BY THE COLONISERS.

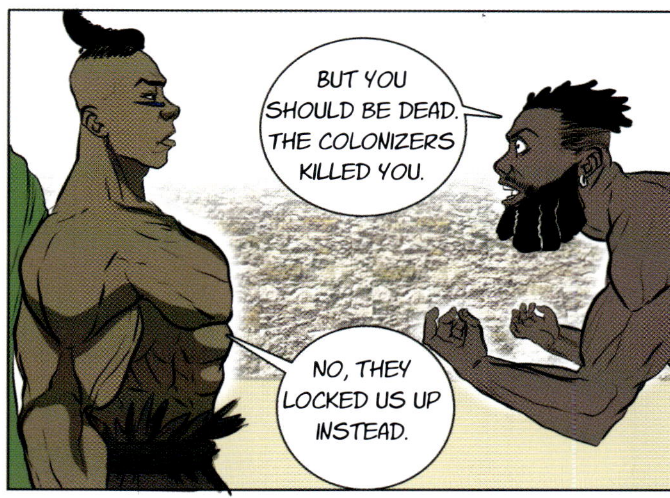
BUT YOU SHOULD BE DEAD. THE COLONIZERS KILLED YOU.
NO, THEY LOCKED US UP INSTEAD.

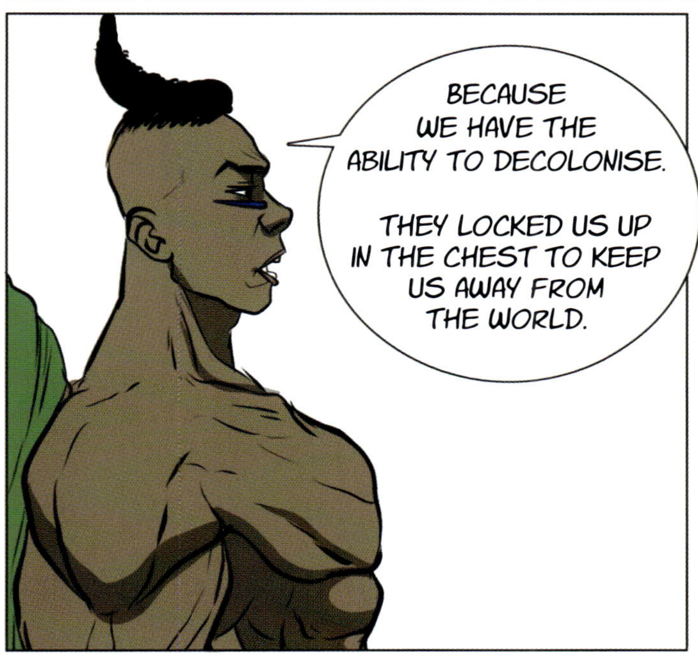
BECAUSE WE HAVE THE ABILITY TO DECOLONISE.
THEY LOCKED US UP IN THE CHEST TO KEEP US AWAY FROM THE WORLD.

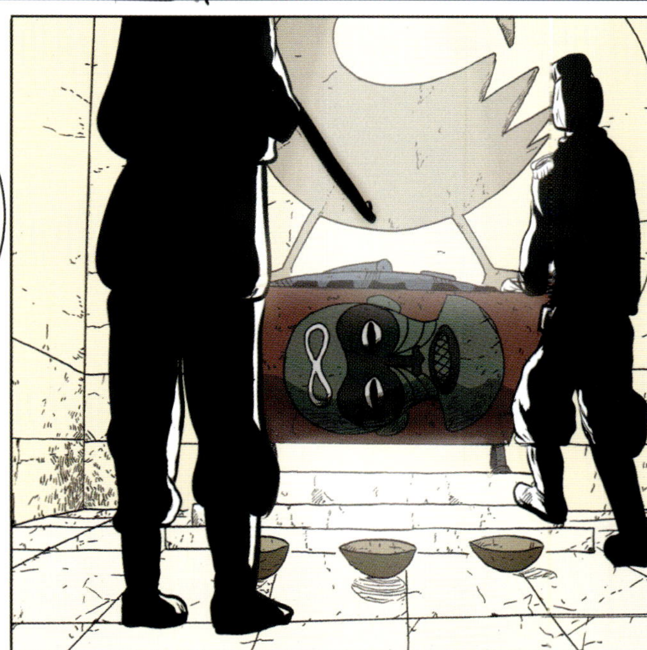

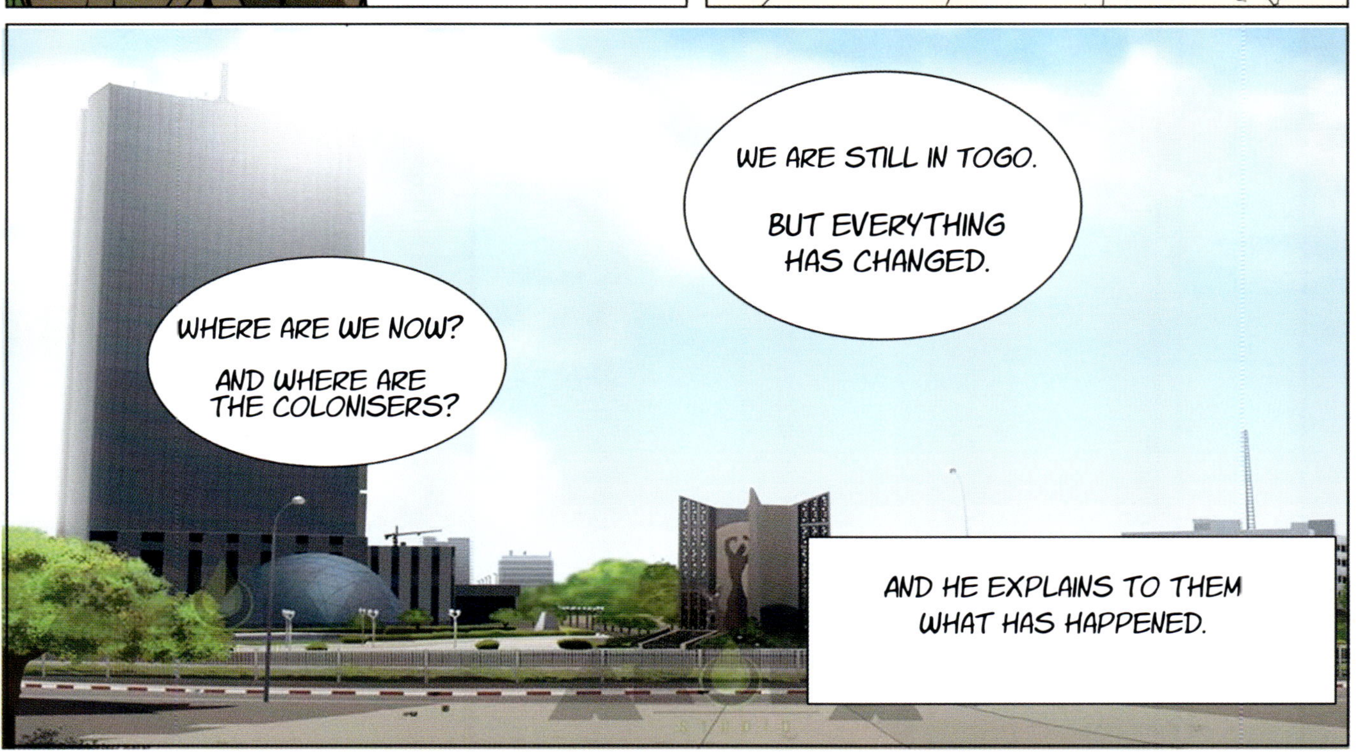
WHERE ARE WE NOW?
AND WHERE ARE THE COLONISERS?
WE ARE STILL IN TOGO.
BUT EVERYTHING HAS CHANGED.
AND HE EXPLAINS TO THEM WHAT HAS HAPPENED.

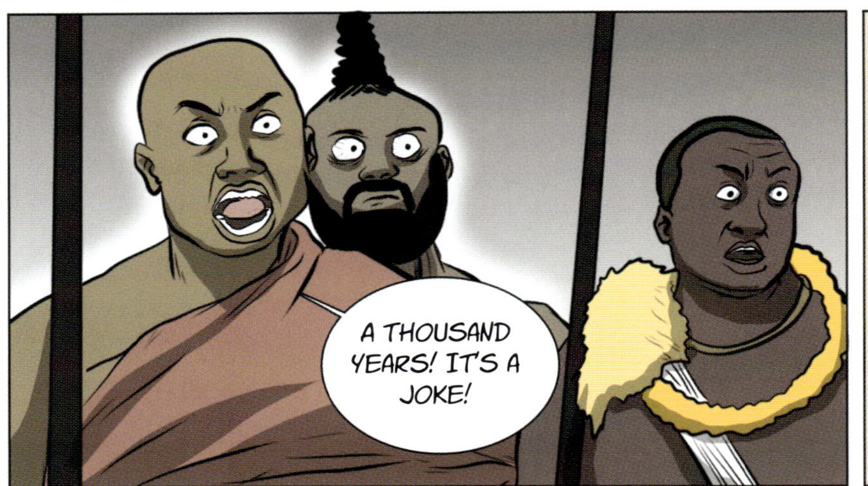
A THOUSAND YEARS! IT'S A JOKE!

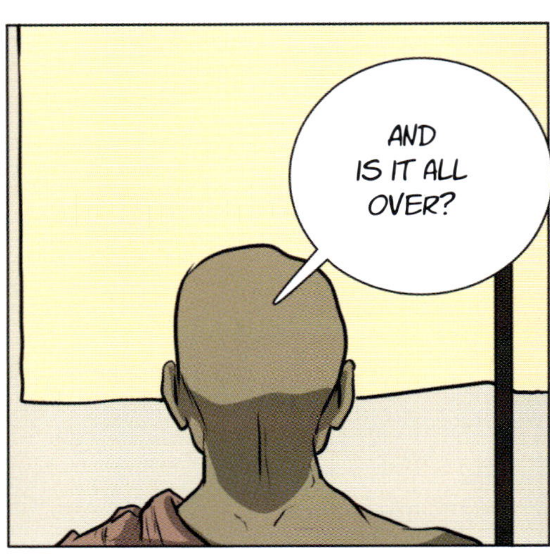
AND IS IT ALL OVER?

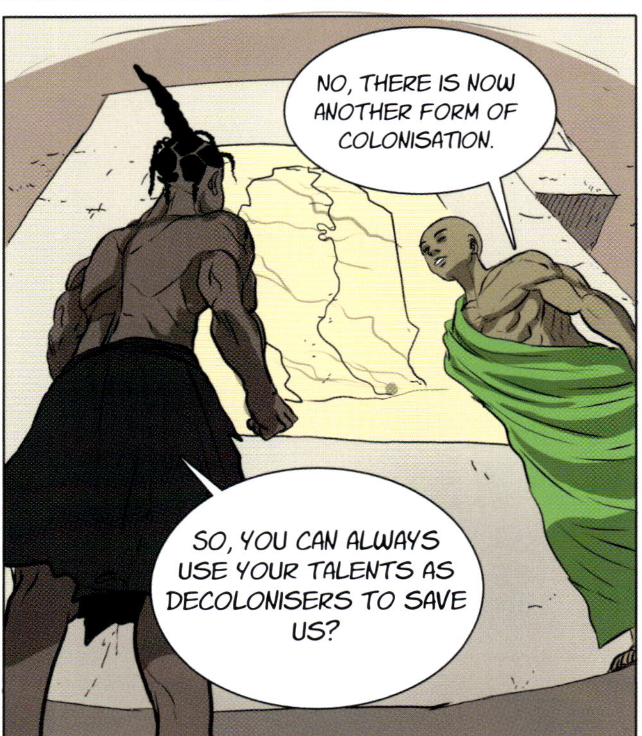
NO, THERE IS NOW ANOTHER FORM OF COLONISATION.
SO, YOU CAN ALWAYS USE YOUR TALENTS AS DECOLONISERS TO SAVE US?

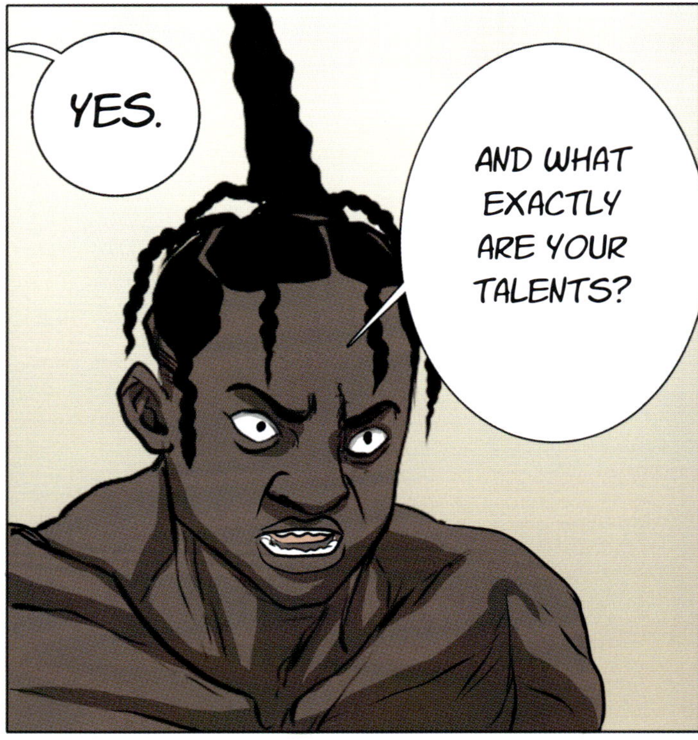
YES.
AND WHAT EXACTLY ARE YOUR TALENTS?

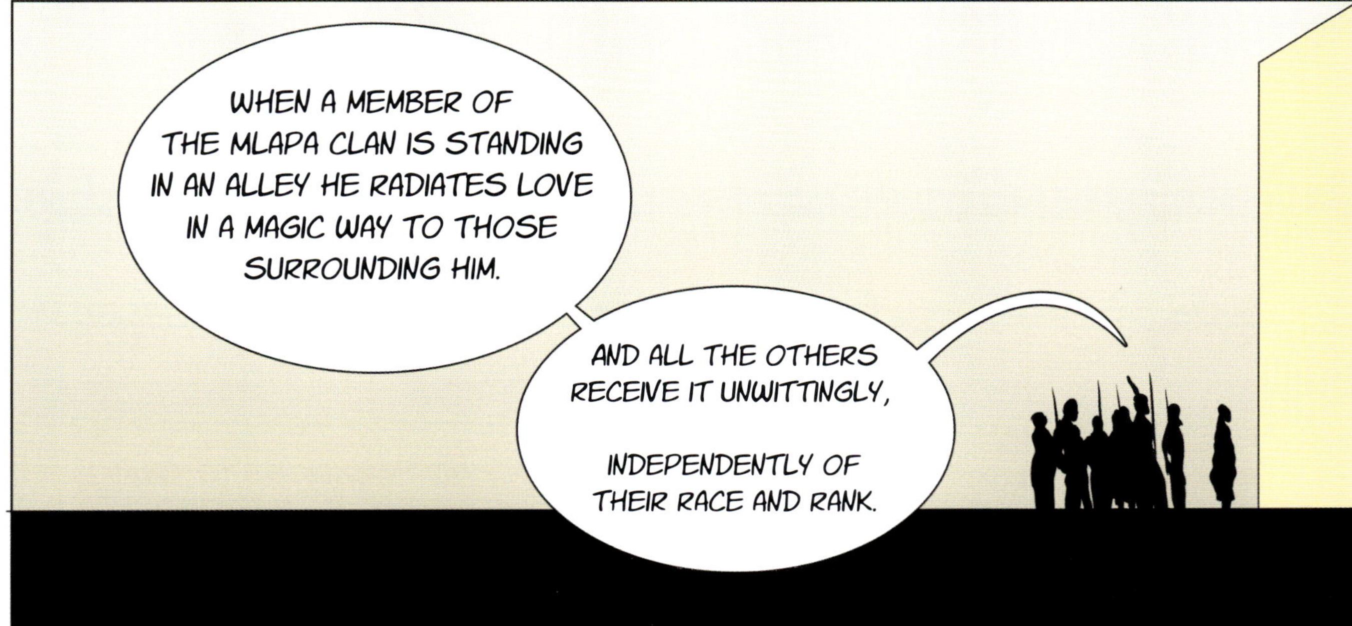
WHEN A MEMBER OF THE MLAPA CLAN IS STANDING IN AN ALLEY HE RADIATES LOVE IN A MAGIC WAY TO THOSE SURROUNDING HIM.
AND ALL THE OTHERS RECEIVE IT UNWITTINGLY,
INDEPENDENTLY OF THEIR RACE AND RANK.

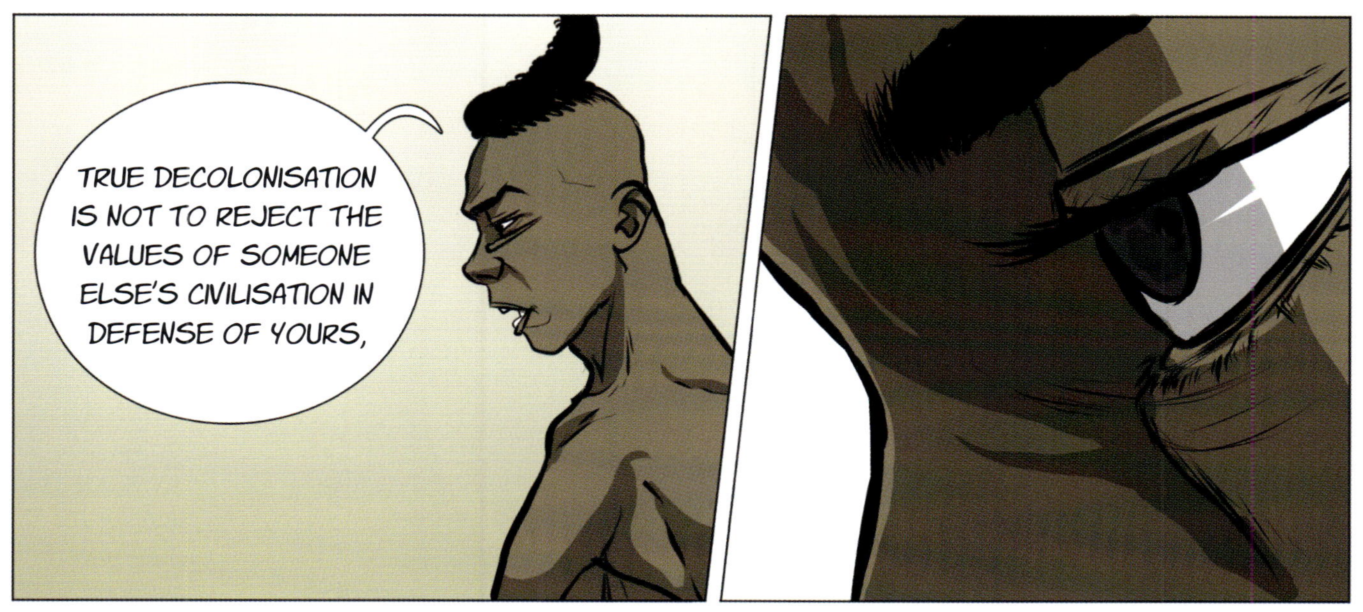

BUT TO LOVE EVERYONE AS THEY ARE –

FOR LOVE GIVES,

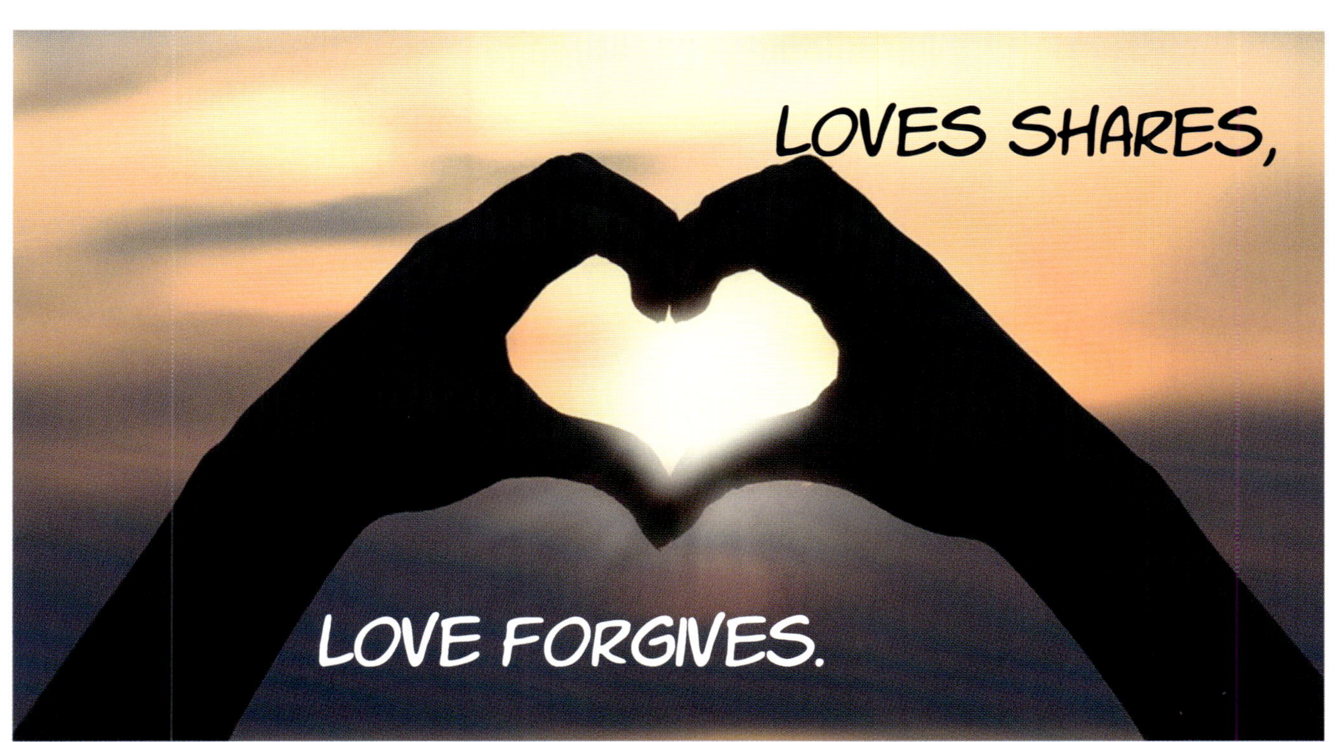

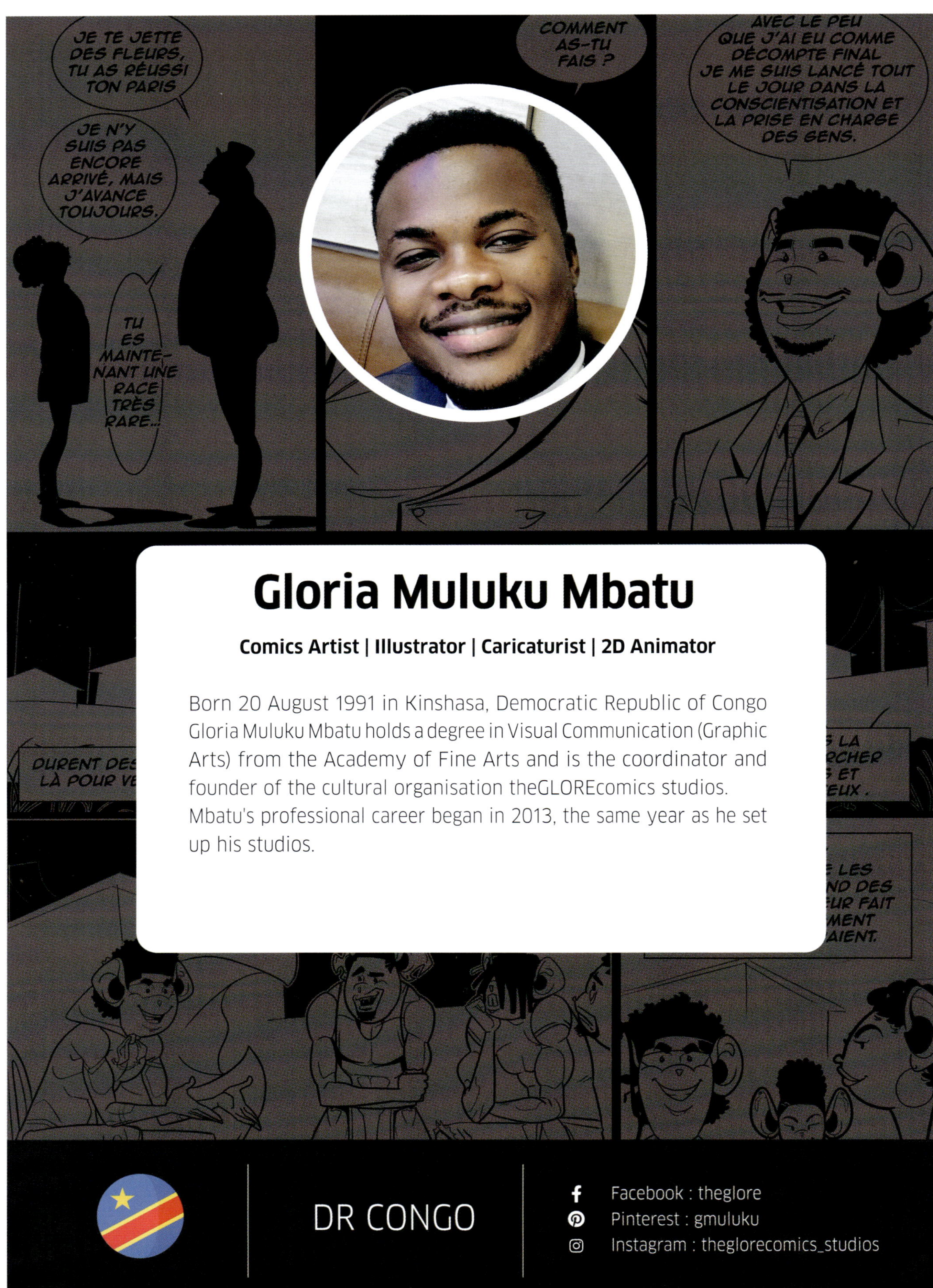

Gloria Muluku Mbatu

Comics Artist | Illustrator | Caricaturist | 2D Animator

Born 20 August 1991 in Kinshasa, Democratic Republic of Congo Gloria Muluku Mbatu holds a degree in Visual Communication (Graphic Arts) from the Academy of Fine Arts and is the coordinator and founder of the cultural organisation theGLOREcomics studios. Mbatu's professional career began in 2013, the same year as he set up his studios.

DR CONGO

Facebook : theglore
Pinterest : gmuluku
Instagram : theglorecomics_studios

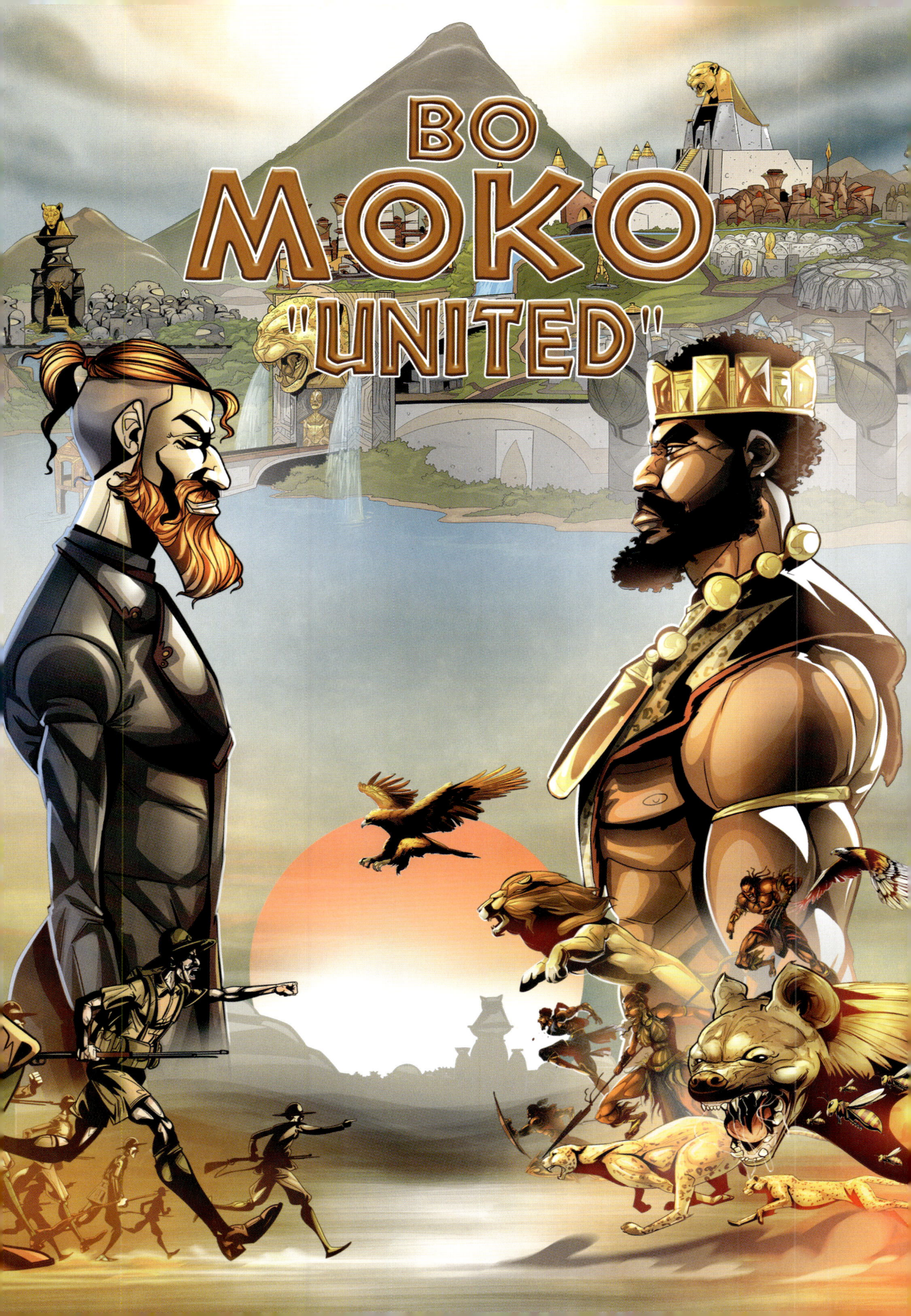
BO
MOKO
"UNITED"

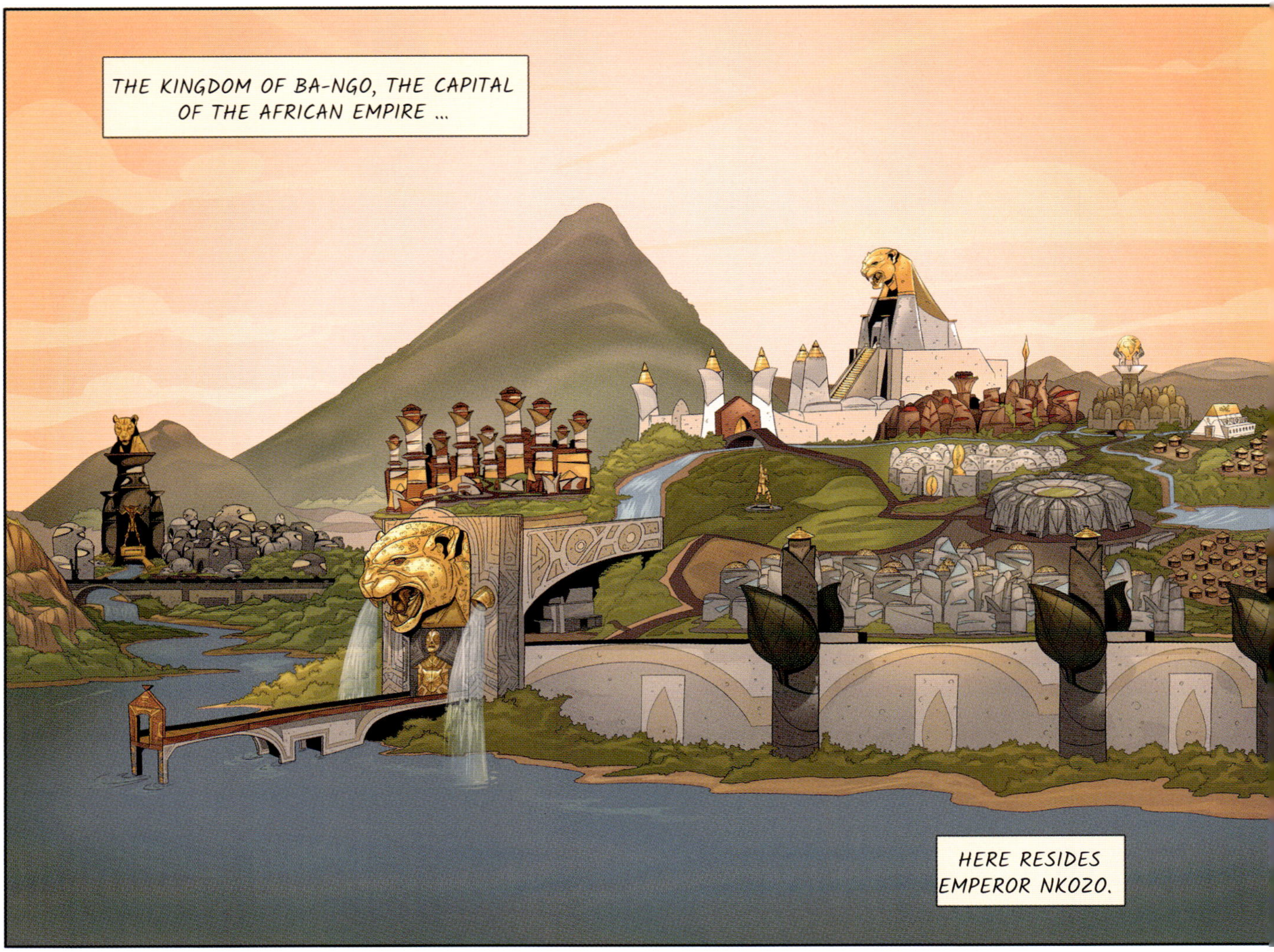

THE KINGDOM OF BA-NGO, THE CAPITAL OF THE AFRICAN EMPIRE ...

HERE RESIDES EMPEROR NKOZO.

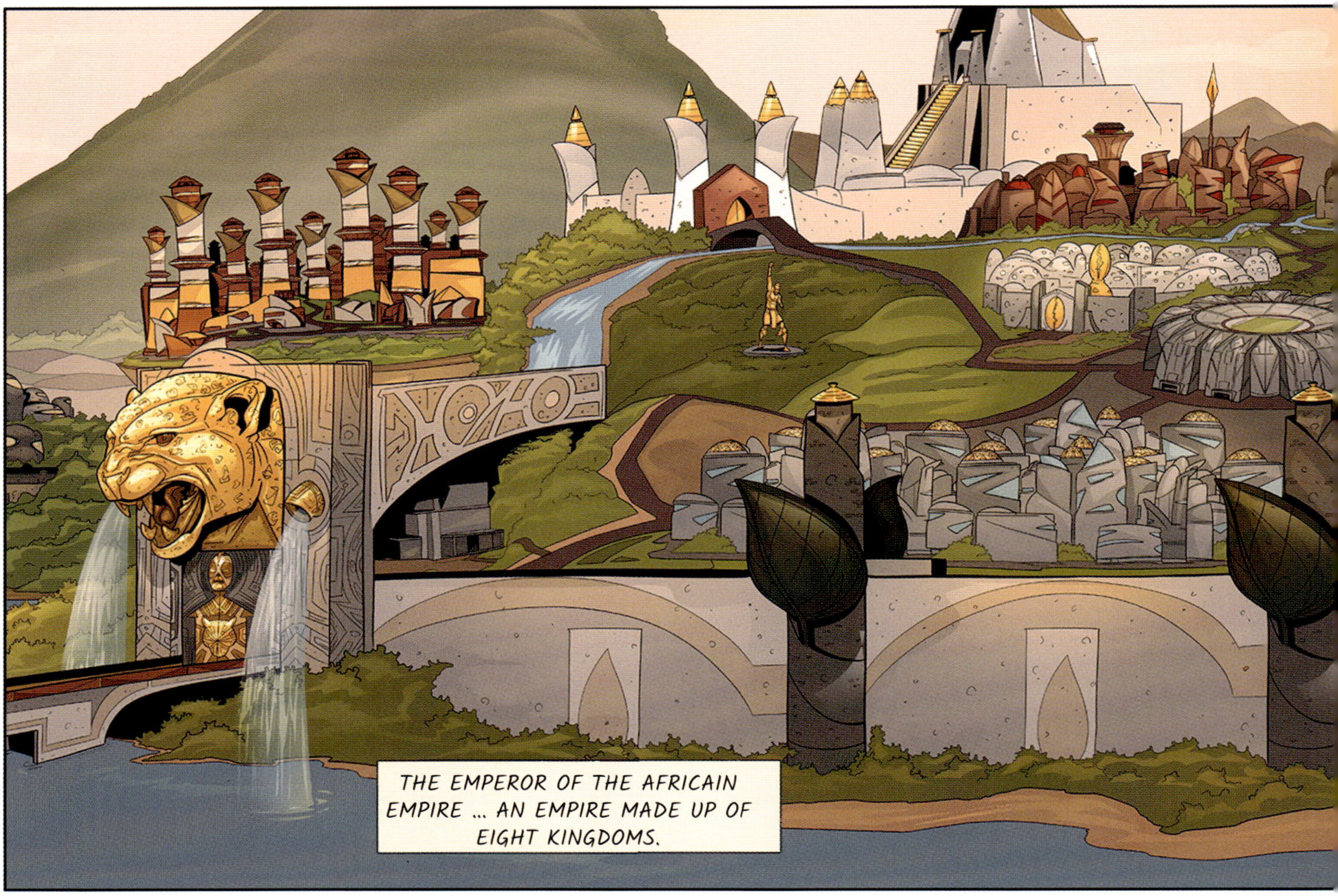

THE EMPEROR OF THE AFRICAIN EMPIRE ... AN EMPIRE MADE UP OF EIGHT KINGDOMS.

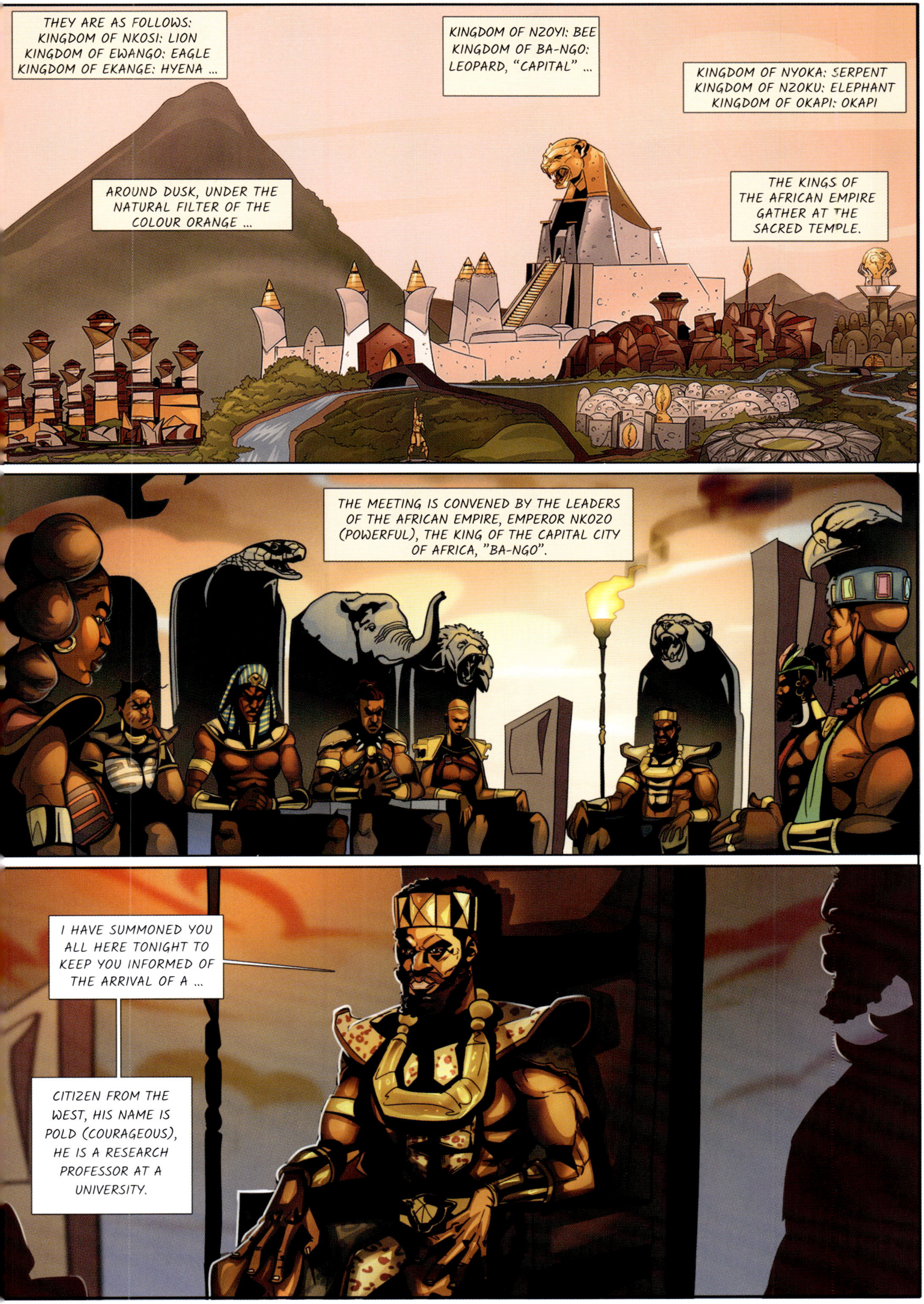

THEY ARE AS FOLLOWS:
KINGDOM OF NKOSI: LION
KINGDOM OF EWANGO: EAGLE
KINGDOM OF EKANGE: HYENA ...

KINGDOM OF NZOYI: BEE
KINGDOM OF BA-NGO:
LEOPARD, "CAPITAL" ...

KINGDOM OF NYOKA: SERPENT
KINGDOM OF NZOKU: ELEPHANT
KINGDOM OF OKAPI: OKAPI

AROUND DUSK, UNDER THE NATURAL FILTER OF THE COLOUR ORANGE ...

THE KINGS OF THE AFRICAN EMPIRE GATHER AT THE SACRED TEMPLE.

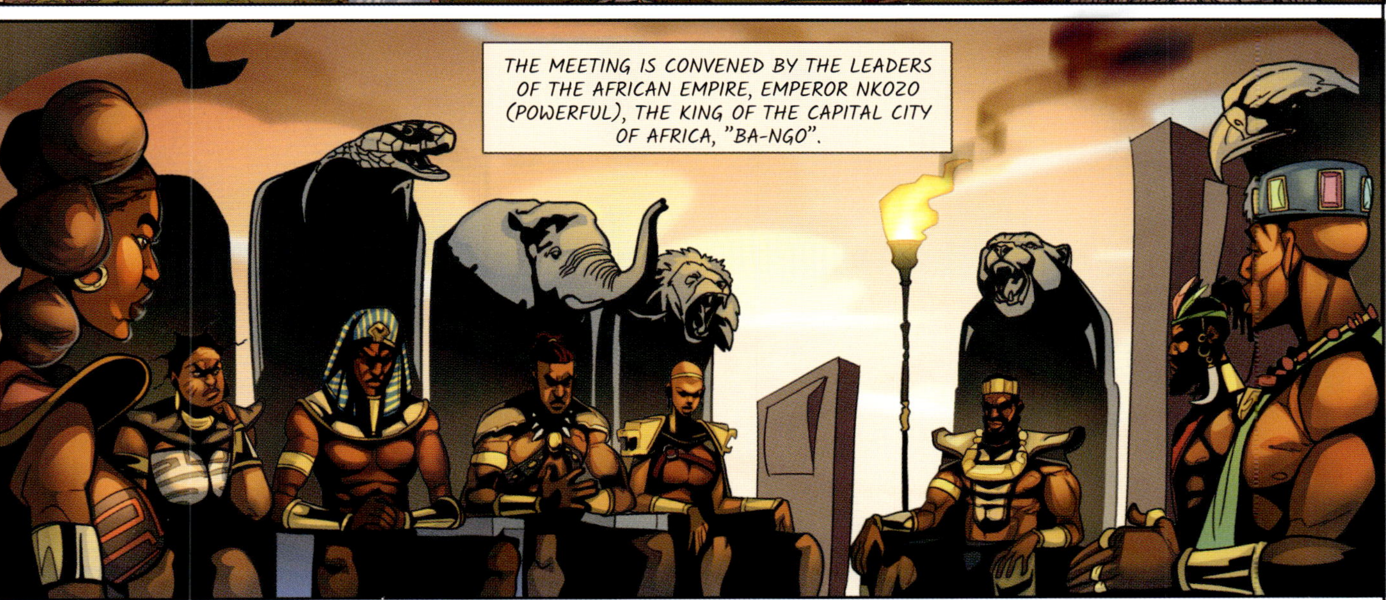

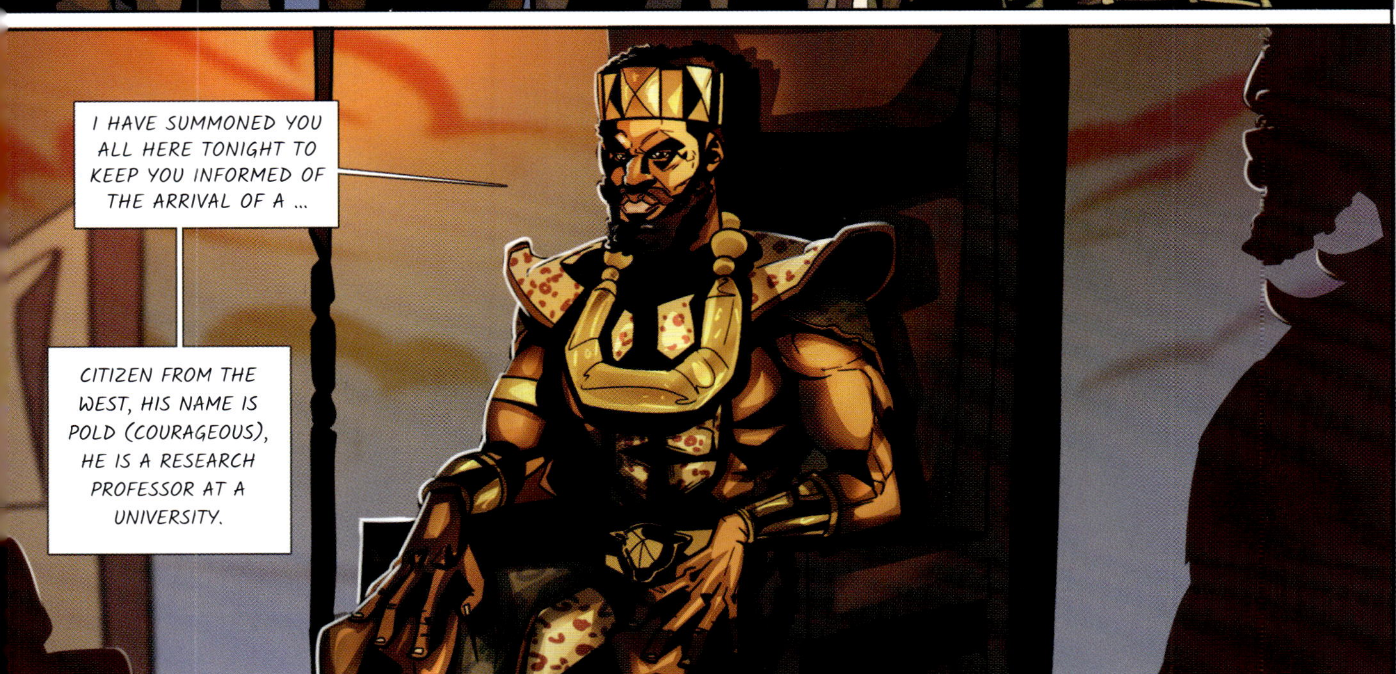

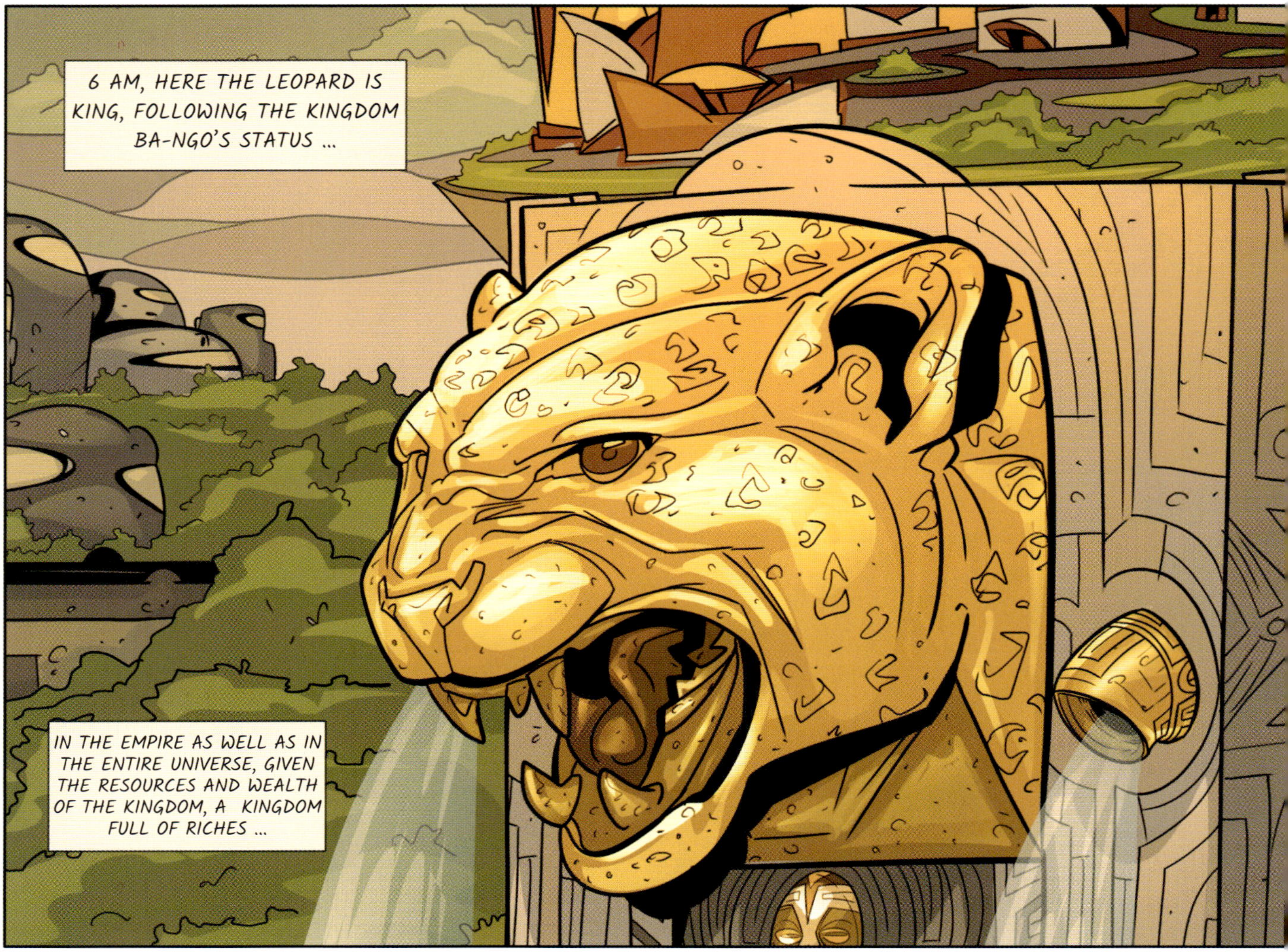

6 AM, HERE THE LEOPARD IS KING, FOLLOWING THE KINGDOM BA-NGO'S STATUS ...

IN THE EMPIRE AS WELL AS IN THE ENTIRE UNIVERSE, GIVEN THE RESOURCES AND WEALTH OF THE KINGDOM, A KINGDOM FULL OF RICHES ...

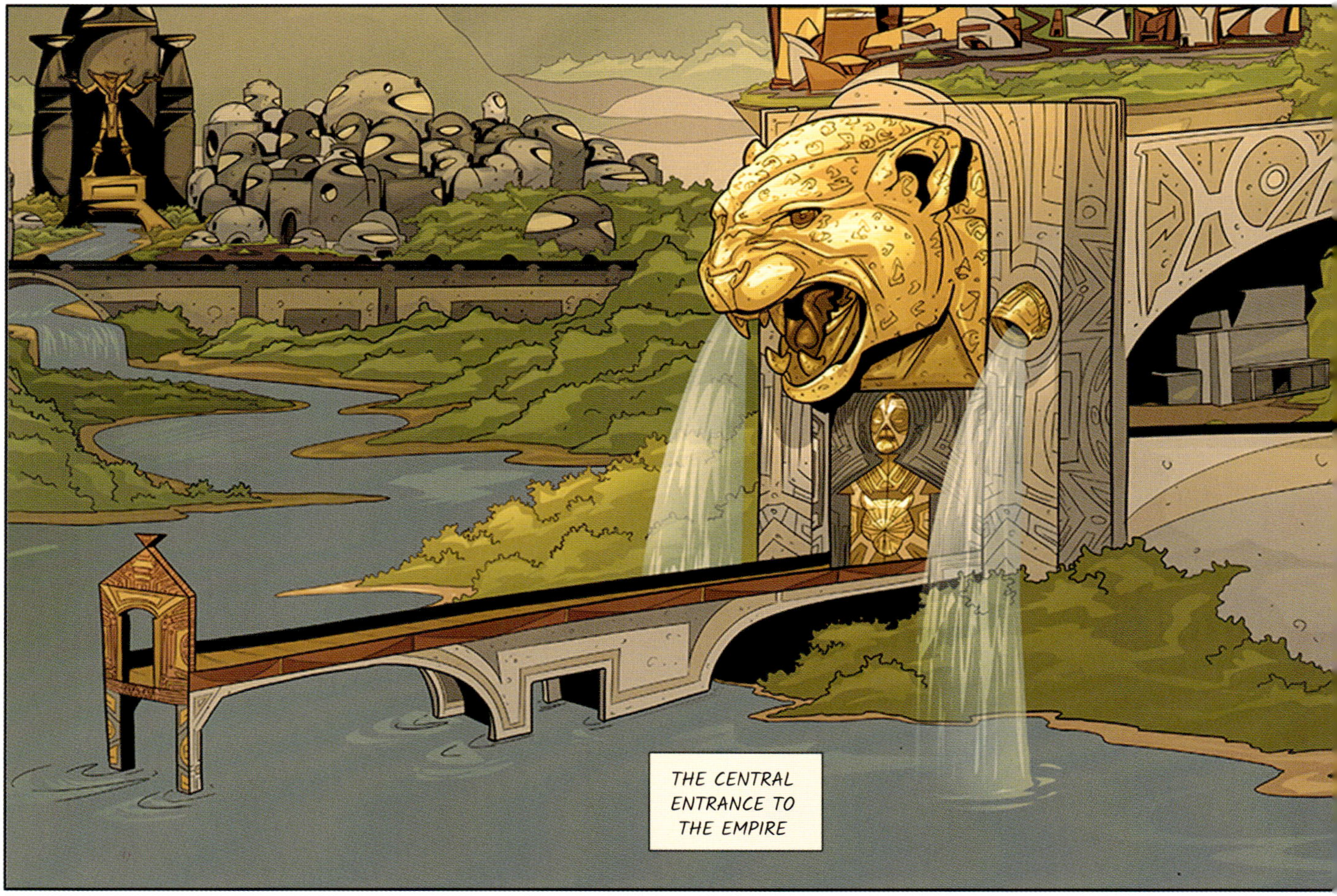

THE CENTRAL ENTRANCE TO THE EMPIRE

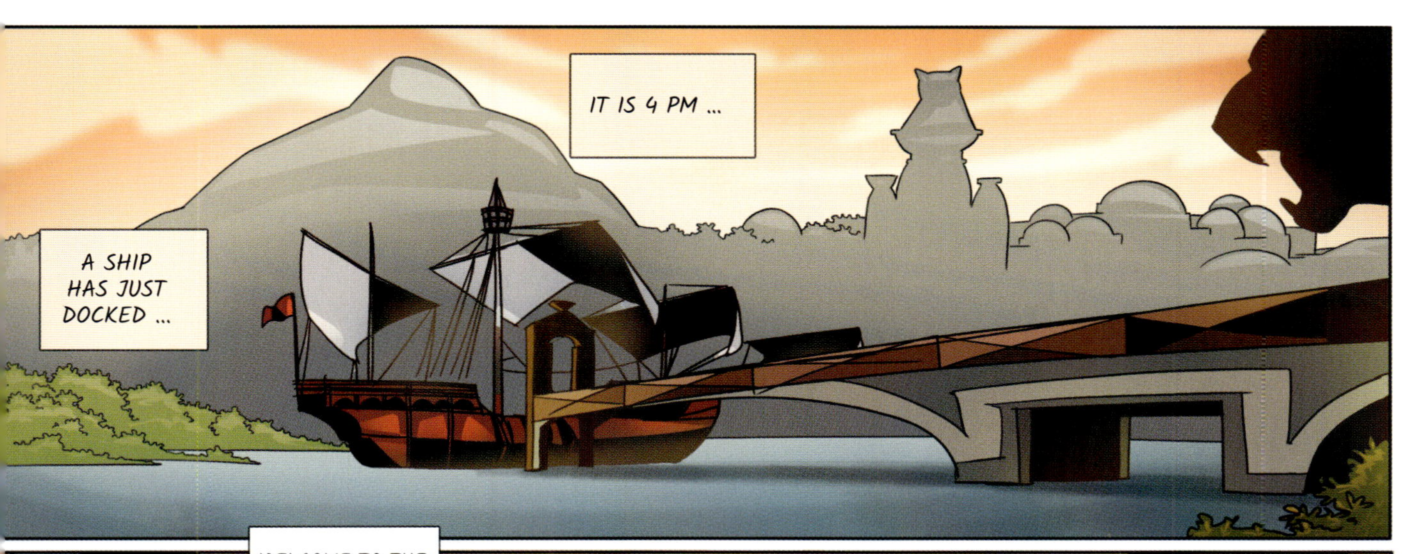

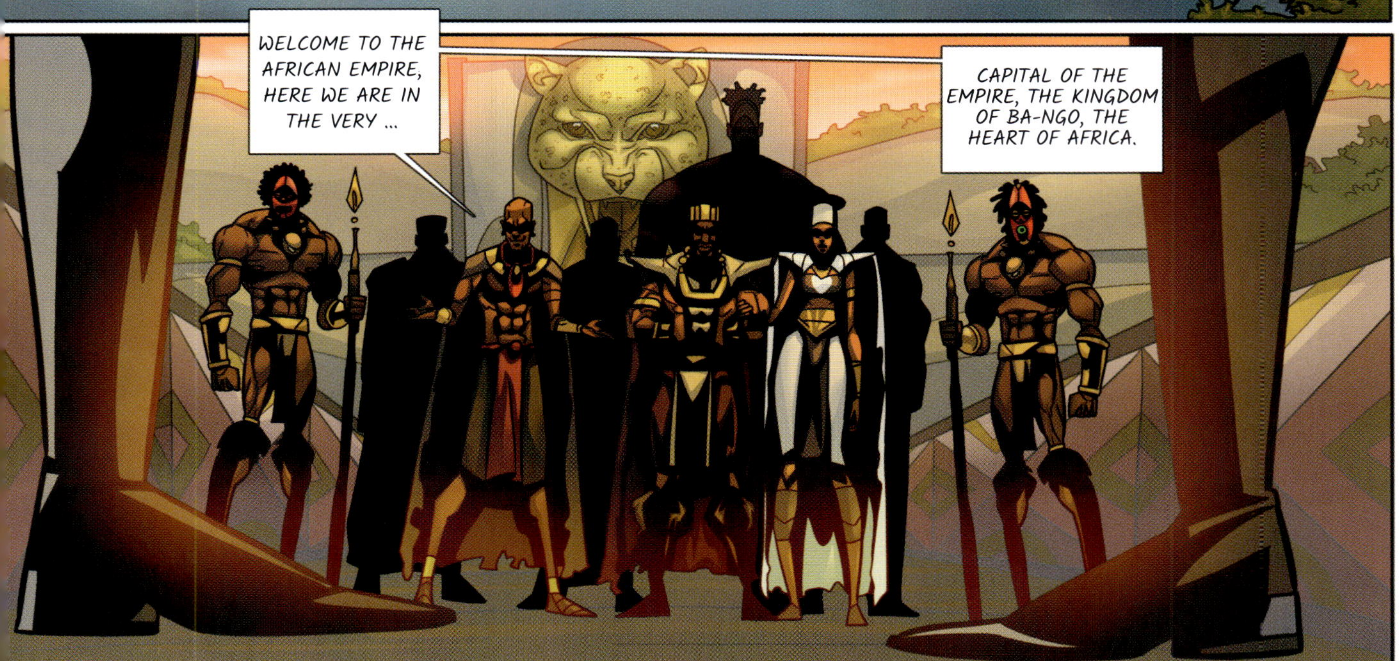

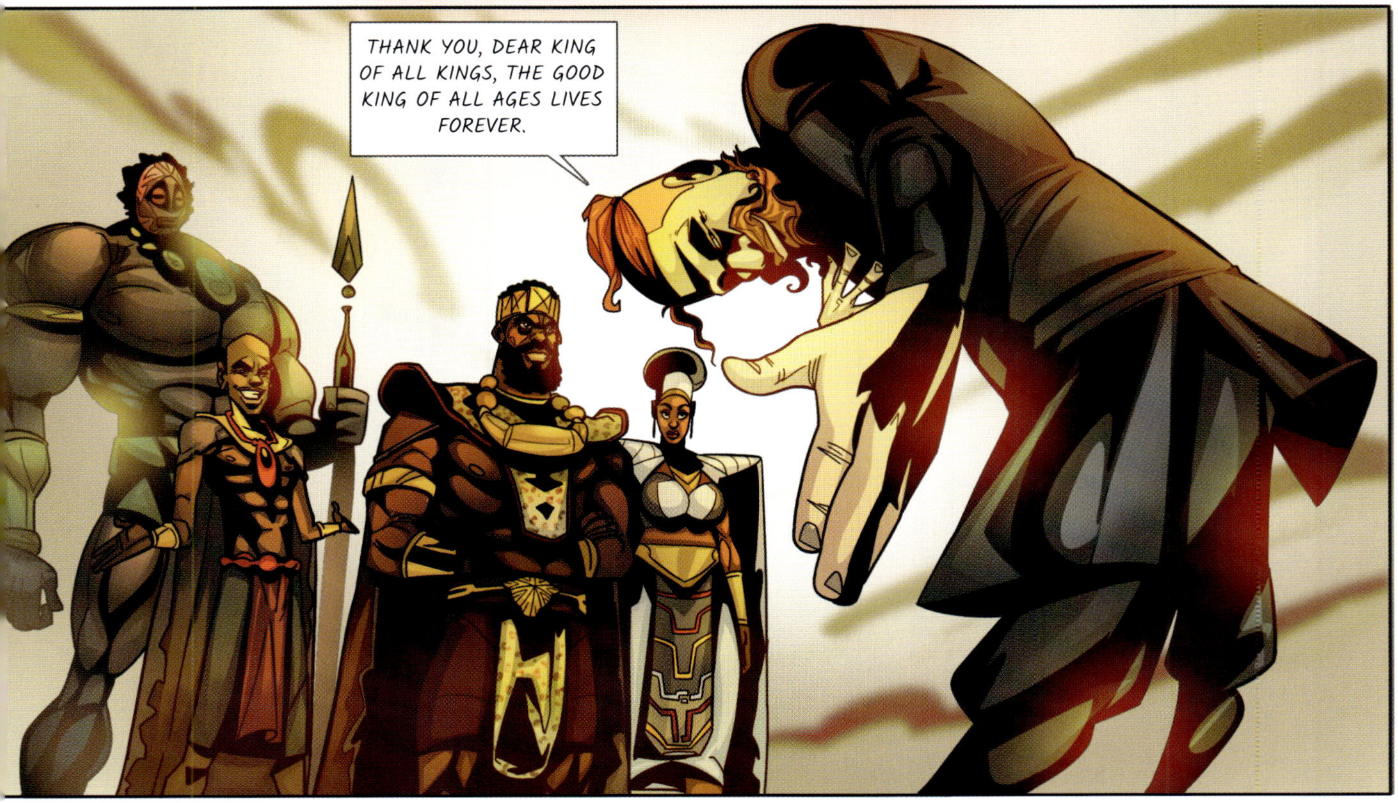

THANK YOU, DEAR KING OF ALL KINGS, THE GOOD KING OF ALL AGES LIVES FOREVER.

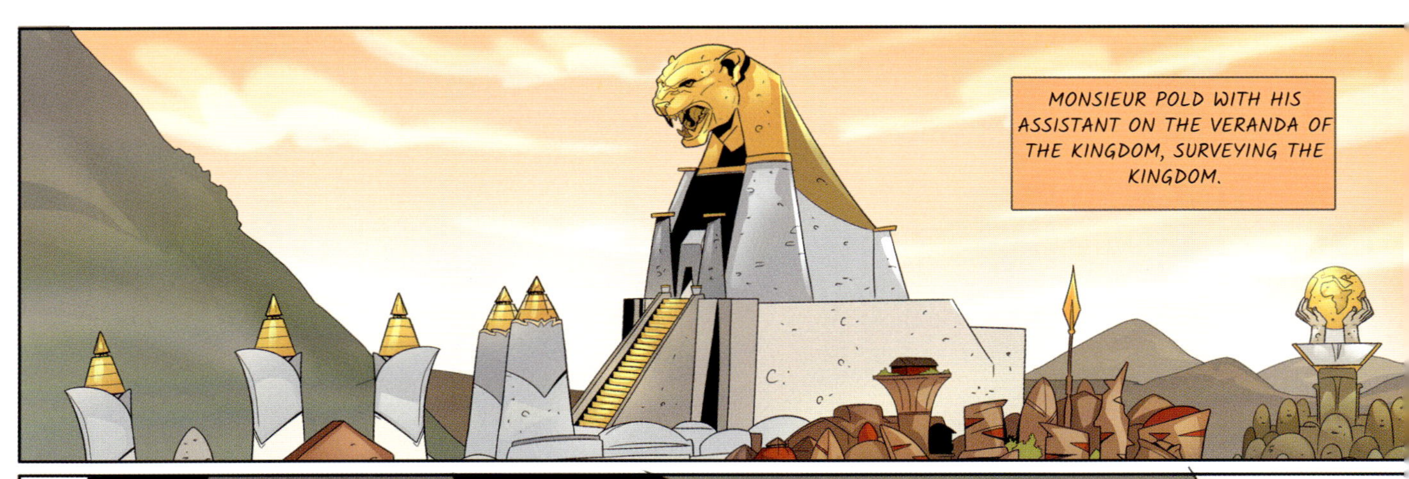

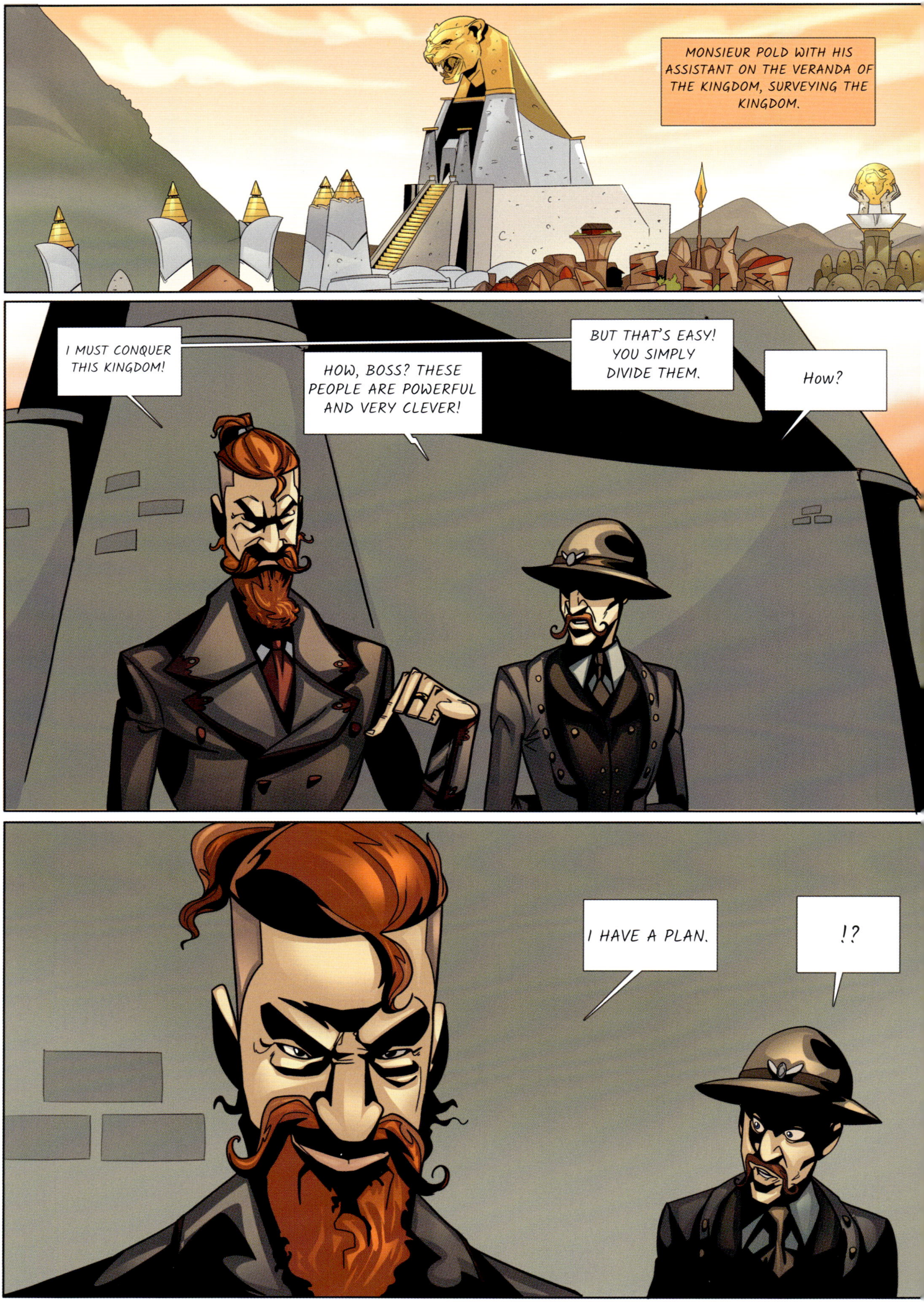

I MUST CONQUER THIS KINGDOM!

HOW, BOSS? THESE PEOPLE ARE POWERFUL AND VERY CLEVER!

BUT THAT'S EASY! YOU SIMPLY DIVIDE THEM.

How?

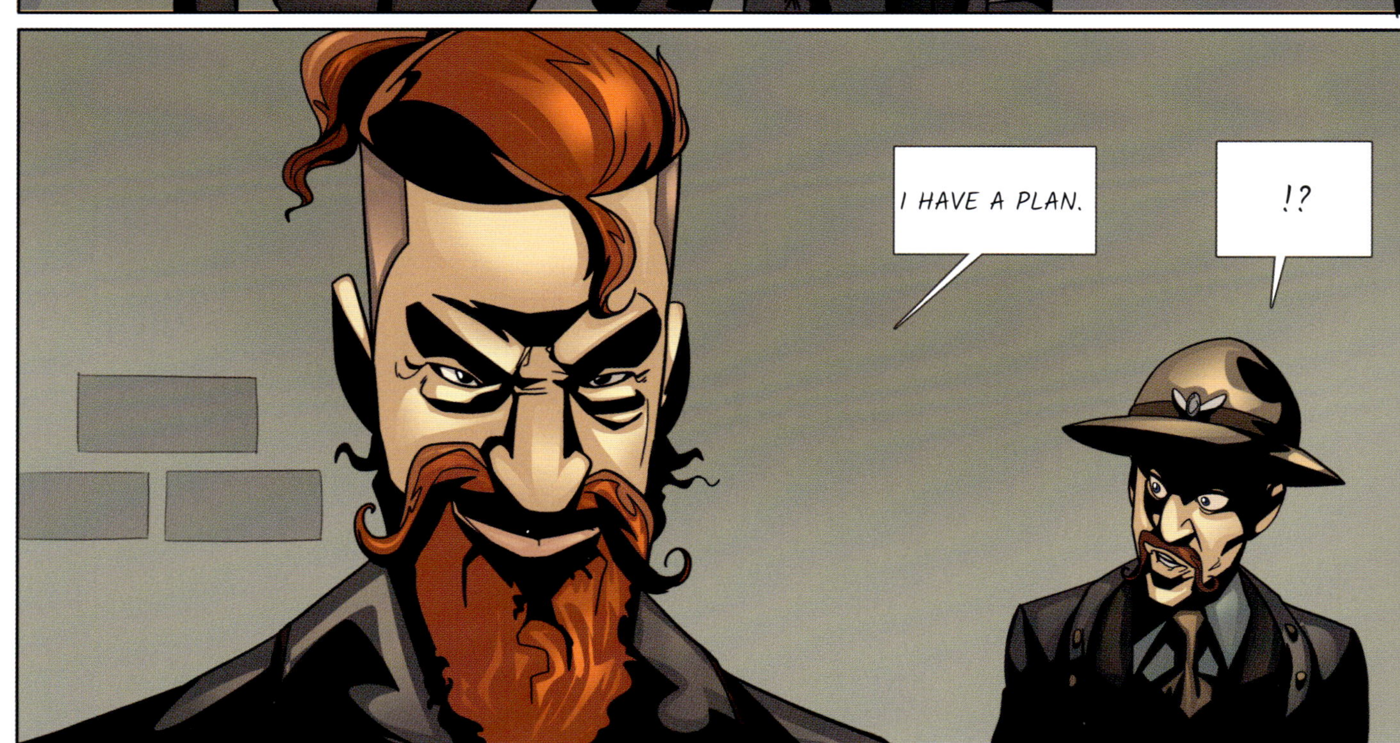

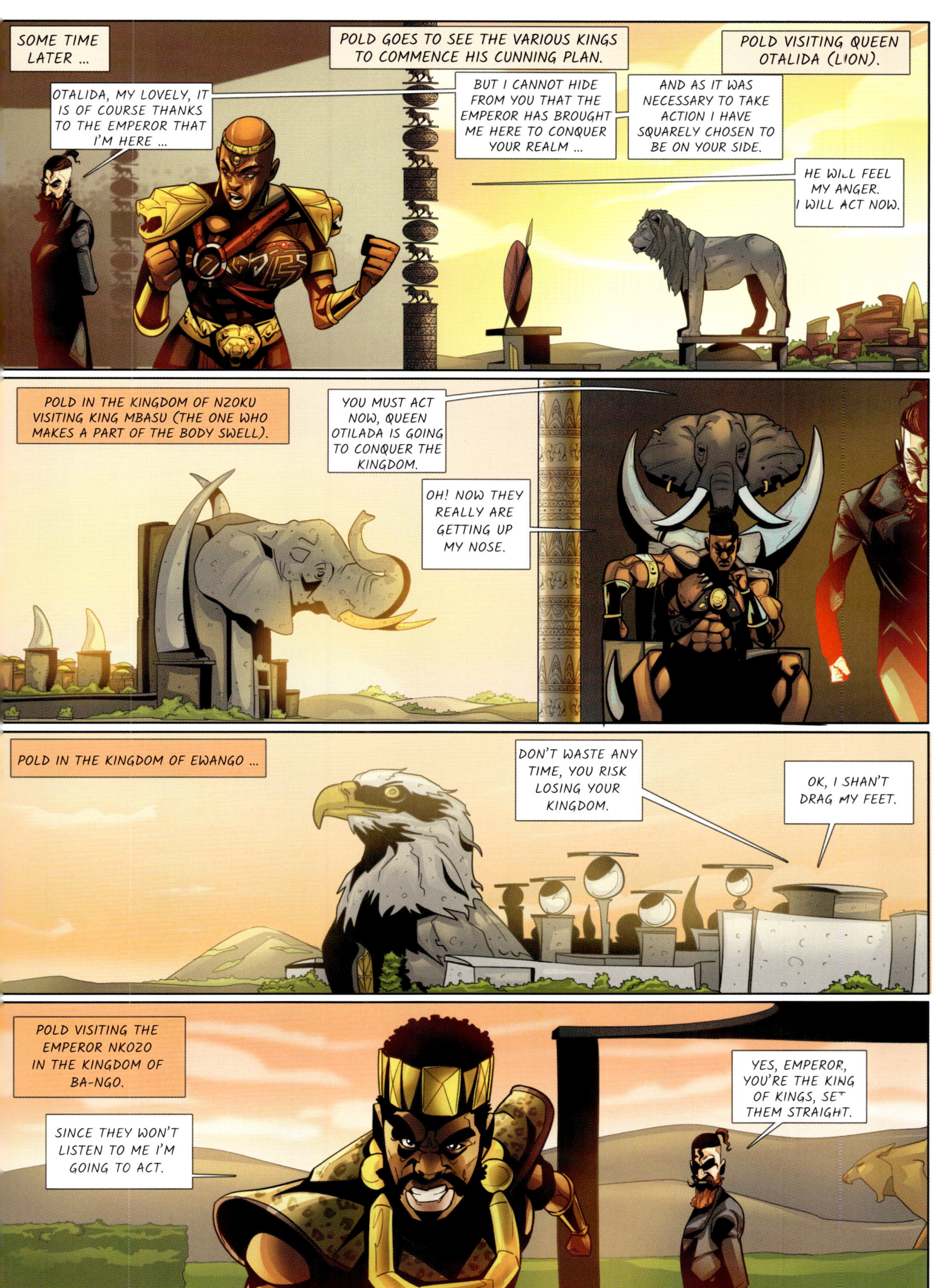
SOME TIME LATER ...
POLD GOES TO SEE THE VARIOUS KINGS TO COMMENCE HIS CUNNING PLAN.
POLD VISITING QUEEN OTALIDA (LION).
OTALIDA, MY LOVELY, IT IS OF COURSE THANKS TO THE EMPEROR THAT I'M HERE ...
BUT I CANNOT HIDE FROM YOU THAT THE EMPEROR HAS BROUGHT ME HERE TO CONQUER YOUR REALM ...
AND AS IT WAS NECESSARY TO TAKE ACTION I HAVE SQUARELY CHOSEN TO BE ON YOUR SIDE.
HE WILL FEEL MY ANGER. I WILL ACT NOW.
POLD IN THE KINGDOM OF NZOKU VISITING KING MBASU (THE ONE WHO MAKES A PART OF THE BODY SWELL).
YOU MUST ACT NOW, QUEEN OTILADA IS GOING TO CONQUER THE KINGDOM.
OH! NOW THEY REALLY ARE GETTING UP MY NOSE.
POLD IN THE KINGDOM OF EWANGO ...
DON'T WASTE ANY TIME, YOU RISK LOSING YOUR KINGDOM.
OK, I SHAN'T DRAG MY FEET.
POLD VISITING THE EMPEROR NKOZO IN THE KINGDOM OF BA-NGO.
SINCE THEY WON'T LISTEN TO ME I'M GOING TO ACT.
YES, EMPEROR, YOU'RE THE KING OF KINGS, SET THEM STRAIGHT.

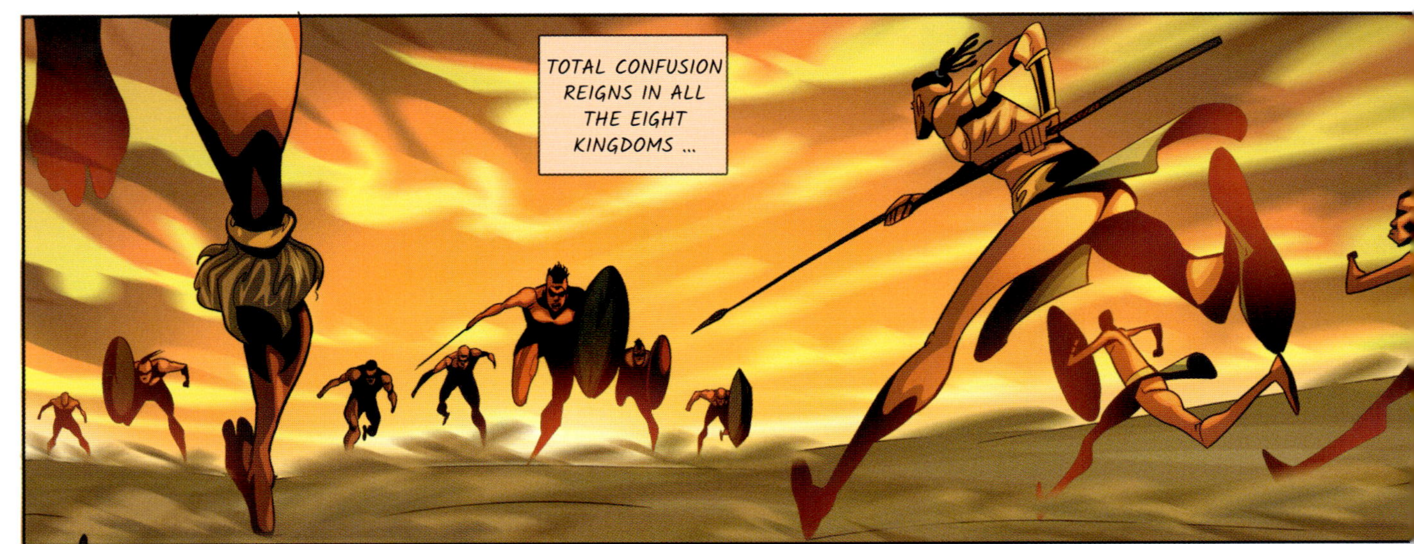
TOTAL CONFUSION REIGNS IN ALL THE EIGHT KINGDOMS ...

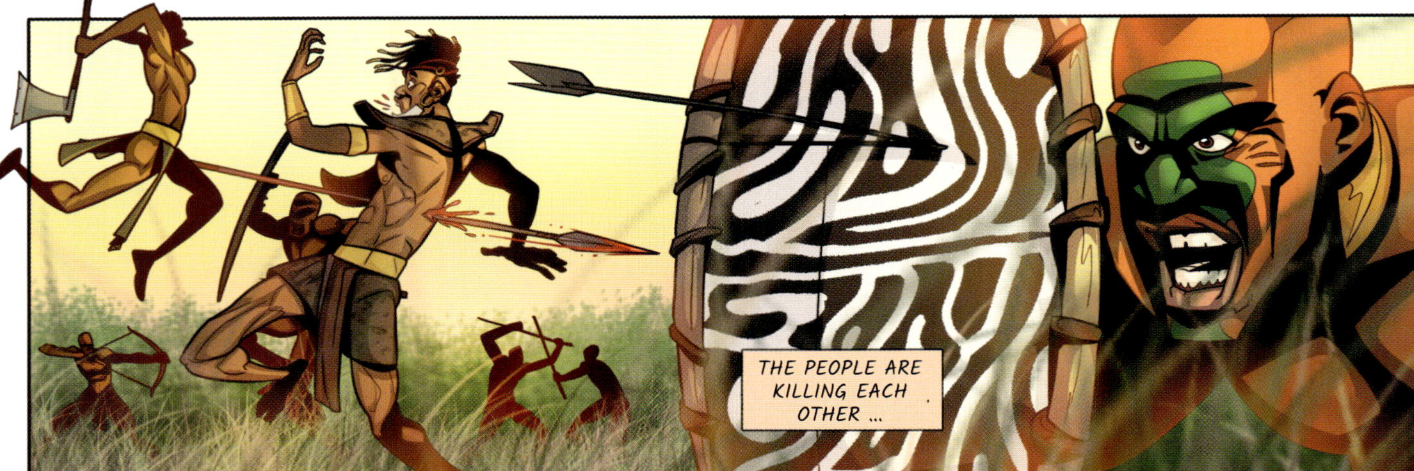
THE PEOPLE ARE KILLING EACH OTHER ...

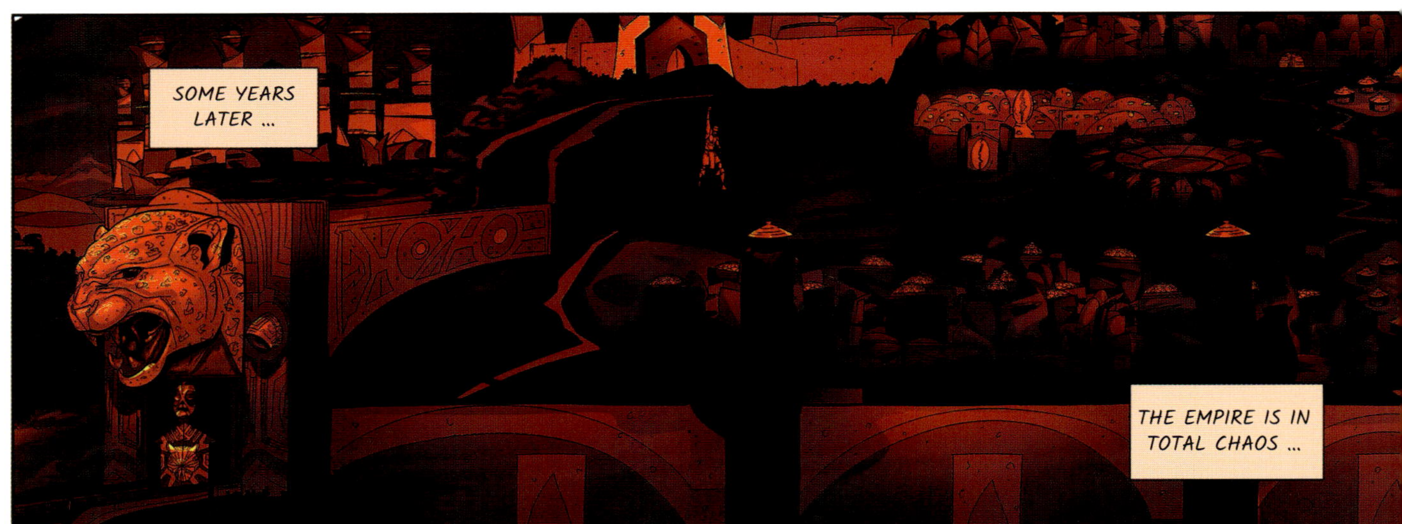
SOME YEARS LATER ...
THE EMPIRE IS IN TOTAL CHAOS ...

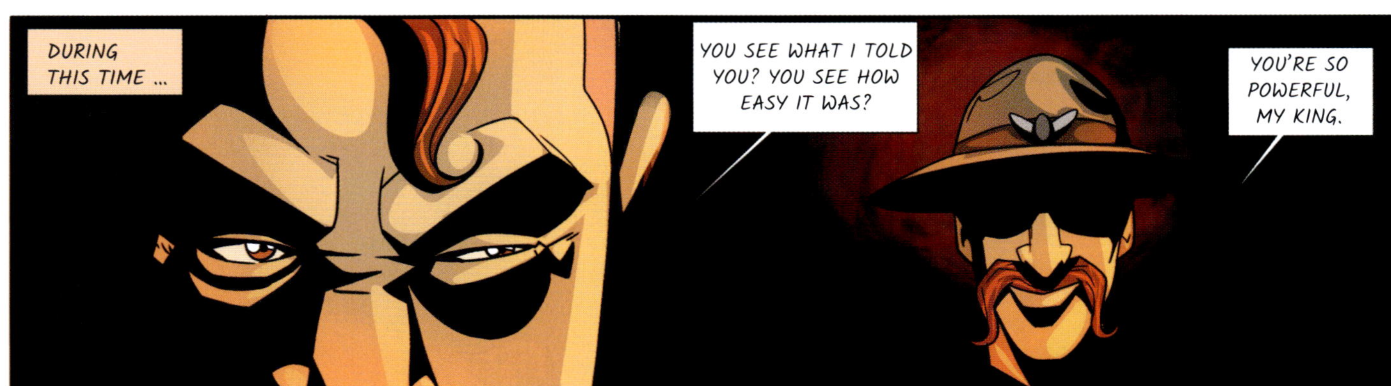
DURING THIS TIME ...
YOU SEE WHAT I TOLD YOU? YOU SEE HOW EASY IT WAS?
YOU'RE SO POWERFUL, MY KING.

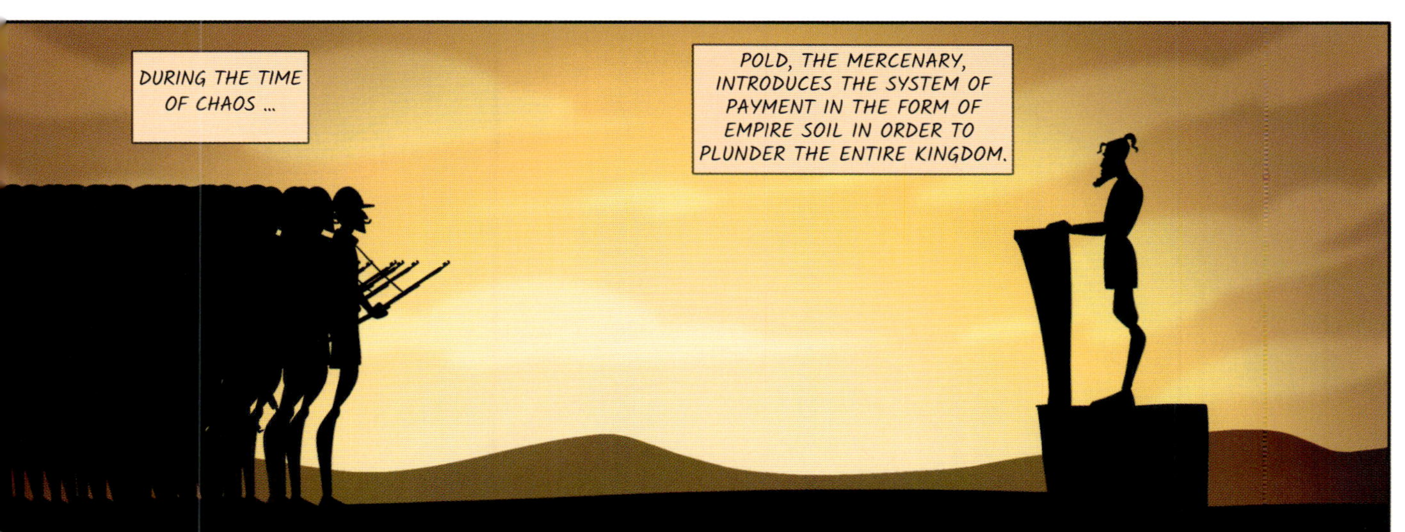
DURING THE TIME OF CHAOS ...
POLD, THE MERCENARY, INTRODUCES THE SYSTEM OF PAYMENT IN THE FORM OF EMPIRE SOIL IN ORDER TO PLUNDER THE ENTIRE KINGDOM.

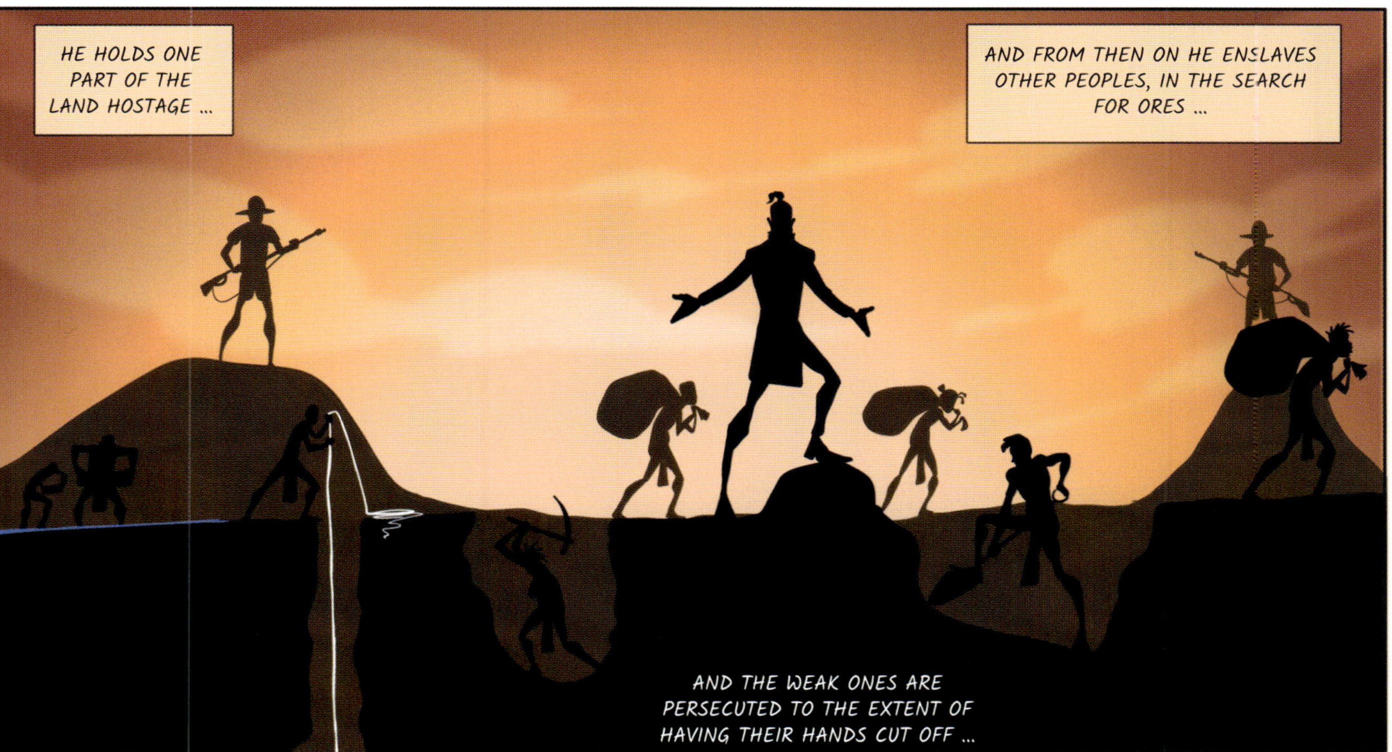
HE HOLDS ONE PART OF THE LAND HOSTAGE ...
AND FROM THEN ON HE ENSLAVES OTHER PEOPLES, IN THE SEARCH FOR ORES ...
AND THE WEAK ONES ARE PERSECUTED TO THE EXTENT OF HAVING THEIR HANDS CUT OFF ...

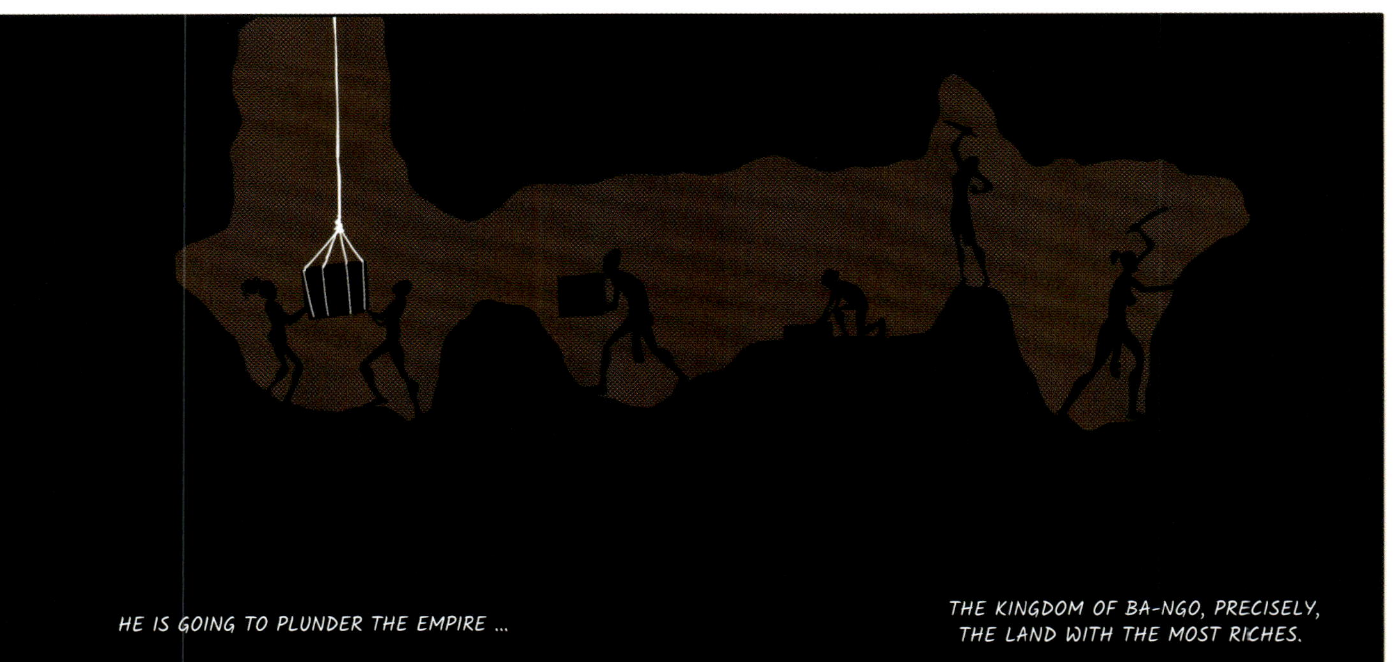
HE IS GOING TO PLUNDER THE EMPIRE ...
THE KINGDOM OF BA-NGO, PRECISELY, THE LAND WITH THE MOST RICHES.

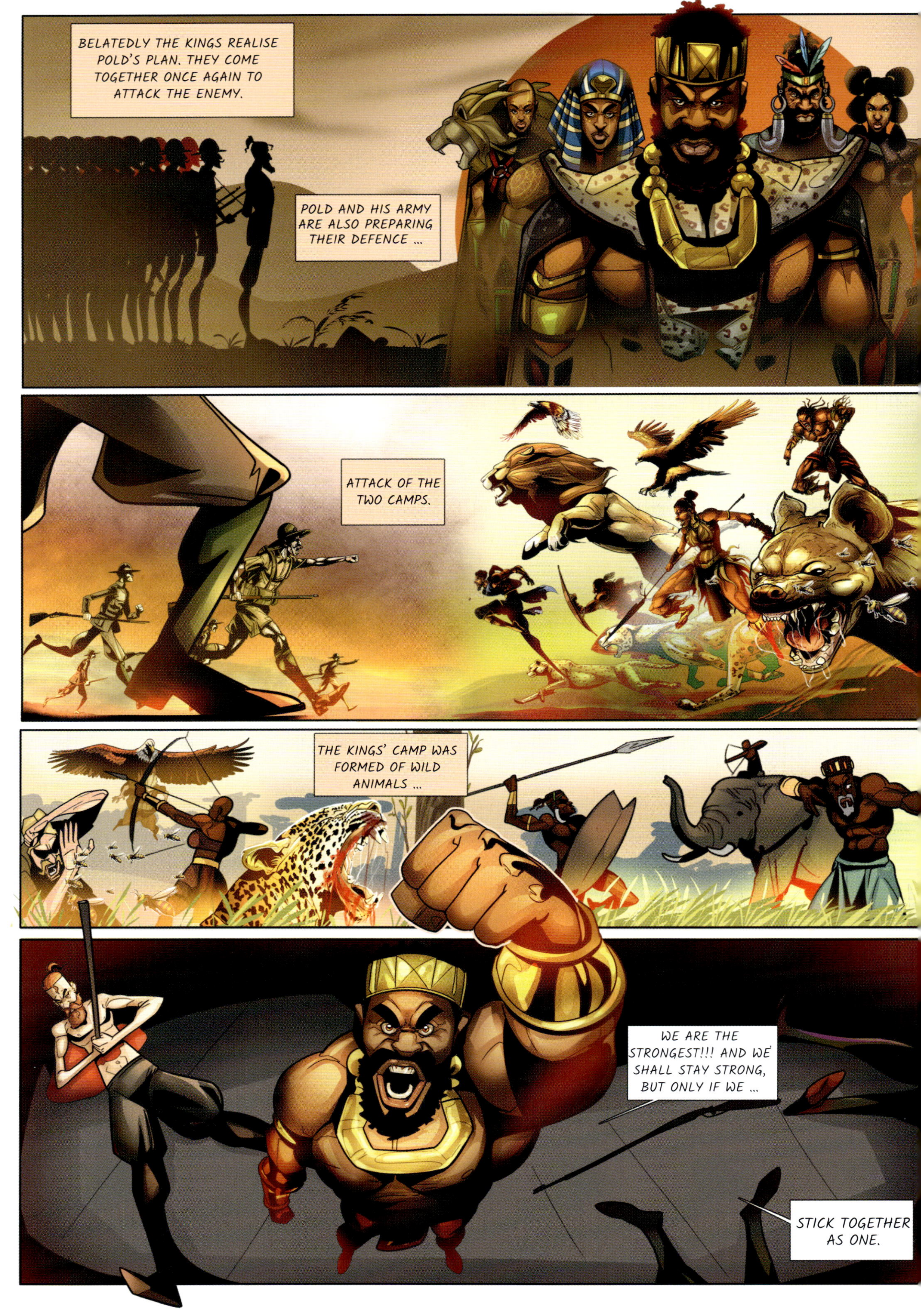
BELATEDLY THE KINGS REALISE POLD'S PLAN. THEY COME TOGETHER ONCE AGAIN TO ATTACK THE ENEMY.
POLD AND HIS ARMY ARE ALSO PREPARING THEIR DEFENCE ...
ATTACK OF THE TWO CAMPS.
THE KINGS' CAMP WAS FORMED OF WILD ANIMALS ...
WE ARE THE STRONGEST!!! AND WE SHALL STAY STRONG, BUT ONLY IF WE ...
STICK TOGETHER AS ONE.

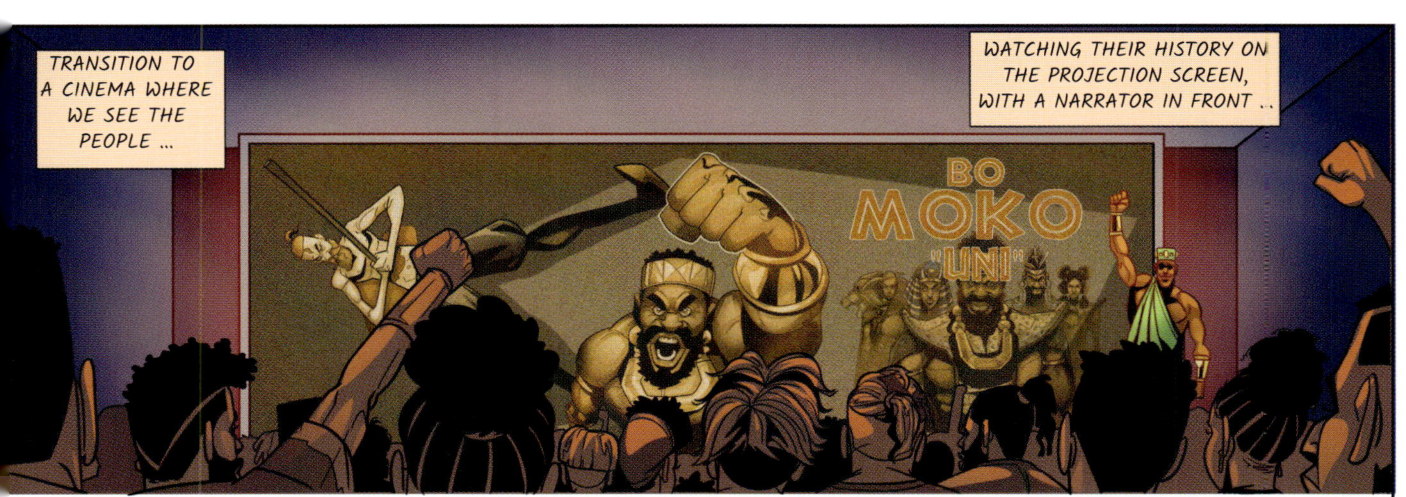

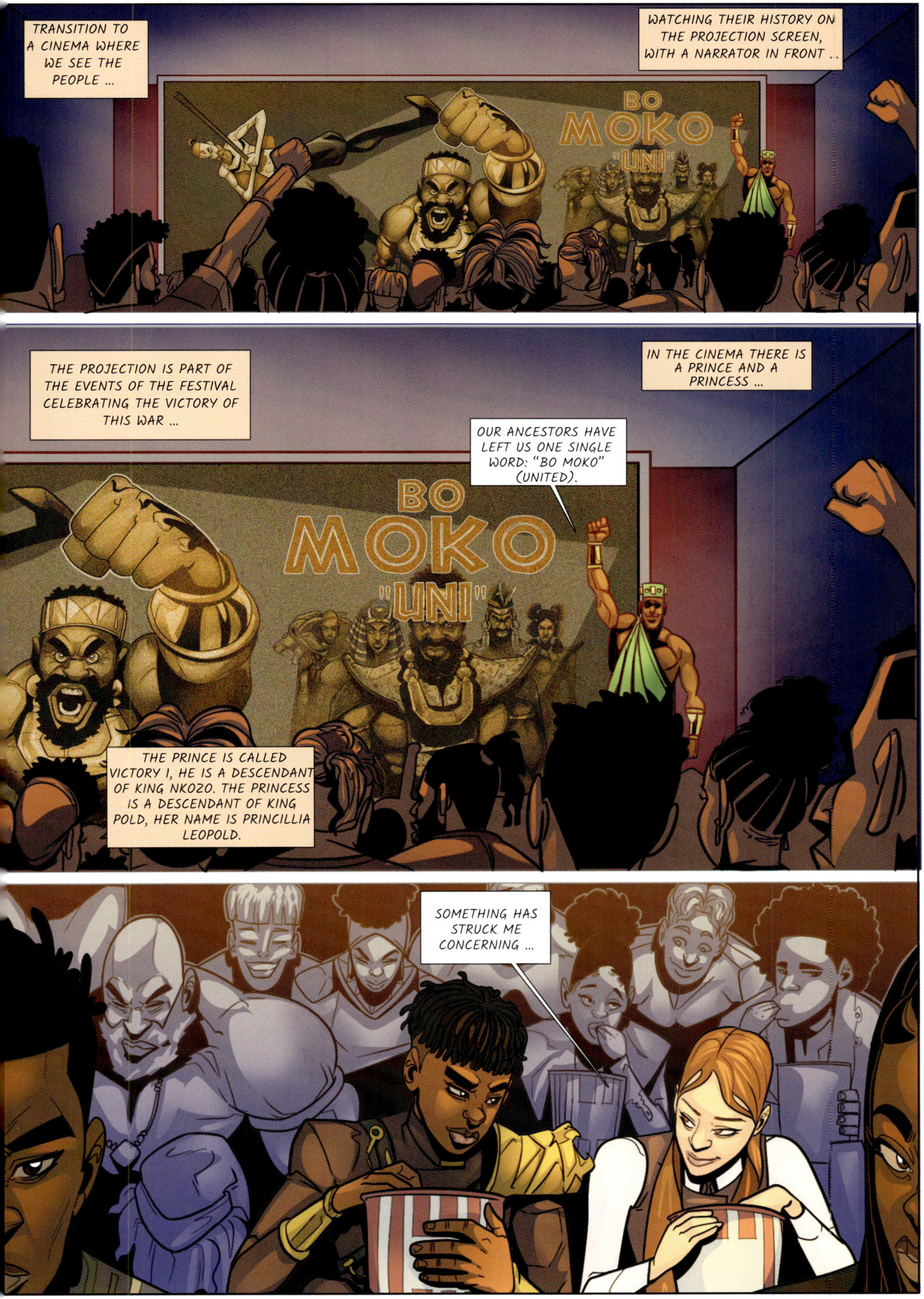

THE PROJECTION IS PART OF THE EVENTS OF THE FESTIVAL CELEBRATING THE VICTORY OF THIS WAR ...

IN THE CINEMA THERE IS A PRINCE AND A PRINCESS ...

OUR ANCESTORS HAVE LEFT US ONE SINGLE WORD: "BO MOKO" (UNITED).

BO MOKO "UNI"

THE PRINCE IS CALLED VICTORY I, HE IS A DESCENDANT OF KING NKOZO. THE PRINCESS IS A DESCENDANT OF KING POLD, HER NAME IS PRINCILLIA LEOPOLD.

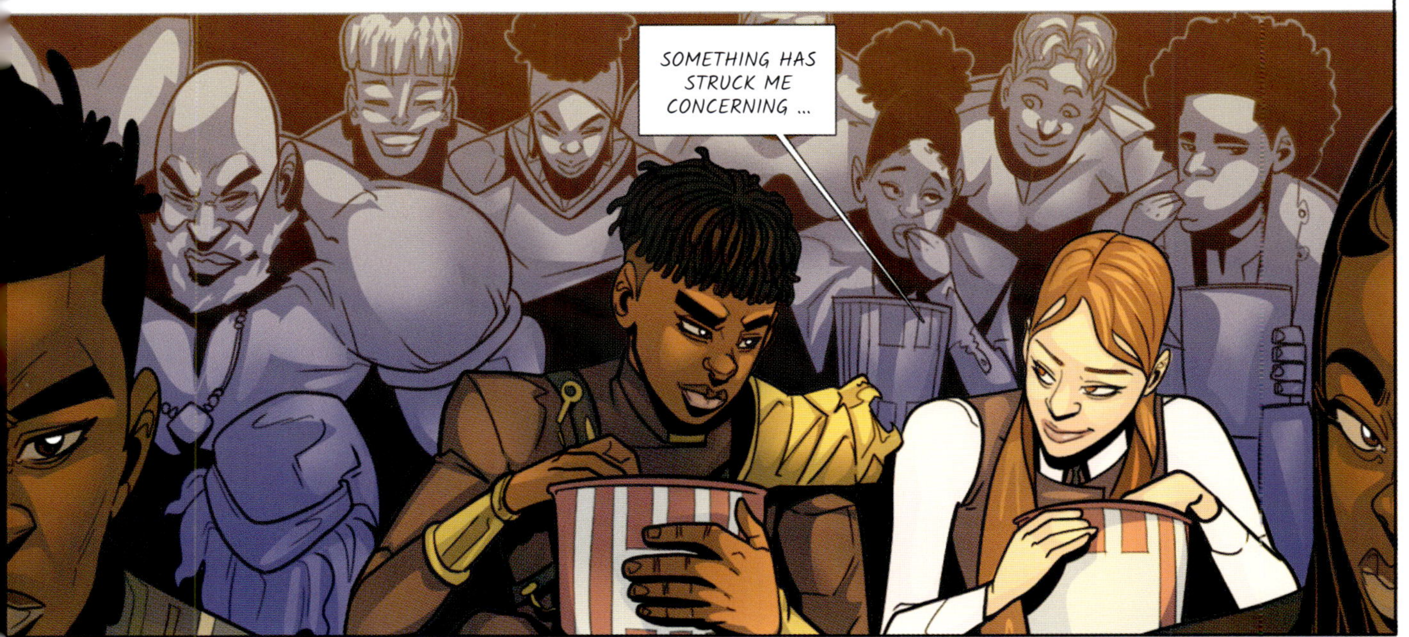

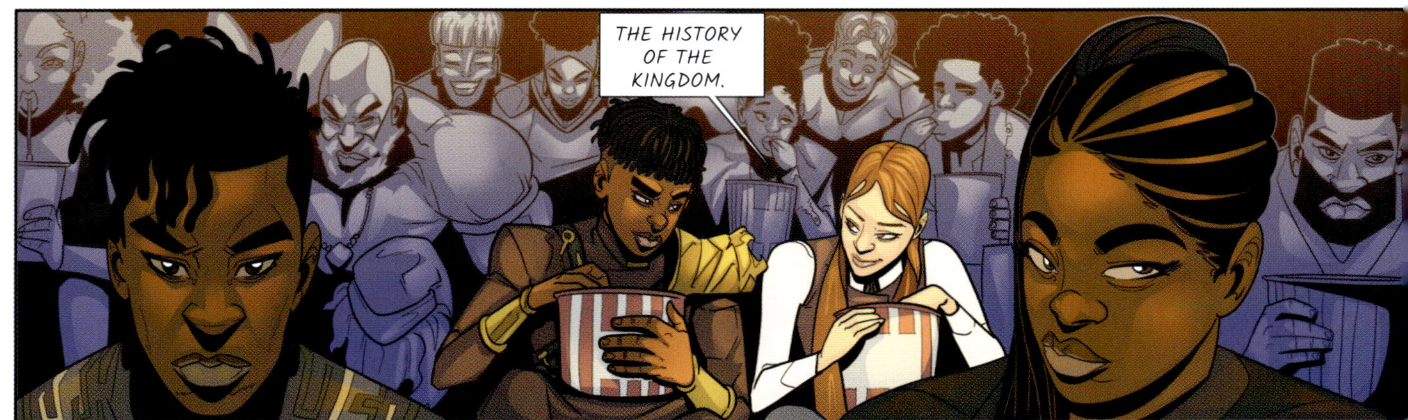

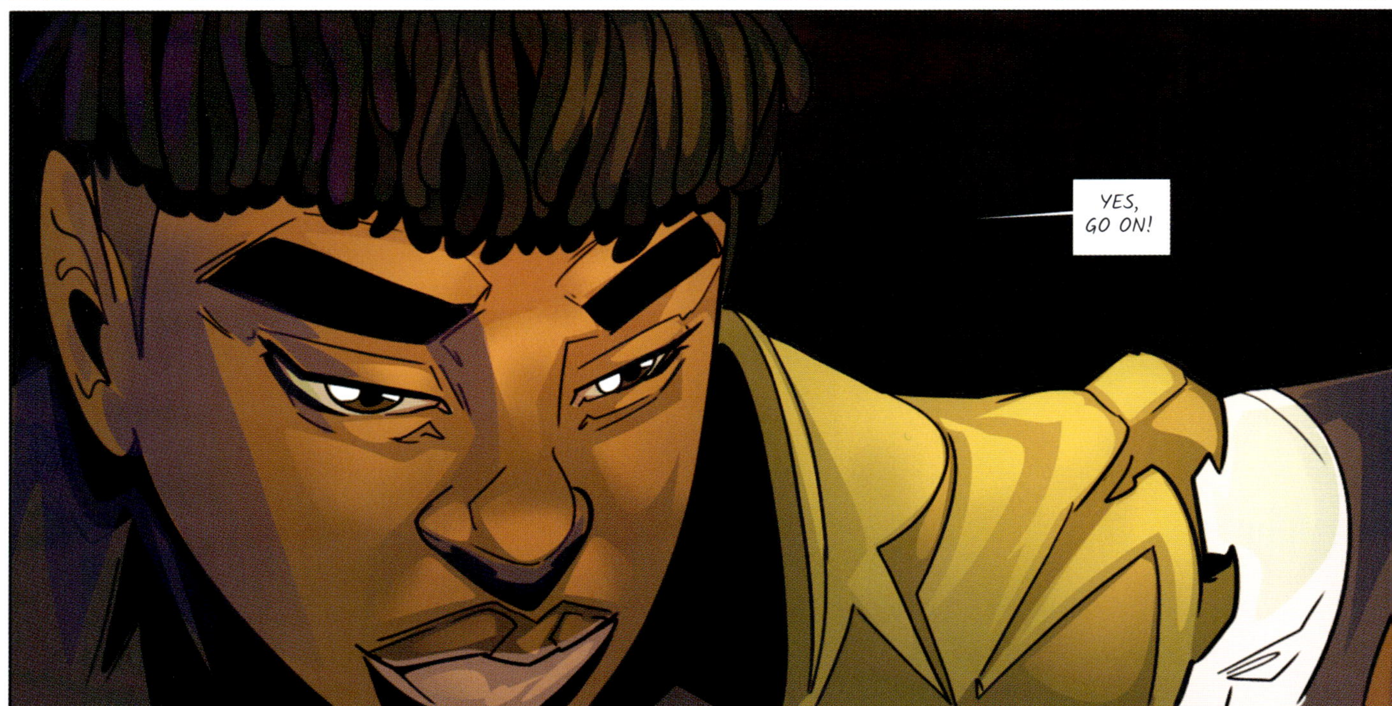

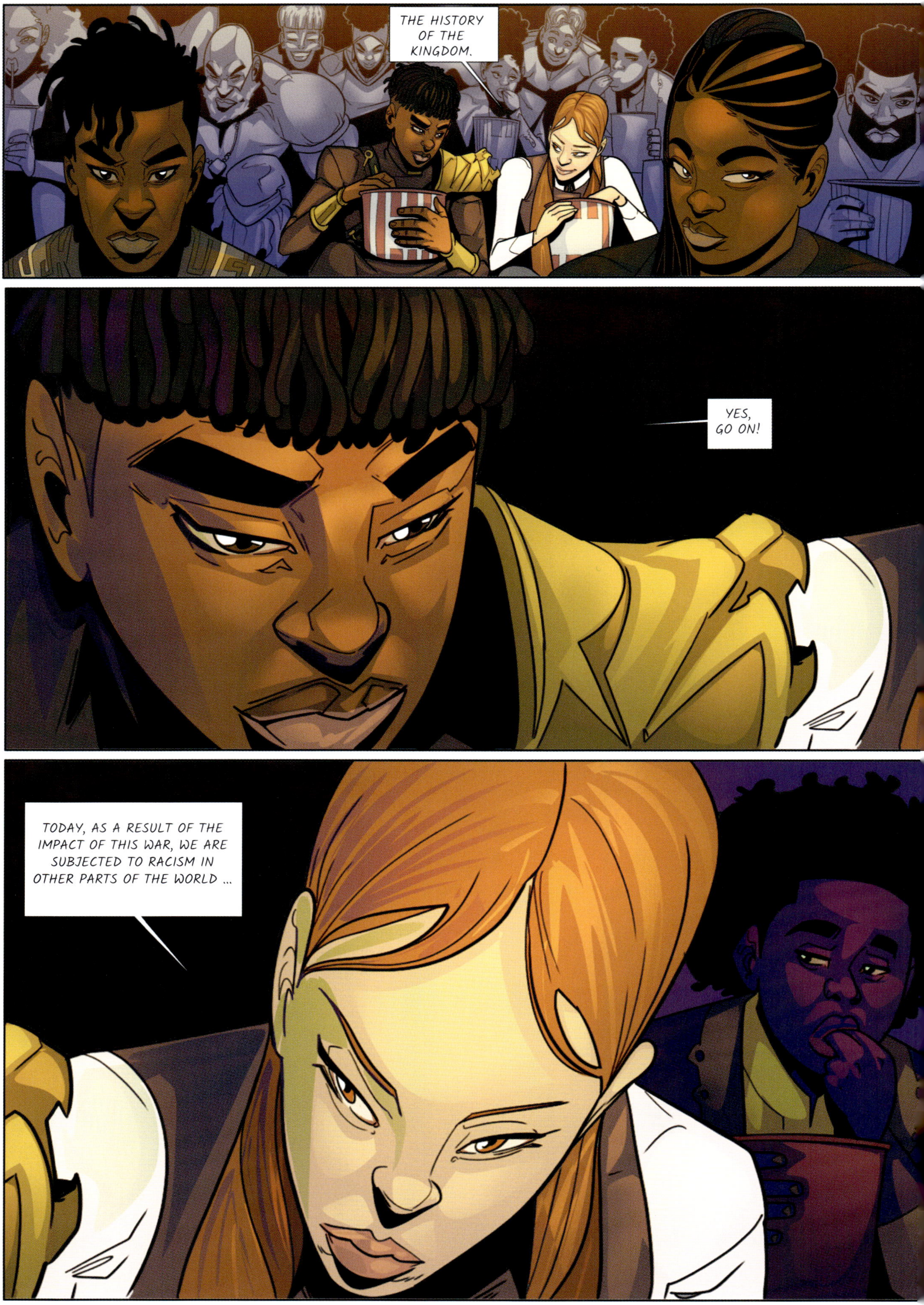

TODAY, AS A RESULT OF THE IMPACT OF THIS WAR, WE ARE SUBJECTED TO RACISM IN OTHER PARTS OF THE WORLD ...

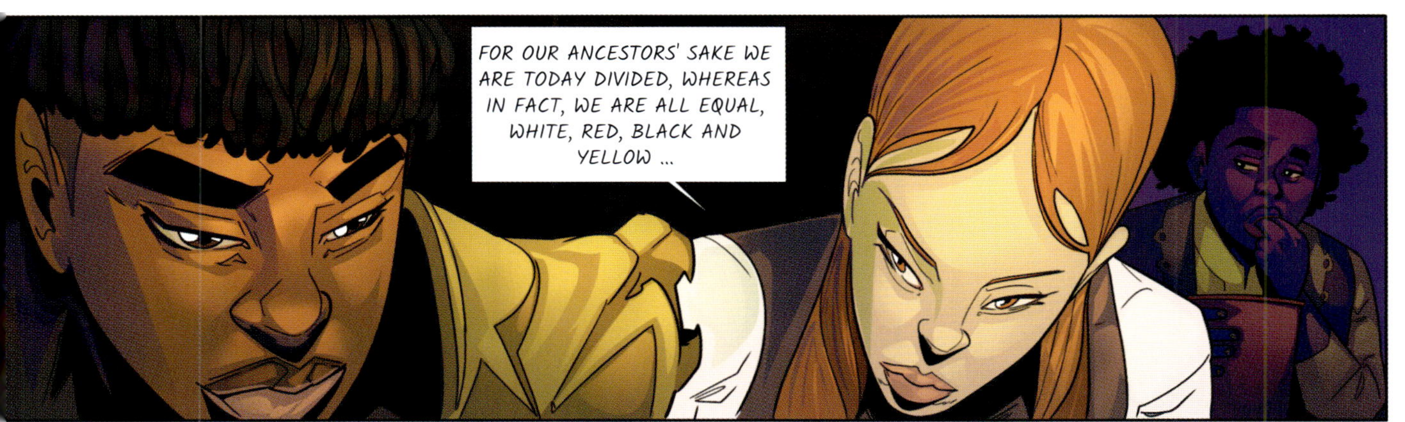
FOR OUR ANCESTORS' SAKE WE ARE TODAY DIVIDED, WHEREAS IN FACT, WE ARE ALL EQUAL, WHITE, RED, BLACK AND YELLOW ...

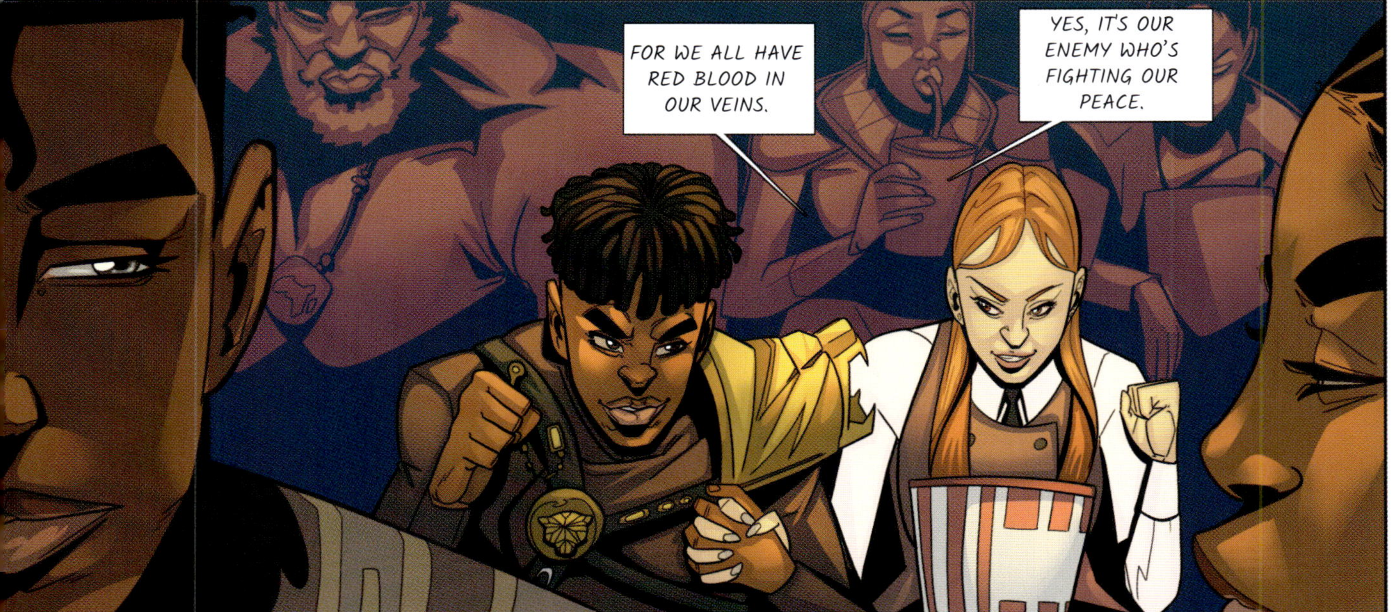
FOR WE ALL HAVE RED BLOOD IN OUR VEINS.
YES, IT'S OUR ENEMY WHO'S FIGHTING OUR PEACE.

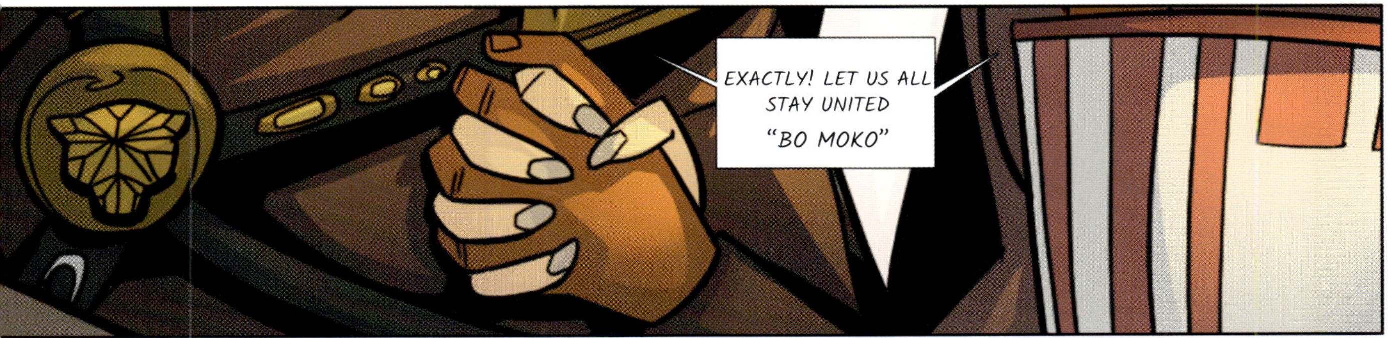
EXACTLY! LET US ALL STAY UNITED "BO MOKO"

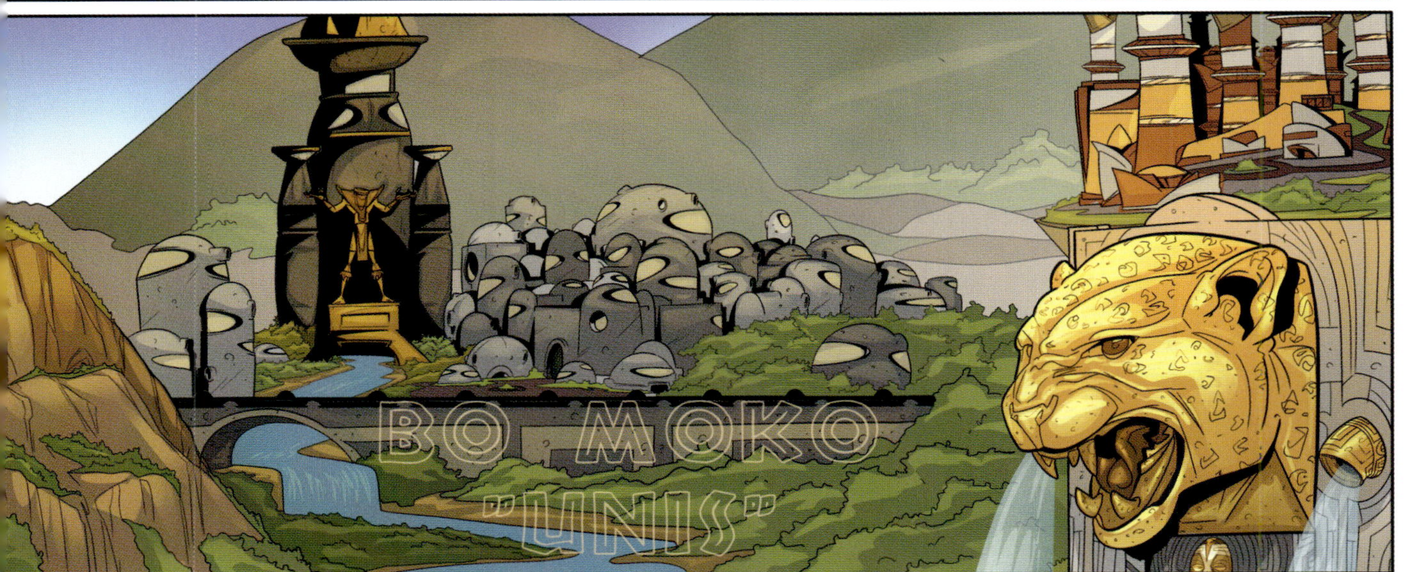
BO MOKO
"UNIS"

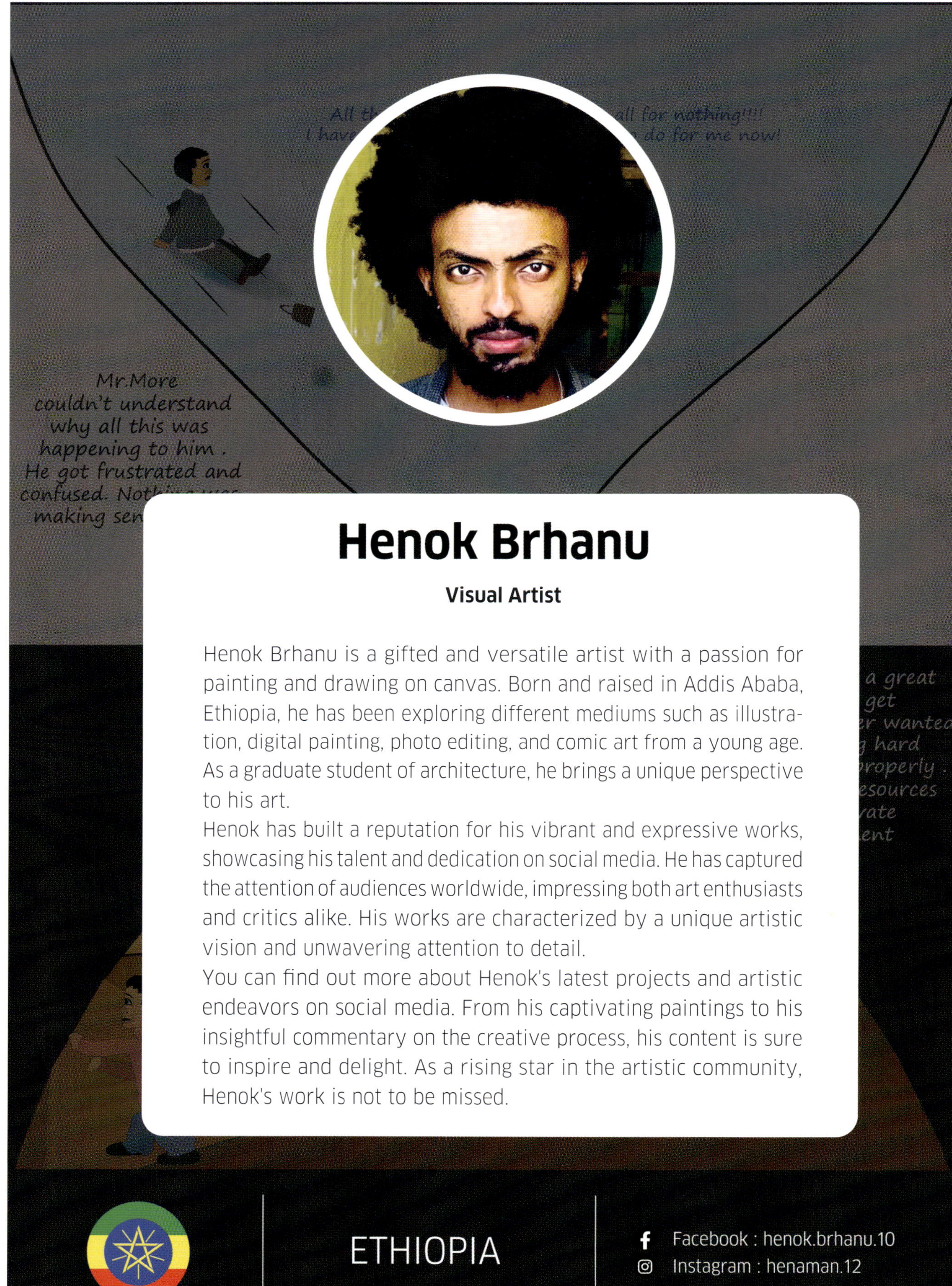

Henok Brhanu

Visual Artist

Henok Brhanu is a gifted and versatile artist with a passion for painting and drawing on canvas. Born and raised in Addis Ababa, Ethiopia, he has been exploring different mediums such as illustration, digital painting, photo editing, and comic art from a young age. As a graduate student of architecture, he brings a unique perspective to his art.

Henok has built a reputation for his vibrant and expressive works, showcasing his talent and dedication on social media. He has captured the attention of audiences worldwide, impressing both art enthusiasts and critics alike. His works are characterized by a unique artistic vision and unwavering attention to detail.

You can find out more about Henok's latest projects and artistic endeavors on social media. From his captivating paintings to his insightful commentary on the creative process, his content is sure to inspire and delight. As a rising star in the artistic community, Henok's work is not to be missed.

ETHIOPIA

Facebook : henok.brhanu.10
Instagram : henaman.12

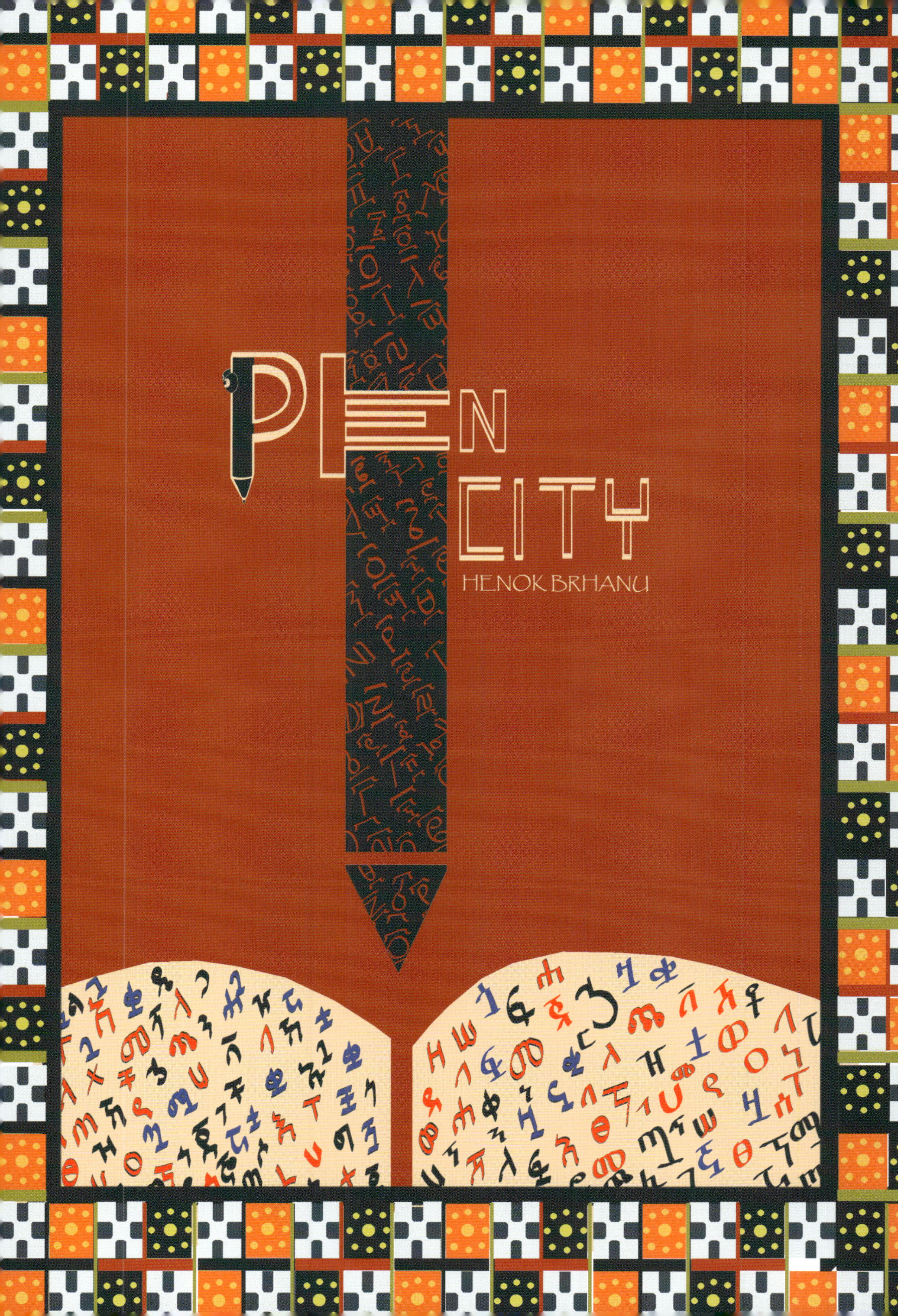
PEN CITY
HENOK BRHANU

CHARACTERS OF PEN CITY

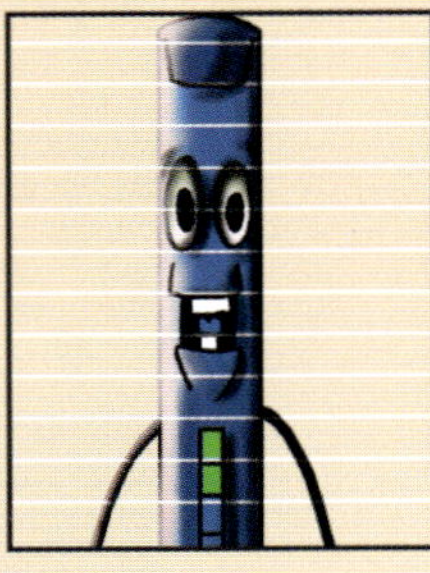

The BLUE PENS

The blue pens are ordinary citizens, who have no power. They can't question anything, not even their own rights. In pen city blue pens live uncomfortable lives in sorrow until their deaths.

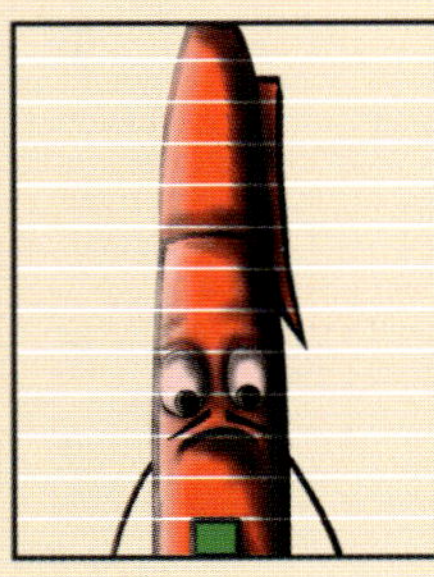

THE RED PENS

The red pens are soldiers and work for the fancy pen.
They are able to control the blue pens and take them wherever they want.

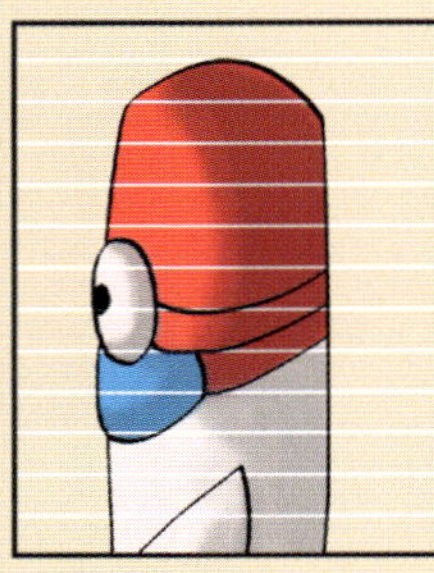

THE DOCTOR PEN

The doctor pens work in the laboratory, which is a secret place in pen city. Only doctor pens and the fancy pen know about it. A collection of ink and filling processes take place inside the laboratory.

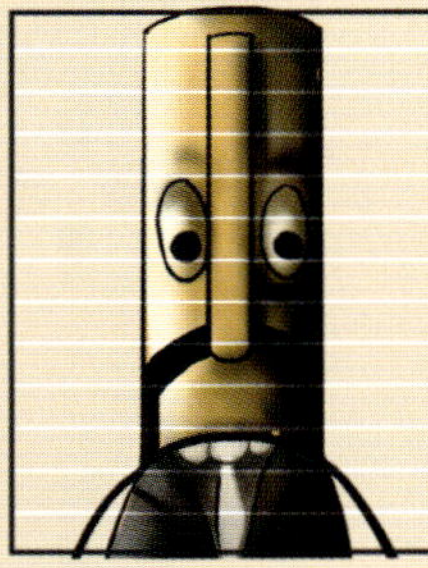

THE FANCY PEN

The fancy pen is the most powerful pen in the city. He has the right to make decisions and has control over the whole city. The red and the doctor pens work for him. No one dares to question his power, since they know what will happen if they do. The fancy pen is the only pen that is not transparent. No one can see his remaining ink.

In this story the key element is the ink, which is the source of conflict, beginning with the consumption of ink. Ink is the life of a pen . If a pen lacks ink, it is of no use or dead. The fancy pen needs the most ink since it has a thick and bold font. In order to be able to live forever, he takes the blue pen's ink by force, to fill his own ink. This is what happens in the laboratory. They extract the ink of the blue pens and store it in big tanks until the fancy pen comes for a fill-up

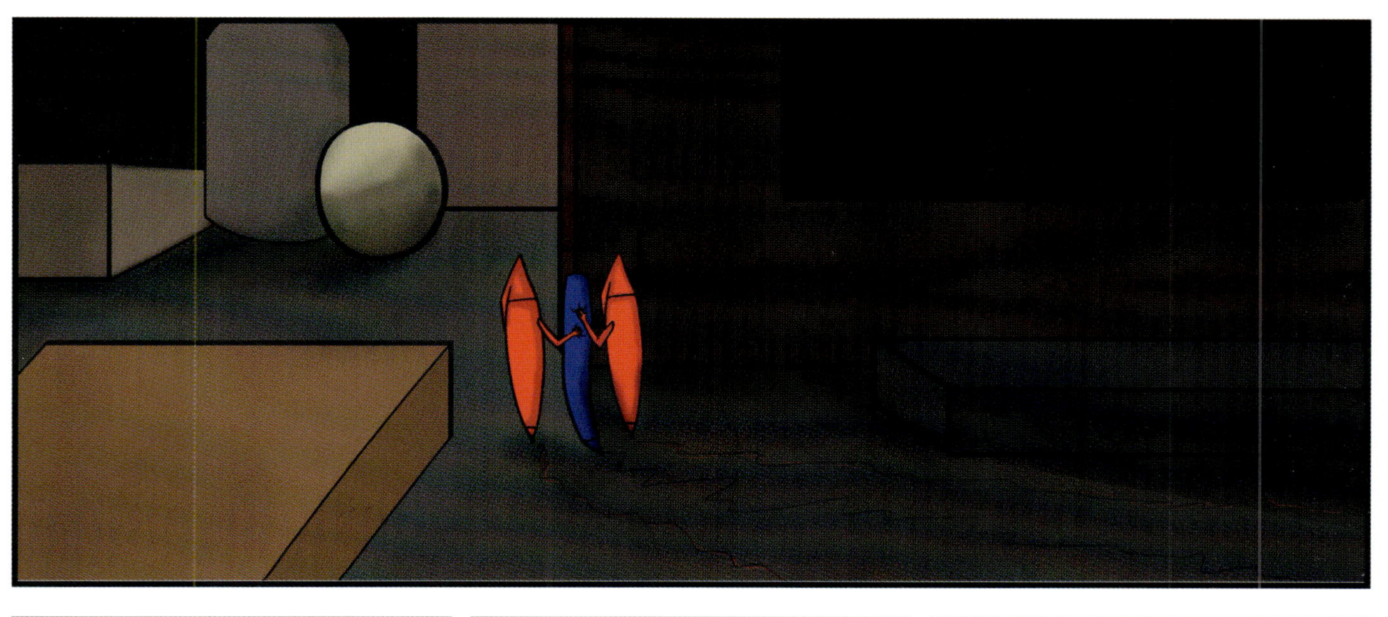

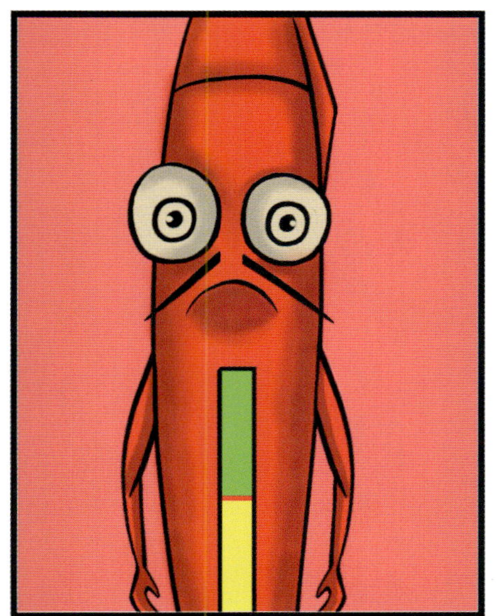

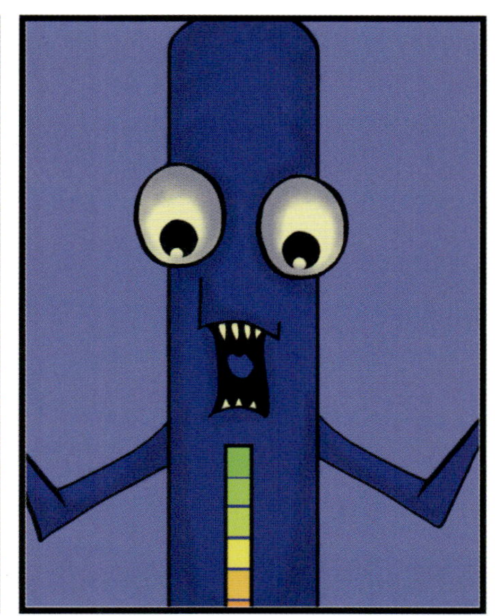

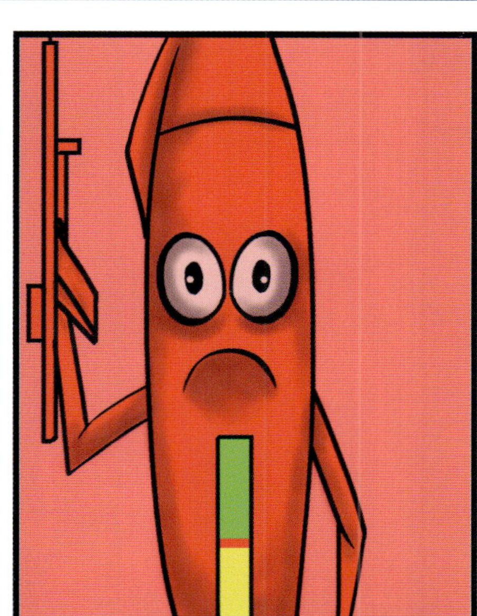

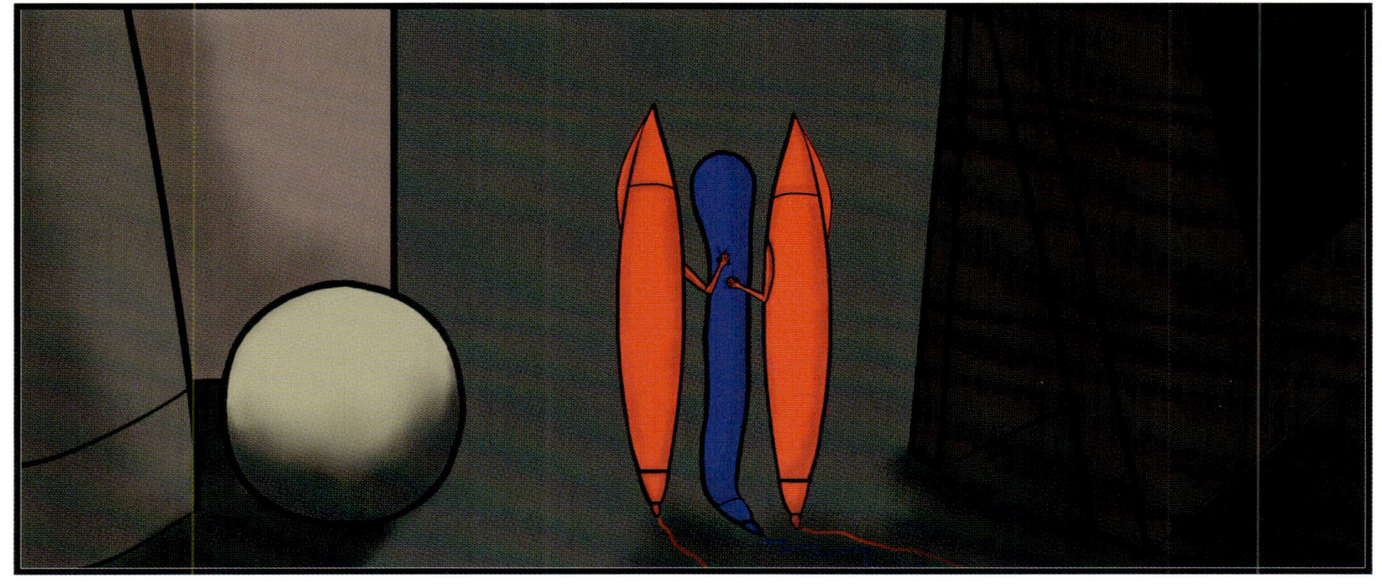

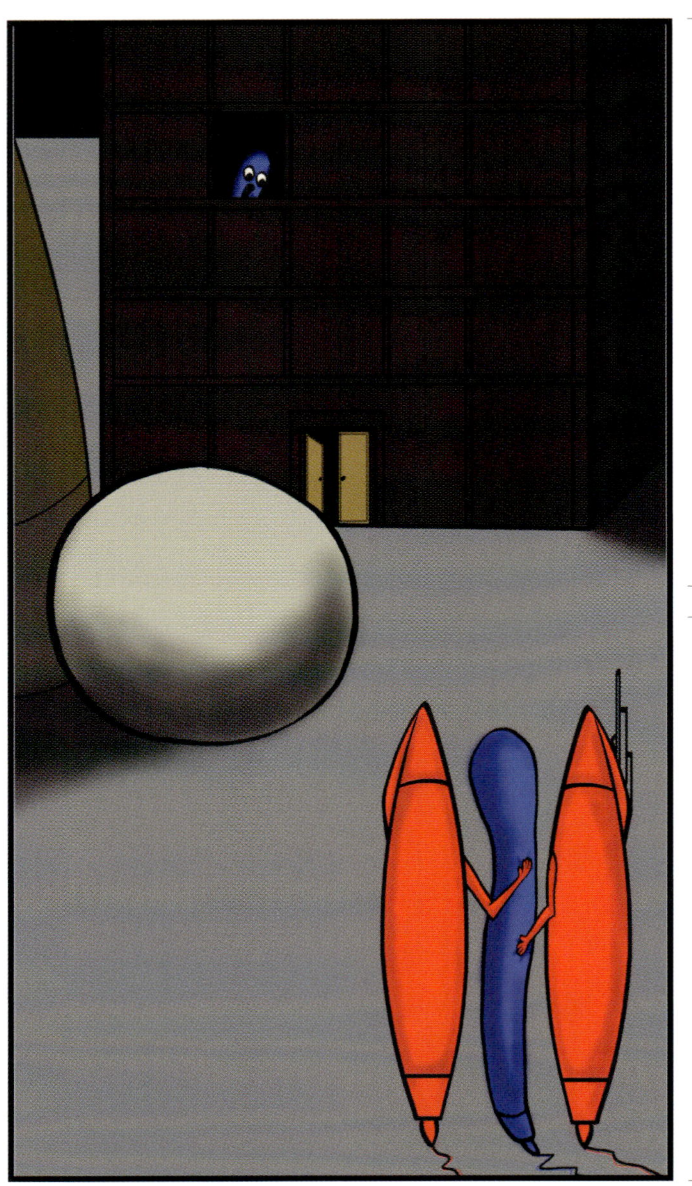
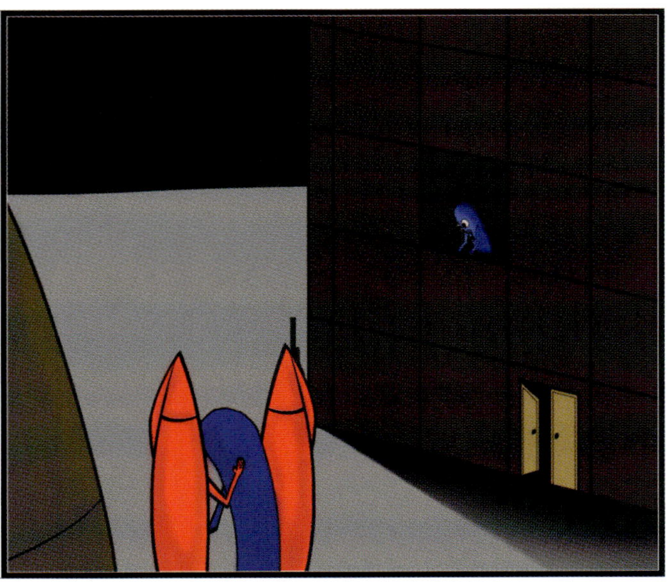
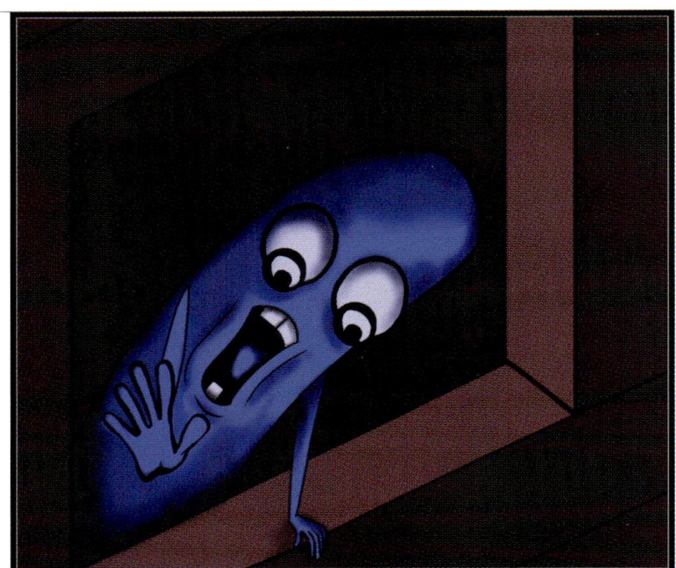
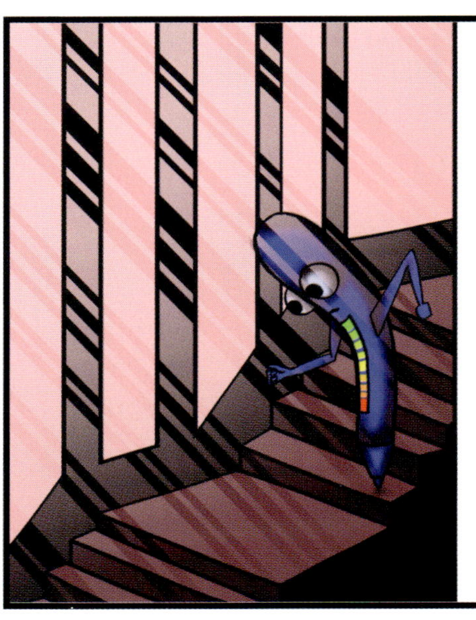
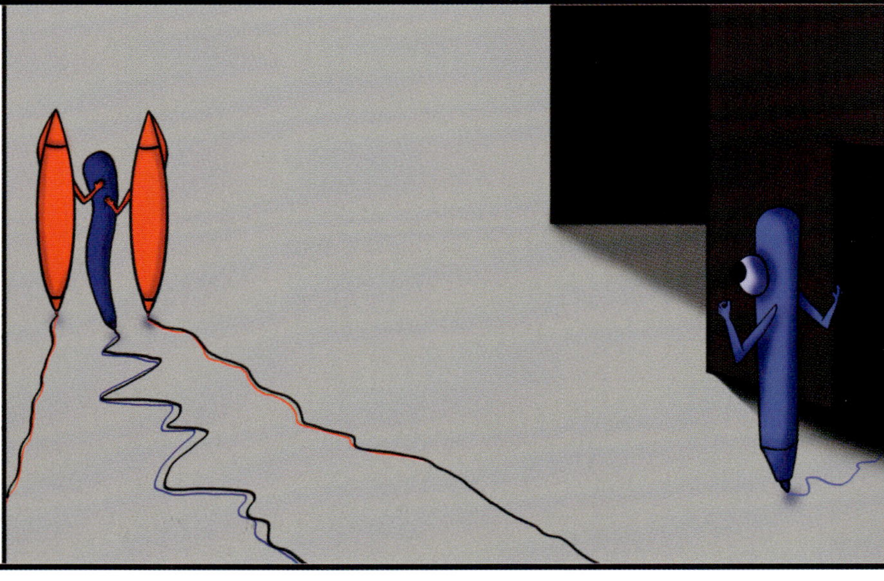

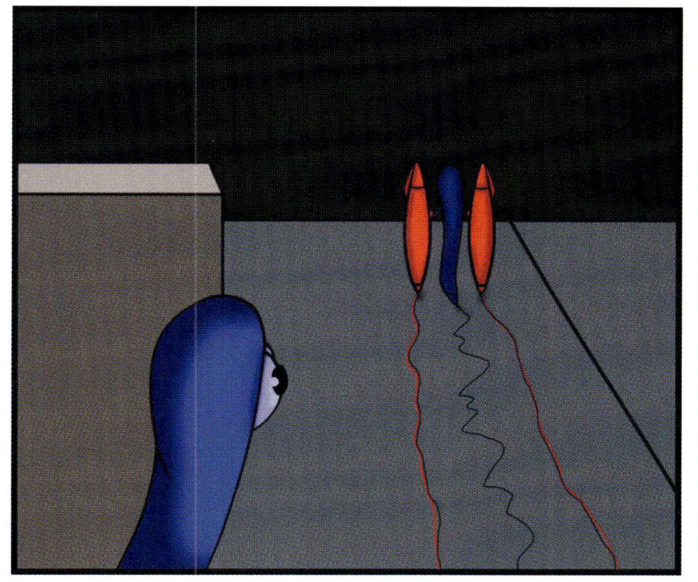
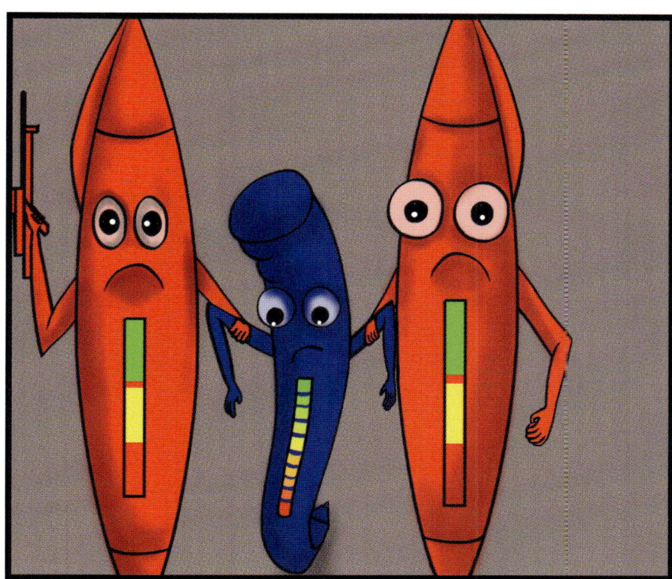
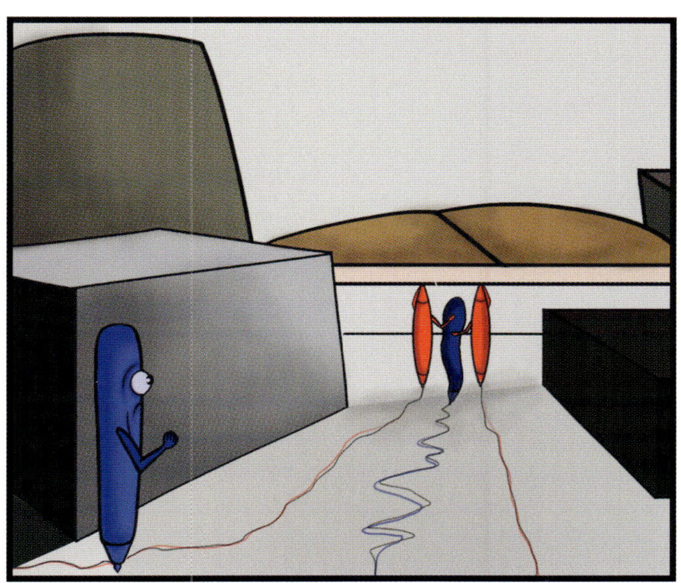
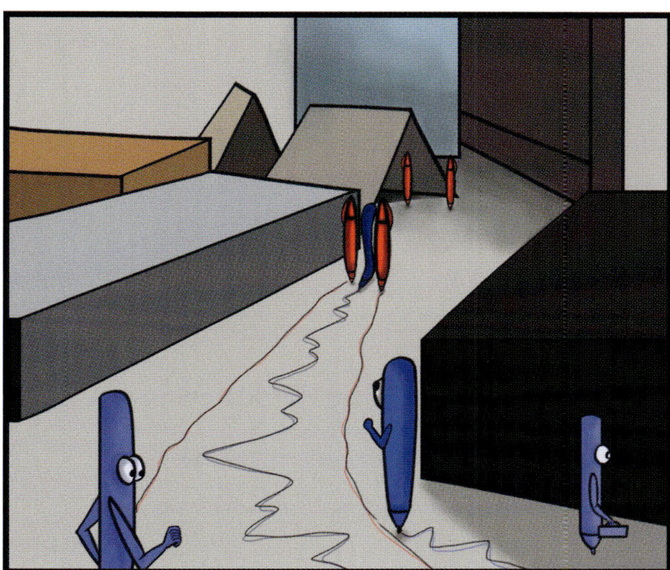
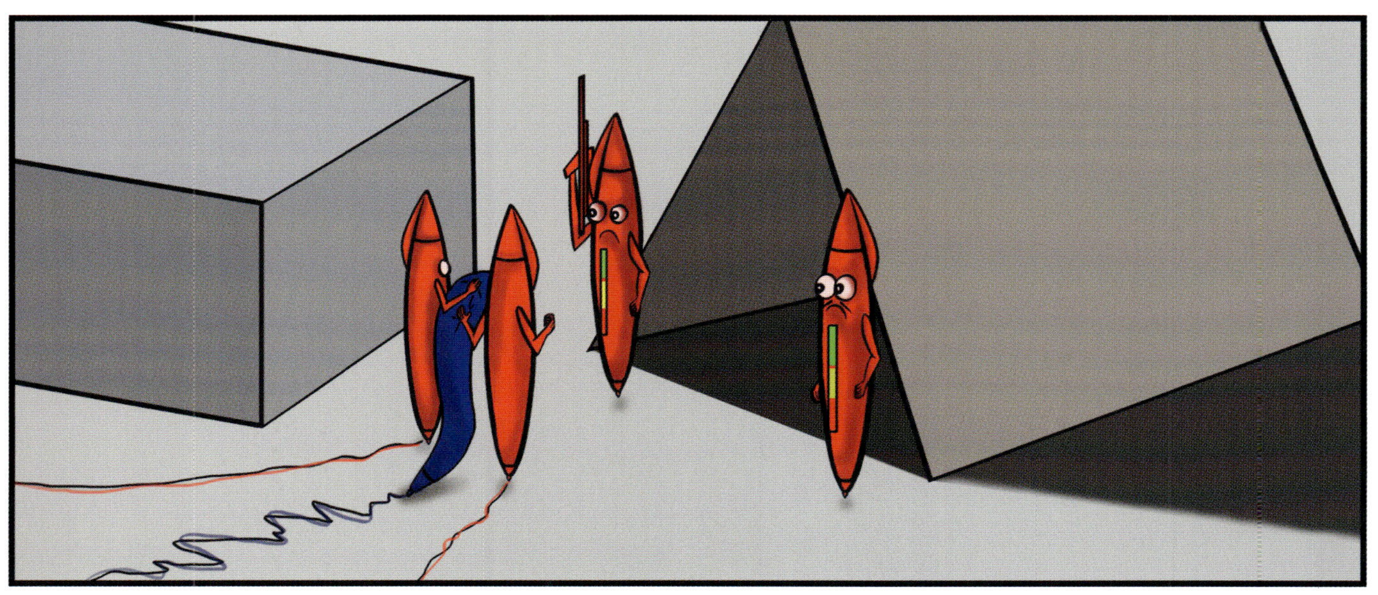

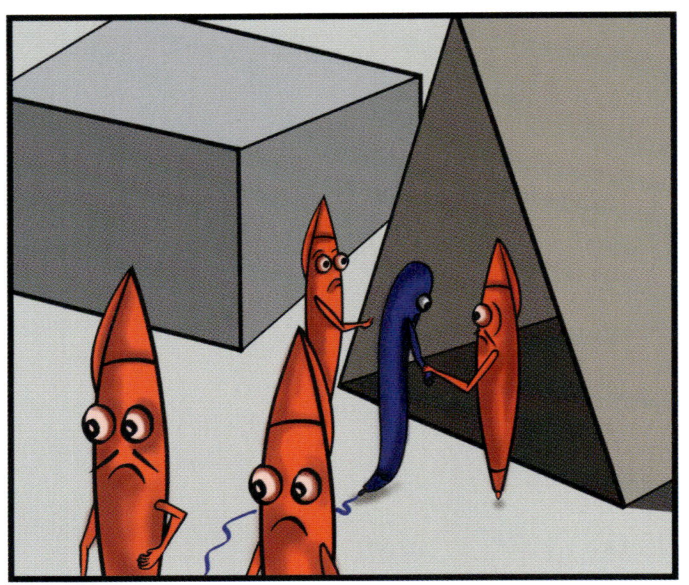
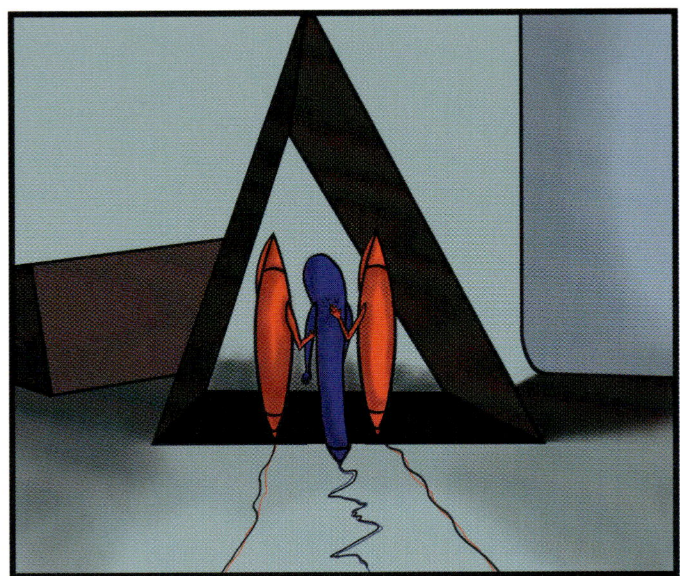
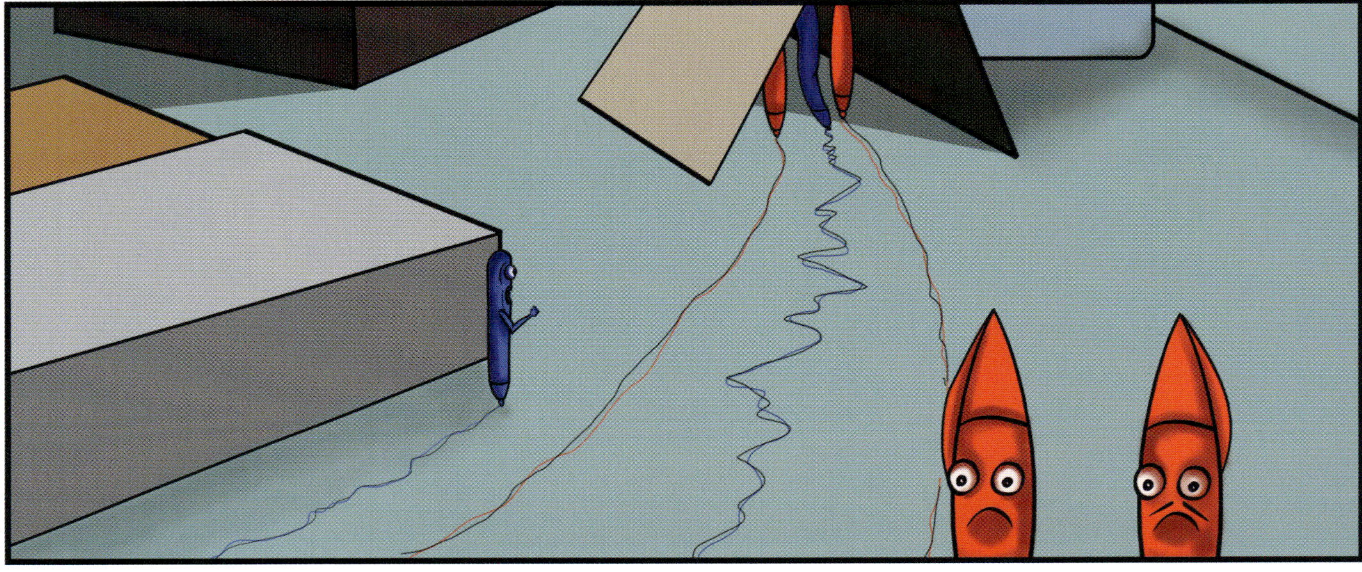
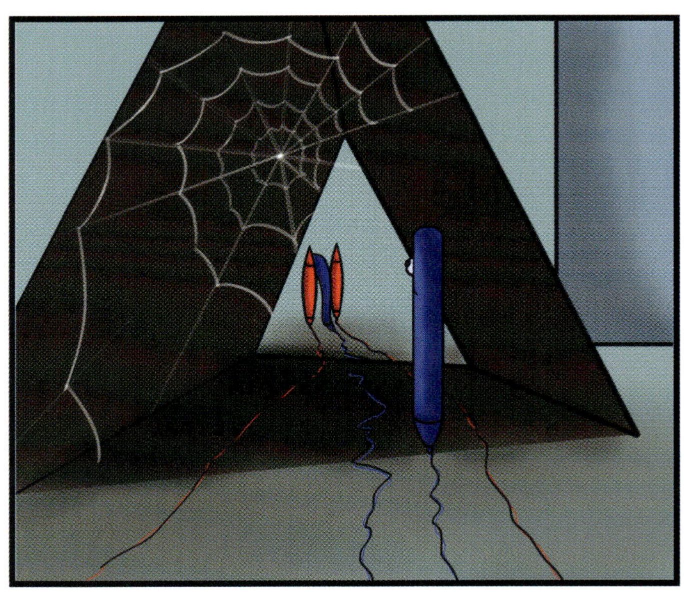
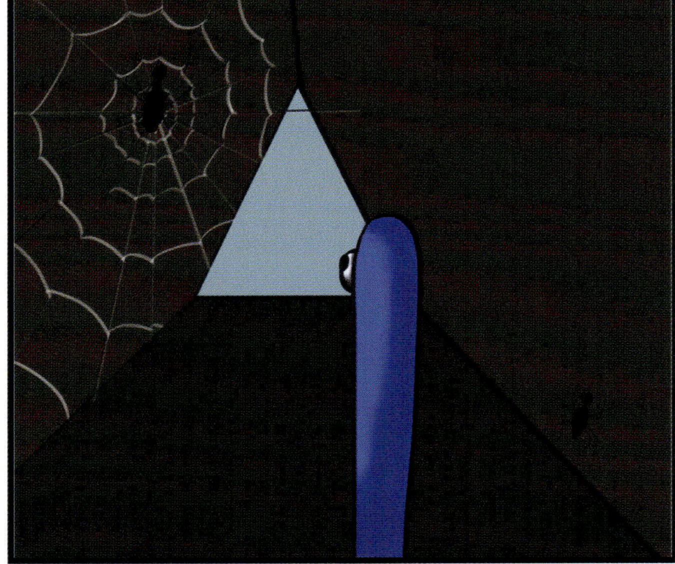

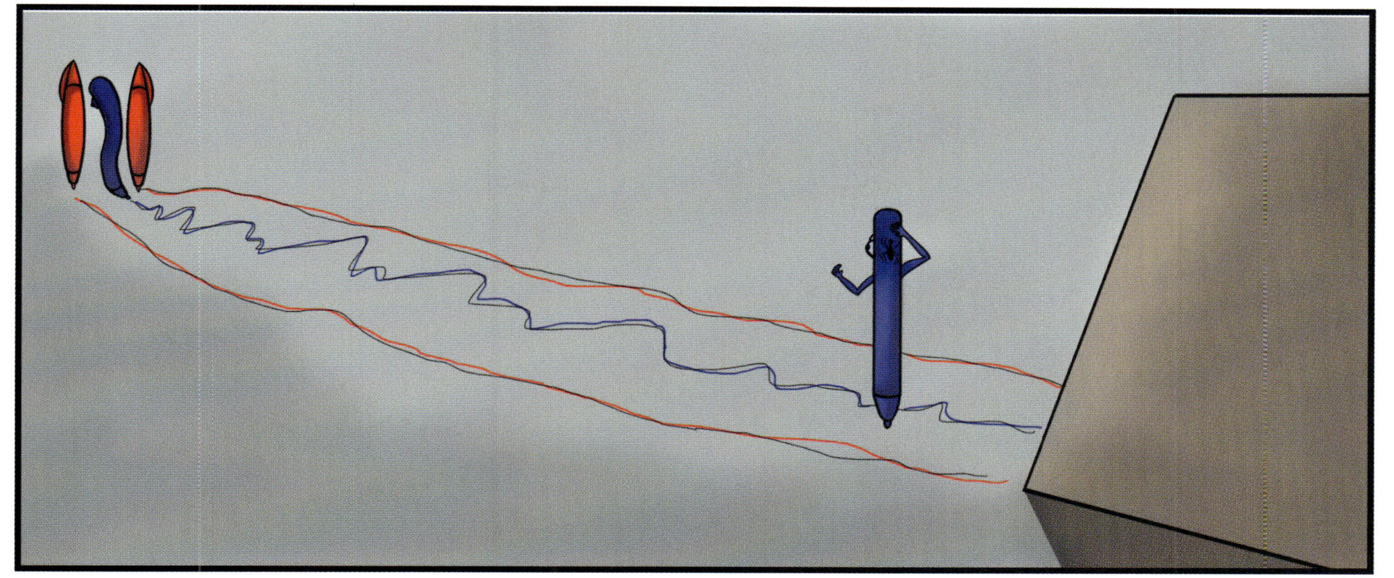
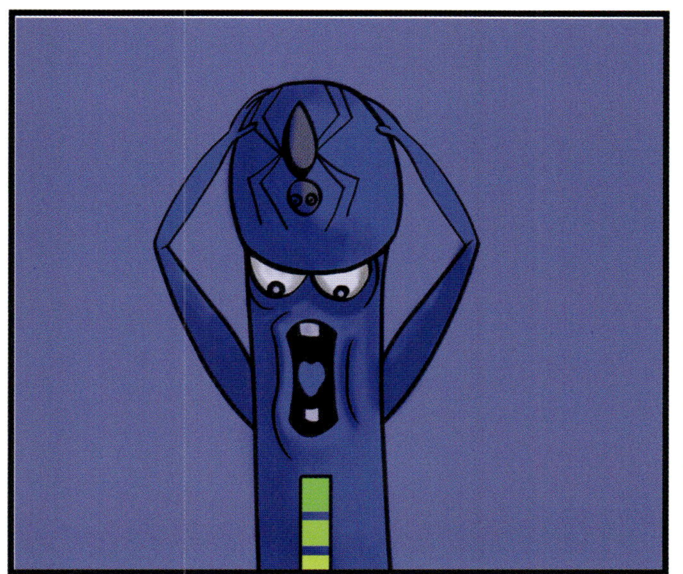
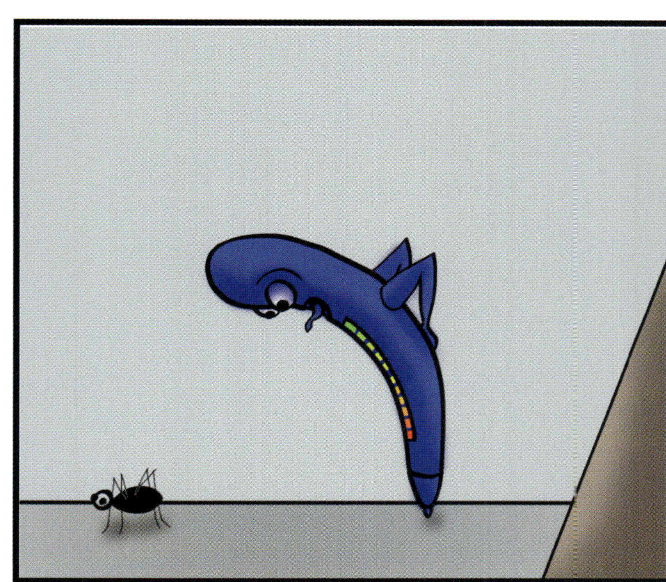
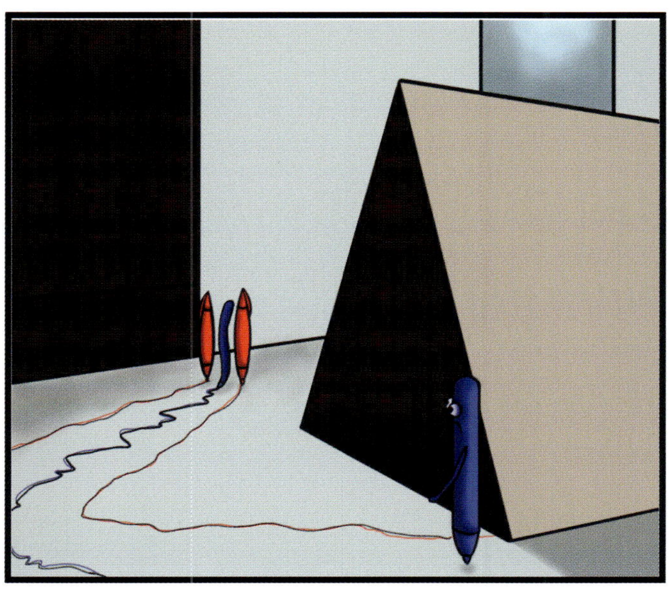
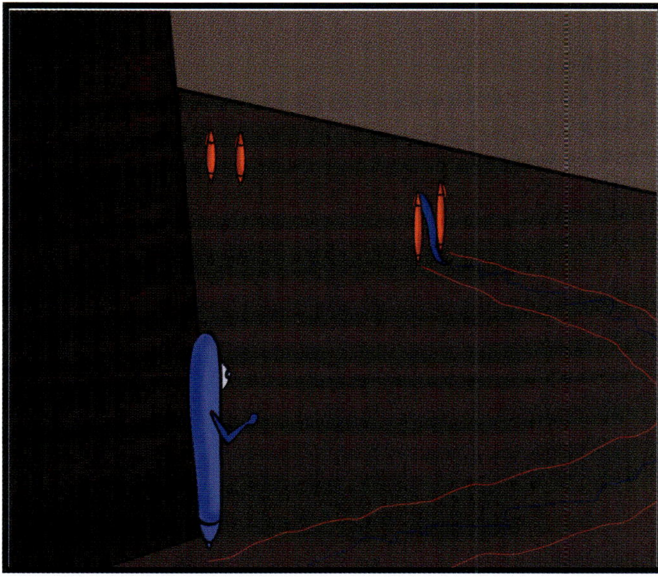

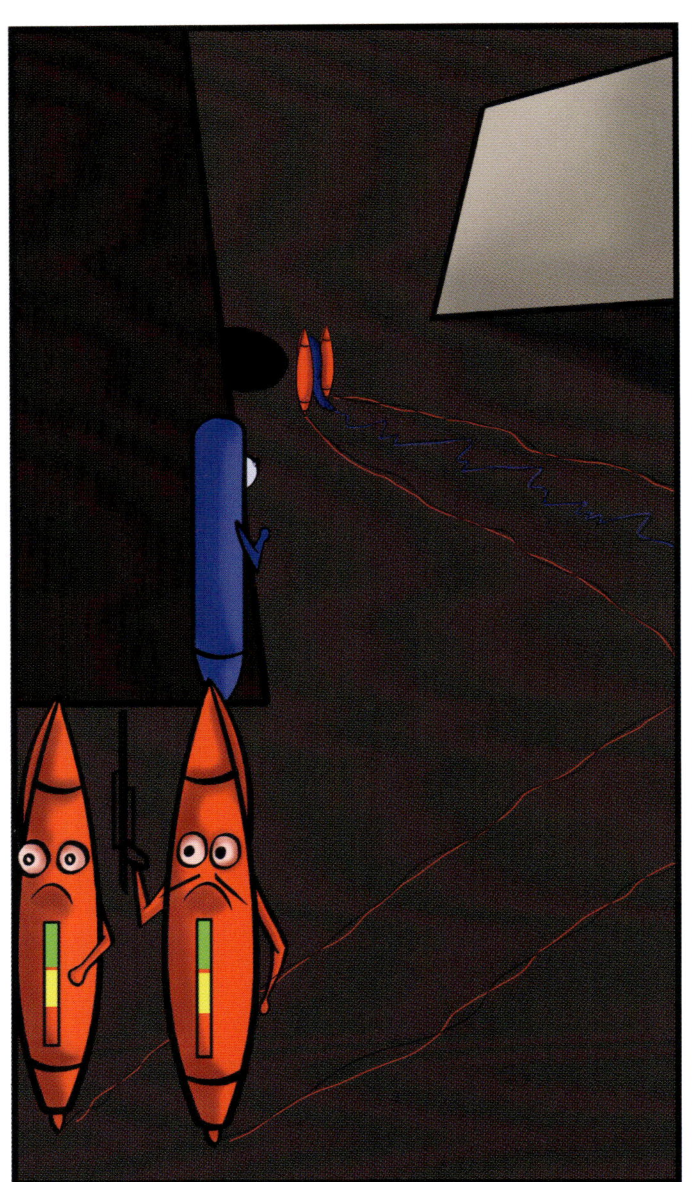
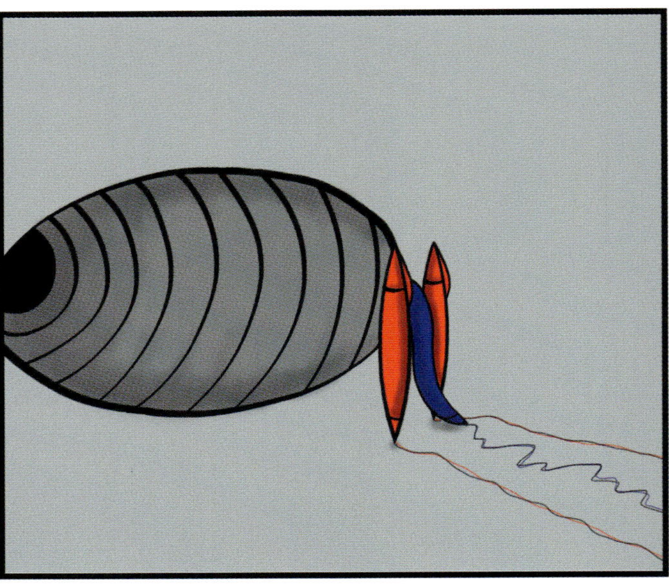
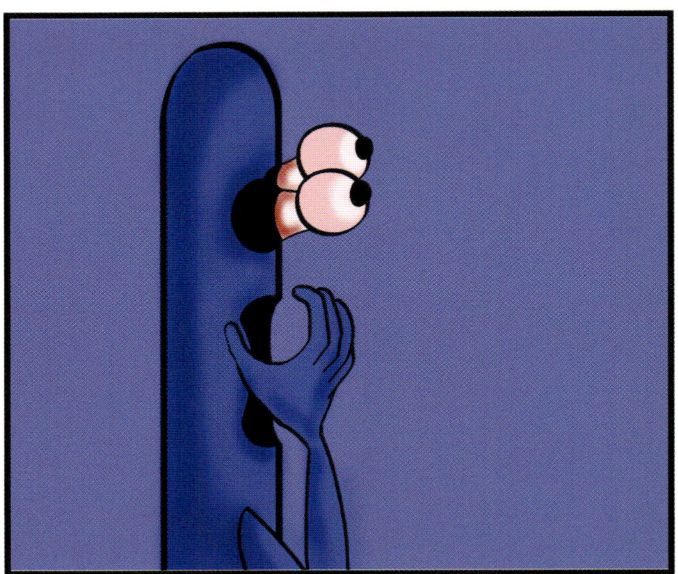
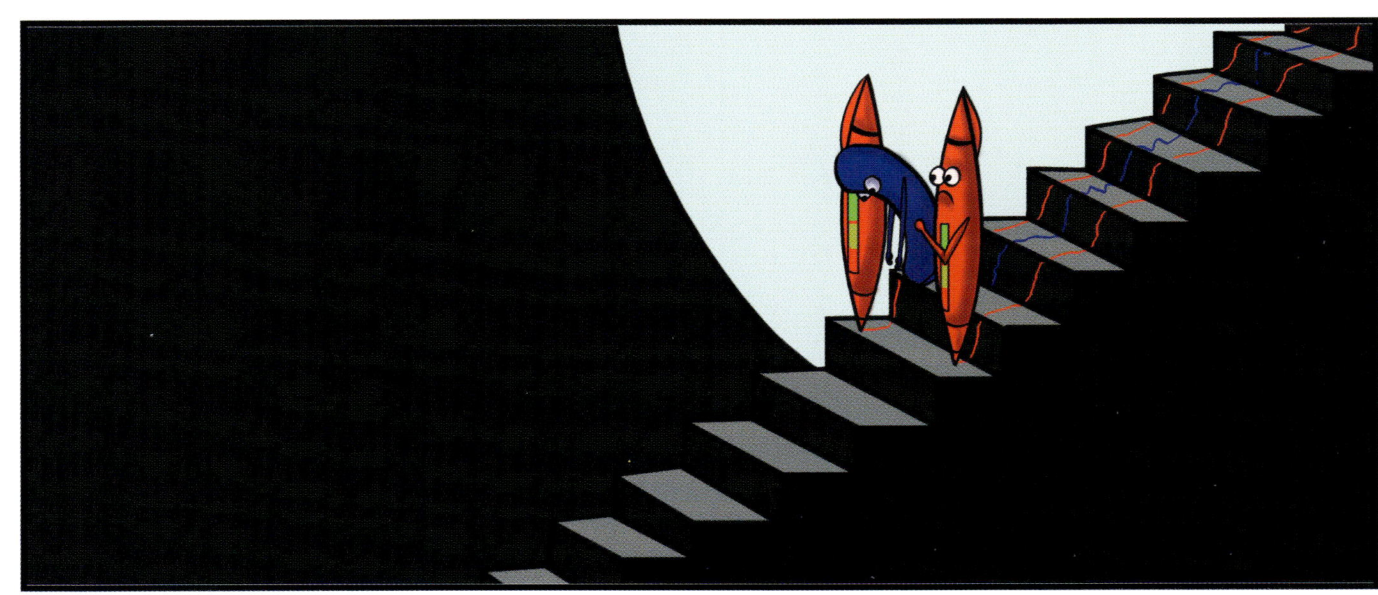

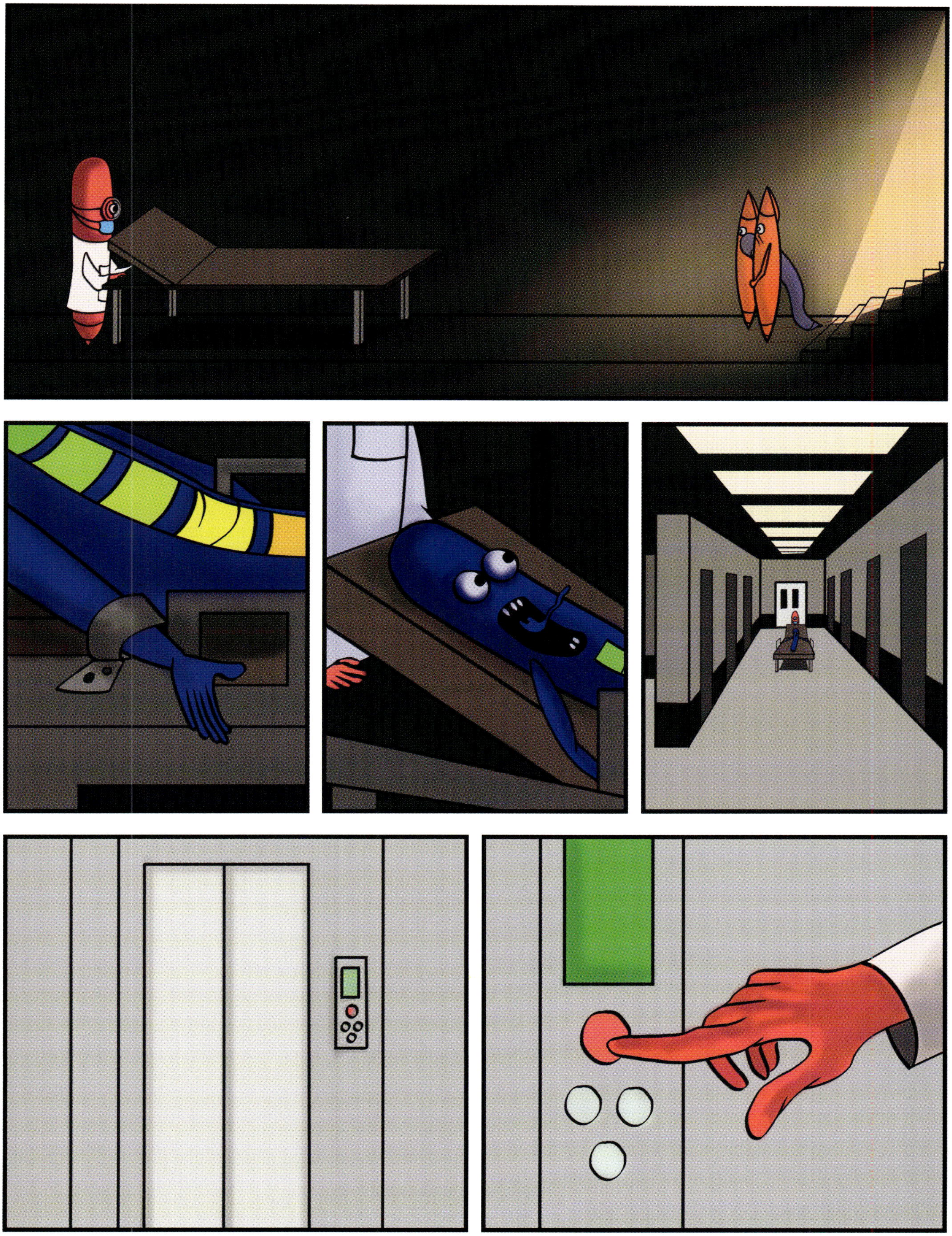

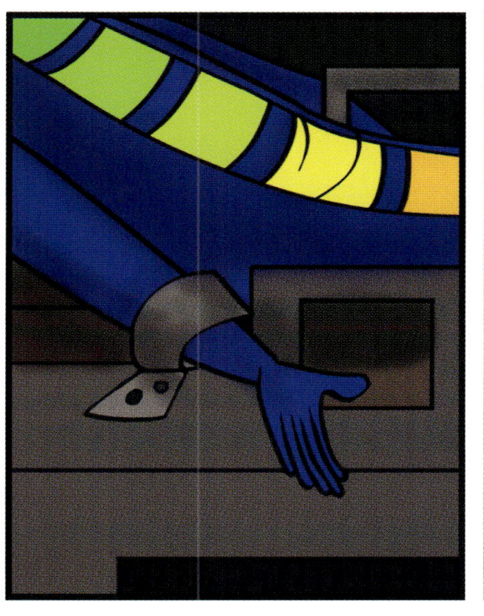
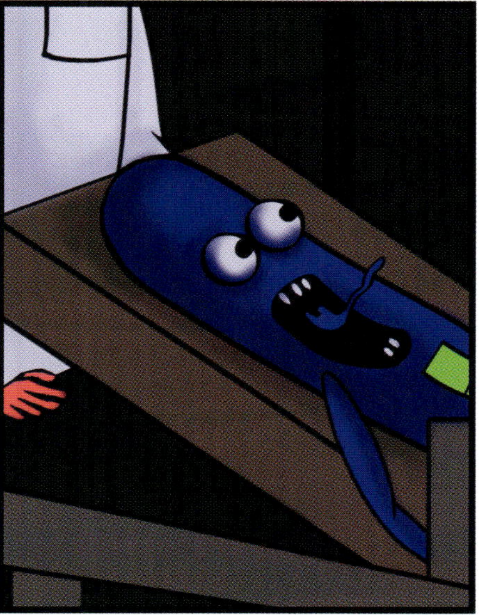
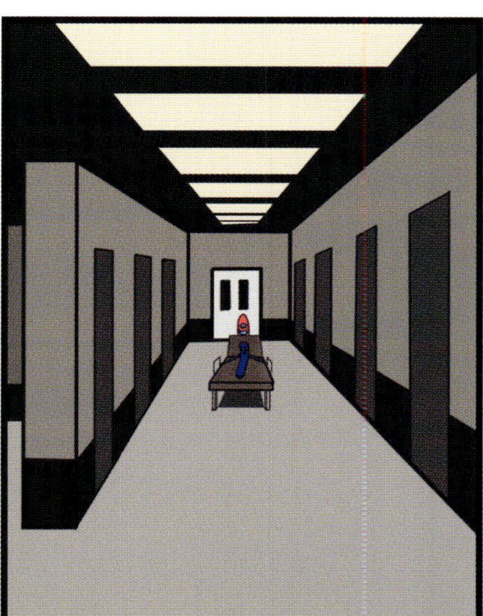
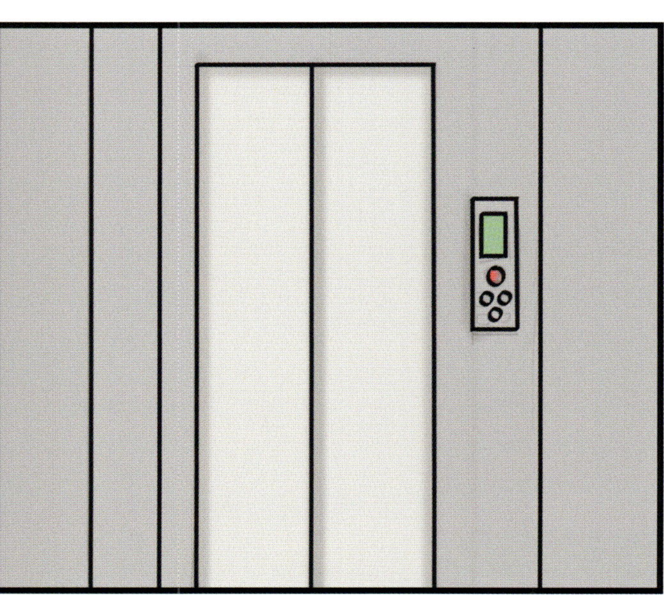
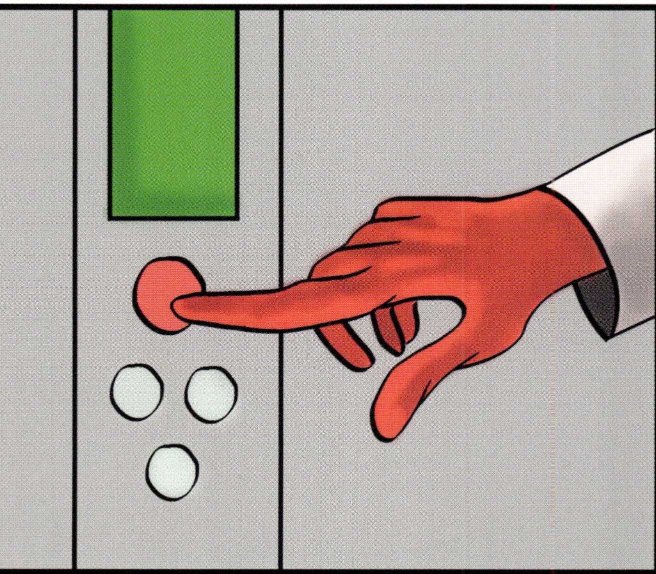

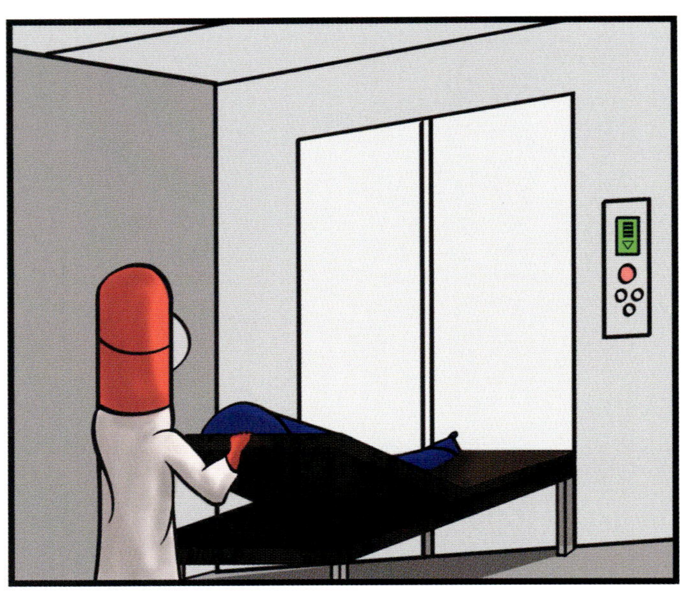
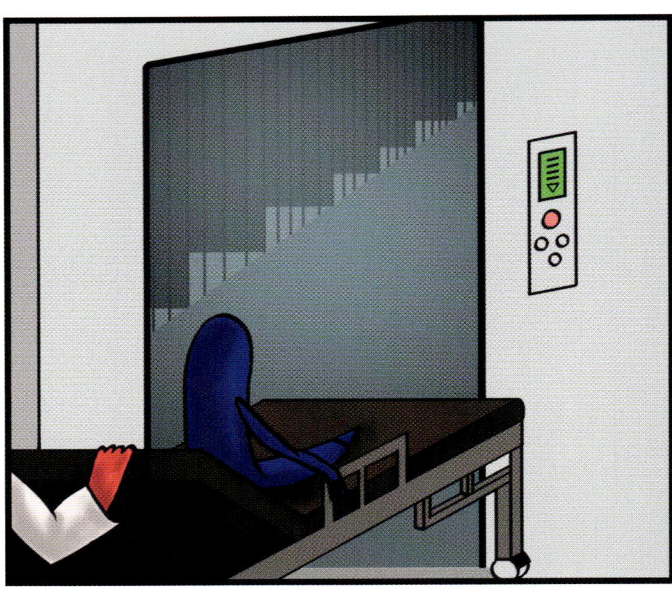
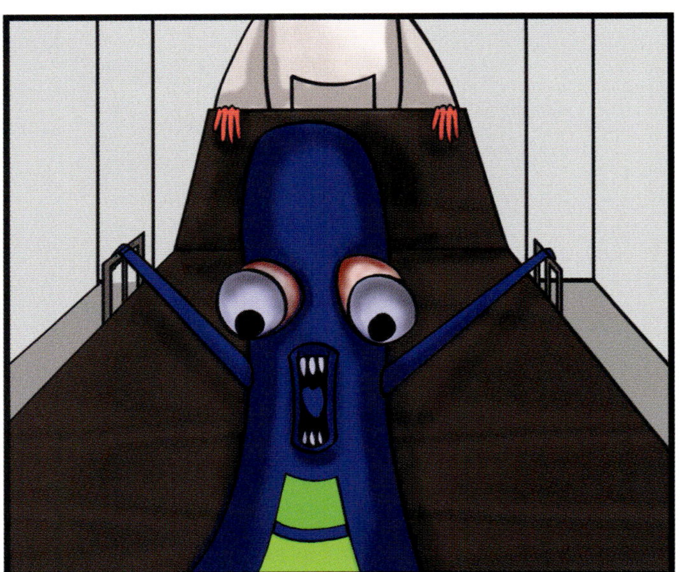
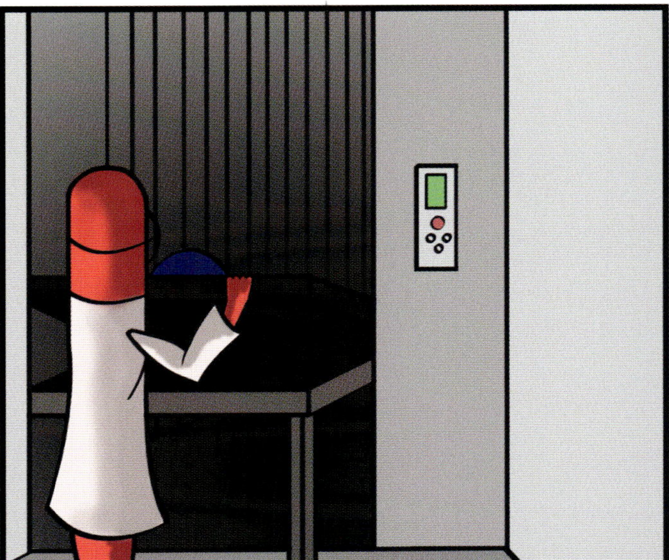
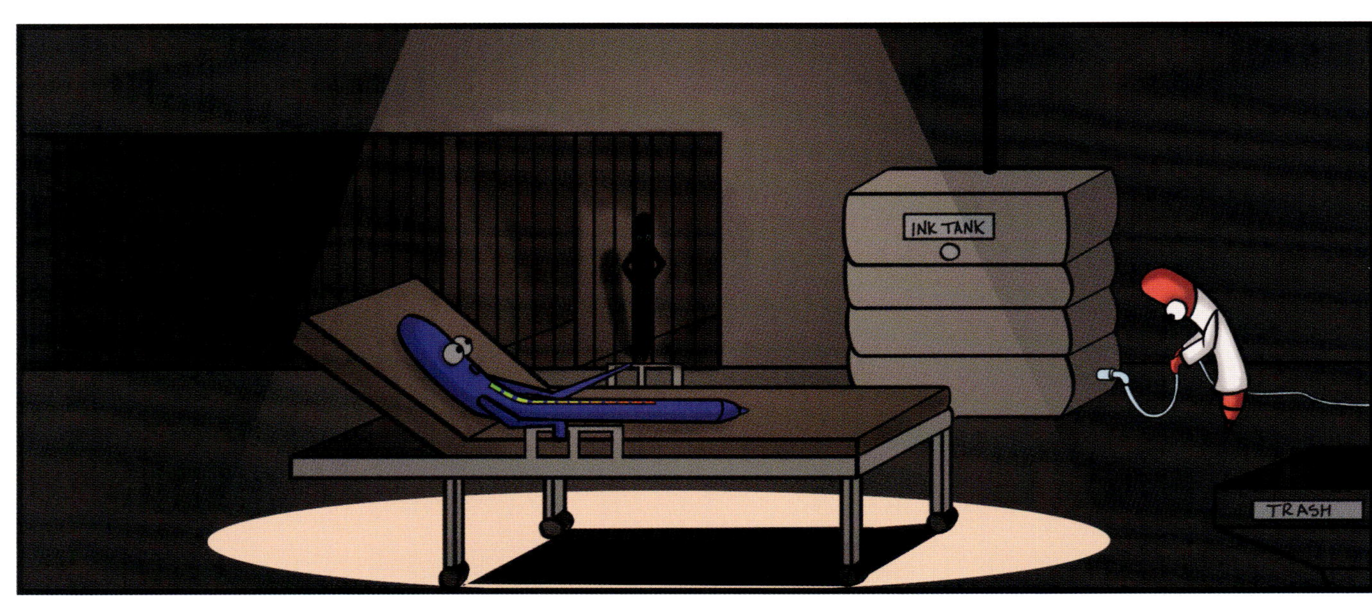
INK TANK
TRASH

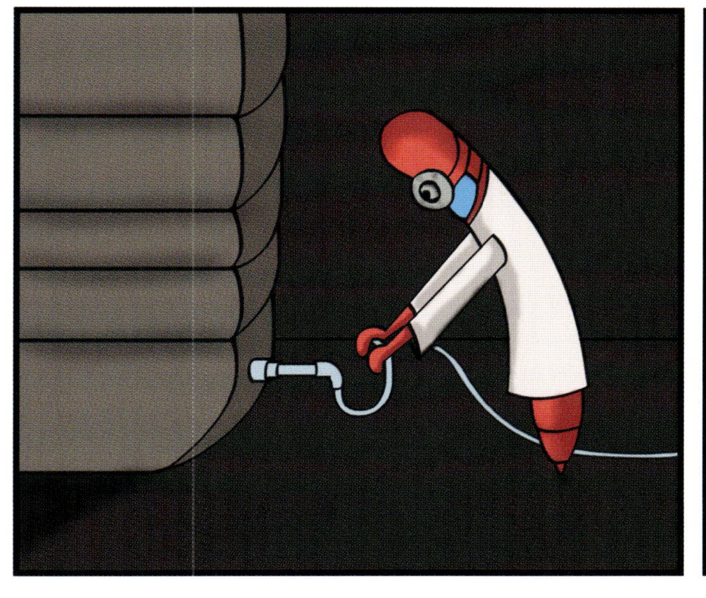

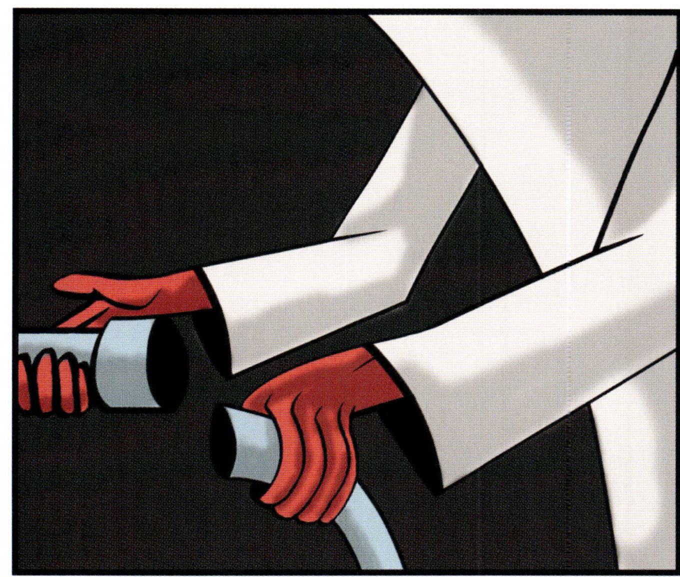

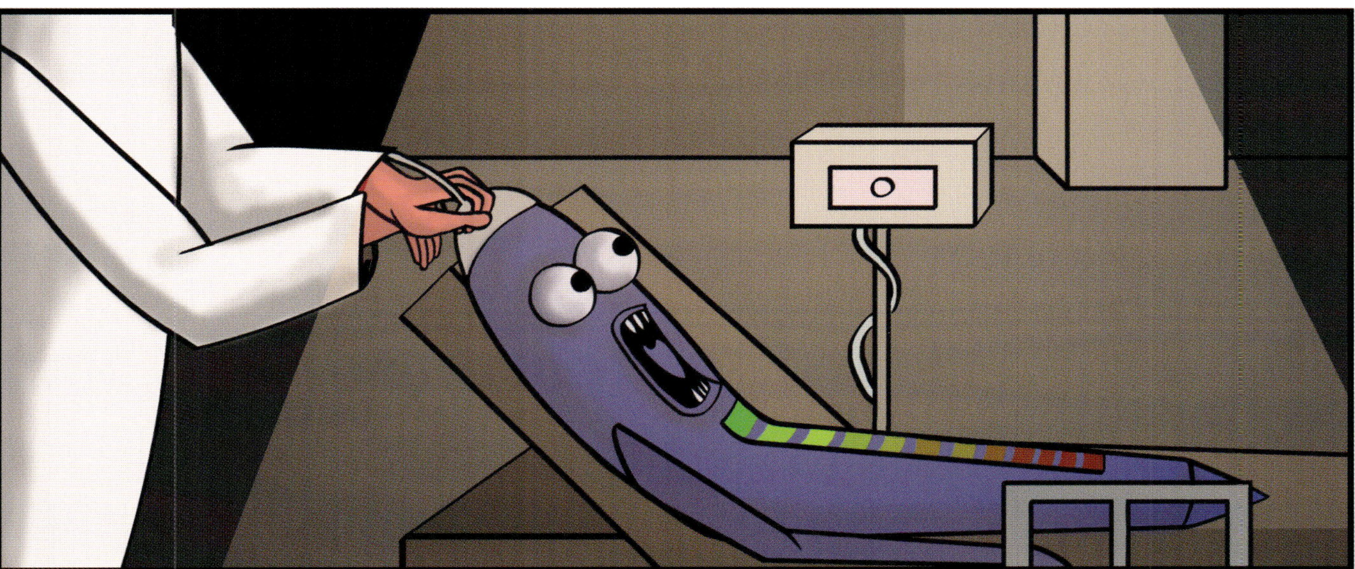

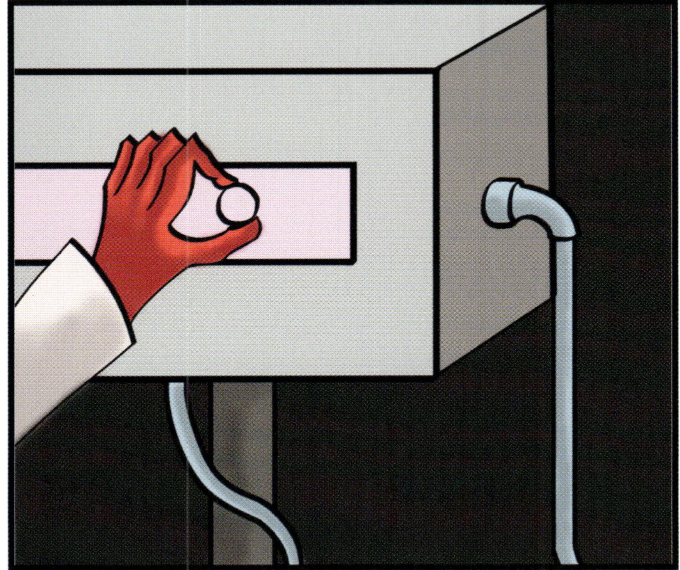

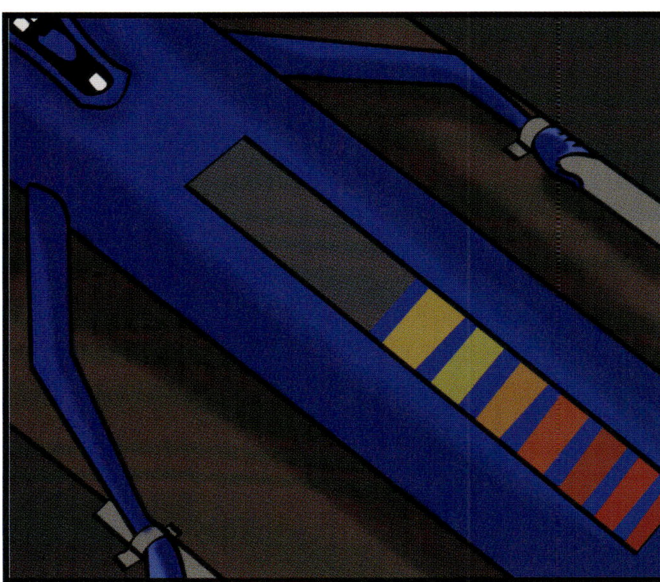

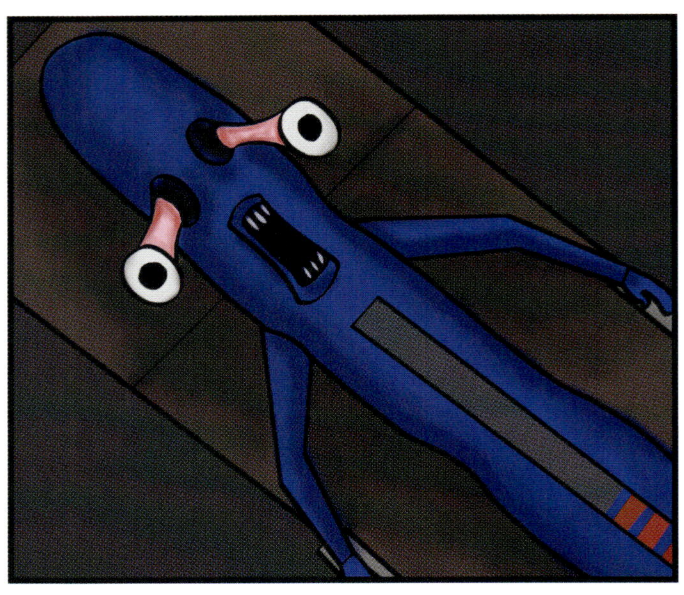

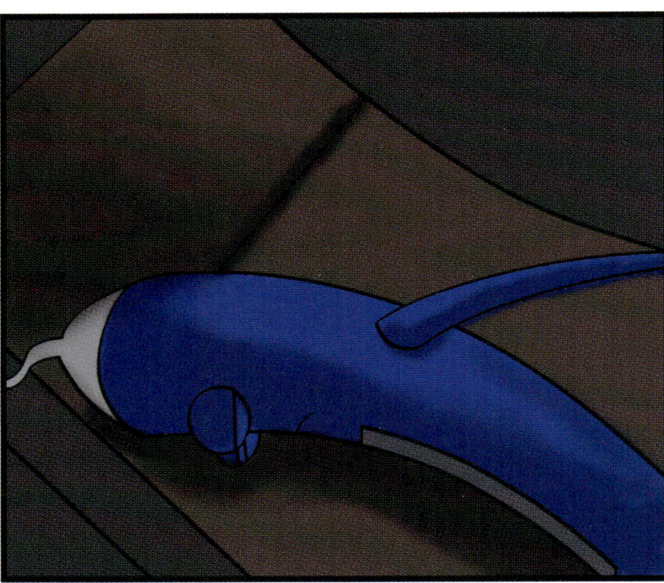

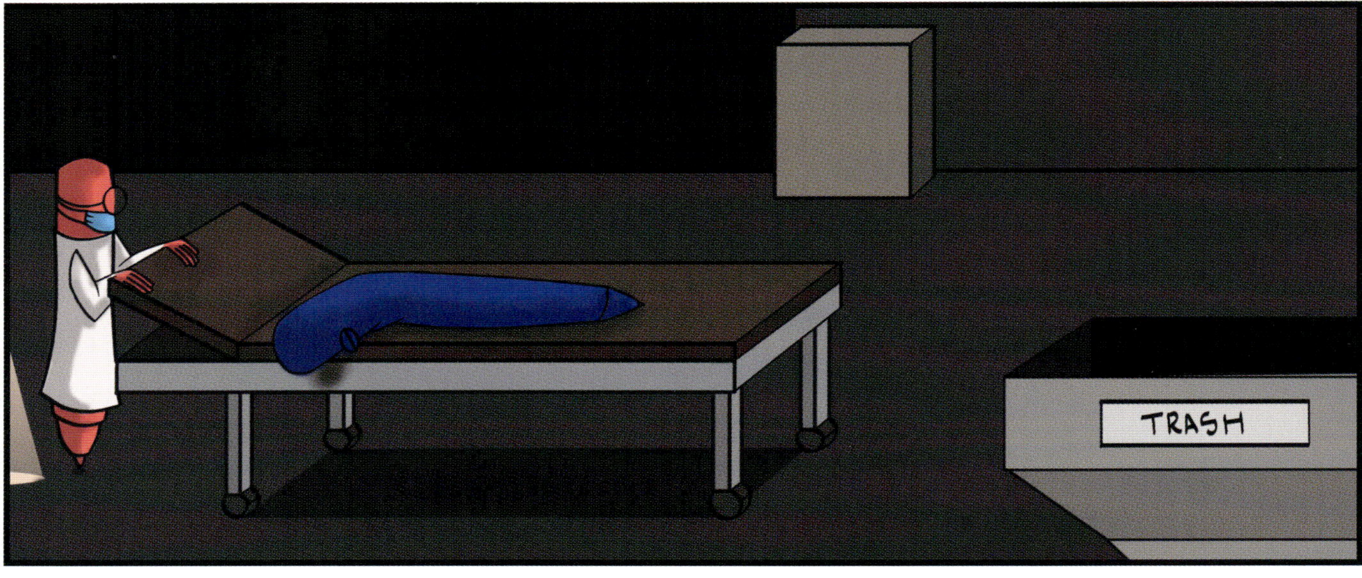
TRASH

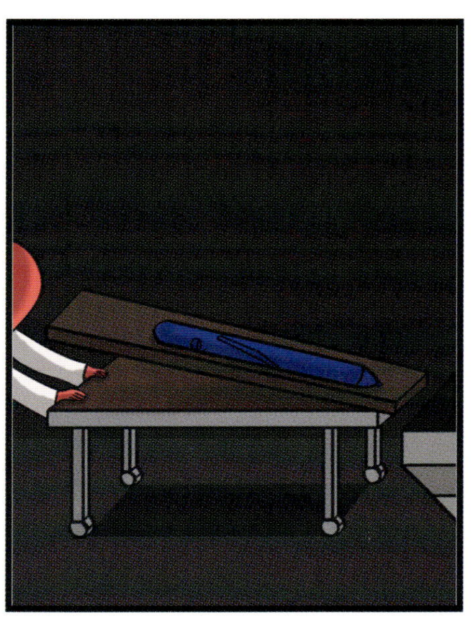

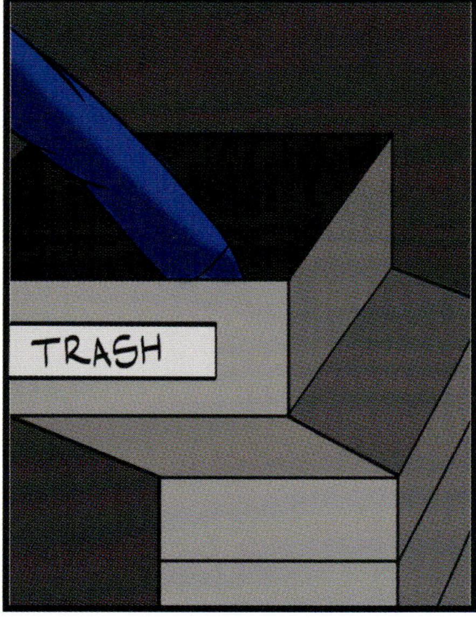
TRASH

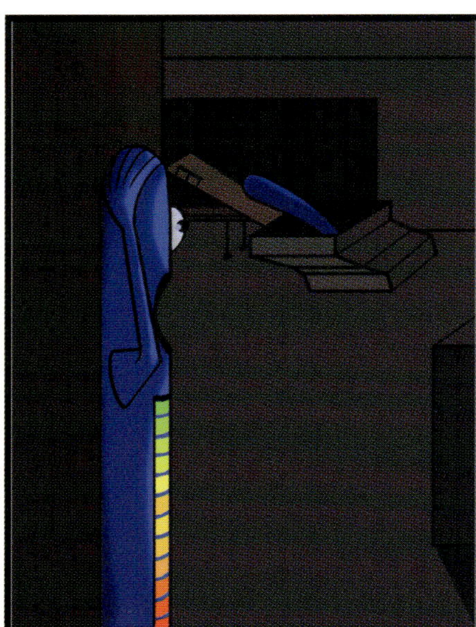

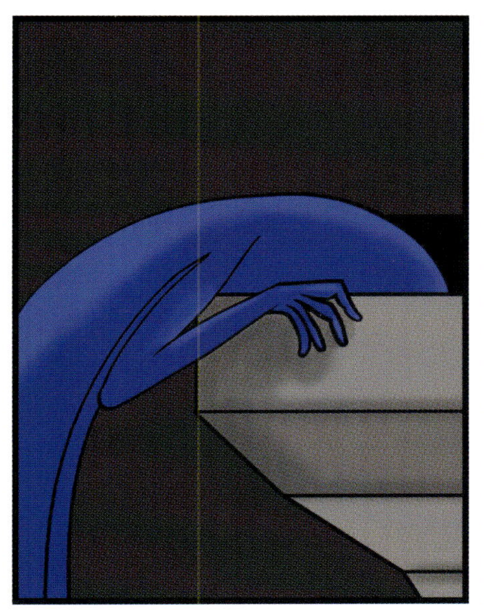
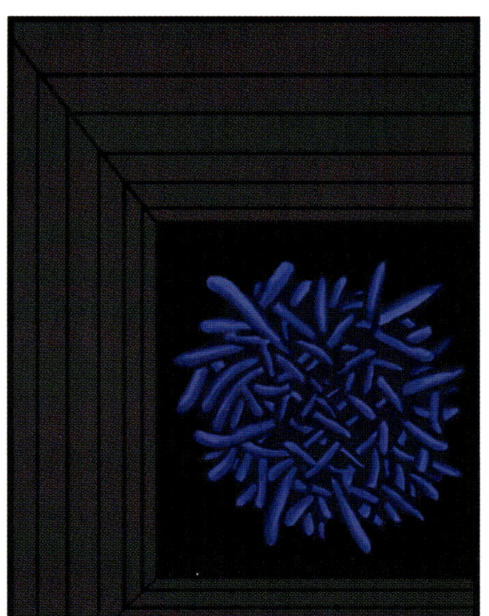
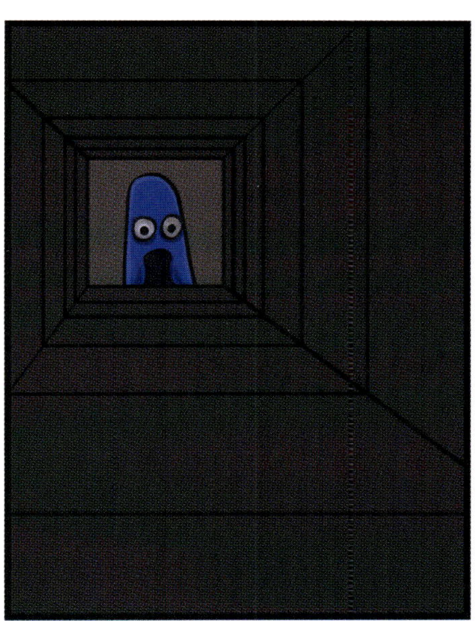
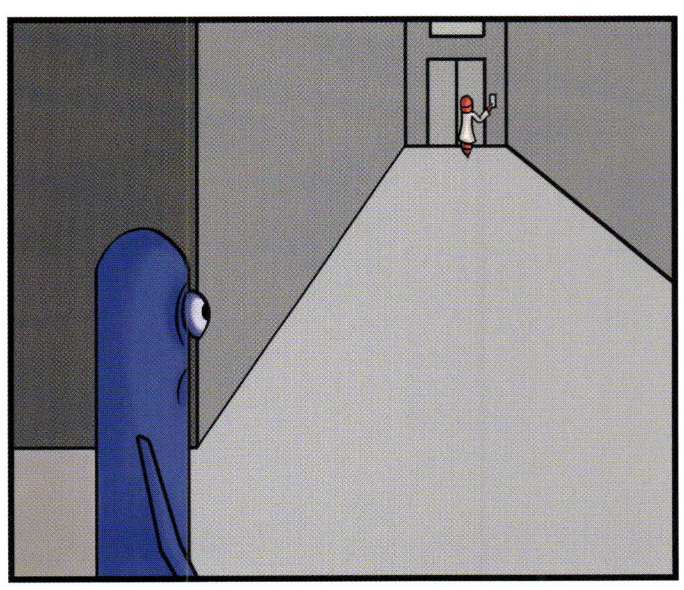
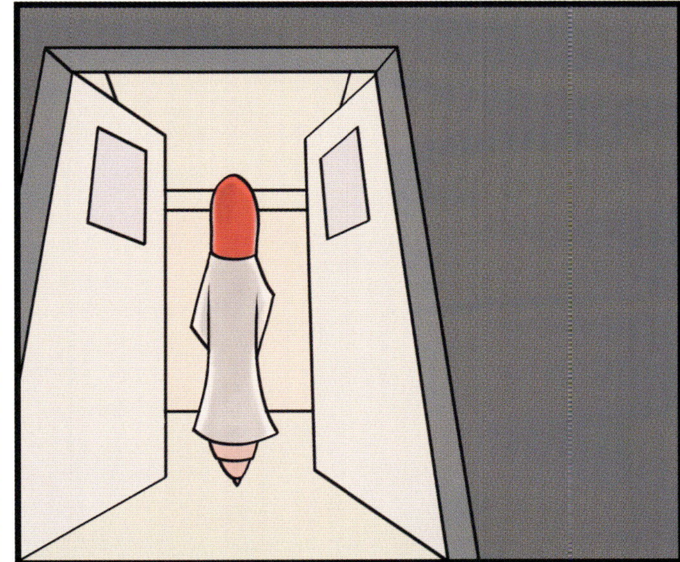
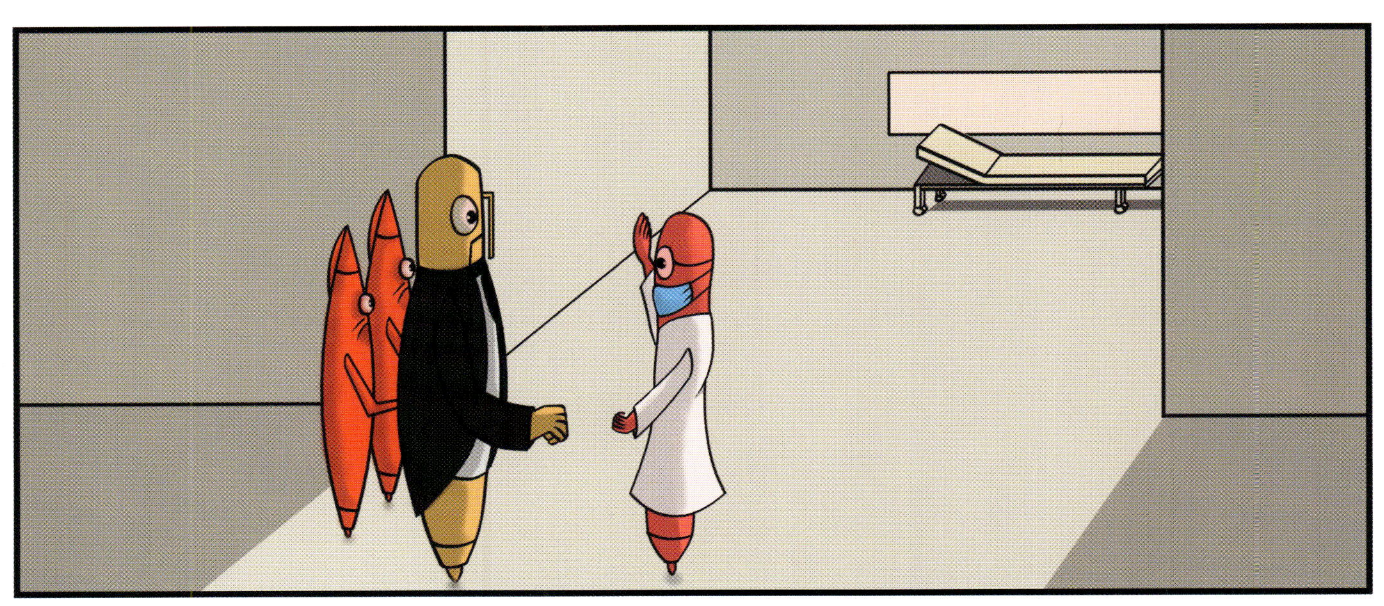

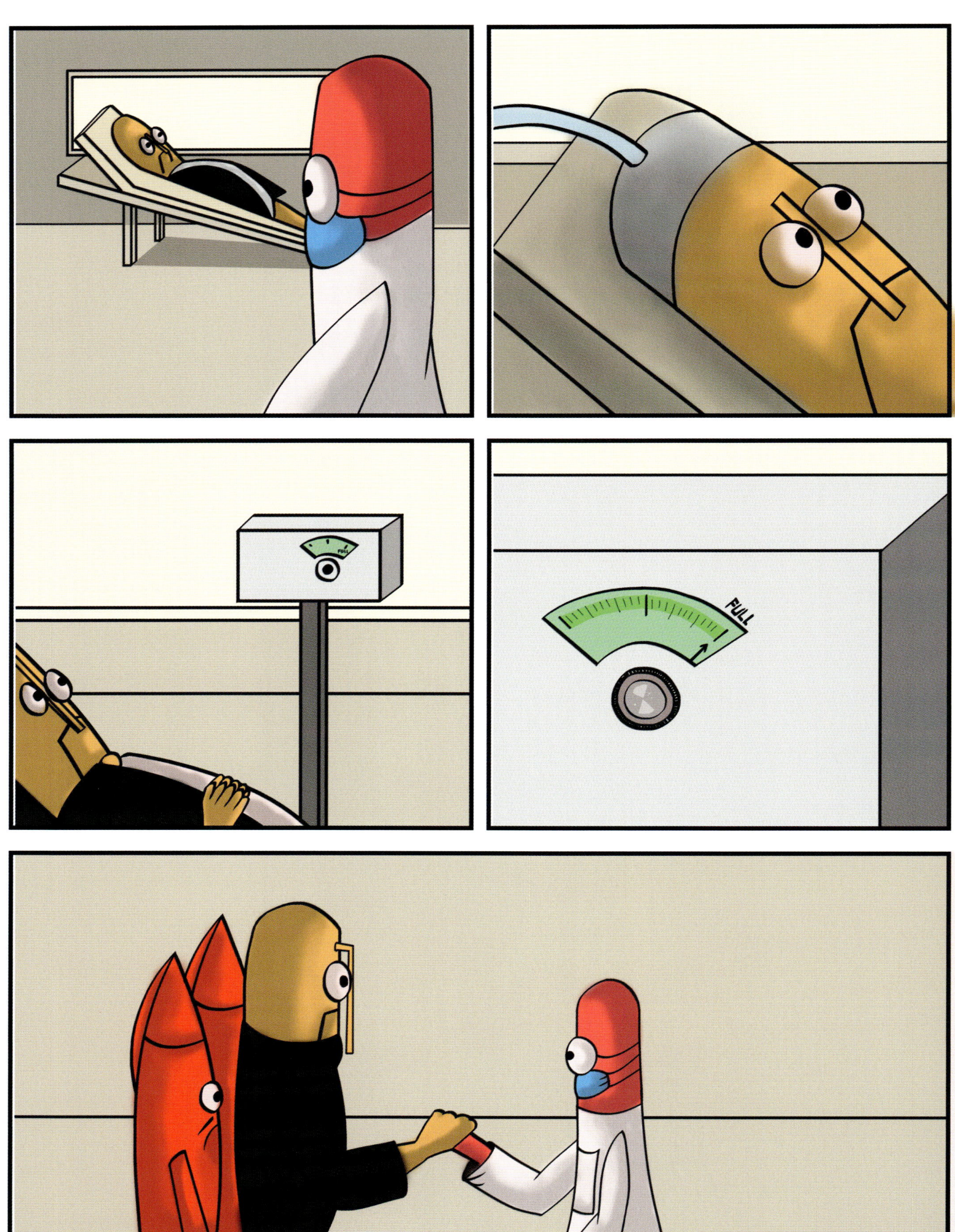
FULL

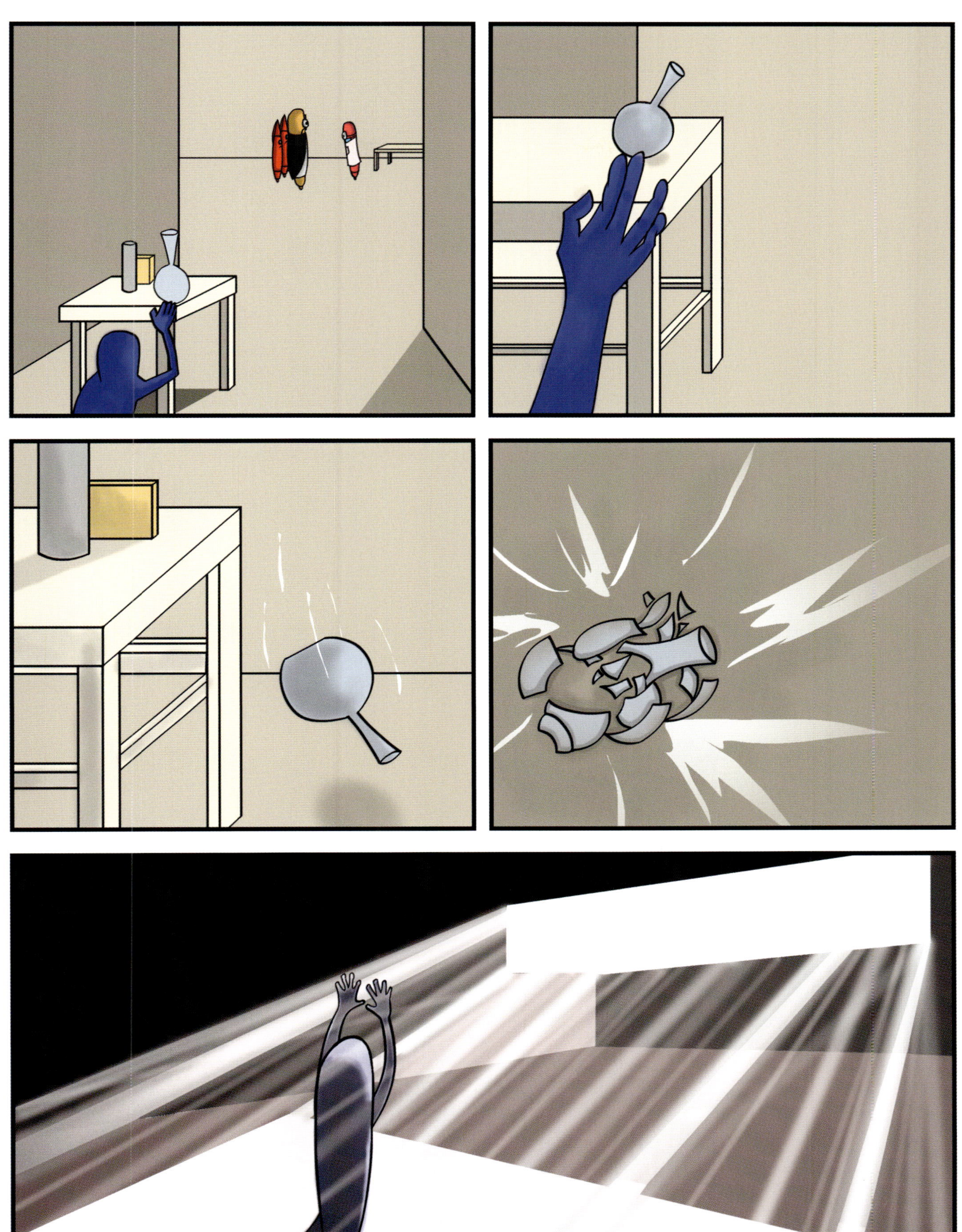

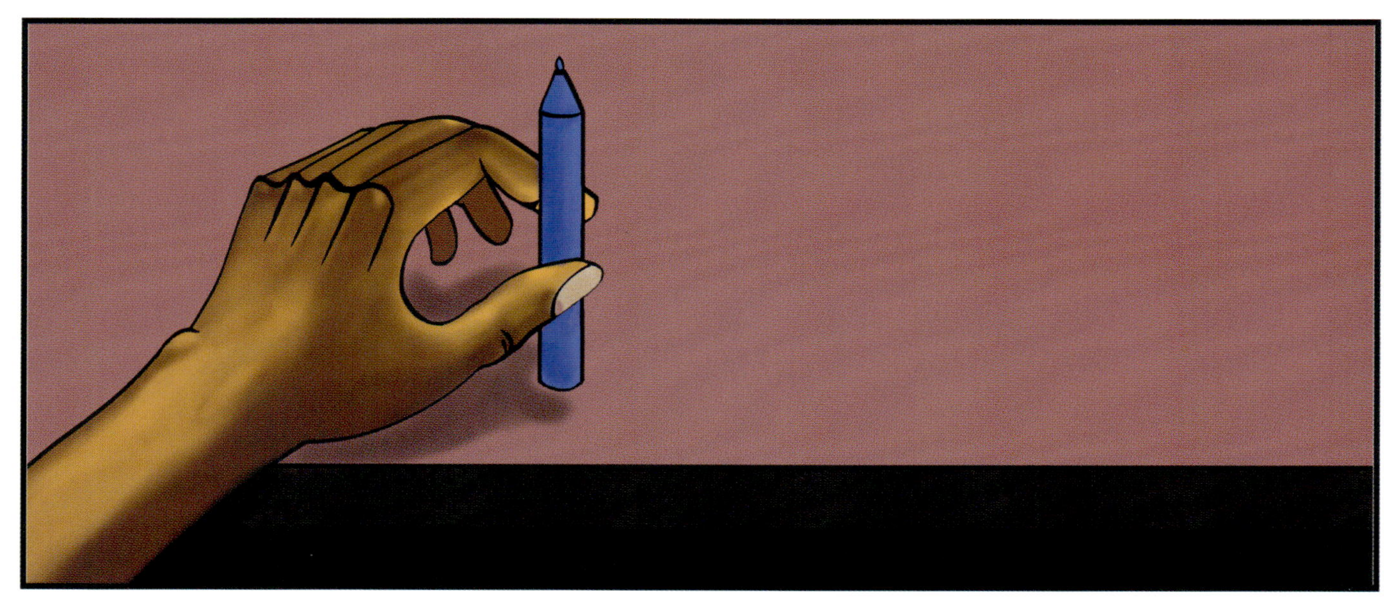

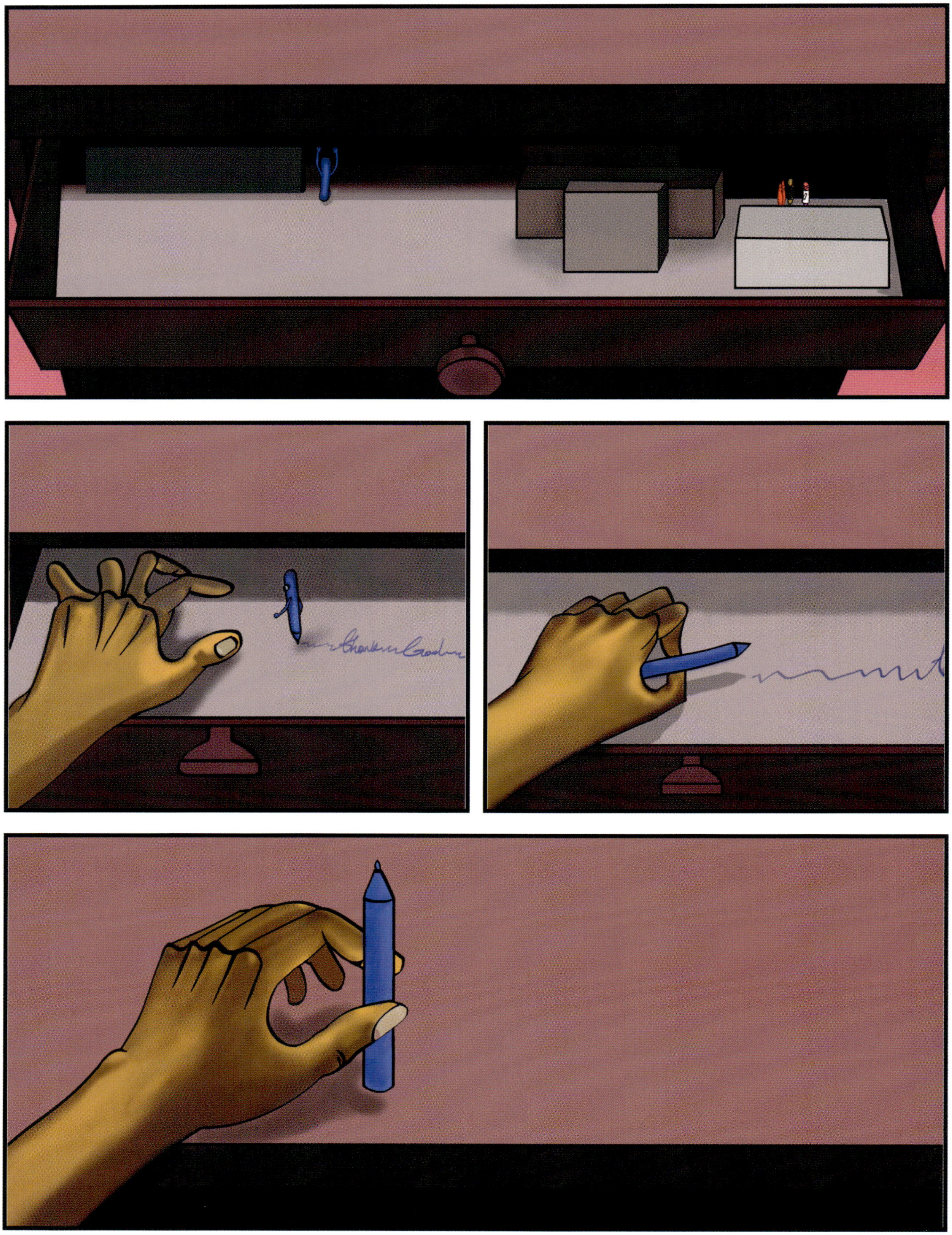

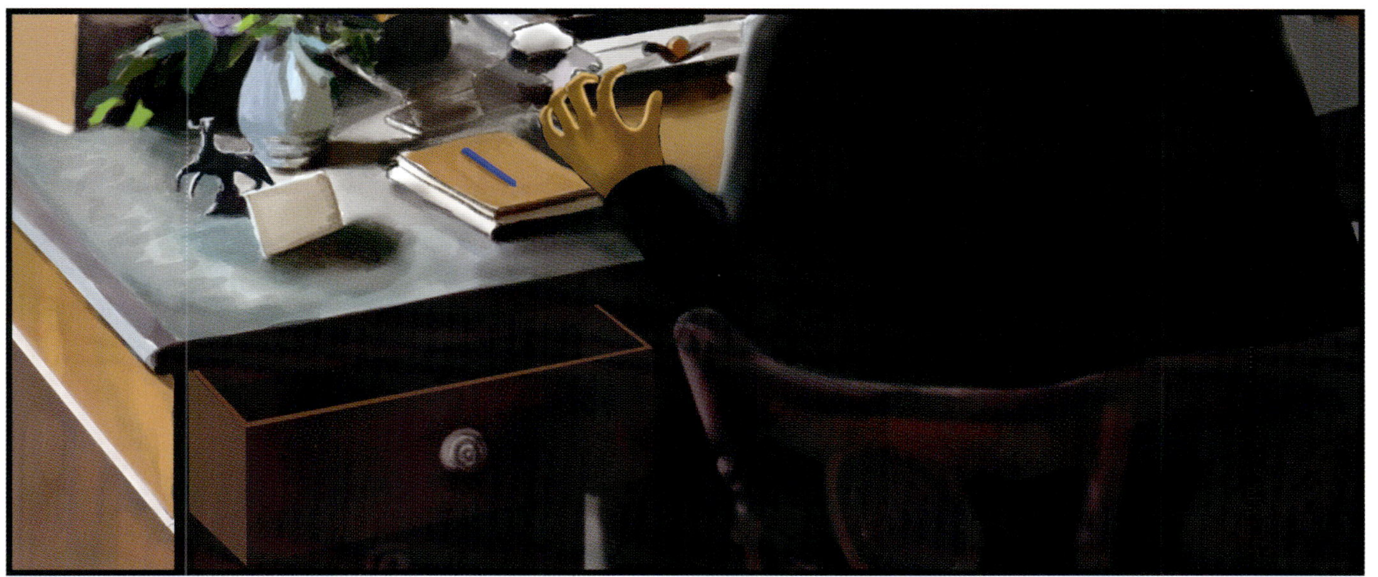

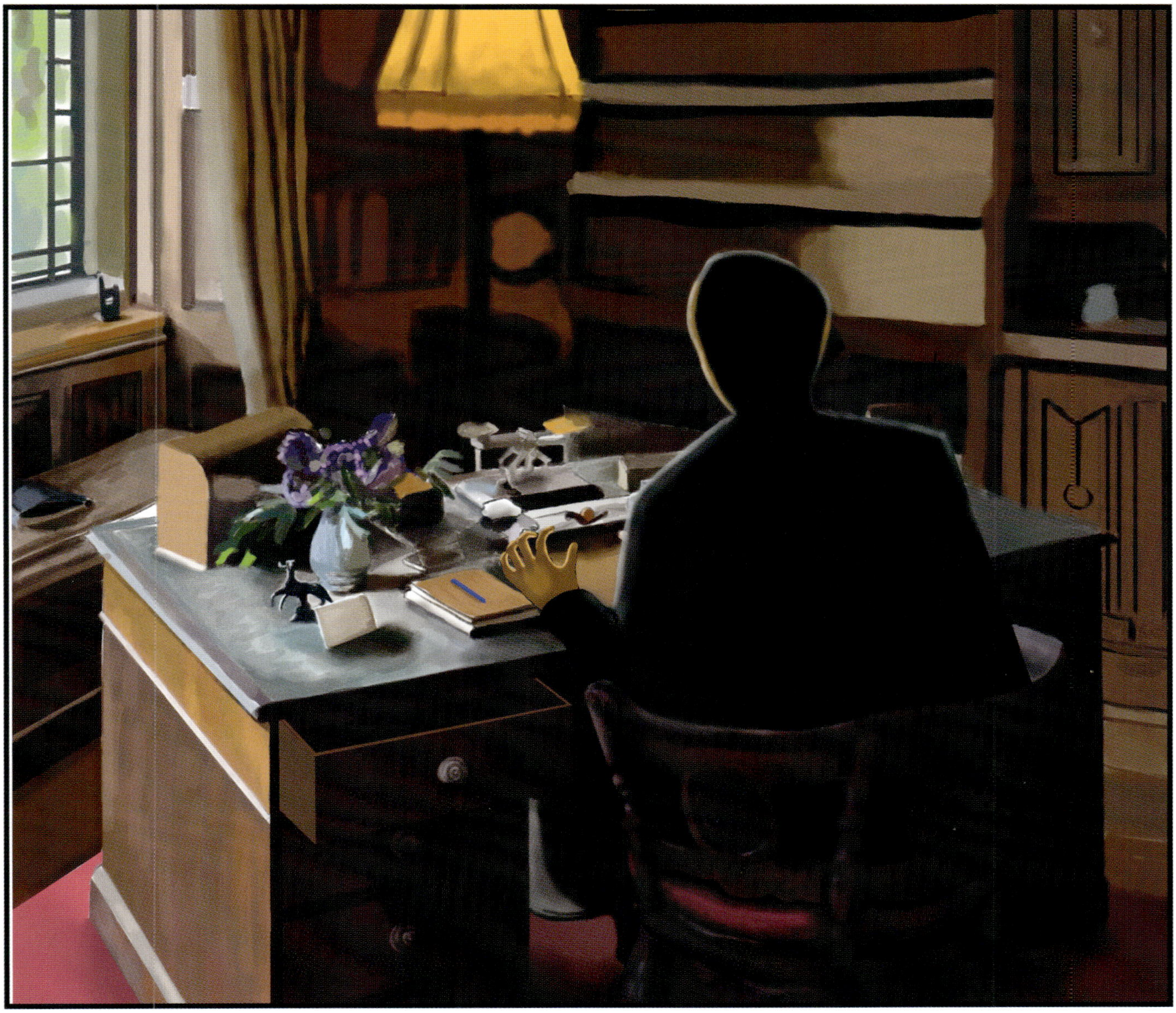

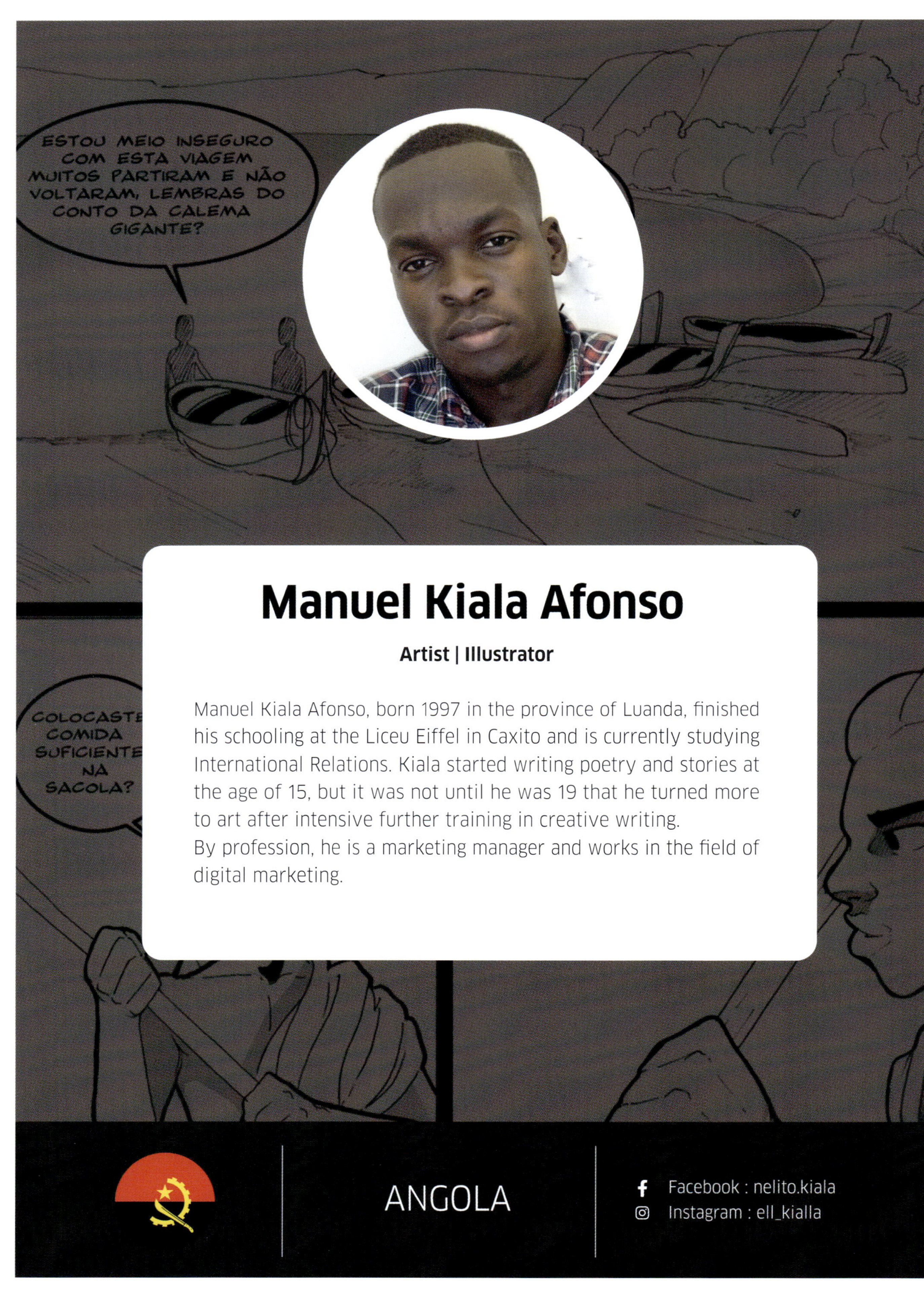

Manuel Kiala Afonso

Artist | Illustrator

Manuel Kiala Afonso, born 1997 in the province of Luanda, finished his schooling at the Liceu Eiffel in Caxito and is currently studying International Relations. Kiala started writing poetry and stories at the age of 15, but it was not until he was 19 that he turned more to art after intensive further training in creative writing.
By profession, he is a marketing manager and works in the field of digital marketing.

ANGOLA

Facebook : nelito.kiala
Instagram : ell_kialla

WE FOR OURSELVES

ART BY: Manuel Kiala Afonso

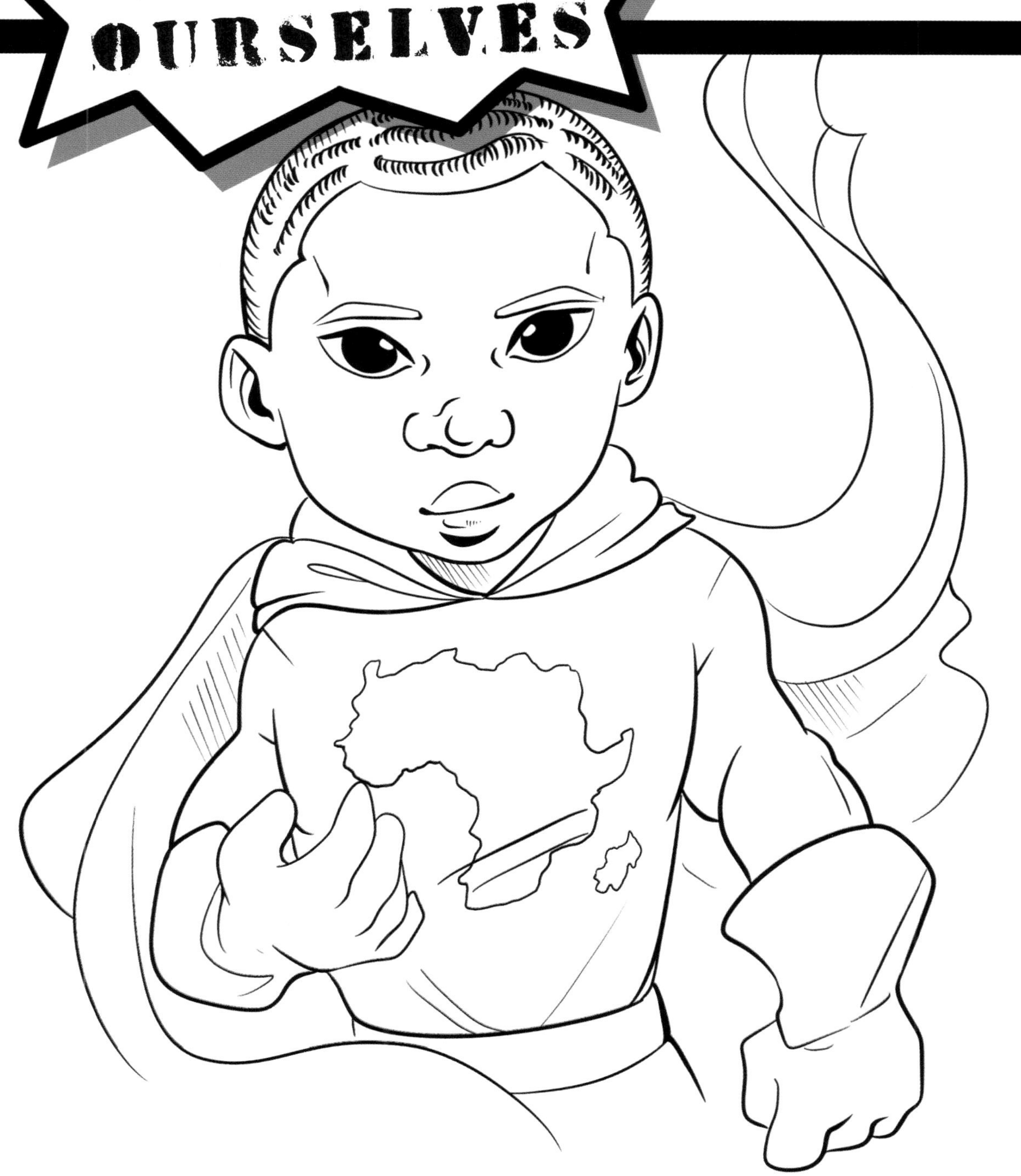

NO HERO WILL COME FROM AFAR TO SAVE
OUR CONTINENT IF NOT OURSELVES.

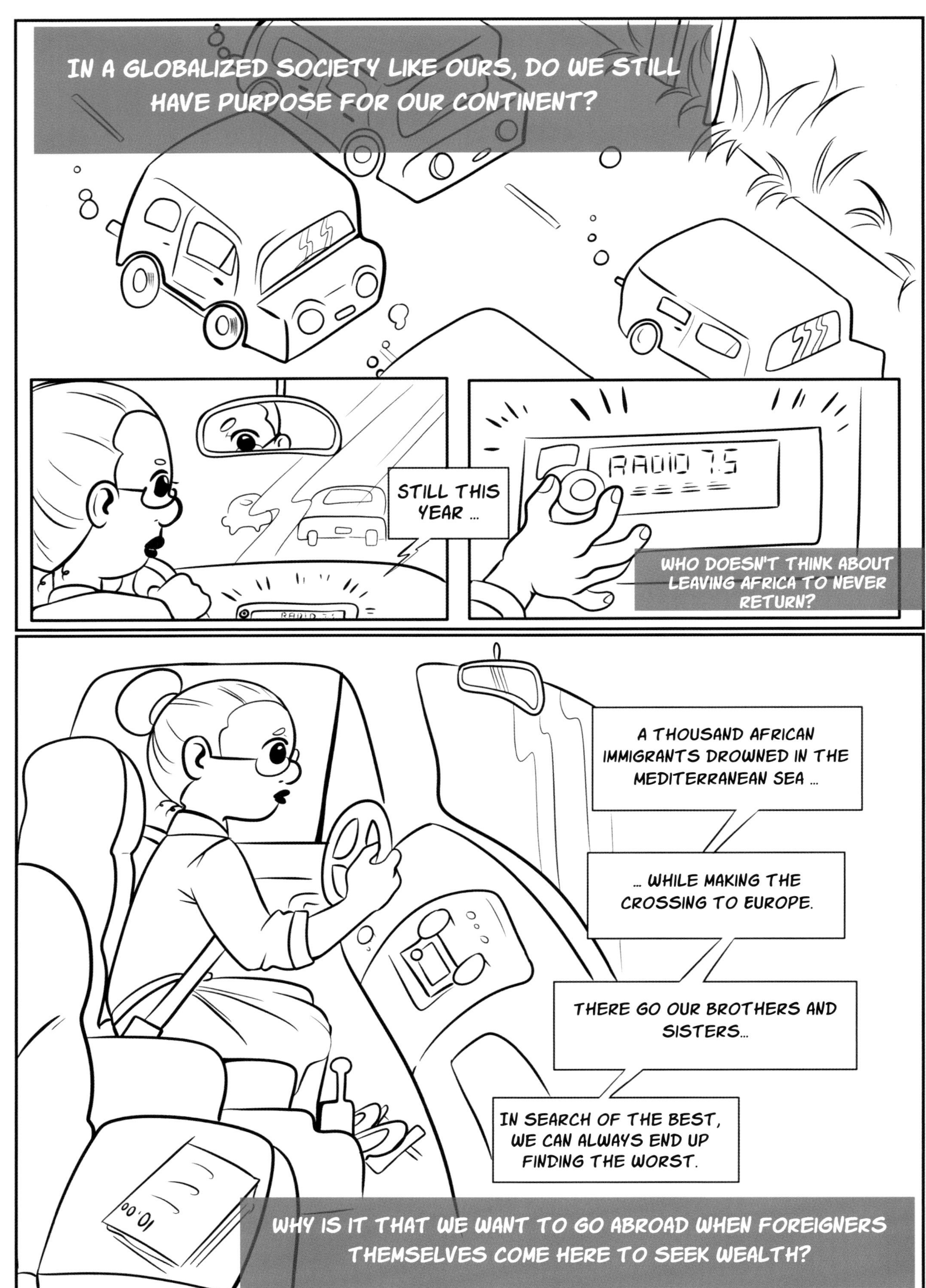
IN A GLOBALIZED SOCIETY LIKE OURS, DO WE STILL HAVE PURPOSE FOR OUR CONTINENT?
STILL THIS YEAR ...
RADIO 7.5
WHO DOESN'T THINK ABOUT LEAVING AFRICA TO NEVER RETURN?
A THOUSAND AFRICAN IMMIGRANTS DROWNED IN THE MEDITERRANEAN SEA ...
... WHILE MAKING THE CROSSING TO EUROPE.
THERE GO OUR BROTHERS AND SISTERS...
IN SEARCH OF THE BEST, WE CAN ALWAYS END UP FINDING THE WORST.
10.00
WHY IS IT THAT WE WANT TO GO ABROAD WHEN FOREIGNERS THEMSELVES COME HERE TO SEEK WEALTH?

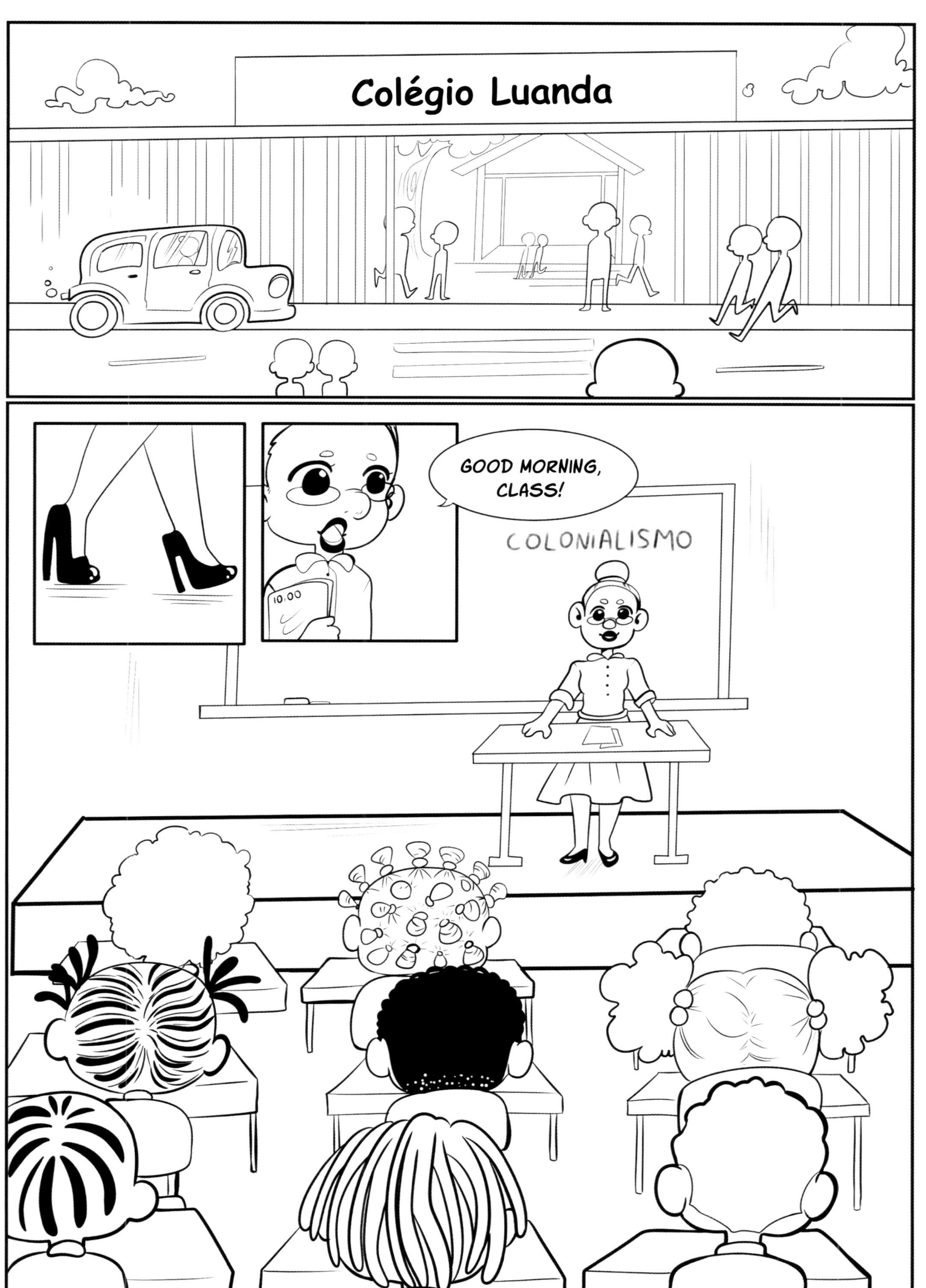
Colégio Luanda
10:00
GOOD MORNING, CLASS!
COLONIALISMO

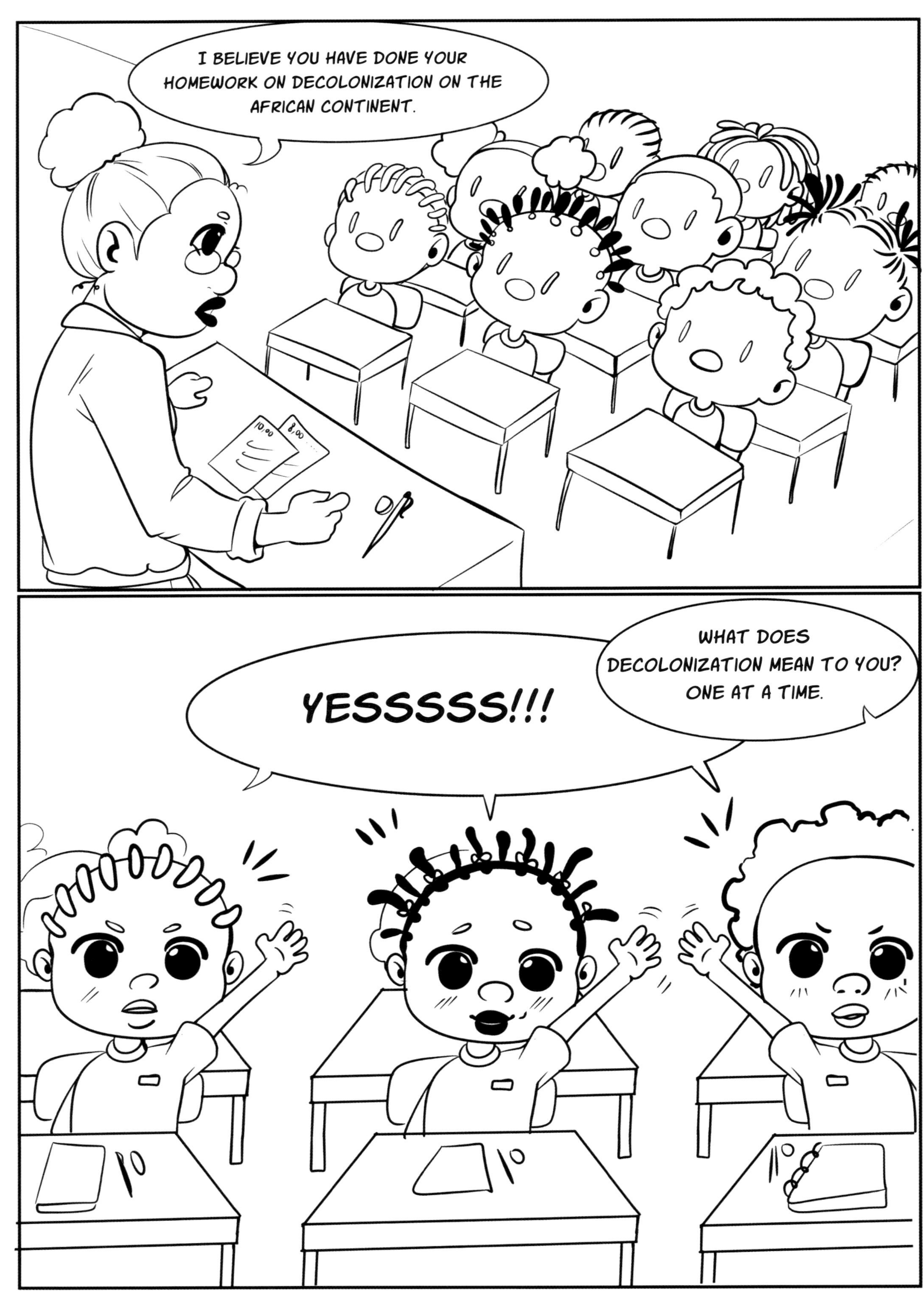
I BELIEVE YOU HAVE DONE YOUR HOMEWORK ON DECOLONIZATION ON THE AFRICAN CONTINENT.
YESSSSS!!!
WHAT DOES DECOLONIZATION MEAN TO YOU? ONE AT A TIME.

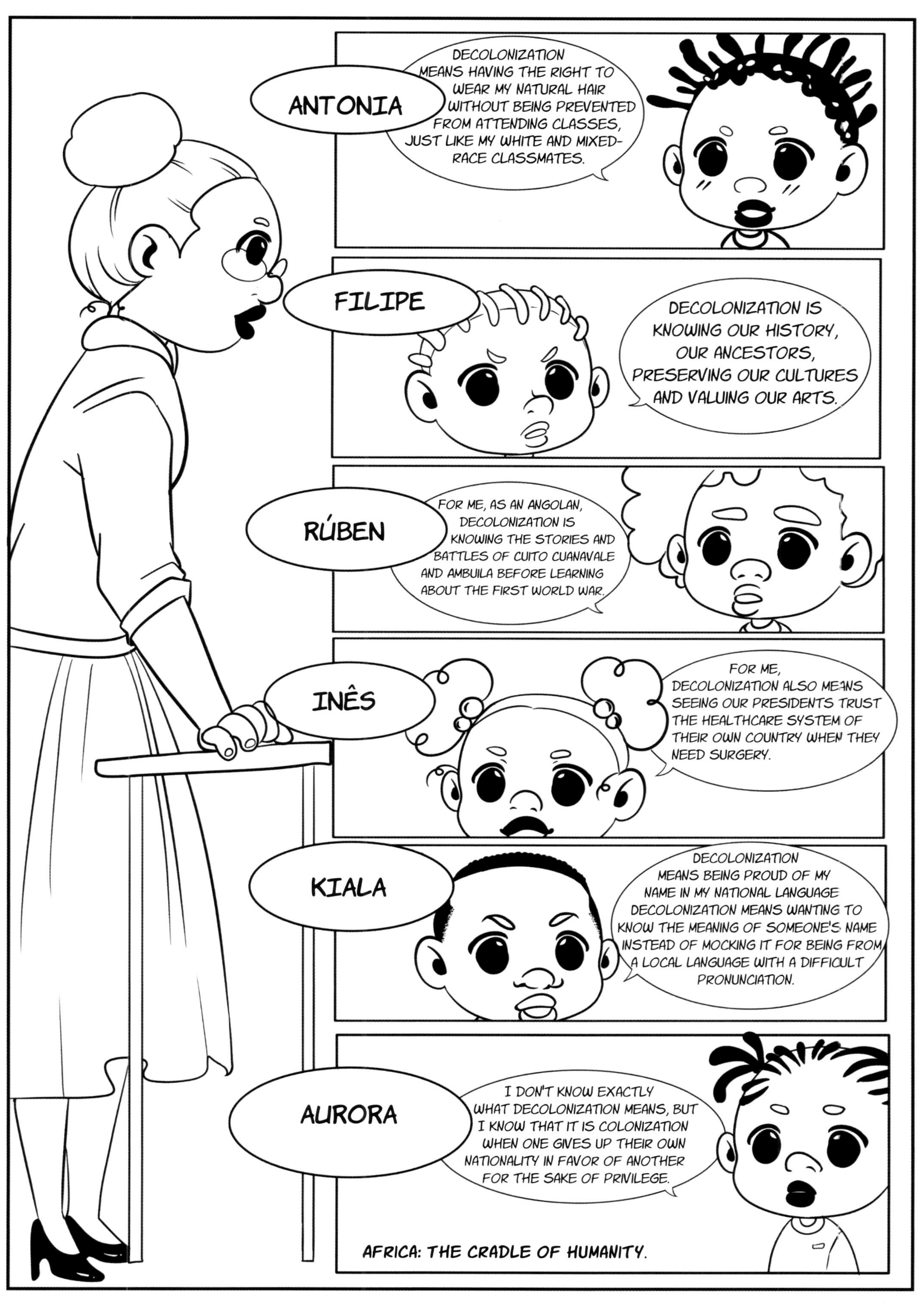
ANTONIA
DECOLONIZATION MEANS HAVING THE RIGHT TO WEAR MY NATURAL HAIR WITHOUT BEING PREVENTED FROM ATTENDING CLASSES, JUST LIKE MY WHITE AND MIXED-RACE CLASSMATES.
FILIPE
DECOLONIZATION IS KNOWING OUR HISTORY, OUR ANCESTORS, PRESERVING OUR CULTURES AND VALUING OUR ARTS.
RÚBEN
FOR ME, AS AN ANGOLAN, DECOLONIZATION IS KNOWING THE STORIES AND BATTLES OF CUITO CUANAVALE AND AMBUILA BEFORE LEARNING ABOUT THE FIRST WORLD WAR.
INÊS
FOR ME, DECOLONIZATION ALSO MEANS SEEING OUR PRESIDENTS TRUST THE HEALTHCARE SYSTEM OF THEIR OWN COUNTRY WHEN THEY NEED SURGERY.
KIALA
DECOLONIZATION MEANS BEING PROUD OF MY NAME IN MY NATIONAL LANGUAGE DECOLONIZATION MEANS WANTING TO KNOW THE MEANING OF SOMEONE'S NAME INSTEAD OF MOCKING IT FOR BEING FROM A LOCAL LANGUAGE WITH A DIFFICULT PRONUNCIATION.
AURORA
I DON'T KNOW EXACTLY WHAT DECOLONIZATION MEANS, BUT I KNOW THAT IT IS COLONIZATION WHEN ONE GIVES UP THEIR OWN NATIONALITY IN FAVOR OF ANOTHER FOR THE SAKE OF PRIVILEGE.
AFRICA: THE CRADLE OF HUMANITY.

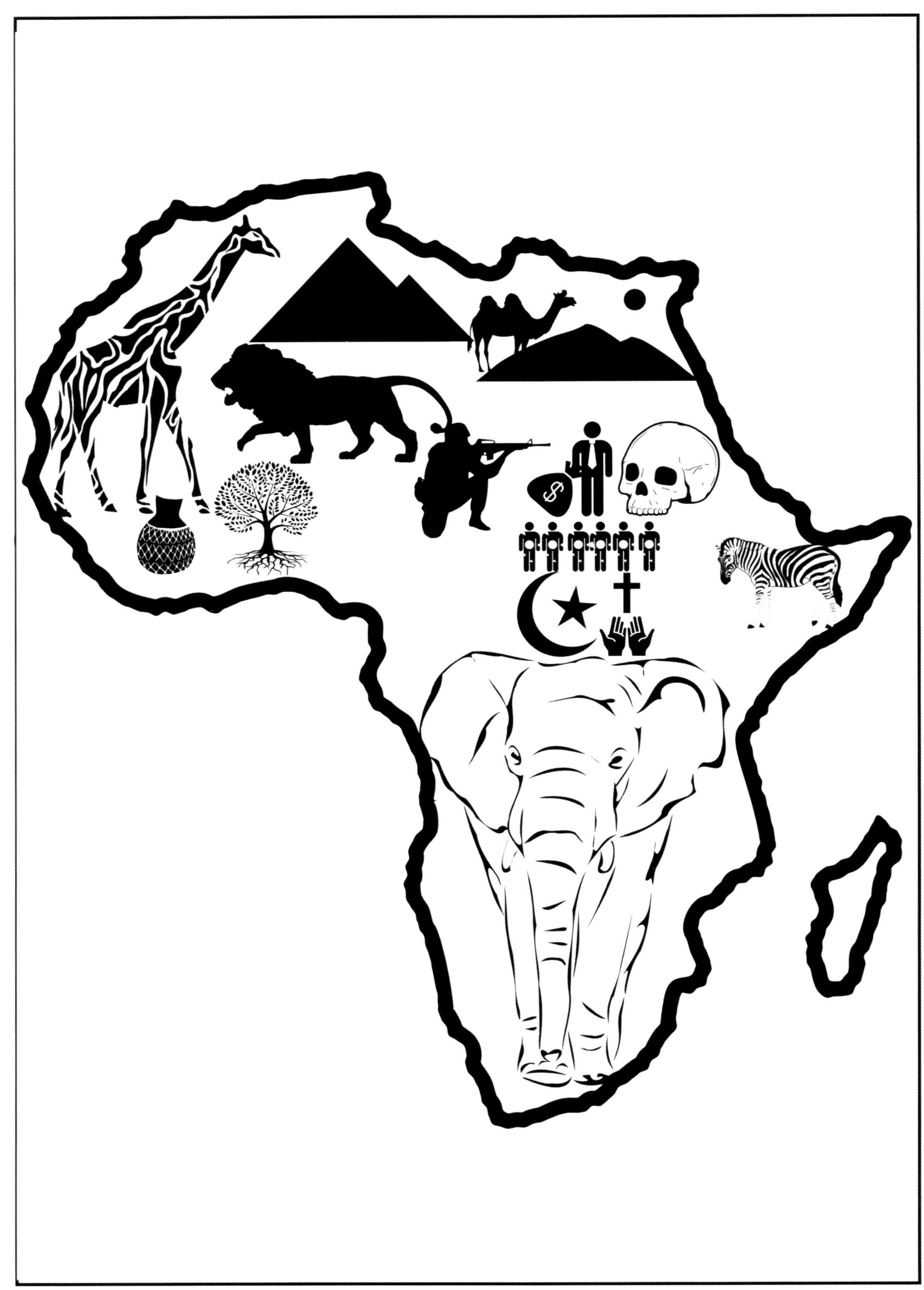

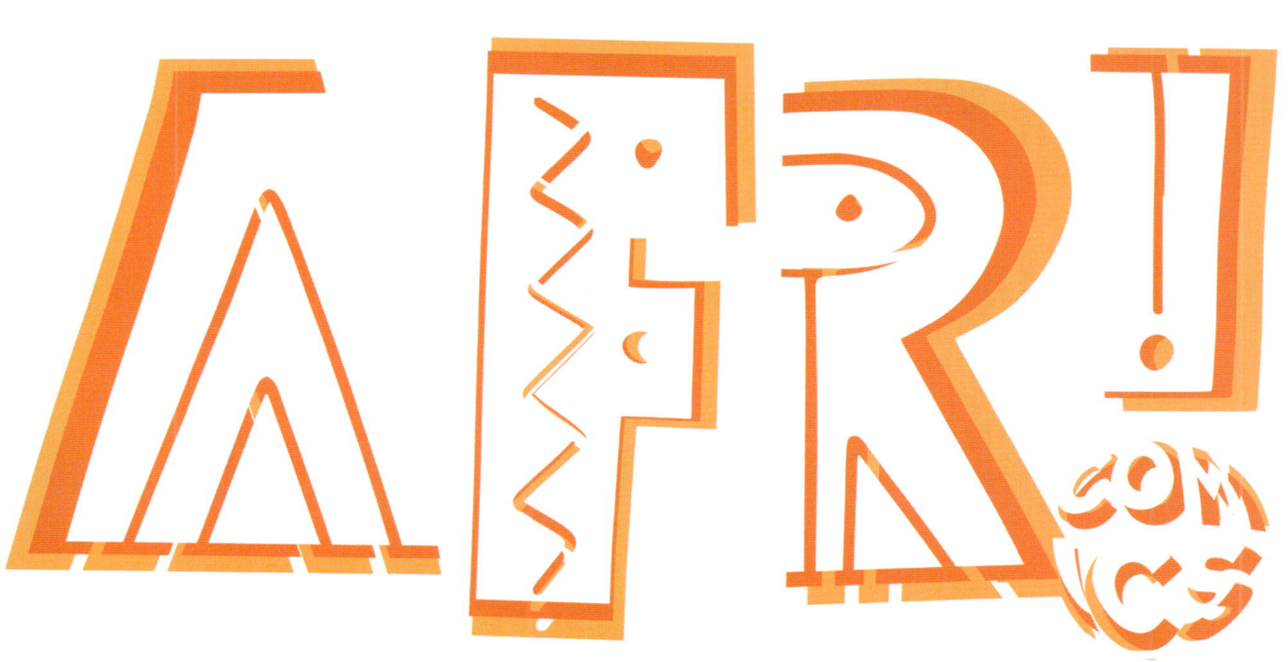
AFRI
COMICS

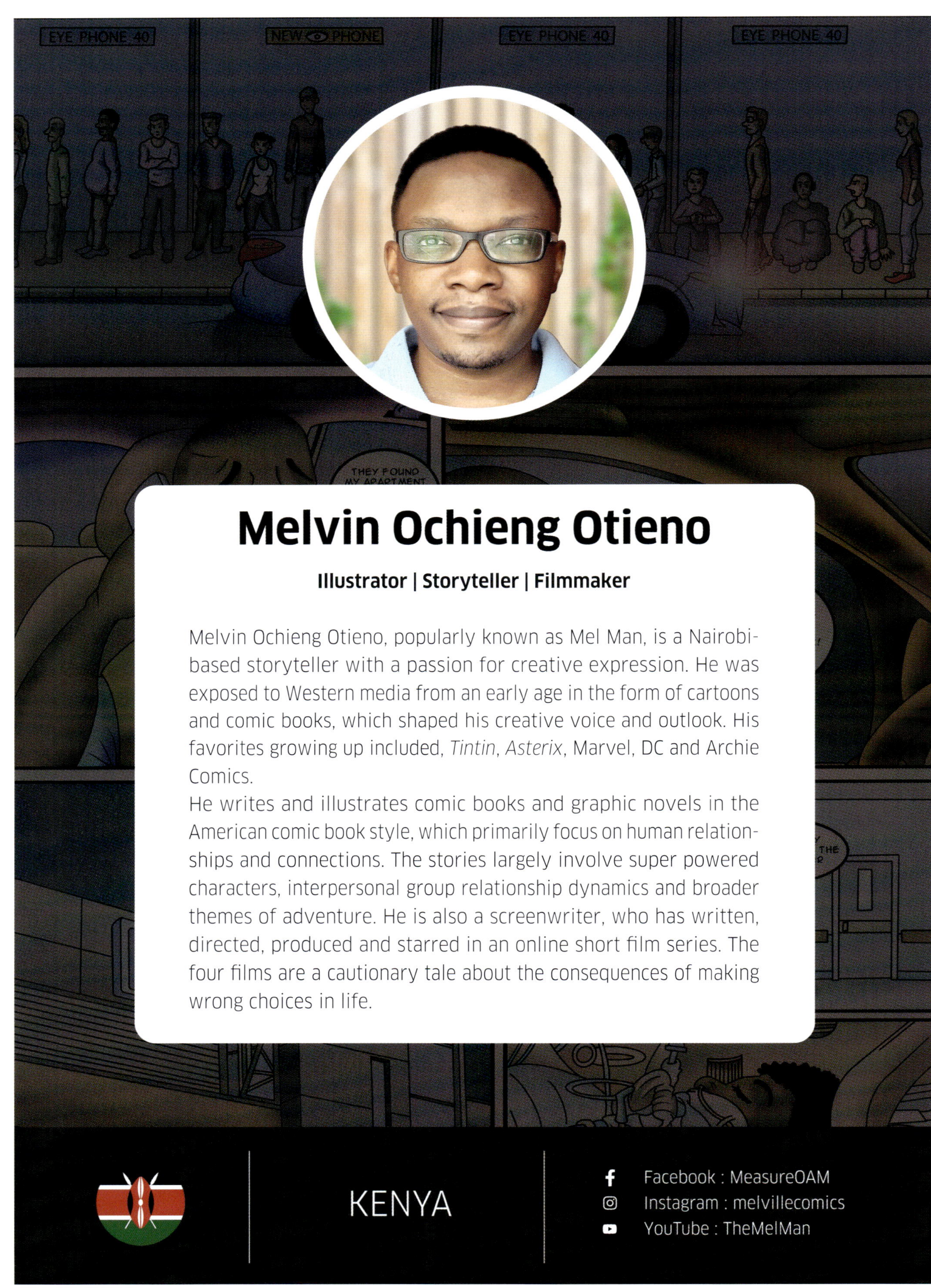

Melvin Ochieng Otieno

Illustrator | Storyteller | Filmmaker

Melvin Ochieng Otieno, popularly known as Mel Man, is a Nairobi-based storyteller with a passion for creative expression. He was exposed to Western media from an early age in the form of cartoons and comic books, which shaped his creative voice and outlook. His favorites growing up included, *Tintin*, *Asterix*, Marvel, DC and Archie Comics.

He writes and illustrates comic books and graphic novels in the American comic book style, which primarily focus on human relationships and connections. The stories largely involve super powered characters, interpersonal group relationship dynamics and broader themes of adventure. He is also a screenwriter, who has written, directed, produced and starred in an online short film series. The four films are a cautionary tale about the consequences of making wrong choices in life.

KENYA

Facebook : MeasureOAM
Instagram : melvillecomics
YouTube : TheMelMan

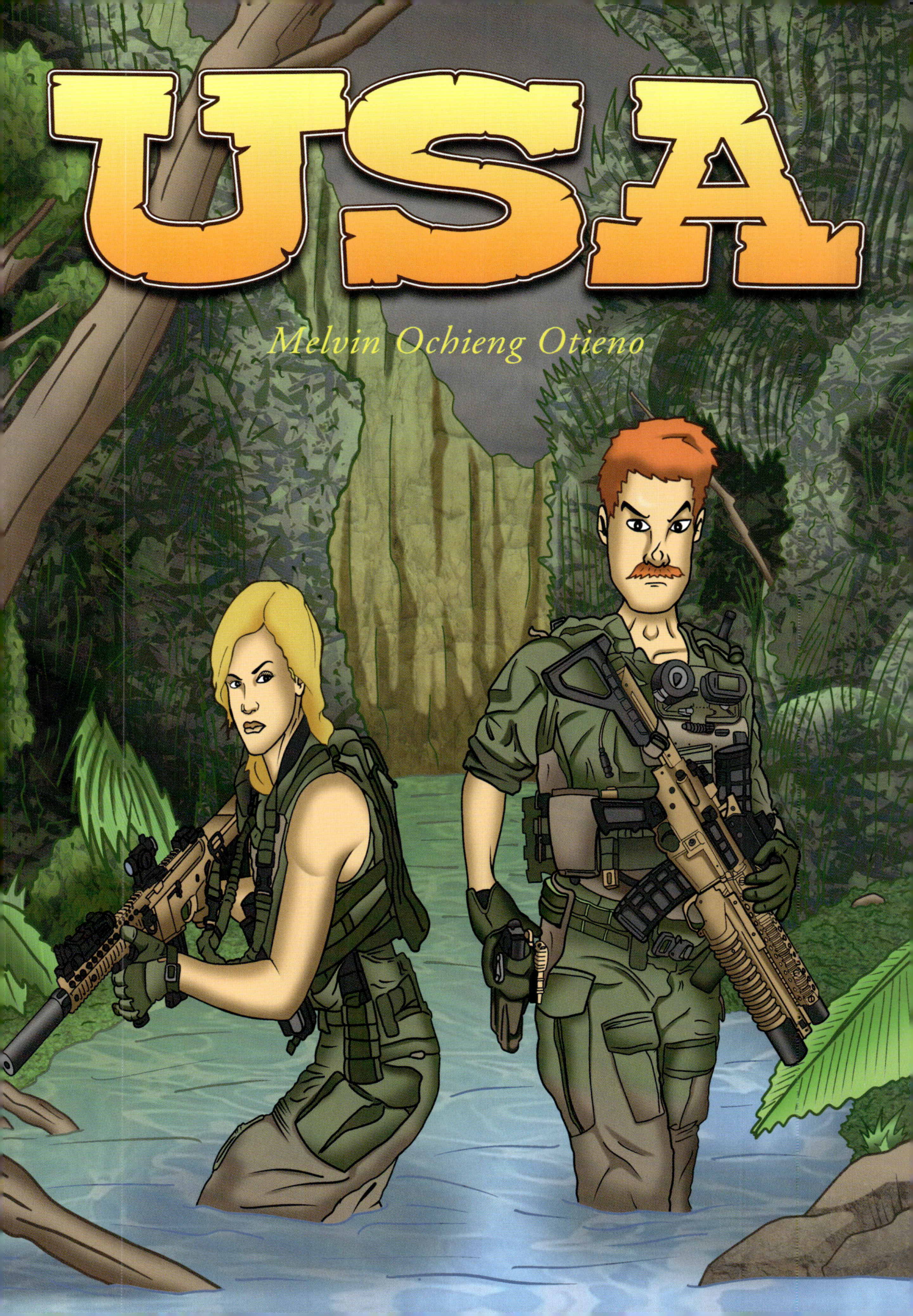
USA
Melvin Ochieng Otieno

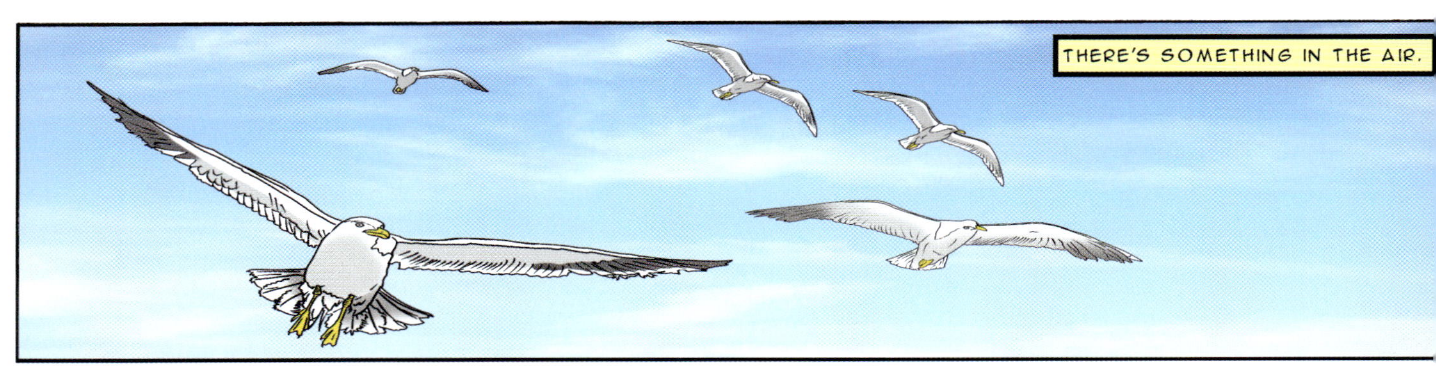
THERE'S SOMETHING IN THE AIR.

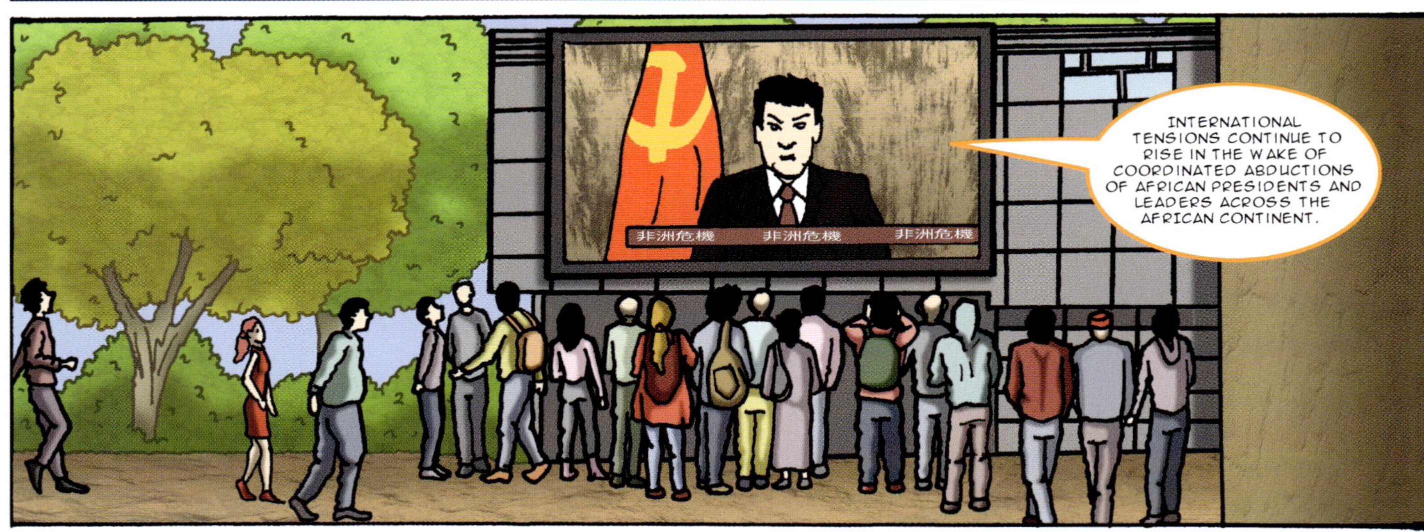
非洲危機 非洲危機 非洲危機
INTERNATIONAL TENSIONS CONTINUE TO RISE IN THE WAKE OF COORDINATED ABDUCTIONS OF AFRICAN PRESIDENTS AND LEADERS ACROSS THE AFRICAN CONTINENT.

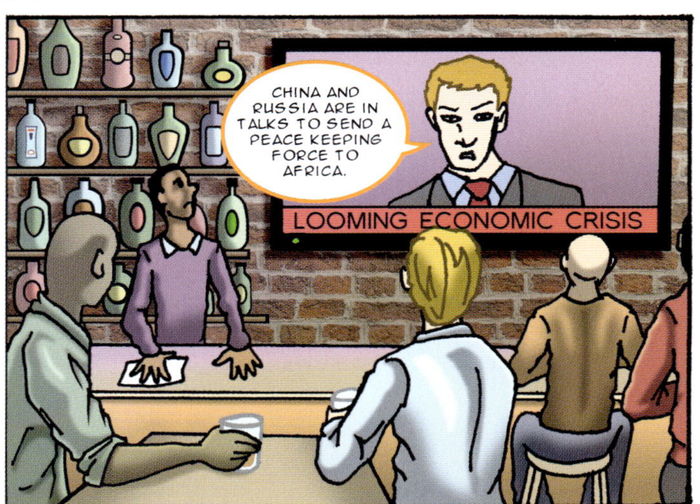
CHINA AND RUSSIA ARE IN TALKS TO SEND A PEACE KEEPING FORCE TO AFRICA.
LOOMING ECONOMIC CRISIS

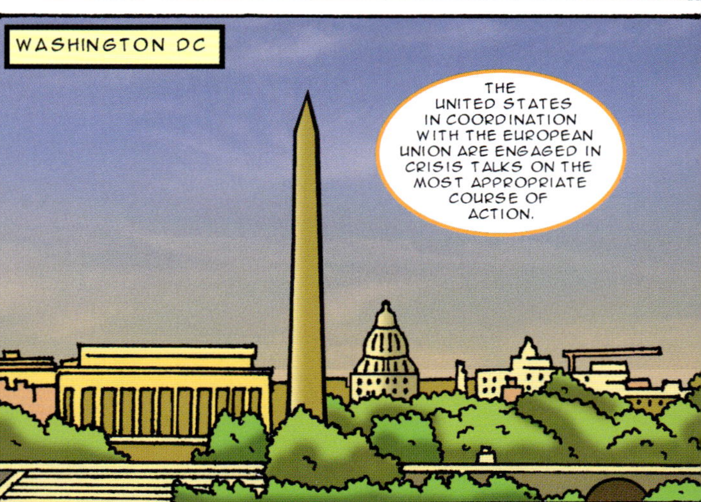
WASHINGTON DC
THE UNITED STATES IN COORDINATION WITH THE EUROPEAN UNION ARE ENGAGED IN CRISIS TALKS ON THE MOST APPROPRIATE COURSE OF ACTION.

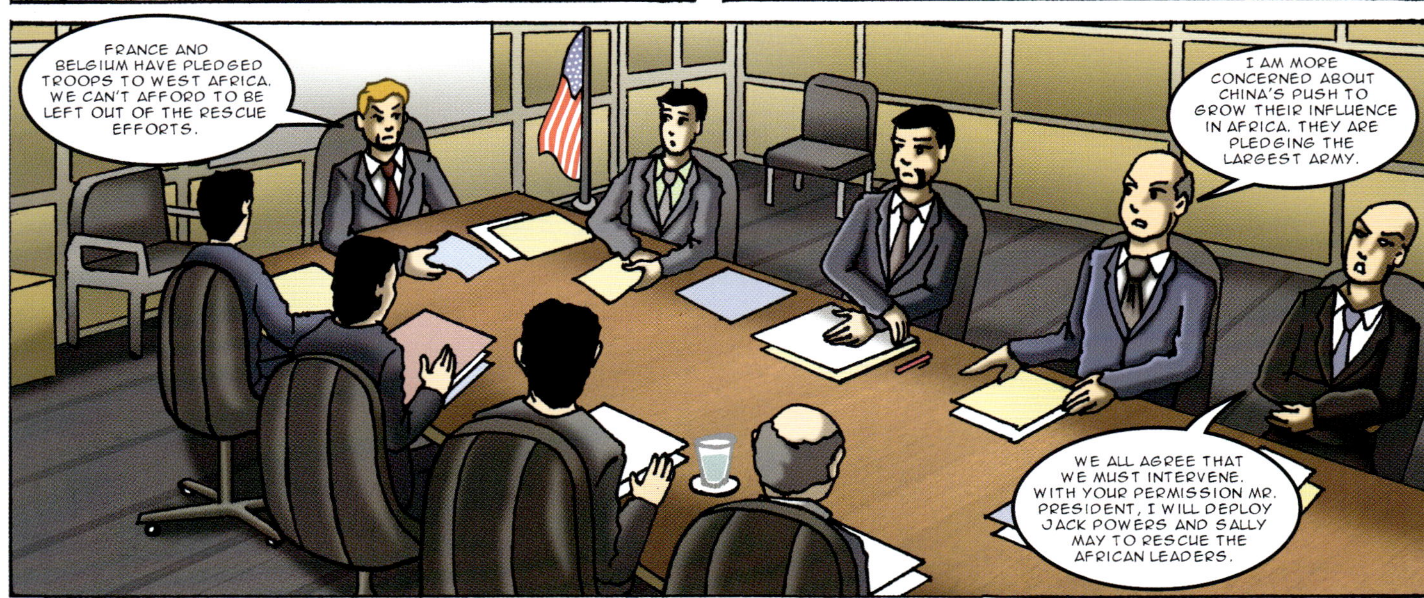
FRANCE AND BELGIUM HAVE PLEDGED TROOPS TO WEST AFRICA. WE CAN'T AFFORD TO BE LEFT OUT OF THE RESCUE EFFORTS.
I AM MORE CONCERNED ABOUT CHINA'S PUSH TO GROW THEIR INFLUENCE IN AFRICA. THEY ARE PLEDGING THE LARGEST ARMY.
WE ALL AGREE THAT WE MUST INTERVENE. WITH YOUR PERMISSION MR. PRESIDENT, I WILL DEPLOY JACK POWERS AND SALLY MAY TO RESCUE THE AFRICAN LEADERS.

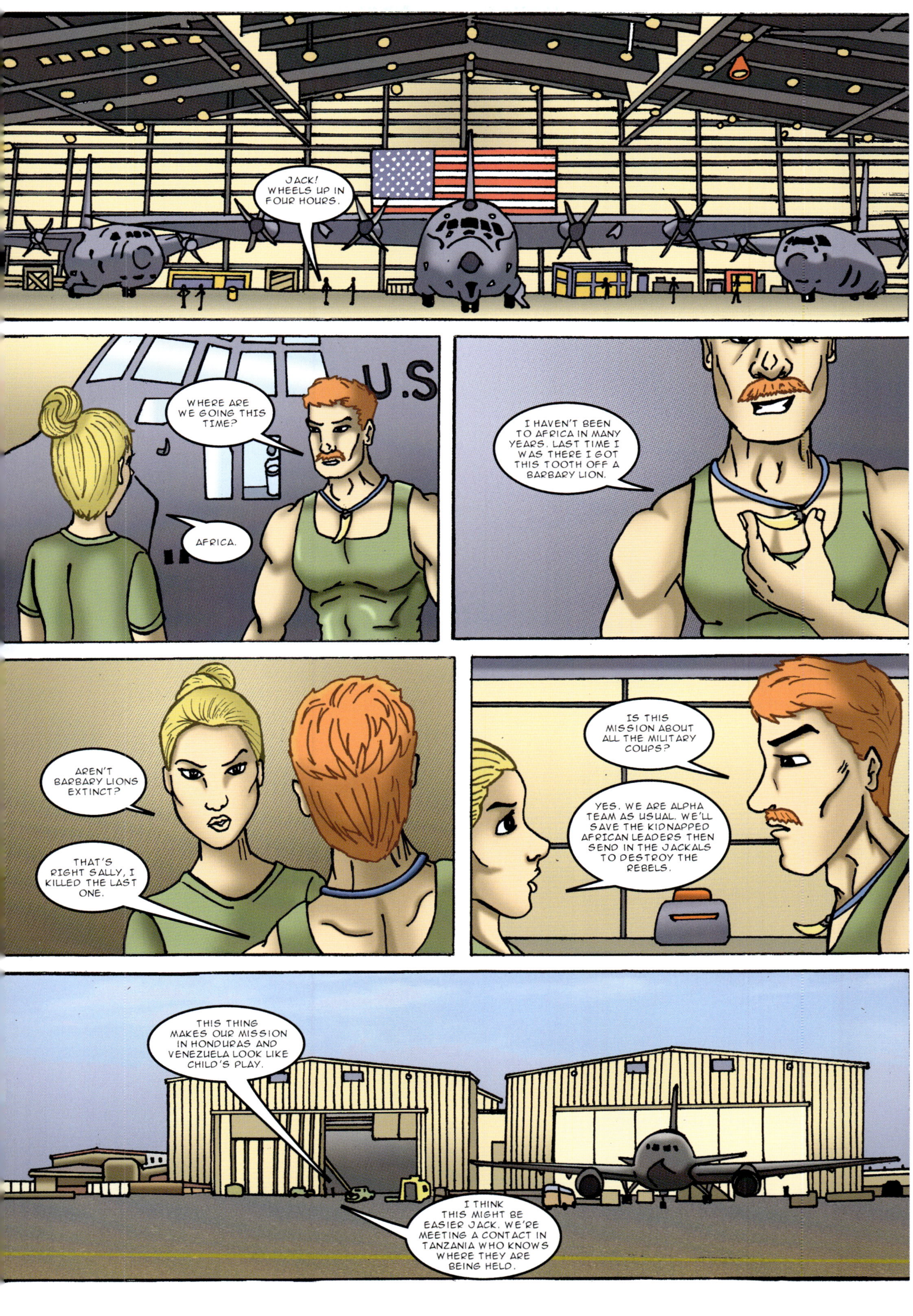
JACK! WHEELS UP IN FOUR HOURS.
WHERE ARE WE GOING THIS TIME?
U.S
AFRICA.
I HAVEN'T BEEN TO AFRICA IN MANY YEARS. LAST TIME I WAS THERE I GOT THIS TOOTH OFF A BARBARY LION.
AREN'T BARBARY LIONS EXTINCT?
THAT'S RIGHT SALLY, I KILLED THE LAST ONE.
IS THIS MISSION ABOUT ALL THE MILITARY COUPS?
YES. WE ARE ALPHA TEAM AS USUAL. WE'LL SAVE THE KIDNAPPED AFRICAN LEADERS THEN SEND IN THE JACKALS TO DESTROY THE REBELS.
THIS THING MAKES OUR MISSION IN HONDURAS AND VENEZUELA LOOK LIKE CHILD'S PLAY.
I THINK THIS MIGHT BE EASIER JACK. WE'RE MEETING A CONTACT IN TANZANIA WHO KNOWS WHERE THEY ARE BEING HELD.

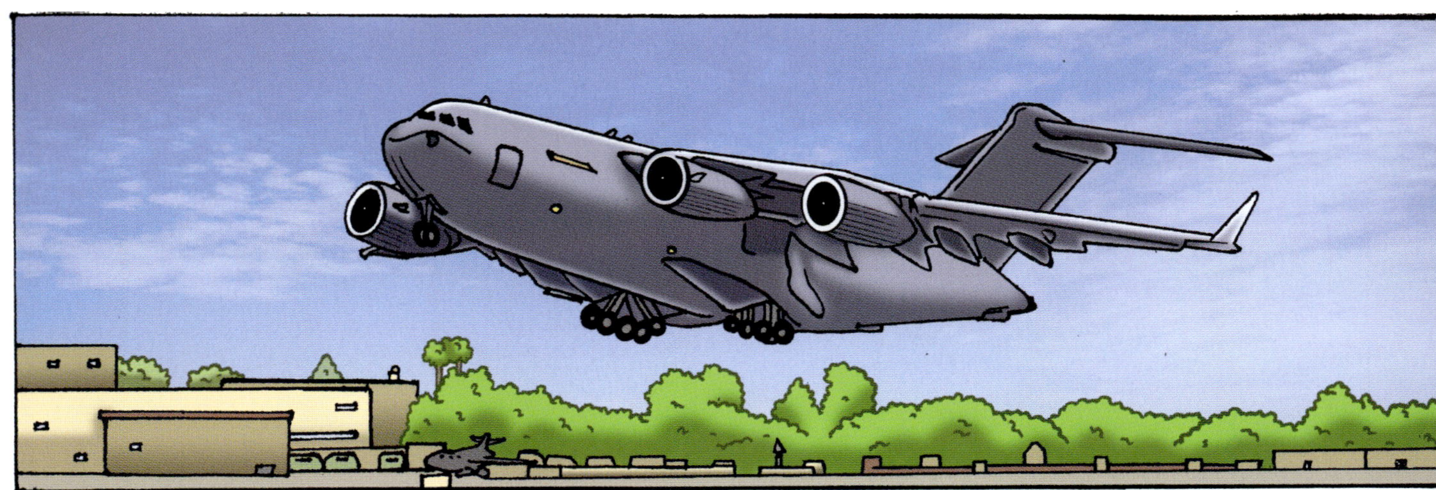

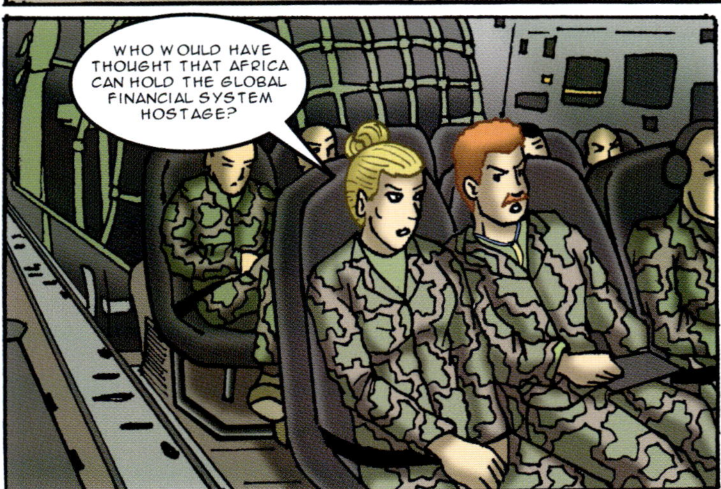
WHO WOULD HAVE THOUGHT THAT AFRICA CAN HOLD THE GLOBAL FINANCIAL SYSTEM HOSTAGE?

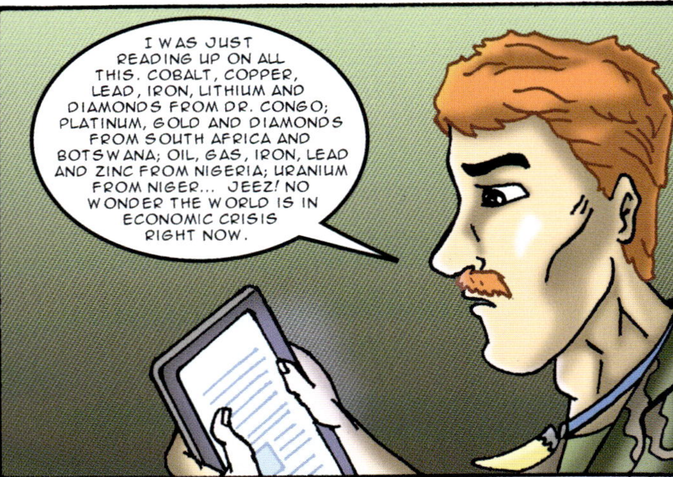
I WAS JUST READING UP ON ALL THIS. COBALT, COPPER, LEAD, IRON, LITHIUM AND DIAMONDS FROM DR. CONGO; PLATINUM, GOLD AND DIAMONDS FROM SOUTH AFRICA AND BOTSWANA; OIL, GAS, IRON, LEAD AND ZINC FROM NIGERIA; URANIUM FROM NIGER... JEEZ! NO WONDER THE WORLD IS IN ECONOMIC CRISIS RIGHT NOW.

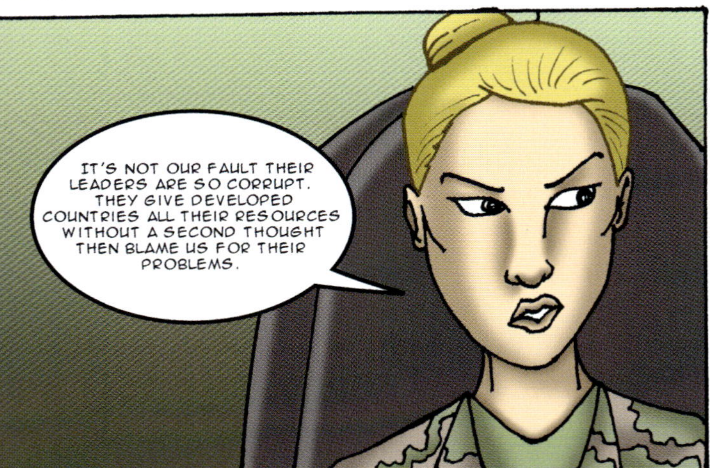
IT'S NOT OUR FAULT THEIR LEADERS ARE SO CORRUPT. THEY GIVE DEVELOPED COUNTRIES ALL THEIR RESOURCES WITHOUT A SECOND THOUGHT THEN BLAME US FOR THEIR PROBLEMS.

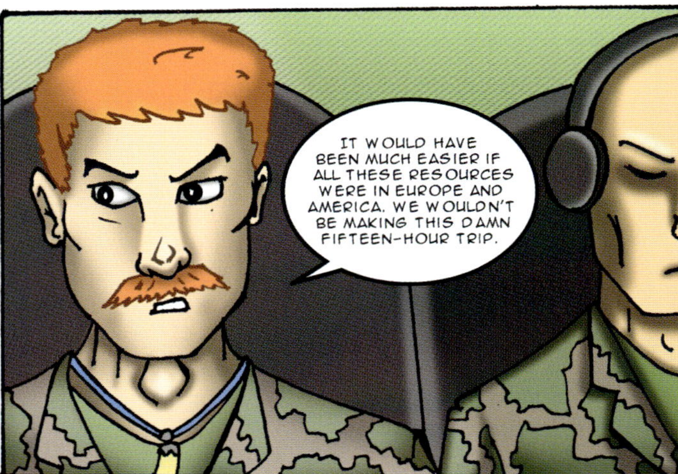
IT WOULD HAVE BEEN MUCH EASIER IF ALL THESE RESOURCES WERE IN EUROPE AND AMERICA. WE WOULDN'T BE MAKING THIS DAMN FIFTEEN-HOUR TRIP.

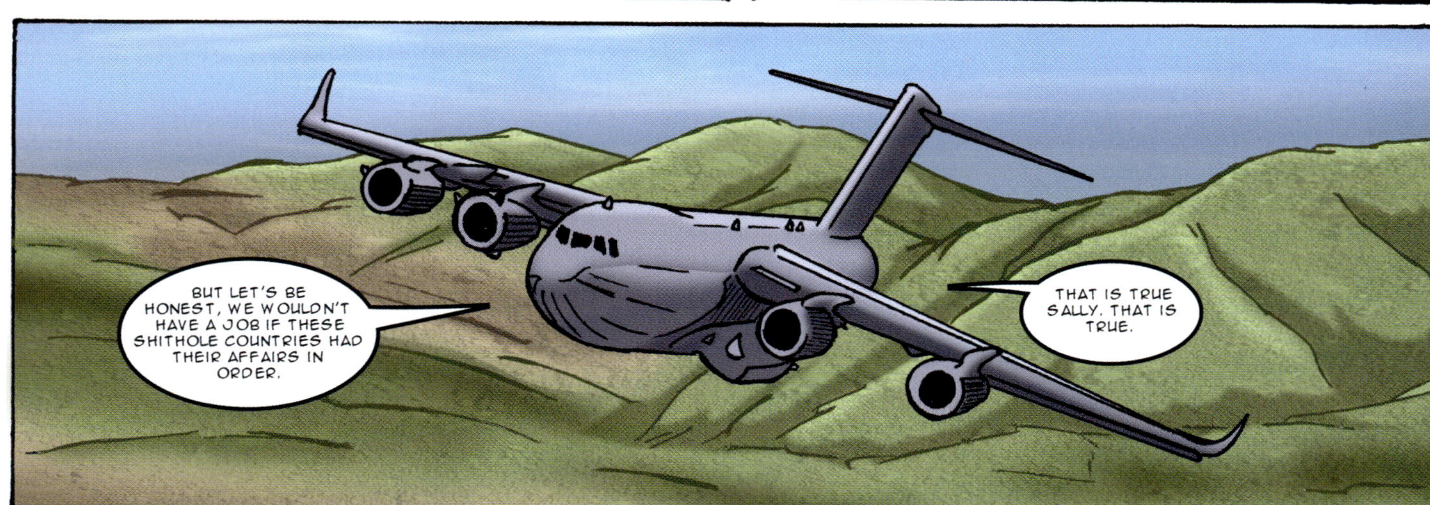
BUT LET'S BE HONEST, WE WOULDN'T HAVE A JOB IF THESE SHITHOLE COUNTRIES HAD THEIR AFFAIRS IN ORDER.
THAT IS TRUE SALLY. THAT IS TRUE.

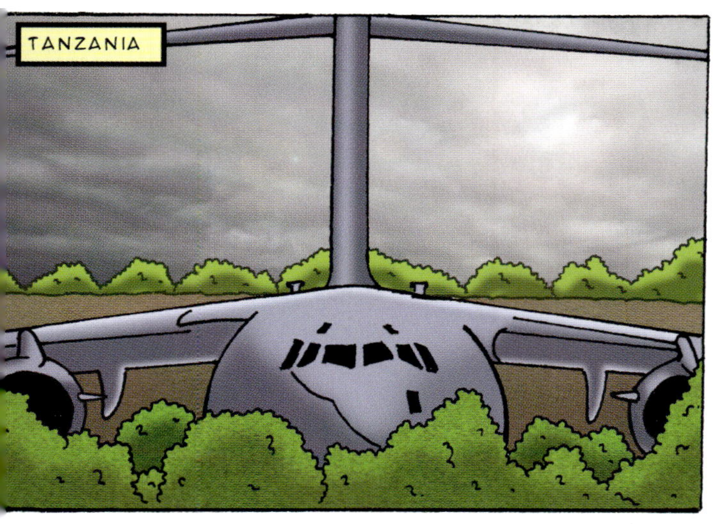
TANZANIA

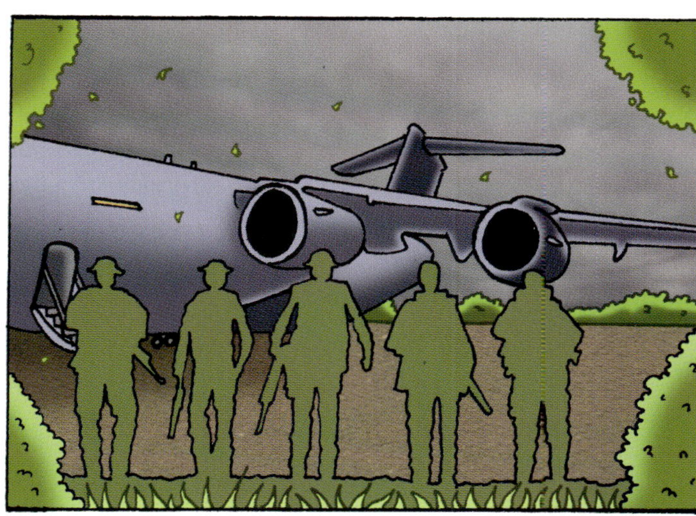

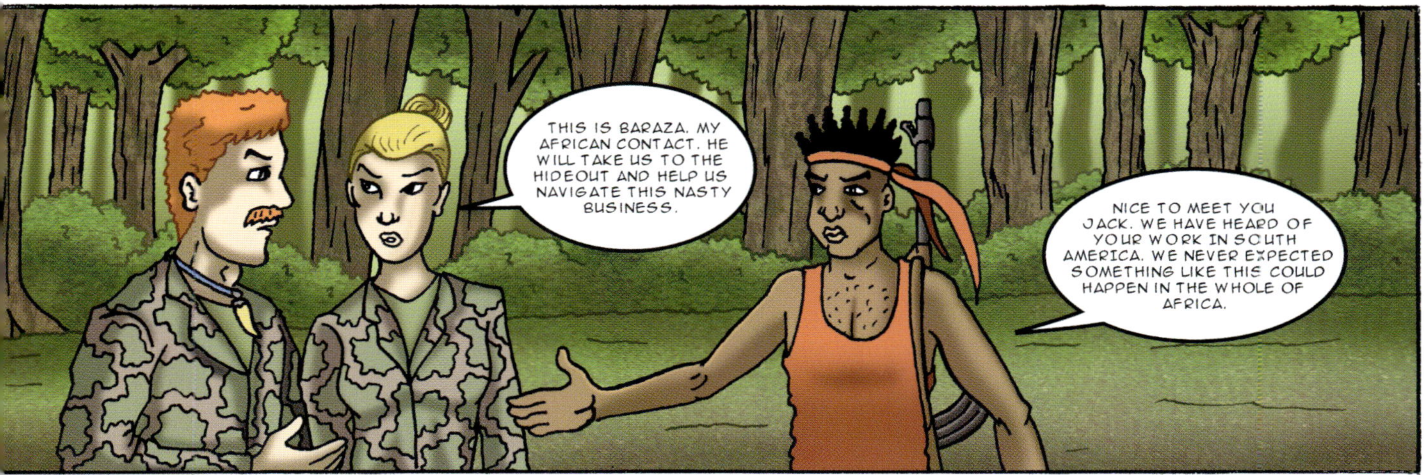
THIS IS BARAZA, MY AFRICAN CONTACT. HE WILL TAKE US TO THE HIDEOUT AND HELP US NAVIGATE THIS NASTY BUSINESS.
NICE TO MEET YOU JACK. WE HAVE HEARD OF YOUR WORK IN SOUTH AMERICA. WE NEVER EXPECTED SOMETHING LIKE THIS COULD HAPPEN IN THE WHOLE OF AFRICA.

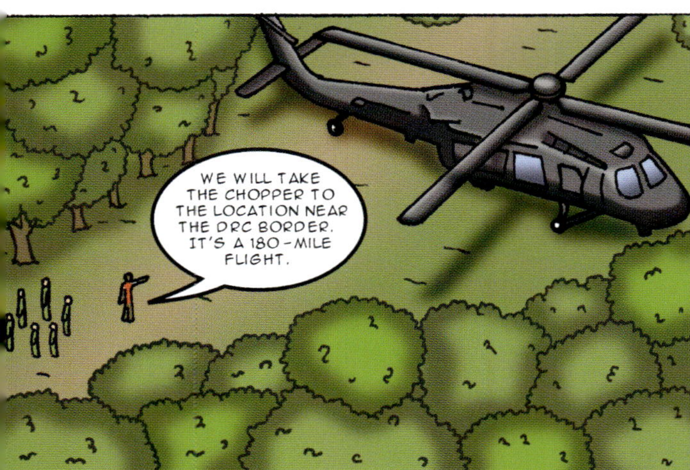
WE WILL TAKE THE CHOPPER TO THE LOCATION NEAR THE DRC BORDER. IT'S A 180-MILE FLIGHT.

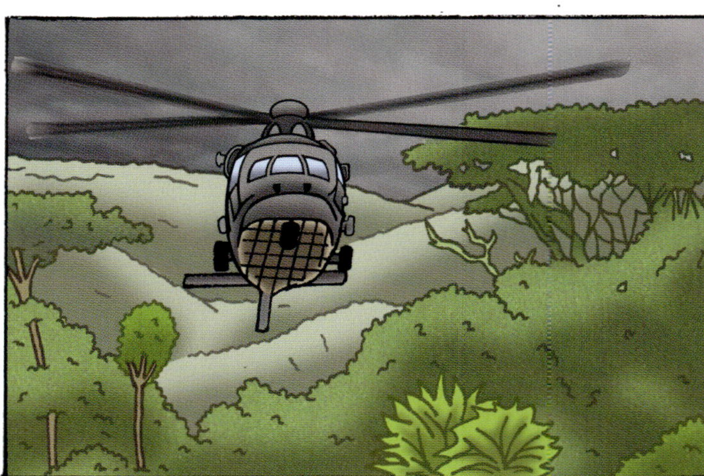

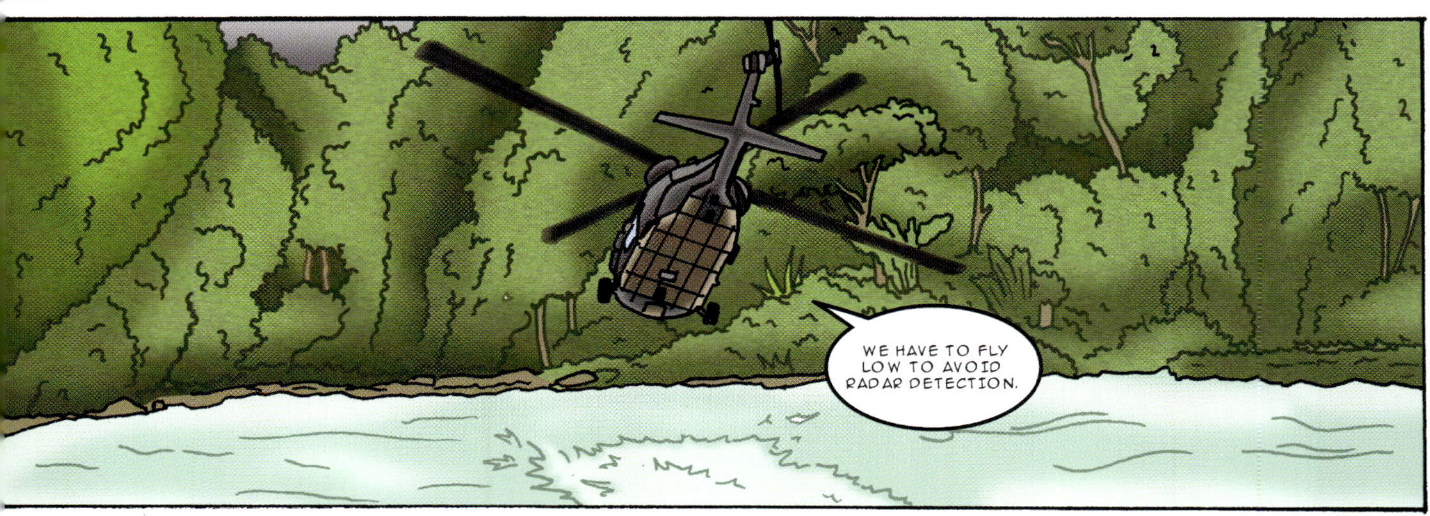
WE HAVE TO FLY LOW TO AVOID RADAR DETECTION.

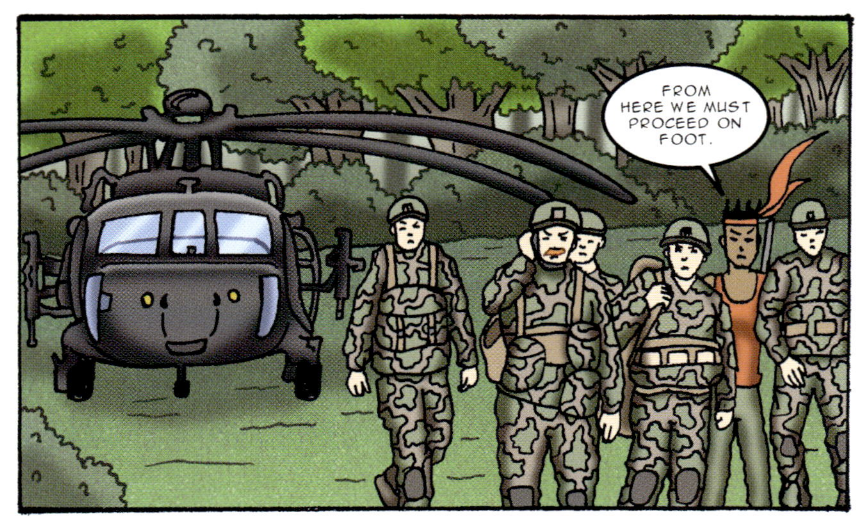
FROM HERE WE MUST PROCEED ON FOOT.
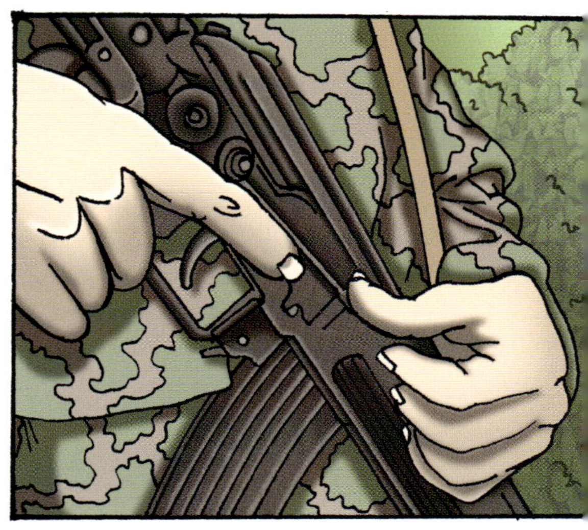
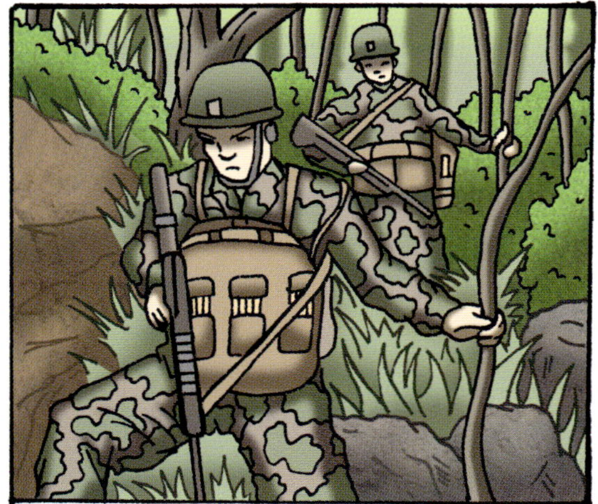
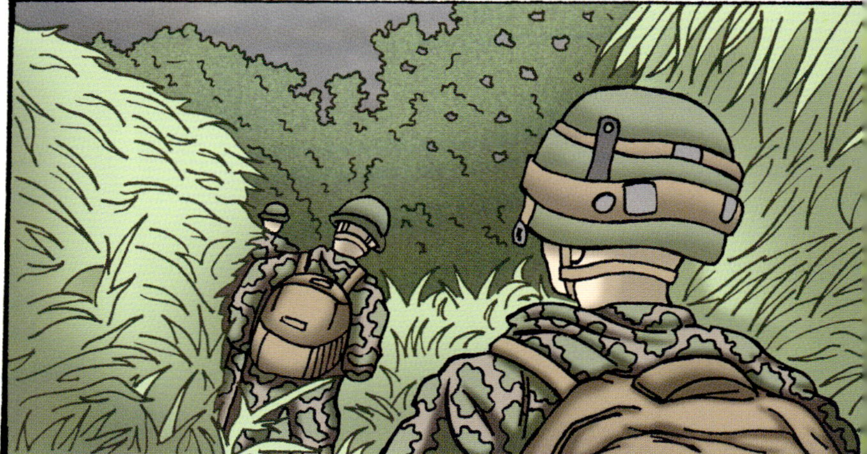
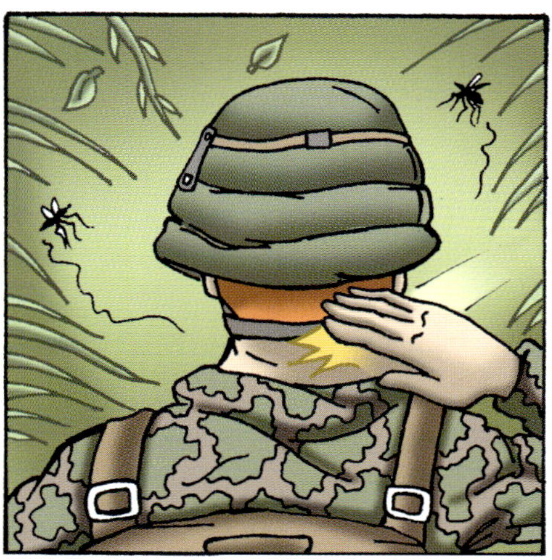
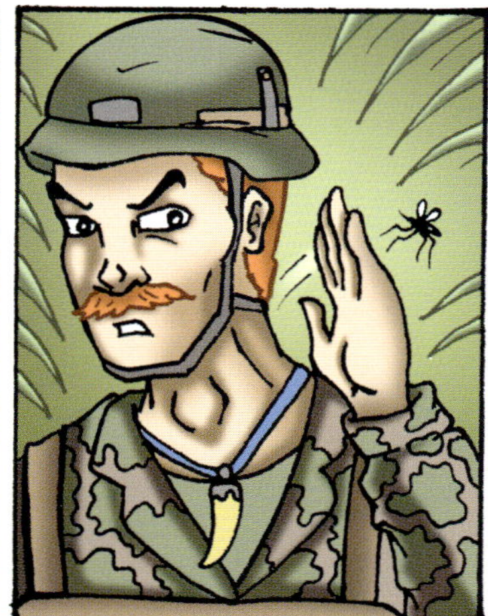
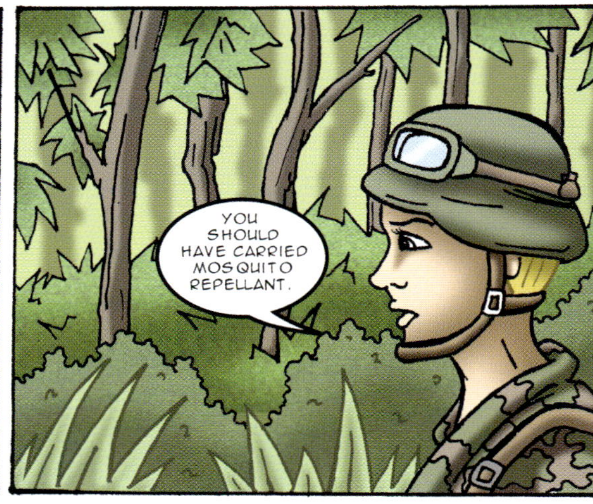
YOU SHOULD HAVE CARRIED MOSQUITO REPELLANT.
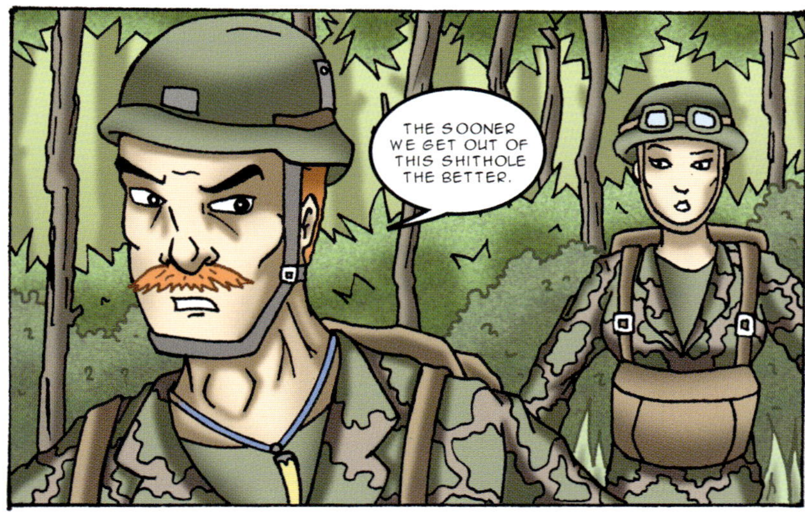
THE SOONER WE GET OUT OF THIS SHITHOLE THE BETTER.
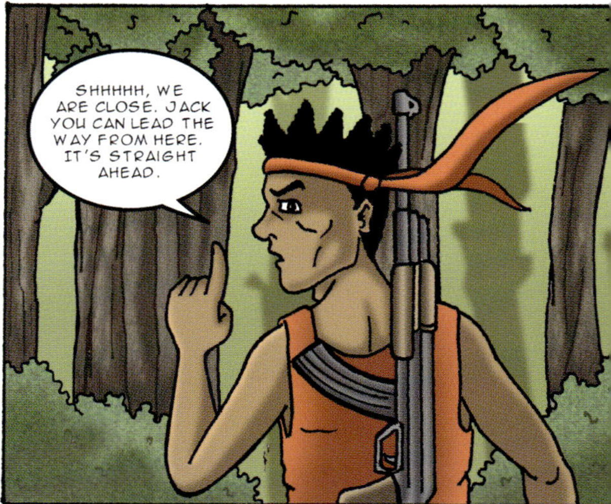
SHHHHH, WE ARE CLOSE. JACK YOU CAN LEAD THE WAY FROM HERE. IT'S STRAIGHT AHEAD.

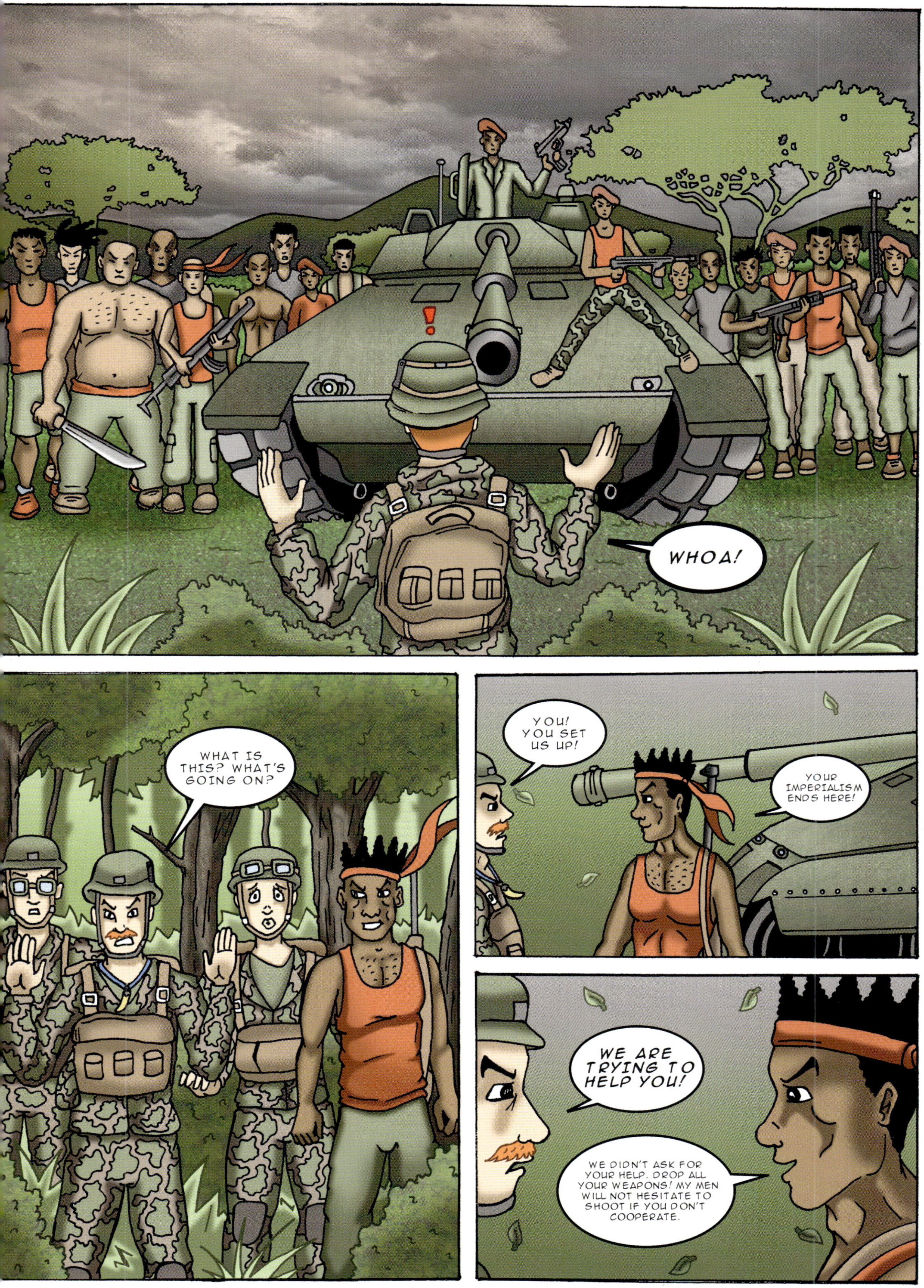

WHOA!

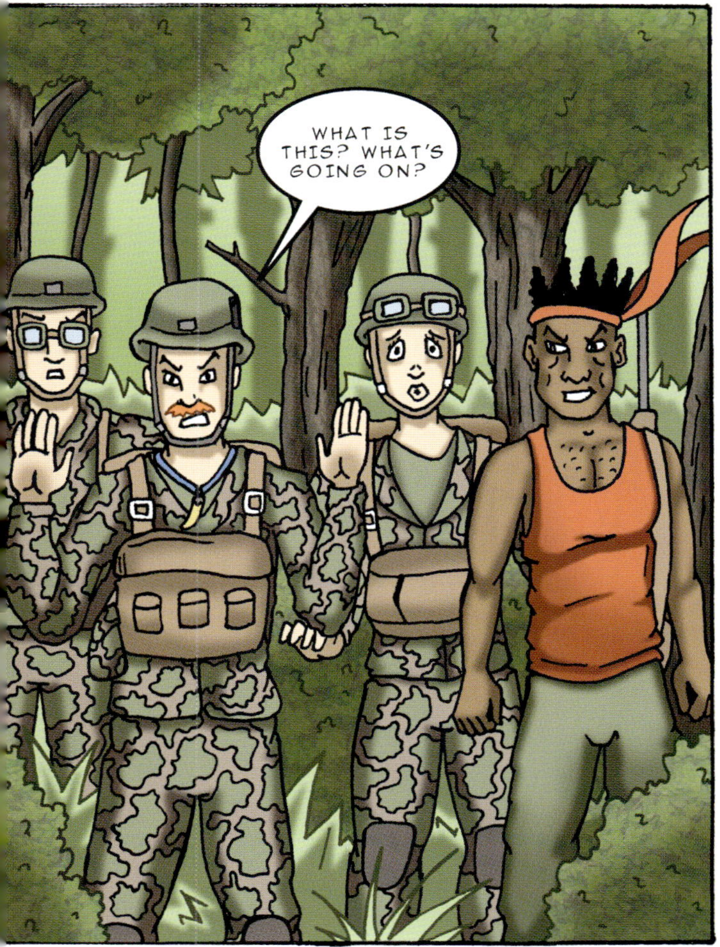
WHAT IS THIS? WHAT'S GOING ON?

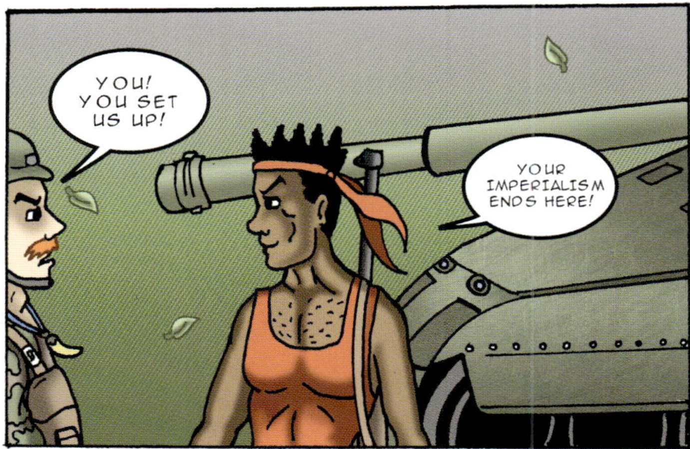
YOU! YOU SET US UP!
YOUR IMPERIALISM ENDS HERE!

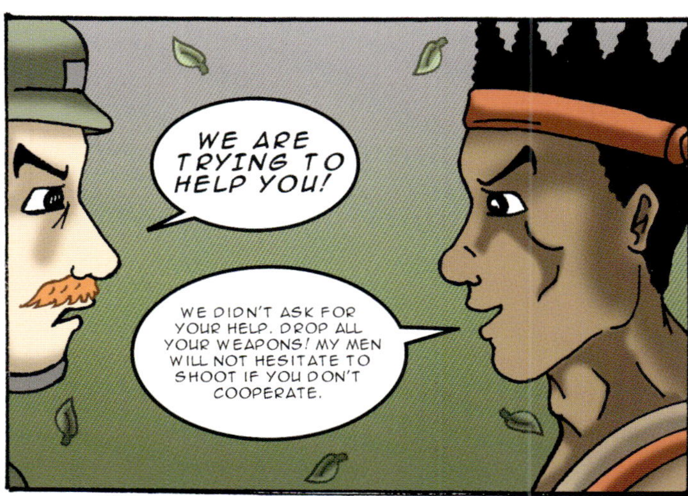
WE ARE TRYING TO HELP YOU!
WE DIDN'T ASK FOR YOUR HELP. DROP ALL YOUR WEAPONS! MY MEN WILL NOT HESITATE TO SHOOT IF YOU DON'T COOPERATE.

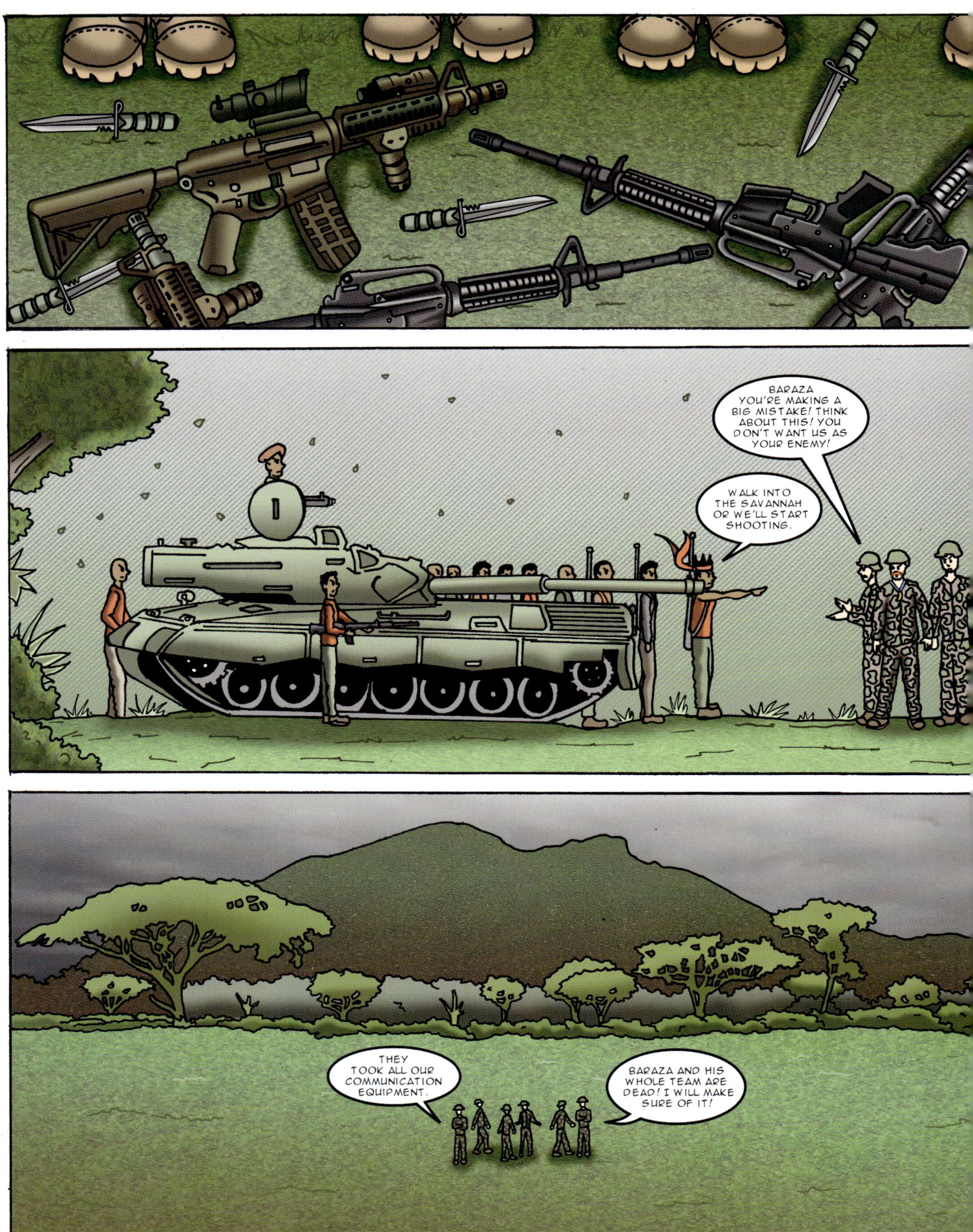
BARAZA YOU'RE MAKING A BIG MISTAKE! THINK ABOUT THIS! YOU DON'T WANT US AS YOUR ENEMY!
WALK INTO THE SAVANNAH OR WE'LL START SHOOTING.
THEY TOOK ALL OUR COMMUNICATION EQUIPMENT.
BARAZA AND HIS WHOLE TEAM ARE DEAD! I WILL MAKE SURE OF IT!

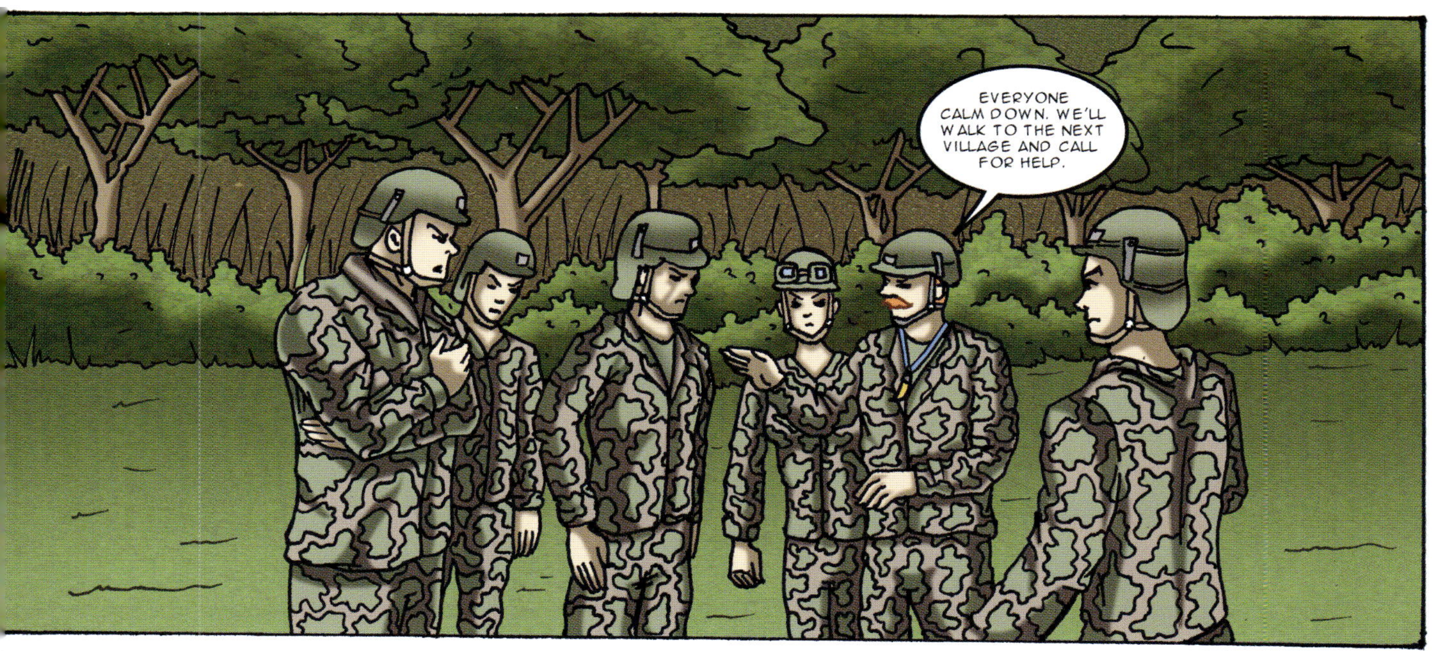
EVERYONE CALM DOWN. WE'LL WALK TO THE NEXT VILLAGE AND CALL FOR HELP.

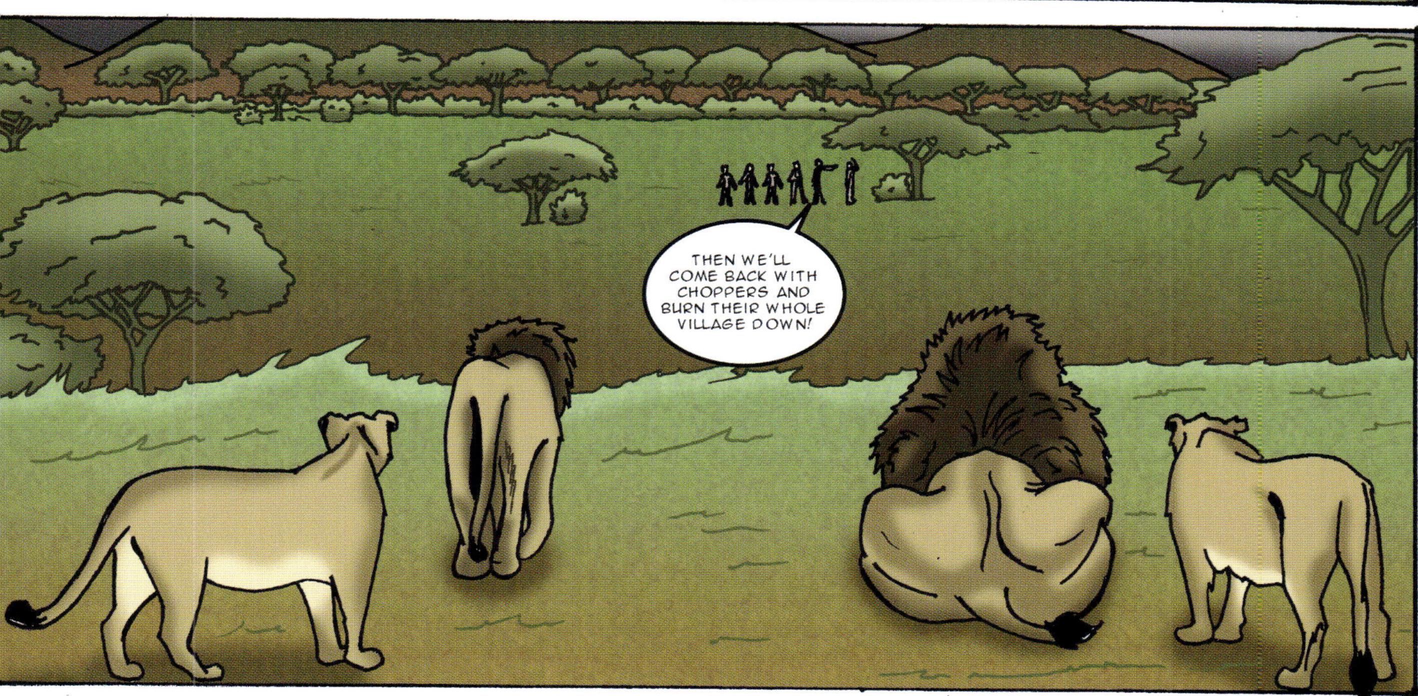
THEN WE'LL COME BACK WITH CHOPPERS AND BURN THEIR WHOLE VILLAGE DOWN!

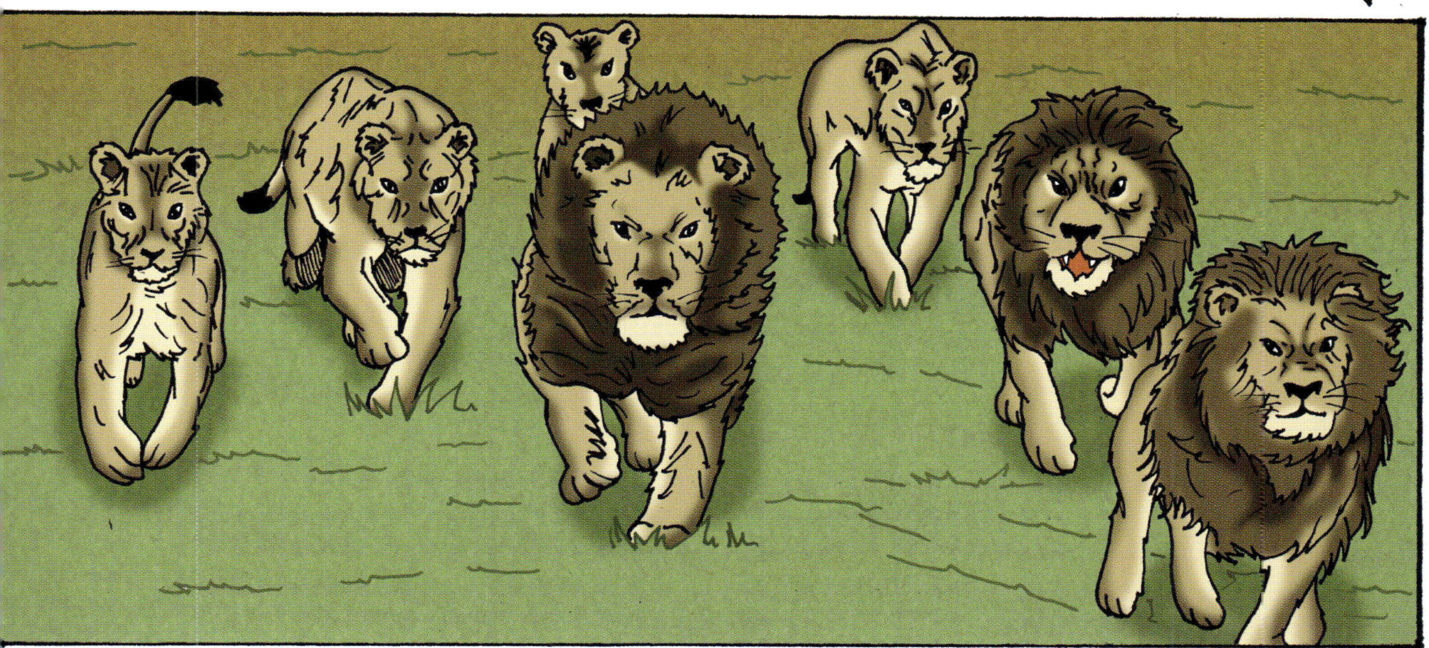

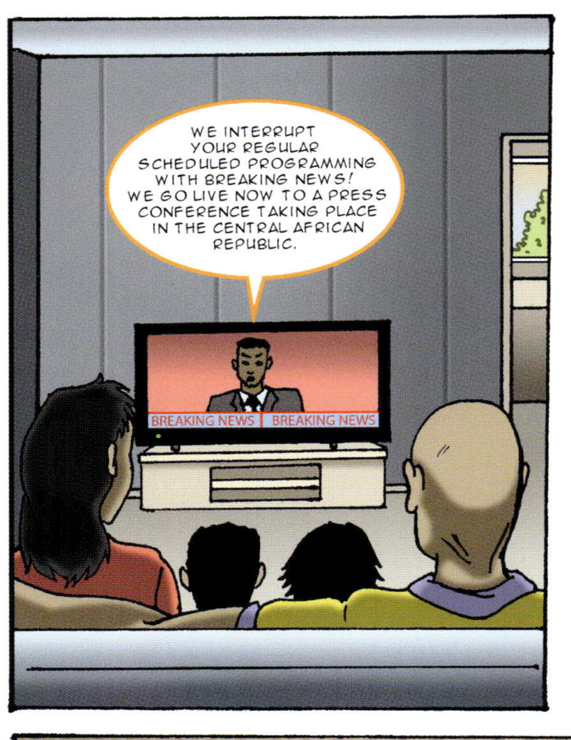
WE INTERRUPT YOUR REGULAR SCHEDULED PROGRAMMING WITH BREAKING NEWS! WE GO LIVE NOW TO A PRESS CONFERENCE TAKING PLACE IN THE CENTRAL AFRICAN REPUBLIC.
BREAKING NEWS
BREAKING NEWS

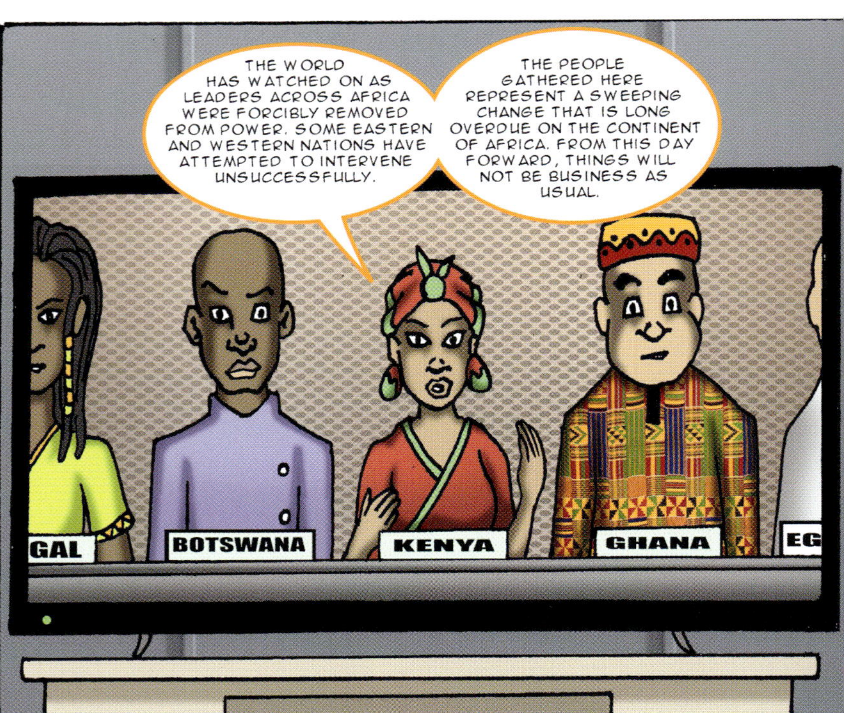
THE WORLD HAS WATCHED ON AS LEADERS ACROSS AFRICA WERE FORCIBLY REMOVED FROM POWER. SOME EASTERN AND WESTERN NATIONS HAVE ATTEMPTED TO INTERVENE UNSUCCESSFULLY.
THE PEOPLE GATHERED HERE REPRESENT A SWEEPING CHANGE THAT IS LONG OVERDUE ON THE CONTINENT OF AFRICA. FROM THIS DAY FORWARD, THINGS WILL NOT BE BUSINESS AS USUAL.
GAL
BOTSWANA
KENYA
GHANA
EG

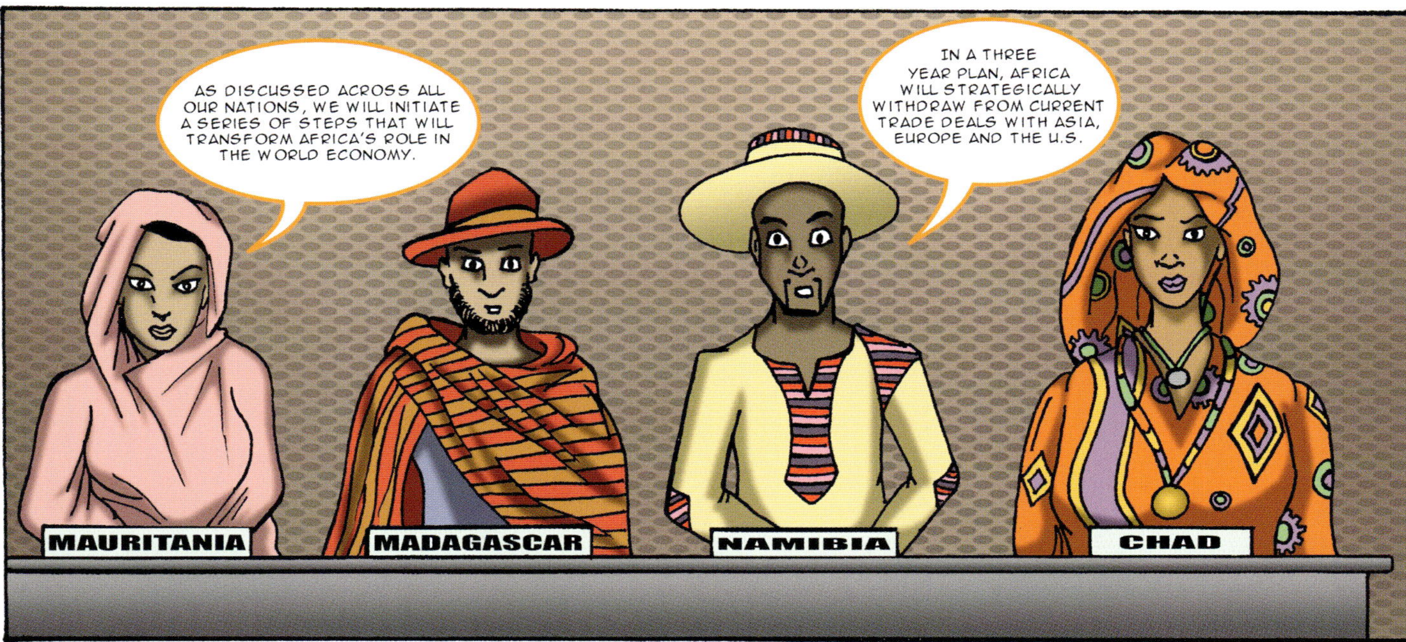
AS DISCUSSED ACROSS ALL OUR NATIONS, WE WILL INITIATE A SERIES OF STEPS THAT WILL TRANSFORM AFRICA'S ROLE IN THE WORLD ECONOMY.
IN A THREE YEAR PLAN, AFRICA WILL STRATEGICALLY WITHDRAW FROM CURRENT TRADE DEALS WITH ASIA, EUROPE AND THE U.S.
MAURITANIA
MADAGASCAR
NAMIBIA
CHAD

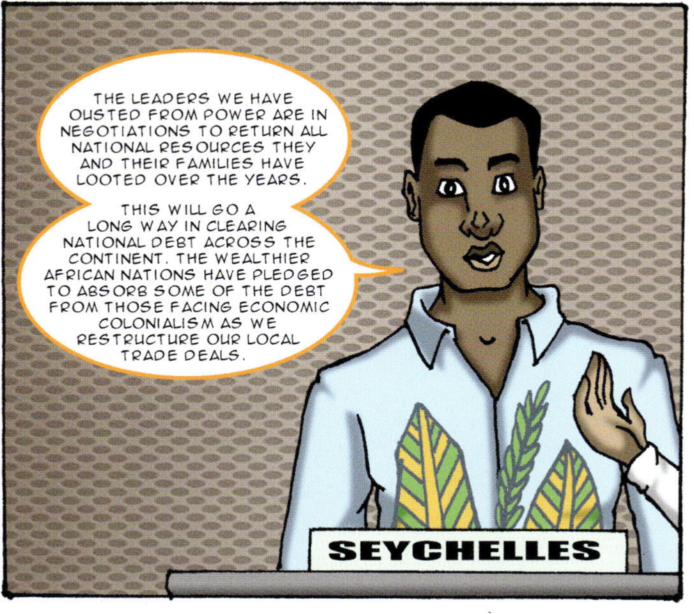
THE LEADERS WE HAVE OUSTED FROM POWER ARE IN NEGOTIATIONS TO RETURN ALL NATIONAL RESOURCES THEY AND THEIR FAMILIES HAVE LOOTED OVER THE YEARS.
THIS WILL GO A LONG WAY IN CLEARING NATIONAL DEBT ACROSS THE CONTINENT. THE WEALTHIER AFRICAN NATIONS HAVE PLEDGED TO ABSORB SOME OF THE DEBT FROM THOSE FACING ECONOMIC COLONIALISM AS WE RESTRUCTURE OUR LOCAL TRADE DEALS.
SEYCHELLES

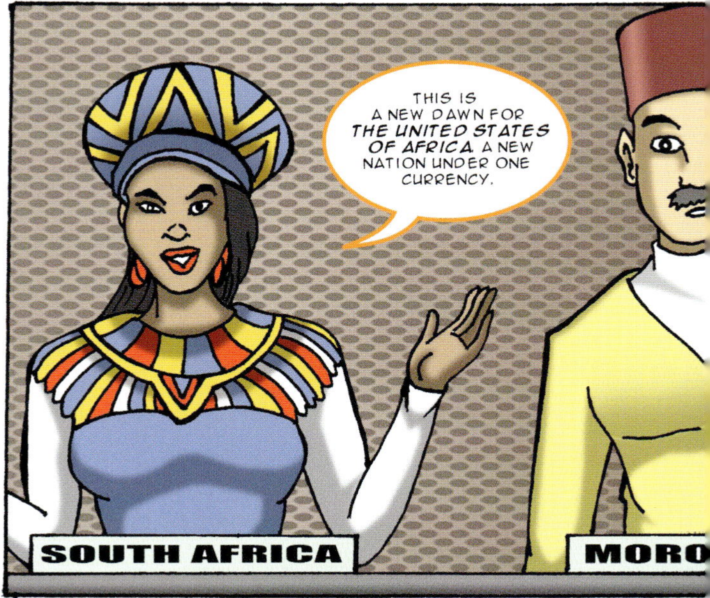
THIS IS A NEW DAWN FOR *THE UNITED STATES OF AFRICA*. A NEW NATION UNDER ONE CURRENCY.
SOUTH AFRICA
MORO

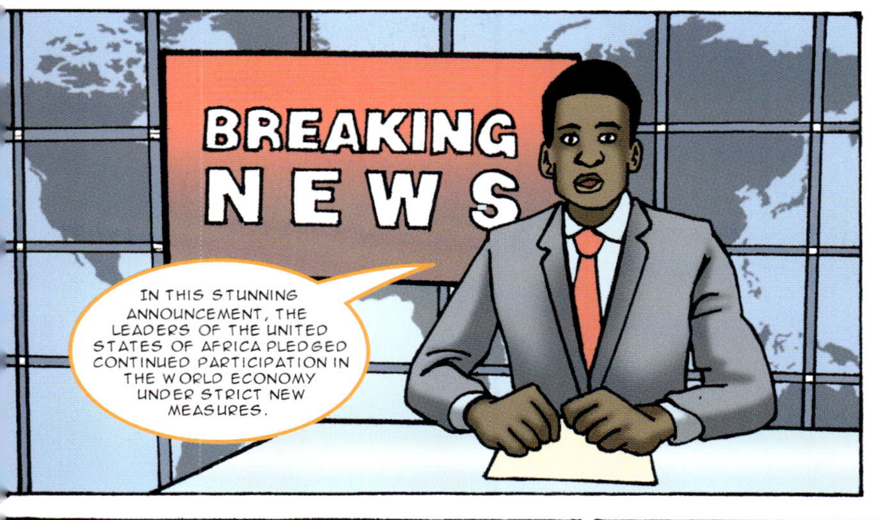
BREAKING NEWS
IN THIS STUNNING ANNOUNCEMENT, THE LEADERS OF THE UNITED STATES OF AFRICA PLEDGED CONTINUED PARTICIPATION IN THE WORLD ECONOMY UNDER STRICT NEW MEASURES.

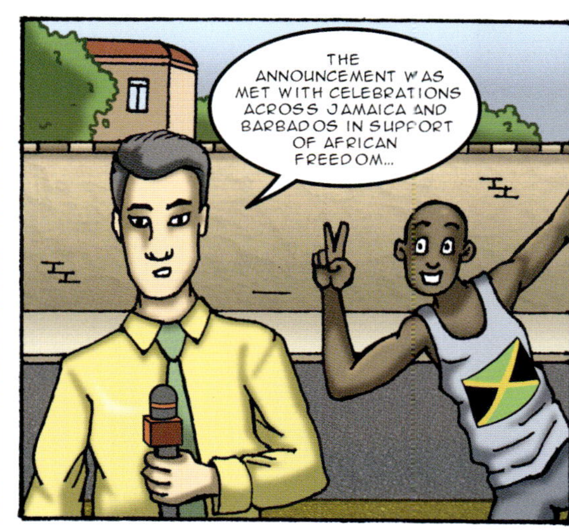
THE ANNOUNCEMENT WAS MET WITH CELEBRATIONS ACROSS JAMAICA AND BARBADOS IN SUPPORT OF AFRICAN FREEDOM...

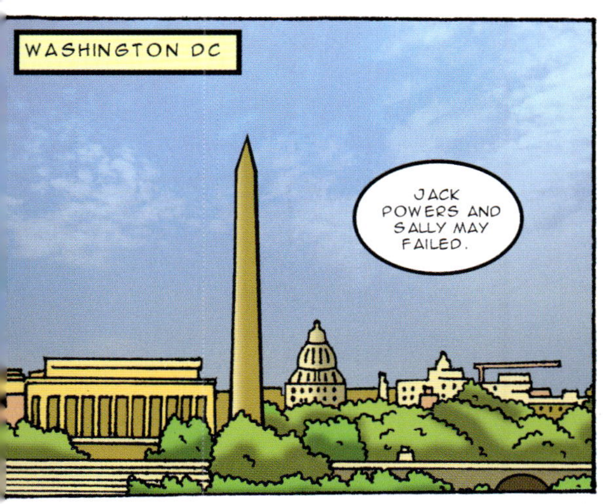
WASHINGTON DC
JACK POWERS AND SALLY MAY FAILED.

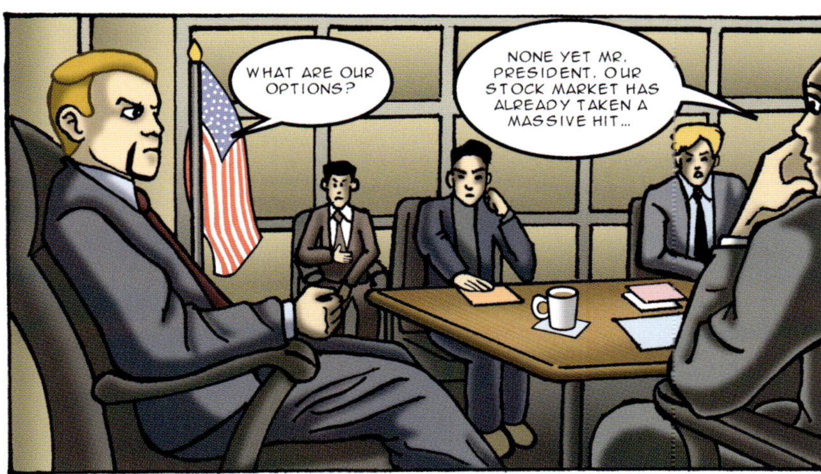
WHAT ARE OUR OPTIONS?
NONE YET MR. PRESIDENT. OUR STOCK MARKET HAS ALREADY TAKEN A MASSIVE HIT...

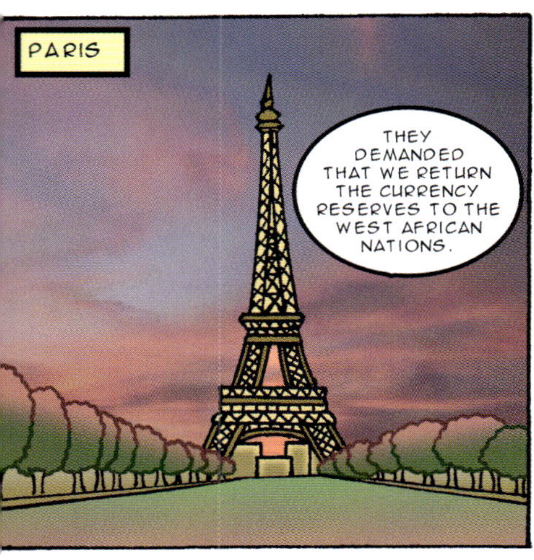
PARIS
THEY DEMANDED THAT WE RETURN THE CURRENCY RESERVES TO THE WEST AFRICAN NATIONS.

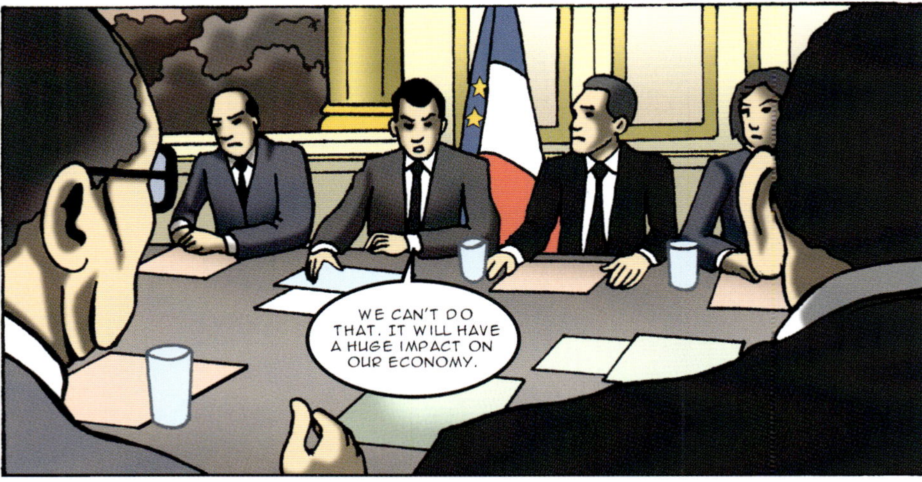
WE CAN'T DO THAT. IT WILL HAVE A HUGE IMPACT ON OUR ECONOMY.

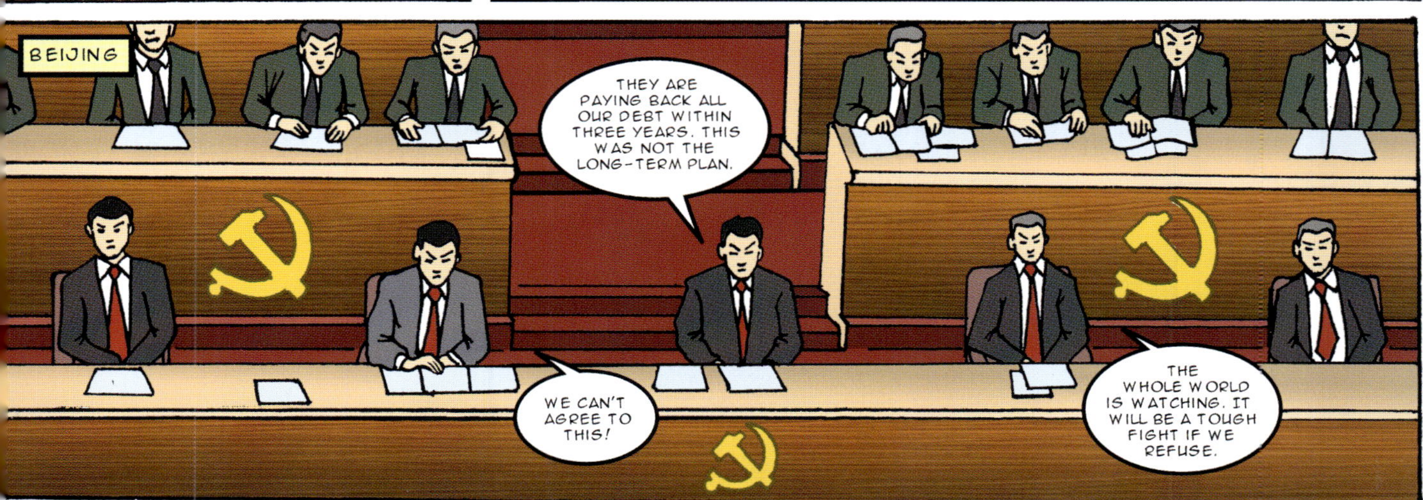
BEIJING
THEY ARE PAYING BACK ALL OUR DEBT WITHIN THREE YEARS. THIS WAS NOT THE LONG-TERM PLAN.
WE CAN'T AGREE TO THIS!
THE WHOLE WORLD IS WATCHING. IT WILL BE A TOUGH FIGHT IF WE REFUSE.

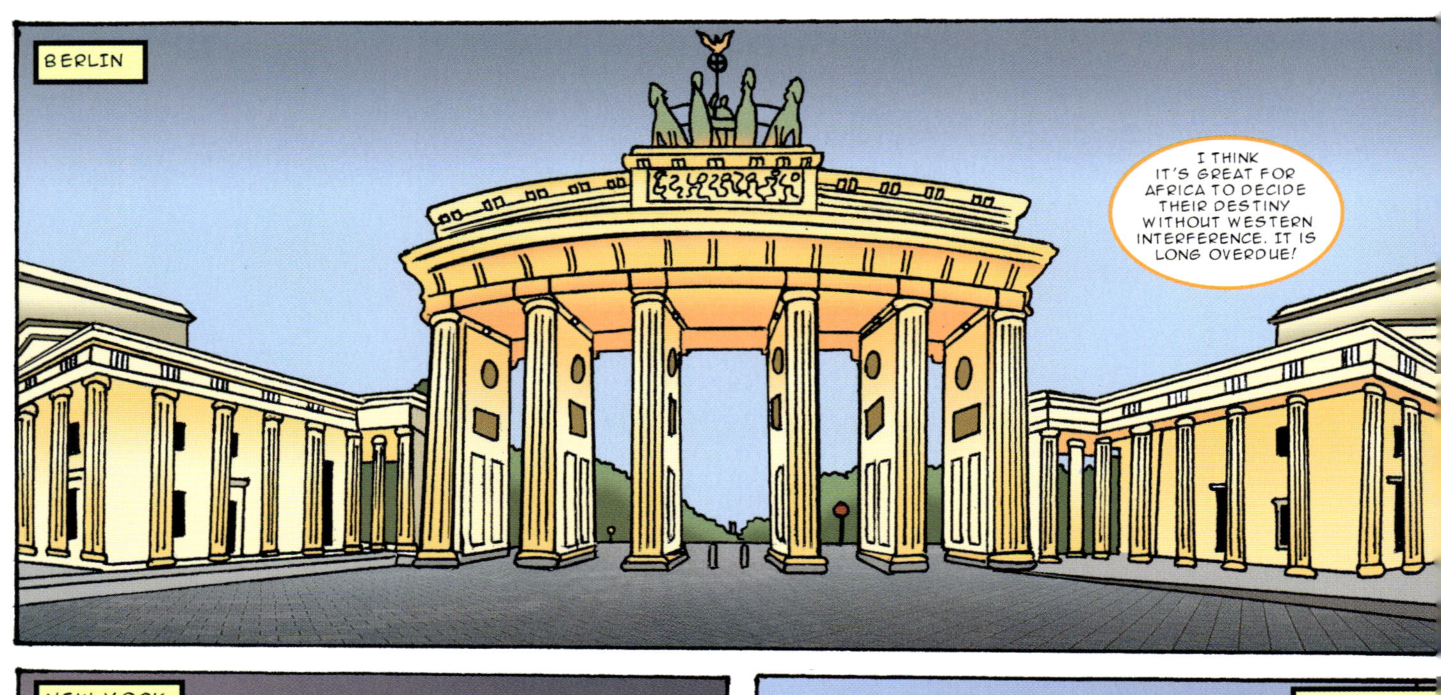
BERLIN
I THINK IT'S GREAT FOR AFRICA TO DECIDE THEIR DESTINY WITHOUT WESTERN INTERFERENCE. IT IS LONG OVERDUE!

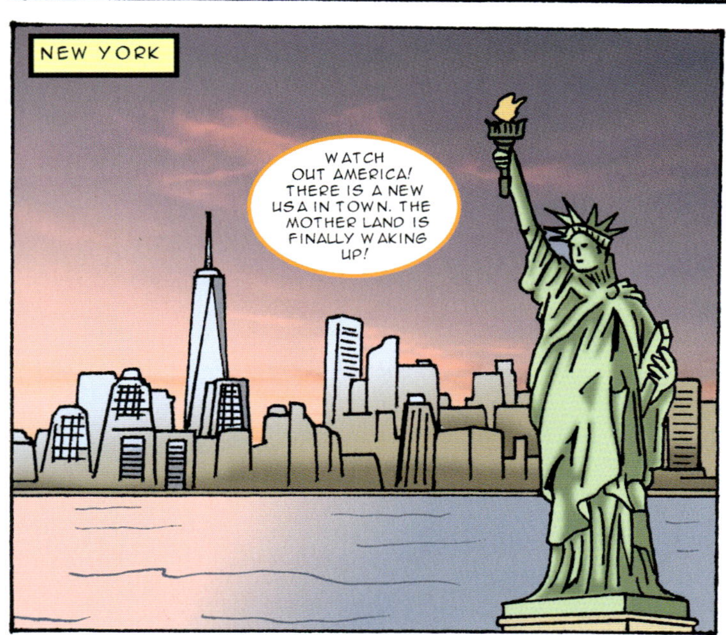
NEW YORK
WATCH OUT AMERICA! THERE IS A NEW USA IN TOWN. THE MOTHER LAND IS FINALLY WAKING UP!

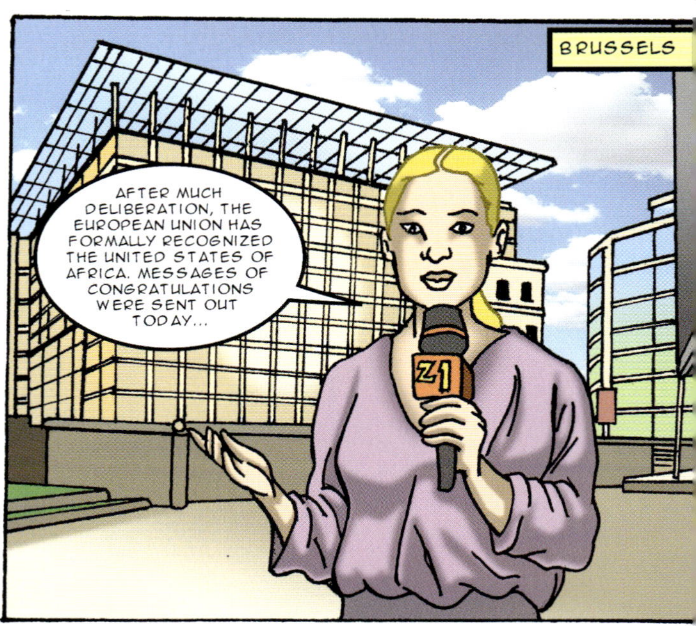
BRUSSELS
AFTER MUCH DELIBERATION, THE EUROPEAN UNION HAS FORMALLY RECOGNIZED THE UNITED STATES OF AFRICA. MESSAGES OF CONGRATULATIONS WERE SENT OUT TODAY...
Z1

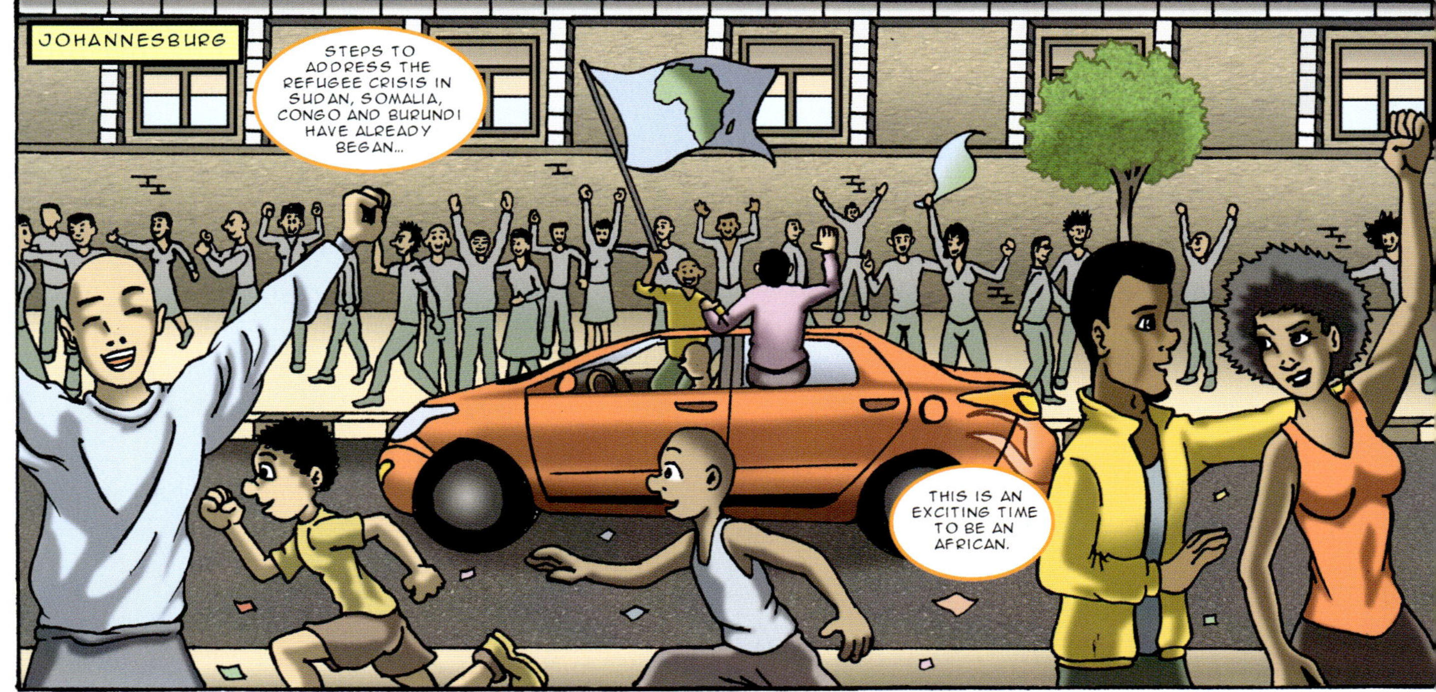
JOHANNESBURG
STEPS TO ADDRESS THE REFUGEE CRISIS IN SUDAN, SOMALIA, CONGO AND BURUNDI HAVE ALREADY BEGAN...
THIS IS AN EXCITING TIME TO BE AN AFRICAN.

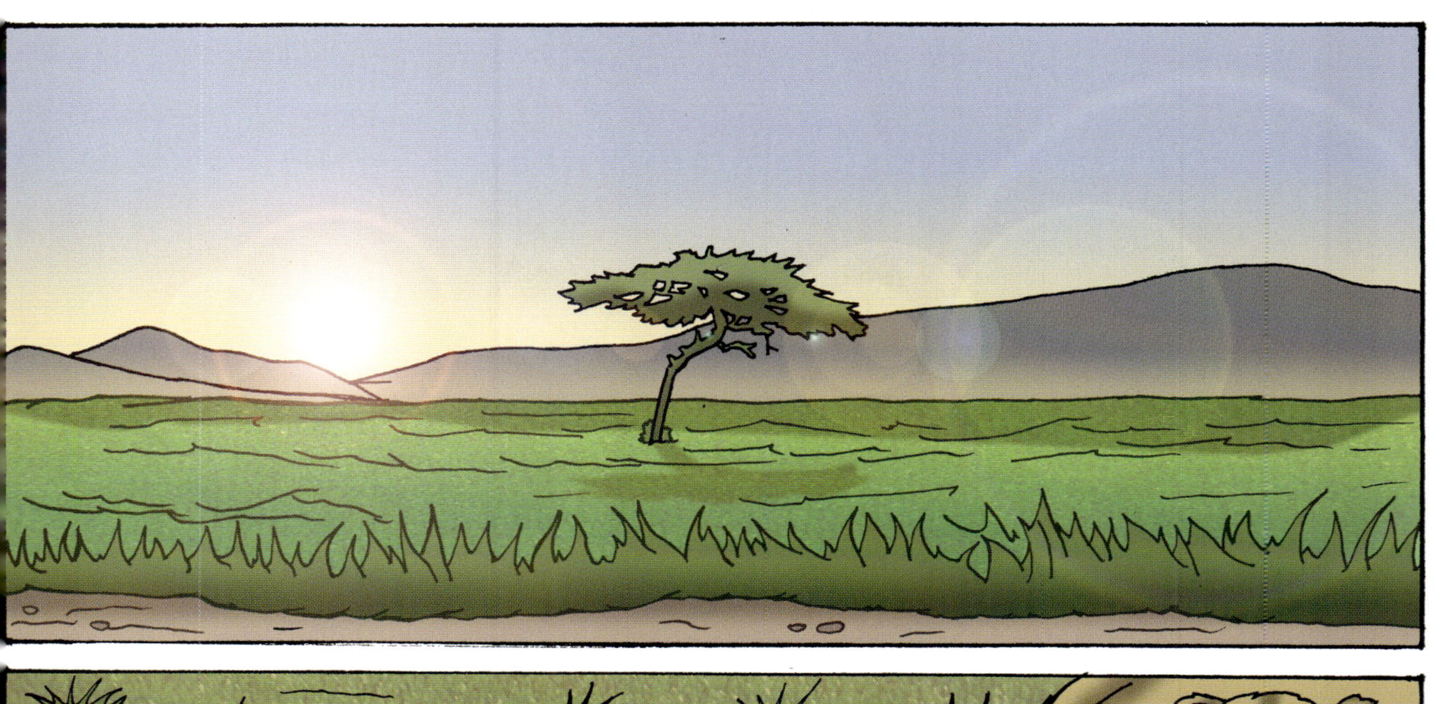

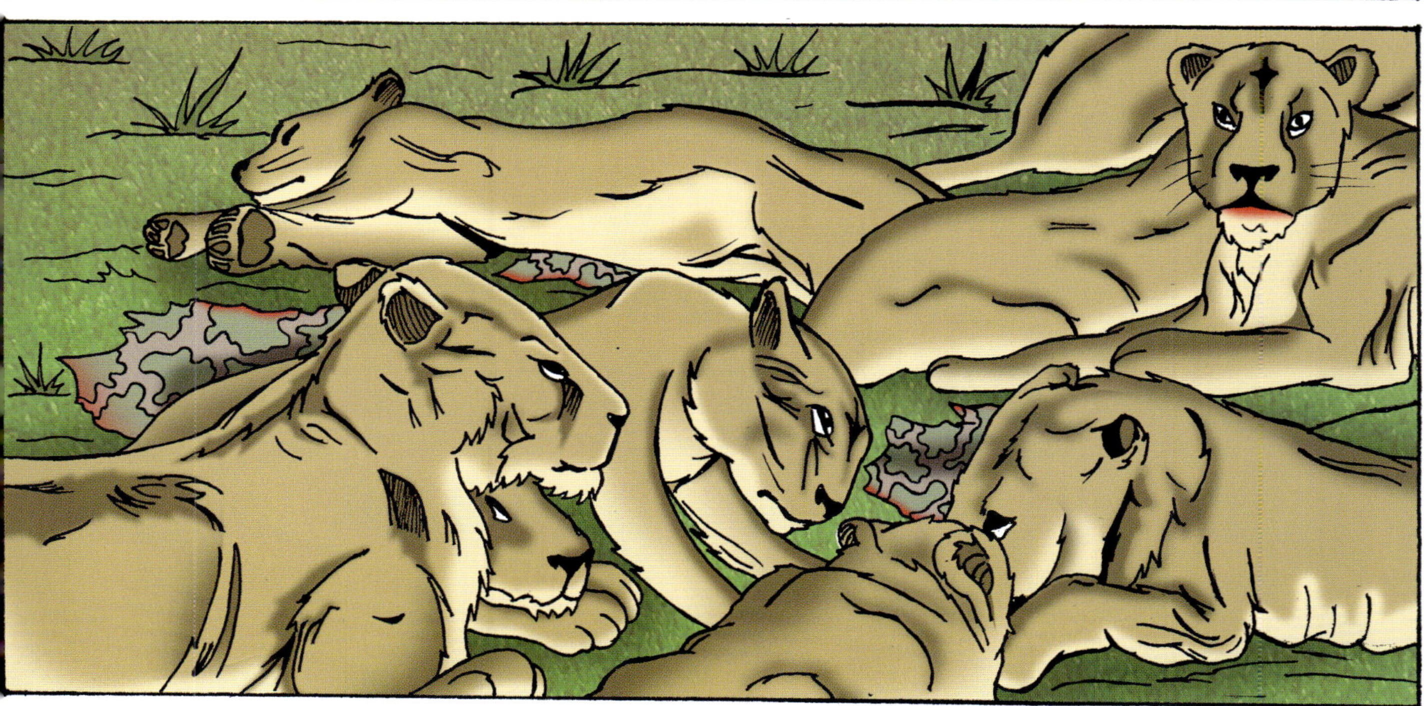

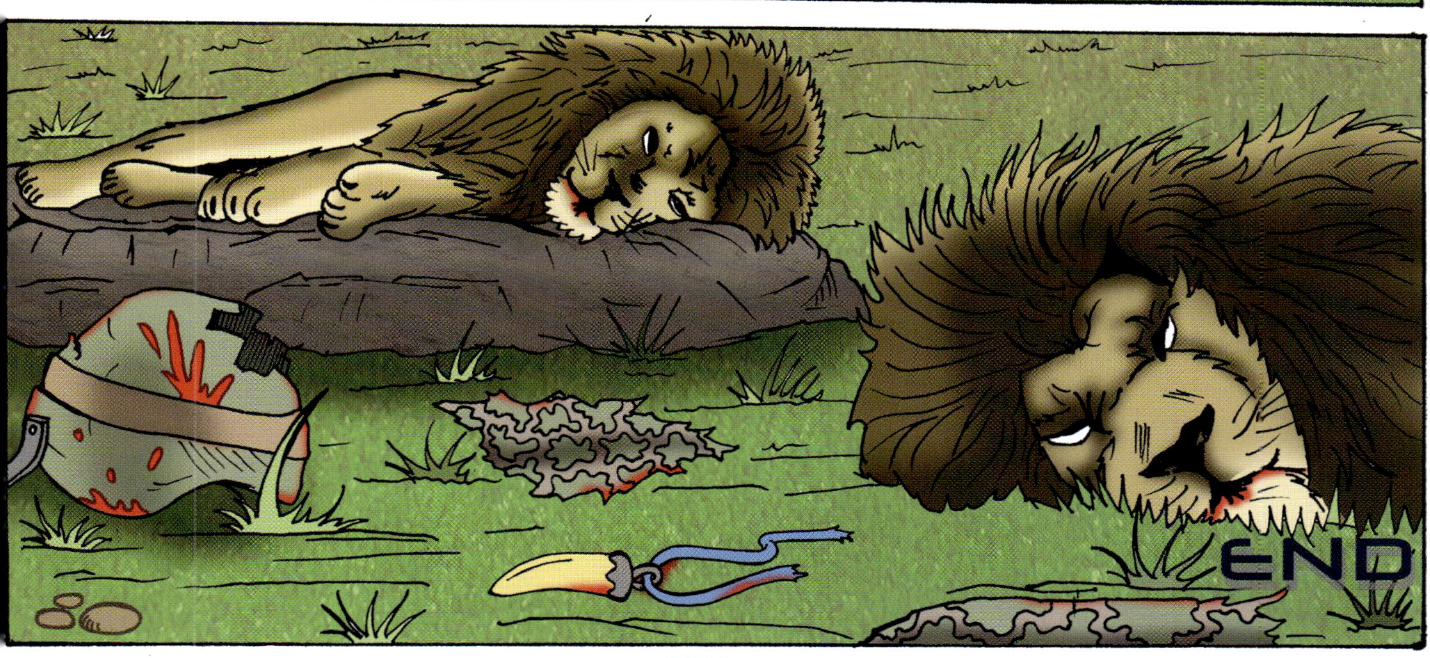
END

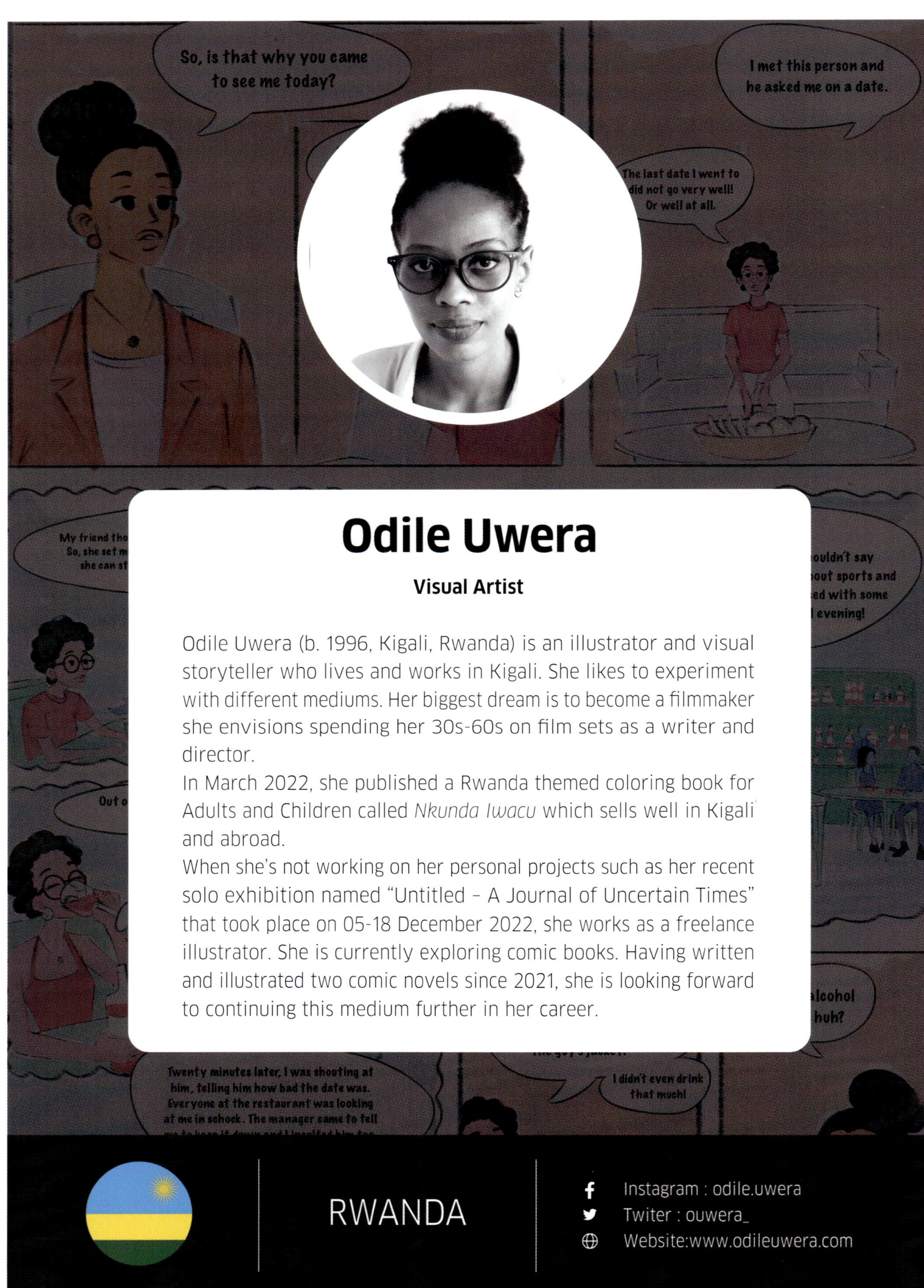

Odile Uwera

Visual Artist

Odile Uwera (b. 1996, Kigali, Rwanda) is an illustrator and visual storyteller who lives and works in Kigali. She likes to experiment with different mediums. Her biggest dream is to become a filmmaker she envisions spending her 30s-60s on film sets as a writer and director.

In March 2022, she published a Rwanda themed coloring book for Adults and Children called *Nkunda Iwacu* which sells well in Kigali and abroad.

When she's not working on her personal projects such as her recent solo exhibition named "Untitled – A Journal of Uncertain Times" that took place on 05-18 December 2022, she works as a freelance illustrator. She is currently exploring comic books. Having written and illustrated two comic novels since 2021, she is looking forward to continuing this medium further in her career.

RWANDA

Instagram : odile.uwera
Twiter : ouwera_
Website:www.odileuwera.com

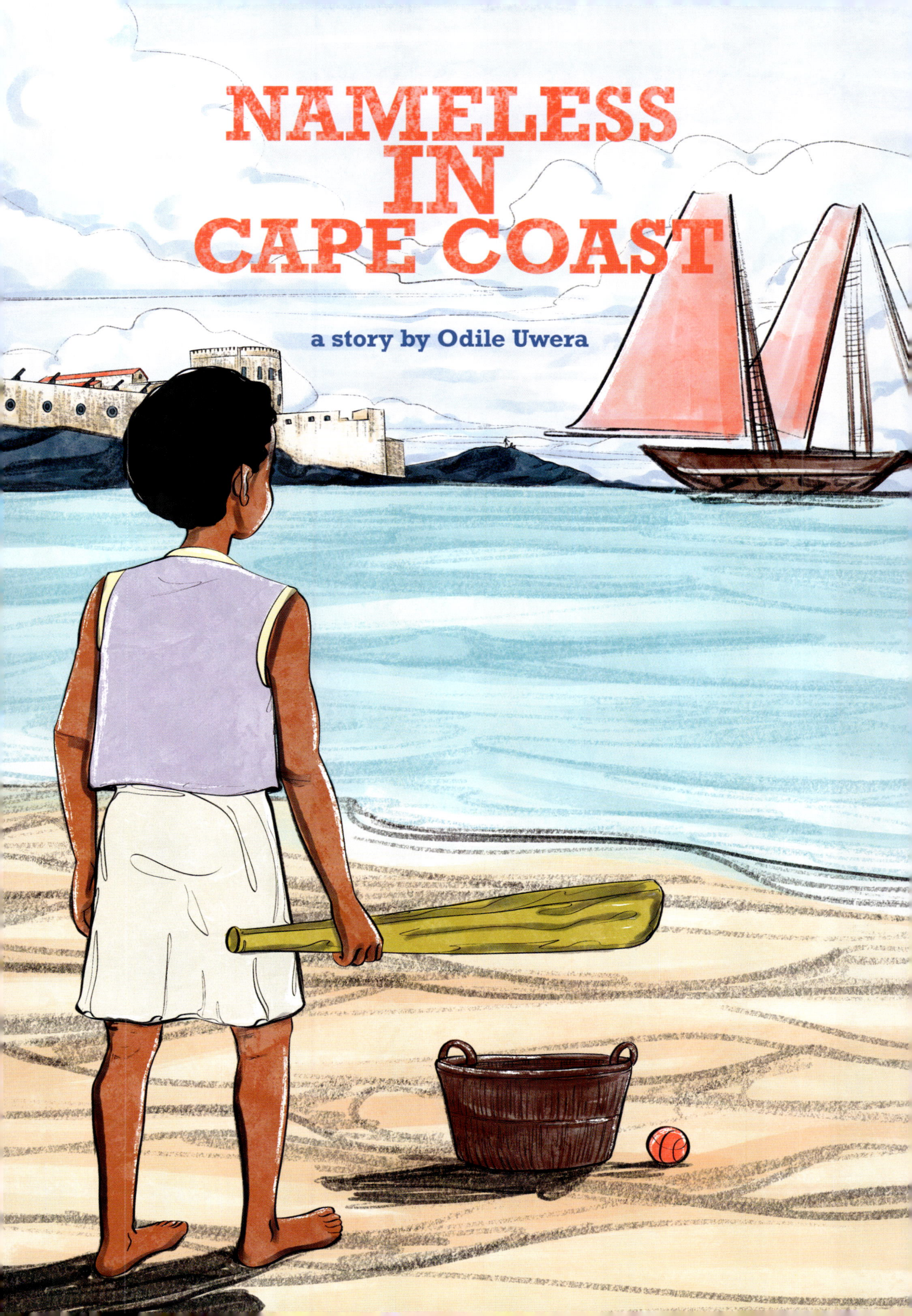
NAMELESS
IN
CAPE COAST
a story by Odile Uwera

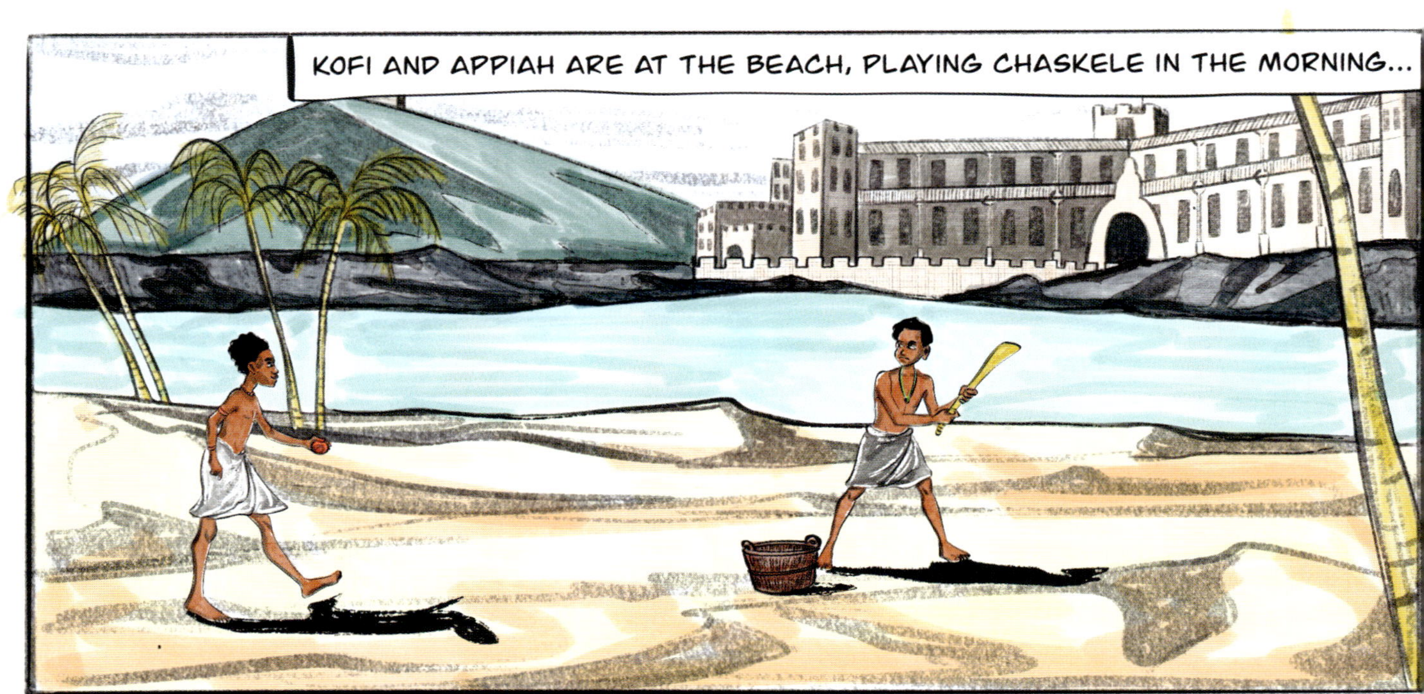
KOFI AND APPIAH ARE AT THE BEACH, PLAYING CHASKELE IN THE MORNING...

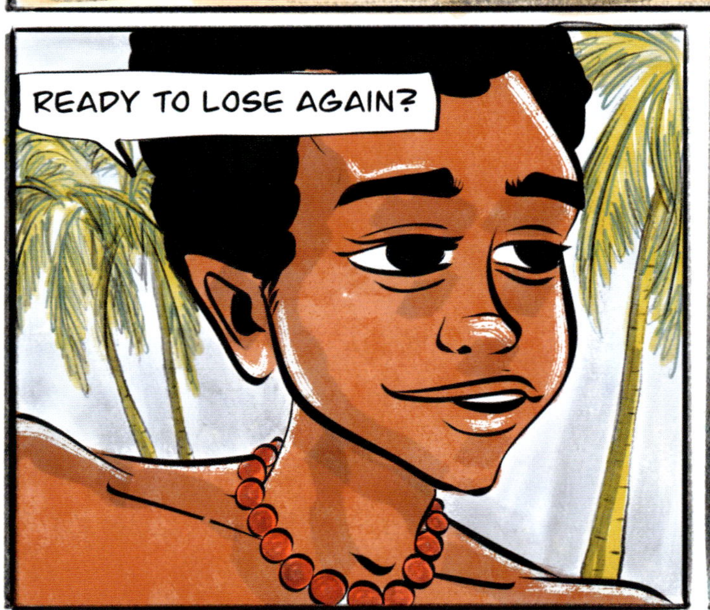
READY TO LOSE AGAIN?

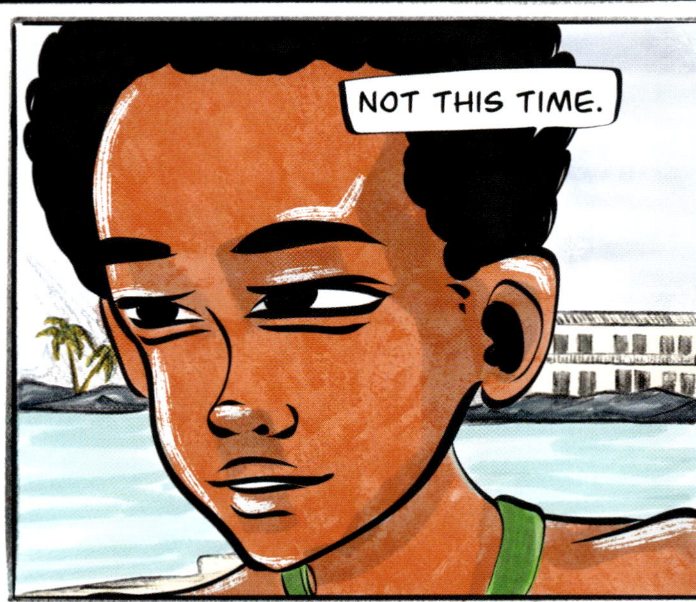
NOT THIS TIME.

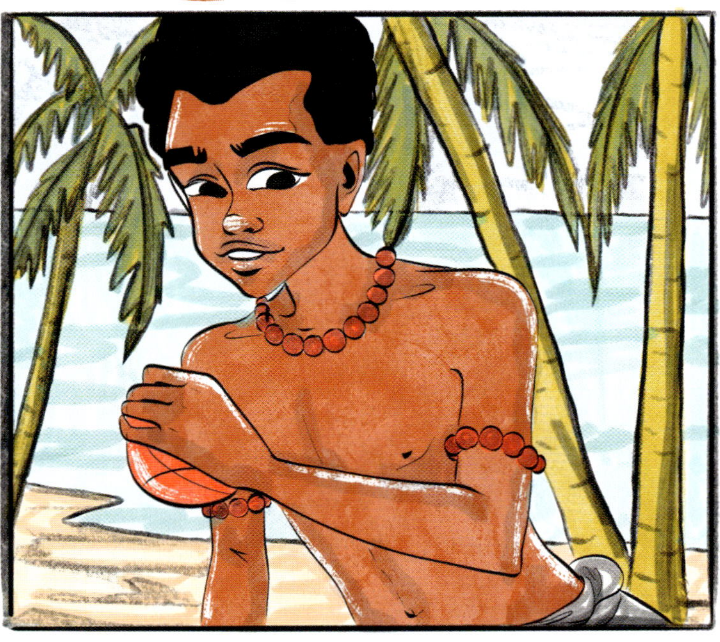

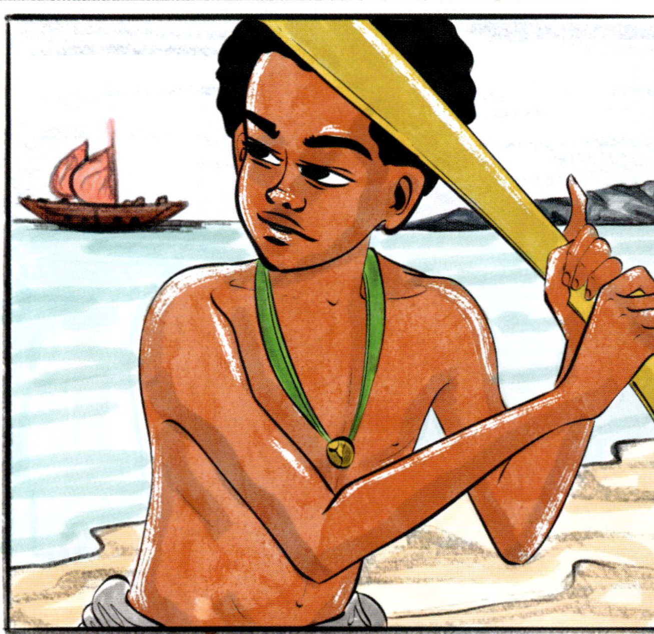

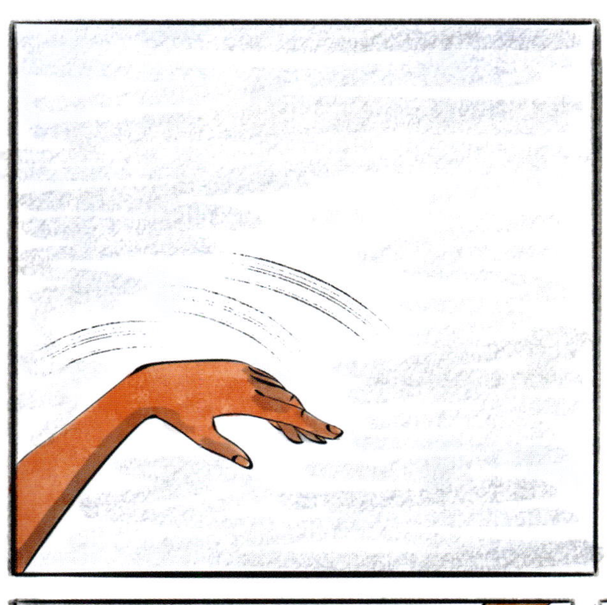
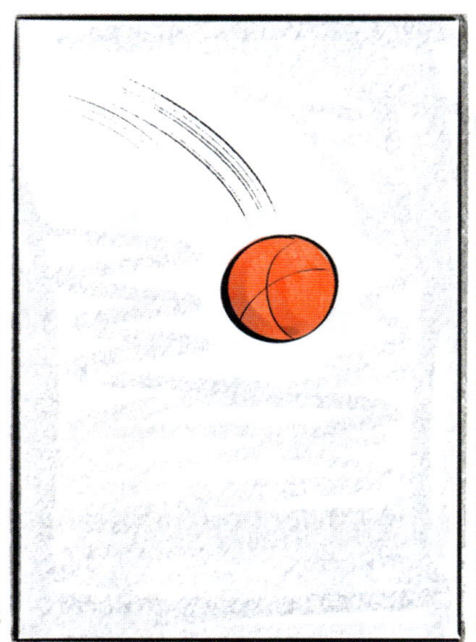
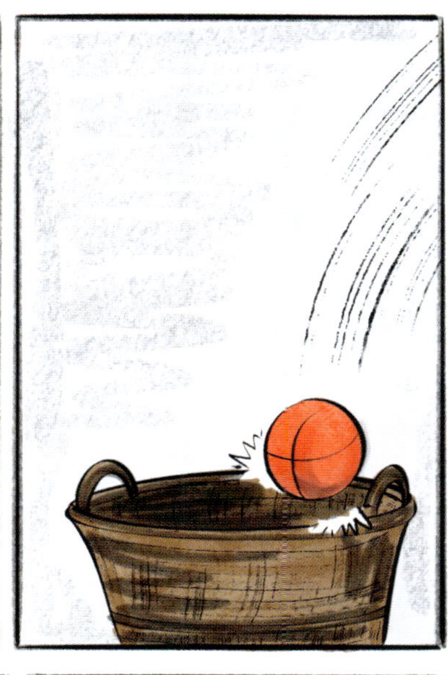
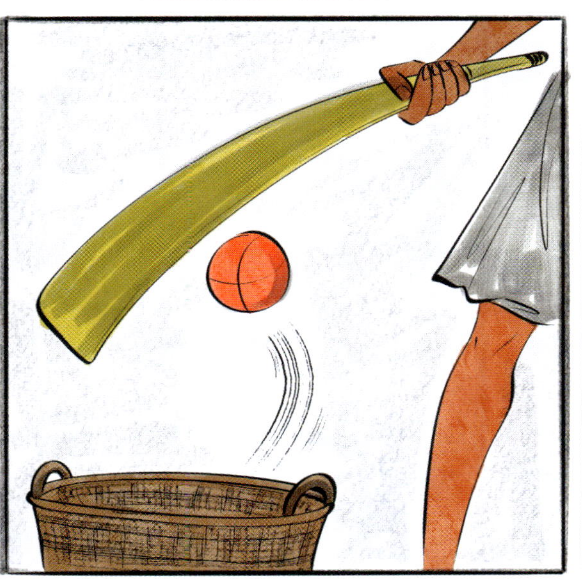
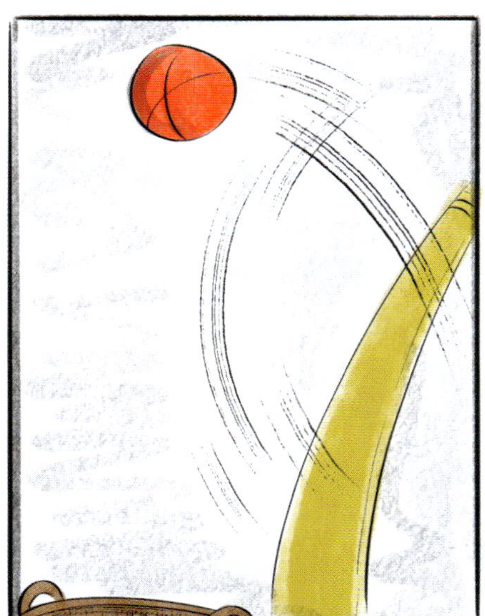
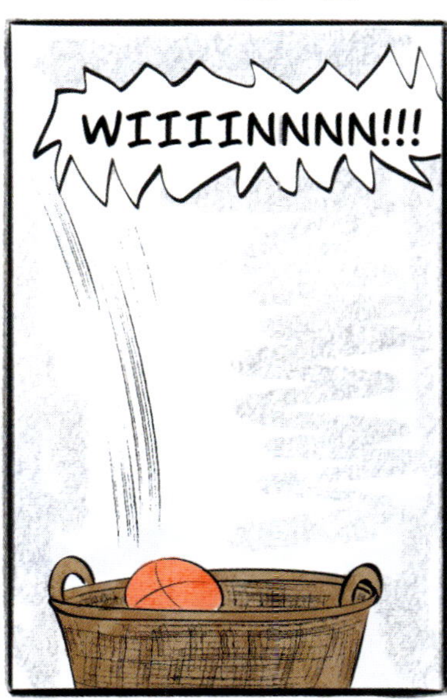
WIIIINNNN!!!
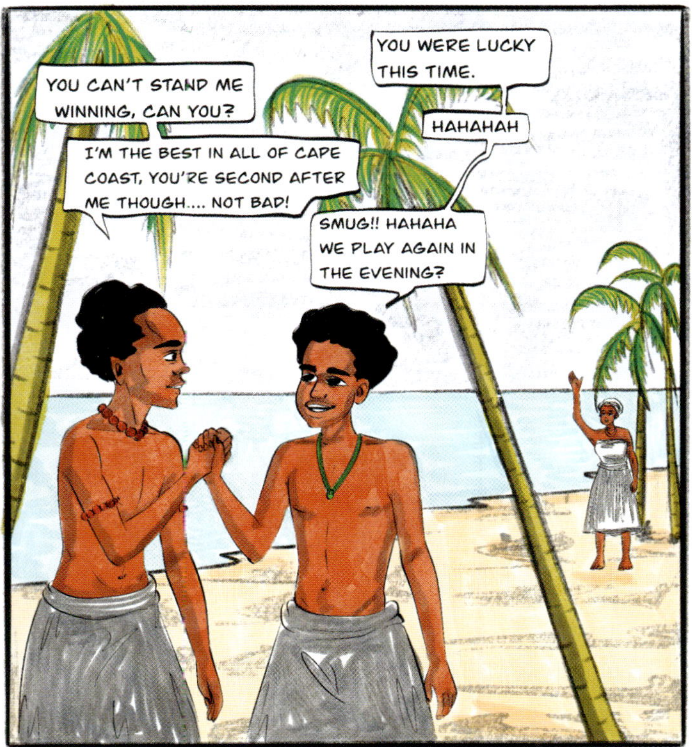
YOU CAN'T STAND ME WINNING, CAN YOU?
I'M THE BEST IN ALL OF CAPE COAST, YOU'RE SECOND AFTER ME THOUGH.... NOT BAD!
YOU WERE LUCKY THIS TIME.
HAHAHAH
SMUG!! HAHAHA WE PLAY AGAIN IN THE EVENING?
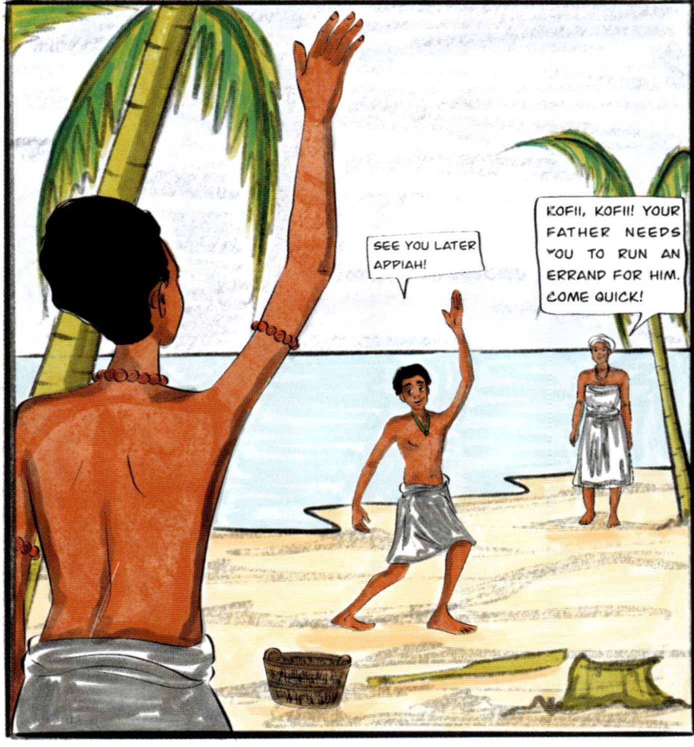
SEE YOU LATER APPIAH!
KOFII, KOFII! YOUR FATHER NEEDS YOU TO RUN AN ERRAND FOR HIM. COME QUICK!

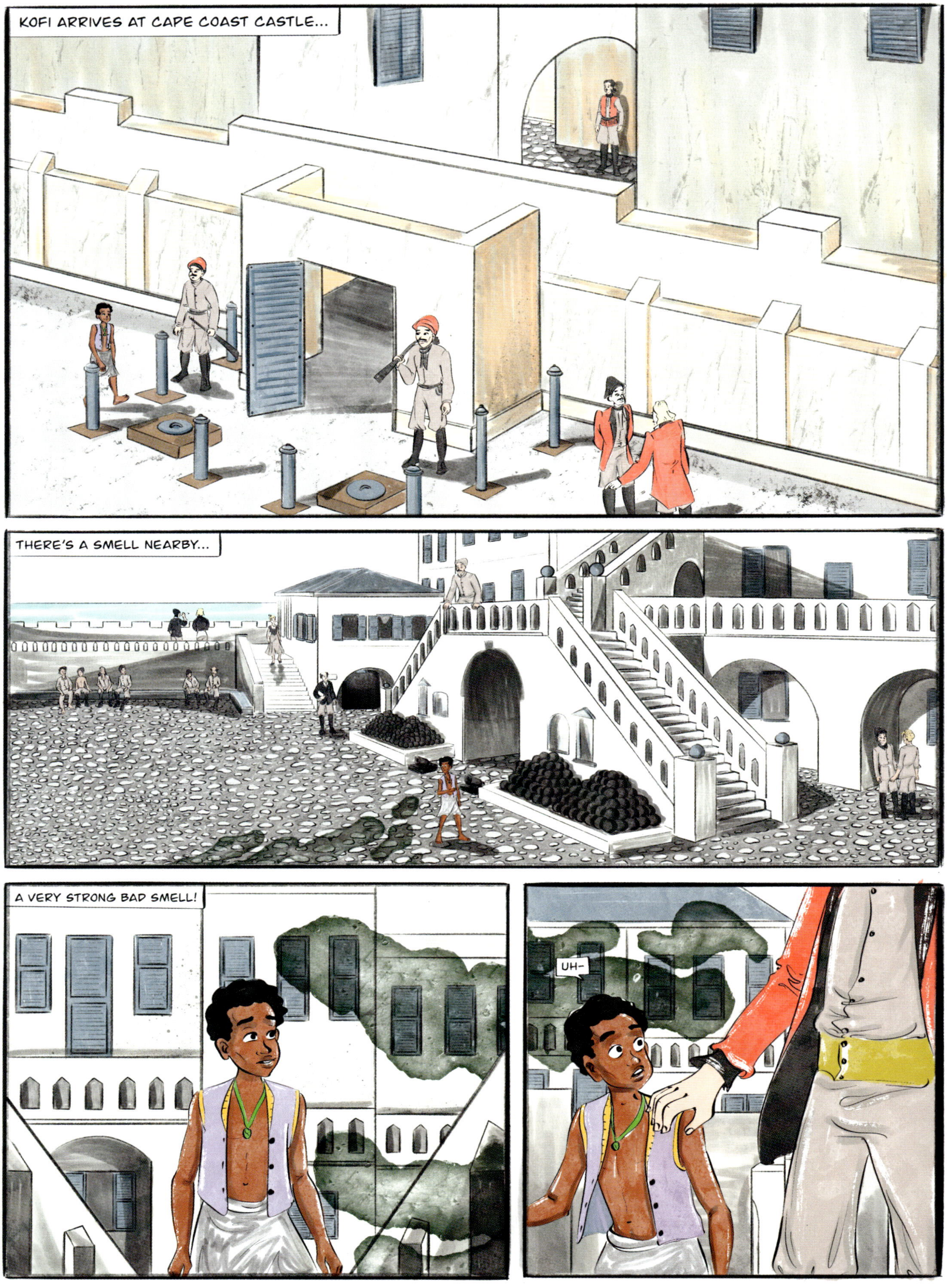

KOFI ARRIVES AT CAPE COAST CASTLE...

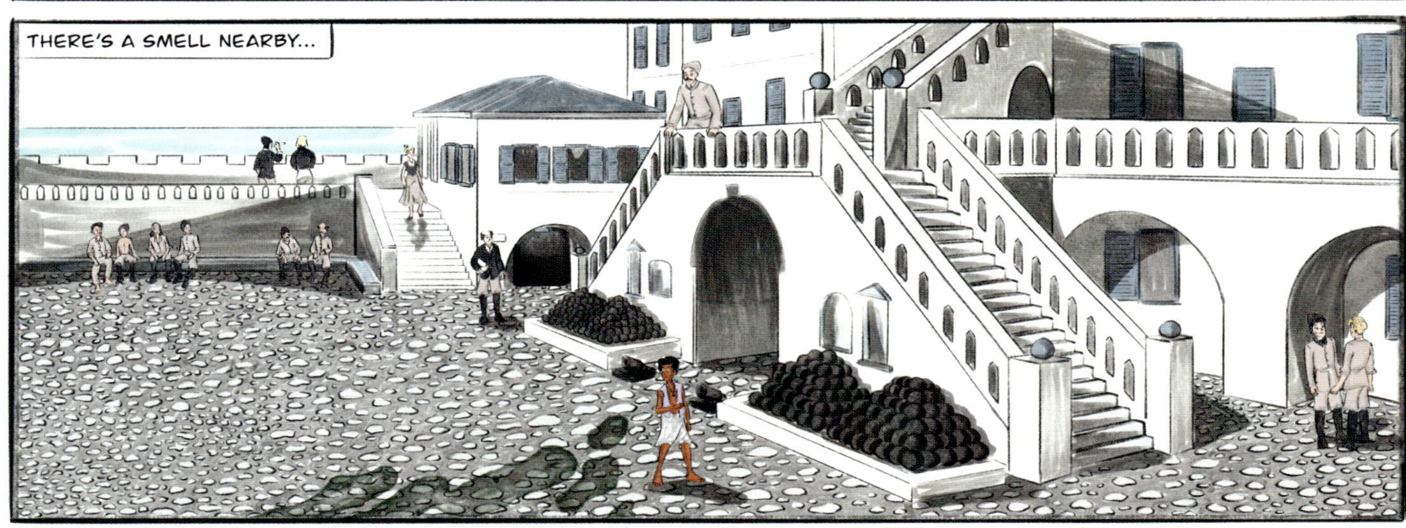

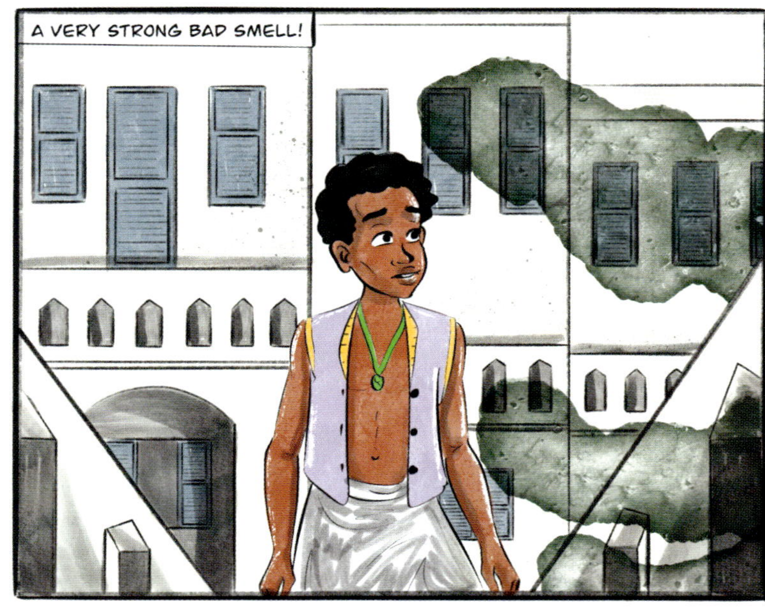

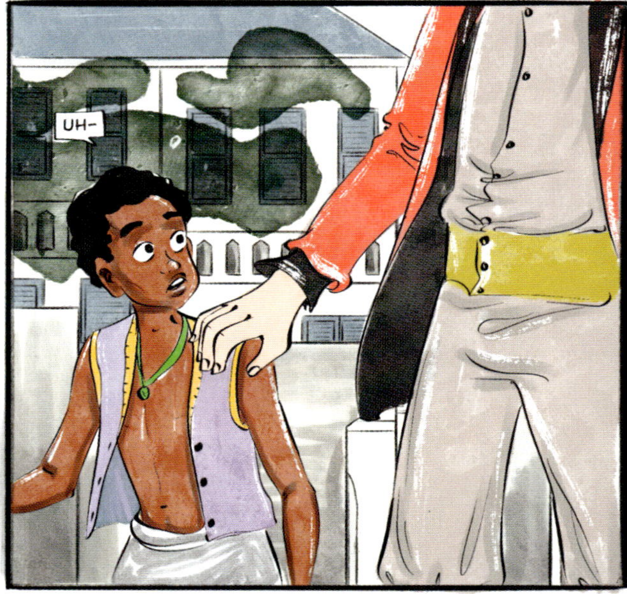

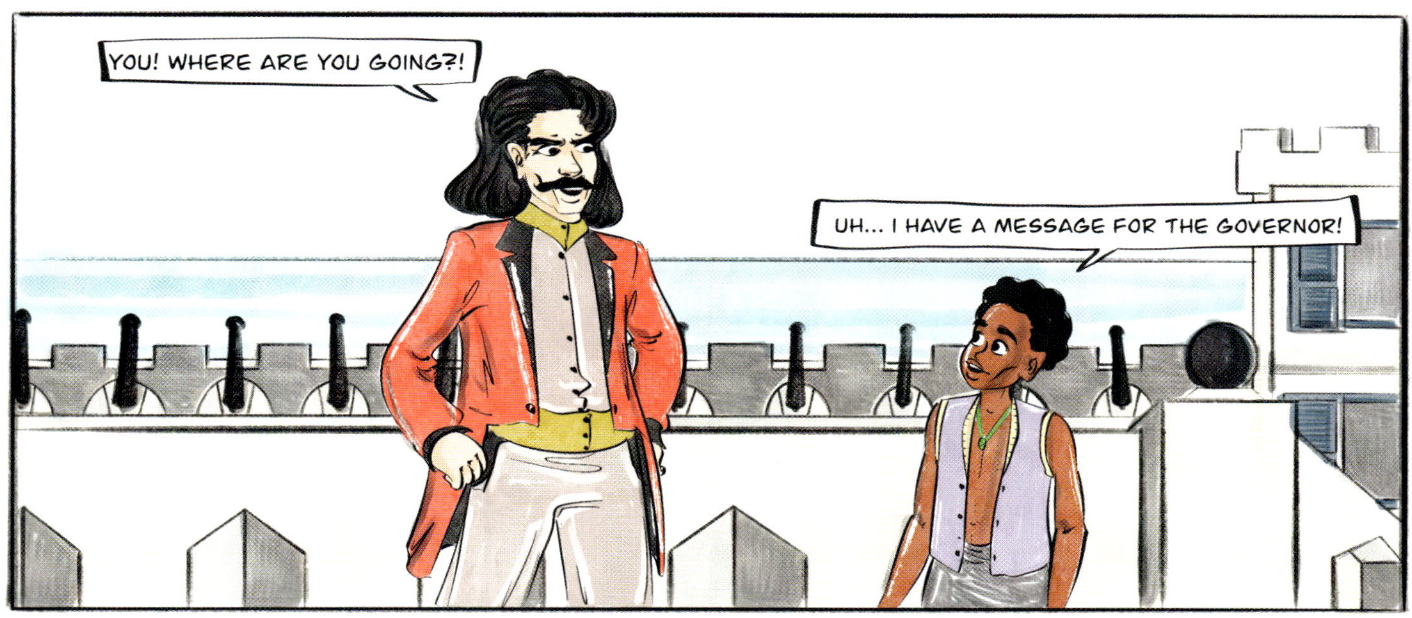
YOU! WHERE ARE YOU GOING?!
UH... I HAVE A MESSAGE FOR THE GOVERNOR!

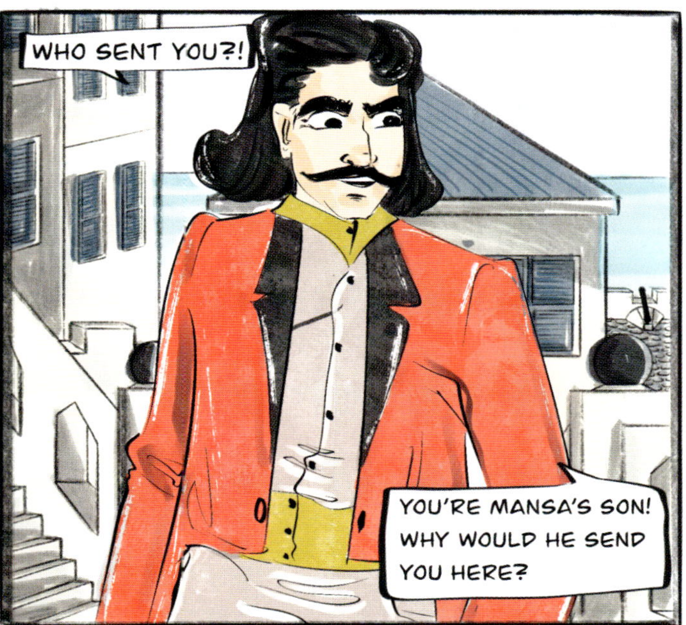
WHO SENT YOU?!

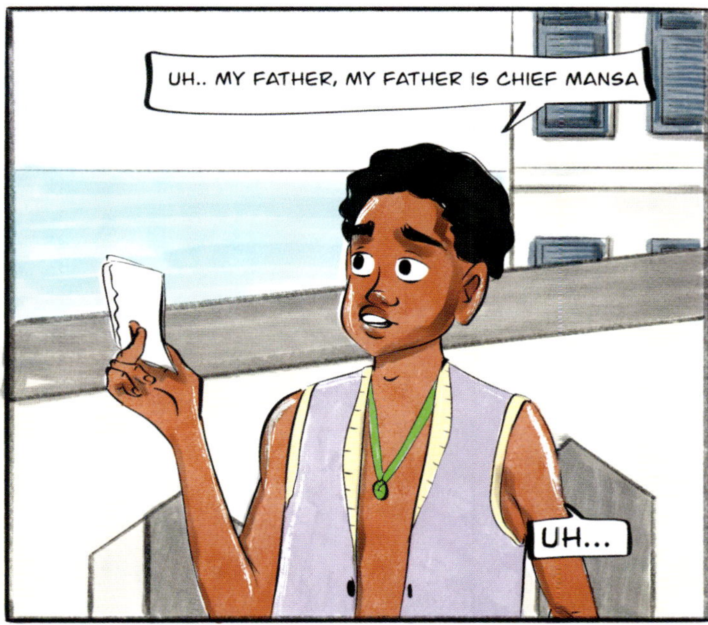
UH.. MY FATHER, MY FATHER IS CHIEF MANSA
YOU'RE MANSA'S SON! WHY WOULD HE SEND YOU HERE?
UH...

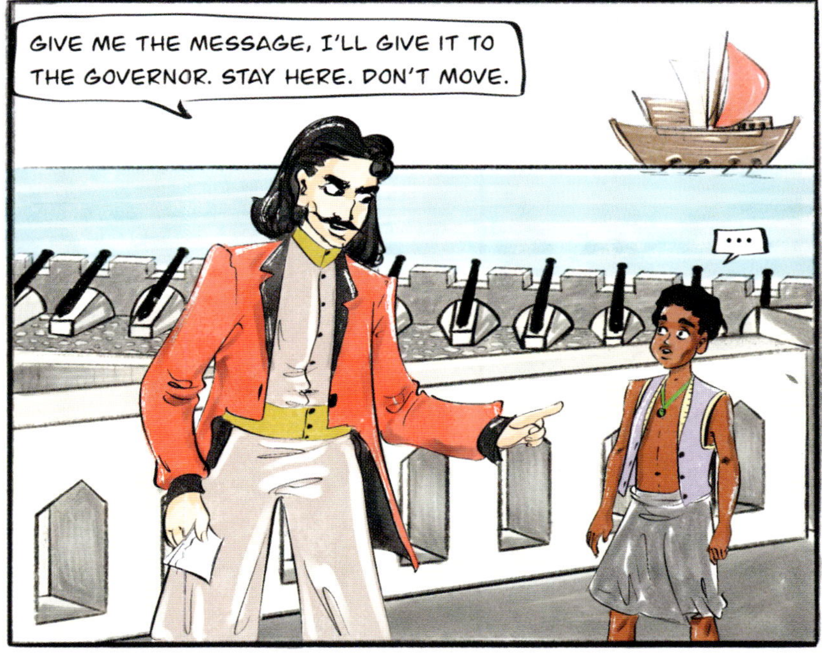
GIVE ME THE MESSAGE, I'LL GIVE IT TO THE GOVERNOR. STAY HERE. DON'T MOVE.
...

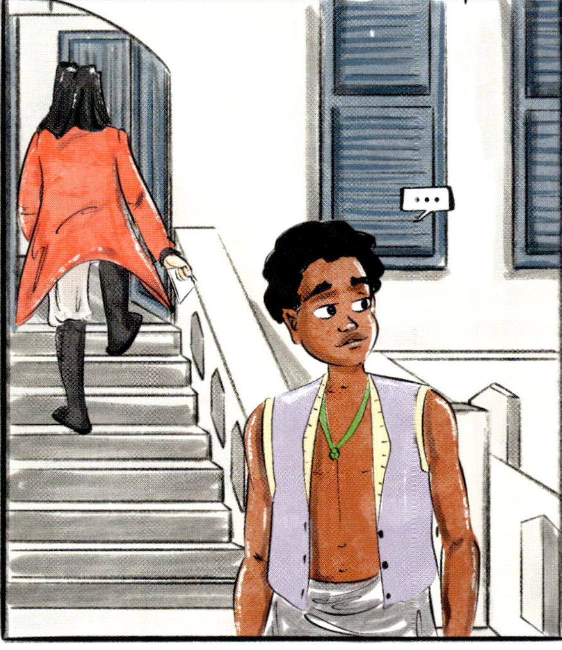
...

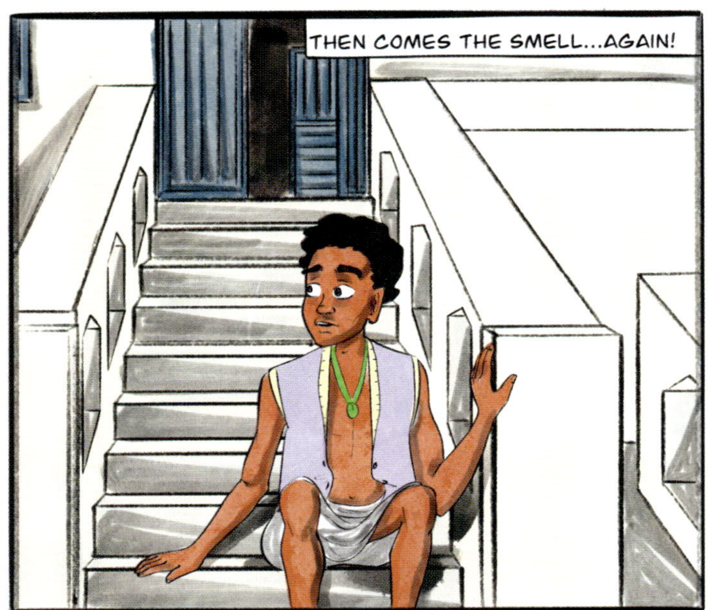
THEN COMES THE SMELL...AGAIN!

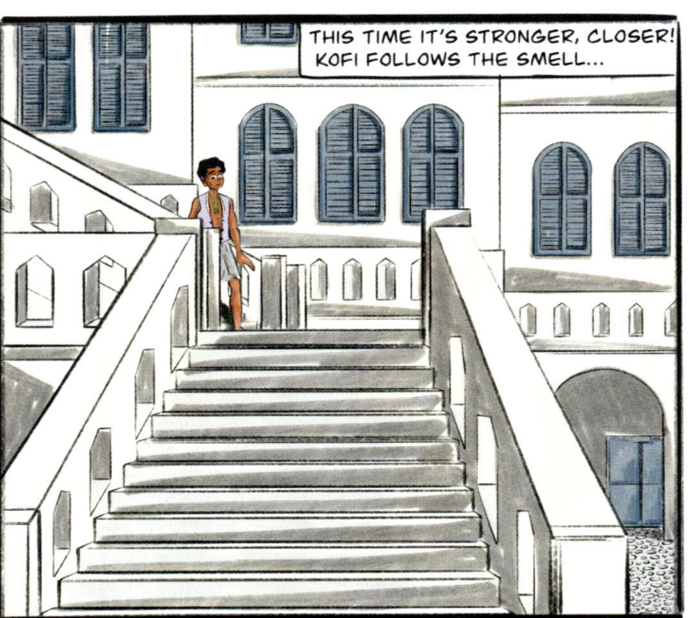
THIS TIME IT'S STRONGER, CLOSER!
KOFI FOLLOWS THE SMELL...

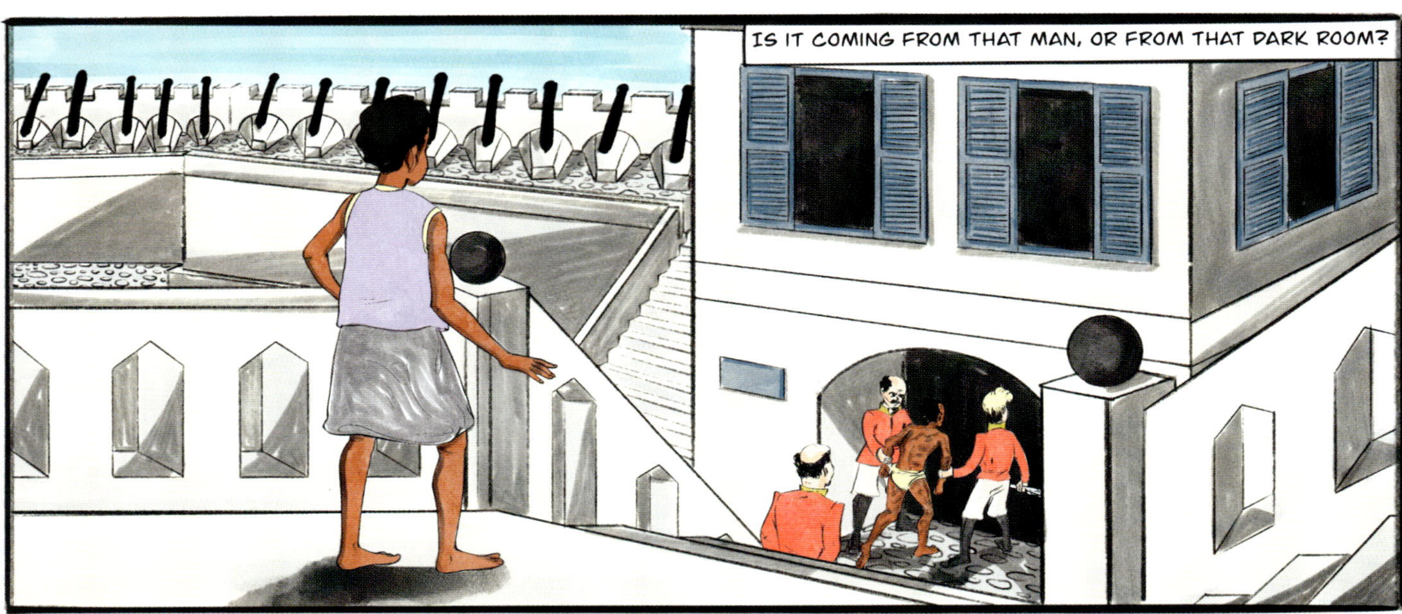
IS IT COMING FROM THAT MAN, OR FROM THAT DARK ROOM?

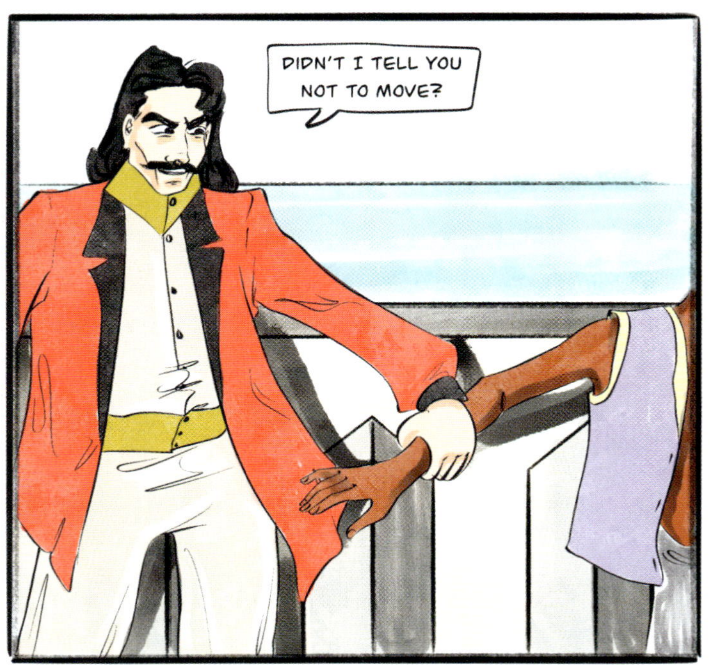
DIDN'T I TELL YOU NOT TO MOVE?

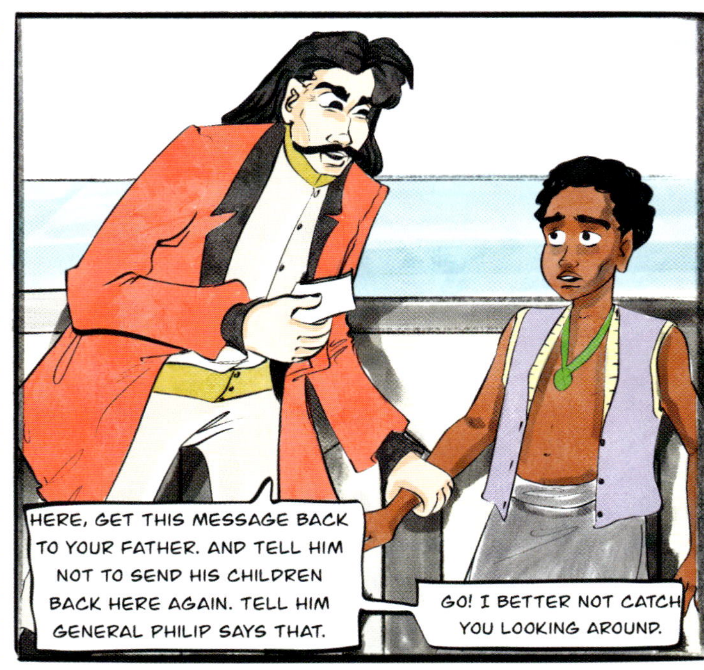
HERE, GET THIS MESSAGE BACK TO YOUR FATHER. AND TELL HIM NOT TO SEND HIS CHILDREN BACK HERE AGAIN. TELL HIM GENERAL PHILIP SAYS THAT.
GO! I BETTER NOT CATCH YOU LOOKING AROUND.

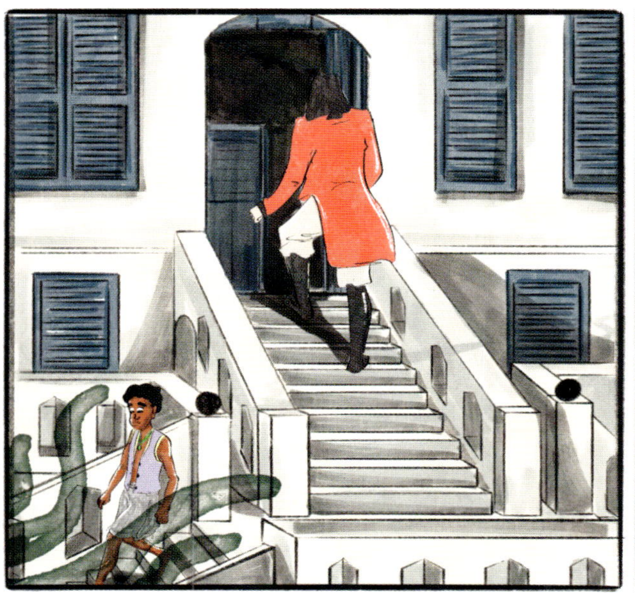
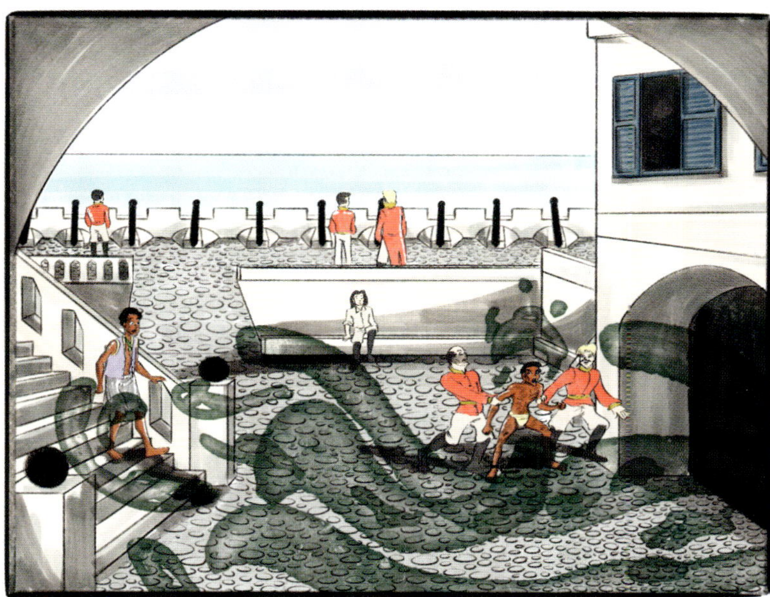
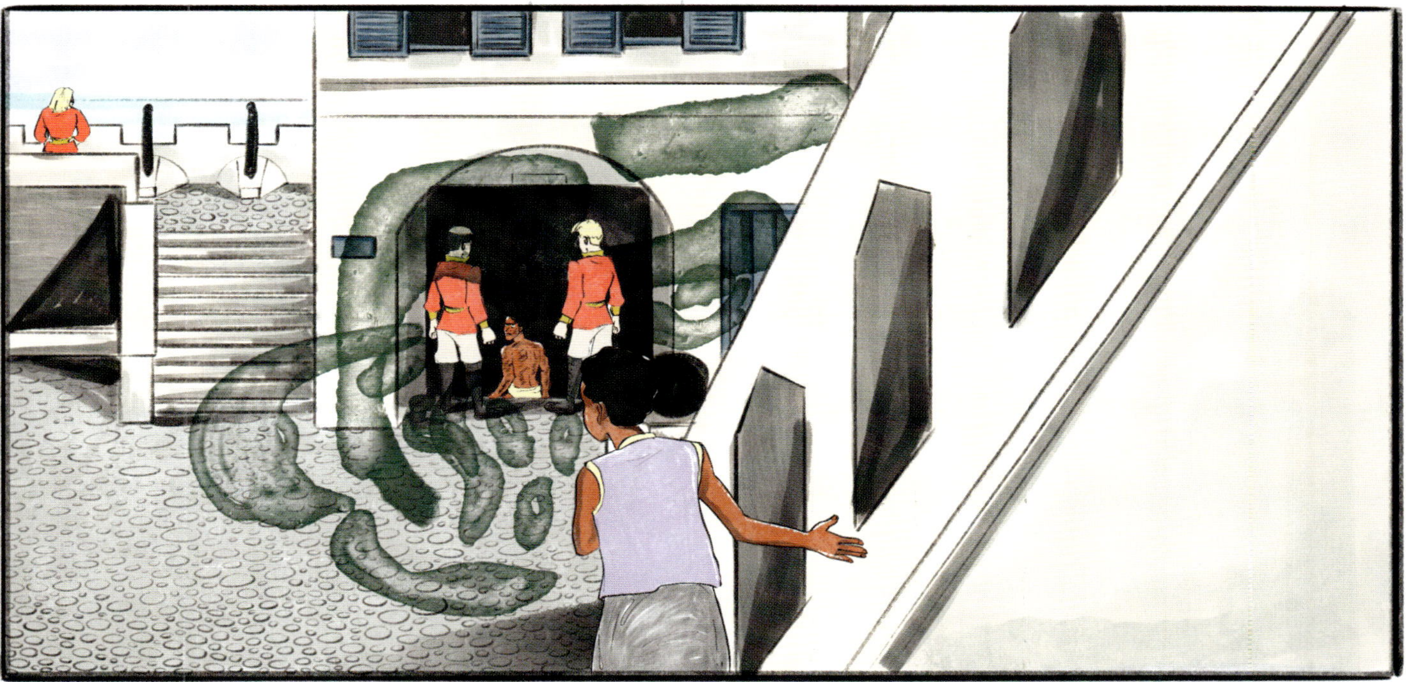
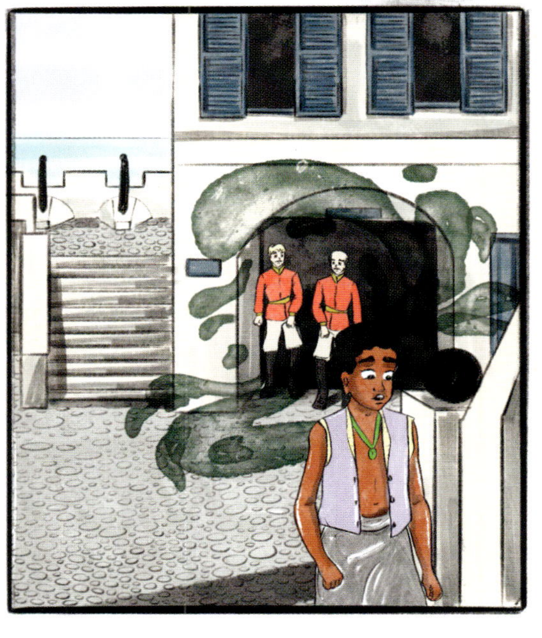
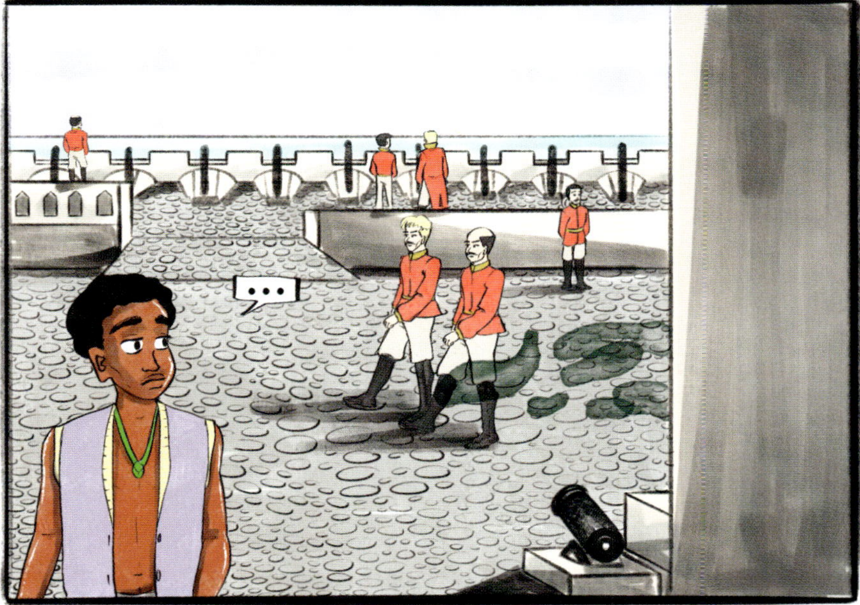

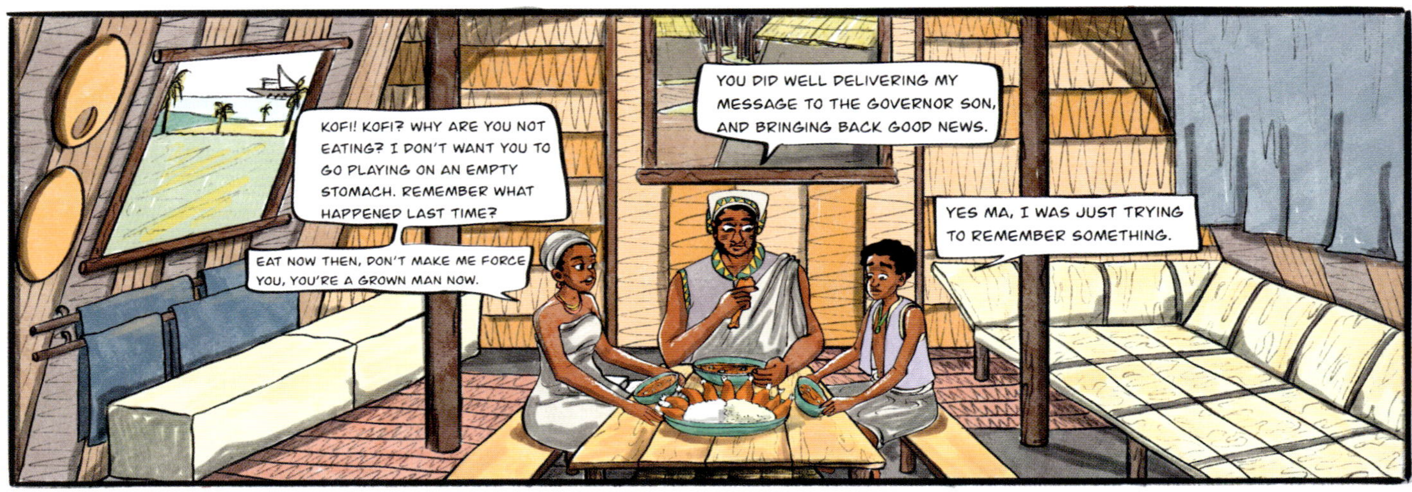
KOFI! KOFI? WHY ARE YOU NOT EATING? I DON'T WANT YOU TO GO PLAYING ON AN EMPTY STOMACH. REMEMBER WHAT HAPPENED LAST TIME?
EAT NOW THEN, DON'T MAKE ME FORCE YOU, YOU'RE A GROWN MAN NOW.
YOU DID WELL DELIVERING MY MESSAGE TO THE GOVERNOR SON, AND BRINGING BACK GOOD NEWS.
YES MA, I WAS JUST TRYING TO REMEMBER SOMETHING.

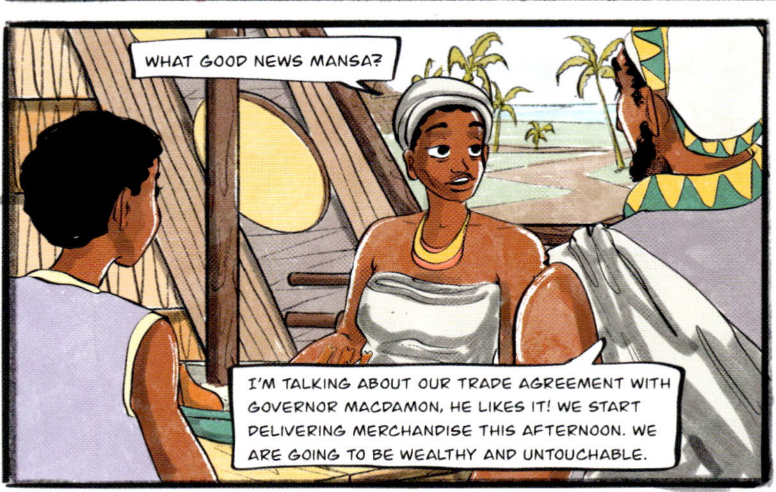
WHAT GOOD NEWS MANSA?
I'M TALKING ABOUT OUR TRADE AGREEMENT WITH GOVERNOR MACDAMON, HE LIKES IT! WE START DELIVERING MERCHANDISE THIS AFTERNOON. WE ARE GOING TO BE WEALTHY AND UNTOUCHABLE.

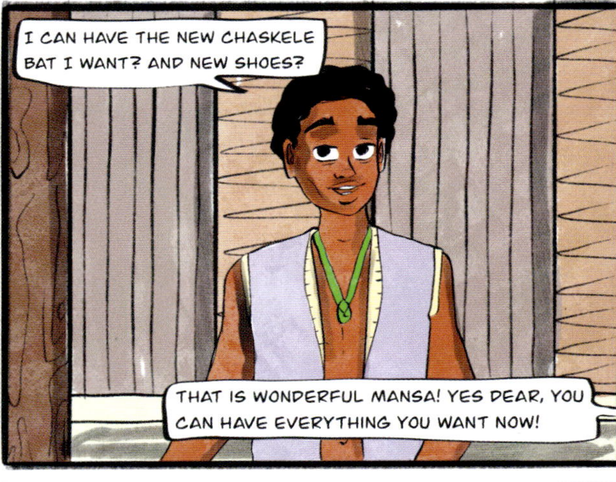
I CAN HAVE THE NEW CHASKELE BAT I WANT? AND NEW SHOES?
THAT IS WONDERFUL MANSA! YES DEAR, YOU CAN HAVE EVERYTHING YOU WANT NOW!

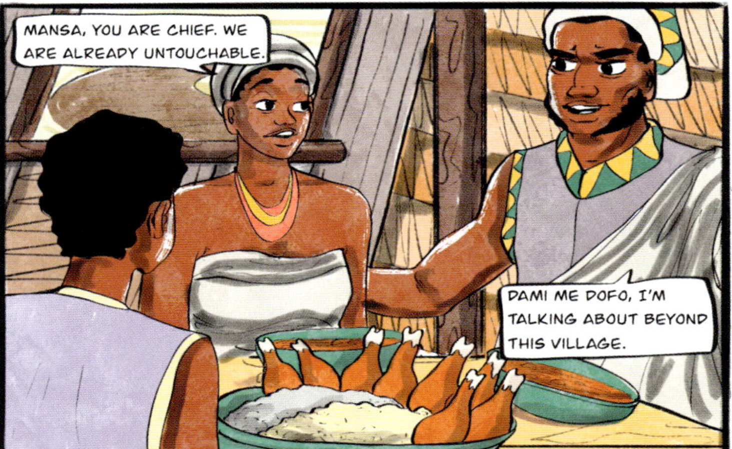
MANSA, YOU ARE CHIEF. WE ARE ALREADY UNTOUCHABLE.
DAMI ME DOFO, I'M TALKING ABOUT BEYOND THIS VILLAGE.

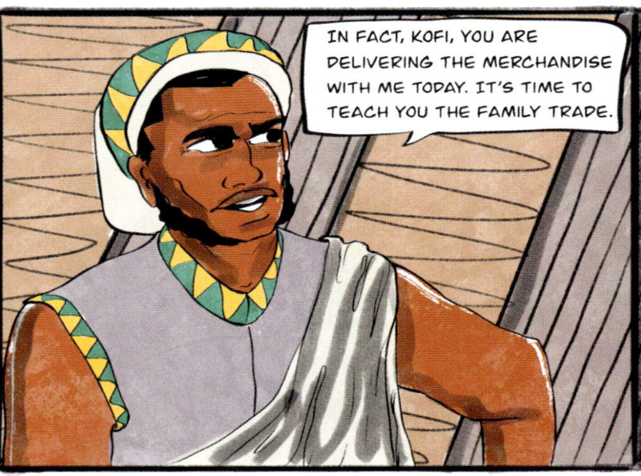
IN FACT, KOFI, YOU ARE DELIVERING THE MERCHANDISE WITH ME TODAY. IT'S TIME TO TEACH YOU THE FAMILY TRADE.

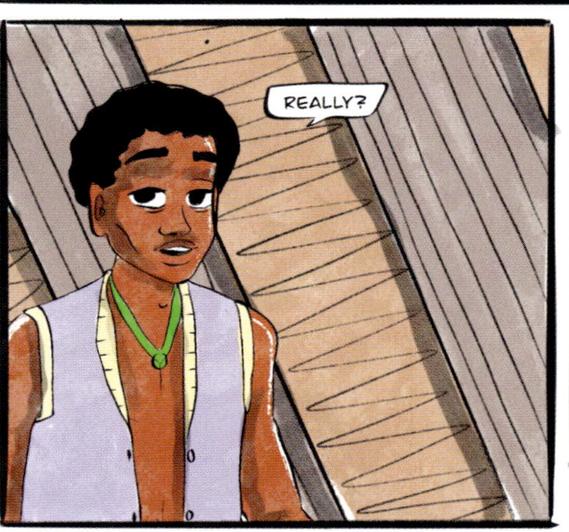
REALLY?

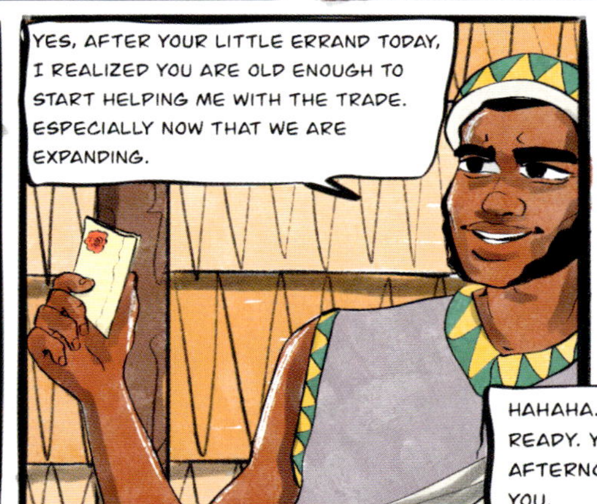
YES, AFTER YOUR LITTLE ERRAND TODAY, I REALIZED YOU ARE OLD ENOUGH TO START HELPING ME WITH THE TRADE. ESPECIALLY NOW THAT WE ARE EXPANDING.
BUT FATHER, GENERAL PHILIP TOLD ME TO TELL YOU NOT TO SEND ME BACK TO THE PALACE.
HAHAHA. THAT'S HOW I KNOW YOU'RE READY. YOU ARE COMING WITH ME THIS AFTERNOON, I EVEN HAVE A TASK FOR YOU.

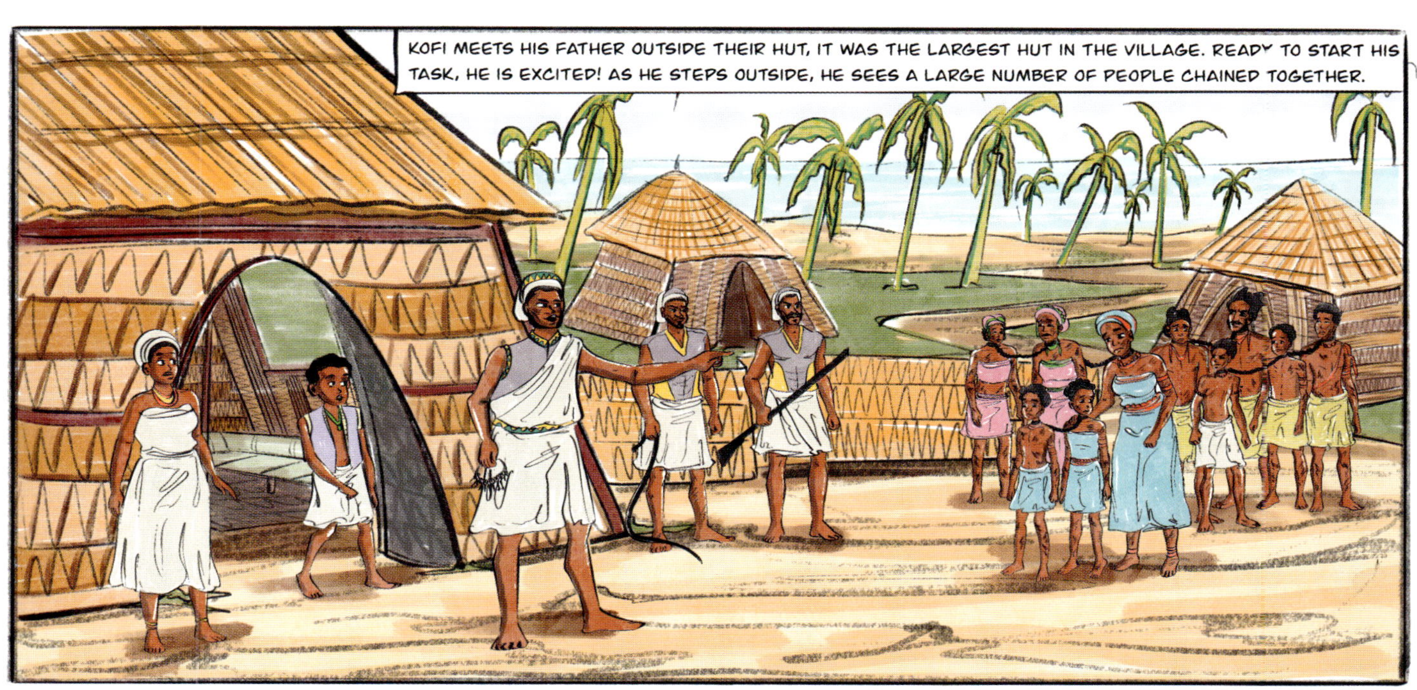
KOFI MEETS HIS FATHER OUTSIDE THEIR HUT, IT WAS THE LARGEST HUT IN THE VILLAGE. READY TO START HIS TASK, HE IS EXCITED! AS HE STEPS OUTSIDE, HE SEES A LARGE NUMBER OF PEOPLE CHAINED TOGETHER.

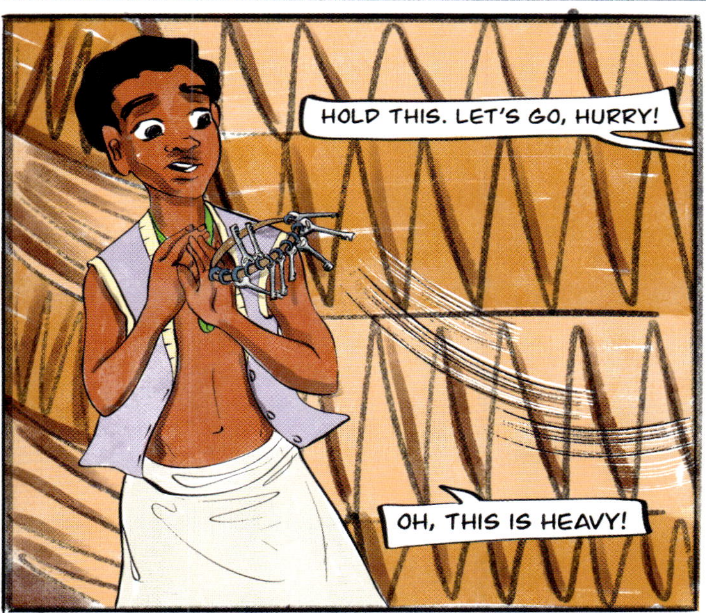
HOLD THIS. LET'S GO, HURRY!
OH, THIS IS HEAVY!

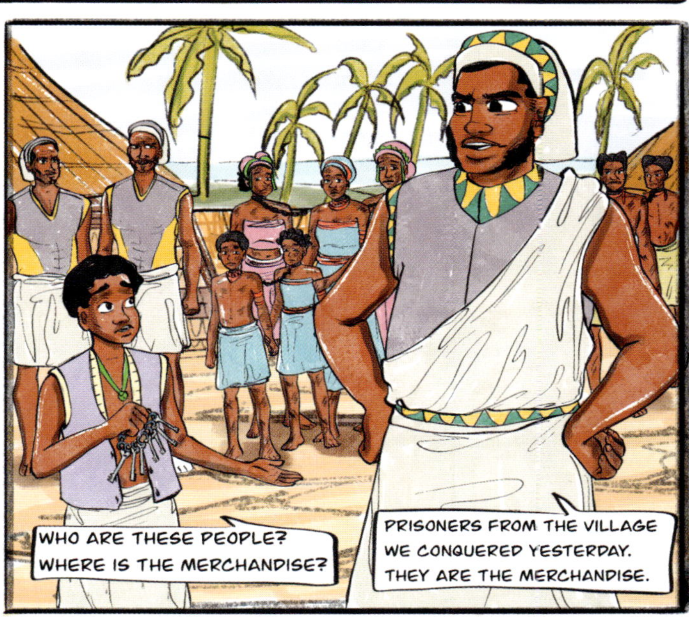
WHO ARE THESE PEOPLE? WHERE IS THE MERCHANDISE?
PRISONERS FROM THE VILLAGE WE CONQUERED YESTERDAY. THEY ARE THE MERCHANDISE.

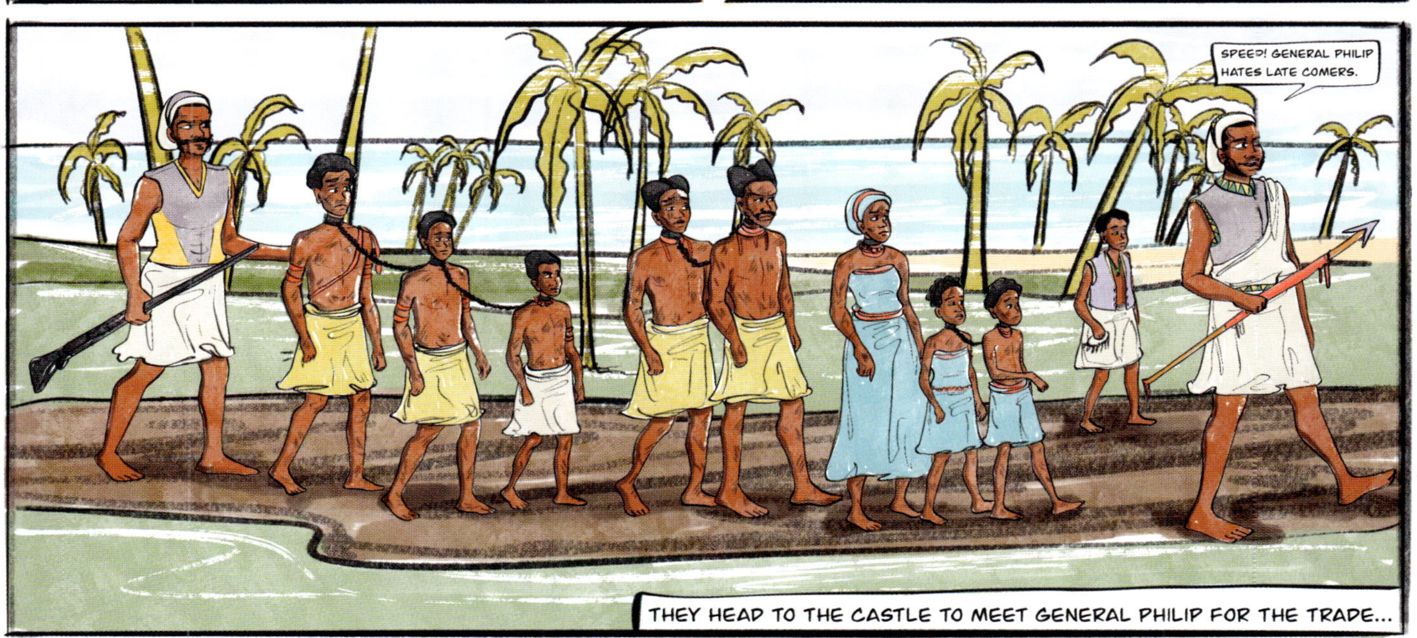
SPEED! GENERAL PHILIP HATES LATE COMERS.
THEY HEAD TO THE CASTLE TO MEET GENERAL PHILIP FOR THE TRADE...

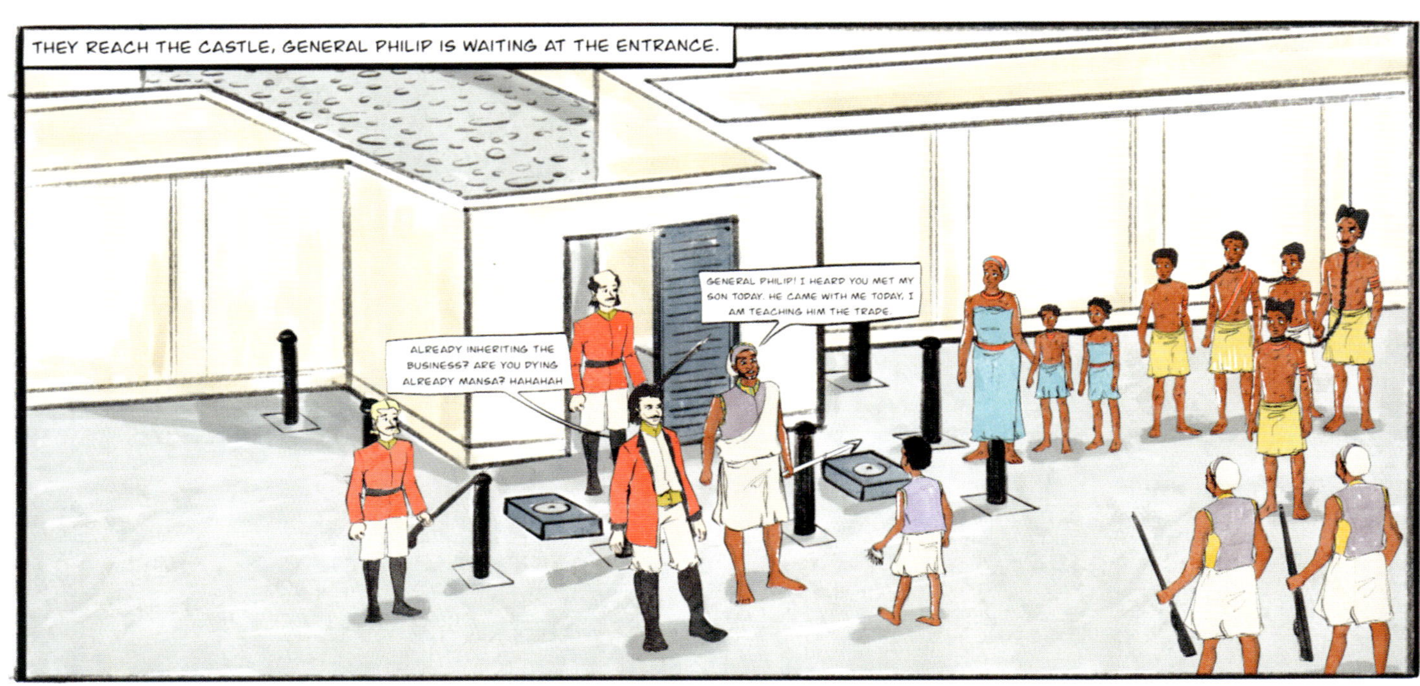
THEY REACH THE CASTLE, GENERAL PHILIP IS WAITING AT THE ENTRANCE.
GENERAL PHILIP! I HEARD YOU MET MY SON TODAY. HE CAME WITH ME TODAY, I AM TEACHING HIM THE TRADE.
ALREADY INHERITING THE BUSINESS? ARE YOU DYING ALREADY MANSA? HAHAHAH

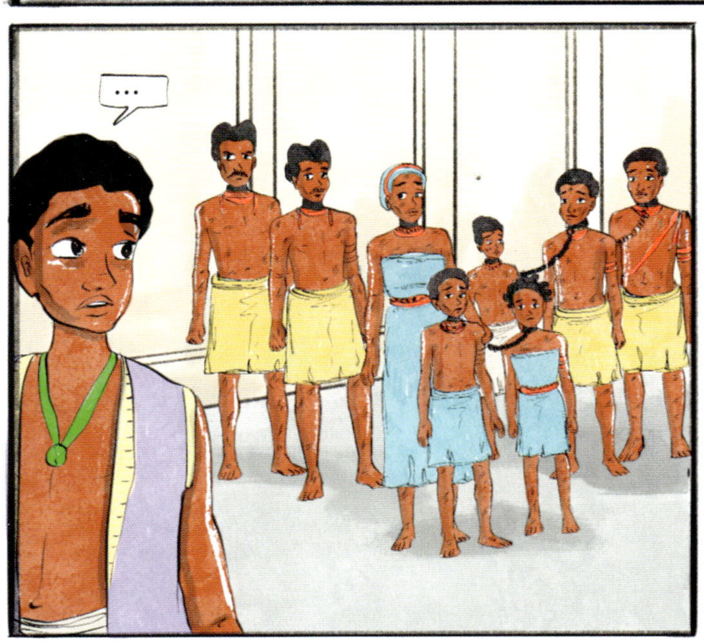
...

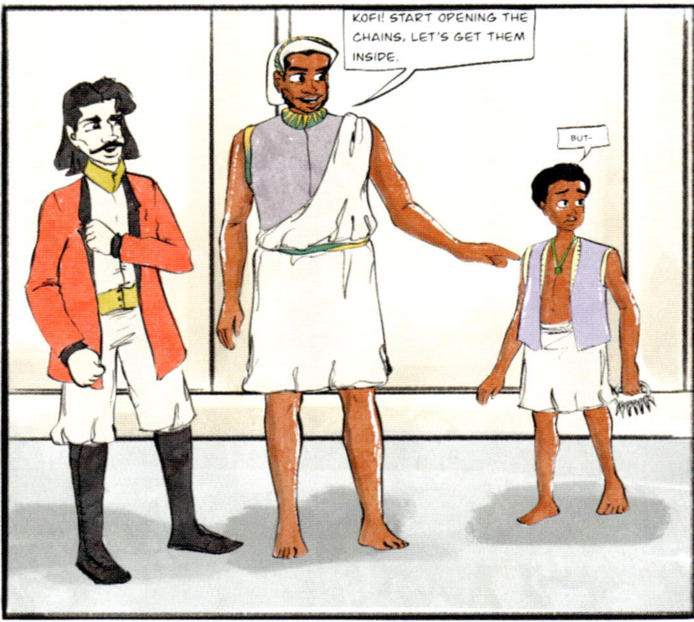
KOFI! START OPENING THE CHAINS, LET'S GET THEM INSIDE.
BUT-

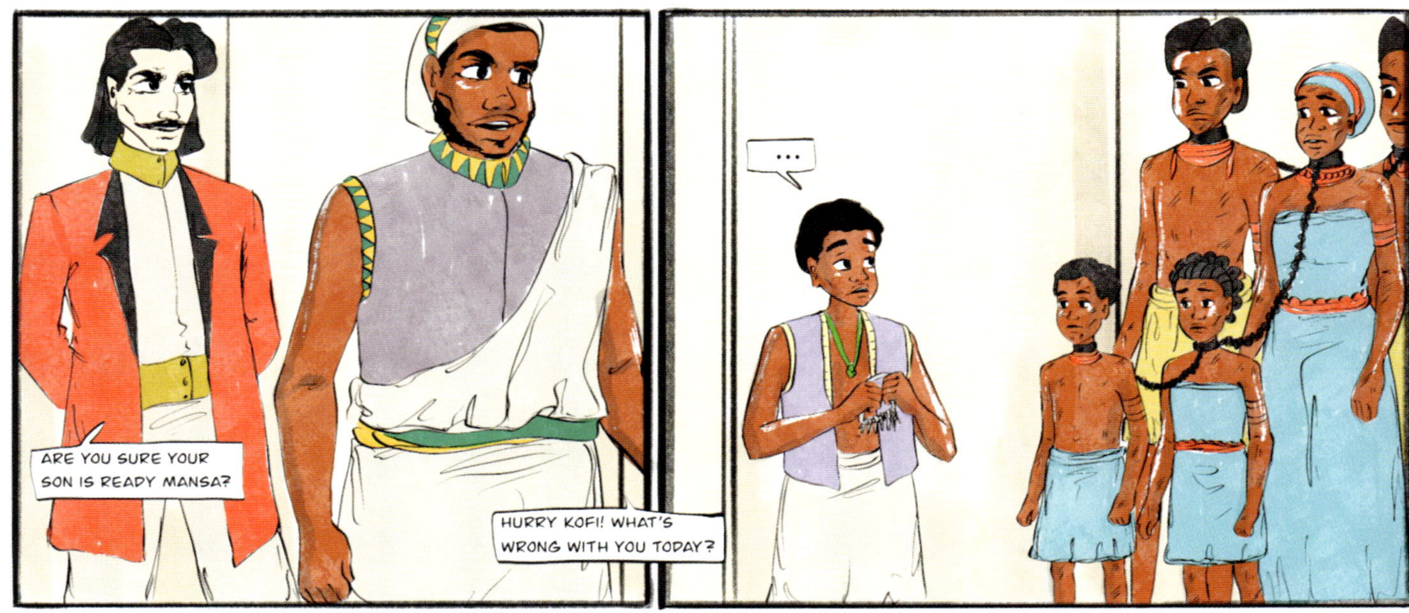
ARE YOU SURE YOUR SON IS READY MANSA?
HURRY KOFI! WHAT'S WRONG WITH YOU TODAY?
...

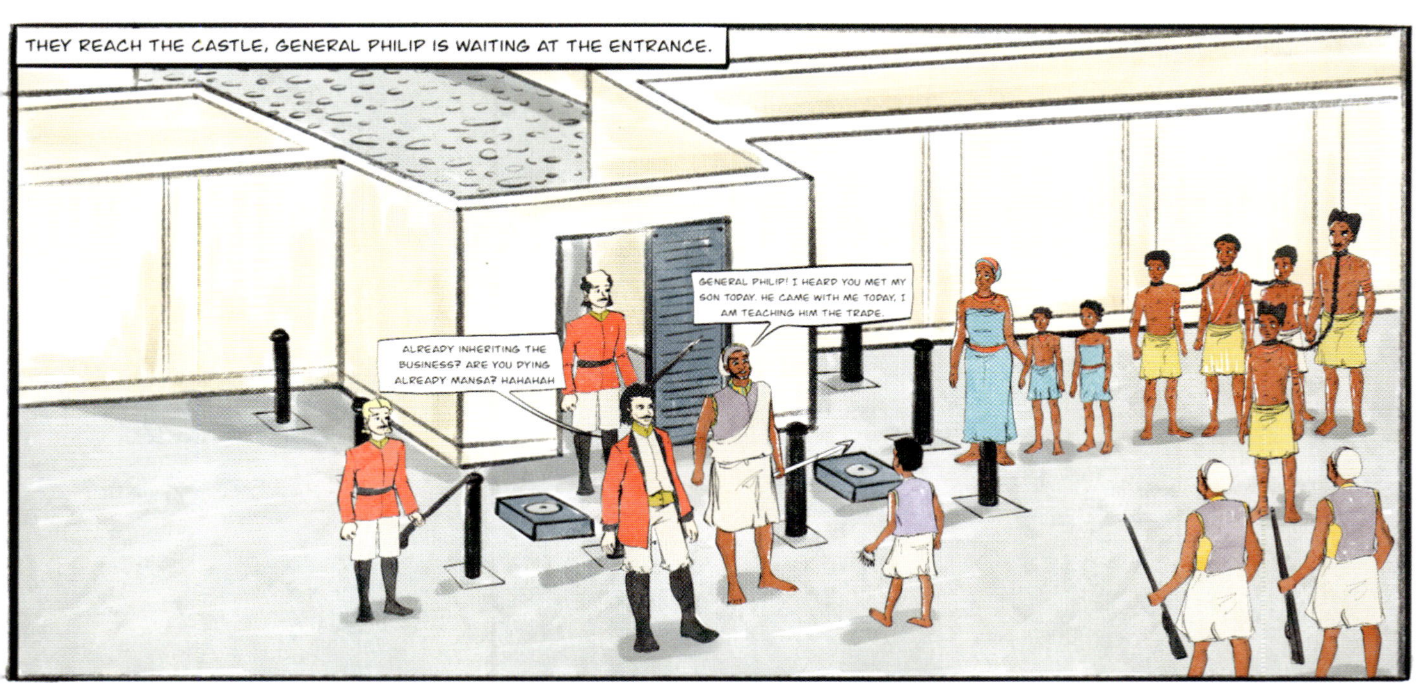
THEY REACH THE CASTLE, GENERAL PHILIP IS WAITING AT THE ENTRANCE.
GENERAL PHILIP! I HEARD YOU MET MY SON TODAY. HE CAME WITH ME TODAY, I AM TEACHING HIM THE TRADE.
ALREADY INHERITING THE BUSINESS? ARE YOU DYING ALREADY MANSA? HAHAHAH

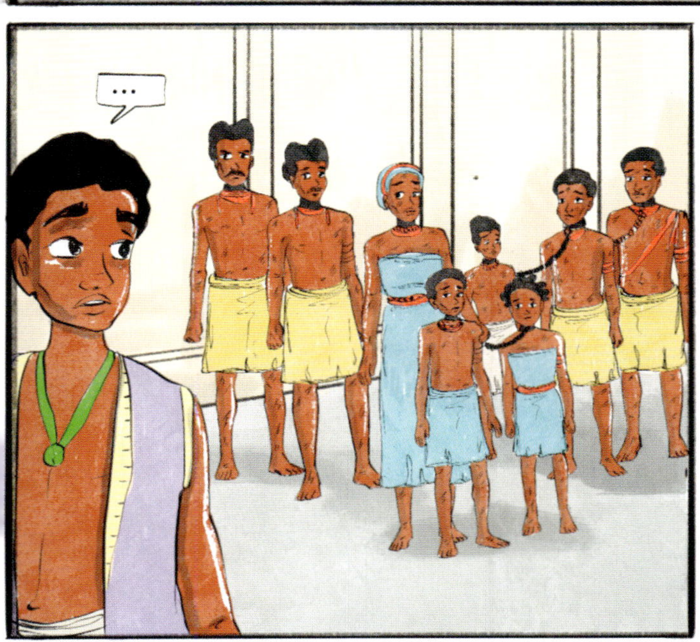
...

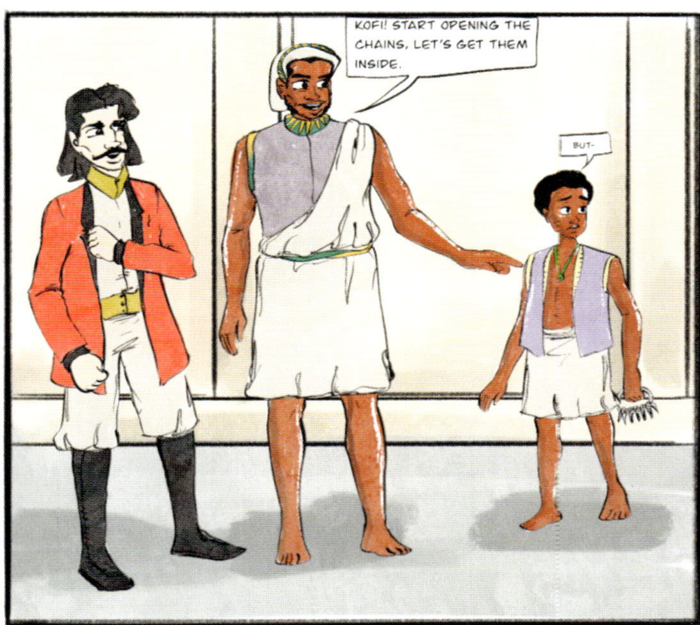
KOFI! START OPENING THE CHAINS. LET'S GET THEM INSIDE.
BUT-

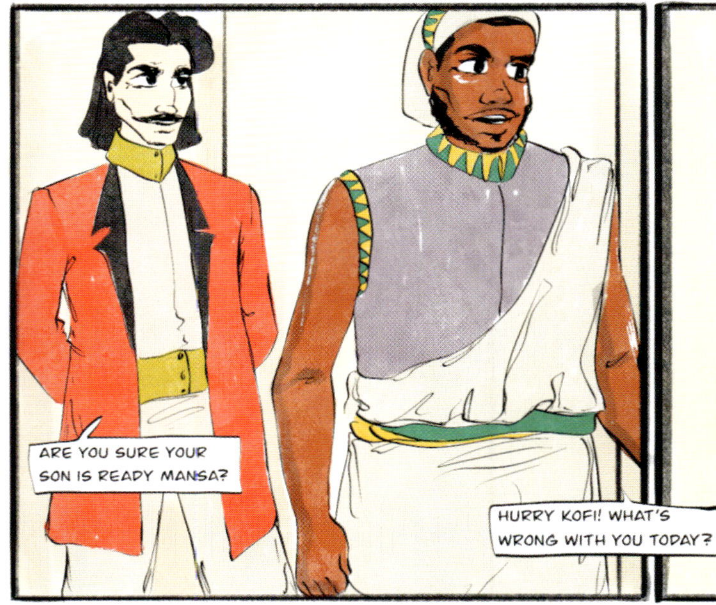
ARE YOU SURE YOUR SON IS READY MANSA?
HURRY KOFI! WHAT'S WRONG WITH YOU TODAY?

...

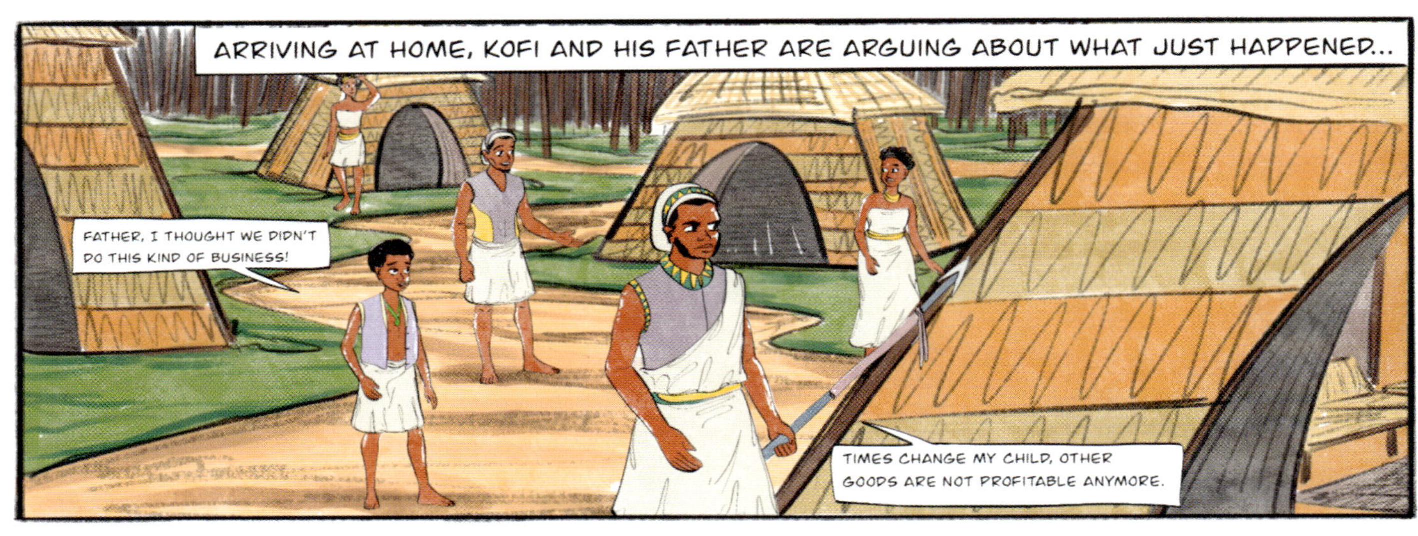
ARRIVING AT HOME, KOFI AND HIS FATHER ARE ARGUING ABOUT WHAT JUST HAPPENED...
FATHER, I THOUGHT WE DIDN'T DO THIS KIND OF BUSINESS!
TIMES CHANGE MY CHILD, OTHER GOODS ARE NOT PROFITABLE ANYMORE.

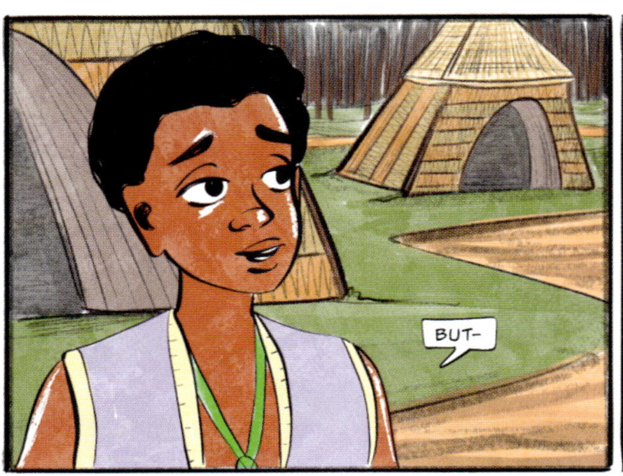
BUT-

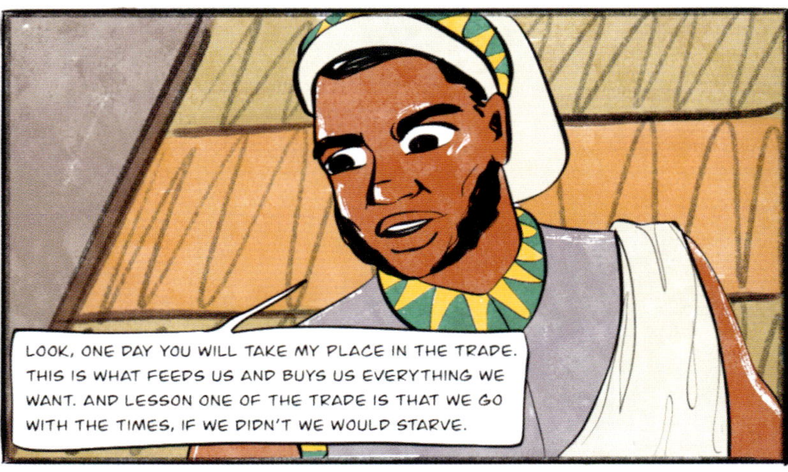
LOOK, ONE DAY YOU WILL TAKE MY PLACE IN THE TRADE. THIS IS WHAT FEEDS US AND BUYS US EVERYTHING WE WANT. AND LESSON ONE OF THE TRADE IS THAT WE GO WITH THE TIMES, IF WE DIDN'T WE WOULD STARVE.

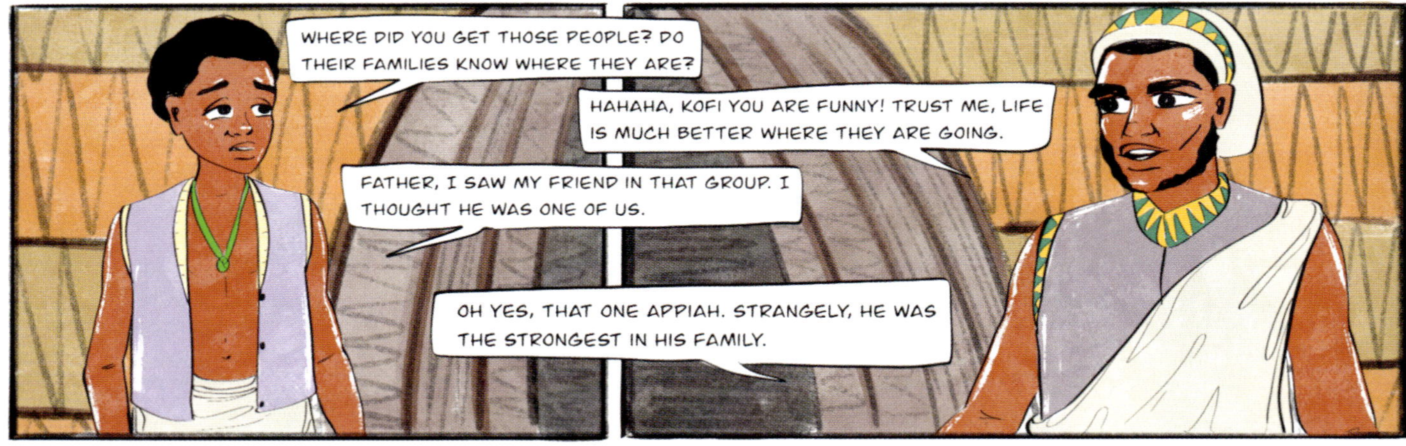
WHERE DID YOU GET THOSE PEOPLE? DO THEIR FAMILIES KNOW WHERE THEY ARE?
HAHAHA, KOFI YOU ARE FUNNY! TRUST ME, LIFE IS MUCH BETTER WHERE THEY ARE GOING.
FATHER, I SAW MY FRIEND IN THAT GROUP. I THOUGHT HE WAS ONE OF US.
OH YES, THAT ONE APPIAH. STRANGELY, HE WAS THE STRONGEST IN HIS FAMILY.

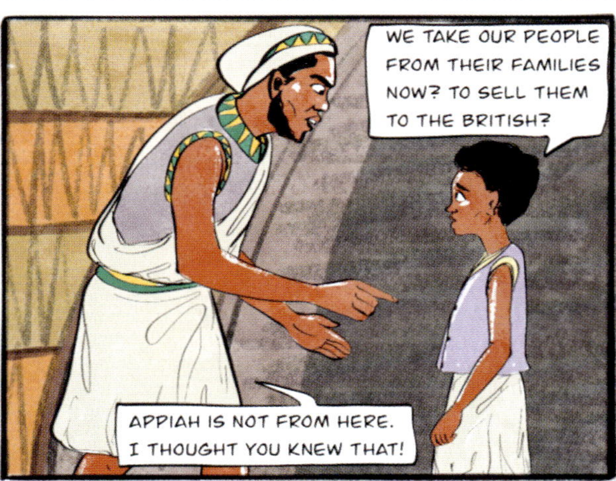
WE TAKE OUR PEOPLE FROM THEIR FAMILIES NOW? TO SELL THEM TO THE BRITISH?
APPIAH IS NOT FROM HERE. I THOUGHT YOU KNEW THAT!

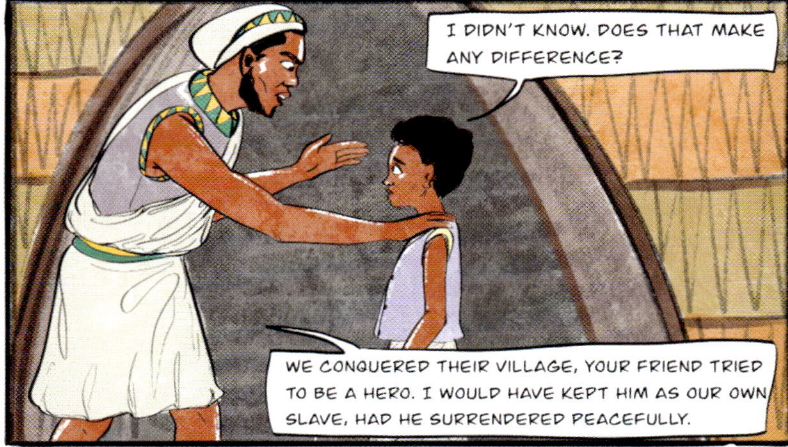
I DIDN'T KNOW. DOES THAT MAKE ANY DIFFERENCE?
WE CONQUERED THEIR VILLAGE, YOUR FRIEND TRIED TO BE A HERO. I WOULD HAVE KEPT HIM AS OUR OWN SLAVE, HAD HE SURRENDERED PEACEFULLY.

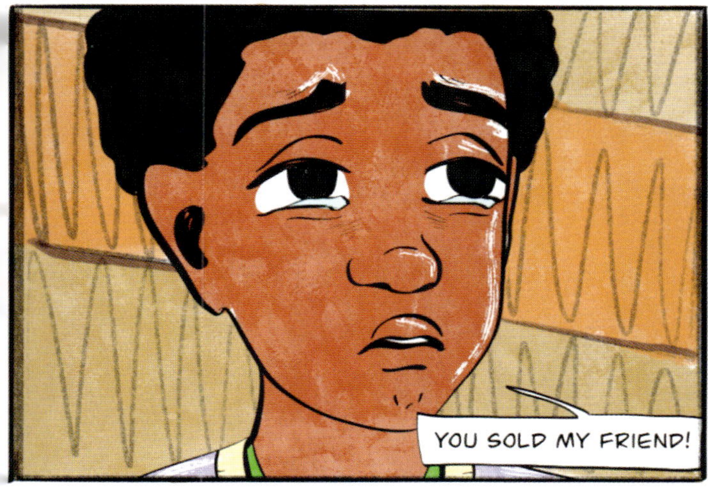
YOU SOLD MY FRIEND!

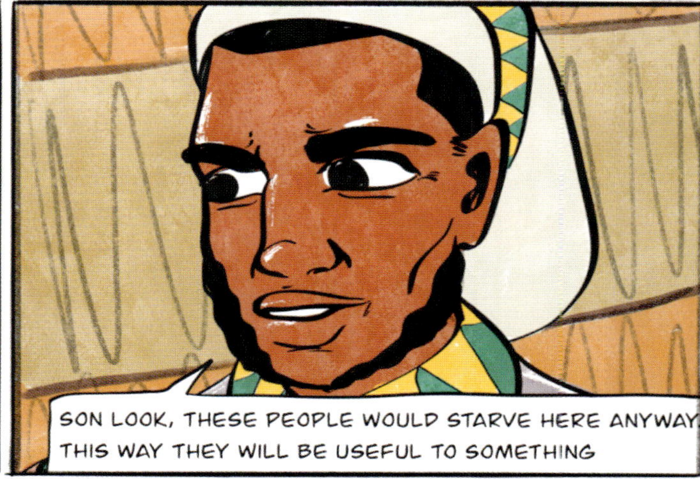
SON LOOK, THESE PEOPLE WOULD STARVE HERE ANYWAY.
THIS WAY THEY WILL BE USEFUL TO SOMETHING

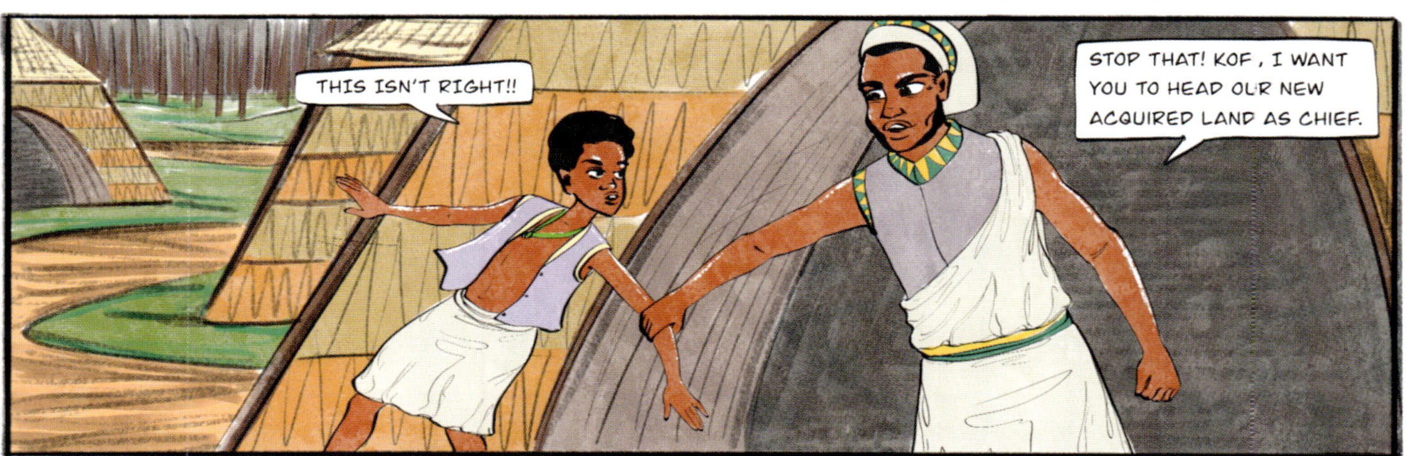
THIS ISN'T RIGHT!!
STOP THAT! KOF, I WANT YOU TO HEAD OUR NEW ACQUIRED LAND AS CHIEF.

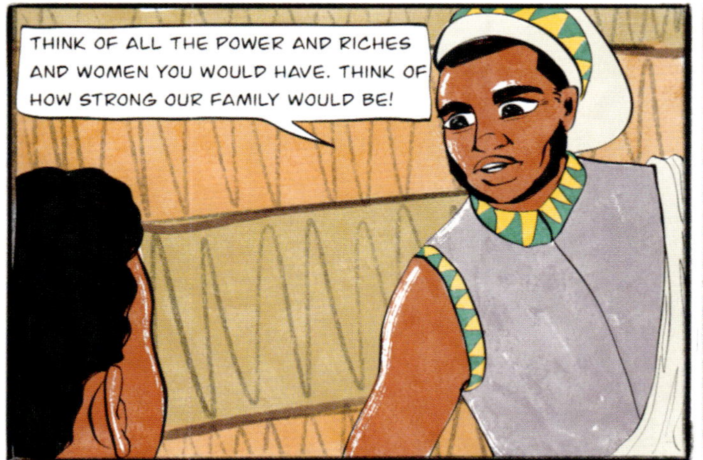
THINK OF ALL THE POWER AND RICHES AND WOMEN YOU WOULD HAVE. THINK OF HOW STRONG OUR FAMILY WOULD BE!

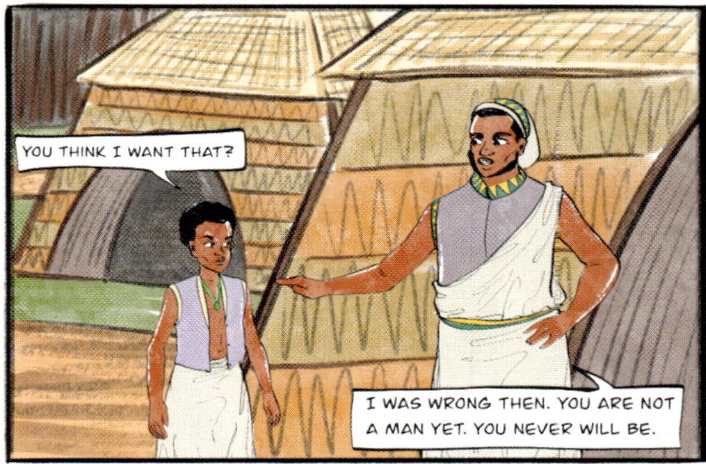
YOU THINK I WANT THAT?
I WAS WRONG THEN. YOU ARE NOT A MAN YET. YOU NEVER WILL BE.

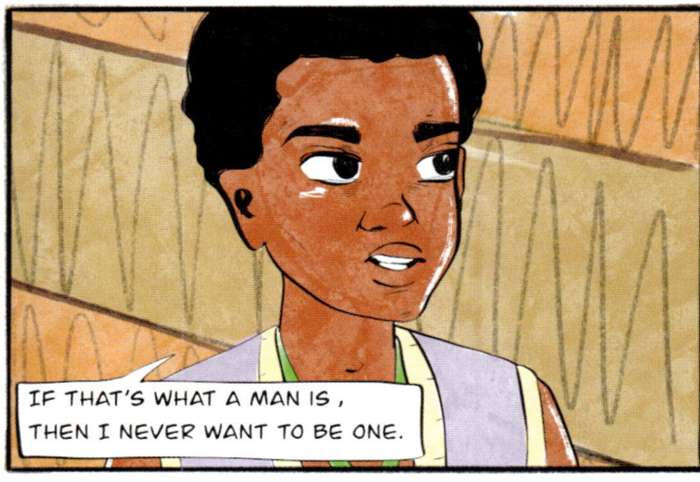
IF THAT'S WHAT A MAN IS, THEN I NEVER WANT TO BE ONE.

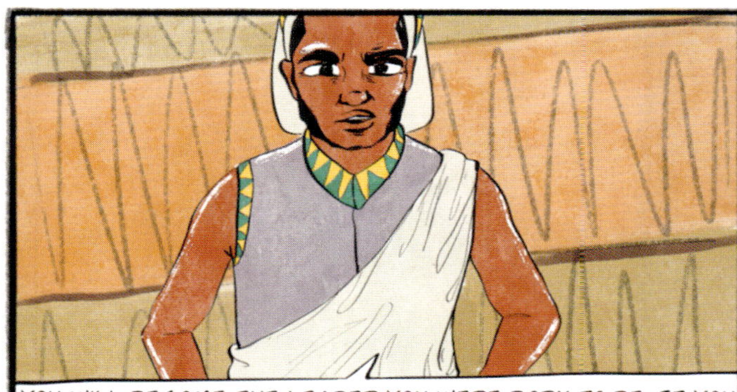
YOU WILL BECOME THE LEADER YOU WERE BORN TO BE. IF YOU OBJECT TO THIS, I WILL HAVE NO CHOICE BUT TO SEND YOU TO EXILE. THERE I CANNOT GUARANTEE YOUR SAFETY AND YOU WILL NOT KEEP MY NAME. YOU WILL BE ON YOUR OWN.

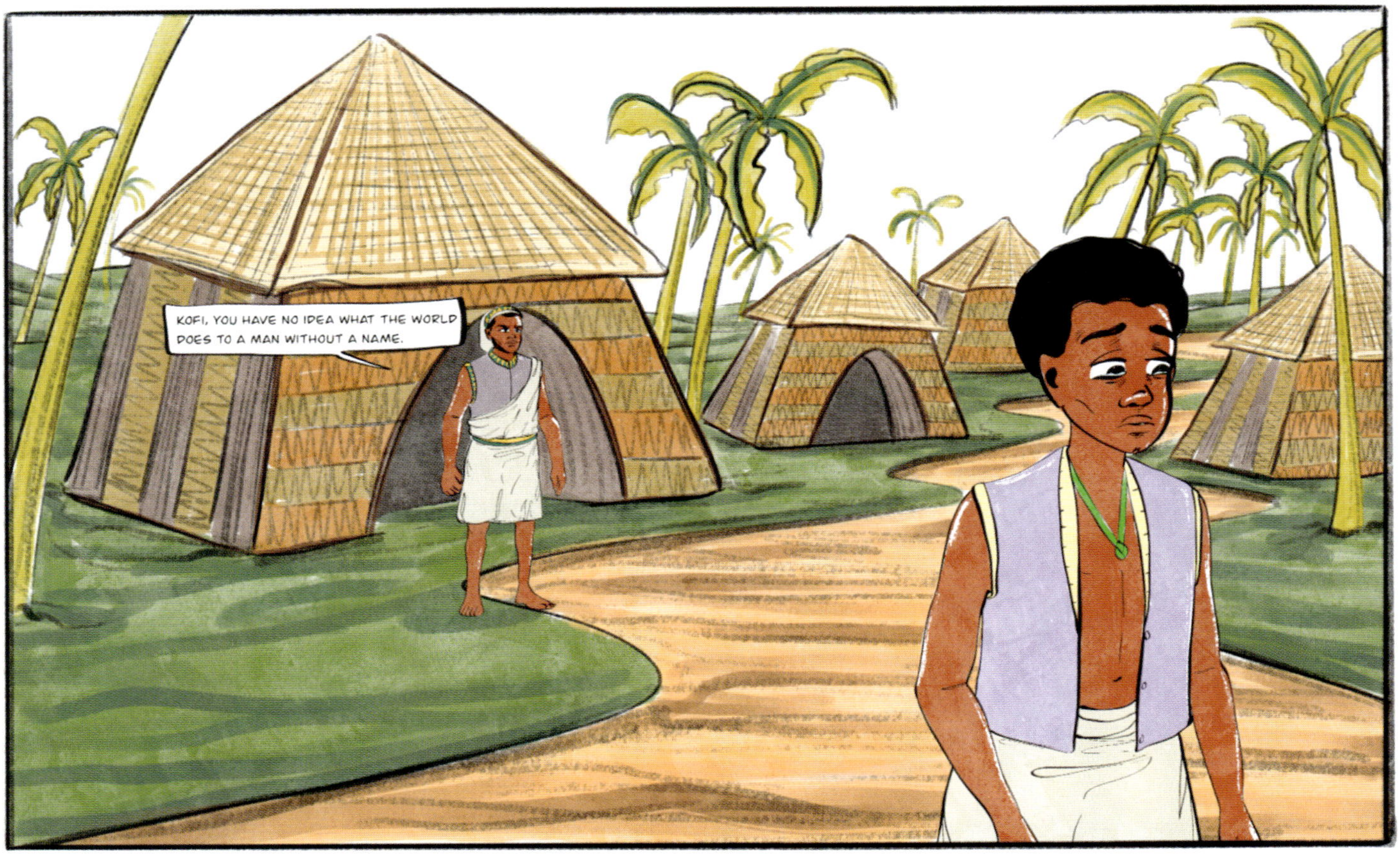

KOFI, YOU HAVE NO IDEA WHAT THE WORLD DOES TO A MAN WITHOUT A NAME.

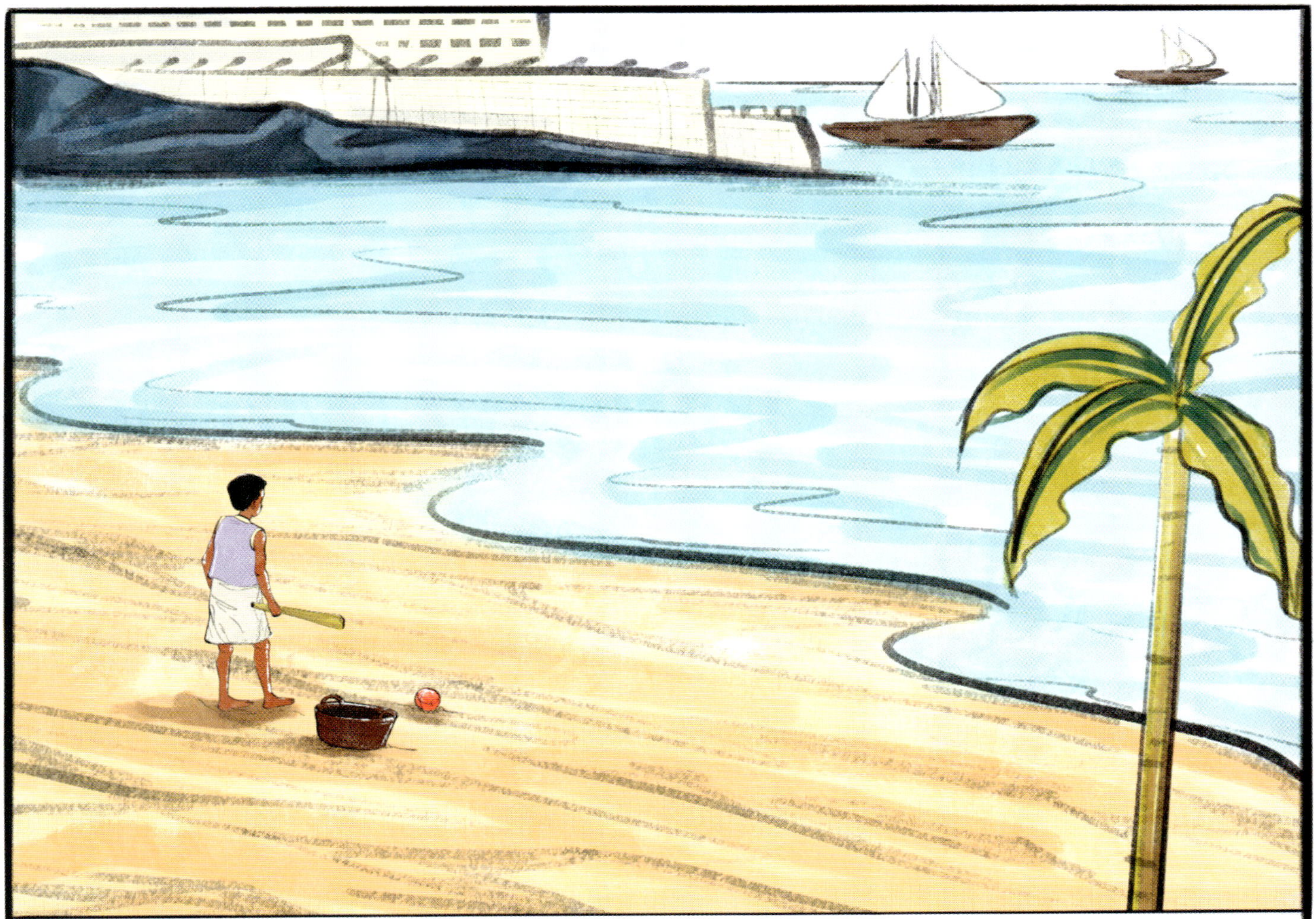

THAT EVENING AT THE PLAYGROUND, WHERE KOFI PLAYS CHASKELE WITH APPIAH, HE STANDS THERE ALONE, UNABLE TO PLAY BY HIMSELF.

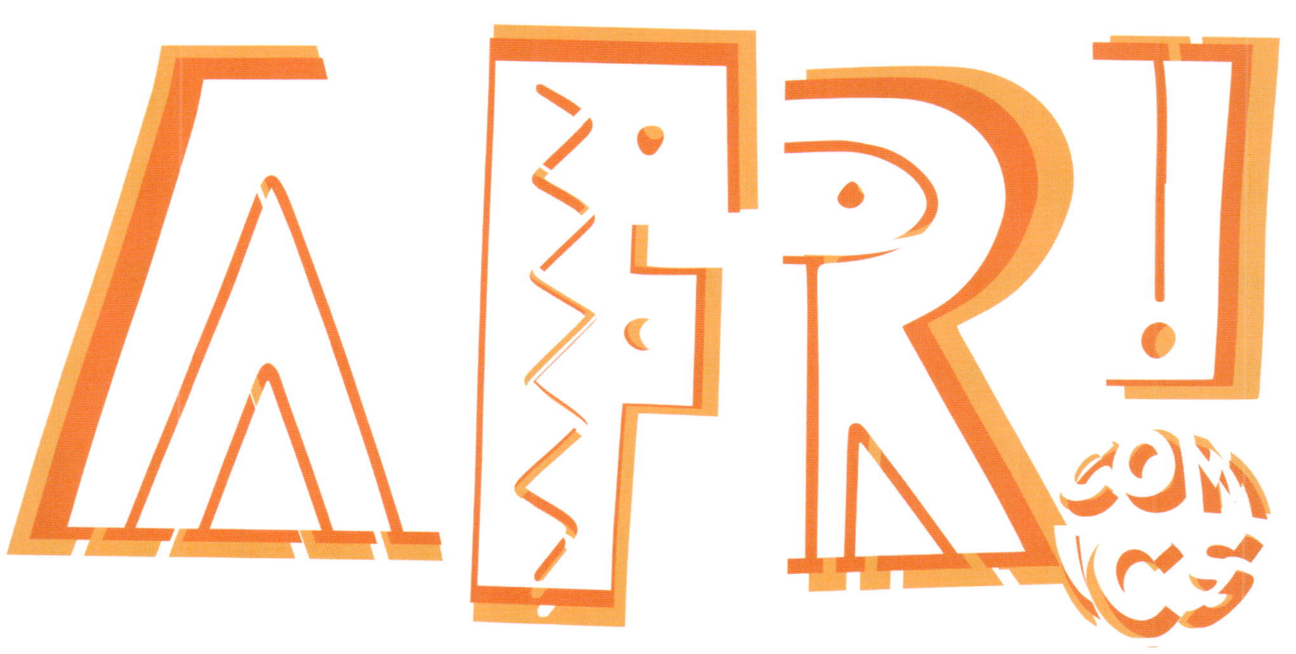
AFR!
COMICS

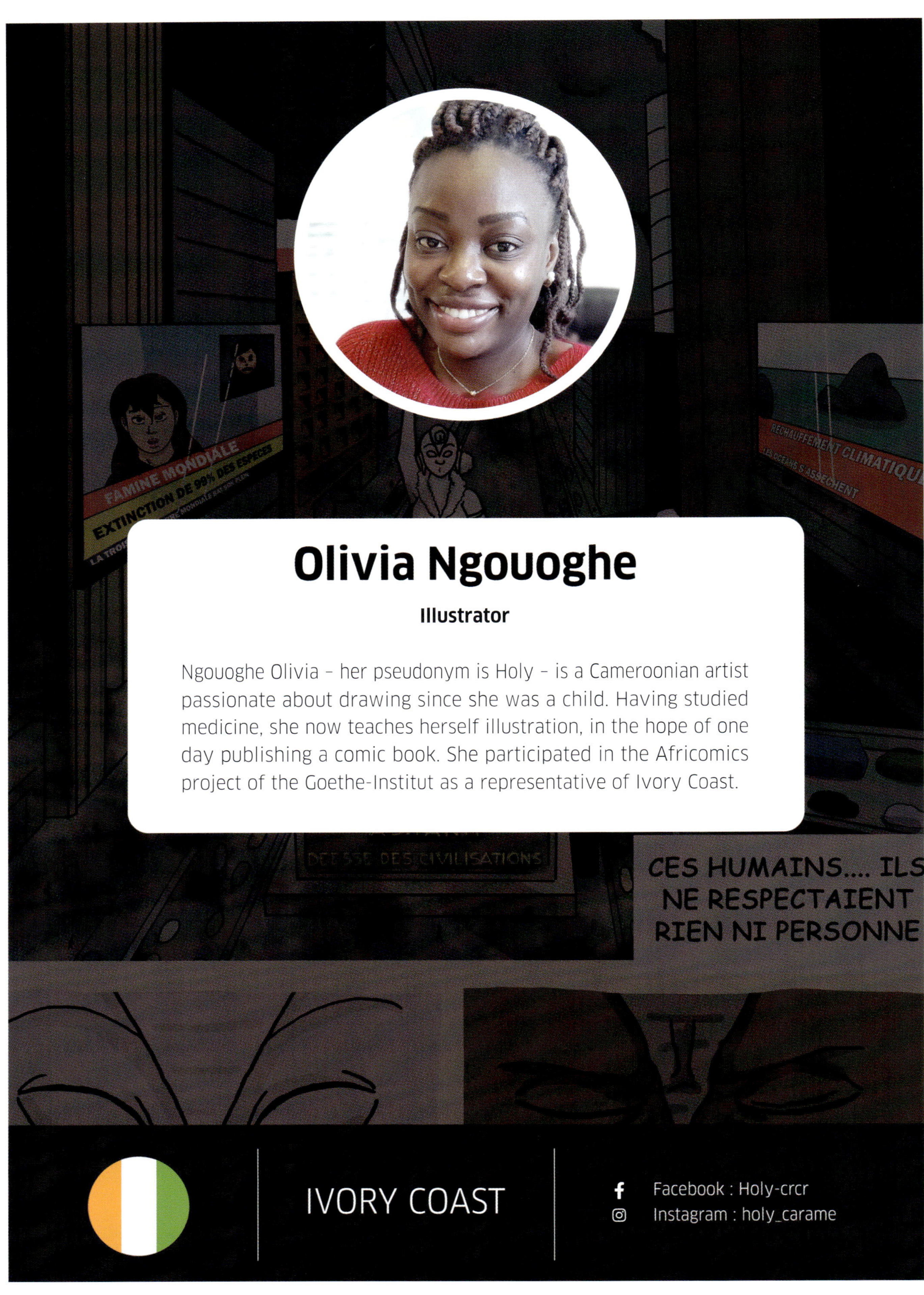

Olivia Ngouoghe

Illustrator

Ngouoghe Olivia – her pseudonym is Holy – is a Cameroonian artist passionate about drawing since she was a child. Having studied medicine, she now teaches herself illustration, in the hope of one day publishing a comic book. She participated in the Africomics project of the Goethe-Institut as a representative of Ivory Coast.

IVORY COAST

Facebook : Holy-crcr
Instagram : holy_carame

THE SUMMIT

Acquire ?

Annul ?

BY HOLY

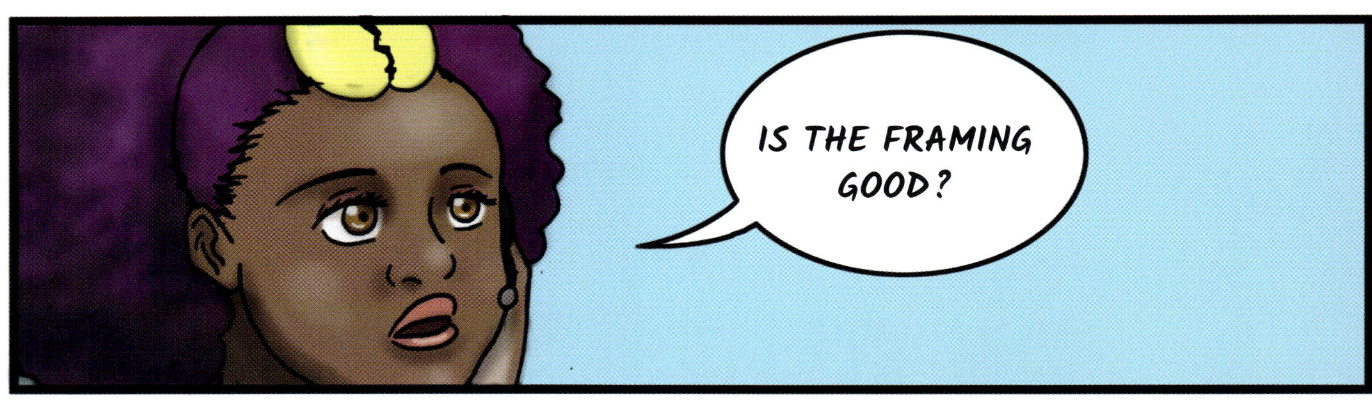
IS THE FRAMING GOOD?
FOCUS OK.
START IN 3 ...
2
1
WE ARE AT THE BEGINNING OF THE 36TH PANAFRICAIN SUMMIT HELD IN BEAUTAFRICA.

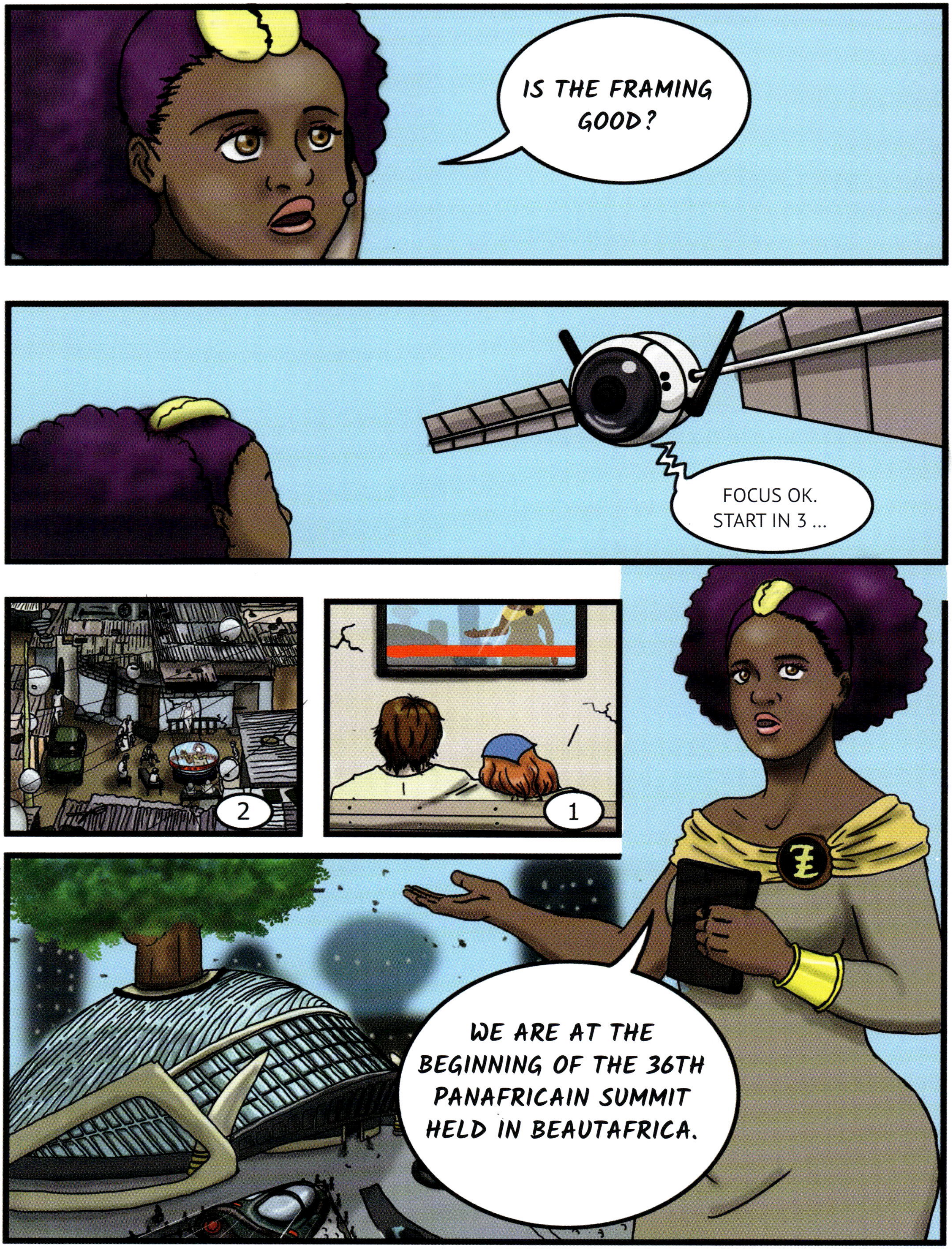

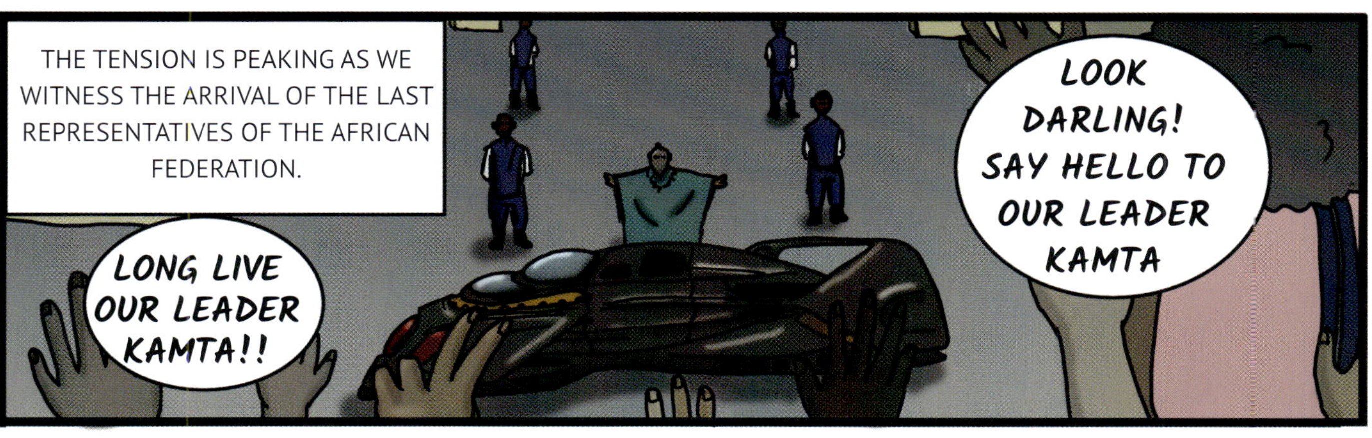
THE TENSION IS PEAKING AS WE WITNESS THE ARRIVAL OF THE LAST REPRESENTATIVES OF THE AFRICAN FEDERATION.
LONG LIVE OUR LEADER KAMTA!!
LOOK DARLING! SAY HELLO TO OUR LEADER KAMTA

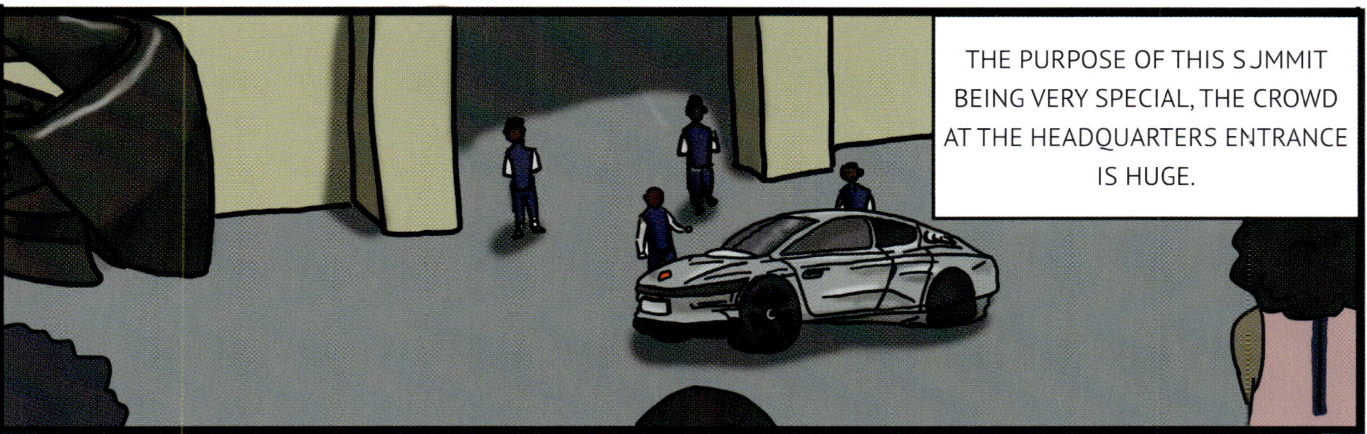
THE PURPOSE OF THIS SUMMIT BEING VERY SPECIAL, THE CROWD AT THE HEADQUARTERS ENTRANCE IS HUGE.

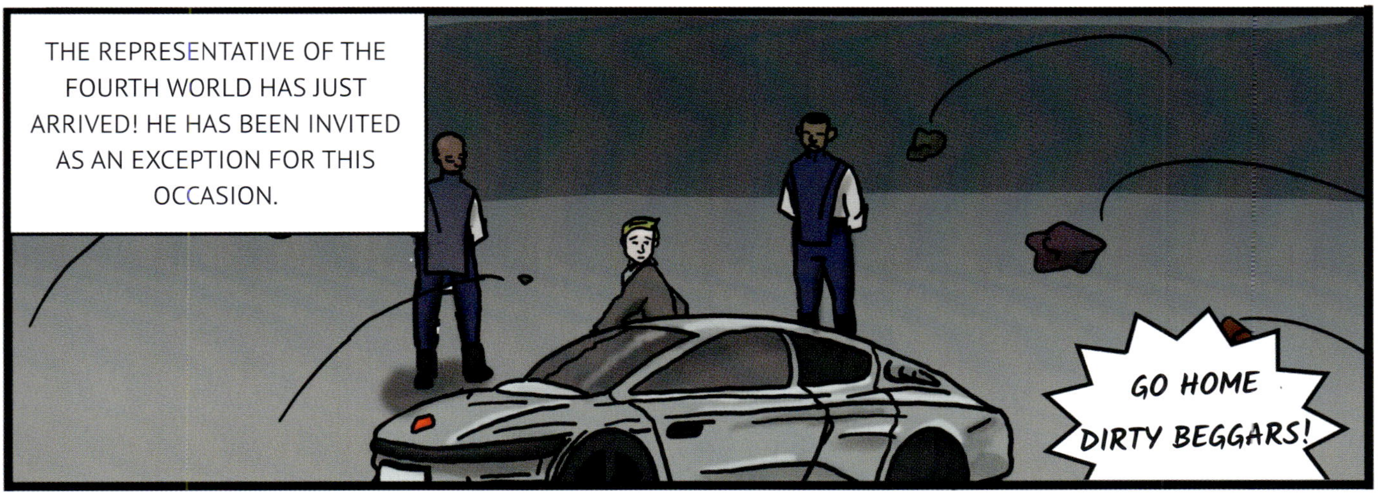
THE REPRESENTATIVE OF THE FOURTH WORLD HAS JUST ARRIVED! HE HAS BEEN INVITED AS AN EXCEPTION FOR THIS OCCASION.
GO HOME DIRTY BEGGARS!

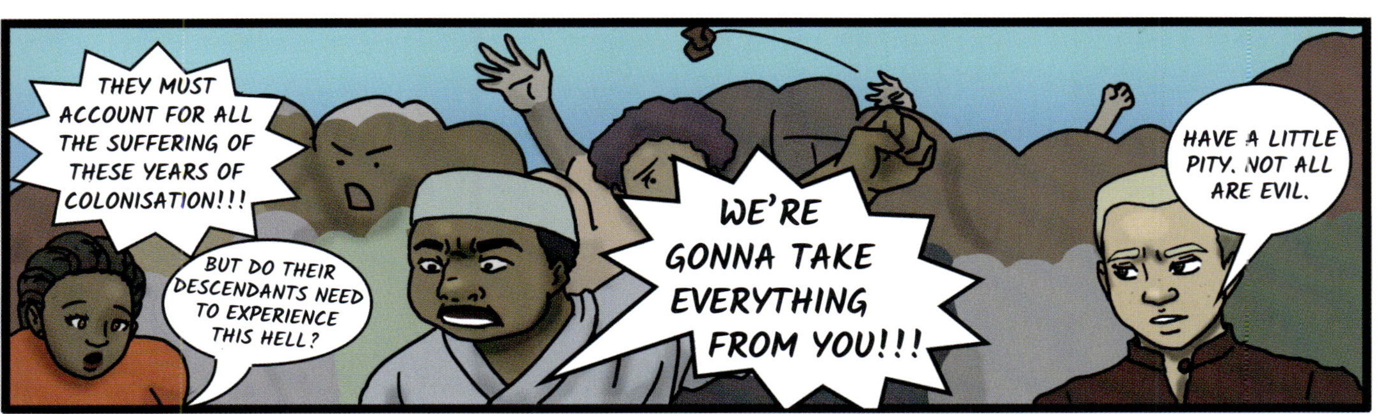
THEY MUST ACCOUNT FOR ALL THE SUFFERING OF THESE YEARS OF COLONISATION!!!
BUT DO THEIR DESCENDANTS NEED TO EXPERIENCE THIS HELL?
WE'RE GONNA TAKE EVERYTHING FROM YOU!!!
HAVE A LITTLE PITY, NOT ALL ARE EVIL.

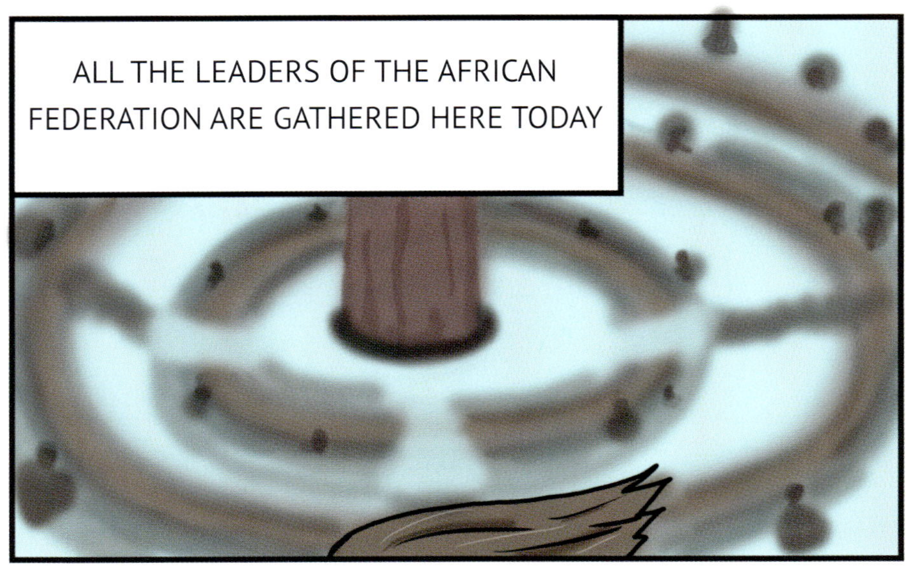

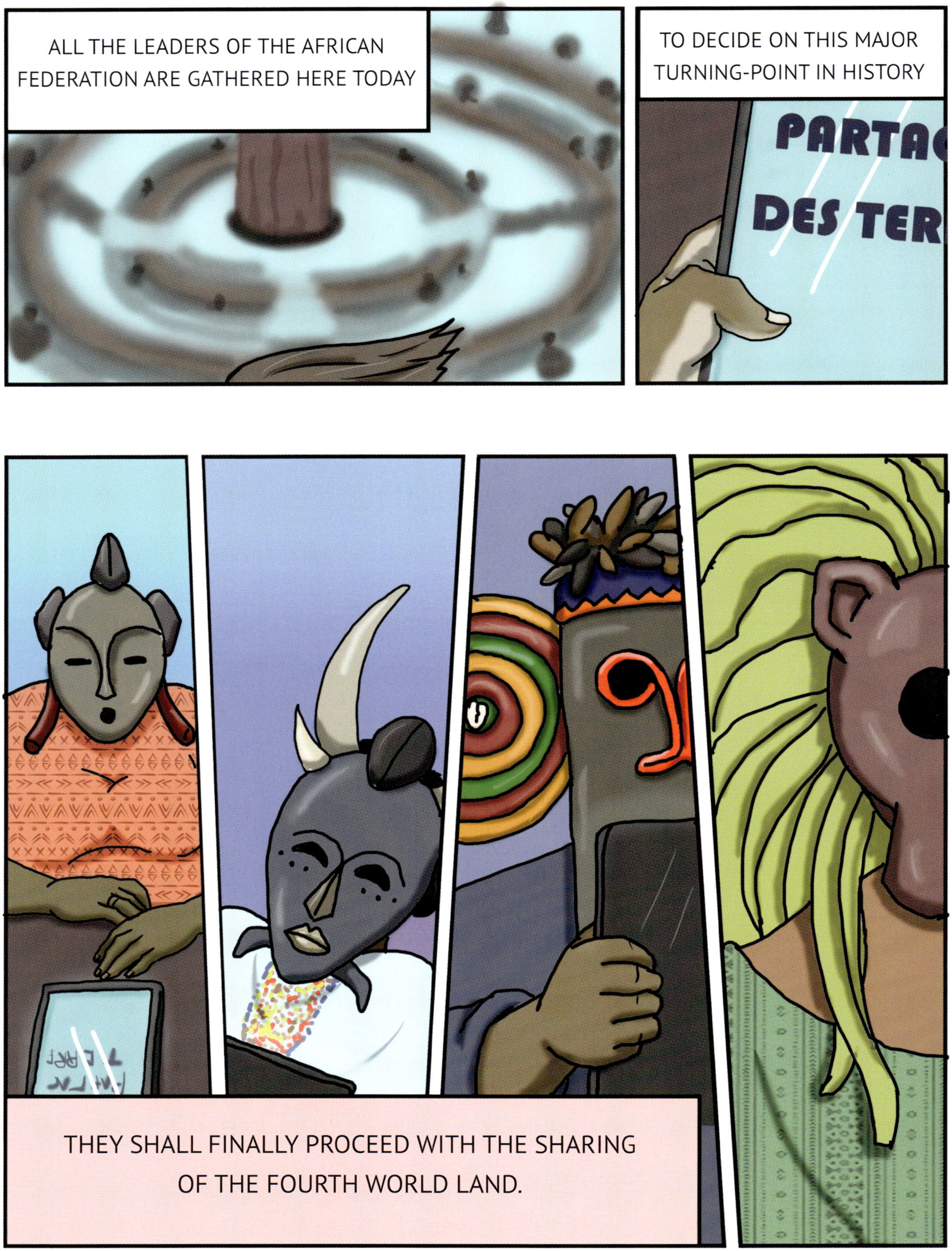

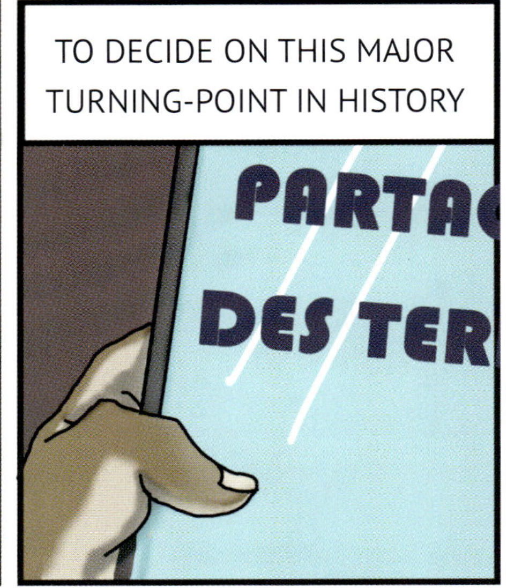

THEY SHALL FINALLY PROCEED WITH THE SHARING OF THE FOURTH WORLD LAND.

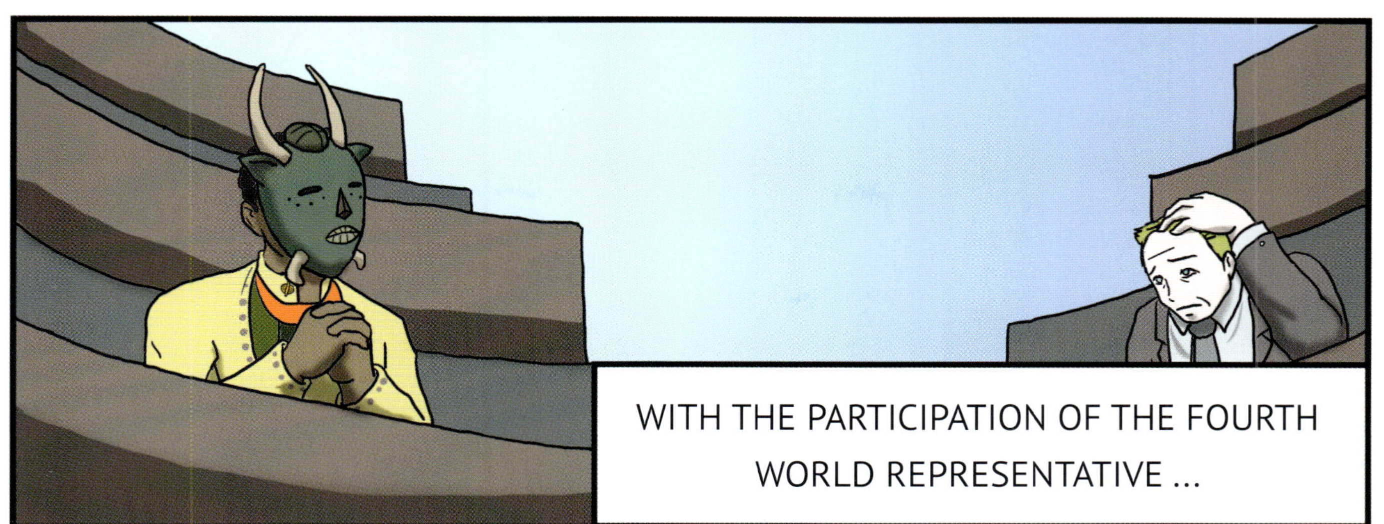
WITH THE PARTICIPATION OF THE FOURTH WORLD REPRESENTATIVE ...

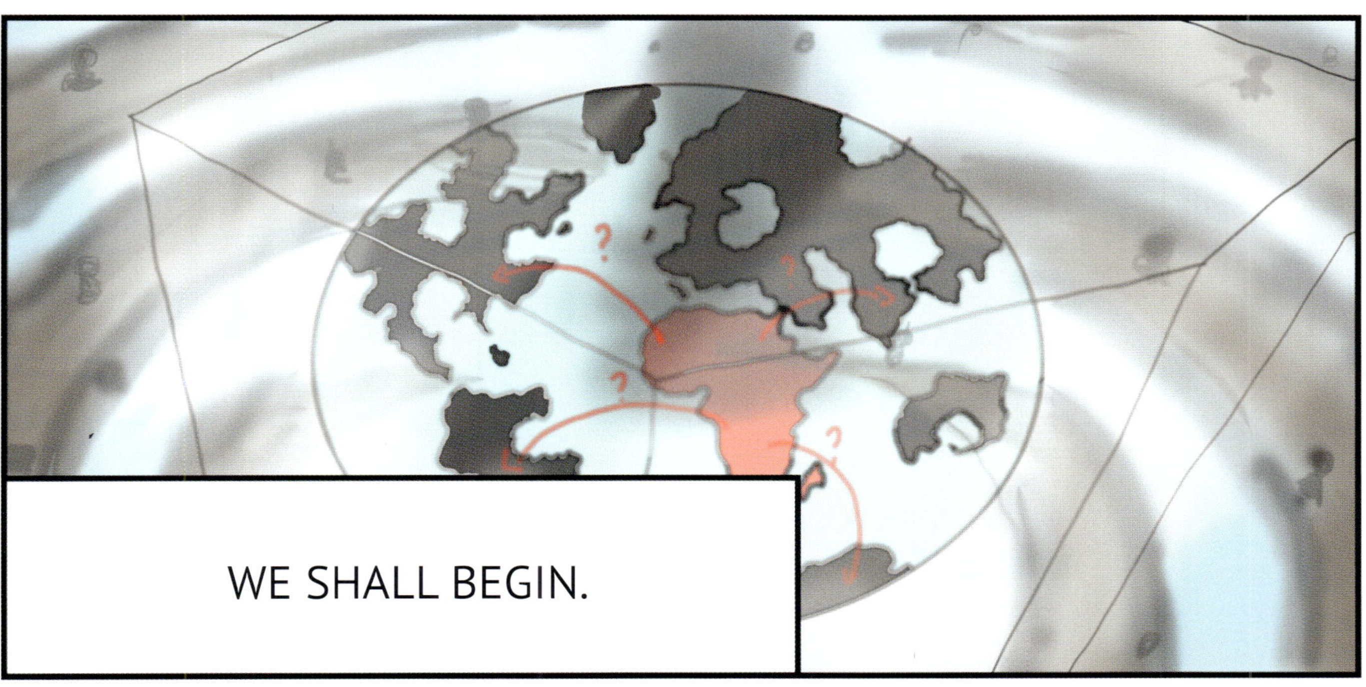
WE SHALL BEGIN.

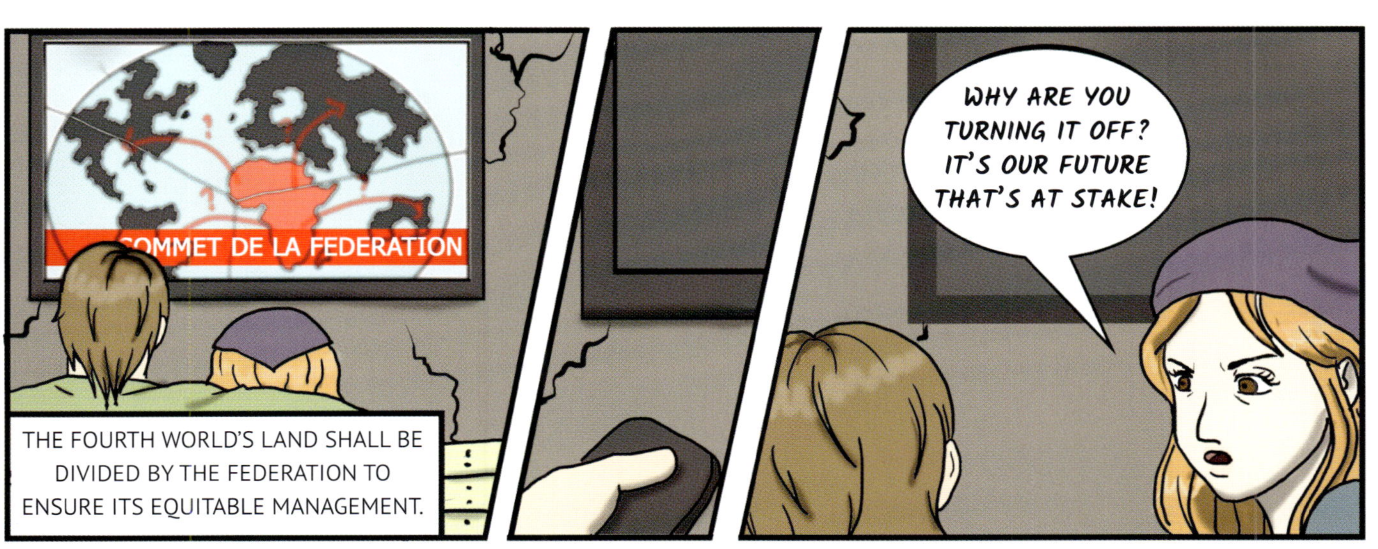
SOMMET DE LA FEDERATION
THE FOURTH WORLD'S LAND SHALL BE DIVIDED BY THE FEDERATION TO ENSURE ITS EQUITABLE MANAGEMENT.
WHY ARE YOU TURNING IT OFF? IT'S OUR FUTURE THAT'S AT STAKE!

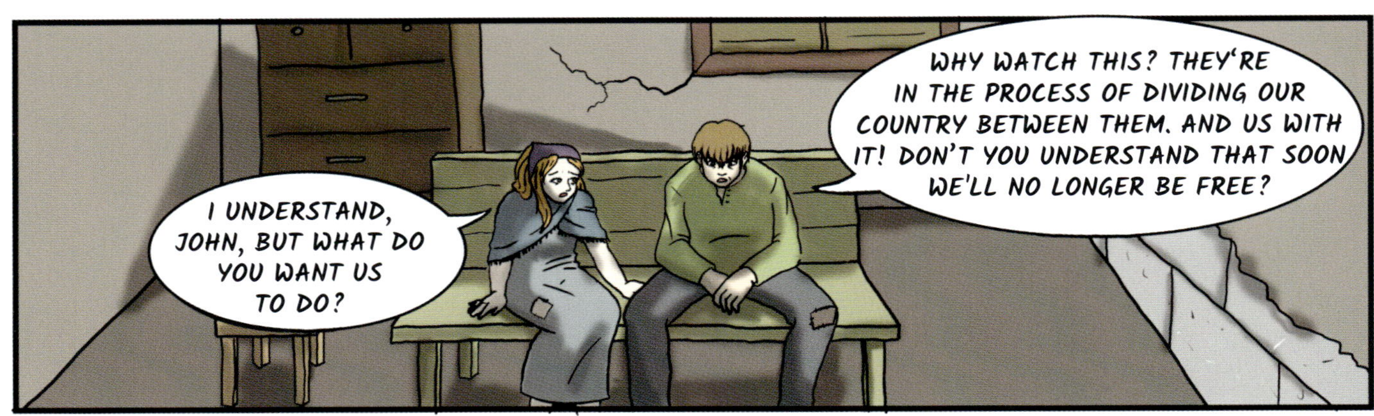
WHY WATCH THIS? THEY'RE IN THE PROCESS OF DIVIDING OUR COUNTRY BETWEEN THEM. AND US WITH IT! DON'T YOU UNDERSTAND THAT SOON WE'LL NO LONGER BE FREE?
I UNDERSTAND, JOHN, BUT WHAT DO YOU WANT US TO DO?

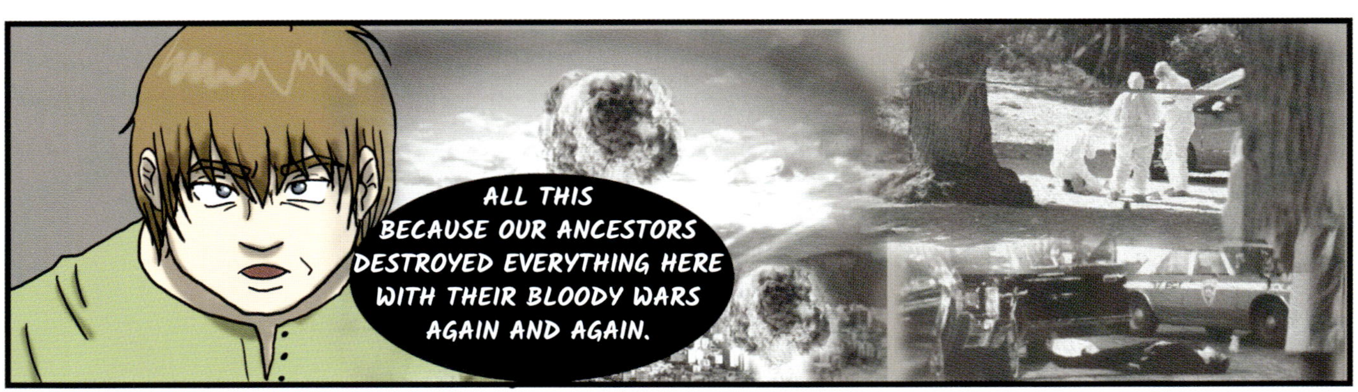
ALL THIS BECAUSE OUR ANCESTORS DESTROYED EVERYTHING HERE WITH THEIR BLOODY WARS AGAIN AND AGAIN.

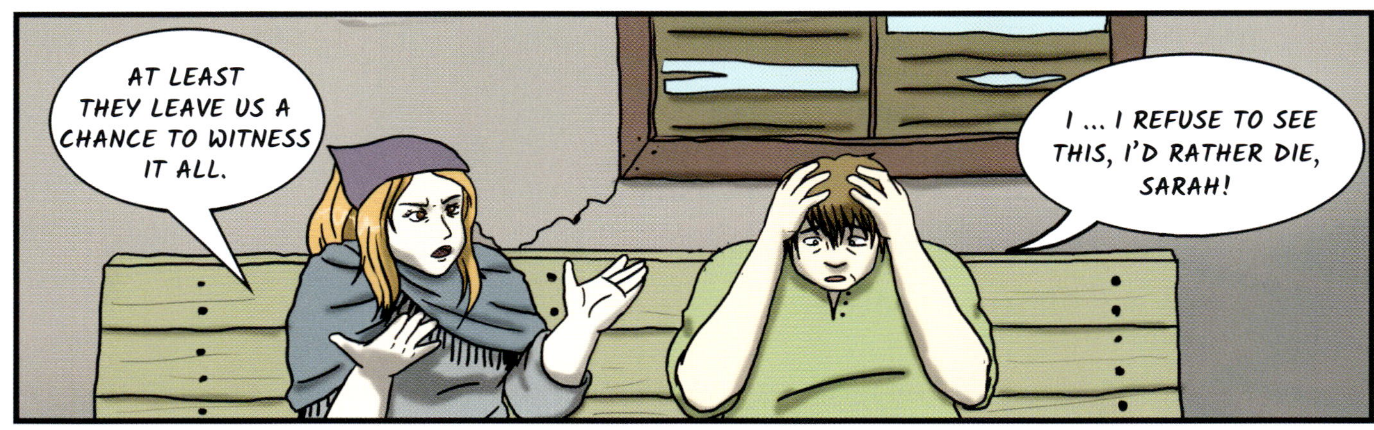
AT LEAST THEY LEAVE US A CHANCE TO WITNESS IT ALL.
I ... I REFUSE TO SEE THIS, I'D RATHER DIE, SARAH!

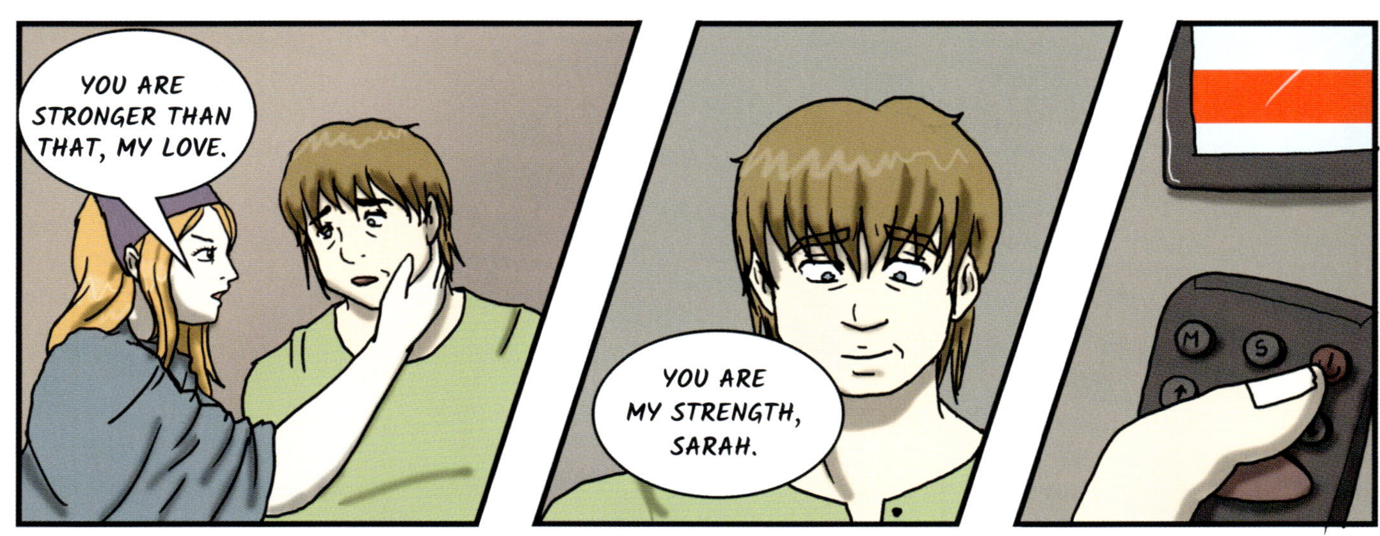
YOU ARE STRONGER THAN THAT, MY LOVE.
YOU ARE MY STRENGTH, SARAH.

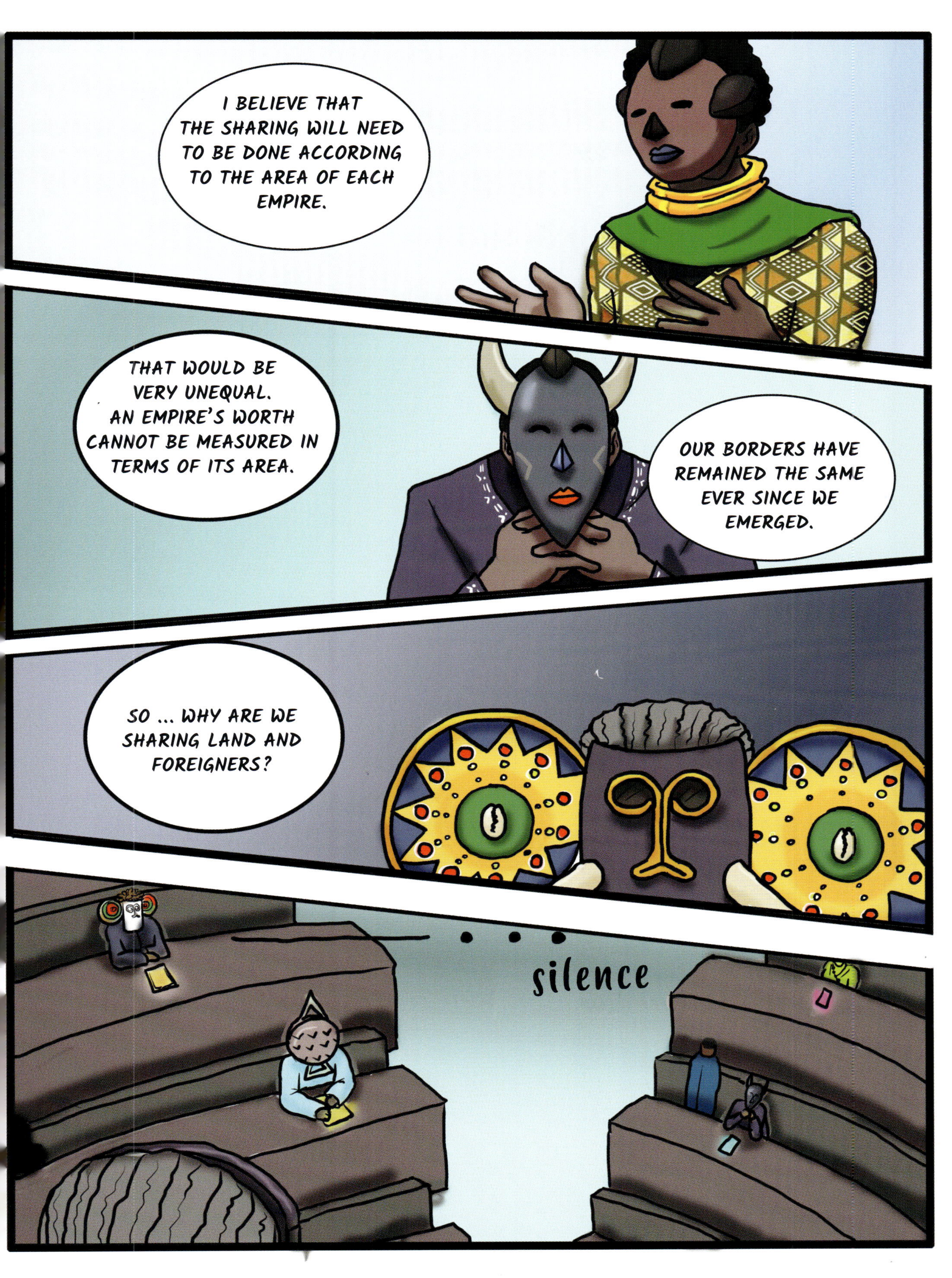
I BELIEVE THAT THE SHARING WILL NEED TO BE DONE ACCORDING TO THE AREA OF EACH EMPIRE.
THAT WOULD BE VERY UNEQUAL. AN EMPIRE'S WORTH CANNOT BE MEASURED IN TERMS OF ITS AREA.
OUR BORDERS HAVE REMAINED THE SAME EVER SINCE WE EMERGED.
SO ... WHY ARE WE SHARING LAND AND FOREIGNERS?
. . .
silence

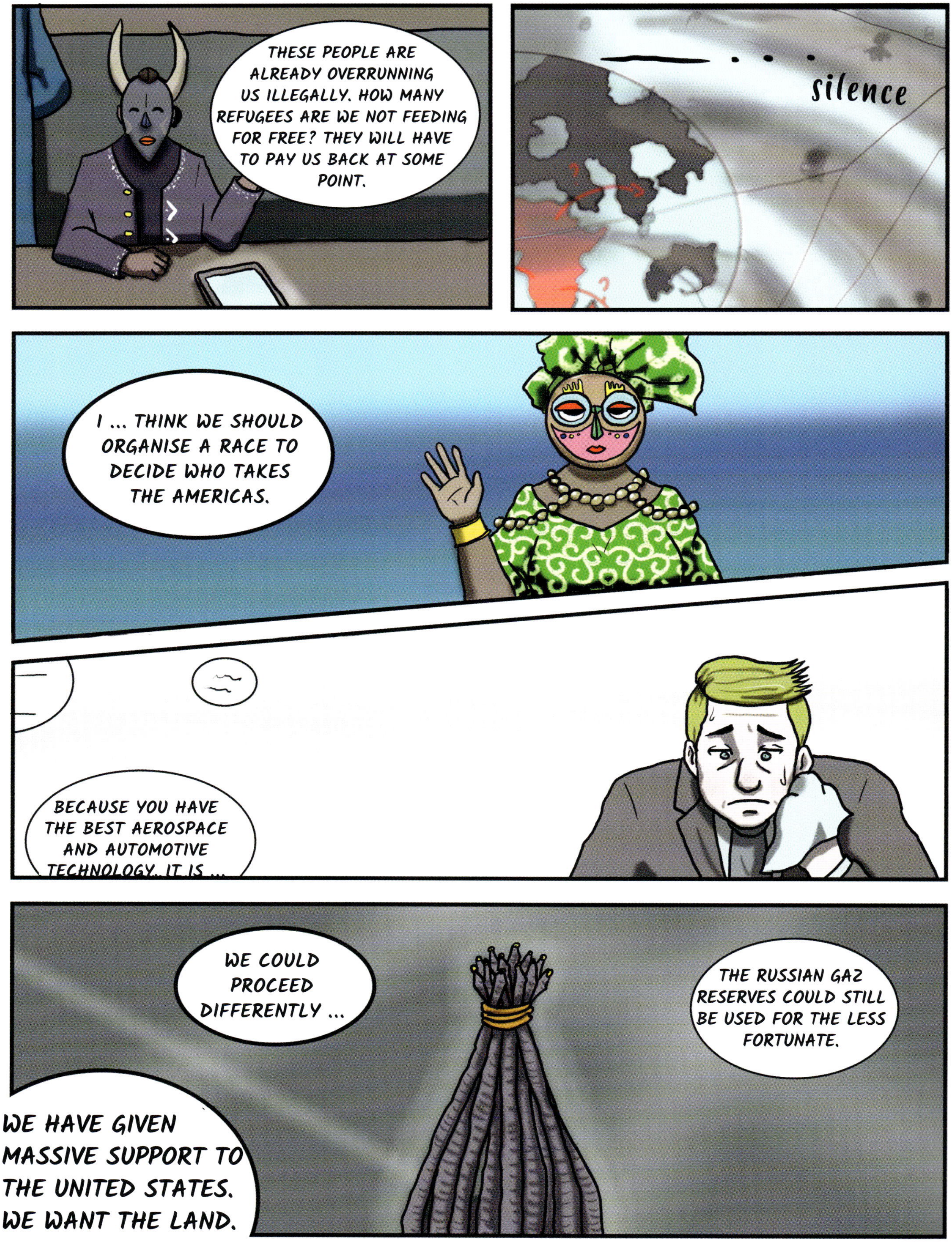

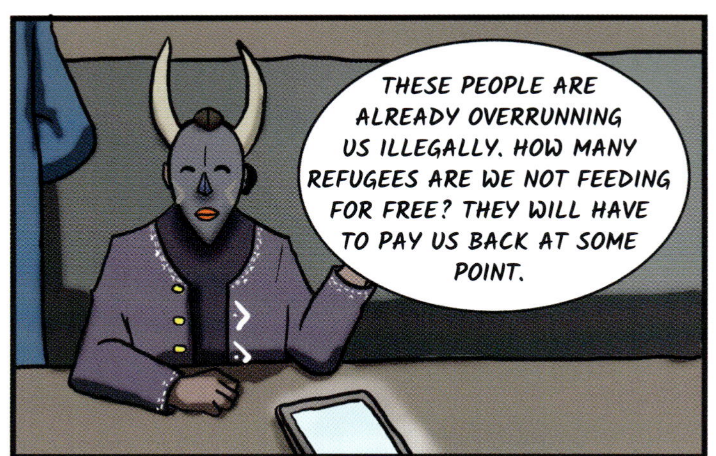

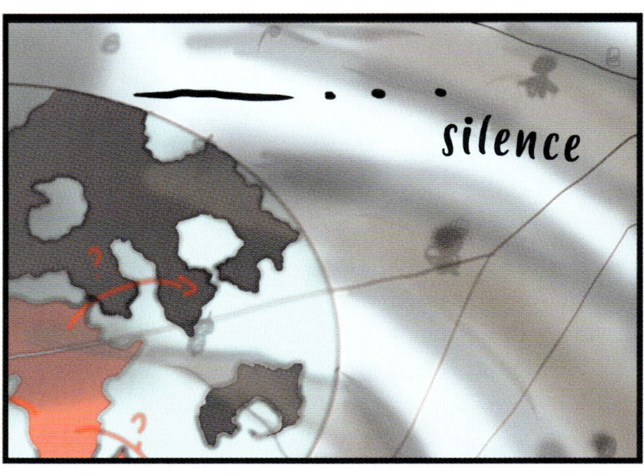

I … THINK WE SHOULD ORGANISE A RACE TO DECIDE WHO TAKES THE AMERICAS.

BECAUSE YOU HAVE THE BEST AEROSPACE AND AUTOMOTIVE TECHNOLOGY. IT IS …

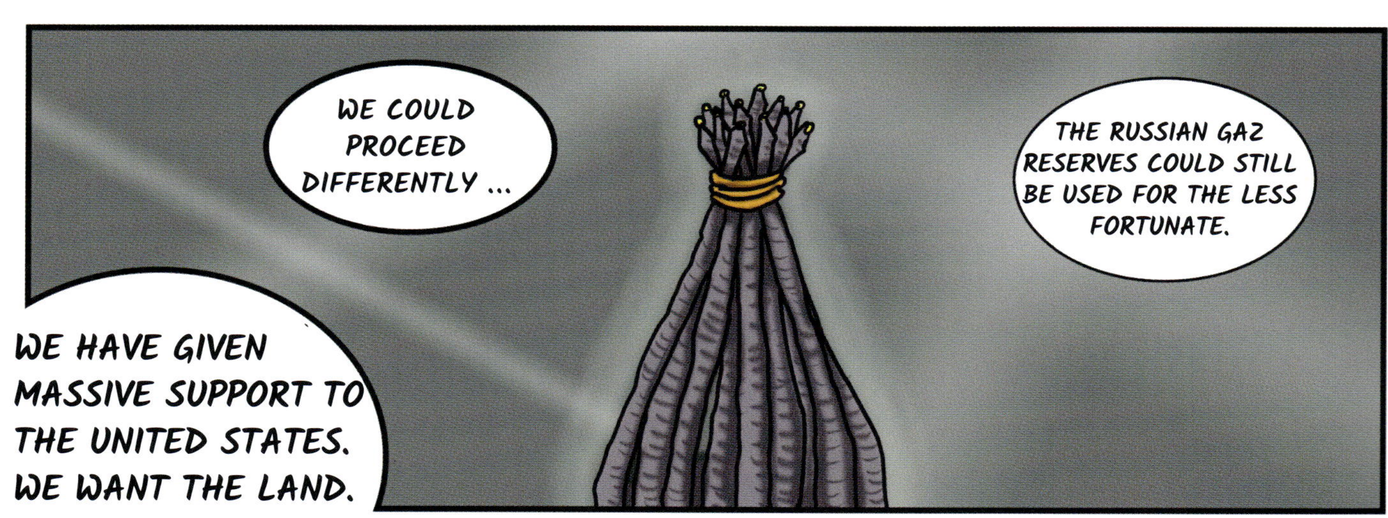

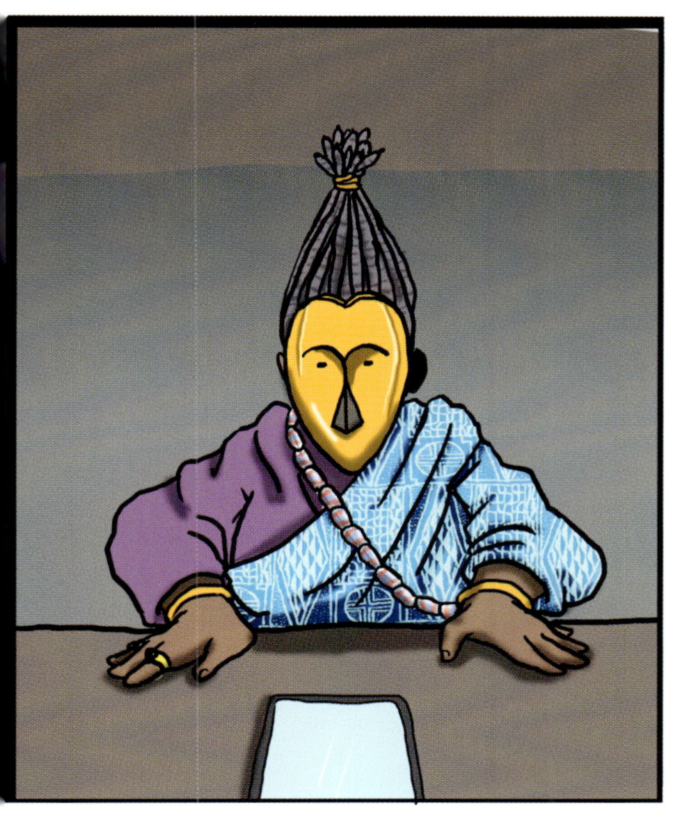

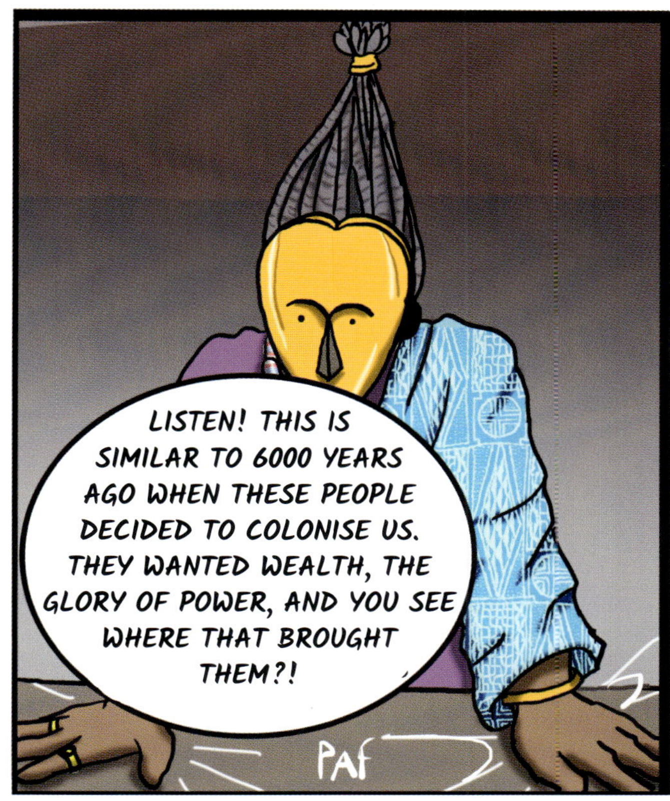
LISTEN! THIS IS SIMILAR TO 6000 YEARS AGO WHEN THESE PEOPLE DECIDED TO COLONISE US. THEY WANTED WEALTH, THE GLORY OF POWER, AND YOU SEE WHERE THAT BROUGHT THEM?!
PAF

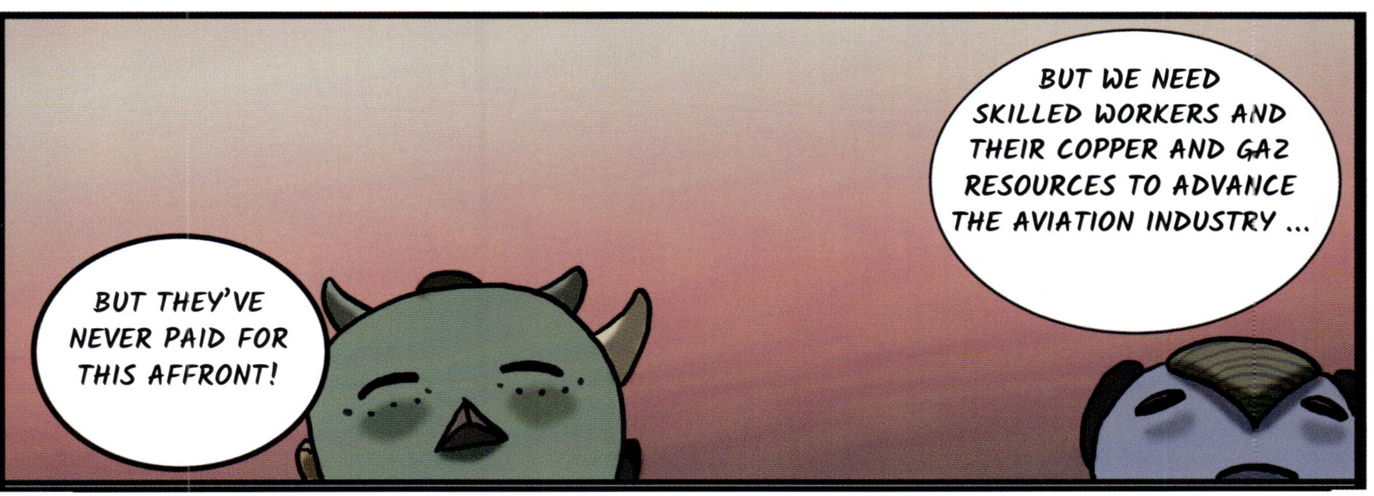
BUT WE NEED SKILLED WORKERS AND THEIR COPPER AND GAZ RESOURCES TO ADVANCE THE AVIATION INDUSTRY ...
BUT THEY'VE NEVER PAID FOR THIS AFFRONT!

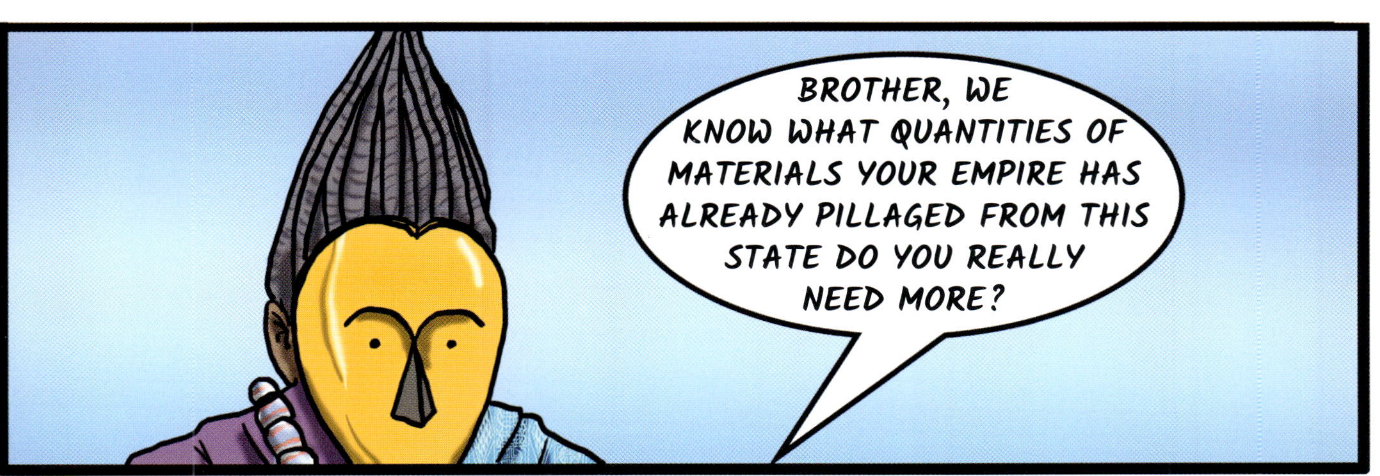
BROTHER, WE KNOW WHAT QUANTITIES OF MATERIALS YOUR EMPIRE HAS ALREADY PILLAGED FROM THIS STATE DO YOU REALLY NEED MORE?

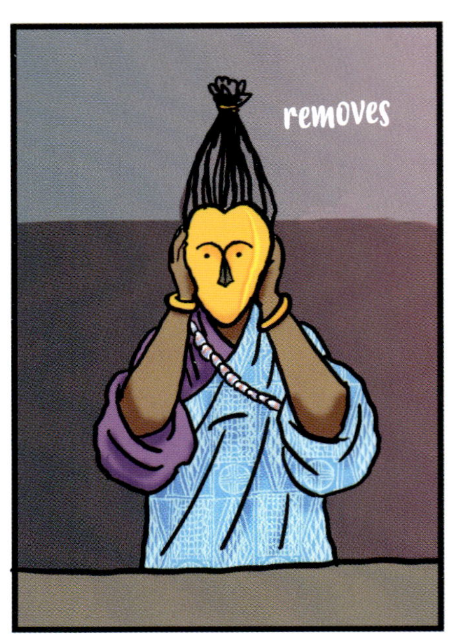

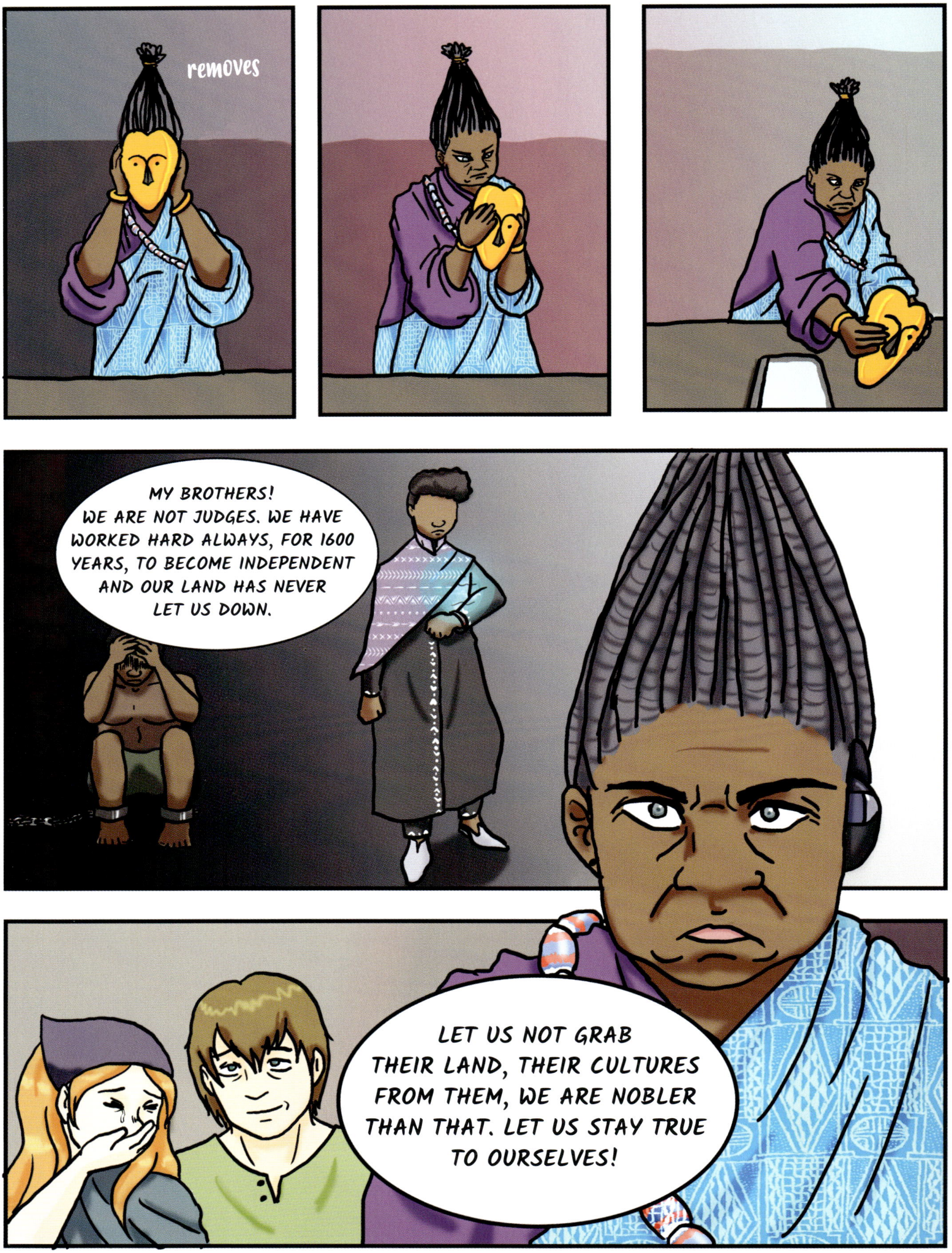

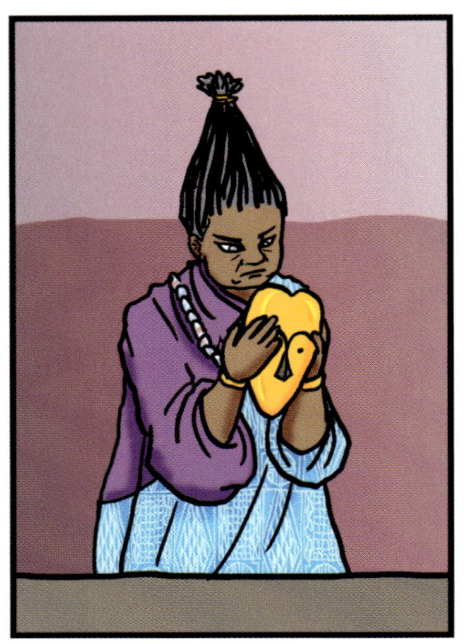

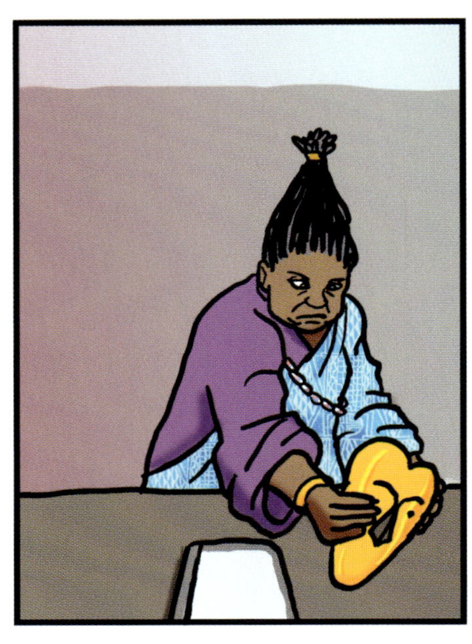

MY BROTHERS! WE ARE NOT JUDGES. WE HAVE WORKED HARD ALWAYS, FOR 1600 YEARS, TO BECOME INDEPENDENT AND OUR LAND HAS NEVER LET US DOWN.

LET US NOT GRAB THEIR LAND, THEIR CULTURES FROM THEM, WE ARE NOBLER THAN THAT. LET US STAY TRUE TO OURSELVES!

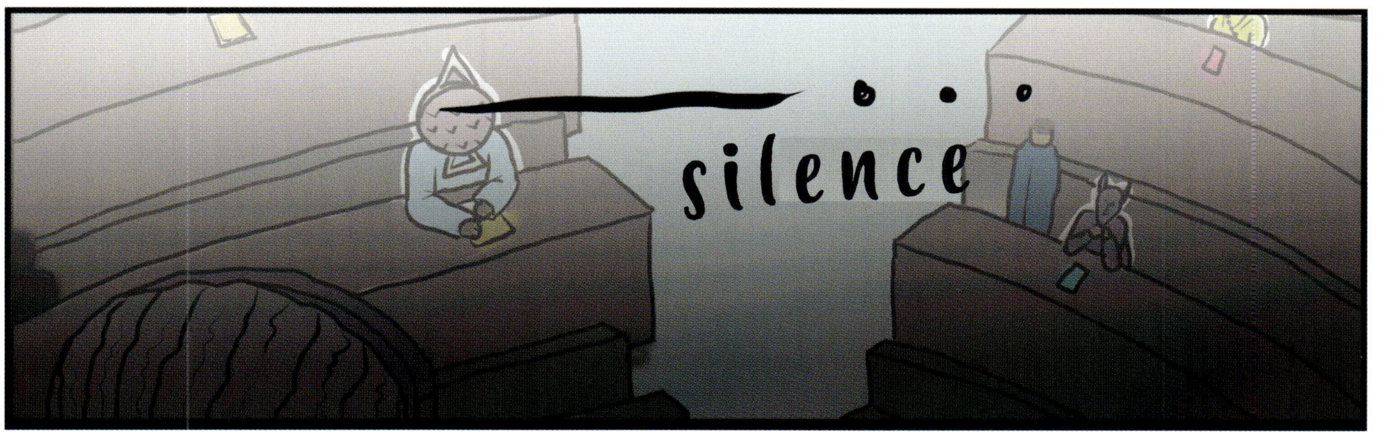
. . .
silence

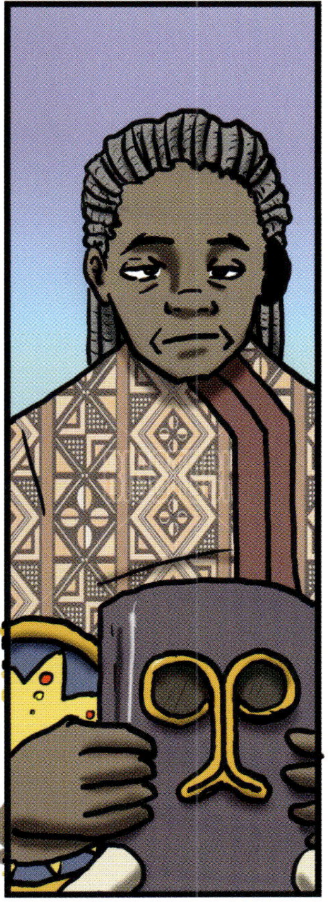

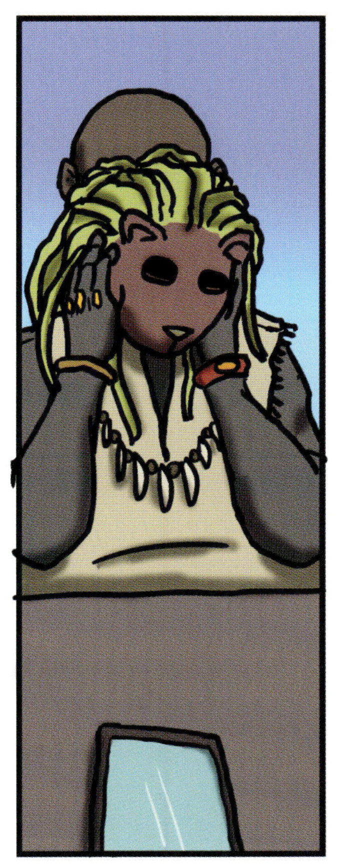

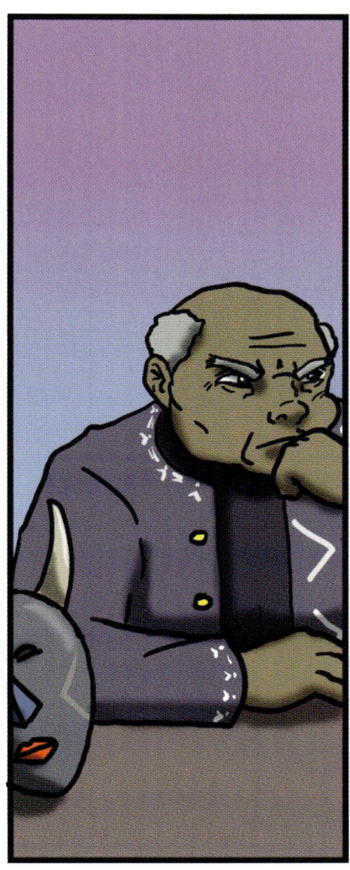

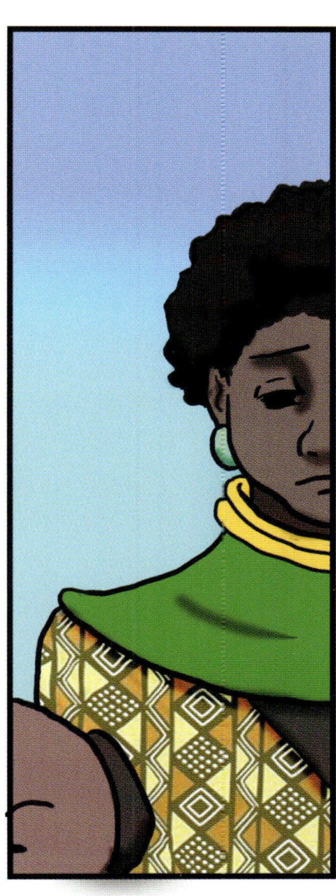

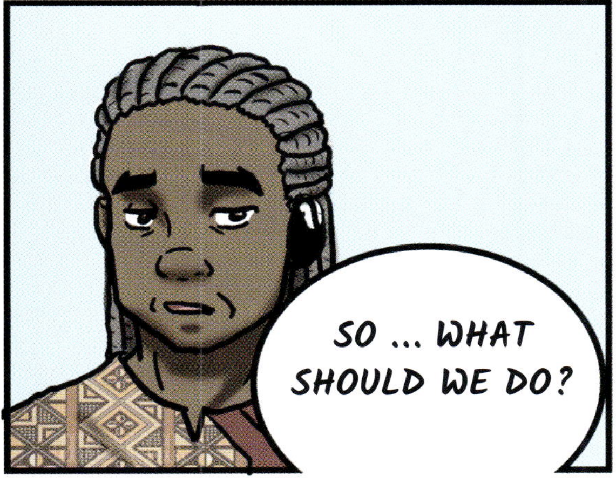
SO ... WHAT SHOULD WE DO?

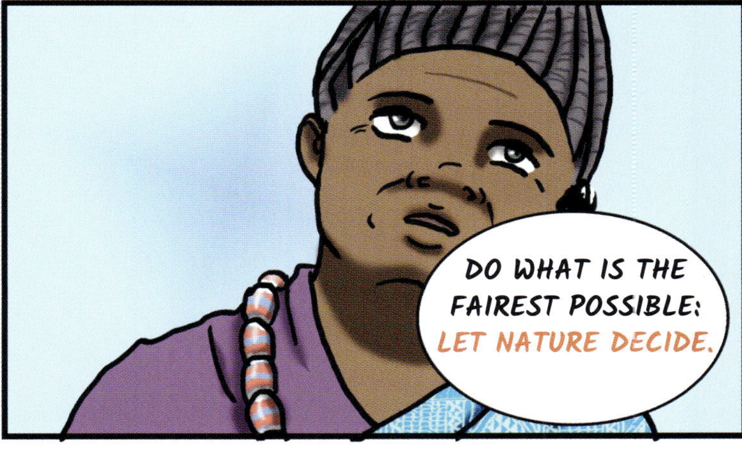
DO WHAT IS THE FAIREST POSSIBLE: LET NATURE DECIDE.

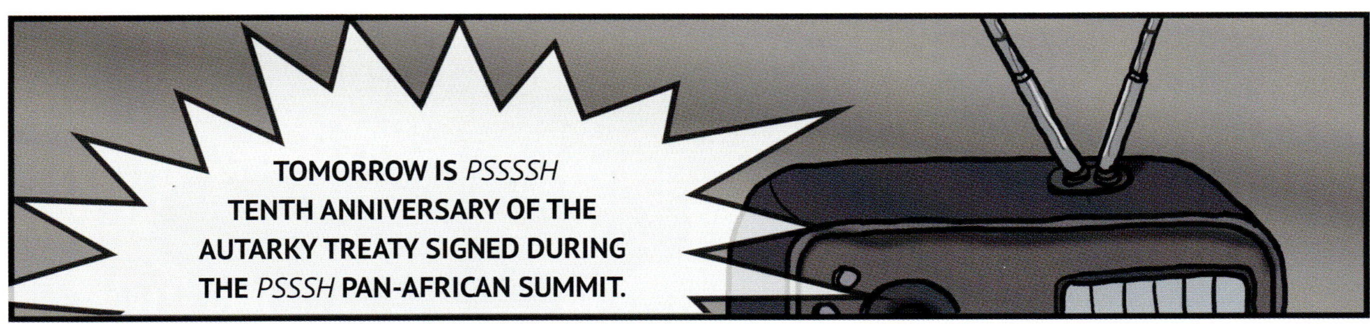
TOMORROW IS *PSSSSH* TENTH ANNIVERSARY OF THE AUTARKY TREATY SIGNED DURING THE *PSSSH* PAN-AFRICAN SUMMIT.

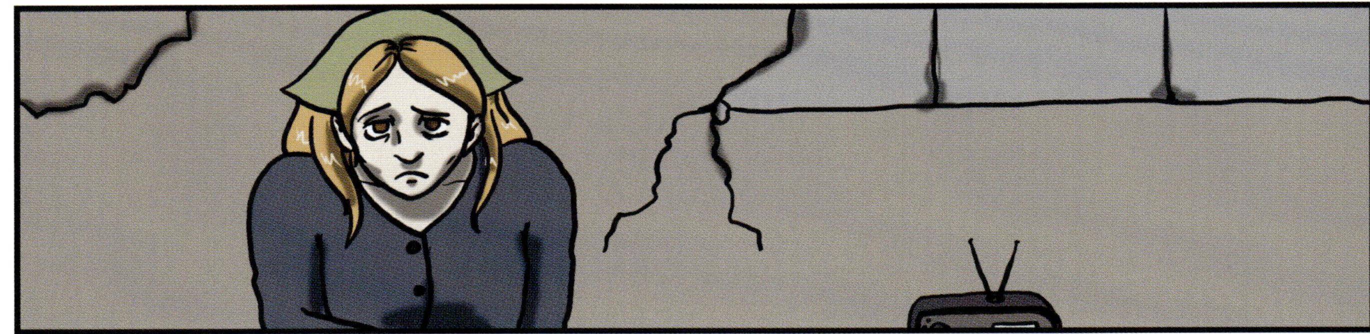

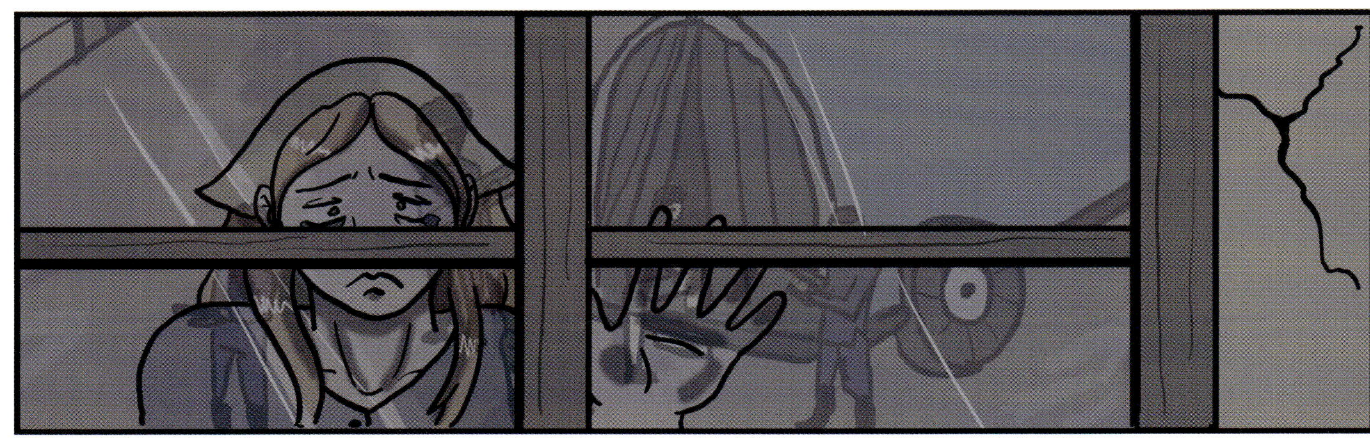

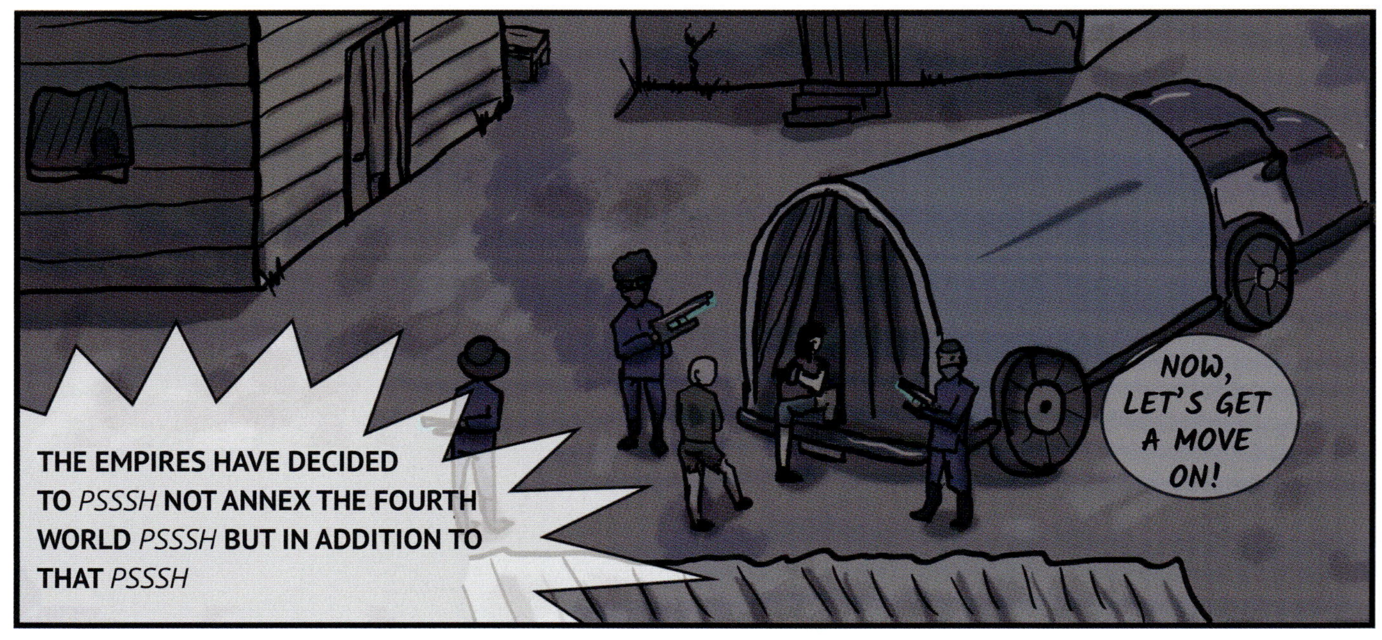
THE EMPIRES HAVE DECIDED TO *PSSSH* NOT ANNEX THE FOURTH WORLD *PSSSH* BUT IN ADDITION TO THAT *PSSSH*
NOW, LET'S GET A MOVE ON!

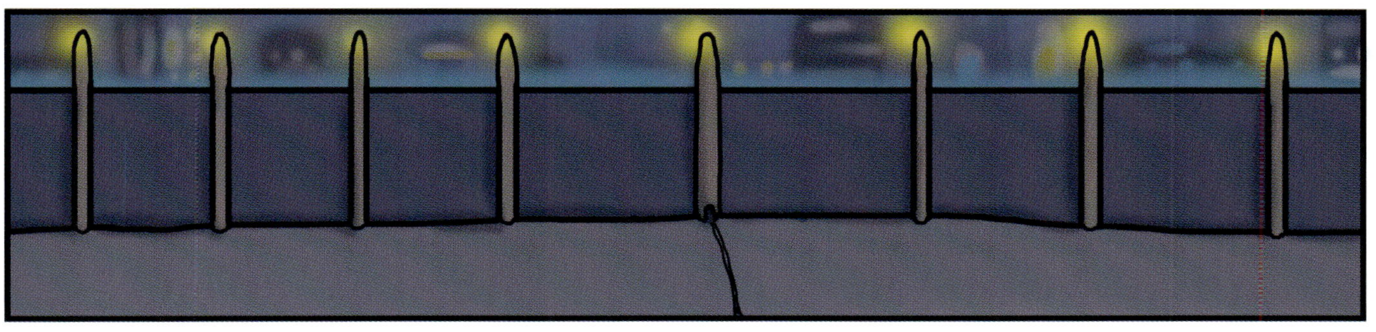

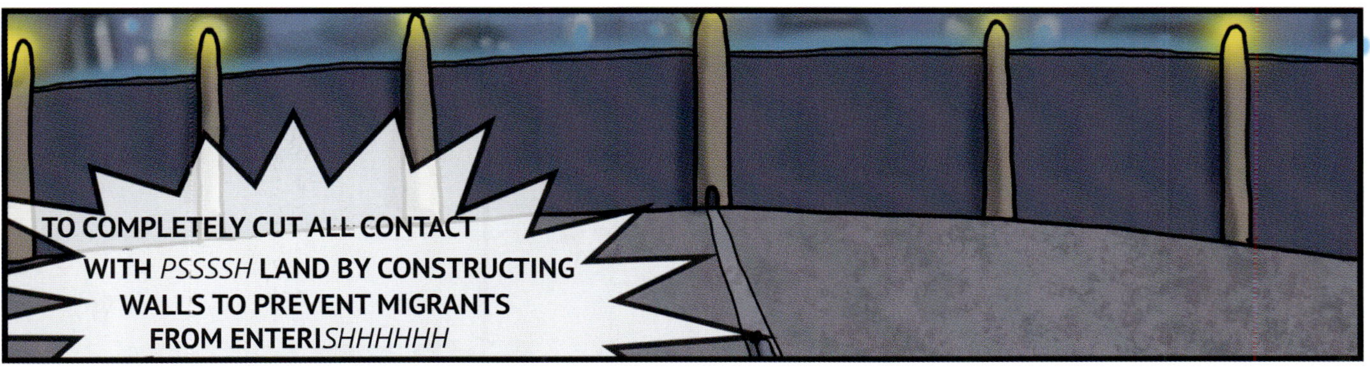
TO COMPLETELY CUT ALL CONTACT WITH PSSSSH LAND BY CONSTRUCTING WALLS TO PREVENT MIGRANTS FROM ENTERISHHHHHH

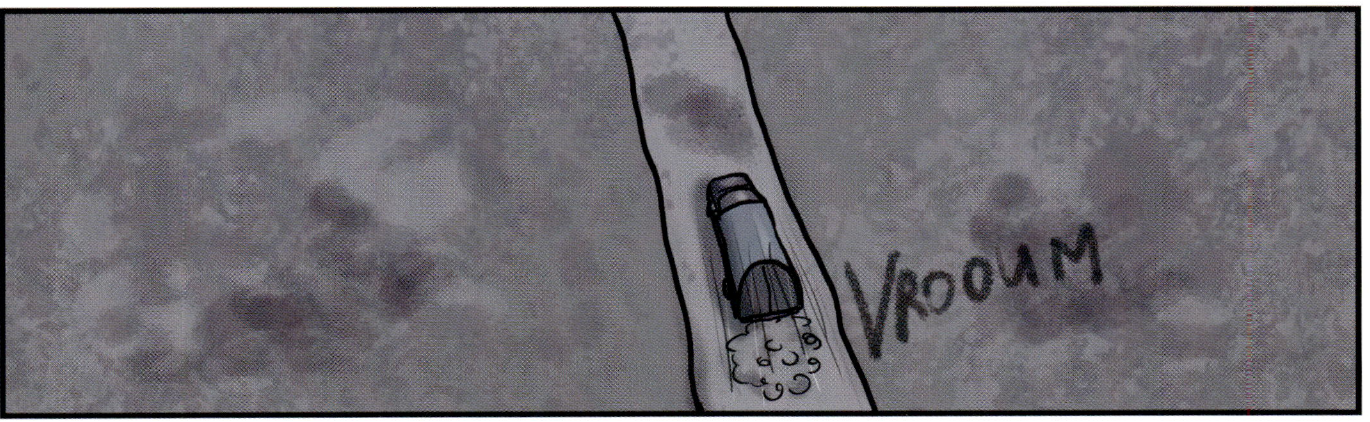
VROOUM

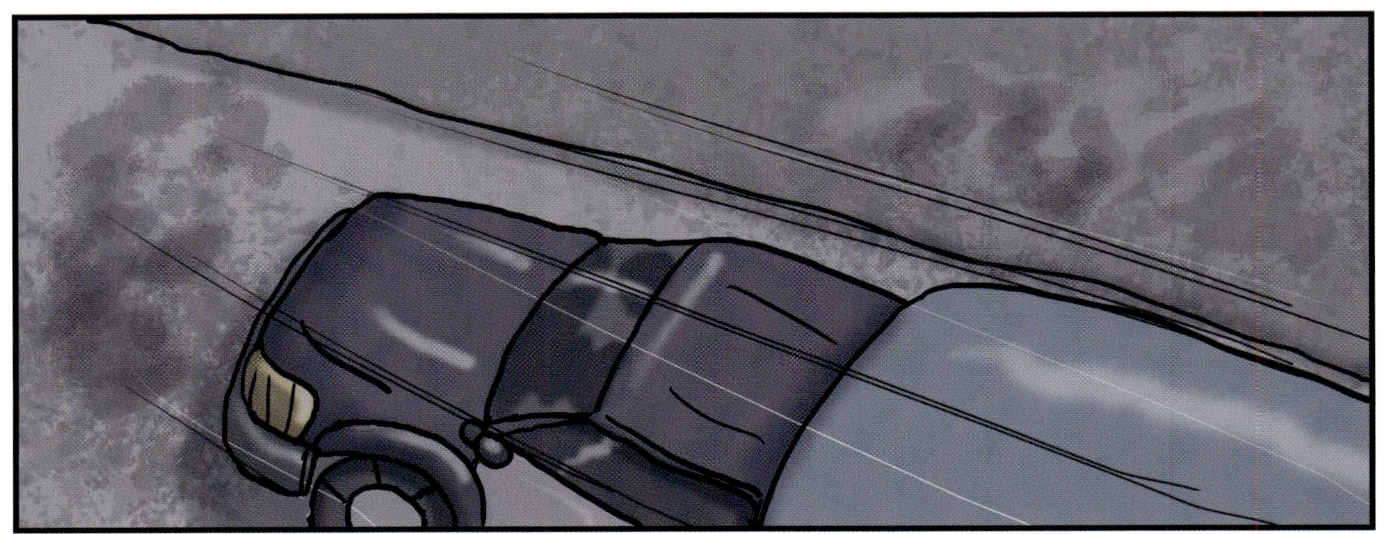

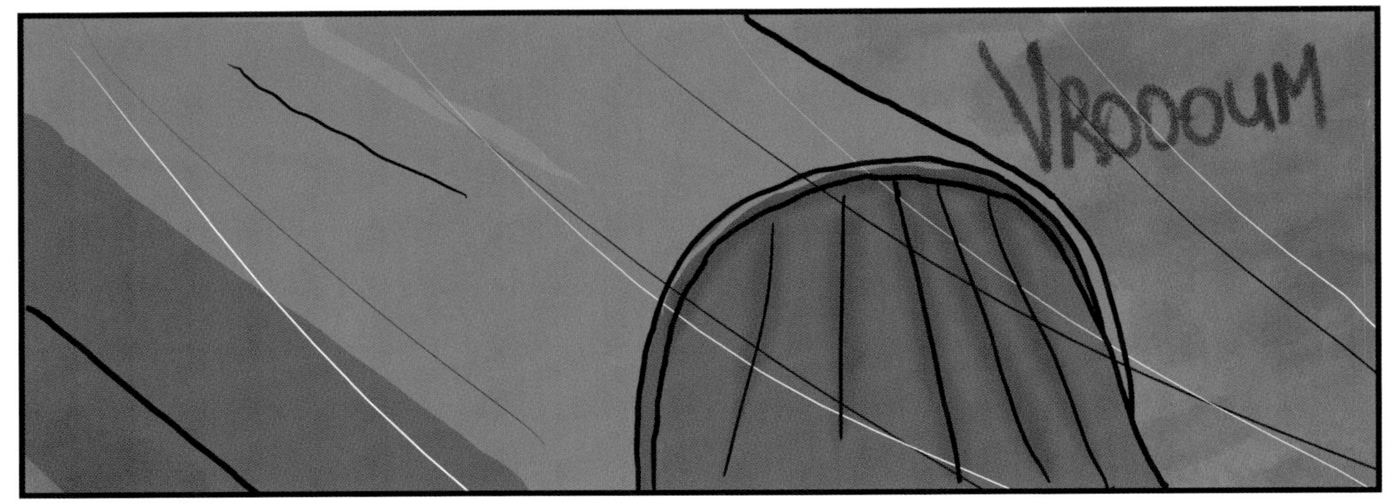

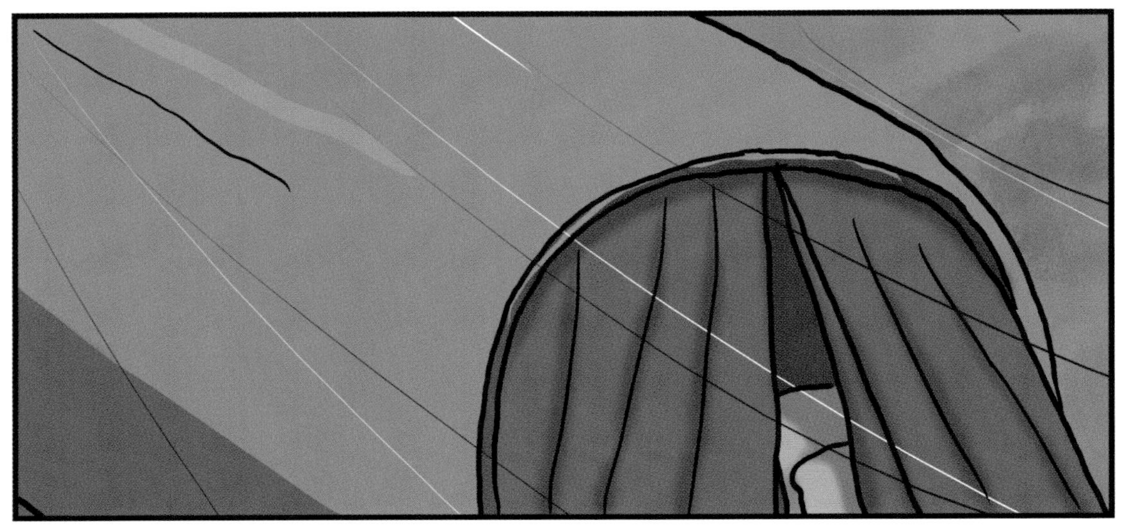

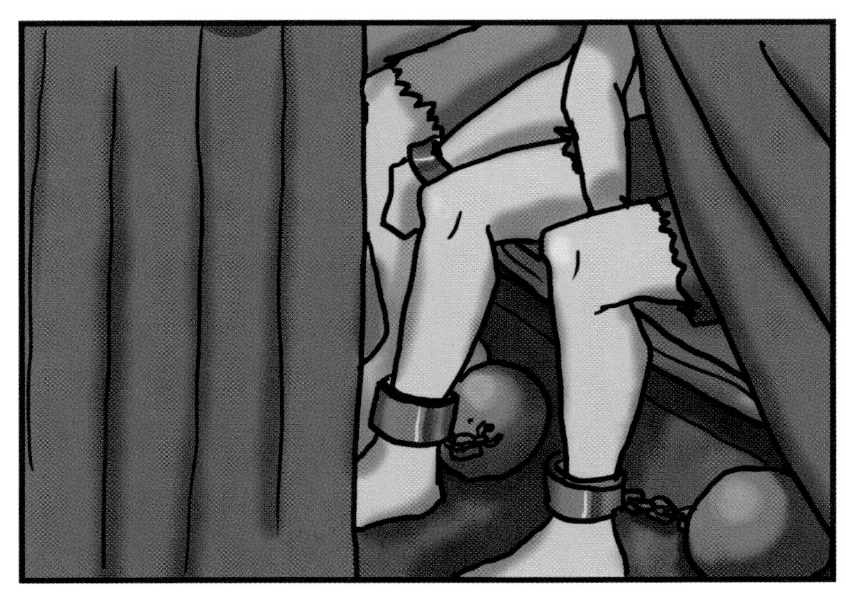

END

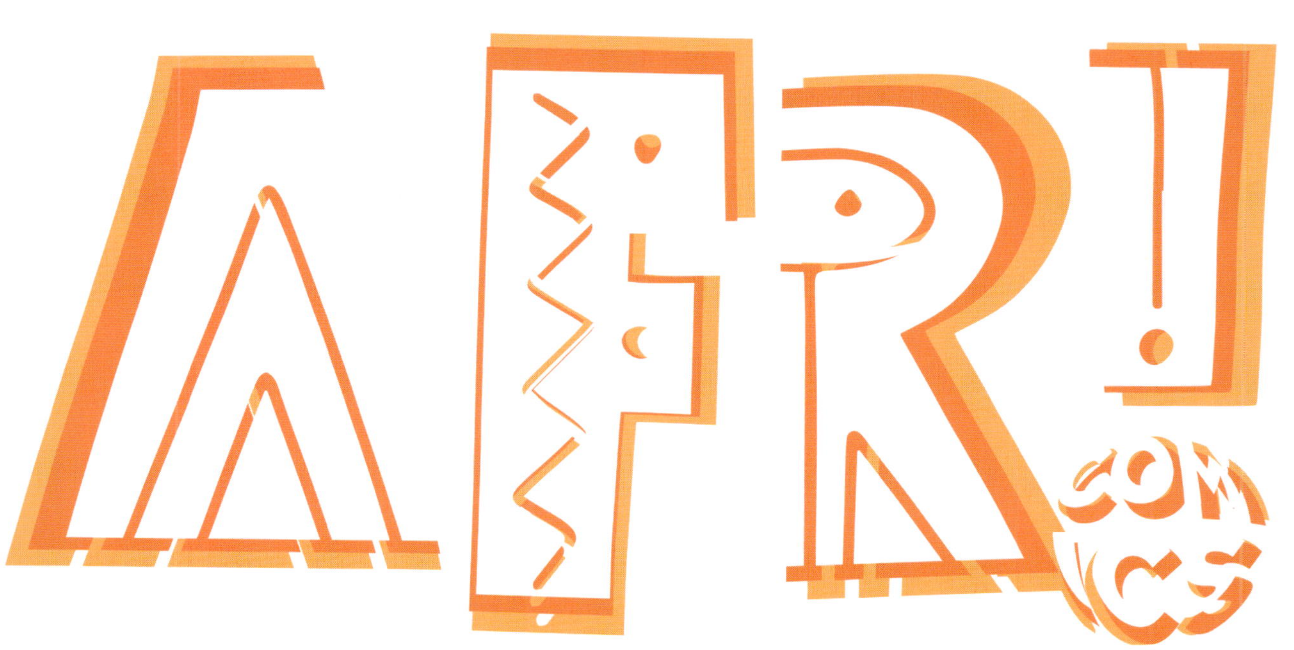
AFRI
COMICS

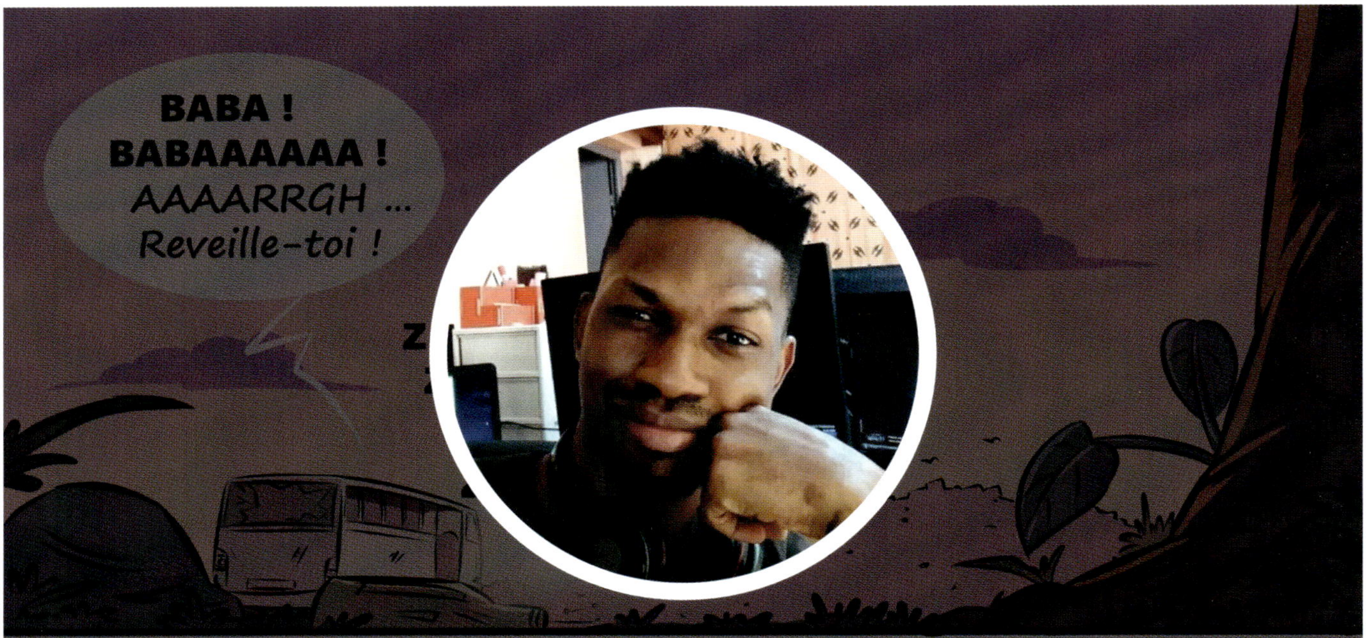

Patrice Mballa Asse

Artist and Illustrator | Comics Creator

Patrice Mballa Asse is a young artist, illustrator and comics creator from Cameroon. Born 1990 in Ebolowa, in the south of the country, he spent his childhood with his grandmother telling him little stories every evening. Passionate about reading from an early age, he read comics such as *Zembla, Blek, Super Picsou, Kouakou*. At the age of 10 he discovered his talent for drawing while scribbling with chalk on the cemented floor in the family house. Having obtained his baccalaureate in literature in 2009, he studied at the university of Yaoundé I, obtaining his degree in Fine Art in 2013 to then enroll for a Masters.

A very talented illustrator and writer, the young artist won fame on the national arts scene when his first comics album *Zog and Mob* was published in 2016, at the time of the Yaoundé international book fair, by Akoma Mba Editions. He is a member of the Cameroonian comic book group "Collectif A3" who since 2010 organise the Festival Mboa BD. Since 2017 he has participated in several international comic book workshops and represented Cameroon at the Africomics Workshops organised by the Goethe Institute in Ghana in 2022.

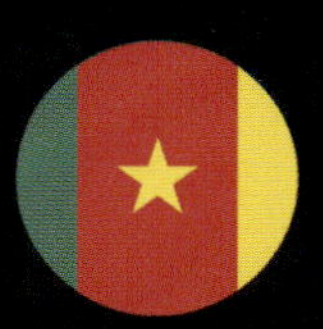

CAMEROON

Facebook : patrice.mbala.79
Instagram : m bal labison

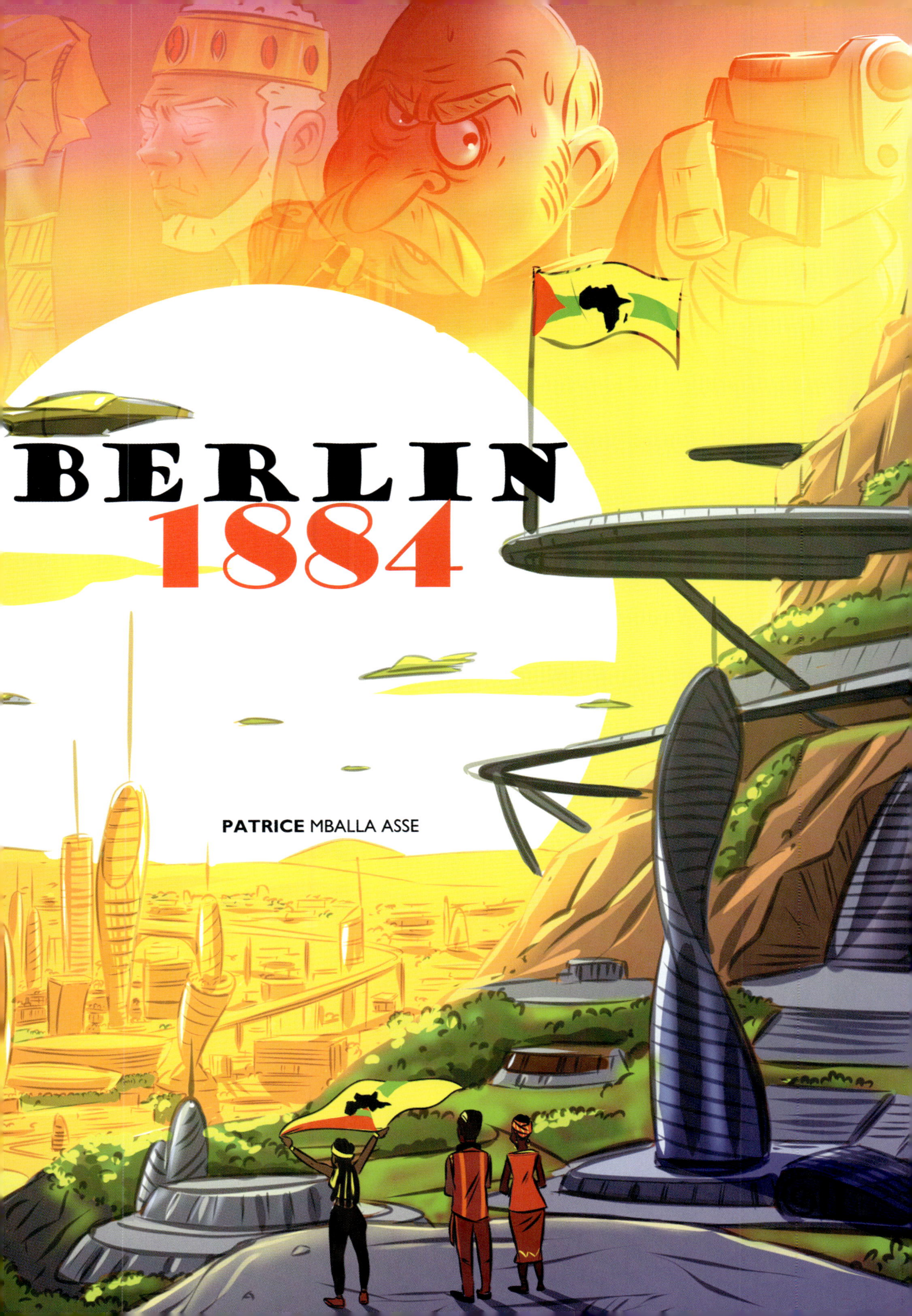
BERLIN
1884
PATRICE MBALLA ASSE

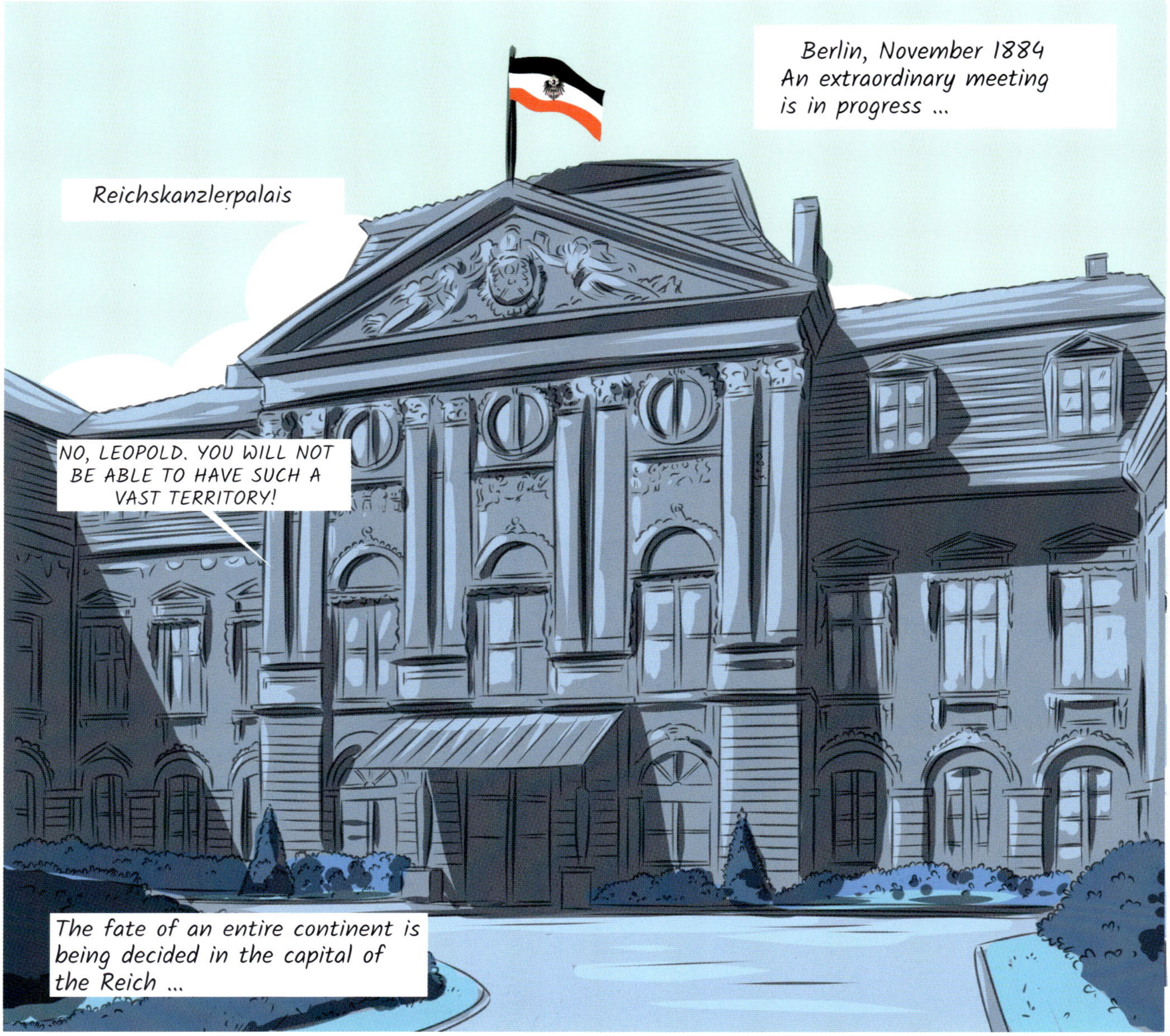

Berlin, November 1884
An extraordinary meeting is in progress ...

Reichskanzlerpalais

NO, LEOPOLD. YOU WILL NOT BE ABLE TO HAVE SUCH A VAST TERRITORY!

The fate of an entire continent is being decided in the capital of the Reich ...

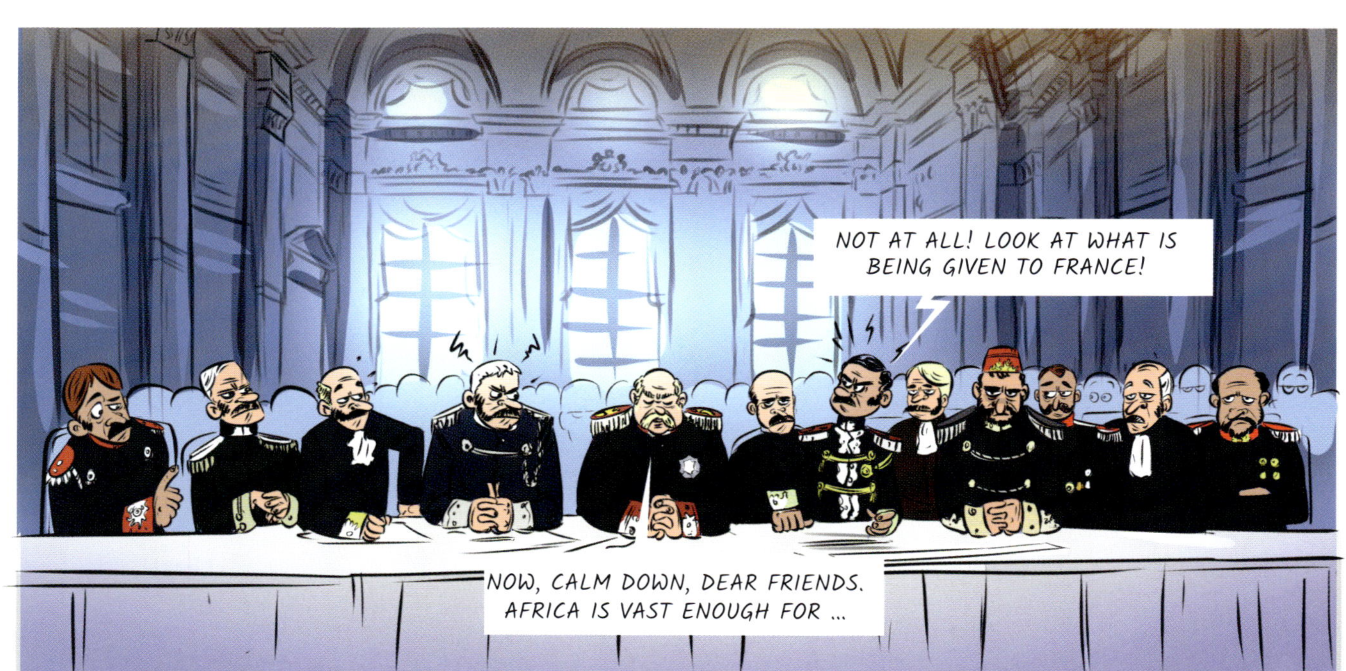

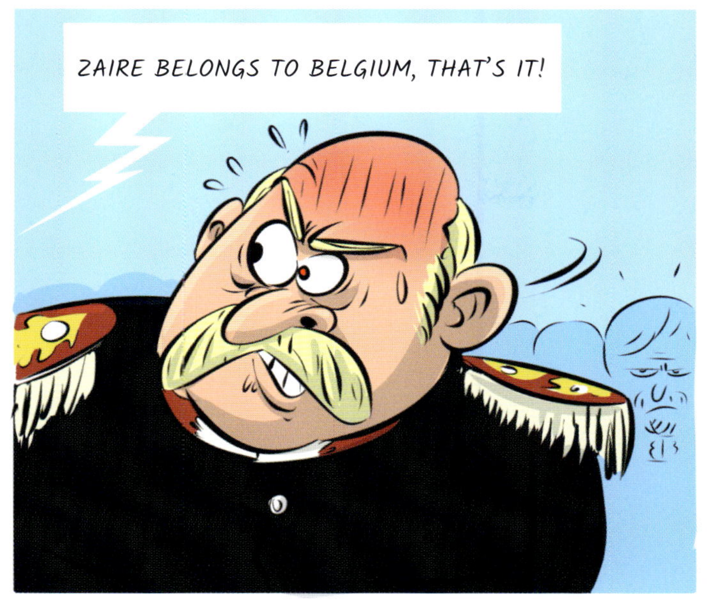
ZAIRE BELONGS TO BELGIUM, THAT'S IT!

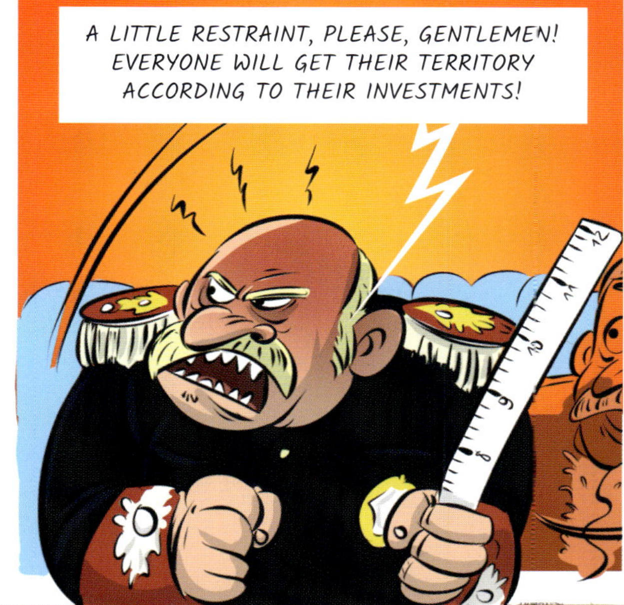
A LITTLE RESTRAINT, PLEASE, GENTLEMEN! EVERYONE WILL GET THEIR TERRITORY ACCORDING TO THEIR INVESTMENTS!

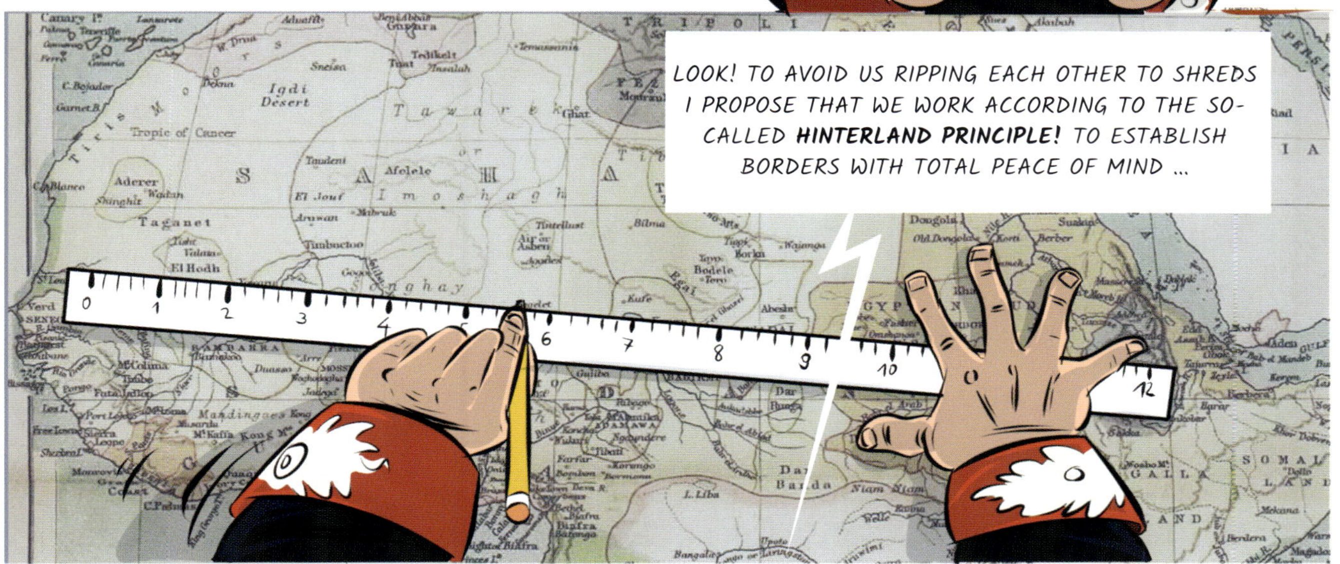
LOOK! TO AVOID US RIPPING EACH OTHER TO SHREDS I PROPOSE THAT WE WORK ACCORDING TO THE SO-CALLED **HINTERLAND PRINCIPLE!** TO ESTABLISH BORDERS WITH TOTAL PEACE OF MIND ...

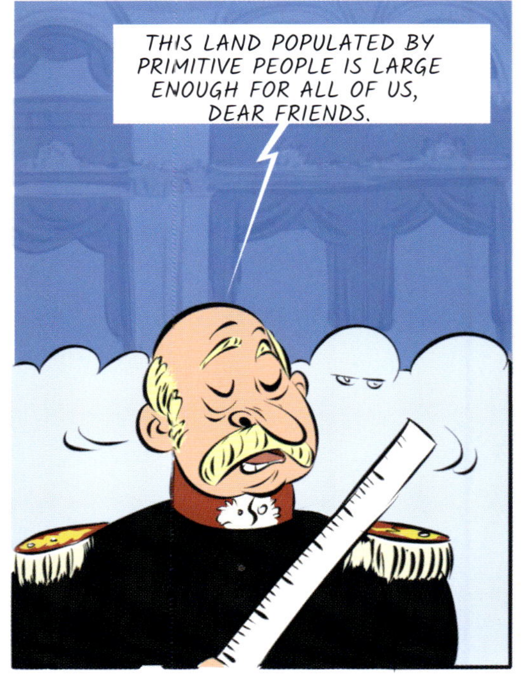
THIS LAND POPULATED BY PRIMITIVE PEOPLE IS LARGE ENOUGH FOR ALL OF US, DEAR FRIENDS.

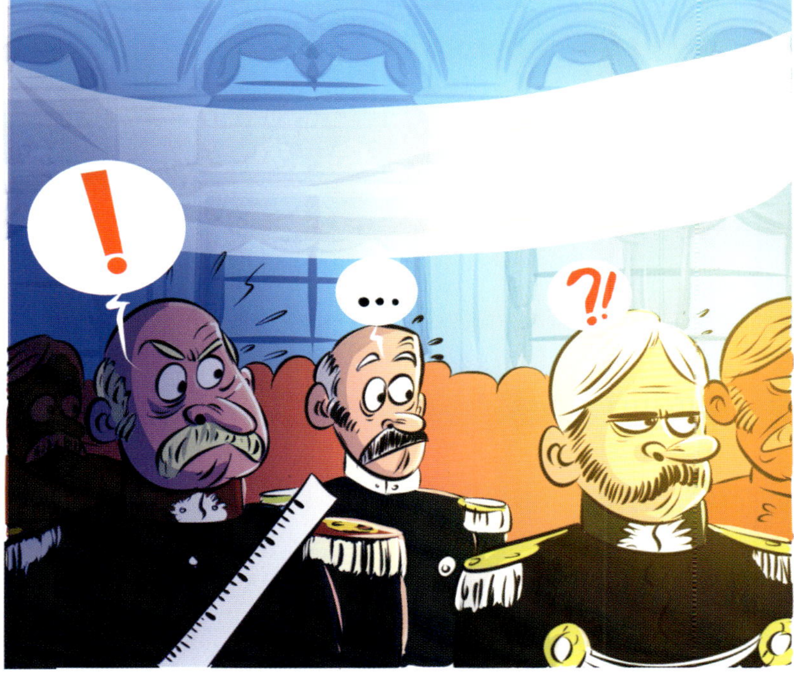
!
...
?!

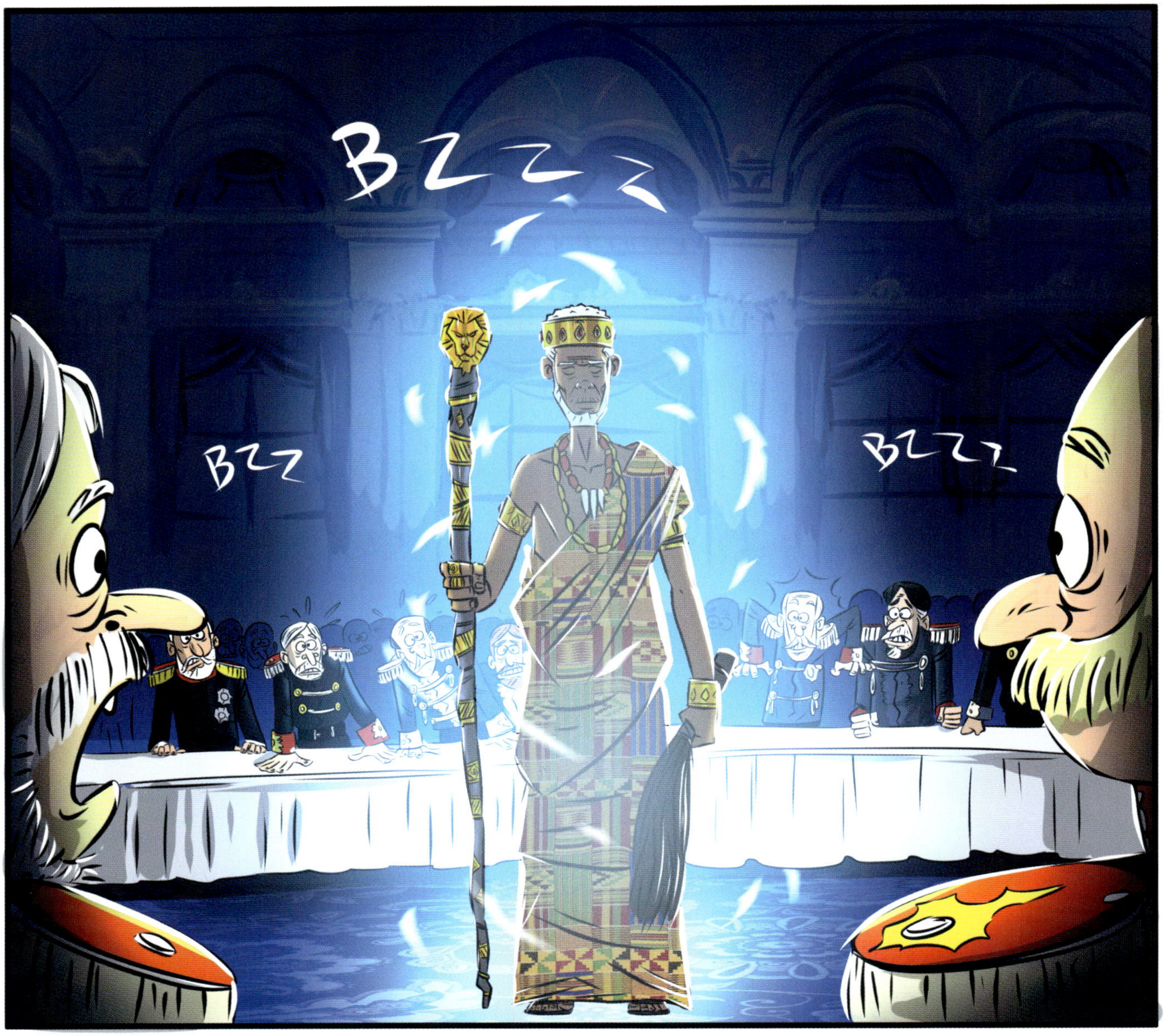

BZZZ
BZZ
BZZZ

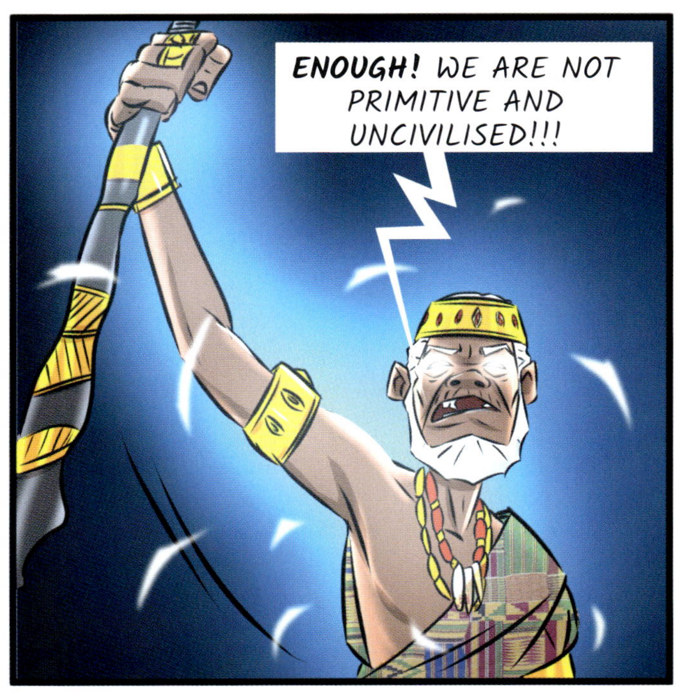
ENOUGH! WE ARE NOT PRIMITIVE AND UNCIVILISED!!!

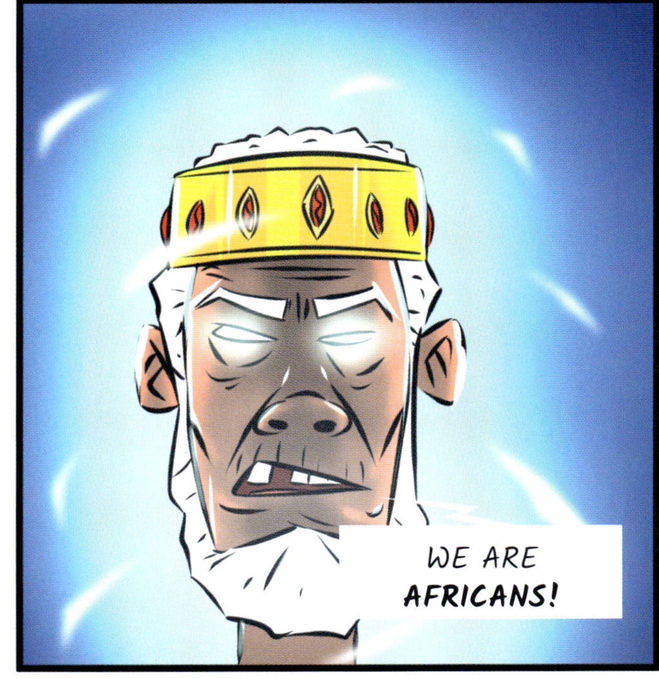
WE ARE AFRICANS!

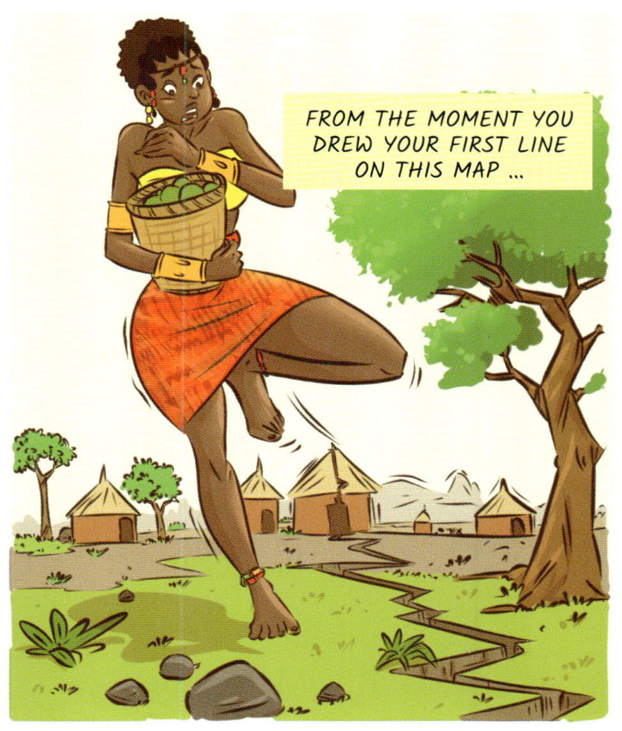
FROM THE MOMENT YOU DREW YOUR FIRST LINE ON THIS MAP ...

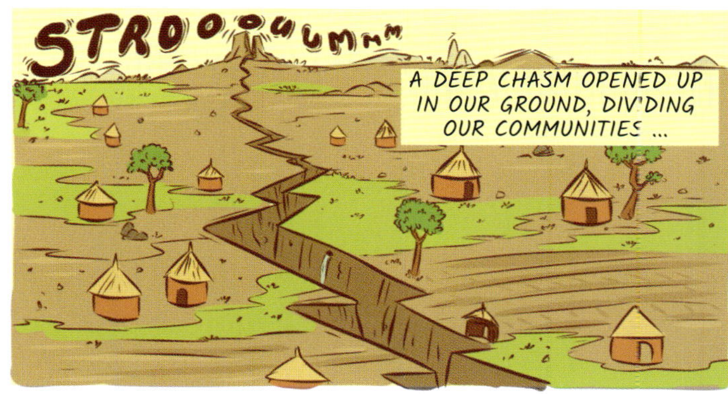
STROOOOUUMMM
A DEEP CHASM OPENED UP IN OUR GROUND, DIVIDING OUR COMMUNITIES ...

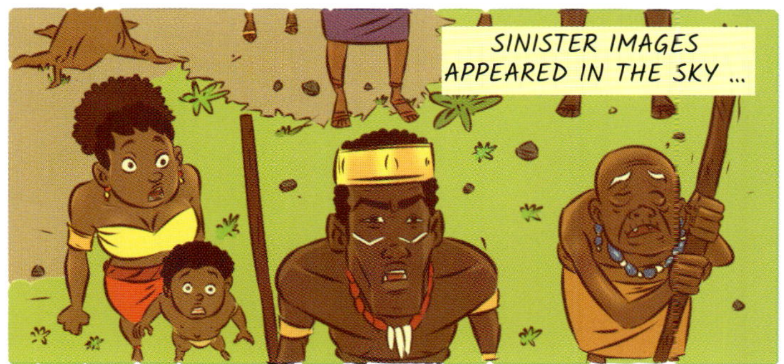
SINISTER IMAGES APPEARED IN THE SKY ...

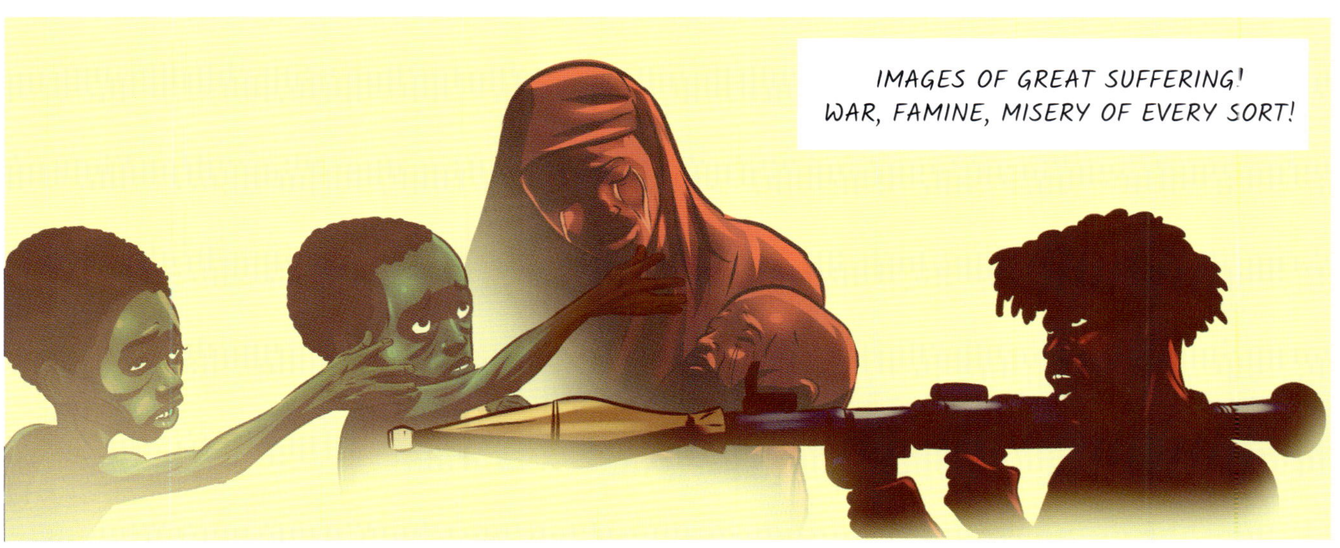
IMAGES OF GREAT SUFFERING! WAR, FAMINE, MISERY OF EVERY SORT!

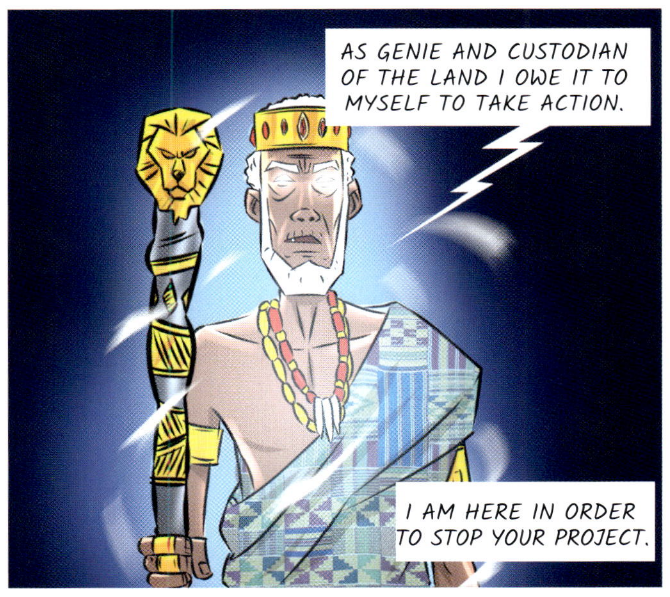
AS GENIE AND CUSTODIAN OF THE LAND I OWE IT TO MYSELF TO TAKE ACTION.
I AM HERE IN ORDER TO STOP YOUR PROJECT.

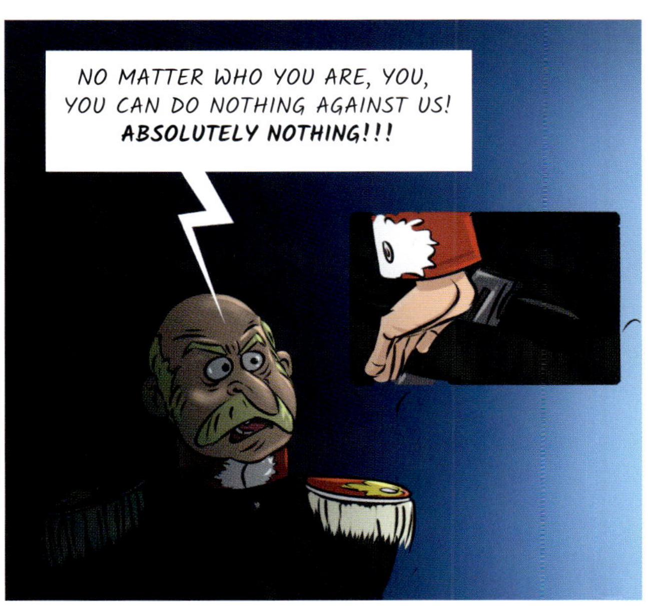
NO MATTER WHO YOU ARE, YOU, YOU CAN DO NOTHING AGAINST US! **ABSOLUTELY NOTHING!!!**

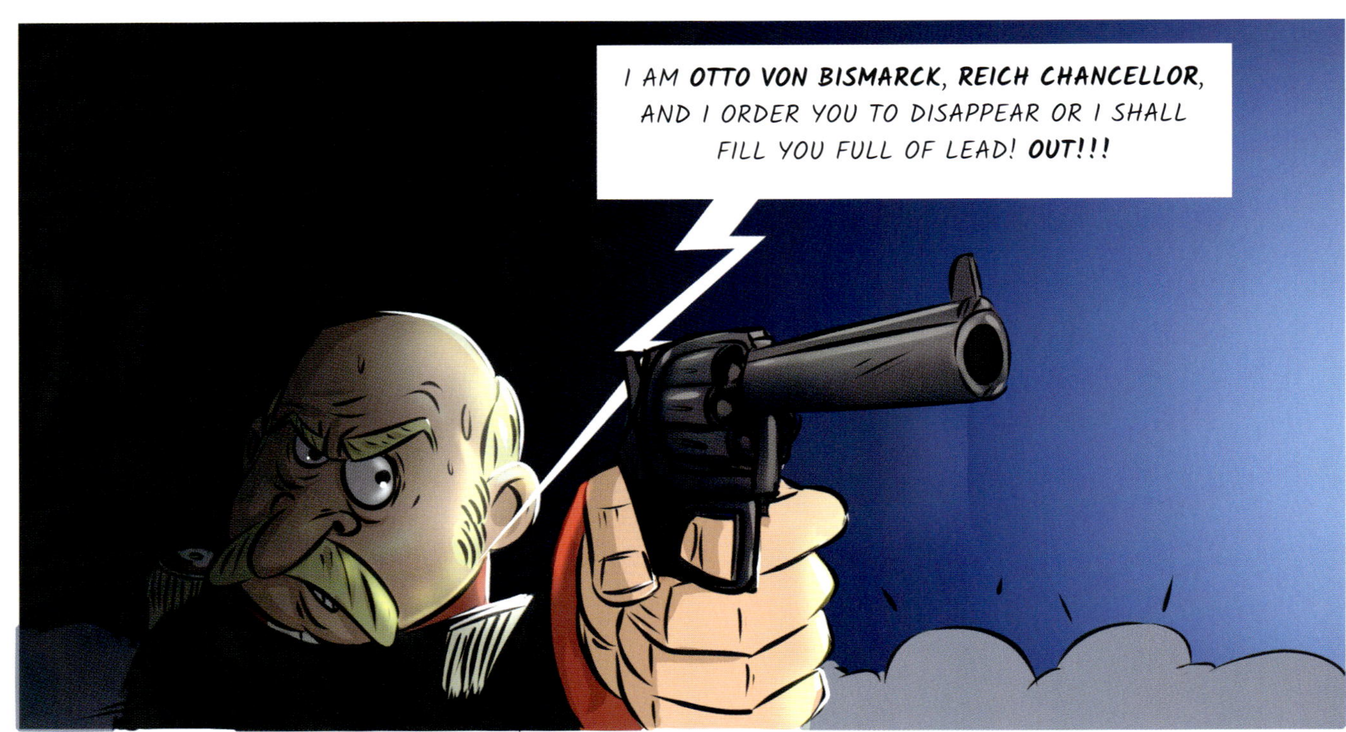
I AM OTTO VON BISMARCK, REICH CHANCELLOR, AND I ORDER YOU TO DISAPPEAR OR I SHALL FILL YOU FULL OF LEAD! OUT!!!

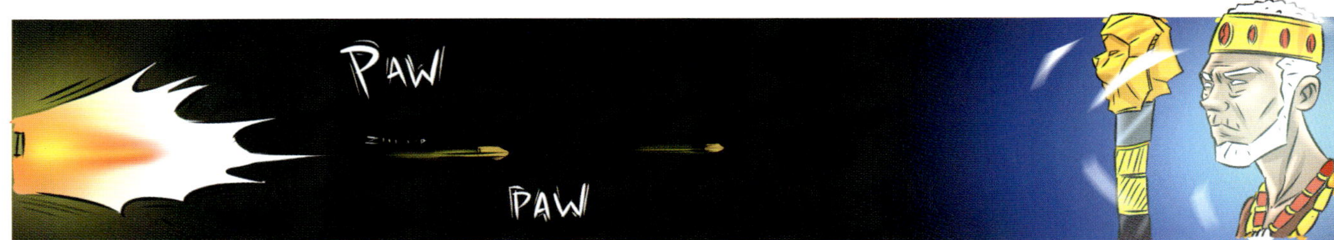
PAW
PAW

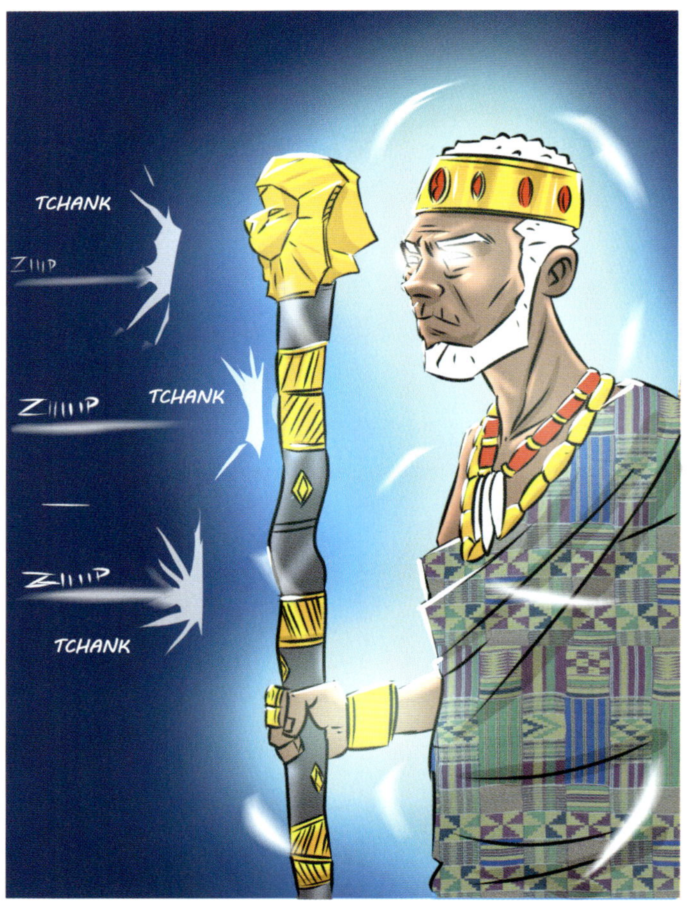
TCHANK
ZIIIP
ZIIIIP
TCHANK
ZIIIIP
TCHANK

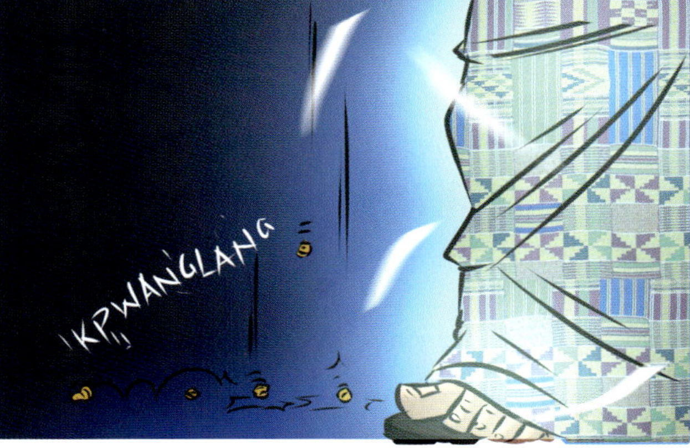
KPWANGLANG

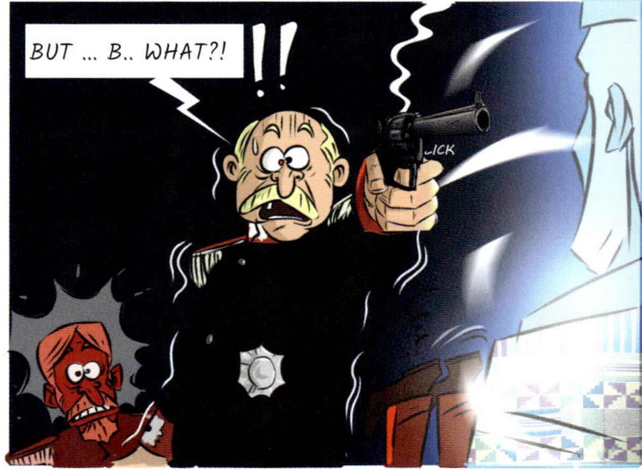
BUT ... B.. WHAT?!
!!

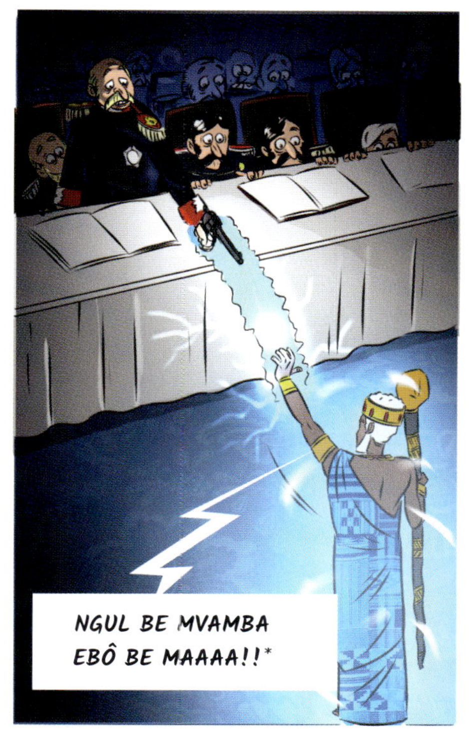

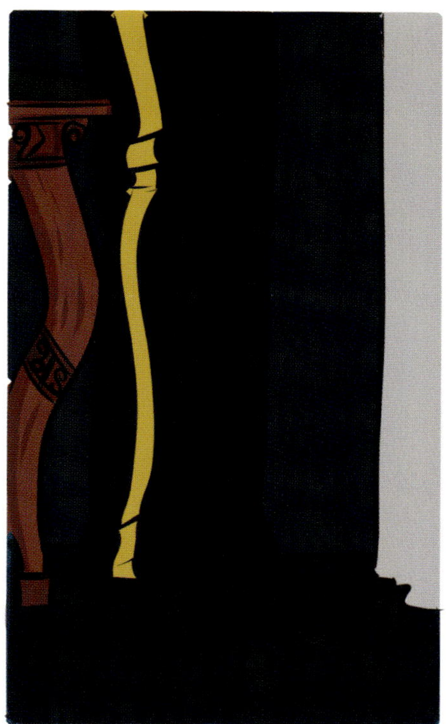
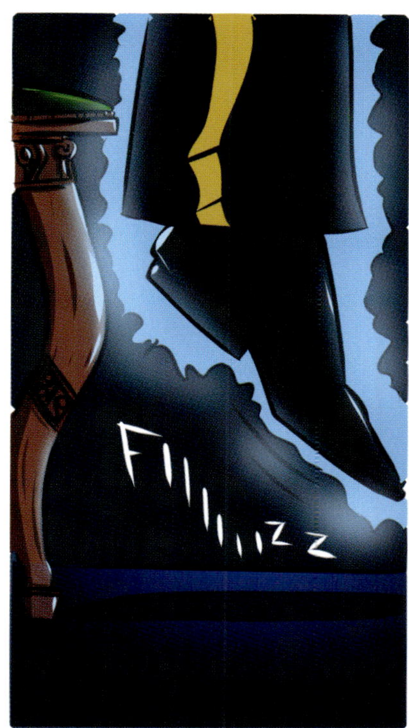

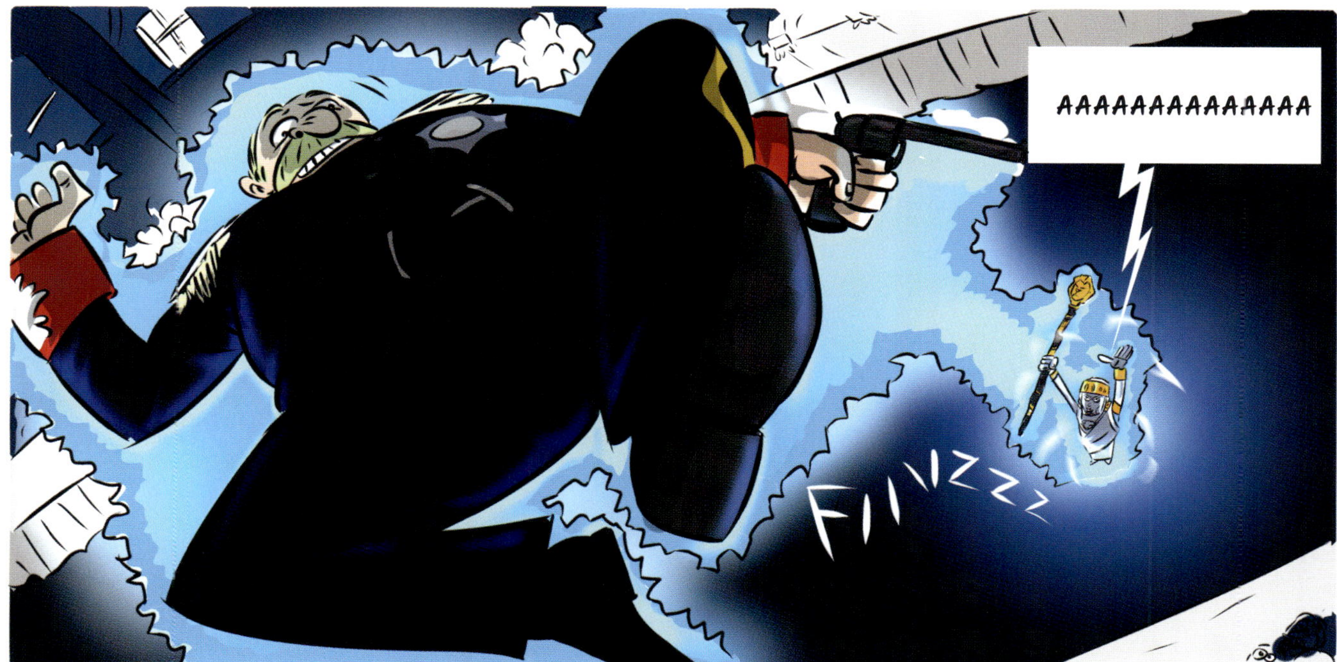

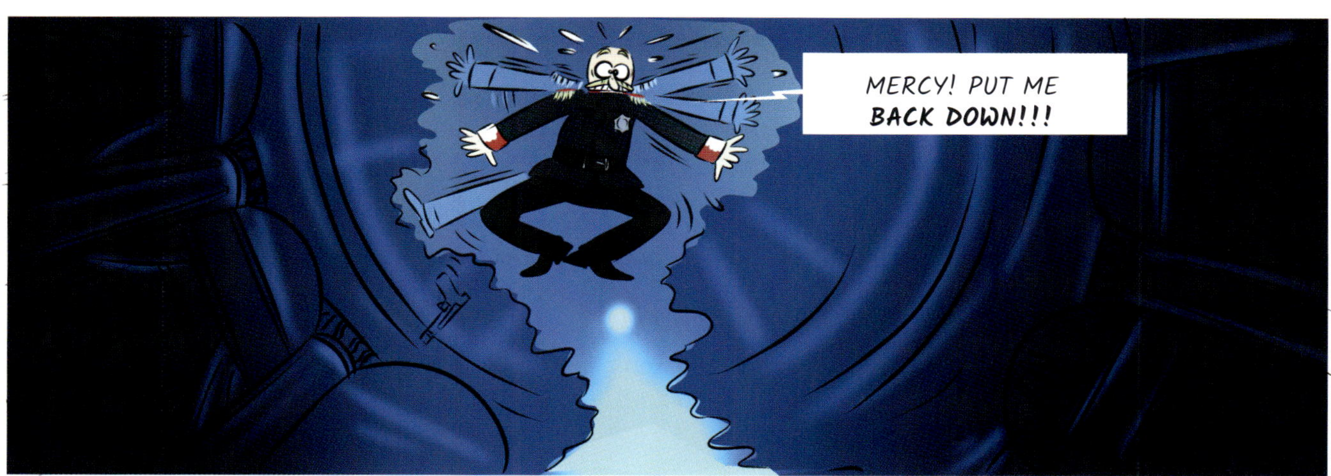

* MAY MY ANCESTORS' FORCE BE WITH ME!

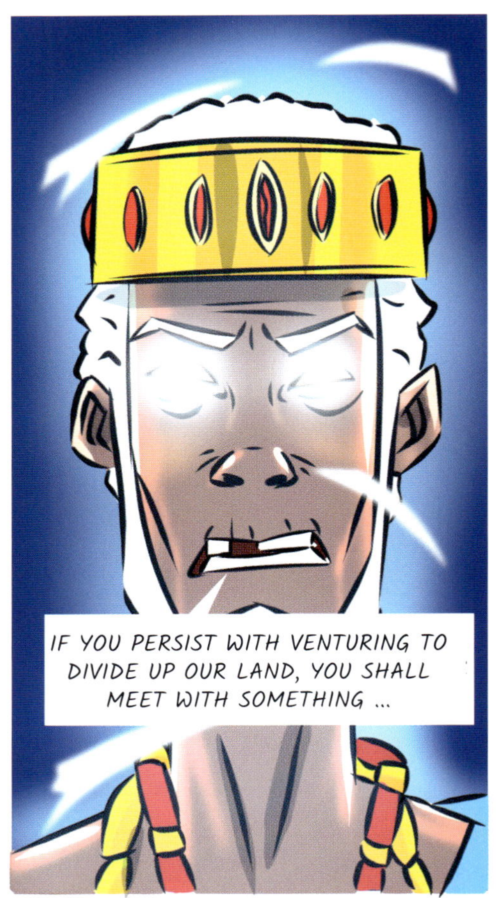
IF YOU PERSIST WITH VENTURING TO DIVIDE UP OUR LAND, YOU SHALL MEET WITH SOMETHING ...

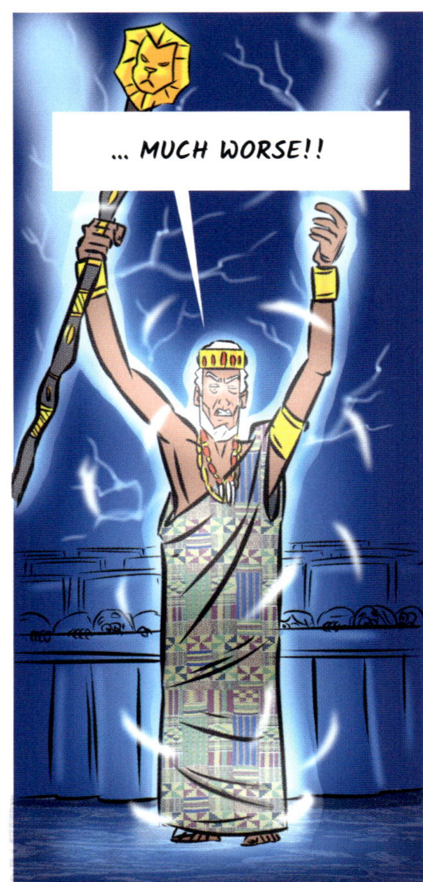
... MUCH WORSE!!

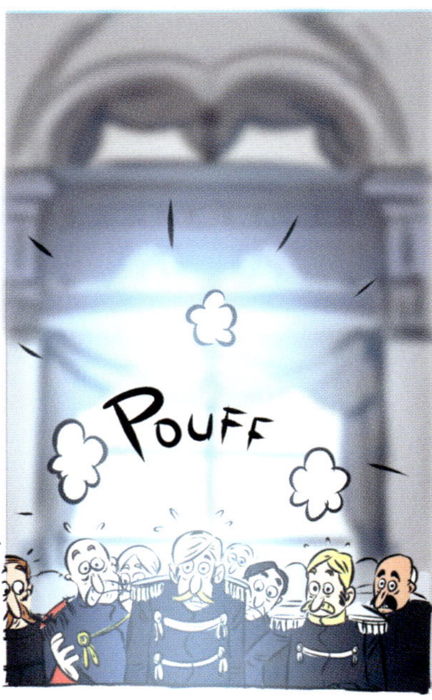
POUFF

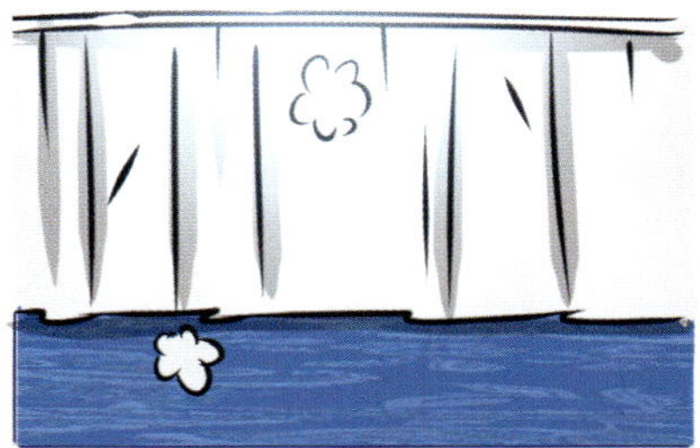

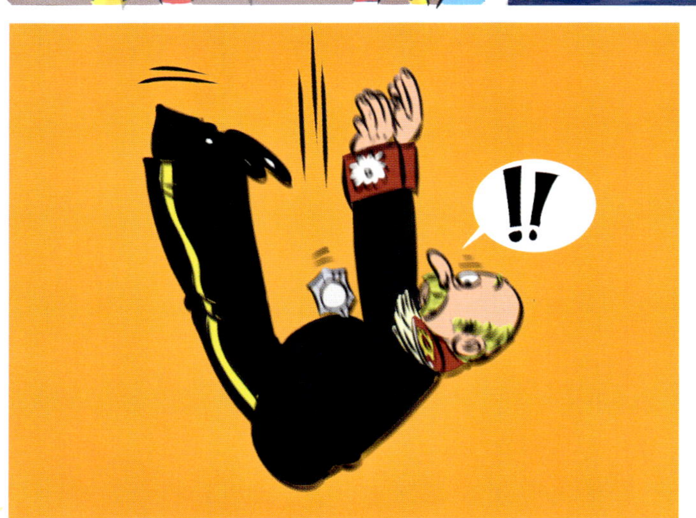
!!

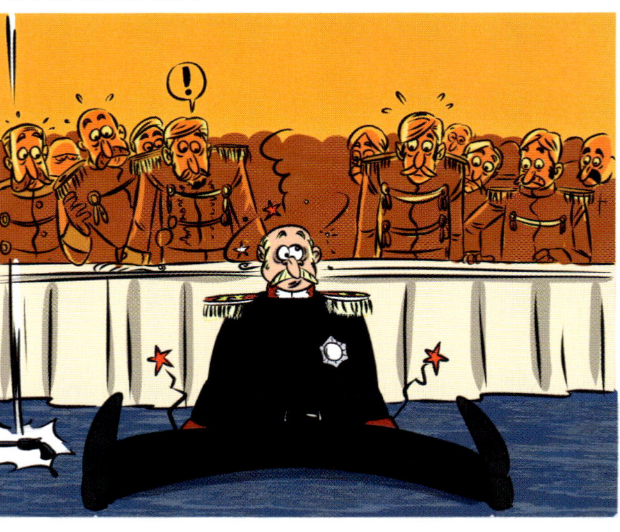
!

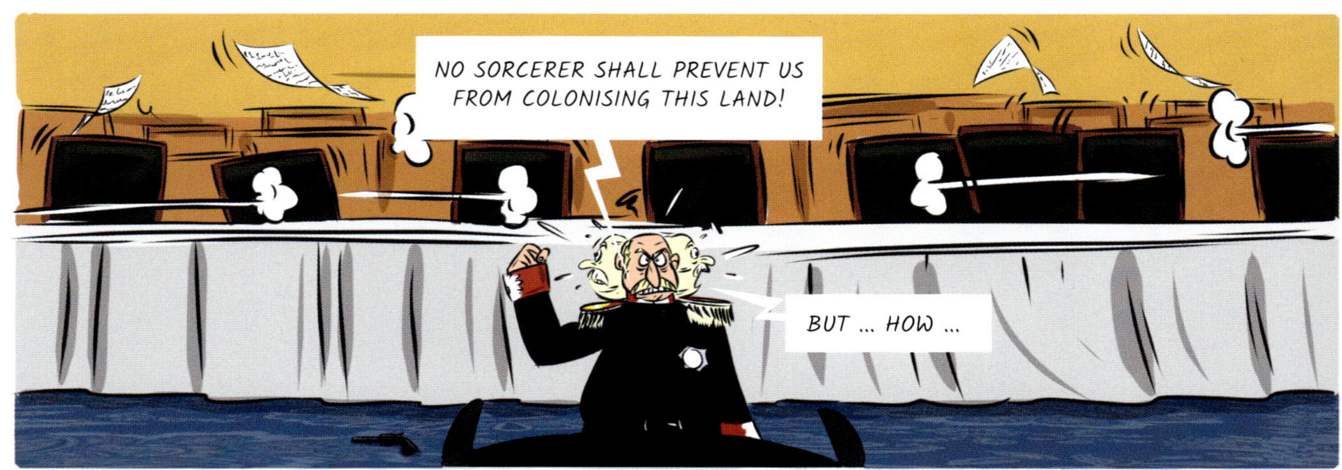
NO SORCERER SHALL PREVENT US FROM COLONISING THIS LAND!
BUT ... HOW ...

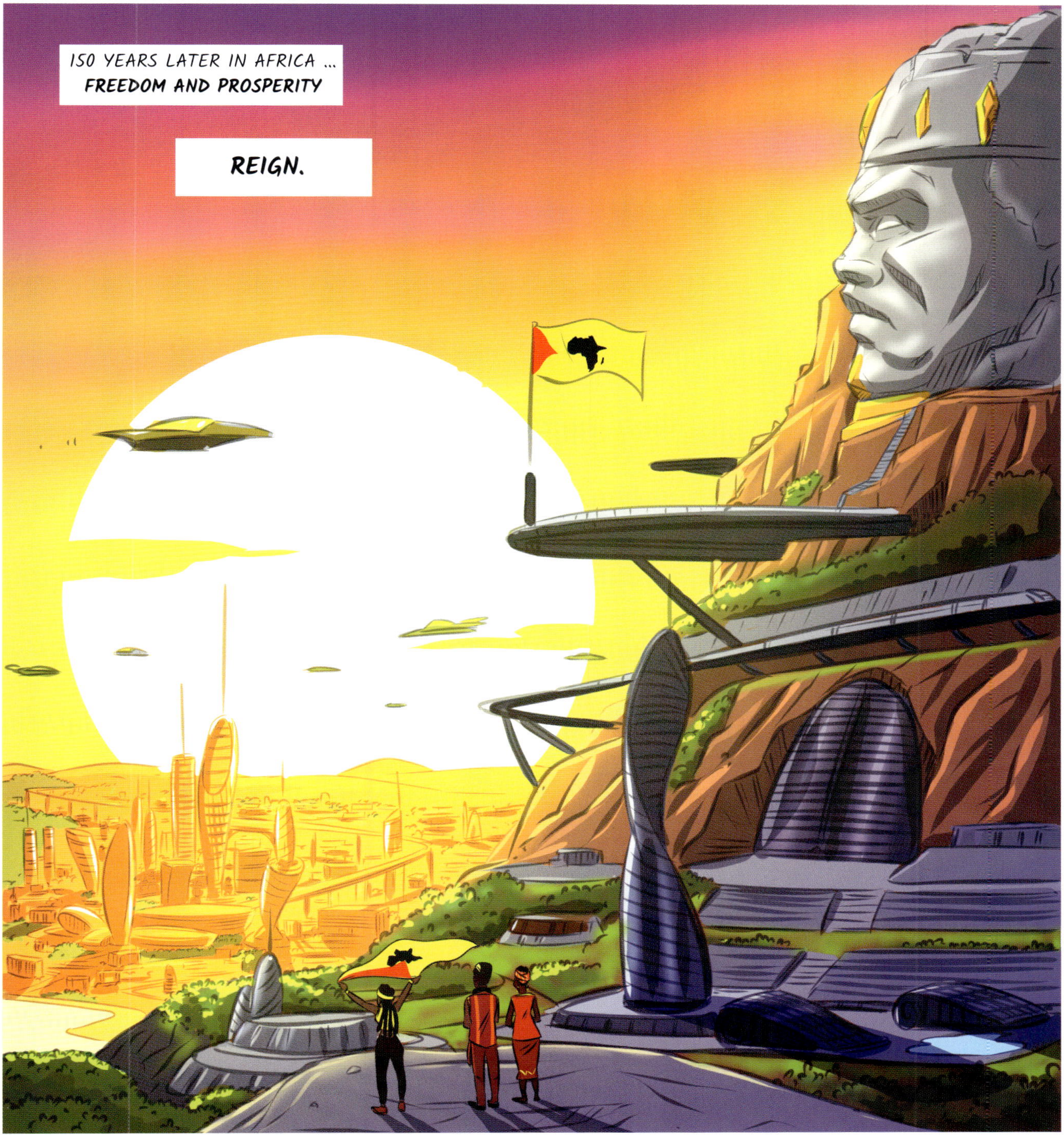

150 YEARS LATER IN AFRICA ...
FREEDOM AND PROSPERITY

REIGN.

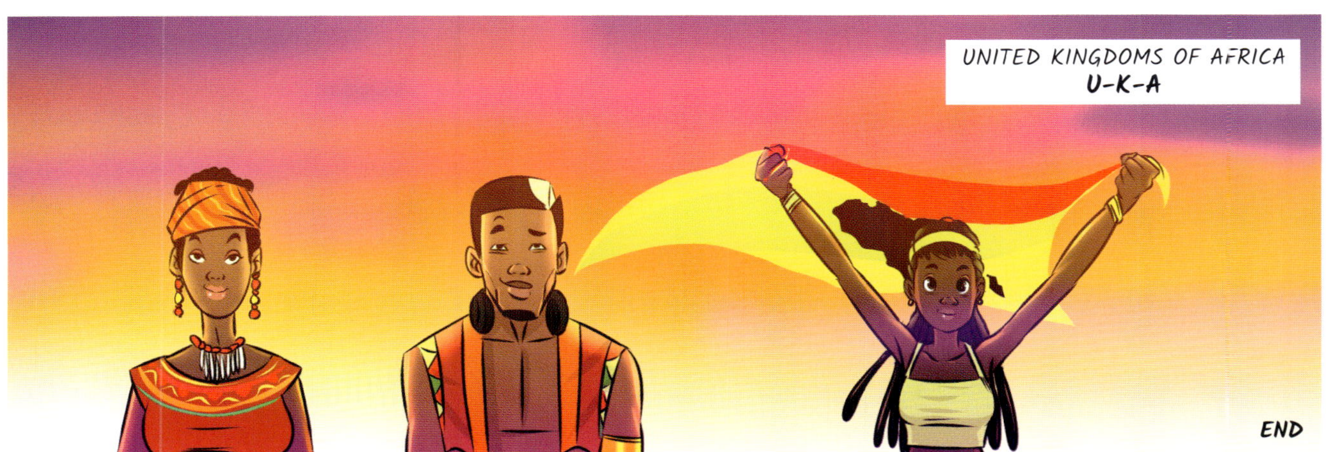

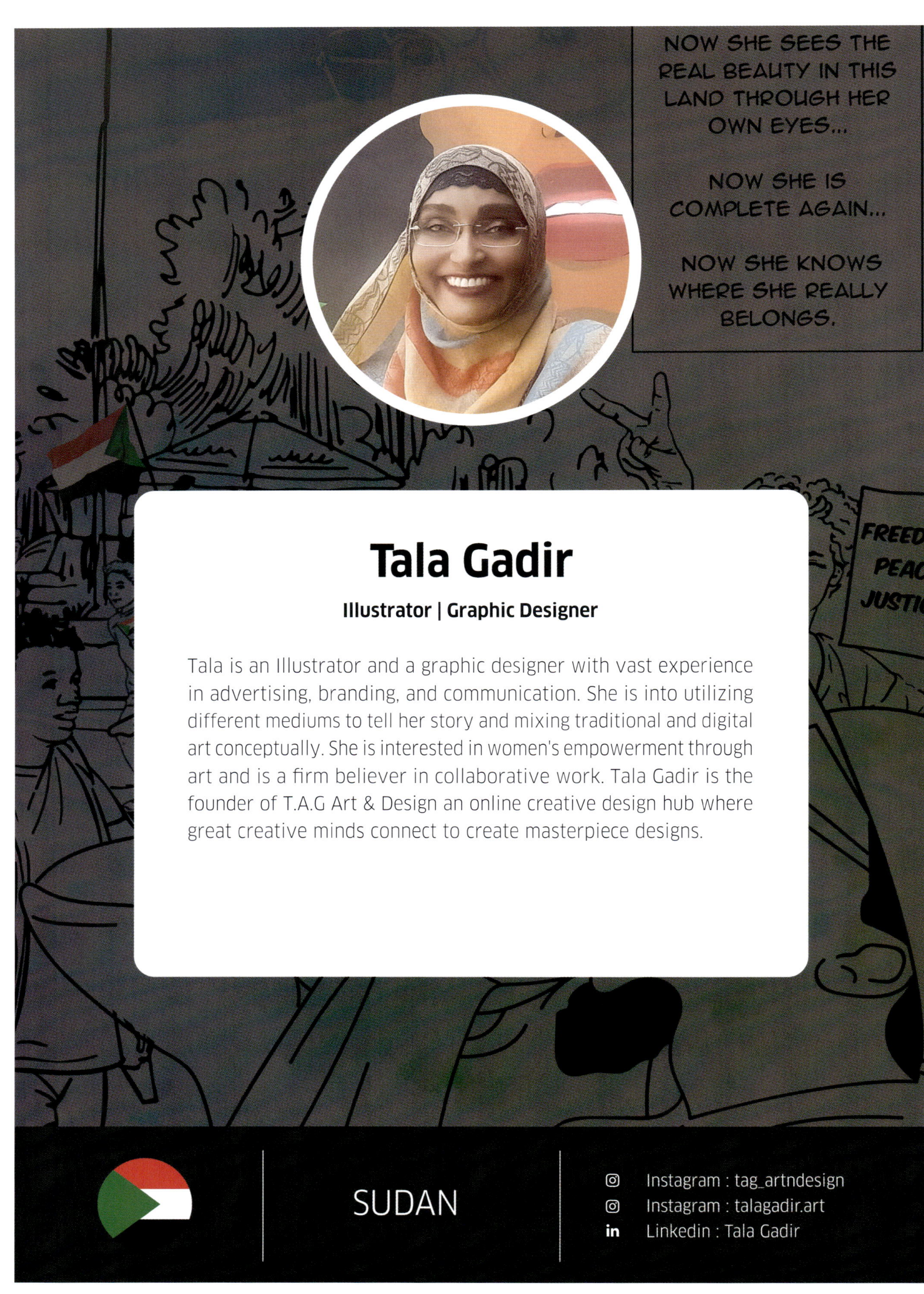

Tala Gadir

Illustrator | Graphic Designer

Tala is an Illustrator and a graphic designer with vast experience in advertising, branding, and communication. She is into utilizing different mediums to tell her story and mixing traditional and digital art conceptually. She is interested in women's empowerment through art and is a firm believer in collaborative work. Tala Gadir is the founder of T.A.G Art & Design an online creative design hub where great creative minds connect to create masterpiece designs.

SUDAN

Instagram : tag_artndesign
Instagram : talagadir.art
Linkedin : Tala Gadir

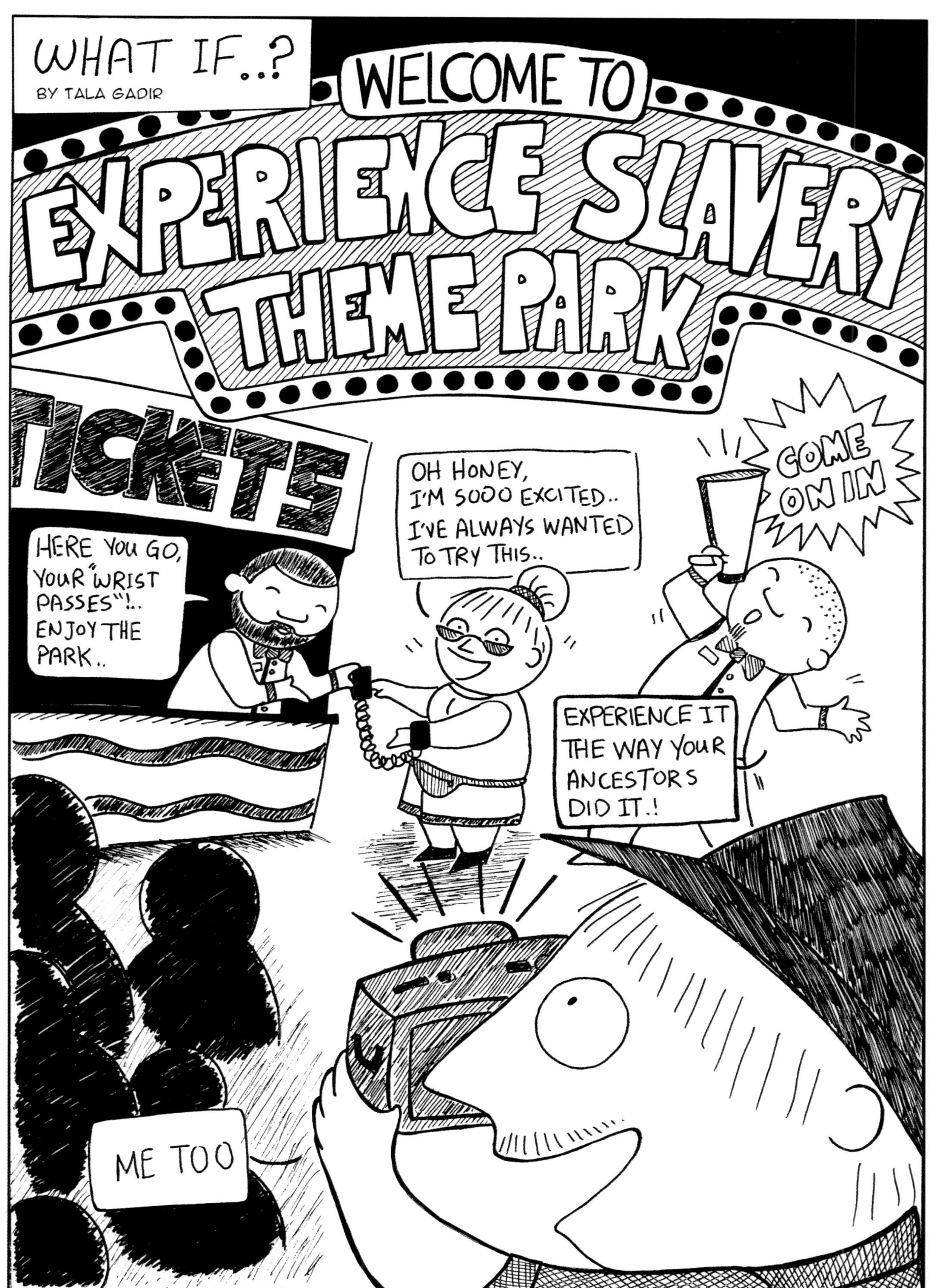
WHAT IF..?
BY TALA GADIR
WELCOME TO
EXPERIENCE SLAVERY THEME PARK
TICKETS
HERE YOU GO, YOUR "WRIST PASSES"!.. ENJOY THE PARK..
OH HONEY, I'M SOOO EXCITED.. I'VE ALWAYS WANTED TO TRY THIS..
COME ON IN
EXPERIENCE IT THE WAY YOUR ANCESTORS DID IT.!
ME TOO

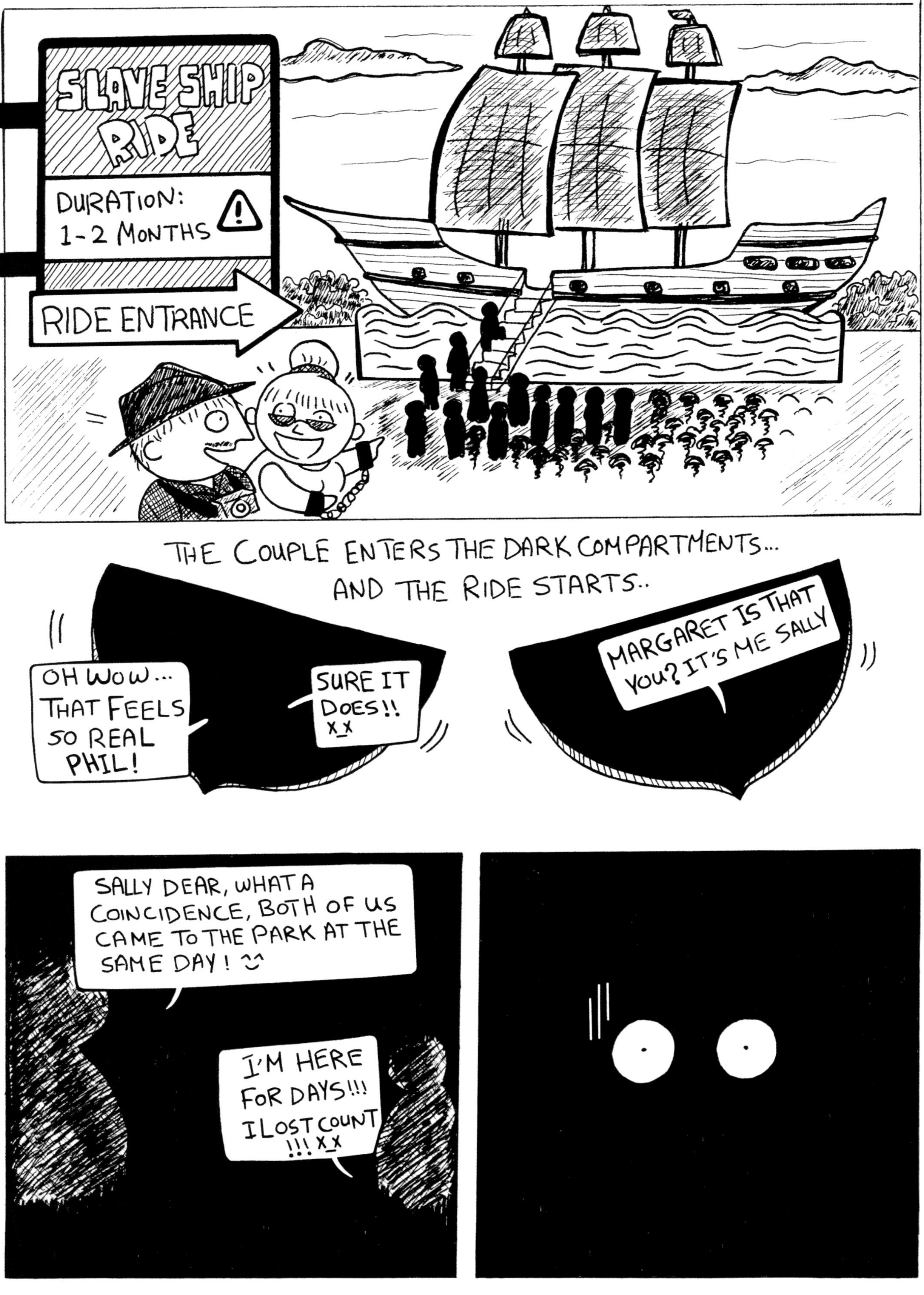

SLAVE SHIP RIDE

DURATION: 1-2 MONTHS

RIDE ENTRANCE

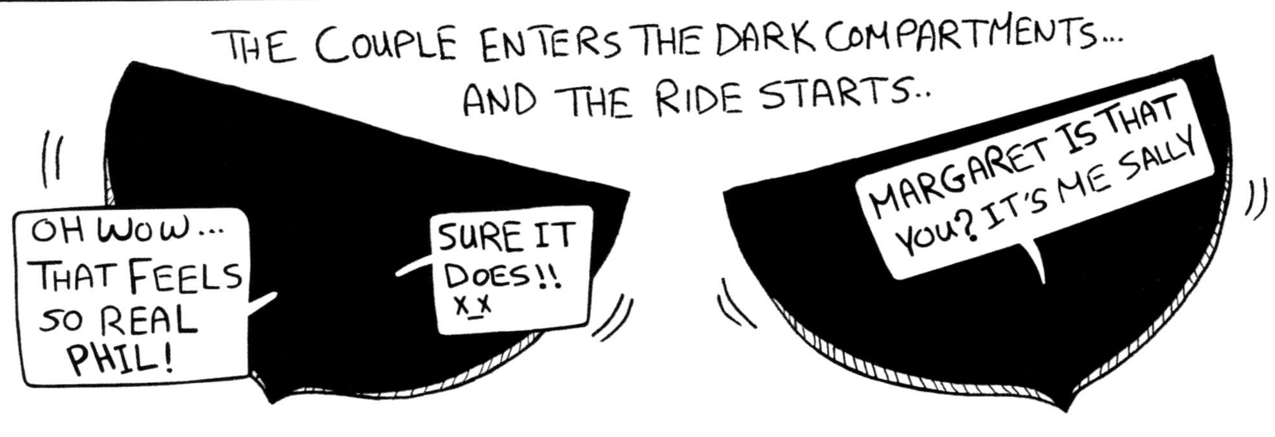

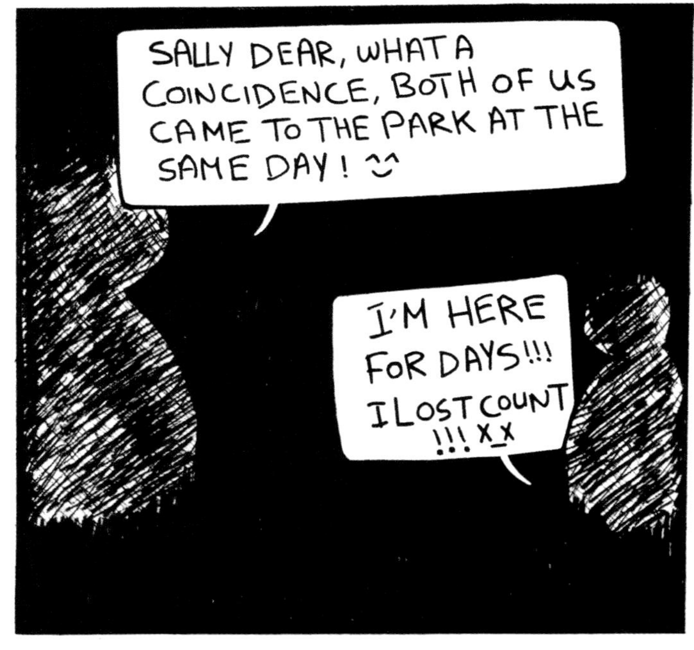

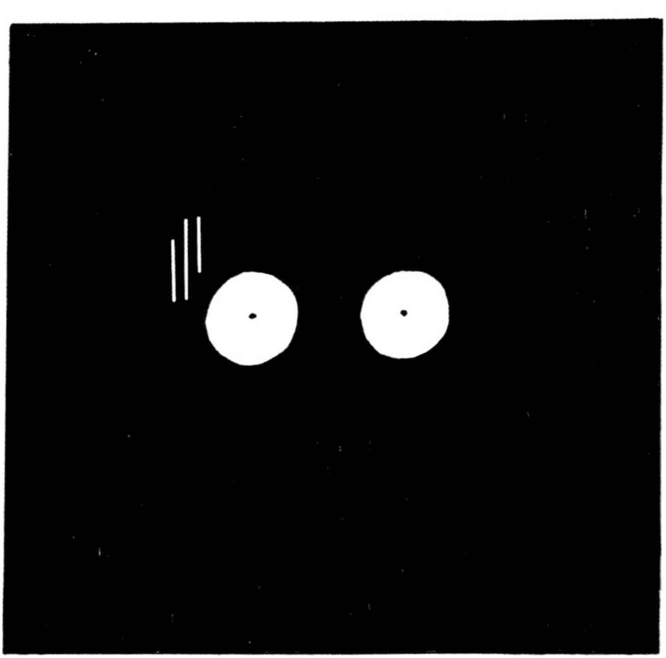

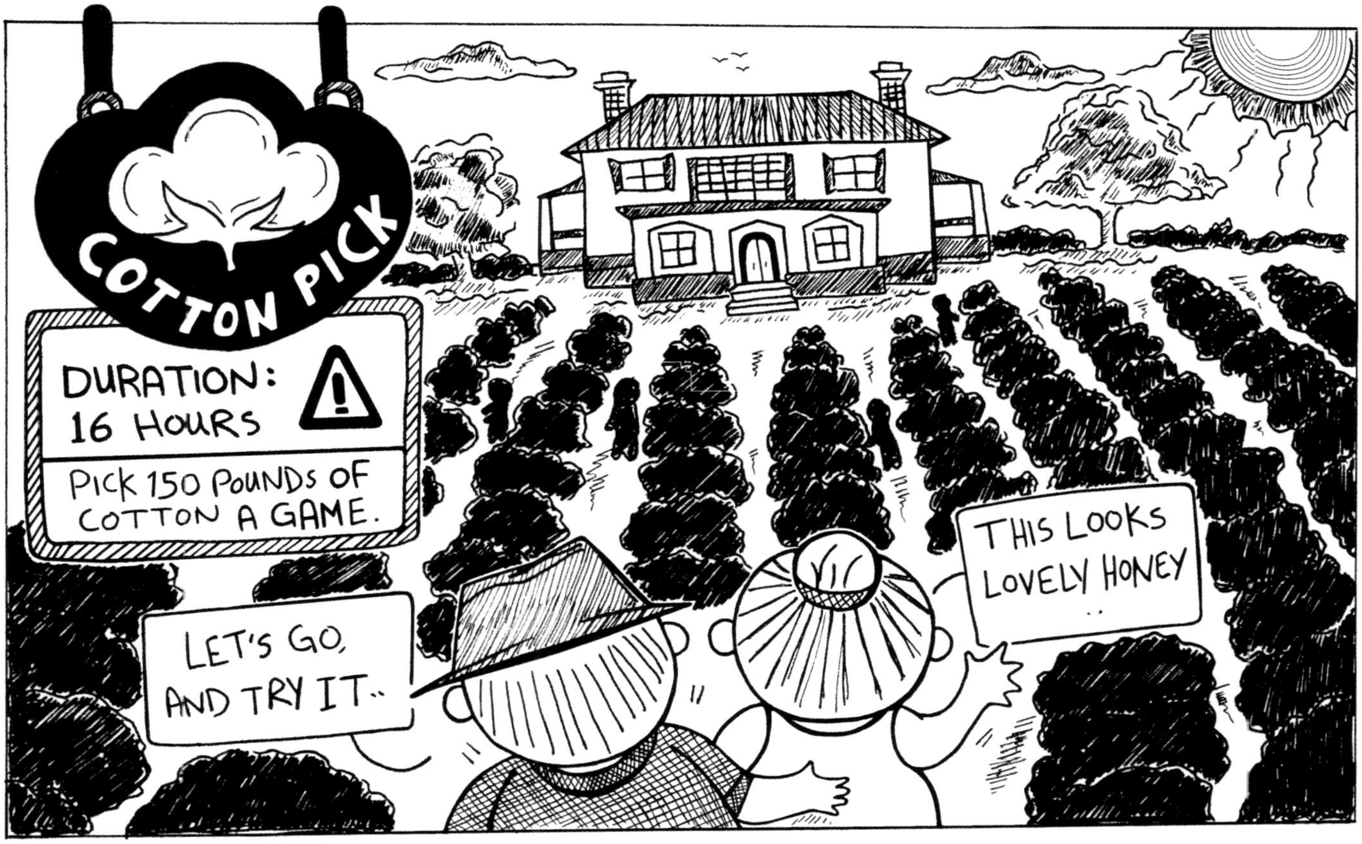

COTTON PICK

DURATION: 16 HOURS

PICK 150 POUNDS OF COTTON A GAME.

THIS LOOKS LOVELY HONEY ..

LET'S GO, AND TRY IT..

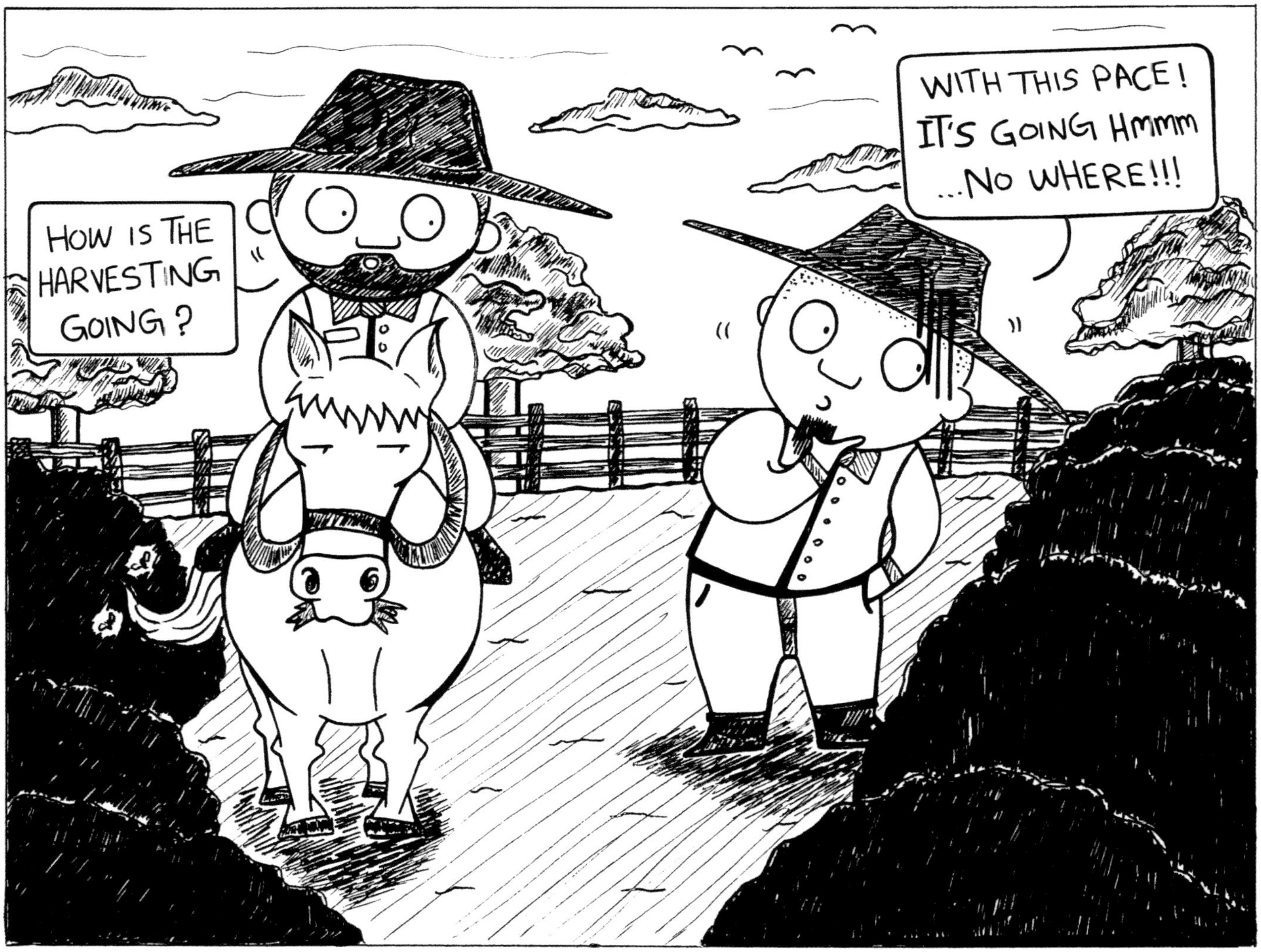

HOW IS THE HARVESTING GOING?

WITH THIS PACE! IT'S GOING Hmmm ...NO WHERE!!!

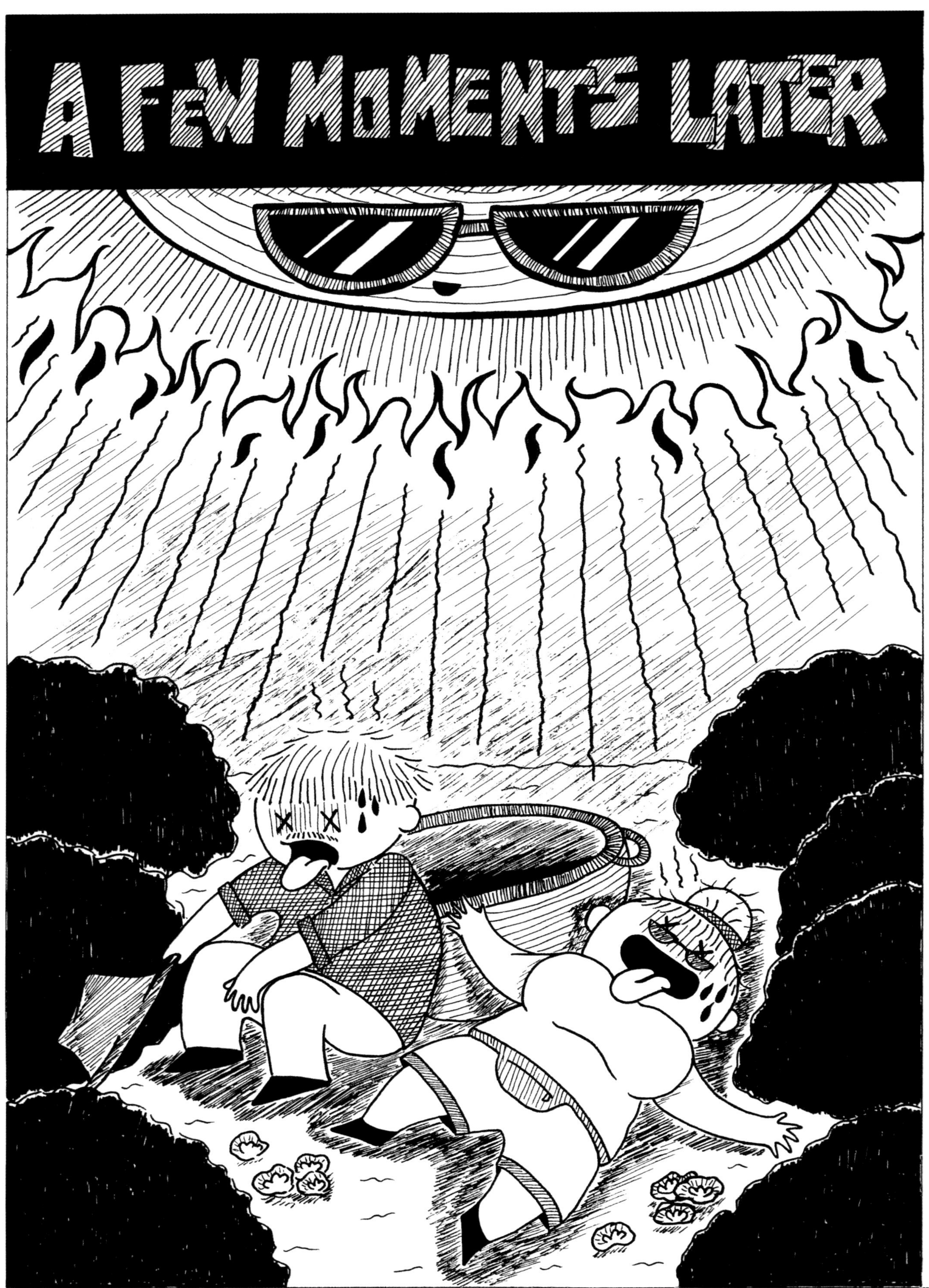
A FEW MOMENTS LATER

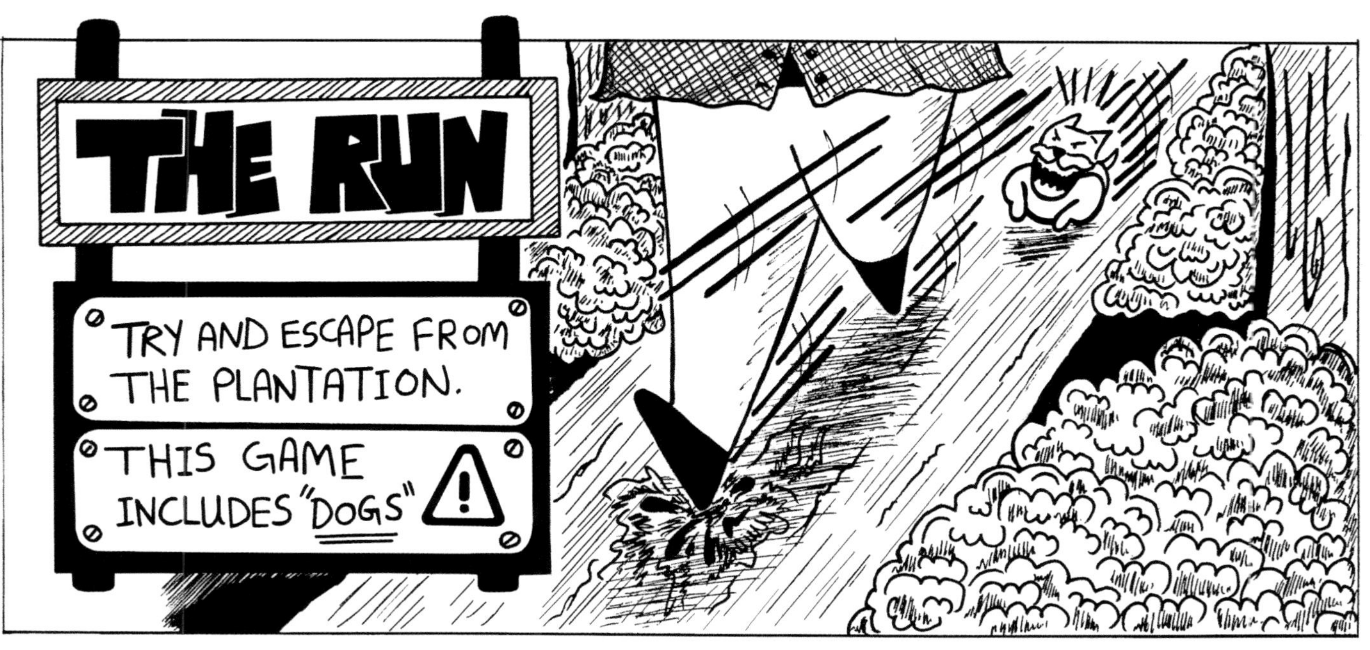
THE RUN
TRY AND ESCAPE FROM THE PLANTATION.
THIS GAME INCLUDES "DOGS"

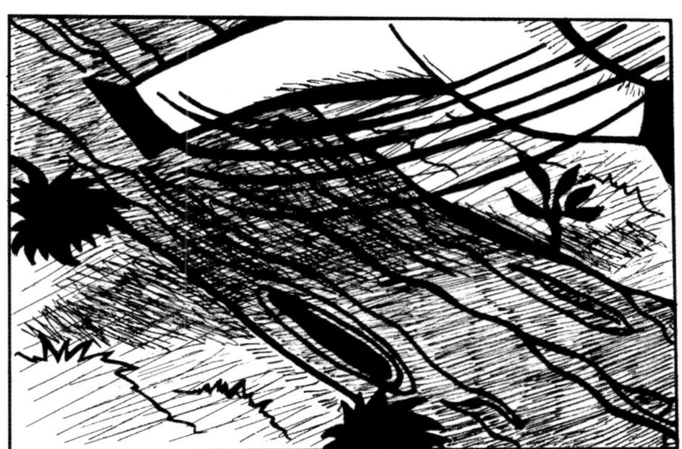

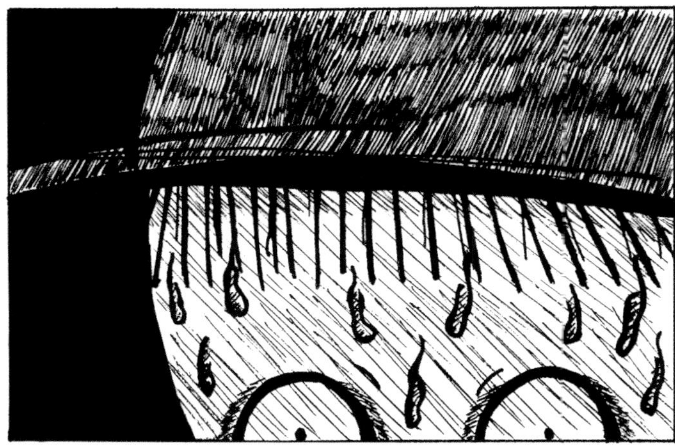

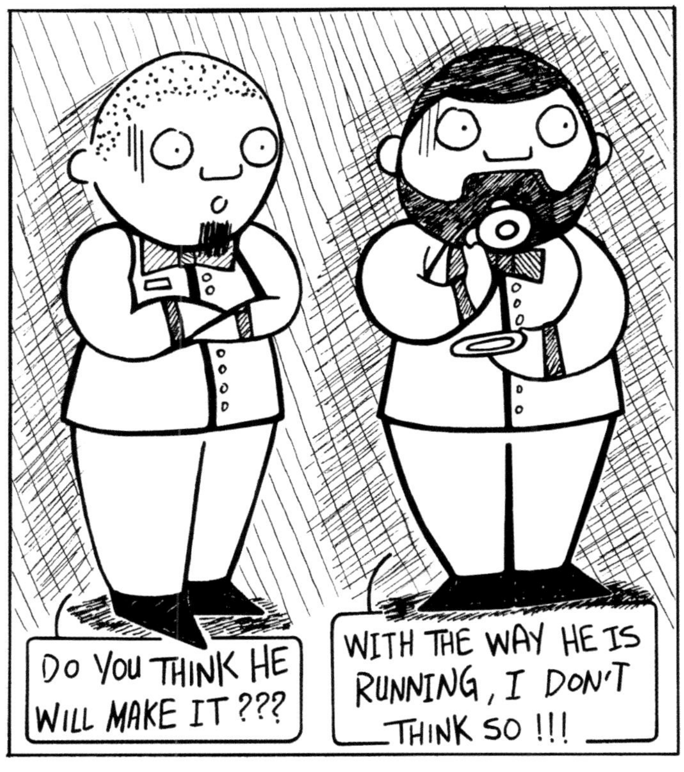
DO YOU THINK HE WILL MAKE IT ???
WITH THE WAY HE IS RUNNING, I DON'T THINK SO !!!

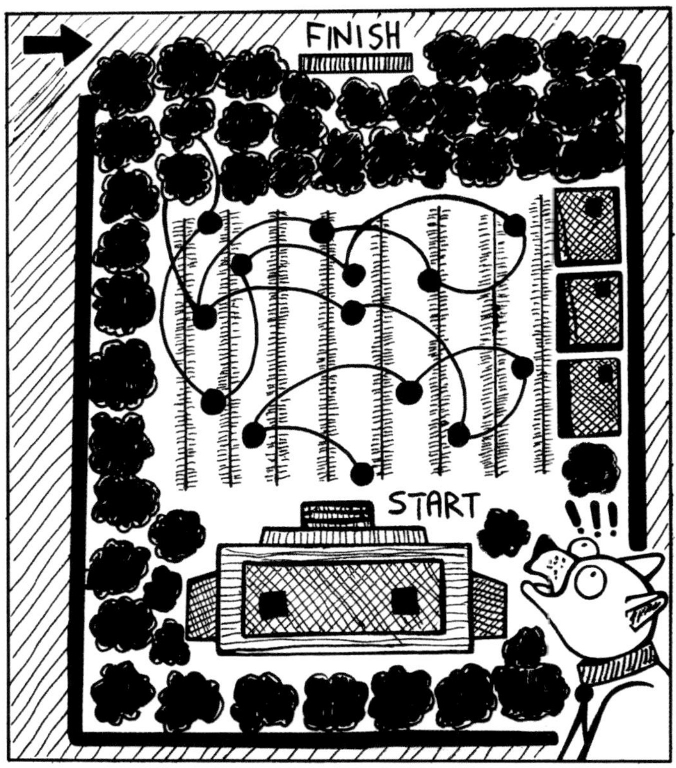
FINISH
START
!!!

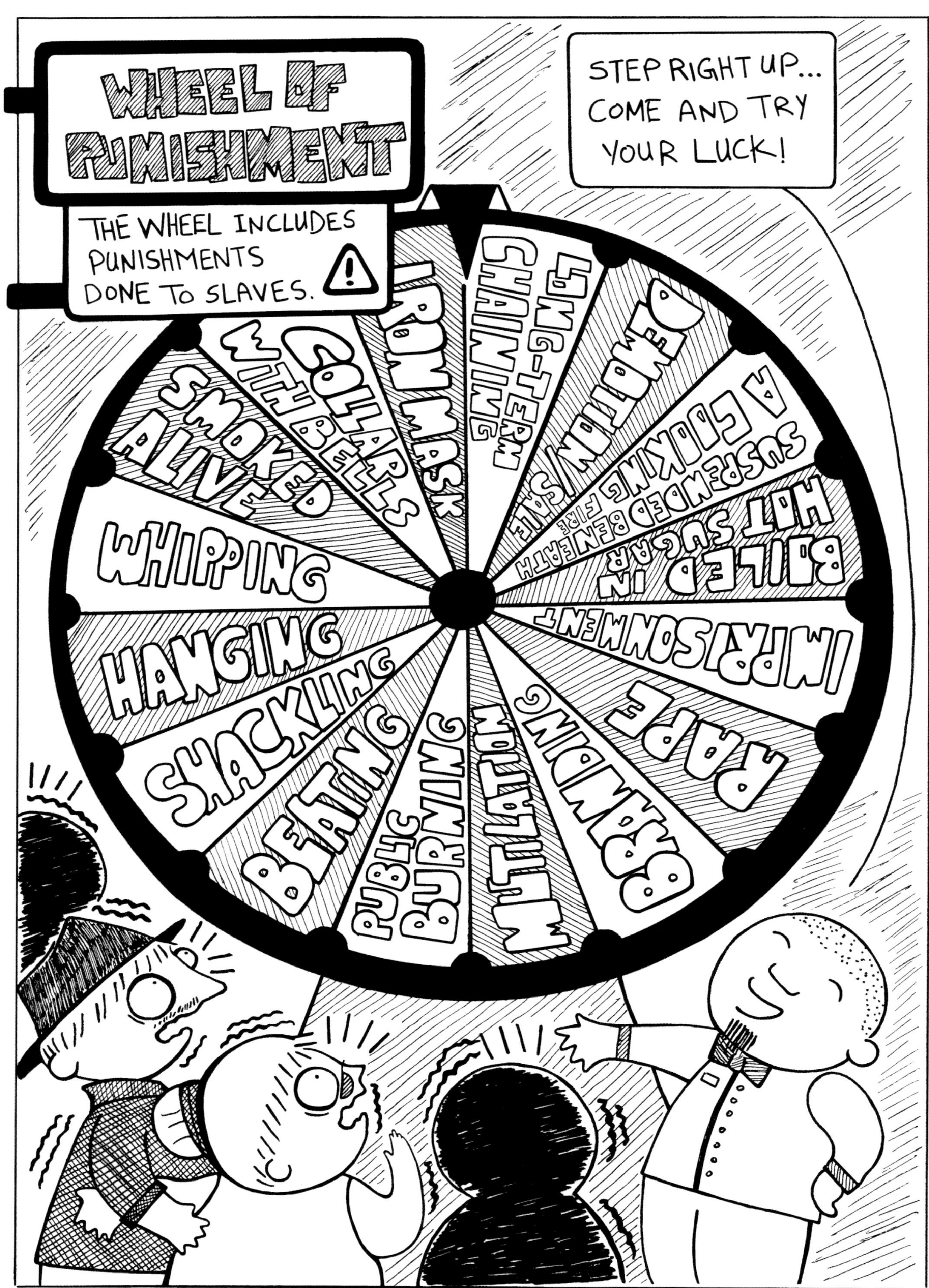
WHEEL OF PUNISHMENT
THE WHEEL INCLUDES PUNISHMENTS DONE TO SLAVES.
STEP RIGHT UP... COME AND TRY YOUR LUCK!
IRON MASK
LONG-TERM CHAINING
DEMOTION/SALE
SUSPENDED BENEATH A COOKING FIRE
BOILED IN HOT SUGAR
IMPRISONMENT
RAPE
BRANDING
MUTILATION
PUBLIC BURNING
BEATING
SHACKLING
HANGING
WHIPPING
SMOKED ALIVE
COLLARS WITH BELLS

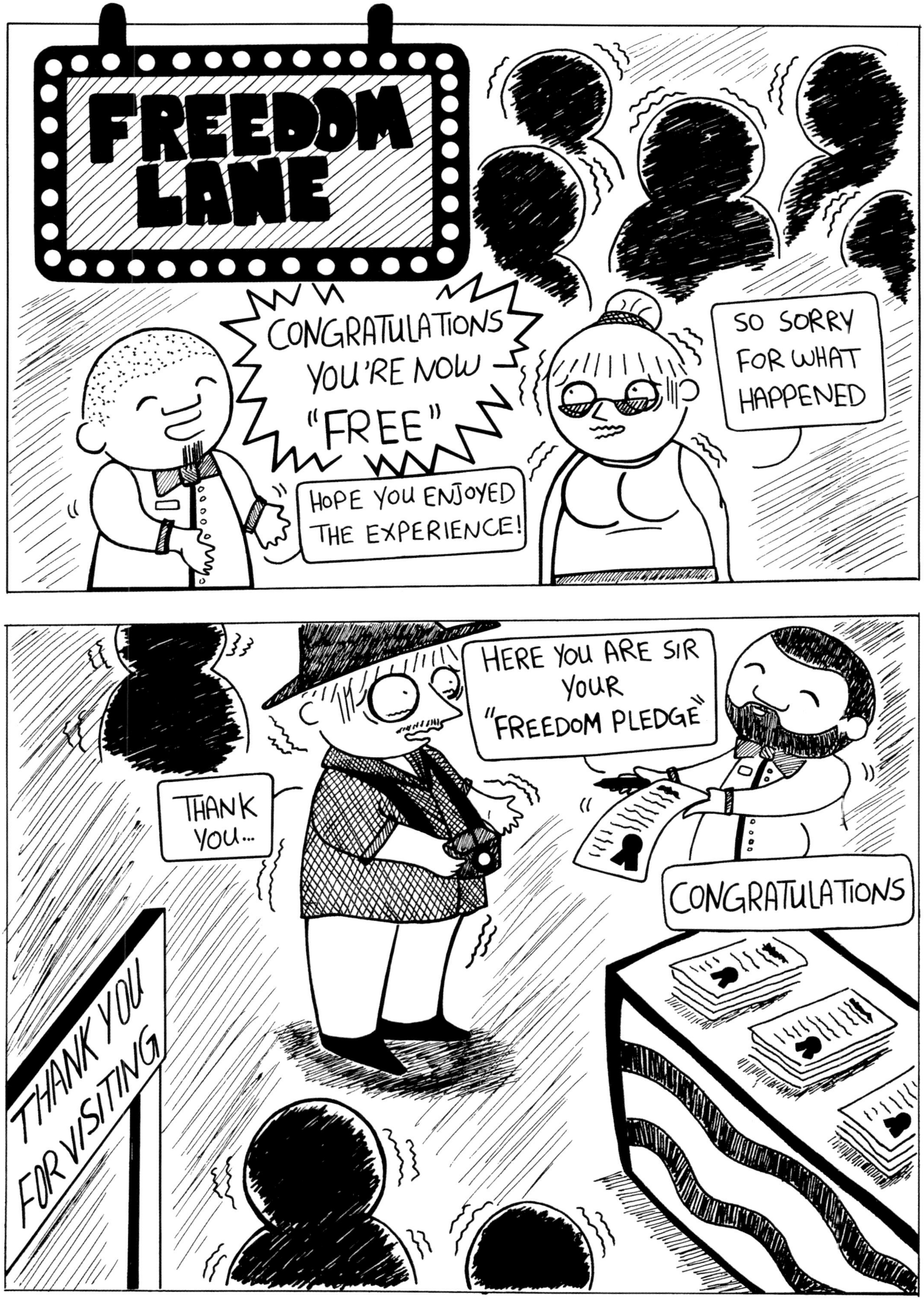

FREEDOM LANE
CONGRATULATIONS YOU'RE NOW "FREE"
HOPE YOU ENJOYED THE EXPERIENCE!
SO SORRY FOR WHAT HAPPENED
HERE YOU ARE SIR YOUR "FREEDOM PLEDGE"
THANK YOU...
CONGRATULATIONS
THANK YOU FOR VISITING

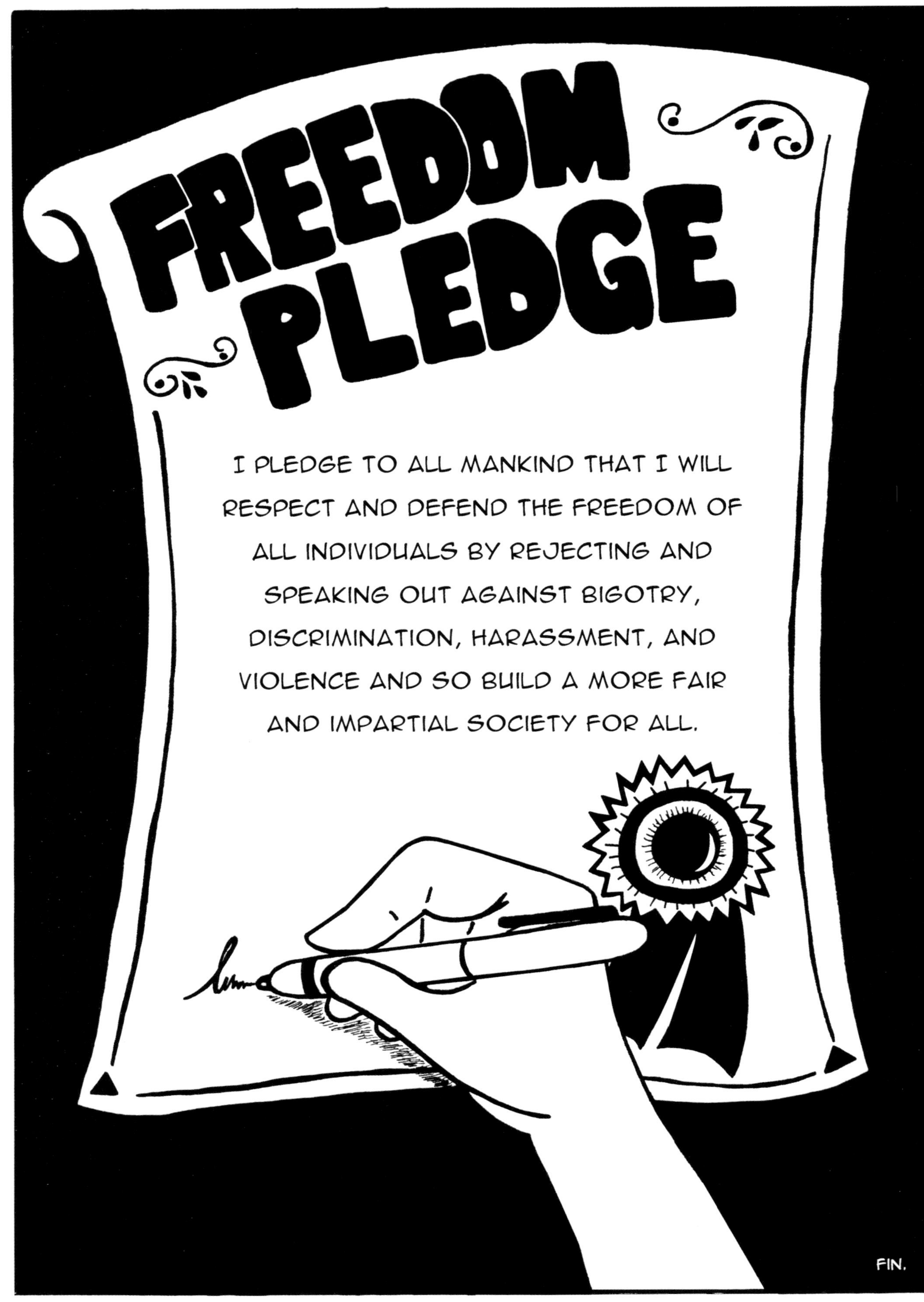
FREEDOM PLEDGE
I PLEDGE TO ALL MANKIND THAT I WILL RESPECT AND DEFEND THE FREEDOM OF ALL INDIVIDUALS BY REJECTING AND SPEAKING OUT AGAINST BIGOTRY, DISCRIMINATION, HARASSMENT, AND VIOLENCE AND SO BUILD A MORE FAIR AND IMPARTIAL SOCIETY FOR ALL.
FIN.

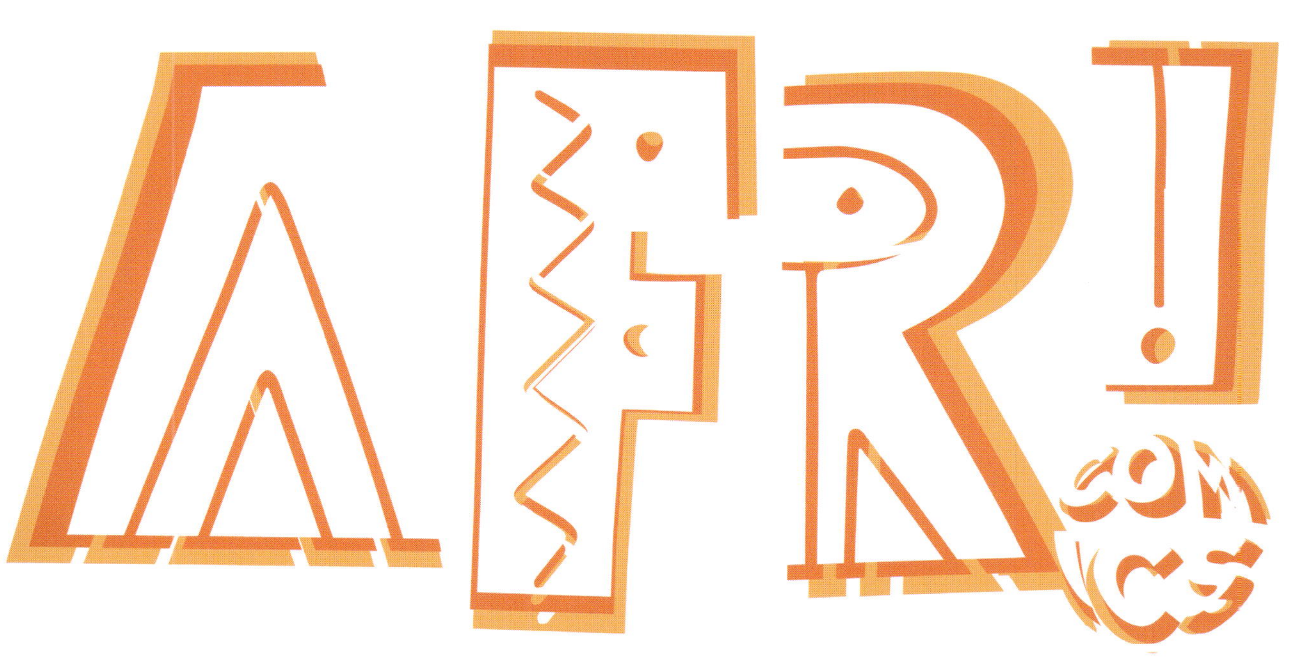
AFRI
COMICS

Acknowledgements

We would like to thank everyone who has contributed to the AfriComics project in one way or another. In particular, these include, in addition to all the artists.

The workshop facilitators: Akosua Hanson (Ghana), Birgit Weyhe (Germany), Déo (Togo), Delfina Bastos dos Santos (Angola), Dolph Banza (Rwanda), Hamed Eshrat (Germany), Hugues Bertrand Biboum (Cameroon), Ib Zongo (Burkina Faso), James Gayo (Tanzania), James Kamawira (Kenya), Jérémie Nsingi (Democratic Republic of Congo), KanAd (Togo), Mikaël Ross (Germany), Nkosingiphile Mazibuko (Namibia), Omar Diakité (Senegal), Roland Polman (Ivory Coast), Sebastian Lörscher (Germany), Yihenew Worku (Ethiopia), and Yousif Elamin Elkhair Elamin (Sudan) for their inspiration and guidance;

The video authors of the video library on the AfriComics website: Akosua Hanson (Ghana), ArtKanoon (Sudan), Bill Masuku (South Africa), Bill Masuku (Zimbabwe), Carnot Júnior (Angola), Goabaone Mogwe (Botswana), Hamed Eshrat (Germany), Inoussa Salogo (Burkina Faso), James Kamawira (Kenya), Jonarol Massengo (Congo), Judith Kaluaji (Democratic Republic of Congo), Kavula Bonolo (South Africa), KanAd (Togo), Lindomar Sousa (Angola), Matatizo Multimedia Productions Company (Tanzania), Matthew Hansen (Ghana), Mola Boyika (Democratic Republic of Congo), Msanii Kimani wa Wanjiru (Kenya), Olímpio (Angola), Omar Diakité (Senegal), Paul-Ivan Andjembe (Cameroon), Prince Ardayfio (Ghana), Ray Whitcher (South Africa), Roland Polman (Ivory Coast), Santa Kakese (Democratic Republic of Congo), Sérgio Piçarra (Angola), Tom Dai (South Sudan), and Yihenew Worku (Ethiopia) for their visual contributions;

The staff of the Goethe Institutes in the Sub-Saharan Africa region in Abidjan (Ivory Coast), Accra (Ghana), Addis Ababa (Ethiopia), Dakar (Senegal), Dar es Salaam (Tanzania), Kigali (Rwanda), Kinshasa (Democratic Republic of Congo), Khartoum (Sudan), Luanda (Angola), Lomé (Togo), Nairobi (Kenya), Ouagadougou (Burkina Faso), Windhoek (Namibia), Yaoundé (Cameroon) for their valuable support;

Special thanks also go to all individuals who contributed to the translations: Annette David, Désirée Schneider, Holger Wolandt, Lea Hübner, Sarah Idrissi, and Sonia da Silva for their effort in translating the comics.

AfriComics - for more see:
www.goethe.de/africomics

SCHILER & MÜCKE